Handbook of Vocational Education Evaluation

Handbook of Vocational Education Evaluation

edited by
Theodore Abramson
Queens College, City University of New York
Carol Kehr Tittle
University of North Carolina at Greensboro
Lee Cohen
City University of New York

 **SAGE PUBLICATIONS**   Beverly Hills   London

For information address:

SAGE PUBLICATIONS, INC.
275 South Beverly Drive
Beverly Hills, California 90212

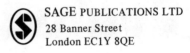

SAGE PUBLICATIONS LTD
28 Banner Street
London EC1Y 8QE

Printed in the United States of America

Library of Congress Cataloging in Publication Data

Main entry under title:

Handbook of vocational education evaluation.

    Bibliography: p.
    Includes indexes.
    1. Vocational education—United States—
Evaluation.   2. Career education—United States—
Evaluation. I. Abramson, Theodore. II. Tittle,
Carol K., 1933-   III. Cohen, Lee.
LC1045.H28   370.11'3'0973   78-24256.
ISBN 0-8039-1078-9

FIRST PRINTING

contents

acknowledgments

The development of this volume has had the support of the New York State Department of Education, and particularly the encouragement of the Office of Occupational and Continuing Education. Lee Cohen, as Director of the Institute for Research and Development in Occupational Education, also supported our efforts to bring this volume to fruition.

In the early stages of planning the chapters, Drs. Helen Spilman and Lois-ellen Datta were a source of many excellent ideas, and provided useful critiques of our early plans. Blanche Berk and Charlotte Fisk bore the burdens of typing much of the manuscript. To all we owe a debt of gratitude.

Theodore Abramson
Carol Kehr Tittle

introduction

The past five years has seen an upsurge of interest in occupational education at all levels of the educational system. At the elementary and secondary school levels career education has become part of the curriculum, and at the secondary and postsecondary school levels increasing numbers of students are enrolling in courses which prepare them for the world of work. As part of this trend there has been increased emphasis on vocational and technical education programs at the high school and junior college levels, accompanied by and perhaps encouraged by greater state and federal levels of funding for such programs.

Concomitantly, in part because of the current economic status of the country there has been a greater stress on the need for accountability and evaluation of social and educational programs. Attempts to meet this need have led to the conclusion that evaluation is a developing field that requires scientific inquiry and rigorous investigation. The recent publication of the *Handbook of Evaluation Research* and the *Annual Review of Evaluation Studies,* as well as new evaluation journals, attests to this need for explicating the philosophy, procedures, methodology, and problems inherent in the evaluation enterprise.

To date, there has been little work that examines evaluation issues in the context of, current vocational education programs and practices. The purpose of this book is to help bridge this gap in the literature by providing a series of chapters designed to assist evaluators, administrators, and policy makers concerned with the evaluation of vocational education programs. Other audiences for the book are those faculty and graduate students concerned with vocational education and evaluation.

This volume is divided into five parts which describe vocational education and its evaluation in terms of: history and goals, evaluation designs and approaches, use of evaluation concepts in program development, measurement and testing issues, and political context and evaluation roles.

We have excluded chapters dealing with some important issues in evaluation and measurement because they have received excellent treatments in other recent publications, and we have provided a selected annotated bibliography in these areas for the reader. For example, there is a chapter on field research methods by Bouchard in the *Handbook of Industrial and Organizational Psychology* (Dunnette, 1976), and chapters on interviewing by Weiss, and on validity, reliability, and special problems of measurement in evaluation research by Nunnally and Durham in the *Handbook of Evaluation Research* (Struening and Guttentag, 1975).

Part One, *Vocational Education: History and Goal Setting,* describes the development and growth of vocational education from the early apprentice system to today, and the role of the Federal government in this progression. The changing approach to and the different roles of the Federal government vis-à-vis evaluation of vocational education are placed in historical perspective. In addition, the setting of goals and allocation of resources at the state and local level are discussed in this section.

Part Two, *Evaluation Approaches and Special Design Issues,* explicates some of the major issues in designing and implementing evaluation studies to provide data that can be usefully, meaningfully, and validly interpreted for program modification or termination. The section also includes chapters on cost-benefit analysis as a means of evaluating vocational education and on conducting follow-up studies. Both of these chapters describe problems with which evaluators deal in conducting studies of vocational education programs.

Part Three, *Program Development and Evaluation Concepts: Linkages in Vocational Education,* discusses methods of carrying out job and task analyses, and the use of behavioral objectives and performance ratings in the development and evaluation of vocational training programs. Although two of these chapters are based on developments by the military, the approach is readily generalizable to civilian programs at the secondary and postsecondary levels. In fact, this work has in large measure been the basis for much of the work undertaken by the Vocational-Technical Consortium of States (V-TECS). The section also includes a discussion of the use, development, and content validity of behavioral objectives in instruction and evaluation of occupational education programs. The last chapter in the section describes the progress and problems associated with attempting to evolve a "grass-roots" competency-based vocational curriculum with teachers who had little experience in writing behavioral objectives and performance measures.

Part Four, *Evaluation Measures and Testing Issues,* includes discussions of general approaches to attitude measurement, and the definitions and uses of job satisfaction measures in evaluating vocational education programs. This latter chapter also describes facet specific and facet free measures, and technical and administrative issues in the use of these measures. Implications of the National Institute of Education's *Guidelines for assessment of sex bias and sex fairness in career interest inventories* for evaluation of vocational education and career guidance programs are presented, including recent research in the areas of the guidelines. A similar discussion is provided of test bias, in general, and its implications for vocational education evaluation in terms of the *Uniform guidelines on employee selection procedures.* Two related areas of concern to vocational education are discussed—evaluation of programs funded under the Comprehensive Employment Training Act (CETA) and Career Education programs. Special problems identified are obtaining appropriate longitudinal outcome data for CETA trainees and the measurement of each USOE learner outcome goal for career education.

The last part of the volume, *Politics and the Evaluator's Role: The Real World of Evaluation,* contains a reprint of Weiss' seminal paper on the political context in which the evaluation research process is embedded. This chapter is followed by a discussion of the evaluator's role when viewed in terms of the motives of the agency or personnel commissioning the evaluation, and a description of the problems frequently faced by evaluators who work as central staff in large city school districts. This section concludes with a case study of an industry-education council, a new approach to the industry-education partnership for the educator and evaluator to consider.

Each of the chapters in the volume, except for the chapter by Carol H. Weiss, were commissioned by the editors and undertaken by each author according to a set of general specifications for the chapter. The editors have also provided concluding remarks for the reader, and a selected annotated bibliography.

The ideas presented in the majority of the chapters should permit evaluators to concern themselves with advancing the state of the art in vocational education evaluation rather than being tied only to the current topics in other areas of educational evaluation. We hope that the concepts, methods, and discussion of issues presented in this volume will help set the course of future developments in vocational education evaluation for the next several years.

Theodore Abramson
Carol Kehr Tittle

VOCATIONAL EDUCATION
History and Goal-Setting

PART I

Major influences in vocational education evaluation for the next decade will be the result of historical issues in vocational education, federal legislation that includes evaluation mandates, and the translation of these issues and mandates into state and local evaluation efforts. Part One provides an overview of the history and goals of vocational education in the chapter by John Gallinelli, *Vocational Education Programs at the Secondary Level: A Review of Development and Purpose.* Federal priorities in vocational education are described by Lois-ellin Datta in her chapter, *Better Luck This Time: From Federal Legislation to Practice in Evaluating Vocational Education.* Federal goals are described in legislation—the Education Amendments of 1976—and made more explicit in evaluation requirements at the federal and state levels. In conjunction with the Education Amendments of 1976, PL 94-482, the National Institute of Education (NIE) will carry out an analysis of state and local compliance efforts for the Act and will examine evaluation practices in vocational education.

The series of studies that form the scope of work for the analysis of state and local compliance and evaluation practice are broader than an input-output model of effectiveness in program evaluation. In the first place, the focus in the studies, as well as in the funding legislation, is on special populations and on coordinating efforts among the various agencies and institutions concerned with vocational education. Second, in addition to describing certain status variables, the methodology for the research includes case studies (NIE, Attachment B, 1978:4). The methods and focus of the NIE studies may be contrasted with those federal level studies carried out under Title I, ESEA, and in the follow-through evaluations. The work to be carried out for the congress through NIE will examine a series of compliance research issues and also the assessments of program quality and their effectiveness as a management tool. In this latter area, the objective of the inquiry is to examine the use of assessments (evaluation) in program management and improvement, the criteria that are being used, and also to examine how the various and overlapping federal requirements for evaluation interact with one another. These were stated in the following series of objectives (NIE, 1978):

(1) "Thus, the first objective of this study is to describe the means now being used to assess program quality and effectiveness and to ascertain whether the results of such assessments are used to manage or improve programs and with what results (p. 19).

(2) "The second objective of the study is to examine the criteria being used to evaluate program effectiveness at the state and local level and to determine what the consequences are of specifying particular criteria in the Act (p. 21).

(3) "Discerning just how the various and overlapping Federal requirements for evaluation will interact with one another, whether they will be complimentary and reinforcing or conflicting and redundant, and what their combined effects on program quality may be constitutes the third objective of the study" (p. 22).

These objectives, along with the compliance objectives, are to be described through the following projects:

(1) "an inventory of information about State legal, administrative fiscal and evaluative practices for the 56 state level jurisdictions;

(2) "a series of ten in depth State case studies focusing upon matters of compliance and State and local administration of vocational education; and a series of ten in depth State case studies focusing upon State and local evaluation practices and their consequences. Five of the States studied for compliance will overlap with five of the States selected for studies of evaluation, while five States will in each instance be different.

(3) "an analysis conducted annually of the implications for matters of compliance, evaluation, and state and local administration of the information to be found in state 5 year plans, annual program plans and accountability reports, SACVE evaluations and other documents produced annually at the state or federal level under the requirements of the Vocational Education Act as amended" (NIE, 1978:23).

The case studies are intended to develop themes, presumably reflecting major issues in vocational education. The themes that appear to be identified by the legislation and the NIE document are legislative compliance, "outputs" of vocational education, and the use of evaluation in rational management. However, there are other themes or issues to be raised in relation to vocational education. These themes are reflected in the historical perspective provided by Gallinelli in the first chapter of this Handbook.

Historically, there was a dichotomy between the traditional classical education which served certain groups as society developed and the apprenticeship or work training that served other groups within western cultures. Gallinelli traces this development and the resulting view of academic versus vocational or practical education in the schools. The attempts to merge the two types of education within the secondary school (and more recently in postsecondary education) have led to a concern with such issues as the purpose of vocational education, its expected outcomes, and the extent to which the schools should serve the industrial or technological society by the preparation of workers. An evaluation of vocational education at the most general level must be concerned with the manner in which vocational education is integrated, or not integrated, into the secondary and postsecondary curricula, and the resulting status of vocational education both within the student's and teacher's perspectives of its outcomes and importance. If vocational educators and evaluators are concerned with the major goals of vocational education as these are reflected in specific programs, the tension between vocational education as *education* and the more specific goal of *education for work* will be reflected in the institutional support for and attitudes toward vocational education.

Another issue that arises within this context is that of the equipment required to teach the practical skills within vocational education, where this equipment should be housed, who should pay for it, and how costs should be entered in cost/benefit analyses. The tension here in costing of equipment is between schools and industry. Gallinelli points out that support for the industrial arts in general education is based on the idea that industry has become more complex and it is difficult for the average person to comprehend the organization, products, processes, and occupations in industry. How, therefore, do schools give students, and do they give *every* student, the opportunity and background to gain such an understanding? This objective, in contrast to the legislated goal of vocational education to provide students with entry level skills, poses a tension for evaluators and schools that arises out of the historical development of vocational education. As there is increasing pressure to evaluate vocational education and to examine its linkages with the goal of employability as reflected in both VEA and CETA programs, evaluators and administrators need to examine again whether all the goals of vocational education are being considered and whether, in fact, evaluation takes place within the broader context of the goals of secondary and postsecondary education.

A second set of issues is reflected in Lois-ellin Datta's chapter examining evaluation requirements in federal legislation and the three federal roles she has described for evaluation in vocational education. One issue is reflected in the theme she has identified as underlying the current federal role in evaluation in vocational education. This theme is the congressional belief that the Executive Branch, state and local agencies "need prodding to keep up with the times and to respond to the needs of diverse groups of citizens." As with earlier federal evaluation requirements in such programs as ESEA, this belief imposes a tension between federal influence exerted through funding and the determination of educational priorities and practices by local education authorities. The evaluation requirements also reflect a belief in rational management and rational decision-making. (An examination of current methodology related to rational decision-making is presented in the last two chapters in Part One.)

A second issue has been delineated by Datta in the three federal evaluation roles that can be identified historically. This issue is concerned with the "state of the art" of evaluation, both conceptually and technically. Evaluation is a newly developing applied social science and many decision makers and evaluators believe evaluation can serve the goals of program change and improvement that are *externally* derived, rather than those goals arising (or not arising) from the problem-solving efforts of local organizations, including schools. Datta's analysis of the federal legislation helps to focus this issue more clearly for evaluators.

According to Datta, the first federal evaluation role is that of gathering information to establish national needs, the second is accountability for legal expenditure of funds, and the third is "galvanizing changes" for program improvement and redirection. Datta provides an optimistic view of the federal effort to insure that evaluation data will be used for planning, improvement and redirection through a variety of attempts to require state and local use of evaluation data. While Datta recognizes the current limitations to evaluation methodology, the reader concerned with vocational education may find it useful to consider other ways of assisting local and state education agencies to identify their own priorities in vocational education. Some of the methods for doing this are provided in a chapter by Carol Kehr Tittle, *Evaluation and Decision-Making: Defining Program Impact for Funding Decisions,* and in the chapter by Alan L. Gross, *Funding Education Projects: Applying Decision Theory to the Problem.*

If federal and state priorities in vocational education are at least partially defined in the programs funded, then an examination of the state level decision process may provide guidance to both evaluators and administrators in vocational education. The chapter by Tittle provides a description of the state level decision-making process for one state, the results of a pilot study suggesting how decision makers may be assisted by defining program impact for evaluation, and the translation of program impact definitions to variables that can be known at the time of funding new programs. Research issues are raised, as well as political concerns for evaluators, in this particular context for decision-making. A brief review of the literature in decision aiding techniques is also included in the chapter. Again, an optimistic view of decision-making as a rational process in management, and of evaluation as a useful adjunct to this management view, underlies the project report by Tittle. However, there is a growing concern about the use of evaluation to aid decision makers and inform policy, particularly at the federal level, and a view that evaluation conceived within this framework is not functional for local organizations. As Pondy (1977) has suggested, more sophisticated evaluation methods may simply encourage further centralization of social programming. He suggests that we might better devote our energies to decentralizing and disseminating existing evaluation skills in a form that permits input of local idiosyncratic information and, indeed, use by local officials.

Major criticisms of federal level evaluations by Meade (1978) and House (1978) have occurred in the context of the follow-through evaluations, questioning conclusions, lack of sensitivity to the program and the participants original purpose, and a narrowness of focus. While evaluators may be able to use decision aiding techniques or decision theory in particular areas, such as assisting in funding decision-making, there is a fundamental concern whether making objectives and values explicit will "improve" the decisions that are made with respect to educational programs. Evaluators and administrators need to consider whether the development of formal criteria will help, for example, to identify the "best" proposals. Past research does not provide satisfactory evidence on this issue and experience with the methods in the field of education is very limited. On the other hand, it may be that there is a use for these procedures in at least some, if not all parts, of the funding decision and evaluation process. The chapter by Alan L. Gross translates the problem of deciding which education projects to fund to a local level example.

Gross has been concerned with formal mathematical decision theory models and particularly with a Bayesian approach. As Gross describes the decision process, he points out several advantages of the decision theory model: There is the definition of relevant variables, the quantification of subjective values and beliefs—bringing this process out into the open—and the synthesis of all relevant information. Gross's description of a local school district decision to select one of three vocational education programs provides a "worked out example" for evaluators and administrators using two procedures. Gross goes on to suggest empirical studies which may provide further information for evaluators and administrators in this developing area of approaches to the systematic specification of goals and priorities in vocational education, and the use of these goals and priorities either in evaluation or in funding decision settings. As he notes, "one of the main limitations is the construction of probability distributions and utility functions for decision theory models." However, he also points out that there have been and will be further efforts to construct computer programs which may assist both evaluators and decision makers.

The chapters in Part One, then, provide an introduction to an important area of concern to evaluation of vocational education programs. Current evaluation of vocational education programs is largely defined by mandated federal evaluation requirements. There are clearly areas of evaluation in vocational education programs that differ from the evaluation of other educational programs. These include the historical tension between vocational education and more traditional goals of secondary and postsecondary education, the cost and currency of equipment needed for practical experiences in vocational education, and the increased emphasis on linking education and work, with resulting efforts to link education and labor force participation. The chapter by David Bresnick (in Part Four) provides a clearer definition of this tension. The other problem for evaluators is the relationship between the evaluation approach taken and its "fit" to vocational education. This relationship is explored in more depth in Part Two of the Handbook.

REFERENCES

House, E. R. 1978. "The objectivity, fairness, and justice of federal evaluation policy as reflected in the Follow-Through Evaluation." Urbana: Center for Instructional Research and Curriculum Evaluation, University of Illinois, February. (draft).

Meade, E. J., Jr. 1978. "Evaluation of evaluations: The case of Follow-Through." Paper presented at the annual meeting of the American Educational Research Association, Toronto, March.

NIE Scope of work: Studies of state and local administrative compliance and evaluation practices for vocational education. Washington, DC: National Institute of Education, 1978. (RFP NIE-R-780012)

Pondy, L. R. 1977. Two faces of evaluation. In H.W. Melton and D. J. H. Watson, eds. Interdisciplinary Dimensions of Accounting for Social Goals and Social Organizations. Columbus, OH: Grid.

VOCATIONAL EDUCATION
PROGRAMS AT THE
SECONDARY LEVEL
A Review of Development
and Purpose

chapter 1

JOHN GALLINELLI | *Glassboro State College*

THE EARLY FORMS OF INDUSTRIAL EDUCATION

Though the vocational education movement did not come into being until the late nineteenth century, vocational education has really existed as long as humankind. It began when parents taught their children the skills necessary for survival in the hunting and gathering bands of primitive people. Children learned the skills of their parents by watching carefully and imitating the process until an exact duplicate could be produced. This method of conscious-imitation was the method by which crafts were "taught" in one way or another until well into the 1400s.

At first all of the simple weapons, tools, and religious and domestic objects were formed by people for their personal use. Later, after people learned to control fire and to smelt metals to form tools, they began to specialize in one of the new crafts that were made possible by these developments. New social developments went hand in hand with new technology and people no longer had to be the jacks-of-all-trades of earlier times. Some could be miners—others smiths, carpenters, masons, or weavers (Bennett, 1926:12).

Craftsmen were eventually brought together by their common interest in a craft to form social groups—and out of these evolved the crafts guilds of the Middle Ages.

AUTHOR'S NOTE: *Special appreciation is extended to Dr. Janice Weaver, Dean of Professional Studies at Glassboro State College for her part in the publication of this chapter.*

The teaching of a trade or craft has traditionally involved a parent-child relationship, and in modern times that relationship has been extended to involve schools. In ancient Jewish culture, the law required parents to teach boys a trade. The boys were to go to the Rabbis for religious instruction in the mornings and learn the father's trade in the afternoon. It was believed that a person with a trade was a useful member of society, and manual work was considered a duty for all persons (Bennett, 1926:14).

The early Christian monks also regarded manual labor very highly and required it of everyone in their communities. It was specified that their time should be divided between prayer and work. (These early monks were attempting to emulate the lives of Christ and the Apostles by their manual labor. Because the monasteries were like small towns, it was necessary to have workers to provide bread, clothing, tend the gardens, and so on; so there was some practical consideration as well.)

While the early Benedictines divided their days between labor and prayer, they added reading to their requirements. It was specified that seven hours a day should be given to work, and two hours a day to reading. This requirement of reading meant that some monks spent their labors copying manuscripts (printing was not invented until the 1400s) and the writing, illustrating, and binding of the manuscripts led to the development of the craft of bookmaking. It was not long before the monasteries became centers of learning and boys were sent to them for education. Because manual labor was so important to them, it was included as part of every boy's education, along with the classical subjects.

Meanwhile, outside the monasteries, crafts were continuing to be taught father to son, and later, father to other men's sons. The craftsmen belonged to associations or guilds which established local control over each trade, and set standards for such things as workmanship and price. The guilds also regulated the training of apprentices and required that when the master took on an apprentice, he was to give him the same training as his own son. He was to instruct the boy in the skills and mysteries of the trade and give him religious and moral training. He was also required to provide housing, food, and clothes for the boy. The boy, in return, was to serve the master faithfully in the trade and in any other household tasks that were required of him. The usual apprenticeship lasted for seven years (Bennett, 1926:27).

Because there was no other schooling available at this time for the great majority, the system of apprenticeship was the primary means of acquiring a trade and along with it a rudimentary education. It also provided the opportunity for gaining a respectable position in the community.

In the 1600s when there began to be some laws providing relief for the poor in England, dependent and orphaned children were given an opportunity to become apprenticed to learn a trade (Edwards and Richey, 1963:21).

Apprenticeships were also used as a means of providing for orphans and poor children in Colonial America. The object was to make them self-supporting so they would not burden society.

In America, as in England, the masters were required by the guilds to take care of the bodily needs of their apprentices and give them instruction in religion, reading, and writing, in addition to the craft. The duties and obligations of the masters were set by the town government, however, because the guilds did not have the same status in the colonies as they did in Europe. When it became apparent that some masters were unable to provide adequate instruction in reading and writing, the state of Massachusetts passed a law requiring communities of over fifty households to appoint a teacher, and it was that 1647 law that marked the beginning of the public school system in America (Edwards and Richey, 1963:56).

The apprenticeship system had functioned very well during the Middle Ages. However, the early nineteenth century with its rapidly developing technology and the factory system of production that came with it, caused the apprenticeship system to collapse. As the small home industries became more like factories, it became difficult to maintain the same type of relationship with the apprentices. There were sometimes as many as fourteen apprentices working under a single journeyman and the work was split up. The apprentice, instead of doing the whole job, as before, worked only in the area where he was most skilled or where he was needed for production. This practice was efficient for production, but the work experience of the apprentice became very limited and tedious. At this same time, the increasing mechanization of industry caused a huge demand for unskilled laborers. Many former apprentices found it advantageous to take these jobs. They were no longer able to learn a whole trade, anyway, only one or more operations—and in the factory they would get paid for doing it.

This mechanization was probably first noticeable in the textile industry. From the beginning, textile work had been a major "cottage industry," but in the course of forty years, all of the elements necessary to bring the textiles out of the home and into the factories had evolved. The flying shuttle, the steam engine, and the spring mule were all invented, and by 1814 the whole process for producing textiles became factory-based. What had once been a woman's home industry was now a factory industry needing large numbers of cheap, unskilled laborers to keep it running.

Women and very young children were put to work in the factories and were shamefully exploited. In the 1860s, two-fifths of all persons employed in New England factories were children (Edwards and Richey, 1963:275). These children were often called apprentices, but, in fact, were not receiving any of the benefits or education that was part of the apprentice system. They were merely workers who toiled for twelve to thirteen hours a day for little pay with no chance for schooling except on Sunday. These terrible conditions were soon causing reformers to call for the regulation of the conditions and hours of work for children.

Technology was developing very rapidly. America was changing the whole continent. In 1835, de Tocqueville observed, "The Americans arrived but as yesterday . . . and they have already . . . joined the Hudson to the Mississippi and made the Atlantic Ocean communicate with the Gulf of Mexico. . . . The longest railroads which have been constructed, up to the present time are in America" (1835, 1956:216). Skilled men were urgently needed to do this work, but the long and slow apprenticeship system simply could not provide them fast enough and, therefore, America looked to Europe for skilled craftsmen.

At the time of the Industrial Revolution, the breakdown of the apprentice system was also occurring in England, Germay, and France. In each case, a system of education was collapsing and there was nothing to take its place. In England, there were some efforts made to regulate the ages and number of hours for children working in factories, and to make provisions for their schooling. Half-time schools were provided in 1844 for children age eight and older, and the children were required to attend school every other day or part of each day they worked in the factory.

The guilds in France had become corrupt and it was very expensive to "buy" an apprenticeship. Therefore, in 1791 the French government abolished the unpopular system of guilds. With no regulations, people were allowed to enter any trade they wished, provided they could obtain a license, and standards of workmanship suffered. The coming of factories further compounded the problems and it was then that France established a system of trade and technical schools as substitutes for the apprenticeship system. They also sought to regulate child labor by requiring children to attend school a certain part of each day (Bennett, 1926:276).

In Germany, the apprenticeship system was not nearly as affected as were those of England and France. Their apprenticeship system still remained firmly placed within the guilds and two systems of goods production developed; the one was based on handicrafts and small-scale production, and the other was the manufacturer with large scale production and factory workers. Apprenticeship training continued as before while a wide range of trade schools slowly developed to fill the needs not being met by the apprenticeship system.

THE NEED FOR PRACTICAL/TECHNICAL EDUCATION

In the early 1800s in the United States, private charity schools and mechanics institutes sprung up in an attempt to meet the educational needs of factory workers. The Boston Asylum and Farm School founded in 1814 was one of the earliest of the charity schools, and it provided education for orphaned boys. It provided a basic education as well as instruction in one of several trades. The mechanic's institutes and lyceums provided further education for their members in both day and night school programs. Technical institutes were also established, such as the Rensselaer Institute founded in 1824, whose purpose was to combine science and practical work for a better understanding of "the interrelationship between chemistry, natural philosophy, and mathematics on the one hand, and agriculture and mechanics on the other" (Barlow, 1967:27).

By 1870, compulsory education laws had become widespread in America, and public education was provided for all children up to the eighth grade. With all classes of children in school, it became obvious that some changes in the curriculum had to be made. Many children could not benefit from the traditional, classical education offered by the schools, and a more practical approach was sought. A strong bias for the practical and the useful in America was noted by de Tocqueville in 1835, and it is still widespread today (1835, 1956:163). People look for the practical value of education; they want to know what they will "get" for their tax dollars. Some of the criticisms of the middle nineteenth century common school curriculum were that it was too "bookish"; it stressed words rather than ideas and there was too little activity. It was also felt, that schools should differentiate between skill and knowledge, and should recognize that skill needed to be practiced. The useful parts of arithmetic should be taught, while skills in composition should replace the grammar. Plain and rapid penmanship should prevail and the "fancy flourishes" should be omitted. It was believed that if such reforms as these were instituted there would be time for teaching the natural sciences and other such things that intelligent working men should know (Barlow, 1967:31).

Around the time of the Civil War, there developed widespread recognition of the need to supplement classical education with education in science and technology. It was an industrial America and complex skills were needed to run it. First, agricultural groups, and later, industrial groups, began to pressure legislators for professional schools of agriculture and the mechanic arts.

Turner was one of the significant leaders in the effort to establish these schools. His plan (Wirth, 1972:6) called for new colleges "designed to help people cope with scientific-technological reality." He based his arguments on the belief that society was divided into two distinct classes. The first, "a small class whose business is to teach the true principles of religion, law, medicine, science, art, and literature, and a much larger class who are engaged in some form of labor in agriculture, commerce, and the arts."

These two classes were called the professional class and the industrial class. Turner felt that 95 percent of the people would be in the industrial class and should have schools to help them understand their work. The type of schools he proposed related the sciences and practical experimental research in agriculture, and the research that would have been generated was to form the basis for an industrial literature. They were also supposed to produce teachers qualified to teach the new curriculum. In short, they were to serve the working classes in the same way the colleges and professional schools had always served the professional classes (Wirth, 1972:6).

Through the efforts of reformers such as Turner, the Morrill Act, establishing land grant colleges was signed into law by President Lincoln in 1862. The goal of these new land grant colleges was to teach subjects related to agriculture and mechanic arts in order to promote the liberal and practical education of the industrial classes. They were aimed at increasing the intelligence of the common people and, thereby, improving the industrial pursuits of the nation (Barlow, 1967:32). The legislation did not specify how its goals should be met however, so the colleges were slow to progress while all kinds of educational questions were debated concerning the curriculum and the manner in which the colleges would operate. One approach was to remove all theoretical study from the curriculum and emphasize the workshop. Under this plan, real work situations were simulated and saleable products were produced. This workshop approach remained with the vocational education movement, but never really took hold in the land grant colleges. The colleges did want to gain stature however, so the tendency was to educate industrial leaders, rather than provide the narrow, practical programs needed by the industrial workers (Fisher, 1967:59).

The schools of engineering were also being established at this time, and seemed to follow the trend of educating the leaders rather than the working men. The Rensselaer Institute trained teachers for the sons and daughters of mechanics when it first began. The classes involved laboratory work as well as demonstrations at nearby farms and shops. By the 1830s, however, the needs of the country were great for trained engineers to do surveying and to build the roads, bridges, and railroads. Because there were few available, Rensselaer began to offer specialized courses in civil engineering and surveying. Rensselaer took as a model the French technical schools, and attempted to provide architects and civil engineers with an education that was both technical and liberal. The number of engineering schools increased rapidly during this period, from five engineering schools in 1860, to approximately eighty-five in 1880 (Fisher, 1967:61).

THE MANUAL TRAINING MOVEMENT

One offshoot of the movement to train engineers was the development of the Manual Training Movement. This came about when John O. Runkle of

MIT and Calvin Woodward of Washington University, who were developing programs to train engineers, discovered that the engineering students lacked rudimentary skills in the use of tools and knowledge of basic mechanics. They were impressed by the methods used by Victor Della Vos, director of the Imperial Technical School of Moscow, which were demonstrated at the Philadelphia Centennial Exposition in 1876. Besides grading projects according to the difficulty of skill, the basic mechanical skills and principles were taught separately from the actual construction of products in the Russian system. This was quite different from the usual American apprenticeship method of instruction, which emphasized specific skill training (Wirth, 1972:10). Woodward had been operating a similar program at the O'Fallon Polytechnical Institute at Washington University. He was head of the Manual Training School there and acclaim given the Russian demonstration gave him the confidence to develop his own program further (Fisher, 1967:68). Woodward felt that manual training would have value to anyone wishing to advance in an industrial society.

Runkle also thought that manual training had implications for general education and should be offered to everyone at all levels of education. He felt this could help restore the dignity of labor, satisfy the demand for skilled labor, ease the conflict between capitol and labor, and aid the development of industries (Fisher, 1967:67). Putting his philosophy to work, Runkle not only developed a new engineering program, but opened a secondary grade school for grammar school students who could qualify. He gave Woodward a great deal of support in his endeavors, but there existed great opposition to the inclusion of manual training in the school curriculum.

E.E. White, then president of Purdue University, thought that some elements of technical knowledge which were clearly of general application could be taught in the schools, but he was firm in his belief that the trades should not be taught in public schools. He saw it as industry subverting the schools to its own use and considered that type of technical education to be a "potential threat to the intellect." He did not believe everyone should learn a trade, as it would crowd the trades and thereby reduce the wages of skilled workers. Furthermore, he felt it would take away from the hard-won education provided the children of the working man who were the ones generally attending the public schools at that time (Barlow, 1967:37).

William T. Harris, U.S. Commissioner of Education from 1889 to 1906, was another prominent detractor of the industrial education movement. He said on numerous occasions, that he had "no patience for those who advocate industrial education at the expense of general education now given in the common school." Although there does not seem to be any evidence that the proponents of industrial education ever intended to do any more than supplement the traditional curriculum, Harris and others persisted in the belief that the traditional curriculum was being threatened. He felt it was preposterous that manual training could be educative in the same sense that arithmetic, geography, grammar, and the natural sciences were educative.

The debate continued for about twenty years, but by the 1900s more and more pressures were coming to bear on the schools to include manual training in their curriculum. There were many, Woodward among them, pressing for the broadening of the curriculum based on the needs of the country for technical training as well as the needs of the students for meaningful studies. Also, private academies and trade schools were springing up everywhere in competition with the high schools to provide people with the practical courses they wanted. This competition eased the way for business and other elective courses to be offered in the high schools. Educators, philosophers, settlement workers, and laborers were also urging a modification of the curriculum, as was the National Association of Manufacturers.

The National Association of Manufacturers (NAM) was established in 1895 and one of its goals was to encourage the schools to teach the skills needed by the new industries. They thought that if American industry was to compete worldwide, more attention had to be given to teaching scientific and technical knowledge. They felt this was so important that money should be diverted from the mainstream of education and put into commercial and technical schools. They based their demands on the idea that industry provided jobs for people so that whatever benefited industry, in turn, benefited the people (Wirth, 1972:23).

The NAM had just struggled out of the 1893-1894 depression and regarded trade unions as their major enemy. They charged the unions with making apprenticeships obsolete and urged the establishment of trade schools. The schools they had in mind were not concerned with developing the "whole child," nor were they the polytechnical schools which provided higher technical knowledge, but rather, trade schools which produced skilled mechanics. They were narrow in scope, and would train workers with those skills needed by industry. At first, the American Federation of Labor (A F of L) was totally opposed to the NAM suggestion of trade schools. They saw the movement as an effort to produce strike-breakers and half-trained workers. They continued instead, to work on their apprenticeship program.

Several of the local unions within the printers union had tried classroom instruction and correspondence work and felt it to be helpful. The object was to broaden the array of skills possessed by the working man and make his chances for advancement better. However, at the national level, little support was given until the NAM established the National Society for the Promotion of Industrial Education. This group was regarded as dangerous by the A F of L, because the type of education it proposed was very narrow and it did not encourage the betterment of oneself. So, in 1907, the A F of L established a position supporting an industrial education that would provide "the best opportunities for the most complete industrial and technical education obtainable for prospective applicants for admission into the skilled crafts of this country, particularly as regards the full possibilities of such crafts to the end that such applicants be fitted not only for all usual requirements, but also for the highest supervisory duties, responsibilities and rewards" (Fisher, 1967:125).

In addition, the A F of L recommended compulsory education for all children until age sixteen, so that they might more fully develop. During that time, they would be given the education that would allow them to advance in industry. This concern for mobility in industry was an element of all A F of L proposals though it varied in intensity from time to time. Business of course, had little interest in mobility; they were concerned mainly with specific trade training.

While organized labor did not fully agree with the directions being taken by the industrial education movement, they did join with the other divergent groups pressing for federal legislation to support it. They felt they could cooperate with the educators and most likely have a strong voice in shaping it more to their interests.

In the early 1900s the state of Massachusetts included public-supported manual training and drawing as part of their public school curriculum. They also established a commission in 1905 to determine the feasibility of establishing industrial schools in the state. The commission subsequently reported that there was great support for vocational education among the people of the state, and recommended establishing a broadened industrial education program (Fisher, 1967:128).

The NAM whose primary goal for education was to provide trained workmen for their businesses, based much of their plan for schooling on the German continuation schools. These continuation schools provided part-time education for young people who were employed, and were between fourteen and eighteen years old. The trade skill learning was done in industrial shops instead of in the schools, so the continuation schools did not cost the public school system very much to run. The German schools were run to service the state, however, and were socially restrictive in that they perpetuated class lines (Wirth, 1972:35). While these schools were attractive in many ways, the underlying philosophy was not suitable for America with its democratic ideal of social mobility.

The labor movement on the other hand, while slow to develop a plan and take an established stand, moved in the direction of encouraging social and economic mobility. At first, they were wary of placing industrial education in public schools because they were uncertain of teachers' attitudes toward labor unions and children of working people. Organized labor finally took the position that if the training of industrial workers was a public necessity then such training should be a part of public education, and labor and others must guard against undue influence and control by industrialists (Wirth, 1972:55).

While labor and management positions were being developed, educational leaders and social reformers were also tackling the problem. John Dewey, Charles Prosser, and David Snedden played significant roles in revising the school curriculum. They all wanted to make schooling more meaningful for the majority, and they wanted the curriculum to include more courses of a technological nature. Their ideas about the ways to accomplish these goals were different, however. The concern of Snedden and Prosser was for vocational education for "social efficiency," while Dewey promoted vocational education as a liberalizing force (Wirth, 1972:159). This notion of social efficiency closely parallelled the NAM's position that vocational education should be oriented toward specific trade training.

Snedden, whose background was in sociology saw the need for differentiated education directed at the "probable destinies" of the different children. He also argued that "human beings fell into the ability levels which paralleled the hierarchical work requirements of modern society. With the aid of new social science intruments, people could be identified and channeled into training that would benefit society and fulfill the individual" (Wirth, 1972:155).

Charles Prosser, a student of Snedden and a follower of his social efficiency philosophy, felt that the purpose of vocational education was to help a person secure a job. He believed that vocational education courses should not be taught by general educators and that vocational education should remain separate from general education (Wirth, 1972:164).

John Dewey rejected the philosophy of Snedden and Prosser and fought against the idea that what was good for industry was good for the people. He wanted to use industry to make schooling more active and more meaningful to students instead of making the schools an adjunct of industry. He thought narrow trade training should be rejected as it was not an "educational experience"; instead he felt education should provide the skills and attitudes for living in an era of science and technology. He was aware that science and technology could either enrich life or debase it and hoped that if the entire population was made technologically aware, they would be able to evaluate the effects of industrial developments. He wanted to train people to challenge the distortions of the system, not simply equip them to meet its needs. Technology was too powerful a force to be set loose without careful social monitoring (Wirth, 1972: ch. 8–10).

INITIAL FEDERAL FUNDING

The many diverse groups interested in having industrial education included in the school curriculum coalesced to form the National Society for the

Promotion of Industrial Education (NSPIE) in 1906. This national pressure group was instrumental in persuading congress to authorize the President to appoint a Commission on National Aid to Vocational Education. The commission, approved in January of 1914, included representatives from congress, labor, and education. According to the Panel of Consultants Report (1964) it was their task to "consider the subject of national aid to vocational education and report their findings and recommendations no later than June 1, next."

In order to do this, the commission set out to answer six basic questions:

(1) To what extent is there a need for vocational education in the United States?
(2) Is there a need for national grants stimulating the States to give vocational education?
(3) What kinds or forms of vocational education should be stimulated by national grants?
(4) How far can the Federal Government aid through expert knowledge vocational education in various States?
(5) To what extent should the Federal Government aid the States through national grants for vocational education?
(6) Under what conditions should grants to the States for vocational education be made? (Panel of Consultants, 1964:20)

After six months of study, the commission's report pointed out the need for a variety of vocational education experiences, but centered their attention on providing vocational education for those common occupations where the greatest numbers of workers were employed. The following quote from the Panel of Vocational Consultants Report (1964) describes the need for vocational education as reported by the commission:

There is a great and crying need of providing vocational education of this character for every part of the United States—to conserve and develop our resources; to promote a more productive and prosperous agriculture; to prevent the waste of human labor; to supplement apprenticeship; to increase the wage-earning power of our productive workers; to meet the increasing demand for trained workmen; to offset the increased cost of living. Vocational education is therefore needed as a wise business investment for this Nation, because our national prosperity and happiness are at stake and our position in the markets of the world cannot otherwise be maintained (Panel of Consultants, 1964:21).

By 1912, Prosser had become the executive secretary of the NSPIE. He promoted a dual system of education where vocational education would be administered by those who understood the world of work, and he promoted narrow trade training. Prosser's position with the NSPIE made him a powerful political force, and it is generally accepted that he was the author of the Smith-Hughes Act, the first major piece of legislation in support of vocational education (Wirth, 1972:162). The Act prescribed specific programs, spelled out administration procedures, and resulted in a vocational education effort concentrating on a narrow range of skill training reflective of the Snedden philosophy.

In February 1917, with the need for increased military production looming overhead, Senate Bill 703, later to become the Smith-Hughes Act (PL64-347) was signed by President Wilson and it remained virtually unaltered until 1963. The provisions of the Smith-Hughes Act called for a Federal Board of Vocational Education which was directly responsible for administering the act. That board was comprised of the Secretaries of Agriculture, Commerce, and Labor, the Commissioner of Education, and three citizens representing agriculture, manufacturing, and commerce. It reported directly to congress. In addition, each state was required to create a state board for vocational education which would prepare a state plan for vocational education describing the program to be provided, the course of study, the methods of instruction, and the schools and equipment. The plan was also to include the qualifications of the teachers and supervisors, and the plans for those training teachers. An annual report showing the funds received, expended, and the services provided was also required.

INDUSTRIAL EDUCATION AS GENERAL EDUCATION

All of the supporters of industrial education were not supporters of the narrow specialized type of trade training that received Federal funding through the Smith-Hughes Act. Many people were still convinced of the importance of including industrial education in general education and they continued to develop programs for doing this. This type of program was unfunded for the most part, but it was also unfettered by rigid Federal guidelines, and had freedom to develop and evolve.

The Manual Training Program begun by Woodward in 1880 was the first stage in the development of a broad-based program of industrial education. The goal was to train the whole boy, not to train mechanics. Woodward's own explanation of his program follows:

> We teach banking, not because we expect our pupils to become bankers; and we teach drawing, not because we expect to train architects or artists or engineers; and we teach the use of tools, the properties of materials, and the methods of the arts, not because we expect our boys to become artisans. We teach them the United States Constitution and some of the Acts of Congress not because we expect them all to

become congressmen. But we do expect that our boys will at least have something to do with bankers, and architects, and artists, and engineers, and artisans; and we expect all to become good citizens. Our great object is educational: other objects are secondary. That industrial results will surely follow, I have not the least doubt; but they will take care of themselves. Just as a love for the beautiful follows a love for the true, and as the high arts cannot thrive except on the firm foundation of the low ones, so a higher and finer development of all industrial standards is sure to follow a rational study of the underlying principles and methods. Every object of attention put into the schoolroom should be put there for two reasons—one educational, the other economic. Training, culture, skill come first; knowledge about persons, things, places, customs, tools, methods, comes second. It is only by securing both objects that the pupil gains the great prize, which is power to deal successfully with the men, things, and activities which surround him (Olson, 1963:3).

This program found its way into a great many high schools and held its place well into the 1920s. Eventually, some weaknesses of the Manual Training Program were brought out, primarily that it was not liberal enough for general education, and that it ignored the relationship with the sciences. Another criticism was that it did not preserve hand skills or concern itself with aesthetic design in the making of projects and models. This latter criticism was reflective of the growing interest in arts and crafts at this period, and the fear that machine production would cause handwork and artistry to be forgotten (Olson, 1963:4).

In 1919, a group of people expressing these concerns and wishing to modify industrial education began a movement termed the Manual Arts Movement, headed by Charles A. Bennett. It was the second stage in the development of a broad-based industrial education program. In his book *The Manual Arts,* Bennett described his proposal for a manual arts program in public schools. He was concerned with the effect of the development of industry on life and wrote the following:

A very important result of this development in the industries is the need of men with a wider knowledge of the materials and processes of industry and the principles upon which the processes and the use of the materials rest. This knowledge is not being handed down from father to son to any great extent, nor from master to apprentice, partly because the factory system does not easily lend itself to education and partly because the knowledge needed is so new that even the masters themselves find it difficult to keep up with the development. But this need for a wider knowledge of the principles and processes of industry is not confined to the workers in these producing industries. Every man who would intelligently use the modern conveniences of his own home, or the labor-saving devices and conveniences of business life, must know something of the materials and principles of industry; and if he is to have any adequate appreciation of the product—if he is to judge the quality of the thing he purchases or uses, he must know something of the process that produced it. In fact, industrial development has been so rapid and so varied in our country—it has affected every man's life to such an extent that if he is to retain sufficient mastery of his environment to make it serve his needs, he is forced to acquire considerable practical knowledge of the materials, principles and processes of industry. And if the school is to furnish it, the school must be equipped with the tools of industry (Olson, 1963:4).

Bennett suggested that the subjects taught in manual arts should be based on a survey of industry, and he recommended graphic arts, plastic arts, textile arts, mechanic arts, and bookmaking arts as being fundamental to civilization, and therefore, justified in being included in the school program.

Industrial arts, according to Olson (1963:5) is the third stage in the evolution of shop work as general education in the public schools, and it is the one industrial education program which is part of general education in most American schools today. It differs from manual arts and manual training by emphasizing the broad aspects of industry as opposed to just the manipulative. Laboratory activities are centered on the development of the individual pupil as opposed to the "project" in manual arts or the mandated exercises in manual training. Further clarification of the goals of industrial arts education has evolved, and examples of these may be found in the writings of Bonser and Mossman (1925); Olson (1963); Wilber and Pendered (1973); Maley (1973).

Support for industrial arts as part of general education came from the 1945 Harvard Committee Report on General Education in a Free Society. The committee wrote that "direct contact with materials, the manipulation of simple tools, the capacity to create by hand from a concept in the mind—all these are indispensable aspects of the general education of everyone" (Wilber and Pendered, 1973:15). Conant (1960), in his book *Education in the Junior High School Years,* also supported industrial arts with his statement that "all girls should receive instruction in home economics and all boys, instruction in industrial arts" (Wilber and Pendered, 1973:15).

Support for industrial arts in general education today is founded on the realization that not only has the world become increasingly technical and industrial, but industry has become more complex. It is difficult for the average person to comprehend the organization, products, processes, and occupations in industry. It is, therefore, up to the schools to give every student the opportunity and background to gain that understanding (Wilber and Pendered, 1973:16). John Dewey expressed a similar view of the relationship of men to technology in the early 1900s. Perhaps it was overshadowed by the tumultuous events of the intervening years, but in any case, it is a need that is still largely unmet today.

RECENT VOCATIONAL EDUCATION LEGISLATION

The Smith-Hughes Act, signed in 1917, remained intact and unamended until 1963, although by then it had become quite apparent that the vocational education system had significant shortcomings for the America of the 1960s.

According to Wirth (1972:163), "the great strength of the Smith-Hughes Act was that it was designed directly to meet a compelling need of America— the need to provide American industry with complicated work skills required in a technological society." Technically skilled persons were provided in two world wars and in an economy where unprecedented technological growth spurred the economy to new heights and produced a standard of living unmatched in the world. However, there were two problems with the legislation: (1) it had not kept up with the fast changing economy, and (2) it concentrated its efforts on the job requirements of industry, and ignored the needs of various segments of the population.

The Vocational Act of 1963 (PL88-210) made an attempt to update vocational education, and provide the mechanisms for correcting the deficiencies seen by modern critics. It provided for a system of vocational education that would meet the needs of a broader spectrum of youth, and it also provided education more suitable for the changing technology. President Johnson signed the bill on December 18, 1963. His remarks made at the signing summarize quite well the intent and major provisions of the bill.

Modern demands upon labor and industry require new skills and an upgrading of old skills, require more education and greater knowledge. It has been said that we need over 100,000 technicians a year just to meet our needs in the engineering field alone but all of our present programs combined, we are told, turn out a maximum not of 100,000 a year but only 20,000 technicians a year. We believe that this new law will help close this gap. Under this law high school students will be encouraged to stay in school. If they need financial assistance, they may receive it under a work and study program.

For the first time Federal funds are going to be available to construct new vocational schools. Demonstration and research projects authorized under this law will vastly improve the quality of our vocational training. Where there is severe unemployment and high numbers of school dropouts, special experimental programs of residential vocational education schools are authorized.

Finally, the extension of the program of aid to schools and districts affected by Federal activities will permit a continuation of Federal assistance where we have a special responsibility. I believe that this measure, together with a Manpower Development and Training Act, places us in a position to make a major attack on one of the most important obstacles to economic growth and productivity. It is a reaffirmation of our conviction that education is the cornerstone of our freedom.

Significant changes were seen in vocational education as a result of this act. There were major increases in the size, number, and breadth of offerings of vocational schools, expanded opportunities for youth with special needs, increased interaction of youth with the real world of work through cooperative work programs, an extended training program for adults which would either upgrade their skills, or retrain them. It also provided for the development of a large number of innovative programs aimed at providing industrial-vocational education for the present as well as the future. The 1963 act laid the groundwork for a broader-based vocational program in the public schools. Five years later, the amendments to it further expanded its provisions to promote guidance and counseling for students. The 1968 amendments also made provisions for contracting for services, to be provided by private institutions, when they could be provided at less cost. Probably the most important and far-reaching provision was the extension of special needs considerations to include the modification of vocational education programs to accommodate the student with special needs.

The Vocational Education Section (Title II) of the Education Amendments of 1976 (PL94-482) became law on October 12, 1976. The major purpose of this act was to extend and revise the Vocational Education Act of 1963. The 1976 act provided for basic grants in continuing vocational education, work study, cooperative vocational education, and extended the grants to new programs in energy education. It also supported efforts to eliminate sex bias in the curriculum, provided special support services for women who enter programs traditionally limited to men, provided day-care services for children of persons enrolled in vocational programs, and gave support to programs in industrial arts education.

The 1917 Smith-Hughes Act provided for evaluation and reporting. However the data reported were not always useful since the system for gathering and reporting was not prescribed in detail. The 1963 Vocational Educational Act, its 1968 amendments, and the 1976 VEA Section of PL94-482 greatly expanded federal efforts to determine the effect of the monies spent. The later evaluation efforts led to: (1) a National Advisory Council on Vocational

Education to review all vocational education programs, (2) a specific reporting and record-keeping system ordered by the commissioner, (3) specific sums of money set aside for services to provide for evaluation at the state and local level, (4) third party evaluation through the Office of Planning, Budgeting, and Evaluation, (5) the Government Accounting Office assessment and report, (6) a National Advisory Council on Vocational Education multiyear study producing "Project Baseline," (7) National Institute of Education evaluations, (8) development of a National Vocational Education Data System, (9) grants for monitoring sex fairness, and (10) a committee made up of representatives from National Institute of Education, US Office of Education, National Center for Educational Statistics and Labor whose task is to coordinate vocational research and evaluation activities. Further explanation and discussion of the history of evaluation and assessment in vocational education can be found in Datta's (1979) presentation in this book.

IN SUMMARY

In this chapter, we have seen that industrial education has been closely interwoven with many of the important social and economic changes in our history. We have seen how the economic need for skilled craftsmen led to the development of the apprenticeship system as a training program for trades, and how it was later broadened to include parental care and schooling. We have also seen the way this system was extended to meet the social need of providing for the poor and lower classes, and how this eventually led to the development of public schools in America. The coming of factories during the industrial revolution made the apprenticeship system obsolete as the sole means of training craftsmen, and public and private schools took on the training task.

We have seen some of the forces that have come into play as the curriculum has been hammered out, especially the needs of industry versus the needs of individuals, and the accommodations that have been made to meet those needs. We have seen how the federal government has stepped in with money to fund this area when it felt it was in the best interest of the country to do so, and more often than not the interests of the government have paralleled the interests of industry. In more recent legislation, there has been some movement toward developing our human resources, from the standpoint of maximizing the potential of the individual, rather than simply providing a work force for the industrial establishment.

While we have seen two diametrically opposed programs of industrial education develop—the narrow specialized trade training on the one hand, and the broad technological awareness programs on the other, we have also seen in the most recent legislation, a recognition of the need for both. There continues to be a great concern for the development of skilled, knowledge-able people able to fill the country's industrial needs, but there is now a greater recognition by industrial educators of the need to build a broader base of knowledge and skill so that the individual will be better able to function in this technological society, and to adapt to the wide variety of changes that will inevitably take place.

REFERENCES

Barlow, M. L. 1967. *History of Industrial Education in the United States.* Peoria, IL: Chas. A. Bennett.

Bennett, C. A. 1926. *History of Manual and Industrial Education Up to 1870.* Peoria, IL: Chas. A. Bennett.

——— 1937. *History of Manual and Industrial Education 1870-1917.* Peoria, IL: Chas. A. Bennett.

Bonser, F. G., and Mossman, L. C. 1925. *Industrial Arts for Elementary Schools.* New York: Macmillan.

Conant, J. B. 1960. *Recommendations for Education in the Junior High School: A Memorandum to School Boards.* Princeton, N.J.: Educational Testing Service.

de Tocqueville, A. 1956. *Democracy in America.* R. D. Heffner (ed. and trans.). New York: New American Library. (originally published in 1835)

Edwards, N., and Richey, H. G. 1963. *The School in the American Social Order.* 2nd ed. Boston: Houghton Mifflin.

Fisher, B. M. 1967. *Industrial Education–American Ideals and Institutions.* Madison: University of Wisconsin Press.

Maley, D. 1973. *The Maryland Plan.* New York: Bruce.

Olson, D. W. 1963. *Industrial Arts and Technology.* Englewood Cliffs, NJ: Prentice-Hall.

Panel of Consultants on Vocational Education. 1964. *Education For a Changing World of Work.* Washington, DC: Government Printing Office.

Wilber, G. O., and Pendered, N. C. 1973. *Industrial Arts in General Education.* 4th ed. New York: Intex.

Wirth, A. G. 1972. *Education in the Technological Society.* New York: Intex.

BETTER LUCK THIS TIME
From Federal
Legislation to Practice
in Evaluating
Vocational Education

chapter 2

LOIS-ELLIN DATTA | *National Institute of Education*

The 1976 Vocational Education Amendments are unusually prescriptive in defining federal roles in vocational education evaluation: establishing a need, assuring funds are spent as intended, and galvanizing program improvement and redirection. This chapter examines (1) how these three federal roles developed and why the legislation is so directive; and (2) the factors that influence the ability (resources) and willingness (political agreement) necessary to carry out these functions in federal, state and local evaluations.

Two themes underlie this analysis. The first theme is that evaluation requirements reflect congressional belief that the executive branch, state and local agencies need prodding to keep up with the times and to respond to the needs of diverse groups of citizens. As Hechinger (1977) saw the tensions among federal, state and local education agencies:

> Control of suburban schools is passing from local school boards to state and Federal governments and teachers' unions. Local governments now pay less than half the education costs and most local funds must also be spent in ways that satisfy a growing number of regulations, standards and restrictions imposed by legislatures, state and Federal agencies, the unions, and increasingly, the courts . . . many of these were a necessary

AUTHOR'S NOTE: *Opinions expressed are the author's. Endorsement by the National Institute of Education is not implied. Helpful critiques of earlier versions of this chapter were generously given by Deborah Bonnet, Ralph Bregman, Robert Harris, Bill Stevenson, and Carol Tittle.*

response to local deficiencies, even irresponsibilities. It is doubtful that teachers' qualifications or academic programs would have been upgraded without state certificate or mandates for minimum instruction. Nothing in the history of American education suggests that most local school districts would have addressed the needs of the disadvantaged or handicapped children without prodding or funding by the Federal government. . . . Yet to abandon the concept of local options because of local failings is comparable to advocating abolition of the Federal government because of its' deficiencies. It is not accident that the framers of the Constitution omitted education as Federal responsibility. They did so not because they valued education less, but because they trusted local responsibility more.

The second theme is that the greatest problems for implementing vocational education evaluation requirements arise from limitations in the state of the art, while the greatest reason for expecting that the new requirements will be met is that achieving these also holds promise for meeting the common educational interests of federal, state and local agencies. If this argument is sound, the picture is at least modestly bright for achieving congressional intent for vocational education evaluations.

THE FIRST FEDERAL EVALUATION ROLE: GATHERING INFORMATION TO ESTABLISH NATIONAL NEEDS

The Constitution, as Hechinger noted, does not establish a federal role in education. Federal involvement can be justified, however, by a national need which could not be met by state or local resources. Facts and figures help prove a national need, and congress sees to it that such data are collected. If needs assessment is considered as part of the evaluation process, then the first federal role in educational evaluation was gathering such information. The origin and fortunes of an 1867 U.S. Department of Education whose missions included establishing needs, disseminating effective innovative practices, and achieving educational equity make almost contemporary reading.

In 1855, Henry Barnard began publishing the *American Journal of Education*, a periodical devoted exclusively to the history, discussion, and statistics of systems, institutions, and methods of education. A year later, Barnard proposed that the Smithsonian Institution or some other agency appoint an official to devote himself exclusively to the increase and diffusion of knowledge on the subject of education. When "An Act to Establish a Department of Education" passed in 1867, the first section defined the purpose of the new agency as "collecting such statistics and facts as shall show the condition and progress of education in the several states and territories, and diffusing such information respecting the organization and management of schools and school systems, and methods of teaching as shall aid the people of the United States in the establishment of efficient school systems." (Cronbach and Suppes, 1969:31). Barnard was appointed the first director of the Department of Education.

The department had a tempestuous beginning. Clark (1974) reports that on July 20, 1868, less than two months after the director submitted his first annual report to congress, the appropriation to the new agency was reduced from $12,000 per year to $9,400, and the appropriations act further undercut the status of the agency by reassigning it as an office in the Department of the Interior. Unable to restore congressional confidence in the new department and faced with rising criticism, Barnard resigned after serving less than two years, and a new director was appointed.

One of Barnard's successors, John Tigert (1924:196), commented:

> It is clear that the expectations of some Congressional advocates of the Department of Education were not realized. It is no wonder. In fulsome speeches, it had been proclaimed that the Department of Education would exert a powerful influence to enlighten the mass of ignorance in the nation, particularly among the freedmen of the South. Two years passed, and the Commissioner of Education with his three clerks had failed to cause the enlightenment of the four million freedmen or to show any appreciable reduction in the sum total of ignorance in the country at large. It was disappointing to the enthusiasts and the reaction had its natural effect.

In the next decades, the Office of Education surveyed colleges, universities, secondary schools, black higher education, teacher training, and school finance. These studies were carried out by national office personnel, rather than through research funds dispersed to educational investigators. National activities until 1945 seldom ventured beyond the information gathering responsibilities assigned to the department in the Education Act of 1867, yet they contributed to development of federal support for education, establishing national needs outside state and local borders.

This federal information-gathering role continues in the National Center for Educational Statistics (NCES), which since 1974 reports to the Assistant Secretary for Education. NCES studies related to vocational education include:

(1) *Studies of learners:* NCES prepares annual reports on student characteristics and enrollments at all levels and for all types of education, including vocational education. The NCES-directed National Longitudinal Study of the Class of 1972 examines the initial status and

subsequent experiences of students who were high school seniors in 1972.

(2) *Studies of what they learn:* The National Assessment of Educational Progress (NAEP) collects data on the educational achievements of large, nationally representative samples. NAEP tests competencies of persons from primary school age through adulthood in science, reading, writing, arithmetic, citizenship, the arts, consumer knowledge, and career preparation. The surveys are repeated at five to seven year intervals providing a national report on the stability, improvement, or decline of knowledge.

Most NCES studies permit comparisons of students enrolled in general, academic and vocational curricula. Designed to give a reliable national picture of educational progress and national need, they cannot be used for accountability evaluation for schools, school districts, or states.

THE SECOND FEDERAL EVALUATION ROLE: ACCOUNTABILITY FOR LEGAL EXPENDITURE OF FUNDS

The federal role in accountability in vocational education began with the 1917 Smith-Hughes Act. This act was the result of almost eleven years of lobbying, studies, and reports that rationalized a need for a national program to prepare trained industrial, technical, and agricultural workers. The basic proposition was that the states, whose schools were academically oriented, could not satisfy this demand (Commission on National Aid to Vocational Education, 1914). Also, the gathering strength of labor unions led to enforcement of the school attendance requirements which some states had enacted as early as 1860. As adults supplanted child laborers in the factories, the acceptability of universal education programs for the presumably non-college-bound children of workers increased (Hawkins et al., 1951; Grotberg, 1976). Serving this different population became a stimulus for educational reform, or at least to philosophizing about new methods for education.

Even in this first act, the federal government did not put the money on the stump and run. An annual report was required for each state recipient of federal aid. The state board report, to be sent to the national board administering the state grants-in-aid, was to include information on the management of the grant, student enrollment in each of the three authorized areas (home economics, agriculture, trades and industries), and data on where the money had gone in purchasing services. Congress was particularly interested in how much nonfederal money was spent on vocational education because the first purpose of the act was to expand the number of vocational education programs.

The chronology below lists some milestones in federal support for vocational education, showing expansion of service and of evaluation. Among the legislative trends were (1) proliferation from 1917 to 1963 of funds designated for training in specific occupations such as practical nursing, fishery work, and defense-related skills and trades, (2) the dispersion of occupational training authorization among several pieces of legislation which resulted in the development of independent, competing education-provider constituencies in the education, commerce, labor, and agriculture departments, and (3) the growing focus on vocational education for groups such as the handicapped, bilingual persons, racial minorities, unemployed, and the underemployed. The vocational education program was initially intended to stimulate the states (SEAs) and local education agencies (LEAs) to use their own tax revenues to prepare skilled personnel for an industrial system seen as threatened with an undersupply of technically trained workers. Later, the vocational education program acquired a purpose of preventing unemployment in times of economic recession and a mission of achieving equity in economic status among groups with special needs.

Chronology of the Development of the Federal Role in Vocational and Technical Education

Date	Event
1906	Formation of the National Society for the Promotion of Vocational Education
January 1914	Congress creates the Commission on National Aid to Vocational Education
June 1914	Commission report recommends federal grants-in-aid to stimulate states to provide vocational education preparing workers for common occupations employing the greatest number of skilled persons
1917	Smith-Hughes Act (PL 64-347) provides $7.2 million annually to promote vocational education in agriculture, trade and industrial education, and home economics in public secondary schools. Purpose is meeting short-term needs for labor. Act to be administered by a Federal Board for Vocational Education responsible directly to congress. Board consists of the Secretaries of Agriculture, Commerce and Labor, the Commissioner of Education and three citizens representing agriculture, manufacturing and commerce. States are required to create State Boards for vocational education; to prepare a state plan showing programs to be provided, schools and equipment, courses of study,

methods of instruction, qualifications of teachers and supervisors, and plans for teacher training. States required to make an annual report to the Federal Board showing work done during the year, receipt and expenditure of funds.

1927   Full authorizations ($8 million) are appropriated for agriculture, trades and industry, home economics, and teacher training.

1936   George-Dean Act (PL 74-673). Adds authorization for distributive education. Annual total authorization, $14 million.

1946   George-Barden Act (PL 79-586). Adds support for two youth organizations (Future Farmers of America and New Farmers of America). Funds for distributive education limited to support of part-time and evening classes for employed workers.

1946   Heath amendments. Add authorization for practical nurse training.

1958   National Defense Education Act (PL 85-864), Title VIII, Area Vocational Education Programs. Adds programs to train skilled technicians in recognized occupations necessary to the national defense.

1961   Area Redevelopment Act (PL 87-27). Adds funds for vocational education for unemployed and underemployed persons living in economically distressed areas to be identified by the Department of Commerce. Persons served to be selected through the Department of Labor. Office of Education grantees may contract with private institutions to provide training.

1962   Manpower Development and Training Act (PL 87-415). Office of Education grantees are to provide training to unemployed persons referred through the Department of Labor. Vocational education appropriations under all acts in force total $79 million.

1963   Vocational Education Act (PL 88-210). Act broadens goals to development of human potential, long-term employment; changes vocational education's purpose from training people in selected occupations to serving the occupational training or retraining needs of persons of all ages in all communities. Strengthens local responsibilities to provide vocational education which is "realistic in the light of actual or anticipated opportunities and which is suited to these persons' needs, interests and ability to benefit from such training," utilizing a variety of educational resources. Adds service to persons with special needs who could not succeed in regular vocational programs and adds research, curriculum development and demonstration authority; establishes program for part-time employment for youth who need the money to stay in school.

Includes requirements for periodic review of vocational education programs and laws, and 1966 appointment of a commission to review program quality. Division of Vocational and Technical Education in USOE reorganized to administer the law, provided with evaluation staff to work directly with the assistant commissioner and with the National Advisory Council on Vocational Education. NACVE directed to review the administration and status of vocational education programs.

1963   The 1963 act required (1) states to conform to record-keeping and reporting procedures specified by the Commissioner of Education, (2) states to evaluate their own performance periodically and report annually to the USOE and NACVE, (3) at least 3 percent of state allotments to be used for ancillary services to assure quality, including periodic evaluation of state and local vocational education programs and services in light of information regarding current and projected manpower needs and opportunities.

Also authorized were funds for research and training (Part C), curriculum development (Part I), and demonstration programs (Part D). Under the first provision (Part C), research coordinating units (RCUs) were authorized, whose role included improving evaluations. All Part C and D funds were allocated on a state formula basis, with half spent at the state's discretion and half at the commissioner's.

1968   Amendments. Expanded definition of vocational education, blurring the distinction between academic and vocational studies, required comprehensive planning, strengthened leadership roles of SACVEs and NACVEs through independent staffs, budgets and authorities. Required a separate SACVE in each state. Detailed state planning mandatory. Amendments also (1) tied funds to performance, (2) encouraged SACVEs to use independent funds for third party evaluations of program effectiveness, administration and operations, (3) authorized state boards to use SACVE evaluations for reporting requirements, and (4) required NACVE to conduct independent evaluations of programs.

1970   USOE reorganizes. All evaluation staff and funds centralized in the Office of Planning, Budgeting, and Evaluation (OPBE). OPBE begins third party, national evaluations of USOE programs, including the management and effectiveness of vocational education programs (Office of Education, 1975).

1972   Appropriations Act (see Senate Report 92-145, June 8, 1971). NACVE responsible for multiyear study of vocational education, which became Project Baseline (Lee, 1977). GAO report, interpreted as critical of vocational education national, state and local administration, released.

1974   GAO report, based on their seven state intensive study of vocational education, concludes funds were not going to areas most in need, that the matching requirements were not met, and that the programs were doing little to reduce the occupational segregation of women, and the handicapped. The report although criticized in its turn by USOE and AVA figured prominently in the reauthorization hearings.

1976   Amendments (PL 94-482). Adds authorization for categories including vocational guidance and counseling, personnel preservice and in-service training, renovation of facilities, grants to overcome sex bias, and funds to assist state planning. Additions to the declaration of purpose are: (1) improve state planning and accountability by involving wide range of agencies and individuals (including representatives of the Department of Labor training programs and more postsecondary representation), and (2) help states overcome sex stereotyping in occupational preparation. A single state board is made the sole agency for administration in a state. Board duties expanded to emphasize planning and accountability. New evaluation and accountability requirements.

Evaluation-related amendments require: (1) annual state accountability reports, (2) continuation of SACVE annual evaluations of the administration and operations of the State Department of Vocational Education (SDVE), (3) continuation of the policy-oriented NACVE annual reports and assessment of USOE administration and operation, (4) a national evaluation of sex fairness in vocational education, (5) NIE evaluations of consumer/homemaking education, studies of resource needs, compliance mechanisms, and evaluation criteria, (6) national vocational education data system (VEDS) to be developed and administered by the National Center for Education Statistics, (7) sex fairness monitoring grants of up to $50,000 per state, (8) extensive federal, state and local involvement in management information systems, (9) annual follow-up studies using criteria for judging effectiveness in terms of employment in training-related occupations, employer satisfaction or continuation in education, (10) authorizes up to $5,000,000 annually for a National Center for Vocational Education Research, (11) establishes a national Occupational Information Coordination Council supervised by USOE, the Department of Labor and NCES, with parallel state committees (SOICCs), (12) requires USOE to evaluate in depth five states annually for the five year period, (13) requires each state to evaluate each funded program in depth at least once in the five years for quality and effectiveness, and (14) establishes a committee to coordinate vocational education research and evaluation activities, with representatives from NIE, USOE, NCES and Labor.

In 1963, the Smith-Hughes Act and related acts were redirected. The Vocational Education Act of 1963 (1) consolidated some of the dispersed occupational training authorities, (2) established the principle of serving the occupational preparation, updating, and second career needs of all persons in a community in contrast to providing training only in specified occupations, and (3) established administration through the U.S. Office of Education (USOE) in conjunction with state advisory councils on vocational education (SACVEs) and a national advisory council (NACVE). Subsequent amendments have (1) reduced further the distinction between academic and vocational programs by emphasizing the general educational value of vocational education, (2) required comprehensive state planning for the consolidated funds, and (3) placed responsibility for state evaluations of accountability on the SACVEs who oversee the annual reports submitted to congress (Office of Education, 1964; Evans, 1969; American Institute of Research, 1976; American Vocational Journal, 1976; Lee, 1977).

Throughout this period, the language of the hearings and the committee reports expressed the assumption that without federal prodding, local vocational education programs would become obsolete and would fail to serve the handicapped, the economically disadvantaged, cultural and racial minorities, and, in a gender-fair way, women. As Mangum (1968) noted, the 1963 act itself was the immediate product of a panel of experts who found vocational education insensitive to labor market changes and the needs of various segments of the population.

Evaluation was seen in these reports and hearings as essential in principle but deficient in practice. The Report of the Advisory Council on Vocational Education (1968:30-31) is illustrative:

We have found it impossible to determine to our full satisfaction what has occurred under the Act. The States may be faulted for the inadequacy of their own internal evaluations but the primary responsibility must rest at the national level. Despite the long foreknowledge of the 1966-68 assignment, no significant studies were undertaken with adequate lead time to produce data for the Council's needs. No significant changes were made in the reporting forms which were designed originally to ascertain whether the States matched the Federal grants-in-aid and spent the monies within the appropriate categories.

Numerous limitations of the present reporting system could be cited but a few will suffice. Although the Act's philosophy refocused effort on people instead of occupational groups, the statistics provide no demographic characteristics beyond the sex of the students. At a time greatly concerned with racial discrimination and poverty, no information is available on age, race, educational and family status. Although groups with special needs were supposed to receive special treatment, there are no data to identify them or to describe the content of courses designed for them. There is no way to determine whether the Act was successful in its intent to encourage training for new occupations. Enrollment data do not indicate the extent of student participation. Participation of one or two days, a week, or a few months is not differentiated from near full-time or full-year attendance. The quality of teachers, equipment, and course content can not be determined from the reporting system. Comparisons of relative enrollments and quality and quantity of vocational education in rural areas, small and medium size cities, suburban areas and large cities can not be made. The only common measure of results is a report of uncertain validity from the vocational education teacher in September on the placement of students who complete a course the previous spring. An 18 month lag for publication of data appears standard. Not only is the extent of non-Federally supported vocational preparation unknown, there is even greater uncertainty as to the total amount spent on Federally reimbursed vocational education. Since states often over-match Federal dollars, it appears to be common knowledge that much of the total state expenditure goes unreported.

The council's report was not without consequences in new legislation (e.g., Senate Committee on Labor and Public Welfare hearings, 1968), yet the 1968 and 1972 changes intended to improve evaluation practice were found inadequate in their turn. Practice continued to founder on lack of uniform definitions, lack of national leadership, lack of authority to achieve state and local cooperation, and lack of funds to create a national evaluation data system (Lee, 1977). The 1976 amendments now require uniform definitions, and provide more authority and funds to create a data system, at least on the federal level. The leadership vacuum continues, however; for over eighteen months, "reorganization" has meant "disorganization" (A. Lee, 1978, personal communication).[1] Yet, failure in 1982 to have better accountability data for congress may well be seen as reflecting unfavorably on evaluation and vocational education itself.

THE THIRD FEDERAL ROLE: GALVANIZING CHANGES FOR PROGRAM IMPROVEMENT AND REDIRECTION

Federal studies prior to the 1960s looked primarily at access and accountability for funds: whether services were provided in the quantity and with the quality intended, whether states were spending enough matching funds on vocational preparation, and whether the funds were spent in allowable categories. These studies might seem to offer some scope to encourage change, but many were not adequately carried out. Those that were did not appear to be effective for program improvement and redirection. Something different seemed to be needed, and it soon arrived.

The vocational education reauthorizations in the 1970s coincided with a general expansion of social science involvement in assisting policy makers to decide what should be done, as well as documenting whether policies were implemented. This section will shift perspective from vocational education alone to the interplay of a broadened evaluation role in federal educational legislation with vocational education.

Before 1960, federal evaluation roles were largely limited to information gathering and accountability; after 1960, the principle of federal support of scientific research which became established during World War II was applied rapidly to the social sciences. In 1940, the total federal research and development expenditures were $.07 billion. In 1950, the total was $1 billion. In 1960, $10 billion was spent, and in 1975, $15 billion. Through this investment and the G.I. Bill, unparalleled numbers of social scientists were trained. During the early 1960s, their attention turned to national policy development. As billions of dollars more were invested in social programs, including education, congress increasingly became concerned with determining how the money was spent, how the programs were managed, what they achieved, and how outcome data were used at the state and local levels to improve or to redirect programs. Evaluation of achievements and evaluation research on what might be achievable under different conditions followed this concern. Under the leadership of Senator Robert F. Kennedy, the Elementary and Secondary Education Act of 1965 (ESEA) set a precedent for massive federal evaluation and research funds for program improvement, requiring an evaluation plan and report for every local grantee (McLaughlin, 1974; Taggart and Levitan, 1976). As Wentling and Lawson (1975) noted, this was the first time all state and local grantees had to evaluate process and product for each federally funded program.

By 1968, however, some of the bloom was off the outcome evaluation rose. Wentling and Lawson (1975:8) commented:

> Evaluation efforts seldom met with the intent of this legislation. One of the identified problems within local education agencies as well as within state agencies was a failure to adequately define evaluation. Although the federal government had required that evaluation be conducted to assess the outcome and the return on the investment . . . , it provided few guidelines on how to conduct an evaluation. With no definition of evaluation, and no guide to evaluative procedure, many people were confused about the requirement.

Referring to vocational educational studies, they (1975:7) stated:

> [T]he approaches taken by various states to evaluate their own programs ranged from statewide follow-up surveys to activities that were focused on assessing the total programs of individual institutions by way of team visits similar to those utilized in accreditation evaluations.

Not suprisingly, given the 1960s enthusiasm for outcome evaluations, the deficiencies reported by the Advisory Council, and the call for stronger federal leadership in specifying uniform standards, the Vocational Education Amendments of 1968 required extensive studies of program effectiveness, an improved national data collection system, and prescribed data utilization.

Outcome data to assist congressional deliberations on the 1976 amendments were not much more interpretable, however, than data collected to inform debate on need and accountability. Although more extensive, better integrated, and better analyzed, the outcome data still suffered from the weaknesses noted in the 1968 Advisory Council report (Lee, 1977; Sparks, 1977). To these uncertainties were added dependence of follow-up studies on training-related placement to prove achievement rather than studies using multiple definitions of effectiveness to suit the multiple objectives of the legislation. There was still variation in sampling procedures, information completeness, and sources of information for the follow-up of spring graduates in the fall. Data were not collected on noncompleters and there was little uniformity in defining a program or a graduate. Under the circumstances, perhaps it is surprising that the vocational education placement rates compared as favorably as they did to those of general and academic program graduates (Sparks, 1977).

The data were collected for different uses, and state variation included outstandingly complete evaluation systems; fairness would celebrate these exemplary states as well criticize inadequate evaluations. For purposes of national aggregation, however, such variations generally are seen as limiting the sturdiness of conclusions (e.g., General Accounting Office, 1977). Lee (1977:5), writing from the perspective of aggregating state-level data for national reports, comments:

> We found great quantities of information, nearly all of it of poor quality. They were compiled in different ways, often from unreliable sources, and were based on different definitions in different states, and even in different school districts within a state. Estimates sometimes bordered on fabrications and sometimes left no doubt about the fabrication. One state reported more black students in vocational education at the secondary level than there were secondary level vocational education students altogether. We also began to find evidence of under-reporting. Schools often preferred to classify their vocational programs as industrial arts or business. None of the enrollments in such programs were being reported. And since under the legislation, each state had to show an increased effort each year, some of them reported less-than-actual expenditures if they were ahead of the previous year in order to keep the total down for the following year.

Ralston (1974), the General Accounting Office (1974), Drewes and Katz (1975), and Ellis (1975) report similar deficiencies in information on program quality, curriculum quality, costs, who was served, staff characteristics, and learner outcomes. These shortcomings, which are reminiscent of criticisms of evaluations of other social programs and hardly unique to vocational education, are discussed also in the evaluation analyses of Bushnell (1975), Christoffel (1975), and the U.S. Office of Education (1975). Evidence that the data were actually used in planning, program improvement, and redirection was even scantier: apparently the data were not influencing what happened next.

The Vocational Education Amendments of 1976 try to ensure that evaluation data will be used for planning, improvement, and redirection through such means as requiring the state planning groups to use reports on learner outcomes for annual revisions of the State Five Year Plan. These provisions, which may seem tyrannous to those unfamiliar with the long history of only modestly interpretable and minimally utilized vocational education evaluations, might better be described as determined and forebearing. In the context of considerable congressional effort to obtain full, accurate information and to encourage federal, state and local use of learner outcomes for program improvement, (Congressional Research Service, 1976; Congressional Budget Office, 1977), and in light of the within-the-fraternity criticisms of vocational education evaluations (Evans, 1976; Lee, 1977), the remarkably prescriptive evaluation requirements of the amendments may be what is needed.

How likely is it that this legislative mandate, which has not been met with equal enthusiasm at the federal administrative levels or by national vocational education leadership, will work? Previous legislation did not change practice fast enough: will this?

There are at least two determinants of the quality and use of evaluations in vocational education programs. These are ability and willingness. Ability means the resource capabilities for evaluation in federal, state and local agencies, and the resources in the state of the art in evaluation. By willingness is meant political agreement: the perceived conflict and compatibility in interests which could thwart or support implementing the law. These are also factors in how the federal, state and local government go about their business of budgeting and administration, and whether secondary and postsecondary, academic and vocational interests in education will be congruent or inhibiting with regard to the practice and use of evaluation. The next sections examine some of these influences and their implications for vocational education evaluation.

FACTORS IN CHANGE: ABILITY

Evaluation reports which are long on methodology and short on unqualified conclusions are failures for most policy purposes. Few evaluations, including vocational education studies, have enjoyed methodologically undisputed conclusions. Technical and practical preconditions for evaluations yielding unequivocal conclusions include: (1) the establishment of criteria for judging success which are related to legislative purposes; (2) the determination of standards for judging acceptable levels of achievement on these criteria; (3) the ability to take process and context into account before reaching judgments on outcomes; (4) the development of levels of tolerable certainty and uncertainty for judgments; (5) trade-offs among agencies in cost, accuracy, and ownership of data collection, analysis, and reporting; (6) establishing evaluation resources—competent staff, with adequate authority and money; and, in a practical sense, (7) use of preexisting nonvocational education data systems at state and local levels.

(1) CRITERIA FOR JUDGING SUCCESS

Considerable effort has been devoted to specifying outcome criteria and uniform definitions for use by the SACVEs and local programs (e.g., Michael, 1966; Sharp, 1968; Songe, 1972; Conroy, 1976; Norris, 1976; Drewes et al., 1977). The Belmont Project was an early effort to design a comprehensive evaluation system (Scientific Educational Systems, 1970). Clary (1970), reviewing the literature on state evaluations of vocational education, reported a Belmont related meeting between NACVE/SACVE representatives and USOE. The conferees agreed on such guidelines as:

- Evaluation should focus on SEA goals and priorities.
- Evaluation should look at all aspects of human resource development.
- Evaluation should report the effects of the legislation for that year.
- The program will be judged effective when the needs of all people are served.
- The evaluation will report opportunities for employment within the state and vocational education services available to meet these opportunities.

A more recent survey by the General Accounting Office (1977:v) of what state and local officials believed most impressed USOE and themselves with regard to effectiveness (in the context of ESEA) showed:

> Although state officials view USOE as being most impressed by standardized norm-referenced test results and local officials view state and USOE officials in the same manner, state and local officials say they are not most impressed by such results. Local officials prefer broader, more diverse types of information on program results and they are more impressed by improvements in curriculum and instructional methods and gains in the affective domain. State officials say they are most impressed by results from criterion-referenced tests.

Among the consequences of such meetings and studies has been a call for widening the focus of vocational education evaluation. To the concern of some that vocational education may be promising to achieve all the outcomes in the Great Taxonomy, many others believe the concept of vocational preparation should be widened to include job-specific skills, basic skills, skills permitting transfer to other occupations, and personal-social development such as good work habits, in addition to reducing the correlations between gender, race, ethnicity, and occupational entry. A second consequence has been a plea to examine what learners need to become employable, and the efficiency and effectiveness of learning out-of-school, on-the-job, and through nonformal education, as well as through in-school classes funded with federal vocational education money. It was hoped that these studies would help distinguish between *employment,* which will be affected by economic conditions, and *employability,* for which educators may feel more responsible.

The trend toward a wider vision of the relation between education and work is also reflected in legislation such as the 1977 Youth Employment and Demonstration Programs Act (YEDPA). YEDPA requires closer relations between schools and city government prime sponsors in planning and service delivery, and allocates a minimum of 20 percent of the funds for YEDPA education to be provided through the schools.

This yearning for expanded outcome criteria in vocational education evaluations seems at odds with the often used criterion of training-related placement, hourly wages, employment rates, and other postschooling outcomes for individuals. What seems like an identity crisis in the purposes of vocational education may be in part historical lag. Before 1963, the purposes of vocational education might have matched such employment criteria closely. If skills were developed in the specified vocational areas, graduates in the expanding postwar economy would find employment in training-related work. (The problem of evaluating home economics education was solved by ignoring these students in follow-up studies of placement in training-related occupations. Studies were limited to students available for paid employment. There has never been a national study on learner outcomes in either better homemaking or more prudent consumer behavior among this large, 23 percent, segment of all vocational education students.)

The transformation of vocational education's mission after 1963 from preparation for a relatively limited number of occupations to preparation for all occupations requiring less than a baccalaureate degree, plus the added mission of serving the handicapped, disadvantaged, bilingual, and minority groups, eventually collided with the problems resulting from a contracting economy. From 1970 to 1976, economic trends made it desirable to keep high school age youth out of the work force, and to raise the age of entry into the primary labor market from eighteen years of age to twenty-one or older. Nevertheless, evaluations continued to focus on employment rates among high school graduates. There was also an unresolved competition between the goal of achieving an educated, employed learner and preventing labor market undersupply, and the goal of remediation of unemployability among hard-to-educate disadvantaged youth. The conflict in these goals has not been reflected in a detailed congressional or administration statement of outcome criteria consistent with the diverse missions implicit in the 1976 amendments.

Table 2.1 is intended as a step toward such a statement. In it are presented criteria and possible measures which seem consistent with the 1976 amendments. The table is intended to be illustrative rather than comprehensive.

Perhaps the most difficult issue in using a table such as this is deciding which data should be collected by whom. One data system may not be able to serve three masters (General Accounting Office, 1977), yet collecting comprehensive data on all outcomes would be costly. An LEA concerned with preventing drop-outs among fifteen and sixteen year olds, a statewide community college system depending on high job placement rates to attract students, an SDVE whose legislature is emphasizing mainstreaming handi-

Table 2.1: Illustrative Criteria for Evaluating Outcomes of Vocational Education (V/E)

Examples of Outcomes	Possible Measures
INDIVIDUAL BENEFITS	

Examples of Outcomes	Possible Measures
1. *Same outcomes* in specific educational objectives for vocational and nonvocational education (e.g., basic skills, good work habits, high school completion). V/E may uniquely help some students whose learning styles and interests are not compatible with general academic preparation.	• *Same* rates of retention, career knowledge and planning, and basic skill achievement for V/E and non V/E students; *more* effective on these criteria for students with a concrete, action-learning style who might otherwise drop out or learn very little.
2. *Unique outcomes* in entry-level skills required for jobs where applicants are expected to be prepared for work (e.g., truck driver, X-ray technologist) includes achievement of sufficient competence to obtain work, even if program is incomplete.	• Competency based measures of preparation for occupations for which trained, achievement of high enough levels of skills, abilities and attitudes adequate for employment.
	• Obtains, holds, and progresses in work needing skills acquired in training, including skills transferrable from one type of work to another.
	• Employer and learner satisfaction with skills, abilities and attitudes believed to be developed in vocational education.
3. *Unique outcomes* in preparation for further training, apprenticeship of on-the-job learning where learner is expected to bring foundation levels of skills, abilities and attitudes.	• Achievement of minimum levels needed to enter further training as measured by competency based assessment.
	• Enters, progresses in and completes further training which requires skills developed during V/E, including skills transferrable from one type of occupational training to another.
4. *Unique outcomes* in consumer competencies and competencies for nonpaid work (e.g., student enrollment in automechanics in order to repair own cars, to be better consumers in purchasing cars and in arranging for car repairs).	• Achievement of minimum competencies required for self-help and prudent consumer choices as measured by performance tests or subsequent learner reports of application of skills.
5. *Same outcomes* for V/E and non V/E students in broad educational objectives (e.g., citizenship, enthusiasm for learning, sense of competency and achievement).	• *Same* rates of achievement on measures of these attitudes, knowledge, and abilities; *more* effective for students with action-learning style.
6. *Supplementary skill outcomes* where skills contribute to or are needed for	• Achievement of minimum competencies required for supplementary use.

Table 2.1: (Continued)

Examples of Outcomes	Possible Measures
other meaningful work (e.g., typing skills may be valuable in further education, provide an extra chance for employment between jobs or during high unemployment, contribute to nonpaid community service work, etc.).	• Application of these skills in situations regarded as meaningful.

SOCIAL BENEFITS

1. *Equity outcomes:* increasing the proportion of minority, bilingual, handicapped persons who are prepared for skilled employment and technical work where there are job opportunities, and where the proportion of such persons in professional and managerial work is not reduced.	• Reduction in correlation between gender, native language, race, ethnicity, handicapping condition, and occupational preparation and entry.
2. *Economic adjustment; supply side.* Skilled technical personnel are neither in over-supply nor under-supply for business, industrial, government and self-employment needs.	• Comparison of occupational competencies and interests in labor pool supplied by vocational education with labor market needs.
3. *Economic adjustment outcomes: demand side.* Modification of the structure of the workplace so the workplace and the nature of work are changed in keeping with changing numbers, skills, values, and interests of the work-force.	• Survey of SACVE/NACVE effectiveness in influencing employer adaptations to changing work-force. • Evidence that vocational education graduates and V/E leaders were effective in changing nature of workplace and working conditions to adapt demand to supply.
4. *Optimum use of vocational education and training resources in schools, business, industry, and government* through coordination of secondary and post-secondary, public and private sector, and DOL/USOE resources.	• Evidence of reduced costs with equally good or better educational quality and access; or evidence of improved quality and greater access with same or increased costs. Greater effectiveness and efficiency in matching where, when, and how training is given with employer and learner needs.
5. *Regional economic development* through preparation of learners for work that does not presently exist, then attracting new industry by the availability of skilled employees; or, preventing loss of industry by remedial training for new population groups who otherwise would not be attractive employees.	• Analysis of the economic situation over a five to ten year period, tracing the attraction of new industries versus loss of existing industries to changes in the calibre and skills of the local work force.

capped adolescents, a federal official administering sex-fair vocational education provisions, and a member of congress with a rural constituency concerned with the drift of its young to the cities may set priorities differently.

Presently legislation does not encourage diversity in reporting learner outcomes or in assessing intermediate outcomes prior to program completion, although some provisions appear to encourage local setting of varied but appropriate objectives. Alternative ways of coordinating the varied goals of the legislation with the narrowness of the specified criterion of results would be (1) widening the outcome criteria to fit the legislative goals or (2) constricting the legislative goals to fit the criteria specified in Section 212(b). (Section 212[b] requires annual follow-up reports on placement in training-related jobs, employer satisfaction or continuation in further education.)

Another criterion issue is the applicability of the costs/benefits paradigm often used to compare the effectiveness of vocational and nonvocational education (e.g., Warmbrod, 1968; Little, 1970; Sparks, 1977). Valuable as these studies can be in stimulating discussion, there is reason to prefer some criteria less quantifiable than such analyses require. Among the other arguments against the cost/benefit paradigm is that it conceals in its technology issues that ought to be more directly accessible to the lay public (e.g., Lovins, 1978).

(2) STANDARDS OF ACCEPTABLE ACHIEVEMENT

Reliable, sensitive, and appropriate measures of most outcomes specified in the 1976 act are possible. Reaching a priori agreement on standards for judging program success and the federal role in setting such standards will also be necessary but politically sensitive steps. As one example, the findings listed below have been cited as evidence of the effectiveness of vocational education programs (NACVE, 1968):

- Enrollment in vocational education increased from 4 million in 1962 to 7 million in 1967.
- Enrollment was greater in home economics, trades and industries and in office occupations.
- Of the 347,370 graduates available for placement in October 1966, 80 percent were placed in fields for which they were trained.

These data may indeed reflect the success of vocational education programs, but without standards for judging how much is enough, they are open to alternative judgments. For illustrative purposes, some hypothetical alternative explanations for each of the three examples of success follow:

(1) Enrollment in all areas of secondary education almost doubled from 1962 to 1967, as a result of the large postwar cohort of children

reaching adolescence and the pressure to keep them in school. The *proportionate* enrollment in vocational education may have stayed the same or decreased. Even if proportionate enrollment increased, what standard of increase would be considered evidence of effectiveness: 10 percent, 20 percent, or anything statistically reliable at the .05 level, an undemanding criterion with national Ns? What if the increase came from low-income students who previously were enrolling in academic preparation programs? Would a diversion of such students from academic to vocational preparation be considered good news? Or would the increase in vocational education enrollments be good news only if proportionately fewer students from all population groups were choosing the general curriculum?

(2) Enrollment may have been greatest in the cited areas due to proportionate declines in agriculture. There may be a roughly constant proportion of students who enroll in vocational education, and a shift into one area is a shift out of another. If so, was the decrease in the losing area so great that the nation would be faced with shortages? Was the increase in trades, industries, and office occupations so large that the nation would have an oversupply in these fields? How much of an increase would be good news and how much would be a future problem?

(3) By 1966, the country was entering a period of economic expansion. In part as a result of the Vietnam war, fewer young men were available to enter the civilian work-force. When this is taken into account, could vocational education be credited with an improvement in placement rates over previous years? Relative to the placement of graduates of academic or general curricula during this period, is an 80 percent placement rate good news or bad news?

As another example, a 1976 report on exemplary consumer education programs for adults living in economically depressed areas cited the following information as the only evidence of effectiveness:

— an individual became a Head Start Center director.
— a former student is working in a day care center.
— the value of vitamins and other health-related items listed for sale by a local store were questioned by class members.
— students who constructed wearing apparel as a class project "have realized the cost/benefits of such."
— a person who began the course with an "exceptionally poor self-concept" took part in the class style show modeling the clothing constructed.
— approximately 9,000 miles were covered by the mobile unit.

Are these outcomes good enough? And have enough of the eligible learners and participating students been affected? Finding out what differences participation has made in people's lives in such practical ways as those cited above may be a better criterion than the information recall or recognition often measured by tests, but without standards of judgment, almost any data are uninterpretable or overinterpretable. Some evaluators would regard pre-specification of goals and standards as traps to be avoided (Deutscher, 1976). Other evaluators are moving toward specifying weights that would be given to various outcomes before data are collected. A few have tried determining whether evaluations sturdy enough to reach firm conclusions about valued outcomes could be conducted under the field conditions, costs and time specified, and have even cancelled studies which would result in uninter-pretable findings (J. Schiller, 1977, personal communication).

Applications of these approaches to prespecifying standards for judging success and failure are scarce. A few studies have used the decision-theoretic approach. None seems to have established a priori criteria of how much of a valued outcome would be enough to increase resource allocations nor, in vocational education evaluations, have the thresholds been stated below which findings would result in withholding or reallocating resources (e.g., Reid, 1972; Ash, 1973; Ralston, 1974; Songe, 1972; Davis and Borgen, 1974; Oregon Department of Education, 1977; Schneider, 1977; Bryam and Rob-ertson, undated).

The need for such standards of acceptable achievement is particularly relevant to the requirement that SACVE's use follow-up studies as a basis for yearly reallocation of funds. What will be regarded as sufficient enough progress in training-related placement? If 85 percent of all those leaving postsecondary occupational vocational education programs who want to work are employed a year later in training related work, earn $5.00 or more hourly, and have less than a month unemployment, will this be evidence of success? Or would this be considered failure if noncompleters who do not go on to further studies also obtained training-related work, earn $5.00 or more hourly and have been unemployed for less than a month? Will success be defined by how much V/E graduates outstrip others? If so, how much better must V/E graduates do in the labor market? Leaving such standards unde-fined until the data are in seems like a game where scoring is decided after time is up. No matter what happens, opponents can claim failure and proponents success. So far, however, evaluators have barely addressed the question of defining magnitude of effects in terms of precommitments to resource allocation decisions by those required in the legislation to use the outcome findings.

(3) TAKING CONTEXT INTO ACCOUNT BEFORE REACHING JUDGMENTS ON OUTCOMES

Once there were two vocational education programs. One program re-ported that gender and race were correlated with staffing, enrollments, and completion. Another program reported the opposite. Is the first program a success and the other a failure with respect to this criterion?

The first program was in a suburb. The federal dollar was only 3 percent of the local education budget. The school board was concerned with declining SAT scores and clearly indicated the superintendent's job depended on ensuring high performance for all children on measures of academic achievement. The community also had a program encouraging minority children to prepare for college, particularly setting their sights on advanced degrees, and there was a program encouraging women to prepare for advanced professional work requiring science and mathematics backgrounds. Only students with great interest in technical work were encouraged to enroll in vocational education, and the vocational education programs set high standards for achievement of all enrollees in academic knowledge, technical skills, work habits, and personal skills. In these programs, enrollment, completion, and staffing were highly correlated with gender and race, being mostly the province of white males except for office occupations and home economics.

The second program was in a rural area where almost all the school funds beyond the minimum required for matching came from the federal government. The district was desperate for educational dollars and the school board had made it clear that the superintendent's job depended on retaining or expanded federal funds. To comply with the sex-fair vocational education regulations, the superintendent transferred into the vocational education programs staff who were of suitable gender and race but were only minimally qualified, mounted an enroll-in-vocational-education campaign targeted to women and minorities, considered as passing work that was marginally acceptable, and placed graduates in whatever job came along that was minimally training-related.

Follow-up studies of program one two years after the students left showed high retention rates in college or on-the-job for vocational education graduates. Over the years, the correlations of gender and race with enrollment, participation, and staffing decreased. The second program showed high enrollment and completion rates, and no correlations of participation by gender or race. However, retention rates were low for students in-college or on-the-job, and there was a decrease in minorities and women preparing for advanced education. In later years retention rates and rates of preparation for advanced education increased.

The first superintendent placed curricular excellence first, working toward expanding vocational education enrollments and staff to be gender and race fair. The second superintendent placed compliance with gender and race fairness expectations first, working toward curricular excellence. This hypothetical example is not intended to illustrate the incompatibility of quality and equality. It is hoped they are compatible: certainly the intent of legislation for achieving both is clear. The example is meant to show that the context in which decisions are made influence what the program does, yielding results where achieving the intent of congress for one objective may mean deferring another.

Evaluation methodology has little to offer beyond case studies to relate process, contexts, and outcomes. There are over 18,000 school districts. When area vocational-technical schools, postsecondary programs, adult programs, work-study projects, cooperative education, and nonoccupational vocational enrollment are taken into account, the methodological problems of placing outcomes in context through case studies becomes almost insurmountable on a national scale.

The aggregated figures on enrollment, completion, and placements offer estimates of program achievement with regard to objectives such as quality, access, and equity of service. Part of the tension, however, between state and local interpretation of the data and national use comes from the inability of evaluations to relate context and consequence technically on a large scale. Studying trends over time, clustered by starting levels among individual programs, rather than measuring each program once in five years might help give some context for progress. This is, however, costly and not presently required.

(4) ESTABLISHING LEVELS OF TOLERABLE UNCERTAINTY AND REASONABLE CERTAINTY

Evaluations are underdesigned if the data do not permit sensitivity to effects with levels of certainty appropriate to the decision being made. They are overdesigned if tolerable uncertainty for the decisions being made has been reduced at a high human and financial cost. Lee (1977) refers to NCES as being caught in a crunch between collecting enough data to satisfy the national legislative requirements and most states' resistance to supplying more than they have to. One could add local resistance to supplying more to meet state legislative requirements than *they* have to.

How much data are necessary depends on how much uncertainty can be tolerated in reaching conclusions. This in turn depends on the seriousness of negative effects and their probability of occurrence, as seen by various users for different purposes. The certainty needed to approve a new pesticide for widespread household use would be different than one proposed for restricted agricultural use where later processing would remove all traces before public consumption. The certainty needed to judge satisfactory progress toward relating proposed vocational courses to locally available work would be lower (due in part to the uncertainties in labor market projections forming a lower limit) than the certainty required before adapting a statewide test for teacher competency.

One way in which this issue is joined in vocational education evaluation is sampling versus total reporting. Current NCES regulations require reporting of total enrollment, staff, facilities, and equipment for each class designated as supported with federal funds. These data are aggregated at building, district, and state levels. Congress typically sees only aggregated national tables, with state data available in an appendix, a considerable overdesign for most purposes.

One reason for the 100 percent reporting requirement is congressional belief that samples would be too vulnerable to a "not in my state, district or school" denial of findings. Another consideration is the cost of obtaining the level of accuracy in local reporting that a sampling strategy might require. On the other hand, sampling is allowed in the annual follow-up study of placement of vocational education graduates to be conducted by the states.

Detailed analysis of the alternatives for sampling versus complete reporting for the various evaluation requirements have not been widely discussed. If most national or state decisions are made on the basis of aggregated data, equal or greater certainty could be obtained for the same or lower costs through sampling.

Information on the unit costs of data collection and the error rates associated with various strategies would be needed to decide wisely on the merits of sampling versus total reporting. Designing evaluations to provide only the minimum levels of certainty needed by decision makers might help reduce resistance to the total data collection load among national, state and local educators, none of whom wants to give or receive more data than are needed.

(5) COST, ACCURACY AND OWNERSHIP IN DATA COLLECTION

Almost all federal reporting systems depend on the classroom teacher and the building principal. To reduce both bias and reporting burden, data systems based on individual student records (to be filled in by the student and cumulated using social security numbers) have been proposed. Arguments against this include (a) cost, (b) impracticality under the Privacy Act, (c) the belief that many educational institutions prefer to retain direct control over statistical reports, (d) the limitations on forms that would have to be designed for use by handicapped, bilingual, or disadvantaged students, (e) the greater difficulty in training many students to use the data forms seriously and accurately in comparison to training the relatively smaller number of teachers, (f) the possibility of systematic bias and underreporting from those less willing or able to complete the forms, (g) the fact that some states do not have the automatic data processing equipment capable of handling these data, and (h) people being more likely to believe data they have participated in collecting than someone else's findings.

Despite these and other objections, a student-based system may be needed if federal and state reporting requirements continue to expand, if nonduplicated counts are wanted, and if extensive cross-tabulations by student, staff, and program characteristics are demanded.

The high-water mark of data demand may, however, have been reached. One influence in that direction is the barrier of clearance procedures for data collection. There are now in the Education Division clearances and reviews by the originating offices, by the Educational Data Acquisition Center (EDAC), by the Chief State School Officers' Committee on Educational Information Systems (CSSO/CEIS), by the Office of Management and Budget reviews, and by their state and local counterparts. These procedures and problems of resolving conflicting congressional directions already are such that only bitter necessity would drive an agency to start another data collection effort.

Another influence in the demand for data is the shift in fashions for social policy analysis and planned change. While state and local groups are now heavily into rational planning models, theorists are becoming skeptical of hyperrationalization of decisions and the possibility of relating diffuse political processes to the directed, linear model of decision-making (e.g., Kneso, 1975; Nay et al., 1976; McGowan and Cohen, 1976; Weiss, 1977; Weiss and Bucuvalas, 1977; and Lovins, 1978). Others object to the institutionalization of distrust implicit in the extensive monitoring apparatus, which sometimes seems to expend millions to catch an occasional ten-cent thief.

Until this issue is more fully examined, who should collect vocational education data probably will emerge as an area where federal preference (which tends toward individual student records), expert advice (ditto), and most state and local practice will differ.

(6) EVALUATION CAPABILITY

A sixth factor influencing implementation of the evaluation requirements of the 1976 amendments is differential capacity. Some states, hand-tabulating reports from mimeographed data sheets, are able to aggregate slowly only the simplest of data. Other states and some school districts have modern computer facilities. In some LEAs, not only enrollment but also daily attendance by age, sex, race, residence, family background, and progress toward completion of competency-based objectives can be transmitted on-line from each school.

A national data system has to be within reach of the states least capable of data collection, and with the least money available for evaluation. Federal vocational education funds for ancillary services including evaluation would be inadequate to install an up-to-date computerized data system for a state now handling its business through hand-tallies. The federal government does

Table 2.2: Part C (Research, Training, RCU) Funds for Vocational
Education Between 1965 and 1976 (Dollars in Millions)

Year	Authorized Funds	Appropriated Funds	State Total	Average State $	Average State $ in 1965
1965	$11.8	$11.8	$ 6.9	$0.14	$0.14
1966	17.7	17.8	8.9	0.18	0.16
1967	22.5	10.8	5.0	0.10	0.09
1968	22.5	13.6	6.8	0.14	0.11
1969	35.5	11.6	5.8	0.12	0.09
1970	56.0	1.1	0.5	0.01	0.00
1971	67.5	35.7	17.8	0.36	0.23
1972	67.5	18.0	9.0	0.18	0.11
1973	67.5	18.0	9.0	0.18	0.10
1974	67.5	18.0	9.0	0.18	0.08
1975	67.5	18.0	9.0	0.18	0.07
1976	67.5	18.0	9.0	0.18	0.06

not pay for the full costs of vocational education data desired essentially for federal purposes, if necessary state and local investments in general use educational data processing systems are included. The states farthest from such ADP systems are among the smallest and the poorest, and receive few federal vocational education dollars. Without more support, there are few incentives to install elaborate data systems, and distinct reasons to keep reporting to a minimum.

The gap between legislative demand and capacity for compliance may not be fully appreciated. As one illustration, Table 2.2 shows funds for Part C of the 1968 act which could be spent to support research, training and research coordinating units, i.e., the development of human resources for conducting evaluations and research necessary to improve evaluation techniques. For the 1965 through 1976 period, the table shows the dollars authorized (by one committee in congress), the total dollars appropriated (under control of a different committee), the total state share (since 50 percent of the Part C funds stayed in Washington), and the *average* state share in both unadjusted dollars and in 1965 constant dollars. In 1976, for example, $67.5 million was authorized and $18 million was appropriated, yielding a total state share of $9 million, an average state share of $180,000 and in 1965 constant dollars, only $60,000 average per state available for all Part C purposes, versus the average state share of $140,000 available in 1965. It has been suggested that congressional authorization committees expect returns to the public commensurate with dream money authorizations rather than returns based on the real money appropriations.

(7) USE OF PRE-EXISTING SYSTEMS

Another consideration in examining evaluation resources is variation among states in the relation between vocational education and state evaluation units. State Directors of Vocational Education (SDVEs) were supported largely through federal funds years before many states had a Chief State School Officer (CSSO). Evaluation offices, however, were created years after the SDVEs and in most states, the evaluation office reports to the CSSO. Since SDVEs rarely have funds to operate full evaluation programs, including reports on students, staff, curricula, facilities, and expenditures required by congress, many SDVEs must obtain the cooperation of the CSSO, competing in the CSSO's evaluation budget with studies of other educational programs. A parallel situation is found in school districts, where evaluation offices may be too understaffed and underfunded to carry out adequate studies of vocational education.

Even though groups such as the CSSO/CEIS (Committee on Education Information Systems of the CSSO) are now negotiating for the states before congressional requirements for evaluation are passed into laws, the design of evaluation and information systems for vocational education programs must accommodate themselves to considerable diversity in LEA and SEA resources and organizations.

The discussion here is not an argument for 100 percent federally funded independent data systems. There are at least four arguments against such an approach: (a) duplication of administrative and technical costs in a federally funded separate system, (b) problems in coordinating data collection to reduce LEA burdens, (c) the need for nonvocational education data to provide a context for interpreting vocational education findings, and (d) the principle that all levels of government should pay for information gathering, accountability, and outcome evaluations. These are more than federal concerns.

There are also at least three arguments for changes to improve the situation: (a) the have-not states reduce the quality of national data; (b) delays of eighteen months or more in obtaining data reduce the utility of information for planning and management, and (c) without some realistic level of guaranteed or required capability at the LEA and SEA levels for vocational education evaluation studies, cutting back on evaluations may be easier than making other accommodations. As postsecondary institutions, less accustomed than LEAs to outcome evaluations, increasingly share the vocational education dollar, the strains on evaluation capacity may become markedly greater.

FACTORS IN CHANGE: WILLINGNESS

A number of reasons are given for previous shortfalls in implementing federal evaluation requirements. People may be unwilling to cooperate with evaluation requirements when they fear the results will be used to close off funds, when they have too many other things to do, and when the rewards are greater for doing something else.

(1) FEAR

There is little evidence that programs are dismantled because of unfavorable evaluations. If anything, evaluators have lamented that demonstrably ineffective programs march on political feet undeterred by evidence. Bad press, however, has contributed to plateauing support for older programs and has made new investments elsewhere seem more attractive. Vocational education has had bad press recently, and vocational educators have felt a chilling lack of confidence in both congress and the administration.

Federal level evaluations, such as the 1974 GAO report, have played some role in this bad press. Local evaluations, with some notable exceptions, tend to accentuate the positive. They tend to be long on process descriptions, contain sympathetic explanations of disappointing results, have recommendations urging program expansion and development, and generally report learner, employer, and staff enthusiasm. One example of such a vocational education evaluation found no evidence supporting twenty-seven hypotheses about program effectiveness, yet the first recommendation in the executive summary urged expansion of the program. National evaluations, with some notable exceptions, tend to accentuate the negative. Even the Project Baseline reports prepared by evaluators who understand vocational education contributed (and accurately) to a negative picture, particularly with regard to sex fairness. The disparity between national and local evaluations leaves some vocational educators feeling that they have unfairly borne the brunt of that part of youth unemployment and occupational segregation due to unfavorable labor market conditions or the effects of nonschool socialization. The result is an attitude toward evaluation that is often "We'll do it if we have to."

(2) OTHER THINGS TO DO

National, state and local evaluation offices design the studies, send out the forms, and analyze the data. Yet much of the total burden of the cumulated evaluation demands for data across all federal and state education-related legislation falls on teachers. They are the ones who collect the daily attendance, administer the tests, describe their facilities and equipment, report their own qualifications, and provide the follow-up records. Along the way, they are responsible for lesson plans, individualization of instruction, and coping with the latest priority (handicapped? gifted? sex fairness? bilingual? basics? reentry women?). Guidance counselors and principals receive the next greatest demands for data, and they also have other things to do. Because a single school may receive funds from CETA, the Bureau of Education for the Handicapped, compensatory education, the Emergency School Assistance Act, as well as vocational education, the "just one more form" has to compete with other demands. The form may get filled in eventually, but as one superintendent said:

> Send me your questionnaire. But if you don't call me personally, I won't answer it. I get a hundred of these things every month and if I answered all of them, I'd be doing nothing else. If I believe you will use these data well, I'll get that questionnaire back to you, but don't just put it in the mail and hold your breath.

The actual documentation requirements for vocational education have not been adequately examined. Some observers believe the problem is irritability and that vocational education staffs do have the time to complete the basic forms required in the legislation. On the other hand, G. Venn (1977, personal communication) reports a doctoral study which found vocational education supervisors place highest priority on keeping up with government requirements, including documentation. While this might seem to leave too little time for educational leadership, there are few empirical studies proving that reporting requirements are the primary reason that more important things receive less than adequate attention.

(3) DIFFERENT INCENTIVES

Money is one source of unwillingness to comply. Some states, for example, pay an LEA more per trades-and-industries student than for a student taking courses which cost less to offer, such as home economics. The incentive is to define as a trades-and-industries student anyone taking a single course, and a vocational home economics student only as one enrolled in required courses for a two-year program. Uniform federal definitions are not likely to change the counts as long as SEAs and LEAs would lose money by adopting these guidelines.

A second source of unwillingness is that SEAs and LEAs legislation, budget allocation, planning, and operations cycles are often out of harmony with the federal system. For example, the SEA cycle of designing data collection forms, approving new forms, training staff to use the forms, adapting computer systems to handle the data, and lead time for collecting data takes six months to a year for each *separate* step, yet federal legislation required implementation of a new comprehensive national data system in a year. If follow-up is added to the immediate participation data, five years will elapse before the new national vocational education data system could return reliable information from all states which would reflect the impact of new legislation. Third, at each node, decision influencers may have different priorities than those expressed in federal legislation. As an example, a Chief State School Officer's priority may be expanding the state community college system; a superintendent and local school board may be most concerned with complying with desegregation requirements, avoiding busing, coping with declining elementary and secondary school enrollments without closing neighborhood schools, and avoiding teachers' strikes when the school budget has not expanded. The incentives for putting a great deal of effort into evaluations of vocational education may be inadequate to the need for improvements.

A fourth source of unwillingness is the debilitating low morale that arises when demands greatly exceed possibility. A. Lee (1978, personal communication) describes these:

> None of the states feel they are doing any real planning as called for by congress and for two very good reasons. One is that they do not have the data yet to plan with, and the other is that OE has once again forced them at the very beginning into a compliance effort which allows little opportunity for realistic planning. . . . Evaluation under these circumstances could hardly be more than simply compounding the frustration already so evident.

Table 2.3 shows these pushes and pulls in another way by illustrating the different purposes similar data may serve at the federal, state and local levels. In theory, the same data (e.g., enrollment figures) ought to be usable at all three levels for several purposes. In practice, it would appear they often are not, or cannot be so used. D. Bonnet (1977, personal communication) points out that the problem in aggregation of program evaluation results at local, state, and finally federal levels is that to be meaningful (1) the definitions have to be the same, (2) the outcomes regarded as important have to be the same or at least comparable for all programs aggregated, and (3) the standards for achievement have to be equally ambitious for all programs, or we have to establish standards for the aggregate. While this might be relatively straightforward for enrollment data, conditions 2 and 3 are particularly difficult for quality and outcome studies. The General Accounting Office (1977) in a report likely to be controversial has urged shifting the evaluation balance of funds and functions from the federal, to state, and particularly local levels. GAO (pp. 64-67) suggests limiting the federal role to assure that local budgets

Table 2.3: Similar Data and Different Functions in Evaluation

PURPOSES AND FUNCTIONS IN EVALUATION DATA

Information User	Establish need	Accountability for funds	Improve programs	Redirect funds
Federal	to justify a federal role at all; establish its' nature and intent	to prevent waste or mismanagement; assure fiscal responsibility	to assess achievement of federal intents regarding expansion of service, innovation, equity, or quality purposes	to judge success of program as a whole: go/no go decisions for expansion, redirection, or "fade-out"; decide among different programs
State	to allocate funds among competing priorities	to comply with regulations; to assure responsible management	to improve service delivery and better serve constituents	to inform or justify program allocation decisions
Local	to develop program requests and meet proposal requirements	to comply with regulations	to improve quality of services to the community; improve efficiency, modify programs	to improve quality of service to the community, modify programs
Examples of data	youth unemployment rates	percentage of funds spent in economically depressed areas	enrollment by gender and race in different voc/ed courses	employment rates of program graduates

and plans include adequate funds and designs for valid, objective evaluations; auditing the evaluations; and developing better measures and methodology. The report also, however, calls for studying the information needs at various levels and what systems would be needed to meet them, if the present aggregate-data-upward system does not.

CAUSE FOR HOPE

Despite these factors limiting willingness to carry out federal evaluation requirements, there are balancing reasons to expect better luck this time. Among these reasons are (1) the common cause among vocational educators at all levels for expanding their share of the educational dollar, retaining their share of the shrinking secondary-school age population and capturing a larger share of the expanding postsecondary age population, and (2) mutual benefits in working together.

COMMON CAUSE

When evaluation data are negative or inadequate, funds for vocational education programs are threatened and new demands for accountability levied. Congressional disfavor with education programs in general and with vocational education in particular, has created a common cause in ensuring vocational education passes inspection in 1982. This perceived congressional threat can bring together vocational educators at all levels to accommodate each other's needs. Although this might also seem like a script for collusion, there are checks and balances:

- The National Advisory Council on vocational education's responsibilities include assessments of USOE administration.

- The USOE program administering vocational education collects only the in-depth monitoring reports from ten states yearly.

- The NCES, although dependent on CSSO/CEIS for cooperation, is accountable to congress for comprehensive information on vocational education, and cannot compromise too much in the data requirements it mandates for the states.

- The sex fair vocational education provisions will be evaluated by the USOE top-level evaluation office reporting independently and directly to the Commissioner; this group has a reputation for tough-minded, disinterested evaluations.

- The NIE, another agency with few organizational ties to programs, will be studying the consequences of the 1976 amendments.

- The General Accounting Office is considering an independent evaluation. GAO in the past has been critical to the point of querulousness over evidence of inadequate management, inadequate programs, and inadequate evaluations.

— Citizen's organizations such as the Lawyer's Committee are taking a strong interest in the new amendments, and will be independently monitoring their implementation and effectiveness.

— New leadership in several professional organizations have incentives to facilitate change rather than defend an orthodoxy.

CONTEXT AND GENERALIZABILITY

Federal level data aggregation permit generalizations about vocational education essential to establish a national interest and accountability. Local and state evaluations and studies, supported through the RCUs, could provide contextual data and quality indicators often lacking in the national reports. While few studies have done this, there is the potential for a mutually beneficial and more complete picture of state and LEA efforts.

Coordination among vocational education studies is facilitated at the national level by three devices: (a) a congressionally mandated committee including the Director of NIE, the Director of NCES, and the Deputy Commissioner for Occupational and Adult Education which has responsibility for annual review of plans for vocational education research, demonstrations, and evaluation; (2) the Federal Interagency Education Committee, whose members are responsible for coordinating programs, and through a subcommittee, for coordinating all educational research; and (3) the Federal Interagency Panels for Research on Adolescence and Adulthood. Formally established coordination groups such as these should facilitate willingness to implement evaluation requirements at the federal level through the attention given to substance and procedures.

Evaluation coordination involving federal, state and local agencies also could facilitate implementing state and local evaluations. Table 2.4 outlines potential links among federal, state and local groups concerned with vocational education evaluation. As an example, improvements in measures of vocational education quality and effectiveness might be enhanced by coordination among the USOE-OPBE, the new National Center for Vocational Education Research, RCUs, and the American Vocational Education Research Association.

Except for the CSSO/CEIS, there are few formally established linkages between federal and other levels. This is not necessarily a bad state of affairs. Formal coordination can become a time consuming ritual, and there are instances of informal links. One example is the conference on criteria for the ten state yearly in-depth studies held by BOAE subcontractors with SDVEs, representatives of community colleges, and professional organizations, a conference not formally required.

Table 2.4: Vocational/Technical Education and Employment Training Evaluations: A Partial Map of Stakeholders and Resources

Activity	Federal[1]				DOL		State		CSSO		Local[2]					
	NACVE	NCES	BOAE	OPBE	ETA	NCVER	SDVE	RCU	CEIS	SACVE	AACJC	AASSP	AASS	AVA	AVERA	AAHE
Improving																
measures				x	x	x		x								
methodology				x	x	x		x								
evaluator training			x												x	x
Deciding on																
criteria	x	x	x	x	x	x	x			x	x	x	x	x		
design		x		x	x	x		x								
sampling		x		x				x								
data forms		x		x				x	x			x	x			
Preparing and conducting																
analysis/reports	x	x		x		x				x	x		x			
utilization/ dissemination	x		x		x		x		x	x	x	x	x	x	x	x
Coordinating																
with general education studies	x	x		x		x			x	x	x	x	x	x		x
with DOL/DOC studies	x		x		x	x	x		x	x	x		x	x	x	

(1) And also NIE, DOC, CRS, GAO, NAS, CBO
(2) And also CETA prime sponsors, LBCM, NUL, NEA, AFT, NSBA, LACVE, ASTD

Table 2.4 also illustrates resources for vocational education evaluators that might be overlooked. As examples:

(1) A local evaluator wants to conduct a needs assessment in a community. The evaluator could turn to the NIE supported ERIC Clearinghouse on Career Education which co-exists with the USOE supported AIM/ARM bank on vocational education research or the USOE supported clearinghouse on adult education. The evaluator could also contact the state RCU or the new NCVER.

(2) A state evaluator wants to follow-up secondary school leavers and completers. The evaluator thinks many secondary school leavers may enter community colleges, particularly in vocational education. To design an efficient follow-up study, the evaluator could contact the USOE/BOAE Planning Office which supports methodological studies such as models for follow-up evaluations, the RCU, the linkage study in vocational education supported through AACJC, the NCVER for additional methodological guidance, NCES or longitudinal study baseline measures, and both NACVE and AVA for information on other related studies.

These examples suggest how knowledge of the major groups concerned with evaluation can assist the individual researcher in developing efficient and effective studies.

PROMISES TO KEEP: A SUMMARY

Three federal roles in vocational education evaluation have been identified: establishing national needs, accountability for spending federal funds to serve the people intended with the programs intended, and finding out how well federally supported programs achieved the results intended, data intended to improve, and to redirect programs. These roles were traced in vocational education legislation since 1917, and have been related to trends in federal support of educational research and evaluation. The modest amount of interpretable data on vocational education, despite high hopes from previous legislation, led to the remarkably specific and extensive evaluation provisions in the Vocational Education Amendments of 1976.

The likelihood that the promise of evaluation in the 1976 act would be better realized for the 1982 reauthorization hearings was considered in terms of two factors: ability and willingness. It was argued that despite reasons why those involved would feel less than enthusiastic about evaluation (fear, other things to do, and competing incentives), willingness to cooperate at national, state and local levels probably would be adequate to implement the evaluation requirements.

Expectations for realizing the evaluation requirements at any level of government were seen as depending less on willingness (important as this is), and more *at present* on limitations in evaluation methodology. Among these limitations, the problems of relating outcome criteria to legislative intents, of establishing a priori standards for progress or failure, of relating context and consequences, and of improving evaluation capability both in terms of ADP systems and human skills were seen as factors likely to define the limits of evaluation for providing interpretable data.

Ascribing limits on evaluation implementation to evaluation technology, and a facilitating role to common political interests may seem upside down and backwards. The July 1977 American Education Research Association Division H *Newsletter* included a resolution that began:

> Local school systems, particularly those located in large cities, have often been overwhelmed by federal data collection and national evaluation efforts, many of which seem non-directed, politically motivated, and not directly beneficial to education (Kean, 1977:1).

The resolution criticizes the federally mandated evaluation instruments, the cost of the studies, lack of interpretability, the destructive use of the data, lack of reporting back to LEAs, and lack of usefulness even if the data were reported back, "due to extreme variation in data collection and quality controls."

Divergent interests can scarcely be overlooked as a source of the Division H resolution, yet the concerns have a familiar ring in the history of vocational education studies. These criticisms have been related here to the limits of evaluation technology, which then are seen more as the causes than as the consequences of resistance to evaluation.

What can be done? One step is to assume good faith among all concerned with vocational education—congress, federal administrators, state and local leadership, teachers, educational staffs, advisory groups, the community, and evaluators—in wanting to help learners. A second step is to recognize the legitimacy of different priorities among these groups, the limitations in evaluation resources and capability, and the state of the art of evaluation in satisfying equally all of the different priorities. There are limits to evaluation, as well as to growth, even if we cannot be sure at present exactly what these limits are. A third step is a determination to work together, through informal as well as formal links, to improve evaluation ability, to define better where evaluation now ends, and the many, many areas in which it is a fruitful beginning. With a little bit of luck, willingness and ability should be adequate this time to take such steps forward.

NOTE

1. The reasons for the eighteen months' vacancy in top leadership in the office responsible for administering the 1976 amendments is another paper. The need to have a suitable mix of gender and ethnicity ("this one has to be a woman"), the vocational education community's vetoes of women unacceptable to them, the unwillingness of the few women acceptable to both the vocational education field and top USOE leadership to accept constraining conditions of federal service, and the less than top priority placed on filling these positions have meant "acting" leadership during the most important period (1976 to 1979) of implementing the new law. Coupled with the dismantling of regional offices and internal OE reorganizations, it may be that the burden of implementing the 1976 law will fall far more heavily on state and local leadership than congress intended.

REFERENCES

Advisory Council on Vocational Education. 1968. *Report of the Advisory Council on Vocational Education.* (ED 021-151)

American Institutes for Research. 1976. *Legislative Mandates for Vocational Education: Study Guide.* Module 5, Vocational Education Curriculum Specialist (VECS). Palo Alto, CA: American Institutes for Research in the Behavioral Sciences. (ED 132-380)

American Vocational Journal. 1976. 200 years of vocational education: special bicentennial issue. *American Vocational Journal* 51:5.

Ash, Lane C. 1973. *Instruments and Procedures for the Evaluation of Vocational/Technical Education.* Washington, DC: American Vocational Association. March 30.

Bryam, H. M., and Robertson, M. *Locally Directed Evaluation of Local Vocational Education Programs.* Danville, Il: Interstate Printers. (undated)

Bushnell, D. S. 1975. *Policy Alternatives in the Evaluation of Vocational Education.* Washington, DC: National Research Council. (ED 130-159)

Christoffel, P. H. 1975. *Vocational Education: Alternatives for New Federal Legislation.* Washington, DC: College Entrance Examination Board. (ED 117-319)

Clark, D. L. 1974. "Federal policy in educational research and development." Graduate lecture at the Center for Vocational Education, The Ohio State University, August 1.

Clary, J. R. 1970. *Review and synthesis of research and developmental activities concerning state advisory councils and vocational education.* Information Series No. 22. Columbus, OH: Center for Vocational and Technical Education. (ED 043-744)

Commission on National Aid to Vocational Education. 1914. *Report on the Commission.* Washington, DC: Government Printing Office.

Congressional Budget Office. 1977. *Elementary, Secondary and Vocational Education: An Examination of Alternative Federal Roles.* Washington, DC.

Congressional Research Service. 1976. *Legislative Oversight and Program Evaluation.* Washington, DC: Government Printing Office.

Conroy, W. G., Jr. 1976. *Recommendations for a Vocational Education Data System— Feedback Book.* Focus: Sections 108, 112, 161, and 161a. Washington, DC: Bureau of Occupational and Adult Education, USOE. November.

Cronbach, L. J., and Suppes, P., eds. 1969. *Research on Tomorrow's Schools. Report of the Committee on Educational Research of the National Academy of Education.* London: Macmillan.

Davis, D., and Borgen, J. 1974. *Planning, Implementing and Evaluating Career Preparation Programs.* Bloomington, IN: McKnight.

Deutscher, I. 1976. Toward Avoiding the Goal Trap in Evaluation Research. Pp. 249-268 in C.C. Abt, ed. *The Evaluation of Social Programs.* Beverly Hills: Sage Publications.

Drewes, D. W., and Katz, D. S. 1975. *Manpower Data and Vocational Education: A National Study of Availability and Use.* Raleigh: Center for Occupational Education, North Carolina State University.

Drewes, D. W. et al. 1977. "Conference on Development of Criteria for Determining Strengths and Limitations of State Administration of Vocational Education." Washington, DC: Conserva, August 30-31.

Ellis, M. L. 1975. *A Report to the Nation on Vocational Education.* Prepared for Project Baseline. Flagstaff: Northern Arizona University. November.

Evans, R. N. 1969. *Education for Employment: The Background and Potential of the 1968 Vocational Education Amendments.* Policy papers in human resources and industrial relations No. 15. Ann Arbor, MI: Institute for Labor and Industrial Relations. (ED 034-861)

———. 1976. *Assessing Vocational Education Research and Development.* Washington, DC: National Academy of Sciences.

General Accounting Office. 1974. *What is the Role of Federal Assistance For Vocational Education?* Report on Congress by the Comptroller General of the United States, December 31.

———. 1977. *Problems and Needed Improvements in Evaluating Office of Education Programs.* Washington, DC, September 8. (HRD-76-165)

Grotberg, E., ed. 1976. *200 Years of Children.* Washington, DC: Office of Child Development.

Hawkins, L. S., Prosser, C. A., and Wright, J. C. 1951. *Development of Vocational Education.* Chicago: American Technical Society.

Hechinger, F. M. 1977. The people and their schools. *New York Times,* August 18.

Kean, M. H., ed. 1977. Division H *Newsletter,* 3,1:1.

Kneso, G. J. 1975. *Program Evaluation: Emerging issues of possible legislative concern relating to the conduct and use of evaluation in Congress and the Executive Branch.* Congressional Research Service, Library of Congress. (JK 421-73-35SP)

Lee, A. M. 1977. Project Baseline: Historiographic Foundations for Vocational Education Statistics. *Educational Researcher* 67 (July-August): 3-9.

Little, J. K. 1970. *Review and Synthesis of Research on the Placement and Follow-up of Vocational Education Students.* Columbus: The Ohio State University.

Lovins, A. B. 1978. Cost-risk-benefits assessments in energy policy. *The George Washington Law Review.*

Mangum, G. L. 1968. *Reorienting Vocational Education.* Policy papers in human resources and industrial relations No. 7. Ann Arbor, MI: Institute of Labor and Industrial Relations. (ED 029-097)

McGowan, E., and Cohen, D. 1976. Rational fantasies: The implementation of innovative federal programs in education. *Policy Science* 7,4(December).

McLaughlin, M. 1974. *The Elementary and Secondary Education Act of 1965, Title I.* Santa Monica, CA: The Rand Corporation.

Michael, B. 1966. Evaluating progress in vocational education. In K. Green et al., *Final Report: Leadership Development Seminar, Vocational-Technical Education.* College Park: University of Maryland. (ED 010-631)

Nay, J. N., Scanlon, J. W., and Wholey, J. S. 1976. Benefits and costs of manpower training programs: A synthesis of previous studies with reservations and recommendations. Pp. 259-261 in U.S. Congress Joint Economic Committee, *Benefit Cost Analysis of Federal Programs.* Washington, DC: Government Printing Office.

Norris, W. R. 1976. *Occupational Education: Report from California Community Colleges.* Sacramento: Office of the Chancellor, California Community College. (ED 121-400)

Office of Education (DHEW) 1975. *Annual Evaluation Report on Programs Administered by the U.S. Office of Education.* FY 75. Washington, DC.

––––. 1964. *Education for a Changing World of Work: Report of the Panel of Consultants on Vocational Education.* Washington, DC (ED 019-500)

Oregon Department of Education. 1977. *Guidelines for Using Data in Vocational Program and Curriculum Planning at the State Agency Level.* Oregon: Career and Education Section, ODE. March.

Ralston, L. W. 1974. "Guidelines for state legislation for vocational education." Ph.D. dissertation, University of California at Los Angeles.

Reid, R. A. 1972. "Guidelines for evaluation activities conducted by state advisory councils for vocational and technical education." Ph.D. dissertation, The Ohio State University.

Reid, J. L. 1976. Involvement to ensure quality is the name of the game. *American Vocational Journal* 51:30-32.

Schneider, E. 1977. *Guidelines for Obtaining and Using Data in Vocational Education Program Planning.* Oregon: Portland Public Schools. January.

Scientific Educational Systems, Inc. 1970. *Joint Federal/State Task Force on Comprehensive Evaluation System: Current Status and Development Requirements.* (Draft) Washington, DC: Scientific Educational Systems, Inc. (ED 042-817 and ED 042-818)

Senate Committee on Labor and Public Welfare. 1968. Notes and working papers concerning the administration of programs authorized under the Vocational Education Act of 1963." March. (ED 021-151)

Sharp, L. M. 1968. *Student Follow-up Study Procedures as a Technique for Evaluating Vocational and Technical Education Programs.* Washington, DC: Bureau of Social Science Research, Inc.

Songe, A. 1972. *Vocational Education: Secondary and Post-Secondary, 1967-1972: An Annotated Bibliography.* Washington, DC: National Advisory Council on Vocational Education. (ED 112-124)

Sparks, D. 1977. *A Synthesis of Research Findings which Describe Selected Benefits and Outcomes for Participants in Vocational Education.* Washington, DC: Office of Education. October.

Taggart, R., and Levitan, S. 1976. *The Promise of Greatness.* Cambridge, MA: Harvard University Press.

Tigert, J. T. 1924. An organization by the teachers and for the teachers. *School Life,* 9 (May).

U.S. Congress. 1976. *Education Amendments of 1976, Public Law 94-482.* 94th Congress. Washington, DC: Government Printing Office.

Warmbrod, J. R. 1968. *Review and synthesis of research on the economics of vocational-technical education: Research Report No. 10.* Columbus, OH: Center for Vocational Education, The Ohio State University.

Weiss, C. H. 1977. Research for policy's sake: The enlightenment function of social research. *Policy Analysis,* 3, 4:531-545.

Weiss, C. H., and Bucuvalas, M. J. 1977. The challenge of social research on decision-making. Pp. 213-233 in C.H. Weiss, ed. *Using Social Research.* New York: Lexington Books, D.C. Heath.

Wentling, T. L., and Lawson, T. E. 1975. *Evaluating Occupational Education and Training Programs.* Boston: Allyn and Bacon.

GLOSSARY

Federal Membership

NACVE	National Advisory Council on Vocational Education
NCES	National Center for Educational Statistics
BOAE	Bureau of Occupational and Adult Education
OPBE	Office of Planning, Budgeting and Evaluation
DOL/ETA	Department of Labor; Employment and Training Administration
NCVER	National Center for Vocational Education Research
NIE	National Institute of Education
DOC	Department of Commerce
CRS	Congressional Research Service of the Library of Congress
CBO	Congressional Budget Office
GAO	General Accounting Office
NAS	National Academy of Science, National Research Council
NOICC	National Occupational Information Coordinating Committee

State Membership

SACVE	State Advisory Council on Vocational Education
RCU	Research Coordinating Unit
CSSO/CEIS	Chief State School Officer, Committee on Education and Information Systems
SDVE	State Director of Vocational Education

Local Membership

AACJC	American Association of Community and Junior Colleges
AASSP	American Association of Secondary School Principals
AASS	American Association of Superintendents of Schools
AVA	American Vocational Association
AVERA	American Vocational Education Research Association
AAHE	American Association of Higher Education
ETA	Prime Sponsors local recipients of education and training grants under DOL legislation, including the Youth Employment Act.
LBCM	League of Big City Mayors—CETA prime sponsors
NUL	National Urban League
NEA	National Education Association
AFT	American Federation of Teachers
NSBA	National School Boards Association
LACVE	Local Advisory Council for Vocational Education
ASTD	American Society of Training Directors
APGA	American Personnel and Guidance Association

chapter 3

CAROL KEHR TITTLE | *University of North Carolina
at Greensboro*

The purpose of the Vocational Education Act (VEA) is to assist states to maintain, extend, and improve existing programs of vocational education, to develop new programs of vocational education, and to provide part-time employment for youths who need the earnings from such employment to continue their vocational training on a full-time basis. Recent amendments in the Education Acts of 1968 and 1976 put increased emphasis on support for program improvement and change, and less emphasis on maintenance of existing vocational education programs. The 1976 amendments specify follow-up studies using such effectiveness criteria as employment in training-related occupations, employer satisfaction, and continuing education.

The VEA legislation and regulations provide broad goals and requirements for vocational education as federally funded, yet leave a wide latitude to the states in allocating funds to local education agencies (LEAs) for programs.[1] One question of interest to evaluators, program developers, and directors of vocational education programs, in terms of the relationship between funding

AUTHOR'S NOTE: *The assistance of Jane Fagen-Steckler, Helen Spilman and Bill Boudreau is gratefully acknowledged. Dr. Fagen-Steckler and Dr. Spilman were colleagues during the first year of the project that forms the basis of this chapter. The paper has benefited from reviews by Bob Stake, Ken Hammond, and Robert Seckendorf. Bill Boudreau clarified funding procedures for the project final report, as well as facilitating the conduct of the project.*

decisions and evaluation data, is, How do state departments of education decide which grant program applications to fund? This chapter has three main parts: (1) *State-level Decision-Making* describes how funding decisions are made at a state level; (2) *Interim Report* presents the procedures and results of a pilot study that suggests how decision makers may be assisted by defining program impact for evaluation, and "translating" these impact definitions to variables known at the time of funding new programs; and (3) *Research Issues and Political Concerns* raises a number of political and research issues for evaluators in this particular context for decision making. For some readers, the present discussion may be better understood in relation to the relevant research and evaluation literature. A separate section (Decision Aiding Techniques) follows Part One, and presents a brief summary of related literature. Other readers may prefer to omit the section on Decision Aiding Techniques, following the main sections of the chapter as presented in Parts One, Two, and Three.

A fundamental concern should be raised at the outset. The work presented here assumes, as does the literature on evaluation, decision theory, and decision aids, that making objectives and values explicit will "improve" the decisions that are made with respect to educational programs. Stake (personal communication), posed the issue of whether these procedures will assist decision makers or intrude on a domain that competent administrators can handle intuitively. Do formal criteria help identify the best proposals? Past research does not provide satisfactory evidence to answer the question, and experience with these methods in the field of education is very limited. Readers may want to keep this issue in mind as they read the present chapter.

The analysis and description which follow are limited by being based on work within one state. However, a review of the literature on the use of systematic procedures to allocate funds within large federal programs indicates that the process may not differ much from the process in other settings. Personal experience in reading program grant applications at the federal level also suggests that the procedures are not atypical. In general, little attention has been paid to developing methods to assist decision makers with the definitions of criteria on which to allocate funds in large-scale, annually allocated funding programs.[2] The interim report given here suggests the value of decision aids to management may be in improving the consistency and, hence, the validity of decision-making in resource allocation in the setting where there are multiple decision makers applying the same criteria. The present chapter will also assist evaluators to gain an understanding of one instance of state level decision-making and the potential use of decision aids in evaluation. As Perloff, Perloff and Sussna (1976) suggested, these methods are apparently useful in developing criterion or outcome variables for evaluation.

1. STATE-LEVEL DECISION MAKING

The Vocational Education Act, as amended, sets constraints for funding decisions for basic grants programs. Federal constraints take the form of setting priorities for state distribution of funds to: (1) economically depressed areas and areas of high unemployment rates which are unable to meet the vocational needs of these areas without federal assistance, and (2) to programs which are new to the areas to be served, and which meet new and emerging manpower needs (Federal Register, 1977:53822). Also, two other criteria are important in distributing funds to LEAs: (1) the relative financial ability to provide needed services, and (2) the relative concentration of low income populations within such agencies. Other constraints in allocating monies include those under fiscal requirements—which target specific percentages of the state's allotment to national priority programs. In the 1976 amendments, these priorities were defined as at least 10 percent of the state's allotment to the handicapped, 20 percent to the disadvantaged, persons of limited English-speaking ability, and students with acute economic needs, and 15 percent to postsecondary and adult programs.

Other constraints are that 80 percent of the funds allotted are used in basic grants—that is, allocations of monies to LEAs for programs. Other sections of the VEA allocate percents or specific amounts to activities such as research, curriculum development and innovative programs, guidance, personnel training, and overcoming sex stereotyping. Although there are federal constraints in general allocation of money at the state level, there are individual decisions remaining in deciding which program grants to fund. In New York State, for example, it is clear that New York City alone could develop vocational education programs that would fit the various special populations and economically depressed requirements for the total amount of the New York State basic grant allotment. There is not enough money to satisfy everyone's needs, because other parts of New York State also meet these regulatory constraints and priorities.

The decision-making process, then, cannot rely solely on federal regulations to allocate funds. And the resulting situation is the decision problem that stimulated the current examination of the relationship between the funding and evaluation processes. The examination received further impetus from the increasing emphasis on evaluation at the federal level that Datta (1979) described. The decision process, as in all resource allocation settings, is subject to external pressures. Superintendents or state legislators, for example, may be asked by their constituents to inquire why particular programs are not funded. These diverse pressures have, in fact, increased state-level support for an examination and discussion of the criteria for allocating funds. Further understanding of the decision process can be gained from an examination of the major decision areas for grant proposals as shown in Figure 3.1.

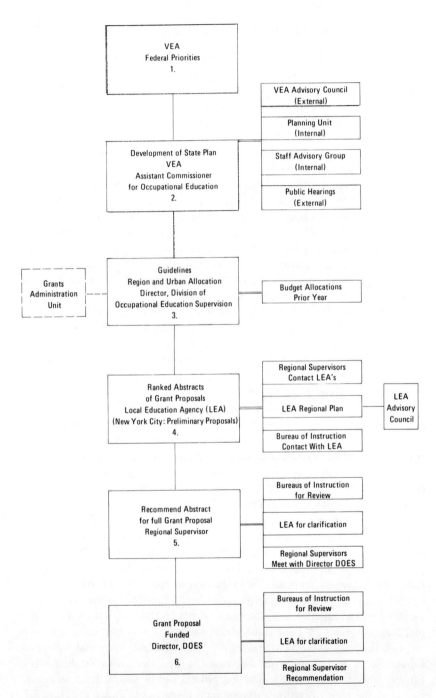

FIGURE 3.1: Major decision areas for grant proposals

Figure 3.1 is based on the decision areas for VEA program grants in FY 1975.[3] As shown, the decision process started with the federal priorities for the VEA. Within the federal framework, each state developed a state plan (long range and an annual program) for the VEA. In New York State the Assistant Commissioner for Occupational Education was responsible for the development of the plan. Several sources provided advice and information for the development of the plan. These sources included the VEA State Advisory Council and public hearings (both external to the SED) and the internal planning unit and staff advisory groups.

The state plan translated state needs and federal priorities into statements of goals and activities for levels of education and population served. (The levels served are elementary and early secondary, secondary, postsecondary, adult and multilevel. The populations served are general, disadvantaged, handicapped, and multi.) Numbers of students to be affected by each goal/activity and costs are given, and in some cases designated by urban/rural areas or for BOCES,[4] Major Cities,[5] and other educational institutions.

The third decision area is the formulation of guidelines for regional and urban allocation. Guidelines for the allocation of funds to individual regions and for each of the five major cities were developed by the Board of Regents, and the Director of the Division of Occupational Education Supervision (DOES). Those guidelines took into account budget allocations from prior years and population statistics. The next decision occurred when the LEAs submitted preliminary proposals—abstracts of grant proposals. These were submitted ranked in order of priority by the LEA.

The steps leading to the submission by LEAs of a set of rank-ordered abstracts of grant proposals may have varied somewhat, but several features appeared common. About December 1, a letter was sent by the Director of DOES to the LEA Directors of Occupational Education. Included with the letter were a list of the tasks to be carried out between December 22 and March 15;[6] a VEA Abstract Form; and an Abstract Summary Sheet (to list the VEA Purpose, Program Title, Budget Total, and LEA priority for each program [within VEA purpose]).

The DOES Regional Supervisor had been in contact with the LEA (typically the agency Director of Occupational Education) prior to January 1, when the abstracts were received by DOES. The contact took the form of assisting LEAs to develop abstracts, identifying priorities of projects, and locating the VEA purpose appropriate for individual projects. Instructional bureau staff may also have worked with LEAs.

By January 31, regional supervisors notified LEAs of the abstracts that were to be developed into full grant proposals. These recommendations were the fifth major decision area. Recommendations were formulated on the basis of several steps:

(1) The regional supervisor reviewed the LEA abstract and applied several types of criteria:
  - conformity with VEA regulations
  - meets state plan
  - meets regional needs (district priorities)
  - clarity of abstract (rationale, objectives, description, evaluation plan)
  - appropriateness of budget (and dollars requested)
  - strength of local staff, likely student enrollment

(2) The abstract may also have been reviewed by the appropriate Bureau(s) of Instruction.

(3) The LEA might have been contacted for clarification or justification of the abstract.

(4) The regional supervisor summarized the requests from all LEAs in the region; dollars requested were totaled by VEA purpose; amounts requested were compared with the guidelines for the region; and decisions were made as to which abstracts to recommend for full development.

(5) The Director of DOES and regional supervisors met. Regional supervisors presented the needs of their regions and the approximate dollar amounts were agreed upon. Some adjustments were made, depending on the dollars available in VEA Purpose categories and regional requests.

(6) LEAs were notified of the abstracts approved for development for full grant proposals.

The sixth decision is the final decision to fund a program. By March, full grant proposals were received in DOES. Typically the grant proposals were sent by the regional supervisor to one or more instructional bureaus for review. During this review procedure the LEAs may have been contacted for revision or clarification of the grant proposal.

Based on a number of criteria (see decision area 5 above), including the review by Bureau of Instruction staff, the regional supervisor recommended approval, deferral, or rejection of the grant proposal to the Director of DOES. The director had final responsibility for the funding decision.

These decision areas describe the general steps of the decision process for FY 1975. However, the development of ideas and local priorities appeared to be a continuous rather than discrete process, because the Director of DOES and regional supervisors were in contact with local districts throughout the year, at DOES-sponsored annual meetings, and on site visits. Also, the funding of VEA proposals did not take place entirely at one time. Proposals were reviewed and funded later in the year due to the availability of additional funds (e.g., some proposals recommended for development were not, in fact, developed, so these funds were released for other projects).

Decisions on priorities and rankings of projects occurred both at the state and local levels, because LEAs were asked to rank order the set of grant applications they submit. The procedures described as part of a pilot study may thus be applicable at both the state and local levels.

The pilot project described in Part Two, *Interim Report,* had several purposes. One purpose was to develop definitions of outcome variables. The outcome variables, when combined, are intended to assist in identifying a "high impact" project: that is, a project which is high on important outcome dimensions for students, employers, or the granting agency. A second purpose was to relate these definitions to funding decisions. For this second purpose, definitions of impact variables (evaluation outcome variables) were translated into "predictive impact" variables that can be determined for each proposal at the time of the application for funding, thus providing some "objectively determined" data to be combined with the other information entering the funding decision making process. A third purpose of the study was to determine the extent of agreement among the major decision makers at the state level on the relative importance of the variables, to determine whether further study of the variables was worthwhile.

DECISION AIDING TECHNIQUES

A brief survey of related research will help in understanding the methods that are presently available to evaluators to assist decision makers to identify the key variables in decision-making, and the utilities (values or weights) that decision makers may assign to the variables. These methods are only part of the set of procedures that would be used by evaluators to present a formal decision theory analysis to decision makers at the state or local level. Gross (1979) described the use of the outcomes of these decision aiding procedures in a Bayesian decision model and used one of the major methods proposed (Edwards' multiattribute utility measurement method). The related research has been identified by topics, and includes evaluation and judgment data, decision-making—decision theory and decision aids, including multiattribute utility theory, social judgment theory, and goal attainment—and impact definitions.

Evaluation and Judgment Data

Davis and Salasin (1975) have summarized many of the issues in the use of evaluation results, including statements by evaluators that their results are not used, and those by administrators that evaluation findings are not available when decisions have to be made. Although there is much discussion of the need to relate evaluation and decision making, there have been few efforts to specify the manner in which this might occur.

Hemphill (1969) provided early examples of the use of educational evaluation data in a formal decision theory model. In one instance, an individual decision maker decided whether to install a new nursery school, and also examined whether to carry out the evaluation study, again within a decision theory framework. Tanner (1971) suggested the use of a Bayesian approach for a hypothetical program evaluation. A review by Stake (1970) focused on the use of judgment data and methods for gathering these data were described. An earlier article by Stake (1967) suggested the need for better methods for processing judgments in evaluation. The work that has gone on in processing judgments has largely occurred *outside* of educational evaluation. This work has been in the area of decision making and preference scaling.

Decision-making

A major function of program evaluation, perhaps the most important, is to provide information needed for policy formulation, program planning, and decision-making. Edwards, Guttentag, and Snapper (1975) took the view that evaluation exists to facilitate decision-making, and presented a "decision-theoretic" approach to evaluation. Weiss (1976) suggested that evaluation designs should be geared specifically to the decisions that were going to be made, although recognizing that there are typically multiple decision makers and interested parties.[7] Work in decision theory and decision aids suggests how this can occur in vocational education evaluation.

A. DECISION THEORY

Decision theory provides a formal model which considers the consequences of a decision in terms of a payoff or loss to the decision maker resulting from the action selected and the state of the world that occurs (Winkler, 1972). The theory of decision-making has been developed largely by economists and applied in business settings, although it is now being applied in other disciplines, including education and psychology. An extensive review of this literature was conducted by Edwards in 1954, and this review was updated by Edwards in 1961.

Slovic, Fischoff, and Lichtenstein (1977) provide the most recent review accessible to those working in educational evaluation. Their review of behavioral decision theory distinguished between two facets, normative and descriptive. The paper included a section in which decision aid techniques were reviewed and discussed. (The work of Edwards et al. [1975] and Hammond et al. [1975b] are placed in the section on aids to decision-making.) Three recent books also provide a series of articles in the area of utilities and decision-making (Cochrane and Zeleny, 1973; Wendt and Vlek, 1975; Keeney and Raiffa, 1976). Einhorn and Hogarth (1978) have provided an interesting review relating studies of human judgment and decisions to studies of learning, especially studies involving probabilities. They presented a model to explain the persistence of the "illusion of validity" in research on clinical judgment: judges consistently displayed great confidence in their (very) fallible judgments. This line of research has implications for decision settings where grants are awarded, and where judgments are used to establish outcomes for evaluation.

B. DECISION AIDS

The application of formal decision theory to some decision-making situations can present practical problems in terms of the time and expertise involved, and the difficulties of casting a real-life decision situation in a decision theory framework, e.g., identifying states of the world, estimating prior and posterior probabilities, and calculating expected payoff or loss values. Recently some components of decision theory have been incorporated into what may be called decision aids—techniques to provide more practical assistance to decision makers. These decision aids are the basis for the present study, but it should be noted that Slovic et al. (1977) cited critics who argue that decision aids require assessments of quantities the decision maker has never thought about, and that these apparently simple assessments may be psychologically more complex than the original decision. Examples of decision aids are multiattribute utility theory and social judgment theory, described next.

Multiattribute Utility Theory:[8] Multiattribute utility theory (MAUT) is a technique which has been developed to aid decision makers to assess values and quantify characteristics of programs or activities for selection among them (Crawford, 1973; Dawes, 1973; Fischer, 1975; Green, 1973; Guttentag, 1973; MacCrimmon, 1973; Guttentag and Snapper, 1974; Edwards, Guttentag, and Snapper, 1975; Mahoney, 1976). In the Edwards et al. (1975:153) description, MAUT employs much of the terminology of decision theory, and includes some similar steps in its methodology:

> The essence of multi-attribute utility measurements . . . is that each outcome to be evaluated is located on each dimension of value by a procedure that may consist of experimentation, naturalistic observation, judgment, or some combination of these. These location measures are combined by means of an aggregation rule, most often simply a

weighted linear combination. The weights are numbers describing the importance of each dimension of value relative to the others.

As they specify MAUT procedures, the steps are: identifying the outcomes or criteria to be taken into account for decisions, assigning a weight to each criteria, locating each project or grant proposal on each criterion scale, and multiplying the project location (scale value) by the weight for that criterion. This last step is carried out for each proposal or project on each criterion. The score is obtained for each project, thus providing a ranking of projects across the multiattributes (criteria) in terms of their value to those defining the criteria (attributes) for decisions. Decision makers can, thereby, identify the projects or grant proposals that are highest across all the attributes of importance. MAUT is said by its proponents to be a more efficient and realistic approach to many program planning and evaluation situations than the use of formal decision theory and utility functions. (Gross' chapter provides a full list of MAUT procedures and an example.)

Some examples of where MAUT has been applied to aid decision-making include: the planning process of the Office of Child Development (Guttentag, 1973; Guttentag and Snapper, 1974), a land-use management problem (Gardiner and Edwards, 1975), the evaluation of suite design proposals for the United States Navy (Hays, O'Connor, and Peterson, 1975), and program planning in a rural community mental health center (Gibson, 1976). Baron (1976, 1977) gives a step-by-step description of the MAUT model, and presents an application to a hypothetical educational program situation. Crawford (1973) provides an example of "impact" analysis using differentially weighted evaluative criteria, similar to MAUT, including expert judgments of probabilities of events. The problem was the analysis of several highway corridor alternatives.

Two studies describing applications of MAUT technology (Guttentag and Snapper, 1974; Gardiner and Edwards, 1975) have reported similar findings concerning comparisons with intuitive decisions. Both found that there was good agreement or high correlation between multiattribute utility measurements and intuitive evaluations, and concluded the model was valid. Slovic et al. (1977:22-23) argue that this is a faulty conclusion because it is essentially circular in reasoning, and recommend more sophisticated approaches to the validity issue.

Social Judgment Theory: Another approach to aid decision-making based on social judgment theory (SJT) has been developed by Ken Hammond and his associates. The SJT approach is concerned both with the decision maker and the properties of the judgment task. Effort is devoted in this method to understanding the relations among cues (dimensions) represented in the judgment task, and to representing the initial ambiguity of the judgment task to the decision maker. SJT is directed toward reducing the ambiguity in the judgment task (as is MAUT), but provides a more realistic task, closer to the actual decision setting, the proposal or items to be judged, than does MAUT.

According to Hammond et al. (1975b) the analysis of the cognitive system of the individual (decision maker) proceeds in four steps:

(1) *Identification of the judgment problem* The substantive and formal properties of the judgment problem are identified.

(2) *Exercise of judgment* The individual makes judgments about a representative set of cases of the judgment problem (presented visually on a computer terminal CRT or otherwise).

(3) *Analysis of judgment* The individual's judgments are analyzed to determine the components of the individual's cognitive system (e.g., weights given to different dimensions in the judgment task).

(4) *Display of results* The results of the analysis are displayed graphically to the individual (ordinarily by interactive computer techniques).

The *identification of the judgment problem* has three parts: (1) defining the judgment to be made, (2) identifying the information (cues) on which the judgment is based, and (3) discovering the formal properties of the set of cue variables in the task (for example, the intercorrelations, distributions, and ranges if these can be found; otherwise the formal properties are constructed on a best guess basis).

The *exercise of judgment* involves using a judgment task that consists of a number of cases representing the judgment problem. Each case (in our decision setting a proposal for funding) has a profile representing a different combination or mix of values on the several cues. The individual rates each of several profiles on a numerical scale. For example, the numerical scale could be a judgment of the overall impact of the project represented in a particular profile, e.g., how would you rate this project in its impact as a VEA project? The *analysis of judgment* data is in terms of multiple regression statistics. The values of the cues are the independent variables and the individual's judgments are the dependent variable:

$$y_{ij} = \sum_{k=1}^{m} b_{ik} \, x_{jk} + c_i + e_{ij}$$

where y_{ij} is the judgment of individual i for profile j, m is the number of cues, b_{ik} is the raw score regression weight for individual i on cue k, x_{jk} is the value of cue k on profile j, c_i is the constant term for individual i, and e_{ij} is the residual error from the model of individual i for profile j. The *display of results* shows the weights and function forms obtained from the analysis of judgment. The display of results can be presented on a computer (CRT), or a printout to the individual after the judgments are made.

Hammond and Adelman (1976) described an actual study in policy-making where SJT was used. They used both expert and citizen judgments (social value judgments) in a policy decision on the type of handgun ammunition to be used by the Denver Police Department. The issue was the question of which bullet was best for the community. The problem was refocused to describe the use of force and injury in enforcing the law. The relative importance of the societal characteristics of bullets (injury, stopping effectiveness, or ricochet) was judged by city council representatives and other citizens, in order to obtain a social policy controlling the selection of police ammunition. Various bullets (N=80) were judged by ballistic experts (blind with respect to the social policy) with regard to their technical characteristics. That is, the judgment task for citizens was the relative desirability of hypothetical bullets, described in terms of the stopping effectiveness, severity of injury, and threat to bystanders. The experts' ratings on stopping effectiveness, for example, showed that three technical characteristics of bullets were important.

The data from citizen and expert judgments were combined in the following way for each bullet:

$$Y_s = W_1 X_1 + W_2 X_2 + W_3 X_3$$

where Y_s is the overall acceptability of a bullet; W_j, j = 1, 3 indicates the weight or relative importance policy makers placed on stopping effectiveness, injury, and threat to bystanders; and X_j, j = 1, 3 are the experts' judgments on that bullet for stopping effectiveness, injury, and threat to bystanders. One of the advantages of the method used in this example is that it makes the dimensions for judgment external and the weights public, and the weights are derived from a judgment task that simulates the complexity of real-world judgments. Comparative studies of weights derived from MAUT, SJT procedures, or validity have apparently not been conducted.

Goal Attainment: Goal attainment scaling is also a decision aid which deals with the quantification of values (Kiresuk, 1975). It was originally designed to measure individual patient progress during or after treatments in mental health settings, but may have wider application. Paine (1977) described applications in the evaluation of children with special educational needs, a college-level psychology class, mental health settings, and also cites mental health program evaluation efforts.

Steps in the goal attainment procedure are as follows:

(1) A set of dimensions or goals are devised for or by an individual.
(2) A scale is developed for each dimension. One example showed a five category scale ranging from "most unfavorable treatment outcome thought likely" to "best anticipated success with treatment." For each dimension each category on the scale is defined.
(3) Weights are assigned among the dimensions. As the scales are weighted relative to one another, any set of numbers can be used.
(4) A set of expected outcome levels are selected for each dimension.
(5) The patient's intake level on each dimension is assessed.
(6) The patient's outcome level is scored by someone not on the treatment center staff.
(7) A score summarizing the outcome across all dimensions is determined, with scores converted to T-scores. A comparison of intake scores and outcome levels provides an estimate of change during treatment.

A critical review of goal attainment scaling was presented by Cytrynbaum, Birdwell, Brandt, and Ginath (1977), including an extensive bibliography. They reached the tentative conclusion that the popularity of goal attainment scaling for evaluation did not appear justified by research to date, but that its usefulness as an *intervention* technique was well established.

Other Ratings for Funding Decisions: Bateman (1968) describes a project evaluation system developed for the Work Experience and Training Program. It includes a rating system whereby projects were ranked according to their ratings on a set of effectiveness measures. One of the intended uses of the ratings was to assist in future decisions. Another scoring model is described by Clark (1976); this model was developed to aid in making funding decisions for grant proposals. Although points are assigned to various categories for raters to use, the scales are not well defined. The Delphi technique is another procedure that has been used to develop lists of objectives or indicators of successful programs, typically using mailed questionnaires. Dagenais (n.d.) used the Delphi technique to identify "most successful" vocational programs on sixteen community college campuses.

Impact Definitions

A critical aspect of program evaluation and determining priorities for funding is the identification and measurement of program impact or outcomes. Papers concerned with the analysis of impact and impact assessment methodology have not always dealt with the issue of the definition of impact (Campbell, 1975; Cook and Scioli, 1975). Representative examples of definitions include: "the capacity of a program to cause changes in those who are exposed to it" (Houston, 1972), and "the difference between what happens with the intervention and what would happen without" (Levine, 1967). Boruch and Gomez (1977:411) defined impact in the following terms:

> By impact evaluation, we mean estimating in the least equivocal and least biased way the relative effect of a program on its target group. The estimate may be made with respect to a control group, a competing treatment group, or to some other standard.

Stein, Hougham, and Zalba (1968) discussed program effectiveness in terms of goals, and provide the following definitions of effectiveness:

- appropriateness of goals
- efficacy of a particular therapeutic technique or service
- extent to which goals are reached without too many intolerable consequences

Cain and Hollister (1972) suggested that measurement of program outputs should be confined to measures of tangible change, such as income and employment. Bernstein and Freeman (1975) dealt with the definition problem by presenting the requirements for impact measurement:

(1) document the extent to which the social action program has or has not achieved its stated goals;
(2) attribute any effects or changes that are discovered to the implementation of the program;
(3) delineate, if possible, the conditions or combinations of conditions under which the program is most effective;
(4) delineate, if possible, any unanticipated consequences or side effects of the program.

This definition assumes a common set of goals across programs, if one objective of evaluation is to permit a comparison of the impact of different programs within a major funding program. Sirois and Iwanicki (1977) have noted the between-program comparison problem, where program goals lack specificity and regularity. The present project is concerned with a somewhat different perspective, because not all programs funded under the VEA can be expected to meet all the goals or priorities of the legislation.

Hu and Stromsdorfer (1975) defined general criteria for measuring the educational and economic impact of research and demonstration projects in vocational education. Two types of impact of vocational education were identified: (1) intermediate impact or goals, and (2) final output or ultimate goals. The first type included: modification or revision of curricula; reallocation of funds within the educational system; effects on students' aptitudes and school performance; number of graduates produced; percentage of graduates working in occupations for which they were prepared; improvement in student attendance; and sense of fulfillment in vocational education teachers after developing a new program. The final output included labor market performance of students (wages, employment, job satisfaction) and educational attainment.

Hu and Stromsdorfer's list can be viewed as a general set of criteria. In addition to the types of variables in their list, the VEA for 1976 provided that training for special populations was also an important goal for VEA programs. The diversity of (legitimate) outcomes means that not all programs will have the same set of objectives. And there is a concern expressed by state decision makers and local program administrators that not every program can meet the same set of standards. When programs serve diverse populations, as in the vocational education legislation, it is probably more realistic to have a set of impact variables to evaluate program impact, not all of which are expected to apply to each program. Projects can be judged to have a high impact by meeting some standards (i.e., being high on some impact scales) but not on all. The same conclusion can be drawn for the predictive impact variables being identified in the project described below. Where federal legislation has multiple goals and groups to be served, a set of important outcomes that are operationally defined may permit identification of "high impact" projects and also permit local needs to be met. Yet, the definition of the impact variables and their use in funding decision making may serve to focus local projects and evaluations on these same outcomes.

In addition to the goal or criterion of maximizing impact in funding, at least two other criteria have been alluded to above. These are: (1) the criterion of giving each community a chance to work its own improvement in vocational education, and (2) the criterion of addressing the greatest needs. Although the present work emphasizes maximizing total impact, the reader should refer to Figure 3.1, presented earlier, and note the decision areas in which funds are allocated to regions of the state (currently on the basis of a formula that takes into account poverty/unemployment data), and the decision area in which the LEA goals are reflected in the submission of proposals ranked in order of local priorities. Impact, then, is one criterion for decision-making. Although the impact variables described below were developed from several sources, it is clear that they are arbitrary. More confidence may be placed in them if they are "validated" through consensus of other groups, including LEA vocational education program directors, as is planned.

2. INTERIM REPORT

This interim report presents a description of the methods and results obtained to date in a pilot project designed to develop definitions of high impact projects, and to examine the agreement among SED staff on the importance of outcome impact variables and on the importance of predictive impact variables (i.e., variables that can be known at the time of funding). The work described here is being followed up with a study of the importance ratings given a revised set of impact variables by LEAs and SED staff.

The work to date has generally followed the Edwards, Guttentag, and Snapper (1975) procedure to develop the impact dimensions. As noted by both Hammond, Stewart, Brehemer and Steinmann (1975b), and Edwards (1976), the most important step is the first one: developing a clear understanding of the decision-making process, and developing the lists of variables to be considered for rating. As noted earlier, interviews were conducted with State Education Department (SED) decision makers to develop a flow chart of the decision process for funding, and to elicit statements defining or critical to high impact projects. In addition, a review of the literature in vocational education was conducted to identify other goals and objectives. An initial list of 104 statements related to the impact of vocational education programs on students, employers, and the SED were sorted and reduced to twelve outcome (impact) statements.[9] These statements were rephrased to nine predictive impact statements by identifying the variables that were known conditions to achieving the outcomes. Table 3.1 shows sample statements used in this pilot study. Rank ordering and ratings of importance (using a twenty-point scale) by SED decision makers were then obtained. The ratings were a modification of the Edwards' procedure. Gibson (1976) and Edwards (1976) both indicate that the use of ratings correlates highly with the more difficult (for judges) procedure of obtaining weights by a ratio method. At the time of the rating, all the dimensions were specified operationally (as shown in Table 3.1), so raters had an idea of what the eventual scale definitions might be, even though on a tentative basis.

Three rater groups were used. The first group consisted of the Director of the SED division responsible for funding decisions; the second group was the set of supervisors who make funding decisions; and the third group was a set of supervisors from related bureaus who also review and have a part in the decision-making process. Agreement among the three groups of raters was measured by Kendall's Coefficient of Concordance (W). The coefficients for the twelve outcome statements were .81 for the ranks and .94 for the ratings ($p < .01$). Agreement was as high for the ranking of the predictive impact statements (W = .81 [.05 $< p <$ .01] for the ranks) but not for the ratings (W = .41 [.50 $< p <$ .30] for the ratings of the importance of the predictive impact statements). We do not know whether there was an error in use of the ratings scales or whether the groups differed that much in their perceptions. Tables 3.2 and 3.3 present the mean rankings for each outcome and predictive impact statement given by the three groups.

Table 3.1: Sample Outcome Impact Statements and Categories[*]

Training Objectives Are Met with Minimal Cost Per Student.

Training cost per student:

| $500 or less | $501 to $1000 | $1001 to $1500 | $1501 or more |

Program Graduates Are Working in Occupations for Which They Were Trained.

Percentage of program graduates employed in occupations for which trained
(within first six months):

| 0-25% | 26-50% | 51-75% | 76-100% |

The Vocational Education Needs of Special Groups Are Met – The Economically Disadvantaged, the Handicapped, and Persons with Limited English-Speaking Ability.

Percentage of students trained who are from these special groups:

| 0-25% | 26-50% | 51-75% | 76-100% |

Students Are Trained for Occupations Traditionally Dominated by the Opposite Sex.

Percentage of students in program who are trained for occupations traditionally
dominated by the opposite sex:[a]

| 0-25% | 26-50% | 51-75% | 76-100% |

[a]Occupations in which the proportion of women is less than 38%

Employers Are Satisfied with Graduates of the Program.

(a) Percentage of graduates that employers rate as satisfactory on entry level skills:

| 0-25% | 26-50% | 51-75% | 76-100% |

(b) Percentage of graduates that employers retain or promote (for a two-year period):

| 0-25% | 26-50% | 51-75% | 76-100% |

[*]Predictive Impact Statements are often the same, with the exception that they are stated in the future tense (. . . will be . . .).

The high agreement among the raters on the set of ratings and rankings of the outcome impact statements was encouraging. It was not clear why there was a discrepancy between the agreement on ranks and that for the ratings for the predictive impact statements, as mentioned above. There has, however, been a revision of the two sets of statements, and a second set of ratings and rankings will be obtained. Revisions were made on the basis of the change in the VEA with the 1976 amendments, and also the two sets are now more

Table 3.2: Mean Ranking of Outcome Impact Statements by Three "Groups" of SED Raters

Outcome Impact Statements	Group Ranking[a]		
	1	*2*	*3*
(A) Training objectives are met with minimal cost per student	2	6	9.5
(B) Large numbers of students are trained	12	8.5	11
(C) Program graduates are working in occupations for which they were trained	1	2	4
(D) Program or product is implemented in widespread geographical area	11	12	9.5
(E) Vocational education needs of special groups are met	7	8.5	7
(F) Students are trained for occupations traditionally dominated by the opposite sex	8	11	12
(G) Training increases student employment options	3	3.5	2
(H) Students learn career planning	9	7	6
(I) Students trained continue their education	10	10	8
(J) Employers are satisfied with graduates of program	4	1	3
(K) Job satisfaction of students trained is increased	6	3.5	1
(L) Students trained have a more positive attitude toward work	5	5	5

[a]Rank based on mean of ranks for the group of raters.

$\underline{W} = .814$

$X^2_{W.} (11 \text{df}) = 26.86 \qquad .01 < p < .001$

parallel. Table 3.4 presents the current list of predictive and outcome impact statements which will be rated by SED staff and LEAs.

A summary of the method to date includes these steps:

(1) Interviews of SED decision makers and surveys of the literature to identify critical aspects of high impact projects;
(2) Developing lists of outcome variables from (1), above;
(3) "Free" sorting of statements by evaluation staff;
(4) For a reduced list (twelve or fewer statements), stating both as outcome and predictive statements; developing operational definitions and sample scales for raters.
(5) Obtain rankings and ratings of the preliminary set.[10]

The ratings or value (utilities) attached to the dimensions can then be used in formal decision theory or a Bayesian decision theory approach (Winkler, 1972; Gross, 1979).

Table 3.3: Mean Ranking of Predictive Impact Statements by Three "Groups" of SED Raters

Predictive Impact Statements	Group Ranking[a]		
	1	*2*	*3*
(A) Training objectives will be met with minimal cost per student	2	5	4
(B) Large numbers of students will be trained	9	7	8
(C) Students will be trained for available jobs.	1	1.5	1
(D) Program will be replicable in other settings	6	3	5
(E) Vocational education needs of special groups will be met	4	6	6
(F) Students will be trained for occupations traditionally dominated by the opposite sex.	5	8	9
(G) Training will be provided to increase students' employment options.	3	1.5	2
(H) Students will learn career planning	7	4	3
(I) New program will serve students' interests (even though jobs are not available locally)	8	9	7

[a]Rank based on mean of ranks for the group of raters.

$\underline{W} = .805$

X^2_W (8df) = 19.31 $.05 < p < .01$

The next steps in the project are to develop forms which can be used to provide the data needed for funding decisions and for evaluation (the predictive and outcome impact statements, respectively). These data will provide the information necessary to change the sample categories given raters to categories based on distribution data. For example, the sample categories for cost per student in Table 3.1 are fictional. In order to know whether a project is high or low on cost per student, actual data must be obtained and grouped for comparable programs. The approach to defining "high" on the impact scales which is planned, is essentially a normative approach. There may be adequate consensus on variables defining a highly effective program, but it is not clear that decision makers have an internal standard of what is "high" or "successful." Datta (1979) has described important outcome variables as seen from the federal perspective, and cited the standards problem as important in judging program success. These standards may, in the long run, be definable only in the comparative or normative sense. The definition of evaluation variables and knowledge of distribution of these variables for comparable programs may serve an *improvement* function, rather than a go, no-go type of decision. Normative standards may serve to identify less effective programs, and to assist both the LEA and SED staffs to improve service.

Table 3.4:   Revised Outcome and Predictive Impact Statements: Statements Applicable to Secondary Programs Eligible for Financing from the State's "Basic Grant" Monies

Outcome Impact Statements

1.   Program graduates are working in occupations for which they were trained.
2.   Program objectives are fulfilled.
3.   No sex discrimination occurred in student selection, training, and job placement.
4.   Training objectives are met in the most cost effective manner.
5.   Large numbers of students are trained.
6.   Training increases student employment options.
7.   Employers are satisfied with graduates of program.
8.   Students trained have positive attitudes toward work.
9.   Students trained continue their education.
10.   Program can be replicated in other LEAs.

Predictive Impact Statements

1.   Students will be trained for occupations where jobs are available.
2.   Project objectives are stated in measurable terms.
3.   No sex discrimination will be made in recruiting and placing students in vocational programs.
4.   Training objectives will be met in the most cost effective manner.
5.   Large number of students will be trained.
6.   Training will be provided to increase students' employment options.
7.   Students will be prepared to meet entry level skill requirements as specified by prospective employers (e.g., employer's ratings of program performance objectives in terms of job requirements).
8.   Program will serve students' interests.
9.   Program is articulated with local postsecondary institutions.
10.   Program will be replicable in other LEAs.

In a continuation of the project we plan to obtain data for past projects on the outcome statements. In order to develop a survey instrument for data collection, LEA Directors of Occupational Education have reviewed and critiqued a draft instrument. We are also planning that a sample of evaluations will be judged as to their overall level of impact by decision makers, and scored on the outcome variables by the evaluators. The relationship between the two measures can be interpreted as one evidence of the validity of the impact dimensions. Also, ratings and rankings of the two sets of impact variables will be obtained from LEA program directors. These data will provide another perspective on the impact statements. Additional sources of related validity data would be rankings of the variables by other groups expert in occupational education, and those concerned with the programs in the status of parents or students. For the long term study of the validity of the predictive impact variables, there will need to be a follow-up rating of the overall level of impact for grant applications that were given predictive impact ratings.

3. RESEARCH ISSUES AND POLITICAL CONCERNS

There are limitations to the method being proposed here. In the first place, much of the validation proposed is circular, as Slovic et al. (1977) have noted for the studies of the other method of aiding decisions. Validity has not been well established for the methods being used to obtain values and objectives. Some validity studies for MAUT have correlated comparisons of MAUT scores with intuitive decisions or wholistic ratings (Guttentag and Snapper, 1974; Gardiner and Edwards, 1975). Both found that there was good agreement between multiattribute utility analysis measurements and intuitive evaluations, and concluded the model was valid. Slovic et al. (1977) argued that this is a faulty conclusion, and recommended more sophisticated approaches to the validity issue. Existing studies have defined validity as examining the results of the MAUT method against the criterion of an overall subjective rating (obtained concurrently). Another view of validity is one that has been proposed for achievement tests—in the area of content validation. Validity can be defined in terms of whether different groups will "construct" the same set of dimensions or variables to define projects that have a high impact on students, employers, or funding agencies. If there is a domain of impact or outcome variables, with various dimensions in it, will decision makers, students (consumers), local teachers and administrators, and/or local advisory councils view the domain and dimensions similarly? Would they construct the same sets of variables for outcome and predictive (funding) evaluation? A comparison of variables developed or weighted by different groups would provide relatively convincing evidence of content validity.

Another view of validity can be derived from the multitrait-multimethod approach to construct validity. Validity might be demonstrated by using two or three methods to develop the important outcome (or predictive) variables, and examining the commonality in the underlying dimensions and weightings (values) attached to dimensions. Methods could include the Delphi, MAUT, and SJT. For the predictive impact variables, a validation study can be designed following the predictive test validity procedures. Projects applications can be scored and follow-up studies made of those funded.

The second limitation is that the impact variables described here, while clearly important for evaluation, are only one part of the information used for funding decisions. Other areas which were rated in funding at the time we examined the decision process included the general management plan for carrying out the project, the proposed staff, and the project evaluation plan. At this stage, it is not known what weight these variables carry in decision-making, or whether they are overriding variables. Unless standards are met in these other areas, projects may not be funded, regardless of impact ratings. Also, as noted earlier, criteria of addressing the greatest need and meeting local solutions for improvement are important criteria for funding.

Other research issues are in terms of comparisons of the various methods of decision aids. Different methods may be better—more feasible, acceptable to raters, practical, and valid—in some types of decision settings than in others. Both the MAUT and SJT, as in the use of the Delphi technique, are first concerned with developing lists of goals, objectives, or impact (outcome) variables. SJT describes this concern well—that the judgment situation be carefully specified, and that the lists of goals, objectives or cues on which the judgment is based are valid—that is, representative of all the cues used by the decision maker. Statements by decision makers and relevant literature can be examined to develop the lists of outcome (and predictive) variables. The most important are identified and importance weights derived. In MAUT this is done by either a rating or ratio scaling procedure; in SJT weights are obtained by a regression analysis of individual judges' ratings of sample cases representing the judgment problem.

In order to develop the sample cases in SJT, the formal properties of the set of cue variables in the task must be known or estimated—in the present example, this would mean knowing the distributions of predictive variables in a representative sample of grant applicants. The use of known distributions of variables and the presentation of representative cases varying on these distributions to obtain importance weights, distinguishes the SJT from the MAUT method. SJT presents combinations of variables as they would occur in real project applications in the decision setting, in order to elicit the utilities or values placed on the major variables by the decision maker. Studies have not yet established the relationship between the outcomes of application of SJT and MAUT. Do the two methods yield the same results? Or, does it matter what weights are derived? Dawes (1973) suggested that unit weights are just as satisfactory. Hammond, Stewart, Adelman and Wascoe's results (1975a) for lay judgments also suggested, that with multiple judges equal weights may result. Perhaps the most important part of the procedure is the first step, common to both: identifying the major dimensions or impact variables to ensure that raters agree on what is important in making a judgment.

There are also political concerns involved in the use of these methods. One political aspect is the relationship between the evaluator and administrative decision makers. The evaluator must be sensitive to staff needs in discussing and describing areas of work that are not typically accessible to outsiders. Particularly important is the need for detailed knowledge of the funding decision-making process as it currently exists (see Edwards, 1976, for similar caveats). A second political aspect is the relationship between decision makers and outside groups, such as state legislators and others with interest in the funding of local projects. From the evaluator's viewpoint, the development of well-defined criteria would appear to have benefits in providing a rationale for funding decisions. From a staff viewpoint, such a development may represent a loss of "degrees of freedom" in their decision-making. From the LEAs viewpoint, there may be a concern that their views are a part of the process to identify high impact variables, as well as an acknowledgment that local needs vary and must be taken into account. Knowledge of the values or importance ratings given to the impact variables by other groups such as LEA project directors or local and state-level advisory councils might lessen this last concern. Evaluators must also examine their roles in this political setting, and determine what interests are being served in the application of the decision aids.

SUMMARY

The significance of the method being developed here is in providing one way in which evaluation and funding decisions can be linked to programs that are continuing and large scale. One characteristic of the programs funded under the VEA is that not every project will meet or be evaluated highly on all major impact dimension. Evaluators can assist decision makers to establish the set of impact dimensions important for funding decisions. In the process, operational definitions of these variables can be established for both evaluators and project directors. Evaluation and decision-making can, in some cases, be more closely related if evaluators clarify the exact decisions to be made, who makes the decisions, timing of the decision, and the nature of the data necessary to make the decision. In the VEA, new programs will not have available past evaluation data at the time of funding, but the use of predictive impact data can, it is hypothesized, increase the likelihood of funding projects that will later be judged as higher in impact.

In this example, and similar settings, evaluators may find that devoting effort to clarifying the types of decisions that can be made and the data that can be provided will increase the use of evaluation results over the long term. Evaluators, however, need to examine further the validity and ethical implications of the methods proposed here for application in vocational education.

NOTES

1. Requirements of the Act include such items as maintenance of fiscal effort by LEAs and that VEA funds are not used to supplant state or local funds.

2. Obvious exceptions are the work of Edwards, Guttentag, and Snapper (1975), and Hammond and his colleagues (1975b) described later in this chapter, and the studies by Bateman (1968), Clark (1976). Studies of the perceptions and attitudes of reviewers

and applicants in peer reviews for research funding have been made by NSF (Hensler, 1976). The peer review studies do not seem directly relevant here, because that review process involves more judges, and is likely to differ also in the knowledge scientific peer reviewers have about past performance and "products" of many research grant applicants. Newhouse (1976) cited work at NIH showing a significant correlation between study section priority scales on research applications and a subsequent criterion of citation index. However, Mahoney (1976) described a study of federal projects where rater assessment of technical research quality for a "bench mark" study (N=239 raters) had a mean of 2.886 and SD of 1.209, suggesting that the project was somewhere between "far above average" and "far below average" on the 5-point scale. The implications of these data are that whether or not a grant may be funded is highly dependent on the rater, if the *same* grant proposal can receive far above average and far below average ratings.

3. Changes have occurred since 1975 due to internal reorganizations or reallocation of responsibility. The presentation here remains based on the FY 1975 grant decision process, since most of the general areas still apply. Among the changes are the setting of a funding formula by the Board of Regents to allocate funds regionally, and the addition of a planning group, and a unit to eliminate sex discrimination and sex stereotyping.

4. Boards of Cooperative Educational Services, established in suburban/rural areas to provide vocational education programs to students in a number of feeder high schools.

5. Major Cities are the five largest cities in New York State.

6. Dates are approximate, based on 1975 schedule.

7. There are competing views among evaluators about the functions of evaluation and the roles of evaluators. One description of alternative views has been given by the Stanford Evaluation Consortium (1976) in their review of the *Handbook of Evaluation Research*. The Stanford group preferred evaluation as a more continuing part of management rather than as a "short term consulting contract" (p. 212). They described a more interactive role for evaluators, e.g., helping an agency to define needs to be met, understanding client populations in formulating a program, addressing research issues as they emerge during a study, and discussing data with program staff as they are available (formative evaluation). This alternate view is not incompatible with the decision aiding approaches, since Hammond is explicitly concerned with identifying different groups and representing those who are stakeholders in policy/decision-making, and some of Edwards studies have also (e.g., Gardiner and Edwards, 1975).

8. MAUT is described more fully in Gross (1979).

9. The initial list of 104 statements is given in the Appendix.

10. There are, obviously, any number of psychological scaling methods available, as well as the methods used in formal behavioral decision theory to obtain utilities (see Slovic et al., 1977). The objective is to obtain a reduced set of statements, and then, to obtain weights for the final set of statements. However, it is not clear that other than unitary weights have great value. For example, Dawes (1973), and Hammond, Stewart, Adelman, and Wascoe's studies (1975a) had results suggesting that with multiple judges equal weights may result.

REFERENCES

Banghart, F. W., and Trull, A., Jr. 1973. *Educational Planning.* New York: Macmillan.

Baron, J. 1976. "A decision-theoretic approach to evaluation research: An explication and application." Paper presented to the Northeastern Research Association, 7th Annual Convention, Ellenville, NY, October 27-29.

——— 1977. "An exploration of the implication of the M.A.U.T.-Bayesian decision-theoretic model for summative and formative evaluation and post-assessment organizational change." Paper presented to the American Education Research Association, New York City, April 4-8.

Bateman, W. 1968. Assessing program effectiveness. *Welfare in Review* 6:1-10.

Bernstein, I. N., and Freeman, H. E. 1975. *Academic and Entrepreneurial Research.* New York: Russell Sage Foundation.

Boruch, R. F., and Gomez, H. 1977. Sensitivity, bias, and theory in impact evaluation. *Professional Psychology* 8, 4:411-434.

Cain, G. G., and Hollister, R. G. 1972. The methodology of evaluating social action programs. In P. H. Rossi and W. Williams, eds. *Evaluating Social Programs: Theory, Practice and Politics.* New York: Seminar Press.

Campbell, D. T. 1975. Assessing the impact of planned social change. In G. M. Lyone, ed. *Social Research and Public Policies: The Dartmouth/OECD Conference.* Hanover, NH: The Public Affairs Center, Dartmouth College.

Clark, R. F. 1976. Scoring model helps determine funding for competitive grants. *Evaluation* 3:45-47.

Cochrane, J. L., and Zeleny, M., eds. 1973. *Multiple Criteria Decision Making.* Columbia, S.C.: University of South Carolina Press.

Cook, T. J., and Scioli, F. P., Jr. 1975. Impact analysis in public policy research. In K. M. Dolbeare, ed. *Public Policy Evaluation.* Beverly Hills: Sage Publications.

Crawford, A. B. 1973. Impact analysis using differentially weighted evaluative criteria. In J. L. Cochrane and M. Zeleny, eds. *Multiple Criteria Decision Making.* Columbia: University of South Carolina Press.

Cytrynbaum, S., Birdwell, J., Brandt, L., and Ginath, Y. 1977. "Goal Attainment Scaling: A critical review." Paper presented at the annual meeting of the American Psychological Association, San Francisco, August.

Dagenais, F. "Identification of most successful educational programs and their characteristics." San Francisco: University of California.

Datta, L. 1979. Better Luck This Time: From Federal Legislation to Practice in Evaluating Vocational Education. In T. Abramson, C. K. Tittle, and L. Cohen, eds. *Handbook of Vocational Education Evaluation.* Beverly Hills: Sage Publications.

Dawes, R. M. 1973. Objective optimization under multiple subjective functions. In J. L. Cochrane and M. Zeleny, eds. *Multiple Criteria Decision Making.* Columbia: University of South Carolina Press.

Davis, H. R., and Salasin, S. E. 1975. The utilization of evaluation. In E. L. Struening and M. Guttentag, eds. *Handbook of Evaluation Research, Vol. 1.* Beverly Hills: Sage Publications.

Edwards, W. 1976. How to use multi-attribute utility measurement for social decision-making. Technical Report 001597 1-T. Los Angeles: Social Science Research Institute, University of Southern California.

——— 1961. Behavioral decision theory. *Annual Review of Psychology* 12:473-498.

——— 1954. The theory of decision-making. *Psychological Bulletin* 51:380-417.

Edwards, W., Guttentag, M., and Snapper, K. 1975. A decision-theoretic approach to evaluation research. In E. L. Struening and M. Guttentag eds. *Handbook of Evaluation Research, Vol. 1.* Beverly Hills: Sage Publications.

Einhorn, H. S., and Hogarth, R. M. 1978. Confidence in judgment: Persistence in the illusion of validity. *Psychological Review.* (in press).

Federal Register. 1977. Vocational Education, State Programs and Commissioner's Discretionary Programs. Washington, DC: Office of Education, DHEW.

Fischer, G. W. 1975. Experimental applications of multi-attribute utility models. In D. Wendt and C. Vleck, eds. *Utility, Probability, and Human Decision Making.* Dordrecht, Netherlands: D. Reidel.

Gardiner, P. C., and Edwards, W. 1975. Public values: Multi-attribute utility measurement for social decision-making. In M. F. Kaplan and S. Schwartz, eds. *Human Judgment and Decision Processes.* New York: Academic Press.

Gibson, K. D. 1976. Rural community mental health center uses decision-making model. *Evaluation* 3:27-28.

Green, P. E. 1973. Multi-dimensional scaling and conjoint measurement in the study of choice among multi-attribute alternatives. In J. L. Cochrane & M. Zeleny, eds. *Multiple Criteria Decision Making.* Columbia: University of South Carolina Press.

Gross, A. L. 1979. Funding Education Projects: Applying Decision Theory to the Problem. In T. Abramson, C. K. Tittle, and L. Cohen, eds. *Handbook of Vocational Education Evaluation.* Beverly Hills: Sage Publications.

Guttentag, M. 1973. Subjectivity and its use in evaluation research. *Evaluation* 1:60-65.

Guttentag, M., and Snapper, K. 1974. Plans, evaluations and decisions. *Evaluation* 2: 58-64; 73-74.

Hammond, K. R. ed. 1978. *Judgment and decision in public policy formation.* Boulder, CO: Westview Press.

Hammond, K. R., and Adelman, L. 1976. Science, values and human judgment. *Science* 194:389-396.

Hammond, K. R., Stewart, T. R., Adelman, L., and Wascoe, N. 1975(a). *Report to the Denver city council and mayor regarding the choice of handgun ammunition for the Denver police department.* Report No. 179. Boulder: University of Colorado, Institute of Behavioral Science. March 25.

Hammond, K. R., Stewart, T. R., Brehmer, B., and Steinmann, D. O. 1975(b). Social judgment theory. In M. F. Kaplan & S. Schwartz, eds. *Human Judgment and Decision Processes.* New York: Academic Press.

Hays, M. L., O'Connor, M. F., and Peterson, C. R. 1975. *An application of multi-attribute utility theory: Design-to-cost evaluation of the U.S. Navy's electronic warfare system.* McClean, VA: Decisions and Designs. October.

Hemphill, J. K. 1969. The relationship between research and evaluation studies. In R. W. Tyler, ed. *Educational Evaluation: New Roles, New Means.* Chicago: University of Chicago Press.

Hensler, D. R. 1976. *Perceptions of the National Science Foundation Peer Review Process: A Report on a Survey of NSF Reviewers and Applicants.* Washington, DC: National Science Foundation.

Houston, T. R., Jr. 1972. The behavioral sciences impact-effectiveness model. In P. H. Rossi & W. Williams, eds. *Evaluating Social Programs: Theory, Practice, and Politics.* New York: Seminar Press.

Hu, T., and Stromsdorfer, E. W. 1975. *An analysis of the impact of applied research and demonstration projects in vocational education.* Office of the Assistant Secretary for Policy, Evaluation and Research, Department of Labor, July.

Humphreys, P., and Humphreys, A. 1975. An investigation of subjective preference orderings for multi-attributed alternatives. In D. Wendt and C. A. J. Vlek, eds. *Utility, Probability, and Human Decision Making.* Dordrecht, Netherlands: Reidel.

Keeney, R. L., and Raiffa, H. 1976. *Decisions with Multiple Objectives, Preferences, and Value Trade-offs.* New York: Wiley.

Kiresuk, T. 1975. Goal-attainment scoring and quantification of values. In M. Guttentag, T. Kiresuk, M. Ogelsby, and J. Cahn, eds. *The Evaluation of Training in Mental Health.* New York: Behavioral Publications.

Levine, A. S. 1967. Evaluating program effectiveness and efficiency: Rationale and description of research in progress. *Welfare in Review* 5:1-11.

MacCrimmon, K. R., 1973. An overview of multiple objective decision-making. In J. L. Cochrane and M. Zeleny, eds. *Multiple Criteria Decision Making.* Columbia: University of South Carolina Press.

Mahoney, B. S. 1976. Policy research planning. In C. G. Abt, ed. *The Evaluation of Social Problems.* Beverly Hills: Sage Publications.

Moskowitz, H. 1975. Some observations on theories of collective decisions. In D. Wendt & C. A. J. Vlek, eds. *Utility, Probability and Human Decision Making.* Dordrecht, Netherlands: Reidel.

Newhouse, J. 1976. Discussion: Research allocation strategies. In C. G. Abt, ed. *The Evaluation of Social Programs.* Beverly Hills: Sage Publications.

Paine, W. S. 1977. "The utility of goal attainment scaling for educational evaluation." Paper presented at the annual meeting of the American Educational Research Association, New York, April.

Perloff, R., Perloff, E., and Sussna, E. 1976. Program evaluation. *Annual Review of Psychology* 27: 569-594.

Sirois, H. A., and Iwanicki, E. F. 1977. "Delphi-discrepancy evaluation: A model for the quality control of federal, state, and locally mandated programs." Paper presented at the annual meeting of the American Educational Research Association, New York City, April.

Slovic, P., Fischoff, B., and Lichtenstein, S. 1977. Behavioral decision theory. *Annual Review of Psychology* 28: 1-39.

Stake, R. E. 1970. Objectives, priorities and other judgment data. *Review of Education Research* 40: 181-212.

––– 1967. Toward a technology for the evaluation of educational programs. *Perspectives of Curriculum Evaluation.* AERA Monograph Series on Curriculum Evaluation No. 1. Chicago: Rand McNally.

Stanford Evaluation Consortium. 1976. Review essay evaluating the Handbook of Evaluation Research. In G. V. Glass, ed. *Evaluation Studies Review Annual, Volume 1.* Beverly Hills: Sage Publications.

Stein, H. D., Hougham, G. M., and Zalba, S. R. 1968. Assessing social agency effectiveness: A goal model. *Welfare in Review* 6: 13-18.

Tanner, C. K. 1971. *Designs for educational planning: A systems approach.* Lexington, MA: Heath Lexington Books.

Weiss, C. H. 1976. The three faces of evaluation: Policy, program and the public. In E. Markson and D. Allen, eds. *Trends in mental health evaluation.* Lexington, MA: D. C. Heath.

Wendt, D., and Vlek, C. A. J. 1975. *Utility, Probability and Human Decision-Making.* Dordrecht, Netherlands: Reidel.

Winkler, R. L. 1972. *An Introduction to Bayesian Inference and Decision.* New York: Holt, Rinehart and Winston.

APPENDIX

Table A1: Impact Statements: Fifty-eight Statements from Interviews

1. How does it impact on people?
2. Is it in line with the law?
3. Greatest impact to get people gainfully employed.
4. Match people's abilities with jobs (even without training).
5. Does it fill a district need?
6. How many people are served?
7. Does program provide training for jobs for which employment possibilities exist?
8. What is wealth of district?
9. LEA not likely to become overdependent on VEA funds.
10. Political aspects: How successful was program?
11. Is it replicable?
12. What program does for an agency?
13. Could elements of program be used by other agencies?
14. Exceeded project objectives.
15. What are you/we doing for kids which is getting them jobs?
16. Has no meaning.
17. Financial need of district.
18. Relative costs of program services.
19. Occupational Education needs of special groups: disadvantaged and handicapped.
20. Is there local employment opportunity?
21. Are there job opportunities in other localities?
22. Regional Plan and Agency Plan.
23. Priority in State Plan.
24. Maintain local effort—no budget decreases.
25. Name identifiable client group.
26. Identify job.
27. Is there need in the area?

Table A1: (Continued)

28. Are we meeting the need?
29. Thinks of it as physical impact, like a gun.
30. Are we training people who can benefit from the program in their own best interest?
31. Local impact *not enough:* program should have widespread use to justify expense.
32. Doesn't like word, uses it only in physical sense.
33. Serving students better.
34. Serve student interests as well as job needs.
35. Update materials and equipment to do job better.
36. Effect on occupational programs in cities.
37. Does it make a difference?
38. Think in terms of student and employment situation.
39. Are you going to have people capable of producing for the state or region and do they?
40. Does it pay off?
41. Is it going to make a difference?
42. Employment opportunity available? No opportunity available?
43. Number of students to be served.
44. Costs per student.
45. Skill training programs for marketable skills.
46. Potential to fill employment gap.
47. Effect change with minimal cost.
48. Students' ability to get or hold job.
49. Replicability under a number of learning settings.
50. Clearly identified components or aspects.
51. Effective delivery system—Review of existing programs and students.
52. Efficiency in use of resources—existing staff and resources available.
53. Effect change with minimal cost (uses existing staff and resources).
54. New or effective method—not repeat.
55. Easily replicated.
56. IMPACT within region.
57. Meet needs of industry.
58. Job producing activity.

Table A2: Forty-Six Impact Statements: From Assessing Vocational Education Research and Development*

1. Influence on the knowledge, skills, or employability of large numbers of students.
2. Prepare students for jobs to meet labor market needs.
3. Meet needs of students and of society.
4. Serve economically and socially disadvantaged students.
5. Increase the flexibility of all vocational-education students in choosing careers and changing occupations.
6. · Prepare students for work.
7. Development of human potential and long-term employment.
8. Better service to the disadvantaged, the handicapped, post-secondary and adult students.
9. Stress career planning.

Table A2: (Continued)

10. Increase employment options available to each person (occupational versatility).
11. Motivate students to learn basic academic skills.
12. Increase the occupational flexibility and decision-making skill of each person.
13. Teach multiple and generalizable skills that will prepare people better for mid-career changes.
14. Equality of access to vocational education programs associated with occupations traditionally dominated by one sex.
15. Help people become responsible citizens by becoming responsible workers.
16. Achieve the level of economic literacy necessary to exercise full rights and responsibilities at work.
17. Job turnover rates.
18. Socio-economic mix of students.
19. **Changes in student self-perceptions.**
20 The extent to which local districts (states) have maintained and implemented previously developed products and results.
21. Are student participants able to identify a greater number of occupations than non-participants?
22. Do students demonstrate more familiarity with tasks and functions associated with selected occupations?
23. Are a greater number of students who have graduated from school employed full-time or engaged in further training than students who did not participate (in the program)?
24. Develop awareness of future job opportunities in young children.
25. Enlarge the vocational self-concept.
26. Engender a work ethic in children.
27. Improve students' attitudes toward their environment.
28. Improve academic achievement.
29. Develop occupational skills.
30. Develop new techniques for teaching the disadvantaged.
31. Students have more positive attitudes toward work.
32. Greater knowledge of careers.
33. Products are widely disseminated.
34. Interest is generated.
35. Initiate exploration of new subjects in vocational education.
36. Students' job satisfaction.
37. Continuation of education.
38. Job mobility.
39. Employers' satisfaction.
40. Savings in training costs.
41. Address needs of groups such as minorities, women, disadvantaged, handicapped, and those for whom English is not their first language.
42. Prepare students for skilled entry-level jobs.
43. Take into account differences in cultural values.
44. Provide manpower data for management of vocational education programs in the state.
45. Wages.
46. Upward job mobility.

Source: *Assessing Vocational Education Research and Development.* Committee on Vocational Education Research and Development, National Academy of Sciences, Washington, DC 1976.

chapter 4

ALAN L. GROSS | *City University of New York*

Generally, one main task of evaluators has been summative or outcome evaluation. This effort has been primarily concerned with collecting data on existing programs in order to make possible judgments of their merit or worth. These judgments in turn have been intended for use by decision makers in deciding whether to continue, modify, or delete current educational programs. More recently, evaluators have become concerned with the process by which decisions are made to fund or not fund proposed projects. In this research, the decision process has been investigated within the context of formal mathematical decision theory models (e.g., Hemphill, 1969; Edwards, 1976). Basically, the decision theory approach consists of first describing the set of possible decisions that are available to the decision maker (e.g., fund project 1, or fund project 2, or fund project 3), second, quantifying the intrinsic worth or value of each possible decision in terms of a utility value (methods of assigning utilities will be described in later sections of the chapter), and third, choosing that decision which possesses the highest utility value. At the present time, it is probably safe to say that the great majority of educational funding decisions are not made within the context of this decision theory model; much more informal procedures are typically followed in educational settings. For the decision maker who has used these informal procedures with "apparent" success it is quite reasonable to raise the question of what exactly is gained by adopting a formal mathematical approach to the problem, and why evaluators need to become knowledgeable about aids to decision-making. One can respond to this question in terms of three advantages of the decision theory model.

(1) Definition of Relevant Variables

In a typical problem where one must decide whether or not to fund a proposed educational program, there may be a large number of relevant variables that need to be considered, e.g., the cost of the program, the number and type of personnel who must be hired, the number of students who will enroll in the program, the number who will graduate, the number of students who can find employment subsequent to finishing the program, and so on. In a formal decision theory approach, the decision maker is required to explicitly enumerate and define all of the variables which he/she considers to be relevant to the funding decision. Consequently, not only are the chances minimized of important variables being overlooked, but in addition the list of relevant variables becomes public knowledge, which can be scrutinized by others.

(2) Subjective Values and Beliefs

The subjective values, priorities, and beliefs of the decision maker can often have a substantial effect upon the funding decision. For example, I may recommend funding an expensive project that I believe to be beneficial to minority group students. However, you, having a different set of priorities and beliefs may choose not to fund the same project. The important point to note is that subjective priorities and beliefs represent an important determinant of funding decisions. Unfortunately, in most instances, the manner in which these subjective inputs affect final decisions is not at all clear. In a decision theory approach to the funding question these subjective values and beliefs are considered as meaningful inputs to the evaluation process. Systematic procedures are followed for quantifying the subjective information and then incorporating it in an explicit manner into the decision-making process. Because this process is "out in the open" it can be readily examined by all concerned parties.

(3) Synthesis of All Relevant Information

Another important aspect of the decision-making process is the analysis of the relevant data or information that are available for each proposed project. This information can be viewed as being of two types, subjective (e.g., the decision maker's subjective priorities and beliefs), and objective (e.g., quantitive data that have been collected in evaluating the project). The decision-making process requires that these two sources of information be combined and weighted together in some fashion. In many cases where the decision-making process is informal, the mechanics of the process are not clearly defined nor are they observable. Furthermore, there is no guarantee that the process will be logically consistent. However, a well-defined, explicit, and logical procedure for combining subjective and objective information and then making final decisions, exists within the framework of the decision theory model. The end result of this process is the computation of the utility or average utility of each possible decision. The decision possessing the highest utility or average utility is then selected as being optimal.

In this chapter, two decision theory models will be described that have been employed by educational evaluators to assist decision makers in making funding decisions. The first procedure, Multiattribute Utility Theory (MAUT), has been described by Edwards, Guttentag, and Snapper (1975). The second approach to be considered is Bayesian Decision Theory (BDT) (Winkler, 1972). Both approaches will be illustrated in terms of hypothetical although realistic examples.

Before considering these examples it is important to point out an important difference between the MAUT model as it has been described by Edwards et al., and the general BDT model. This difference has not been made clear in past educational applications of the MAUT and BDT models.

The problem of deciding whether or not to fund a proposed educational project is basically a multivariate or multiattribute problem. In other words, funding decisions are typically based upon the values of an entire set of variables which characterize the proposed projects. In many instances these variables can be viewed as unknown statistical parameters. In the Bayesian model, a systematic statistical procedure is available for investigating these unknown quantities. The method consists of quantifying one's prior beliefs concerning the parameters in terms of "prior" probabilities, and then revising these beliefs using observed data. These revised beliefs are represented by a "posterior" probability distribution. (The procedure is based upon the notion of conditional probability and will be described in detail later in the chapter.) Once information is available concerning the value of each unknown parameter, the overall worth or utility of each project can be computed. For example, suppose for simplicity there are only two parameters that need be considered in evaluating the fundability of a proposed project, the proportion of students in a given school who will graduate from the program (π_1) and the proportion of graduates who will find employment (π_2). If one knew the exact values for π_1 and π_2, the overall worth or utility would be given as $U = W_1\pi_1 + W_2\pi_2$ where W_1 and W_2 are weights which express the decision makers' perception of the importance of each attribute. Because one does not know the exact values of the parameters, the expected or average utility value (EU) is computed by replacing π_1 and π_2 in the formula for U with Bayesian estimates or π_1 and π_2. These estimates are computed from the posterior distributions, or from the prior distributions if no data are available. The decision to fund or not to fund is then made in terms of the EU value.

How does this procedure differ from the MAUT model? Basically the difference lies in the manner in which the information on the relevant attributes is obtained. In some applications of the MAUT model (e.g., Baron, 1977), the values of the unknown parameters (e.g., π_1 and π_2) are *not* statistically estimated within the Bayesian framework of computing prior and posterior probability distributions. Rather, estimates of π_1 and π_2 are provided by simple educated guesses of the standing or scale value of each project on each dimension.

In other instances (e.g., Guttentag and Snapper, 1974), the underlying parameters are not quantified but are defined as only qualitative dimensions. For example, in the MAUT model, one might consider the political feasability of a proposed project. In this instance, one also provides only educated guesses as to the standing of each project on this qualitative parameter.

In summary, one can view the MAUT model as a modification of the general Bayesian decision theory model. When the MAUT model is used in conjunction with the Bayesian estimation procedures, the MAUT and BDT procedures basically become one and the same. Examples of the use of both procedures will now be considered.

MAUT MODEL

Suppose a local school district needs to decide which of three vocational education (VE) programs should be funded. The MAUT approach provides a systematic and quantitative procedure for determining the overall worth or utility of each project. The program having the highest utility value is selected for funding.

Following Edwards et al. (1975), the determination of the utility of funding each project consists of five stages. These stages can be implemented by evaluators to formalize the local decision-making process.

(1) Forming the Decision-Making Team

The evaluation of any project will be influenced by the subjective values and priorities of the decision makers, and therefore, it is important that the team be representative of all individuals who have a stake in the evaluation. If certain individuals are excluded from the team, certain viewpoints may also be excluded. Thus, the team might include school board members, the principal, teachers, parents, and perhaps students.

(2) Identification of Relevant Dimensions of Importance

In determining the overall worth of each VE project there are certain relevant variables or dimensions which must be considered. For example,

(a) the number of students who can be enrolled in the program
(b) the number of graduates who can be expected to find jobs
(c) the number of teachers who must be assigned to the project
(d) teacher satisfaction with the program
(e) student satisfaction with the program

The enumeration of these dimensions represents a group effort by the team of decision makers.

(3) Quantifying the Importance of Each Dimension

The relative importance of each dimension is assessed in the following manner:

(a) The five dimensions are ranked in importance.
(b) The least important dimension is assigned an importance weight of 10. The second most important dimension is assigned a weight which reflects (in a ratio sense) how much more important it is than the least important variable. For example, the assignment of an importance weight of 20 to the second dimension reflects the belief that the second is twice as important as the first. The process continues until all dimensions are assigned an importance weight. Due to disagreements among members of the team, several repetitions of this procedure may be necessary.
(c) Each importance weight is now rescaled by dividing it by the sum of the importance weights and then multiplying by 100. The resulting importance weights are denoted as W_1, W_2, ..., W_5 where $\Sigma W_j = 100$.

Suppose for example, the following scaled importance weights are computed: student enrollment (20), graduates finding jobs (40), number of teachers assigned (25), teacher satisfaction (10), student satisfaction (5). Needless to say, this assignment of importance weights reflects the specific values of the team.

(4) Rating Each Project in Terms of Each Dimension of Importance

Each VE project is now rated on each dimension of importance. These ratings reflect the standing or utility of the project in terms of the given dimension. Edwards et al. (1975) suggest a simple scaling procedure for computing these standings. Basically the assigned values represent educated guesses by the team.[1] The standing or utility of project i on dimension j is denoted as U_{ij}. In the problem under consideration, there are three projects

Table 4.1: An Application of the MAUT Model

Dimensions Importance Weights	1 20	2 40	3[a] 25	4 10	5 5	$U_i = \Sigma W_i U_{ij}$
Project 1	30	80	15	50	60	4975
Project 2	70	70	30	20	20	5250
Project 3	90	30	70	10	30	5000

[a] Since the number of teachers may be considered as an undesirable cost factor, the fewer the number of required teachers, the higher the utility value.

and five importance dimensions. Thus 15 U_{ij} values would be assessed, as indicated in Table 4.1.

In making these assignments, anchor points of 0 (lowest possible standing or utility) and 100 (highest possible standing or utility) are used. For example, suppose project 1 is given a utility value of 80 on the dimension of employability of graduates (Dimension 2 in Table 4.1). The value 80 reflects a judgment by the evaluation team that project 1 is highly desirable or has a high standing in terms of this dimension. Suppose the following assignments were made as shown in Table 4.1.

(5) Computation of Overall Utility Values

The overall utility value for each project is computed from Table 4.1 as a weighted linear combination of the W_{ij} values.[2] In other words, U_i is computed as $U_i = \Sigma W_j U_{ij}$. For example, the overall utility of project 1 is assessed as

$U_1 = (20) (30) + (40) (80) + (25) (15) + (10) (50) + (5) (60) = 4975.$

Because project 2 has the highest utility rating it becomes the project to be funded.

In summary, when deciding in which program to invest, the MAUT model can provide evaluators with a systematic rating procedure to assist decision makers to assess the overall utility of a program when several variables or dimensions must be considered. The procedure provides for a systematic inclusion of the values and priorities of the decision makers in the process. Finally, the entire decision-making process is "out in the open."

BDT MODEL

In general there are three aspects to any Bayesian decision problem: (1) a specification of the set of possible decisions that are available to the decision maker; (2) a specification of subjective probabilities associated with relevant "states of the world" (i.e., the relevant variables); and (3) a specification of a subjective utility function which quantifies the decision-making team's values and priorities. In the Bayesian approach one computes the average or expected utility associated with each possible decision. The optimal decision is that which possesses the highest expected utility. To better understand the mechanics of the Bayesian approach a simple "single attribute" decision problem will be presented. In other words, whereas in the MAUT example five attributes (dimensions of importance) of each project were considered, in the first BDT example a problem will be presented where only one attribute is considered by the decision-making team. Following this simplified example, the previously described multiattribute example will be reexamined within the framework of the general BDT model.

Suppose a school system must make one of two possible decisions, d_1 = fund a new vocational education project, or d_2 = do not fund the project. (In this example, d_1 and d_2 represent the set of possible decisions.) Suppose further, that the school board or decision-making team, decides that the decision to fund or not fund the project should depend only upon the proportion (π) of the student body who will potentially enroll in the program. In this example π represents the relevant state of the world. The decision to fund or not fund the project would be relatively simple if the school board knew the exact value of π. However, in general π will be an unknown parameter which describes the population of students in the school. Although π is not known with complete certainty, it is reasonable to assume that the school board or team does possess some information concerning its value. This information may come from past experience with similar vocational education programs, and may be in the form of subjective beliefs. In the BDT model these beliefs are quantified in terms of a subjective probability distribution, referred to as the prior probability distribution of π, $[p'(\pi)]$. Various procedures for quantifying beliefs are described by Winkler (1972). One such method would consist of asking the school board a series of questions of the form, "What do you think are the chances that π is between 0.0 and .10 and .10 and .20, . . . , .90 and 1.00"? The school board would further be instructed that the sum of the 10 responses must equal 1.0. Suppose the school board jointly agreed upon the following responses to these questions (see Table 4.2). The probabilities given in column two of Table 4.2 represent the school boards prior probability distribution for π. If one were to graph the probability distribution, its shape would be triangular. This type of distribution expresses the general belief that the value for π is quite low, because most of the probability is concentrated about the small values of π. For example the probability that π is greater than or equal to a value of .60 is computed to be only .16 in Table 4.2.

In most Bayesian analyses it is mathematically convenient to express prior beliefs using continuous rather than discrete (as in Table 4.2) probability

Table 4.2: Prior Probability Distribution of the Unknown Proportion (π)

π	"Chances" that π is in the interval	Beta Probabilities
0.0 to .10	.20	.19
.10 to .20	.17	.17
.20 to .30	.14	.15
.30 to .40	.12	.13
.40 to .50	.11	.11
.50 to .60	.10	.09
.60 to .70	.07	.05
.70 to .80	.05	.05
.80 to .90	.03	.03
.90 to 1.0	.01	.01

distributions. In the present example the most mathematically convenient continuous distribution is given by a member of the beta family of distributions. (A thorough and readable discussion of the use of beta distributions to represent prior beliefs is given by Novick and Jackson [1974].) Thus, one would select a beta distribution which closely approximates the discrete prior probability distribution. In the current example, a good approximation would be provided by a beta distribution with parameter values 1 and 2. The formula for this beta distribution can be written as

$$P'(\pi) = 2(1 - \pi).$$

The prior mean or prior expected value of this beta distribution is given as

$$E'(\pi) = 1/(1+2) = .33.$$

If one were to graph this beta distribution using the formula $2(1 - \pi)$ the distribution would be seen to have a triangular form, which closely approximates the original discrete prior distribution. The accuracy of this approximation can be seen in the last column of Table 4.2, which gives the prior probabilities (computed from the beta distribution) of π being in each interval. Each of these prior probabilities is computed as an area under the beta distribution in a given interval. The original discrete probabilities and the probabilities computed from the beta distribution closely agree.

The third input into the decision problem is the specification of a utility function, (U). This function basically quantifies the subjective values and priorities of the decision-making team in terms of the consequences of making a given decision when a certain state of the world occurs. Since in this example there are two possible decisions, d_1 = fund, and d_2 = do not fund, two functions $U(d_1,\pi)$ and $U(d_2,\pi)$ are specified. The function $U(d_1,\pi)$ for example, expresses the utility or intrinsic worth to the decision team of making the decision to fund (d_1), if the state of the world were to be some specific value of π. It is convenient to construct linear utility functions, although other functional forms are possible (Winkler, 1972). For example, suppose $U(d_1,\pi) = 3(\pi - .30)$ and $U(d_2,\pi) = -2(\pi - .30)$. The utility function for funding, d_1, expresses the feeling that as π increases, i.e., as a greater percentage of students enroll, the utility of d_1 increases. For $\pi < .30$, d_1 is undesirable because $U(d_1,.30) < 0$. For $\pi > .30$, d_1 is desirable because the utility is positive. For the decision not to fund, d_2, the utility decreases as π increases beyond .30 and increases as π decreases below .30. Not funding is desirable for $\pi < .30$ because U is positive, but undesirable for $\pi > .30$ which leads to a negative utility. The point $\pi = .30$ represents the "breakeven" point where $U(d_1,\pi) = U(d_2,\pi) = 0$. We also note that the slope for $U(d_1,\pi)$ is larger than for $U(d_2,\pi)$, expressing the feeling that changes in utility are greater for d_1 than d_2 per unit change in π.

If the value of π were known with certainty, the decision makers would know exactly which decision to make; for $\pi < .30$ choose d_2, for $\pi > .30$ choose d_1, for $\pi = .30$, flip a coin to decide. However, π is known only with uncertainty. This uncertainty is quantified by the prior beta distribution. To decide between d_1 and d_2 the decision maker must compute the expected or average utility for d_1 and d_2. This expected utility value (EU) is computed over the prior probability distribution for π. Since the utility functions have a linear form, the expected utility values (EU) are computed by substituting the prior expected value of the beta distribution $E'(\pi) = .33$ for the value of π appearing in the utility function. For the above example, replace $U(d_1,\pi)$ $= 3(\pi - .30)$ by $EU(d_1) = 3(E'(\pi) - .30) = 3(.33 - .30) = .09$ and similarly $EU(d_2) = -2(.33 - .30) = -.06$. Because $EU(d_1) > EU(d_2)$ the optimal decision is to fund. Actually, it is sufficient to compare the value of prior mean $[E'(\pi)]$ to the breakeven point .30 in choosing between d_1 and d_2. In other words, if $E'(\pi) > .30$ choose d_1, if $E'(\pi) < .30$ choose d_2.

The Bayesian model also makes it possible to postpone a decision until some data have been collected. The data are used to revise or update the prior beliefs concerning π by transforming the prior beta distribution into a posterior beta distribution. For example, suppose a random sample of $n = 10$ students are asked if they would enroll in the VE program and $x = 2$ respond "yes" and $n-x = 8$ respond "no." These data are used to revise the evaluator's prior beliefs concerning π through the application of Bayes Theorem (Novick and Jackson, 1974), which provides the statistical basis for the construction of the posterior distribution. In general, suppose one's prior beliefs are represented by a beta distribution with parameter values b_1 and b_2 and prior mean

$$E'(\pi) = b_1/(b_1+b_2).$$

The general form of this distribution is proportional (denoted by the symbol φ) to

$$P'(\pi) \varphi \pi^{b_1-1} (1-\pi)^{b_2-1}$$

In the present example $b_1 = 1$ and $b_2 = 2$.

After the data (x,n) are observed, the updated or posterior beliefs are represented as a beta distribution with parameters b_1+x and b_2+n-x. The updated beliefs thus reflect not only one's prior beliefs (as given by b_1 and b_2) but also the observed data (x,n). The expected average posterior belief concerning π has a value of

$$E''(\pi) = (b_1 + x)/(b_1 + b_2 + n).$$

In the present example, $E''(\pi) = (1 + 2) / (1 + 2 + 10) = .23$. Because this value is less than the breakeven point, d_2 would now have the greatest expected utility. If desired, the decision makers can still delay making a decision and collect additional data. In this case, the previous posterior distribution is treated as a prior distribution, and is updated by the second data set. The technique of "Pre Posterior Analysis" (Winkler, 1972) provides the evaluator with a procedure in Bayesian analysis for deciding when the data collection should cease and the final decision be made.

The Bayesian model can also be extended to the case where there are more than two possible decisions, and more than one relevant state of the world, i.e., in MAUT language more than one dimension of importance. Using the MAUT example, suppose the set of possible decisions consists of $d_i =$ fund project i, $i = 1,2,3$.

The problem facing the decision team is to choose a single project to be funded. Further, suppose, relevant states of the world are:

π_1 = proportion of students who will enroll in project 1.
π_2 = proportion of students who will enroll in project 2.
π_3 = proportion of students who will enroll in project 3.

π_4 = proportion of students graduating project 1 who will find jobs.
π_5 = proportion of students graduating project 2 who will find jobs.
π_6 = proportion of students graduating project 3 who will find jobs.

π_7 = proportion of current faculty who will be assigned to project 1.
π_8 = proportion of current faculty who will be assigned to project 2.
π_9 = proportion of current faculty who will be assigned to project 3.

π_{10} = proportion of faculty satisfied with project 1.
π_{11} = proportion of faculty satisfied with project 2.
π_{12} = proportion of faculty satisfied with project 3.

π_{13} = proportion of students satisfied with project 1.
π_{14} = proportion of students satisfied with project 2.
π_{15} = proportion of students satisfied with project 3.

The gene al Bayesian analysis would consist of simultaneously specifying a joint prior distribution for all fifteen unknown parameters. In addition, the general approach requires the specification of a utility function for each of the three possible decisions. These two tasks can be extremely complicated when the number of unknown parameters is large, as in the present case. However, some simplifying assumptions concerning the form of the utility function can lead to a workable analysis. First, suppose the evaluator is willing to assume that the utility of making decision d_i ($i = 1,2,3$) is only a function of the parameters describing project i. For example, the utility of making decision 1, only depends upon the parameters $\pi_1, \pi_4, \pi_7, \pi_{10}, \pi_{13}$. Second, suppose each of the utility functions can be expressed as a simple linear combination of the respective parameters, i.e.,

$$U_1 = U(d_1, \pi_1, \pi_4, \pi_7, \pi_{10}, \pi_{13}) = A\pi_1 + B\pi_4 + C\pi_7 + D\pi_{10} + E\pi_{13}$$
$$U_2 = U(d_2, \pi_2, \pi_5, \pi_8, \pi_{11}, \pi_{14}) = F\pi_2 + Gk_5 + H\pi_8 + I\pi_{11} + J\pi_{14}$$
$$U_3 = U(d_3, \pi_3, \pi_6, \pi_9, \pi_{12}, \pi_{15}) = K\pi_3 + L\pi_6 + M\pi_9 + N\pi_{12} + O\pi_{15}$$

where the values A through O (importance weights) are determined by the decision-making team in accord with their priorities and values. Again, the reader is referred to Keeney and Raiffa (1976) for the theoretical rationale for these utility functions. It should be noted that the specification of the utility functions could be even further simplified if one were willing to introduce a third assumption, and assign equal importance weights to all three decisions, i.e., assume that A = F = K, B = G = L, C = H = M, D = I = N, and E = J = O. Given this assumption one need only consider one utility function rather than three utility functions. The five importance weights could be determined in the same exact manner as they are in the MAUT model, i.e., following steps 1-3.

The expected utility of each decision is computed by replacing each value by its average value as computed from the respective univariate prior distributions. As in all Bayesian analyses, if data were available, the fifteen prior distributions could be updated using Bayes' theorem and the posterior means used in computing the expected utility values. That project possessing the highest expected utility is funded.

The computation of the expected utility values closely parallels the computation of utility in the MAUT example; in both cases utilities are computed as linear composites. The main difference is that in the BDT model, prior or posterior means are used as estimates of the unknown parameters, whereas, in the MAUT model as described by Edwards et al. (1975) the standing of each project on each dimension of importance is determined using a simple rating procedure.

To make the current example more concrete, suppose the decision-making team's prior beliefs concerning the 15 unknown proportions (π_i, i = 1,2,...,15) are expressed in terms of 15 beta distributions.

Table 4.3 represents these prior beliefs in terms of the parameters (b_1 and b_2) of the beta distributions, as well as the prior means. It is informative to consider in detail the prior beliefs of the decision-making teams.

In Table 4.3, there is one case where the prior beta distributions have b_1 and b_2 values equal to 1. This distribution can be viewed as reflecting a state of "prior ignorance" concerning the parameter. When a beta distribution has parameter values $b_1 = b_2 = 1$ its shape is rectangular or flat. In other words, the area under the distribution between, for example, the points 0.0 and .10, .10 and .20, .20 and .30, ... .90 at 1.00 is a constant value of .10. Thus when the beta distribution specified by $b_1 = b_2 = 1$ is chosen to represent one's beliefs, one is admitting that in a certain sense every value of the parameter is

Table 4.3: Prior Distributions of $\pi_1, \pi_2, \ldots, \pi_{15}$

	Parameter	b_1	b_2	Prior Mean $E'(\pi) = b_1 / (b_1 + b_2)$
P	π_1	4	6	.40
R				
O	π_4	7	3	.70
J				
E	π_7	1	5	.17
C				
T	π_{10}	1	1	.50
1	π_{13}	2	1	.67
P	π_2	7	3	.70
R				
O	π_5	8	2	.80
J				
E	π_8	1	3	.25
C				
T	π_{11}	1	5	.17
2	π_{14}	1	5	.17
P	π_3	9	1	.90
R				
O	π_6	1	4	.20
J				
E	π_9	5	1	.84
C				
T	π_{12}	1	5	.17
3	π_{15}	2	6	.25

"equally likely." Consider now the meaning of the remaining prior distributions where b_1 and b_2 are not both equal to 1. These distributions represent various degrees of knowledge concerning the unknown parameter. When b_1 exceeds b_2, the beta distribution is skewed to the left, i.e., π values above .50 have a higher probability of occurrence than π values below .50. The situation is reversed when b_2 exceeds b_1. Further, the larger the values chosen for b_1 and b_2, the less in general will be the variance of the beta distribution. Smaller variance can in turn be interpreted as representing greater information concerning the unknown parameter. For example, the prior distribution for π_8, ($b_1 = 1$, $b_2 = 3$) and π_{15}, ($b_1 = 2, b_2 = 6$) have the same mean (.33), but the variances are .038 and .027 respectively. In other words, the decision-making team can be described as being more "sure" about the value for π_{15} than the value for π_8.

The same "fractile" procedure described in the previous single attribute Bayesian example could be applied fifteen separate times in constructing each of the prior beta distributions. Obviously the procedure can become quite tedious with a large number of parameters. Recently, an interactive computer program has become available that greatly simplifies the problem of specifying the b_1 and b_2 values of each beta distribution (Novick, Isaacs, and Dekeyrel, 1977). Basically, the program consists of a series of simple questions posed by the computer to the decision-making team concerning their beliefs concerning each π_i value. The responses to these questions provide sufficient information for a unique beta distribution to be "fit" to the decision team's beliefs. The entire process can be accomplished in a relatively short period of time.

Continuing with the present example, suppose the decision-making team's utility functions with respect to each possible decision are specified as:

$$U_1 = 20\pi_1 + 40\pi_4 + 25\pi_7 + 10\pi_{10} + 5\pi_{13}$$
$$U_2 = 20\pi_2 + 40\pi_5 + 25\pi_8 + 10\pi_{11} + 5\pi_{14}$$
$$U_3 = 20\pi_3 + 40\pi_6 + 25\pi_9 + 10\pi_{12} + 5\pi_{15}$$

The expected utility of each possible decision is computed by replacing each π_i value by its prior mean.

$EU_1 = 20(.40) + 40(.70) + 25(.17) + 10(.50) + 5(.67) = 48.60$
$EU_2 = 20(.70) + 40(.80) + 25(.25) + 10(.17) + 5(.17)\ \text{-}54.80$
$EU_3 = 20(.90) + 40(.20) + 25(.84) + 10(.17) + 5(.25) = 49.95$

Since project 2 possesses the highest expected utility, it would be selected as the project to be funded.

Suppose the decision-making team considered the question of whether the final funding decision should be delayed until some pilot studies could be conducted and actual data collected for each proposed project. The Bayesian technique of preposterior analyses enables the decision-making team to answer this question. The technique basically consists of first considering all of the possible sets of sample data that theoretically might be observed if pilot studies were to be run; second, considering the means of each of the hypothetical posterior distributions that would be computed following the observation of each potential data set; third, computing the expected utility of each of the three decisions in terms of these posterior means; fourth, selecting the largest of the three utilities; and finally, averaging these largest utilities over all of the possible data sets. If and only if, the average utility (adjusted for the effort of running a pilot study) exceeds the current maximum utility value (EU_2 = 54.8), is it worthwhile to conduct the pilot studies. If pilot studies are conducted, the resulting data would be used to revise the 15 prior beta distributions by constructing posterior beta distributions. The expected utility of each proposed project would now be computed in terms of the 15 posterior means.

SOME UNANSWERED QUESTIONS AND FUTURE RESEARCH

There are a number of important unanswered questions with respect to the application of formal decision-making models to educational funding problems. If evaluations are to assist decision makers in vocational education, these questions need examination. One basic question involves the choice of a decision model; in a given problem, should the MAUT or the BDT model be chosen? A second basic question pertains to the feasibility of the decision theory approach in general. In other words, will or can the approach ever become widely implemented in educational settings?

In answering the first question it is useful to distinguish between those problems where the relevant variables (dimensions of importance) are treated as basically qualitative variables, e.g., political feasibility of the proposed program, or the extent to which the proposed project "reflects prevailing public and social thinking," (Guttentag and Snapper, 1974), and those problems where the relevant variables are basically quantitative (e.g., proportion of students graduating from the program who will be able to find employment). In the former case, the MAUT model is directly applicable, because the location of each project on each dimension simply requires the subjective specification of a scale value. In other words, the decision makers would judge the political feasability of each proposed project on a scale from 0 to 100. On the other hand, the Bayesian approach is not directly applicable, because the specification of a prior probability distribution with respect to a given dimension basically requires that the variable be quantitative. Of course, one can argue that in any decision problem, each relevant variable should be operationally defined in such a way that it can be readily quantified. For example, the variable, "political feasability" could be represented as the proportion of the eligible voters in a given state who would support (i.e., vote yes) the proposed project. This proportion could then be treated as an unknown statistical parameter and estimated within the Bayesian framework. However, if one insists upon only a qualitative definition of the relevant variables, the MAUT model alone is applicable.

One can next consider the class of decision problems where the relevant variables are expressed in quantitative terms. In light of the previous discussion, one can in theory consider every decision problem as a member of this class. Which model, MAUT or BDT, should be selected by the educational evaluator to assist decision makers? From a theoretical point of view one can argue that the BDT approach is clearly superior. The Bayesian procedure of quantifying prior beliefs, updating these beliefs as data become available, and estimating the unknown parameter in terms of some characteristic (e.g., the mean) of the prior or posterior distribution is a highly systematic procedure strongly grounded in statistical theory. The MAUT procedure of locating or determining the standing of a given project on each dimension presents only a simple, convenient rating method. In some situations, of course, the MAUT ratings and the BDT estimates may be similar; however, in other problems the results may be quite different. One would expect greater similarity in problems where no data are available, i.e., only a prior distribution is specified in the BDT model. However, in problems where data become available, the Bayesian method of updating one's beliefs by computing posterior distributions would likely lead to very different estimates than those provided by the MAUT ratings. A further consideration is that the MAUT procedure is quite simple to implement, whereas the use of a Bayesian model can be quite time consuming. Which model should then be used? It is difficult to answer this question in the absence of empirical studies which compare the two procedures in the context of educational funding decisions. Clearly then, this is an area for future research.

The second question involves the entire feasibility of the decision theory approach, be it the MAUT or BDT model. In other words, can or will the procedure ever gain wide acceptance by educational decision makers? As previously noted earlier in the chapter, this acceptance is not evident at the present time. The present situation stems in part from a lack of familiarity by educational evaluators and decision makers with the entire area of decision theory in general. However, the primary reason for the limited use of decision theory models is most likely the difficulty involved in constructing prior probability distributions and constructing utility functions. Both of these tasks can be quite time consuming when done by hand. Fortunately, there have been attempts in recent years to construct computer programs which greatly facilitate these two tasks. One such program, Computer Assisted Data Analysis (CADA) has been developed at the University of Iowa (Novick, Isaacs, and Dekeyrel, 1977). As previously noted, the program allows for a relatively simple, step by step specification of prior probability distributions, and also the construction of utility functions. Using these programs, a decision theory analysis of educational funding problems becomes quite feasable. It is hoped that as increasing numbers of educational evaluators and decision makers make use of this available technology, the decision theory approach will be seriously considered in educational settings.

NOTES

1. It should be noted that in the Bayesian model described later in the chapter a rather different approach is taken. The standing of project i on dimension j is treated as an unknown statistical parameter. The value of each of these parameters can then be studied within the standard Bayesian framework of specifying a prior distribution, and updating beliefs as data become available.

2. The theoretical justification for this type of utility function is thoroughly discussed in Keeney and Raiffa, 1976.

REFERENCES

Baron, J. 1977. "An exploration of the implication of the M.A.U.T.-Bayesian Decision Theoretic Model for summative and formative evaluation and post-assessment organizational change." Paper presented to the American Educational Research Association, New York City.

Edwards, W. 1976. *How to use multiattribute utility measurement for social decision-making.* Technical Report 001597-1-T. Social Science Research Institute, University of Southern California.

Edwards, W., Guttentag, M., and Snapper, K. 1975. A decision theoretic approach to evaluation research. In M. Guttentag and E. L. Struening, eds. *Handbook of Evaluation Research.* Beverly Hills: Sage Publications.

Guttentag, M., and Snapper, K. 1974. Plans, evaluations and decisions. *Evaluation* 2:58-64, 73-74.

Hemphill, J. K. 1969. The relationship between research and evaluation studies, In R.W. Tyler, ed. *Educational Evaluation: New Roles, New Means.* Chicago: University of Chicago Press.

Keeney, R. L., and Raiffa, H. 1976. *Decisions with Multiple Objectives, Preferences and Value Tradeoffs.* New York: Wiley.

Novick, M. R., and Jackson, P. H. 1974. *Statistical Methods for Educational and Psychological Research.* New York: McGraw-Hill.

Novick, M. R., Isaacs, G. L., and DeKeyrel, D. F. 1977. *Computer-Assisted Data Analysis-1977: Manual for the Computer-Assisted Data Analysis System (CADA) Monitor.* Iowa City, University of Iowa.

Winkler, R. L. 1972. *An Introduction to Bayesian Inference and Decision.* New York: Holt, Rinehart and Winston.

EVALUATION APPROACHES
AND SPECIAL
DESIGN ISSUES

PART II

Vocational education programs constitute a unique set of interests and values within the school environment. Generally the programs contain the goals espoused by the people who make up the traditional constituencies of the school, i.e., school personnel, parents, students, and also the goals of industry and labor who comprise the industrial/technical world of work. Vocational education, as a hybrid, must therefore satisfy the interests and needs of the *school* world and the *world of work.* The historical perspective presented in Part One of this Handbook describes the special federal legislation and funding of vocational education, and especially in the chapter by John Gallinelli describes and traces this dual role and purpose of vocational education. Evaluation of vocational education programs must, therefore, also preserve this duality, must be viewed within the context of the school setting in which the programs occur, and simultaneously must take into account the relationship of the programs to the work environments for which the graduates are being prepared.

Although the definition of program success has recently been expanded to include continued education as an acceptable goal for the graduates of vocational education programs (PL 94-482, section 212 [b]), it is still true that the major goal of vocational education is to prepare its graduates with entry-level job skills, that is, to immediately enter the labor force if they so desire.

Vocational education evaluation considers the school context by examining program goals, objectives, processes, and outputs in terms of vocational and traditional school objectives. Concurrently, vocational education must be evaluated in terms of what happens to its graduates if and when they enter the labor force. Thus, evaluation of vocational education programs must be examined in terms of general approaches to evaluation that have been applied to traditional school programs, and unique approaches to evaluation that are specifically undertaken to examine the relationship between vocational education and the world of work.

In examining vocational education evaluation, therefore, the following questions come to mind: (1) What are some of the issues and approaches to evaluation of general educational programs that are equally applicable to vocational education? (2) Which approaches or types of evaluation studies have been applied almost exclusively to vocational education? (3) Within the schools and the world of work, which evaluation methodologies have been and will probably continue to be most fruitful?

This section of the Handbook discusses and describes general issues and approaches to evaluation, and cost-benefit analysis and follow-up research as two of the approaches to evaluation that are more regularly applied to vocational education programs than to other educational programs.

The chapter by Theodore Abramson, *Issues and Models in Vocational Education Evaluation* reviews the general issues that are currently being discussed by evaluators, describes the major approaches that have been developed and used in evaluating educational programs, synopsizes some of the reviews of the literature in vocational education evaluation, and describes a few of the approaches to vocational education evaluation that recently have been proposed. The chapter describes the difficulties in attempting to define evaluation and to apply traditional experimental approaches to evaluation studies, and notes the quasi-experimental approaches which have recently been discussed. In addition, secondary analysis of evaluation data and meta evaluation approaches are briefly discussed. Evaluation models that are included in the chapter are the CIPP model developed by Stufflebeam and his colleagues. Two other examples of decision-oriented models, those of Provus and Alkin are also presented. The ideas of Stake, Scriven, and Borich are described in terms of judgment-oriented approaches to evaluation. Congruence models of evaluation based on Tyler's ideas are also discussed. The chapter concludes with a brief description of three approaches to evaluation developed expressly for use by vocational educators at the local level.

In doing program evaluations it is frequently impossible to impose a true experimental design that includes random assignment for the purpose of making causal inference statements. Yet many people maintain that true evaluations must contain procedures that lead to causal relations between the program and outcomes in order to make judgments of the values or worth of the object or program being evaluated. Such approaches normally presuppose comparisons of the object under study with absolute or relative standards. How does one approach evaluation in instances where the assumptions underlying traditional experimental causal models have been violated? Edgar F. Borgatta, in his chapter *Methodological Considerations: Experimental and Nonexperimental Designs and Causal Inference* discusses these issues.

The chapter begins by presenting the reasoning behind the usual experimental model through a description of a simplified approach to experimentation in the social sciences, and includes the logic of experimentation based on equivalent groups. It also includes a section on internal and external validity—those factors which limit the logic of the experiment in terms of its immediate conclusions, and those factors which limit the generalizability of the findings, respectively. These issues are, of course, important whether or not the study follows the classic, quasi, or nonexperimental approaches. Quasi-experimental or nonexperimental designs are described in terms of their relationship to an ideal design. The discussion gives examples of the pitfalls that one must be aware of in attempting to interpret the findings of these kinds of studies. In addition, the chapter describes the use of "trace measures" as evidence for program outcomes in relationship to its stated objectives, and concludes with discussions of causal inference models based on descriptions that grow from theoretical assumptions. In particular, regression analyses and path analyses are described.

One of the major functions of evaluation is to provide information for program modification or termination. Presumably, if a program is found to be partially successful, program modification considered likely to lead to greater program success would be implemented. This presupposes that the relationship between the variable(s) manipulated within the program and its (their) relationship to program outputs is clearly understood. This assumption, as the literature points out, is more of a hope than a reality. A prerequisite to understanding the relationship of program inputs and outputs is a thorough and meaningful description of the variables that theoretically and empirically have the greatest effect on the program's results.

The chapter by Elizabeth C. Proper, *Documentation of Program Implementation,* investigates the state of the art in this crucial area, and points out that no matter what the origin of the innovations, ultimately a new program when implemented in the schools is a function of the instructional strategies and procedures of the teachers who are charged with carrying out and attaining the objectives of the program. Without a thorough description of the activities of the teachers implementing the program, the evaluation does not provide information as to the amount of innovation or whether the innovation was actually carried out. In terms of the evaluation models and experimental or quasi-experimental designs described in the earlier two chapters in this section, the basic question revolves around whether or not the comparison between the experimental and treatment groups is, in fact, a meaningful one. Without information specifying the amount of treatment in the experimental group, or the amount of or lack of treatment in the control group, the comparisons on the outcome variables are meaningless. Differences, should they be found, are uninterpretable in terms of the variable(s) of interest. This chapter provides a review of selected observation instruments developed to assess the effectiveness of particular programs and to aid in program monitoring. The reliability and validity data for each of these instruments are described. The chapter concludes by pointing out that the implementation information required by different groups varies. The type and level of such information required by the developer, the evaluator, the administrator, and the policy maker, may be different and, thus, depending on the requirements, different instruments must be selected and used.

An obvious concern in today's economy is that of the costs of educational programs. Vocational education traditionally costs more than the more academically oriented or general high school program for a number of reasons. First and most obvious is the cost of specialized equipment, and the need for specialized shops or laboratories to conduct instruction. Second, there is the need for constant updating and modernization of equipment as it wears out and as it becomes obsolete. Third, there is a limit to the number of students that can be accommodated at any one time, due to the need for simulating as closely as possible the real world of work for the students as they learn the knowledges and skills required within their particular vocational program. Thus, a major concern in evaluating vocational education programs, especially during the last fifteen years, has been that of cost benefit analysis. That is, over and above the usual evaluation questions pertaining to inputs, processes, and products, vocational education has looked at the costs of the program, the benefits accruing to society, and to the individuals who have gone through and graduated from vocational training programs. The chapter by Teh-Wei Hu and Ernest W. Stromsdorfer, *Cost-Benefit Analysis of Vocational Education,* examines the issues of obtaining accurate cost and benefit estimates in attempting to evaluate the differences between vocational and general education programs. The chapter also presents major cost benefit analysis studies of vocational education programs that have been undertaken during the last fifteen years. Hu and Stromsdorfer conclude that although most of the studies show higher costs for vocational education, the benefit analysis tended to show that it pays off economically.

In evaluating vocational program outcomes, true measures of the effects of the program often cannot be seen immediately, and can only be fully assessed at a time subsequent to the student's participation in the program. Although this is true for all educational and social programs, vocational education programs are much more often evaluated through the use of follow-up studies to ascertain the effect of the program on its graduates than are other programs. This is probably due to the clear perception of vocational education as preparation for entering the world of work. The issues in conducting such studies as a means of evaluating programs are described in the chapter *Follow-Up Research as an Evaluation Strategy: Theory and Methodologies* by Jonathan Morell. The issues discussed relate to the quasi-experimental designs that are used and to drawing inferences from these data. Problems related to attrition and missing data are described as well as the determination of program effects, the collection of data, late data, and nonrespondence. Procedures for dealing with these issues are discussed. The chapter also includes a section describing statistical approaches to analyses of follow-up data, the cost of doing follow-up studies, and the selection of relevant variables and their interpretation. The point is made here too, that follow-up studies should include more than the measures of wages and earnings, as suggested in the analyses by Hu and Stromsdorfer. The chapter concludes by pointing out that evaluation studies are important because they are the only known method that can give us information as to the longevity or staying power of a particular treatment.

Part Two of this Handbook, then, was designed to provide information on the various approaches to evaluation of vocational education. In addition, this section includes chapters on cost benefit analysis and follow-up studies. The difficulties in arriving at appropriate estimates of costs and benefits are described, as are the issues in attempting to interpret follow-up study data based on quasi-experimental approaches. The issues related to defining appropriate variables and designing evaluation research studies were presented in terms of experimental or quasi-experimental designs.

The process and outcome variables that are studied should represent the relationship between the world of work, and the skills and knowledges obtained by students in vocational education programs as a function of the curriculum and instruction they are given. Part Three of the *Handbook* deals with the curriculum and its relationship to the world of work.

chapter 5

THEODORE ABRAMSON

*Queens College,
City University of New York*

Evaluation as a field of inquiry has grown up during the past decade. It has now become big business and academically acceptable as a field of endeavor for social scientists. Freeman (1977) estimated that in the period between 1970-1976 hundreds of evaluation studies with budgets in excess of $100,000 were undertaken annually. Publication of the *Handbook of Evaluation Research* (Guttentag and Struening, 1975), *Evaluation Studies Review Annuals* (Glass, 1976; Guttentag, 1977), and the publication of refereed journals devoted almost exclusively to evaluation of social programs are an indication of the increased growth of evaluation research. The status of evaluation has changed from a second class status, typically given to all applied disciplines by academics, to that of an emerging discipline in its own right.

Much of this growth is probably directly attributable to federal legislation embodied in the ESEA Act of 1965, and the amendments of 1968 and 1976 (Wentling and Lawson, 1975; Datta, 1979). Paradoxically, along with this growth and insistence on evaluation studies concurrent with social program funding, has come an increase in awareness and scope of problems associated with evaluation activities. Some of these issues are rather general in nature and are not dependent on specific types of programs, while some issues are specific to evaluation of vocational education programs. The purpose of this chapter is to provide an overview of some of the current major issues in evaluation, summaries of some of the major evaluation models that have been developed, and a discussion of implications for vocational education program evaluation.

The chapter presents these ideas in three main sections. The first one deals with general evaluation issues and briefly outlines current status in terms of problems associated with definition of evaluation, experimental methods, secondary analysis, and meta evaluation. The second section presents some of the major models that have been developed in the conduct of program evaluation, such as those based on the work of Scriven, Stake, and Stufflebeam. The final section of the chapter refers to some of the major reviews of vocational education evaluation studies, and concludes with projections for future work in the field of evaluation of vocational programs.

GENERAL EVALUATION ISSUES

Definition of Evaluation

Evaluation as a field of endeavor, which has only recently started to receive a good deal of attention by social scientists, suffers from the lack of consensus definition. The problem is not new, and a decade ago Guba (1969) in discussing some of the major problems with evaluation identified the lack of definition as a major concern. The three types of evaluation definitions that Guba (1969) identified were (1) measurement, (2) congruence between performance and objectives, and (3) professional judgment. Worthen and Sanders (1973) in describing a framework for the planning of evaluations presented eight different evaluation models and their associated definitions. Not surprisingly, most of these definitions can be subsumed under the terms used by Guba (1969), although two new definitional emphases were added: evaluation as description and judgment, and evaluation as provider of information for decision-making. Suchman (1967), in discussing the lack of a consensus definition, made the basic distinction between "evaluation" and "evaluative research." He considers evaluation to be the process of judging the worth of a product, process, or a program which does not necessarily require systematic procedures or evidence supportive of the judgment. Evaluative research on the other hand is "utilization of scientific research methods and techniques for the purpose of making an evaluation ... evaluative research refers to those procedures ... which increases the possibility for proving rather than asserting the worth of some social activity" (Suchman, 1967:8). Scriven's (1967) work also defines evaluation as judgment of the value of a thing, as does more recent work (Webster and Stufflebeam, 1978). Freeman (1977) and Guttentag (1977) argue that the most important aspect of evaluation research is the relationship of its findings to the decision-making processes, and consider data related to program value as *research* rather than as evaluative research. Wentling and Lawson (1975), in a book on evaluating occupational education, discuss some of these definitional problems and present two definitions: (1) "Evaluation is the process of delineating, collecting, and providing information useful for judging decision alternatives" (Stufflebeam, Foley, Gephart, Guba, Hammond, Merriman and Provus, 1971), (2) "Evaluation is the determination of the worth of a thing. It includes obtaining information for use in judging the worth of the program, product, procedure, or objective or the potential utility of alternative approaches designed to attain specified objectives" (Worthen and Sanders, 1973). While the two definitions are not mutually exclusive, there is a difference in their emphasis with the first definition stressing data collection for presentation to decision makers, and the second accenting data collection accompanied by value judgments. Some of these definitional problems are briefly described by Flaherty and Morell (1978).

Perhaps some of these issues may be reconceptualized in terms of a distinction between the terms evaluation, program evaluation, and evaluative research, where the first and last terms would follow Suchman's distinction, and program evaluation would be a term not quite as broad as evaluation but broader than the concept of evaluation research. Program evaluation would be seen as a series of activities which may or may not require rigorous scientific research (experiments) procedures, and would include instances which do not incorporate rigorous social science methodologies. Program evaluation may thus be seen as incorporating evaluation research, and what Freeman (1977) refers to as "para-evaluation activities." From the perspective of practitioners at the local level, this definition of program evaluation would be less restrictive than the concept of evaluation research, and more rigorous, data based, and decision oriented than the more global concept of evaluation.

Experimental Issues in Evaluation

A debate that goes back a number of years about the need for experimentation in evaluation is still raging. Suchman (1967) and more recently Freeman (1977), as mentioned above, have indicated their strong preference for maximizing rigorous experimentation within evaluation studies of social programs. On the other hand, there are those (Cronbach, 1963; and Guttentag, 1977) who argue that educational and large scale national or state programs cannot be considered independent variables subject to traditional experimental models. It has also been pointed out that when experimental models are applied to evaluation studies the emphasis is generally only on those measures which are easily objectified, related, and achievement oriented, and excludes relevant organizational variables (Berk and Rossi, 1977). Linn (1978) in discussing the validity of the proposed Title I RMC Evaluation models, finds them to be based on narrowly conceived approaches to evaluation limited to the measure of cognitive achievement gains. The problem is not basically related to the advantage of experimentation but whether there is ultimate payoff in imposing the experimental models on most program evaluation designs. The question is not "to experiment or not to experiment" but whether strict adherence to experimental models is the most fruitful and useful approach to evaluation research.

Campbell's (1977) work using regression analysis and quasi-experimental designs (Cook and Campbell, 1976), investigated possible solutions to some of the design and statistical problems in evaluation research. Morell,[1] for example, in discussing follow-up evaluation gives a number of examples in which experimental or quasi-experimental designs can and should be incorporated into follow-up studies, an area which frequently has not attempted to apply experimental or quasi-experimental designs. Hollaway and Carrier (1978), as another example, have proposed possible use of aptitude by treatment interactions as a means of evaluating programs.

There are a number of other important research issues regardless of whether or not the evaluation design is cast in an experimental mode. Datta (1979) raises the issue of how much of the treatment must be operational before the program can be said to be implemented. Bridgeman (1978) in dealing with this problem, described a multiple linear regression approach in which the amount of program implementation was considered a categorical variable and included in the analyses. He found a significant result which was absent when program implementation was excluded from the analysis. The question of the inclusion of policy makers in evaluation research is also currently being debated. Rippey (1973) in describing transactional evaluation, felt that all constituencies must be included within the evaluation team so that the ultimate results of the evaluation will be more decision-relevant and thus be implemented. Those whose approach to evaluation is more purist tend to exclude policy makers from inclusion in the evaluation effort.

There has also been work on developing in a specific way the goals and objectives of the program to be evaluated. The paper by Kromhout (1978) was one recent example of the use of multiattribute utility theory in arriving at needs assessment and prioritization for a statewide vocational curriculum system. Finally the issue of the role of the evaluator in evaluation research has received some attention with many writers advocating greater and earlier involvement of evaluators. For example, Borich (1977) describes structured hierarchical decomposition as a technique that is useful in interrelating the planning, designing, developing, and evaluating roles. This issue of evaluator roles in evaluation is discussed in a separate chapter in the book.[2]

Secondary Analysis

A major issue of some concern in the recent literature is that of secondary analysis of psychological and measurement data. This concern has obvious ramifications for the use of evaluation data. Bryant and Wortman (1978) indicate three major reasons and uses for secondary analysis of psychological data. The first is the assessment of the credibility of the findings. Availability of evaluation data for secondary analysis or independent reanalysis would make it possible to validate the statistical procedures and conclusions of the initially reported data. Second, the knowledge that the original data would be subject to secondary analysis would probably lead to a more careful original analysis. At the least, many of the clerical errors in collecting, tabulating, and reporting the data might be more carefully checked and removed. Third, a routine procedure for availability of original data would tend to make available a greater number of longitudinal studies. One of the basic assumptions in the reanalysis of data for longitudinal studies is the comparability of the data to be collected over the period of time of the study. A similar concern would be for studies in which different samples supposedly representative of the population would be examined under a set of similar conditions. In dealing with this latter problem Light and Smith (1971) and Salasin (1977) have developed and discussed a concept known as cluster analysis.

In the discussion reported by Salasin (1977), Light describes cluster analysis as an approach in which the results of several contradictory studies are broken down into smaller units of analysis so that the results may be examined for subject by treatment interactions, differences in allocations across treatments, and results of study designs. This approach to secondary analysis permits a combination of the results of a number of related studies, and leads to the possibility of understanding results that appear to be contradictory. Thus, the fourth reason for secondary analysis would be the resolution of contradictory findings.

In a recent paper, Glass (1976) proposes another approach to integrating data from a series of studies which does not necessarily require access to raw data, or to data collected from the same or similar instruments. In this analysis, called "meta analysis," Glass showed how imperfect or weak studies that do not meet the criteria of rigorous designs can be incorporated and lead to appropriate conclusions when aggregated. This approach leads to a fifth reason for secondary analysis, in that it permits judgments about social action programs or bodies of psychological studies which vary on a number of dimensions, and on the data collected using different instruments. Data integration of large numbers of studies, some of which vary in terms of the rigor of the designs used, may well lead to valid conclusions rather than to calls for more integrated reviews of the literature and better research.

Meta Evaluation

Another area which has recently received a good deal of attention is that of evaluation of evaluations, or what Scriven (1969) called "meta evaluation." Studies reporting reanalyses of data from earlier program evaluations are a subset of meta evaluation, and these types of reports have recently started to appear in the literature. Cook and Gruder (1978) describe summative meta evaluation research in terms of models that are analogous to a three factor analysis of variance design. The three factors are: (1) the point in time when meta evaluation is conducted—subsequent to or simultaneous with primary evaluation, (2) manipulation of evaluation data—data are or are not reanalyzed, (3) number of data sets to be examined—single or multiple. They describe each model and the ways in which they might be used to improve the quality of some of the evaluations and some of the weaknesses of each of the models. On a more mundane level, Sanders and Nafziger (1976) developed a checklist to determine the adequacy of evaluation designs. The use of their checklist prior to the actual conduct of an evaluation study would lead to better evaluation designs that would provide more useful information to the group for which the evaluation is being undertaken. The checklist is made up of four general sections that deal with the evaluation planning, collection and processing of information, adequacy of the reporting of information, and ethical considerations and appropriate interface mechanisms.

Gowin and Millman (1978) argue, that in addition to meta evaluation insuring that the evaluation will be carried out adequately and efficiently, and exposing the strengths and weaknesses of completed evaluation studies, there are four areas in which meta evaluation will increase our understanding of the evaluation process. These areas are: (1) the practice of evaluation, (2) the concept of value, (3) the criteria for judging evaluations, (4) the procedures for conducting meta evaluations. That is, not only does meta evaluation provide information about evaluations that have been conducted, they also provide further explication of the evaluation process itself.

EVALUATION MODELS

A description of the models and frameworks for conducting evaluations is meant to describe and emphasize general procedures of evaluations, the audiences to which they are addressed, and the activities to be undertaken by the evaluators. In describing program evaluation there are a number of different classification schemes that are possible. The major distinction between decision oriented and judgment oriented evaluations is based on the ideas of Worthen and Sanders (1973). In considering evaluation models and designs one must be cognizant of the basic distinction between models and theories. Models are basically judged on the basis of a continuum of usefulness. Theories are judged along a continuum of truthfulness. Thus, facts which cannot be incorporated into theory and serve as counter examples of what the theory predicts are generally fatal, and lead to the demise of the theory. Models on the other hand do not pretend to subsume all facts and, thus, are more robust and are not necessarily destroyed by facts which are inimical to the ideas which are embodied in the model. Borich (1974:145) points out that evaluators frequently tend to use models that are general in nature rather than using models that are too specific because of the complexity of the systems that they are attempting to evaluate. In addition, he states that:

> In contrast to the scientist, the evaluator usually spends much less time verifying his model than he spends using it. The evaluator sees his models as a means to an end; if it works reasonably well in achieving that end, the evaluator rarely takes the time to document the effectiveness of the tool that got him there.

Thus, in summarizing the ideas embodied in the models described below, two things must always be kept in mind. The first is that the models at best describe and represent only a part of the phenomenon under study, in our case, the vocational education program, and secondly, that the model must be considered in terms of its usefulness. Therefore, in deciding which evaluation model and design one should employ in studying the effectiveness of a program, it becomes important to consider the uses to which the evaluation data are to be put, and the questions for which the data are meant to provide answers.

Wiley (1978), for example, in describing the RMC models to Title I evaluations indicates that their major functions and the uses to which the data are to be put relates to political issues resulting from the legislative provisions for Title I. With respect to local districts' needs he maintains that the model's function is to provide for the development of more effective Title I projects, as called for in the legislative mandates. The national policy need for the measurement of effectiveness and program characteristics leading to effectiveness, led Wiley to conclude that evaluation effort at the local level should consist of student sample data collection, reporting of program characteristics, and testing data. Major studies, analyses, and interpretation of findings should be done at the national level to feed into policy decision-making. Perhaps in terms of the RMC models such an approach might be justified because the RMC models only deal with a single major issue in evaluation, measuring the cognitive achievement gains of students (Horst, Tallmadge and Wood, 1975).

While it is possible to categorize evaluation designs according to the uses to which the data are to be put, it is also possible to examine the models in terms of the philosophical and methodological positions taken by their proponents. There are those whose approach to evaluation is based on Tyler's (1942) ideas, and who, therefore, view evaluation as a measure of the congruence between performance and objectives that have been stated prior to program implementation. Stufflebeam (Stufflebeam et al., 1971; Stufflebeam, 1969) basically perceived evaluation as a series of activities that provide data to decision makers. Still others consider evaluation as the means to establish the worth or value of a program (Scriven, 1967). Stake (1967) suggests that a description of the project as well as a judgment of the project's value are the two basic components of evaluation. Borich (1977) in extending some of Stake's ideas about the use of judgments collected about antecedents, transactions, and outcomes described the purpose of evaluation as a revision, deletion, modification, and or confirmation of the effectiveness of the program. Wholey (1976) in discussing program evaluation from the perspective of policy science indicates that the basic issue with which program evaluation is to be concerned is the assessment of program outcomes. That is, the major emphasis of program evaluation should be a judgment of the value of program outcomes—what occurred as a result of the program that would not have happened in its absence.

The three sections that follow briefly describe approaches that are categorized as decision oriented evaluation, judgment oriented evaluation, and other approaches to evaluation.

Decision Oriented Evaluation

Stufflebeam et al. (1971) developed an evaluation model whose major purpose is to provide data to decision makers that are relevant to the judgments that are to be made. The model is thus conceptualized in terms of the *decisions* for which the evaluation is to provide information. Decisions are classified along two dimensions: (1) ends-means, (2) intentions-actualities. A 2 x 2 matrix of these dimensions yields four cells: intended ends, intended means, actual means, actual ends. In educational settings, these four types of decisions and their associated evaluations are classified as: (1) planning decisions (intended ends)—context evaluation, (2) structuring or programming (intended means) decisions—input evaluation, (3) implementing decisions (actual means)—process evaluation, (4) recycling decisions (actual ends)—product evaluation. Thus, the four types of evaluations in this model are: context, input, process, product (CIPP).

Context evaluation is concerned with identification of needs, conditions, and problems within a defined and operating educational environment. This description of the setting gives rise to the goals and specific objectives of the program. Data from theoretical and empirical studies which compare the intended and actual system performance lead to analysis of possible discrepancies. (Coster and Ihnen [1968], in their review of program evaluation in vocational education found that studies of goals and objectives were usually conducted by asking panels of "experts" to judge the appropriateness of existing objectives.)

Input evaluation is concerned with the identification and assessment of the system's capabilities and strategies for overcoming difficulties in meeting project objectives. Cost-benefit analyses of human and material resources in terms of alternative strategies for achieving project objectives provide the basic data for making comparisons and decisions. Thus, input evaluation is concerned with resource, budget, and time requirements necessary for achieving the desired goals as identified in context evaluation. (Coster and Ihnen [1968] review some cost-benefit studies of vocational education programs.)

Process evaluation is concerned with the relationship between actual program operation during its implementation stage and the original program design. Process evaluation data help determine whether the program is being implemented as it was originally planned. These data also indicate whether the goals and problems identified in context and input evaluation and their suggested solutions are occurring as planned. This type of evaluation is basically interested in examining the day-to-day management of the project in terms of those areas which may give rise to project failure. These areas include personnel, resources, and allocation problems.

Product evaluation is concerned with the relationship between program outcomes and program objectives, and the relationship between these outcomes and the context, input, and process evaluation data. Student outcome data are generally collected for this type of evaluation, and these data are interpreted and related to the context, input, and process data. It is interesting to note that although Stufflebeam et al. (1971) described four types of evaluation in their CIPP model, there is only one evaluation approach for the conduct of all four types of evaluations. The structure of the evaluation consists of six major components: (1) focusing the evaluation; (2) information collection; (3) information organization; (4) information analysis; (5) information reporting; and (6) administration of evaluation.

Focusing the evaluation requires identification of the decision-making level(s), definition of the decision situations within the levels, specification of variables that define the criteria within the situations, and description of the policies to which the evaluator must adhere. Data collection requires specification of subjects, instruments, sampling, administration procedures, and scheduling. Information organization and analysis requires appropriate data processing format, selection of and means for data analysis. Reporting of information requires specification of the audience(s) for the evaluation reports, the means, and schedule of dissemination activities. Administration of the evaluation requires planning and conducting the evaluation design by specifying resources, schedules, personnel, and budget. The CIPP model and its corresponding design provides program managers with information that leads to informed decisions. Context evaluation provides data for the determination of the appropriate goals and objectives of the program, and provides the wherewithal for planning decisions. Input evaluation provides the data necessary for appropriate allocation of resources to meet the defined program goals and objectives; thus serving and structuring decisions. Implementation decisions are served by the consulting program monitoring that results from process evaluation. Finally, product evaluation provides the data necessary for recycling decisions through its measurement and interpretation of the degree to which project objectives were met.

A second approach to evaluation as a means for providing school administrators with information leading to appropriate decisions was developed by Provus. In this model Provus (1969:245) described the purpose and processes of evaluation as follows:

> The purpose of program evaluation is to determine whether to improve, maintain, or terminate a program. Evaluation is the process of (a) agreeing upon program standards, (b) determining whether a discrepancy exists between some aspect of the program, and, (c) using discrepancy information to identify the weaknesses of the program.

This model which has come to be known as the Discrepancy Evaluation Model (DEM) is conceptualized in terms of four major stages resulting from program development. The stages basically consist of a program definition, program installation, program implementation processes, and program goal attainment or products. Within each of these stages the DEM is conceptualized as consisting of continuously repeated sequences of questions through implied criteria, new information, and ultimately a decision. Simply put, the DEM evaluation always consists of a comparison of Performance (P) against Standard (S) which yields the Discrepancy (D) information. D then serves as the basis on which judgments are made and decisions rendered. Each stage of the program goes through a series of SPD cycles in attempting to provide the necessary information to the program personnel. The initial series of questions in each stage are as follows: Is the program defined?, Is the program installed?, Are the enabling objectives being met?, Are the terminal products achieved? SPD cycles are continuously repeated within each stage until appropriate decisions can be made. The function of the DEM evaluator is to serve the needs of the program staff through constant communication that provides the data necessary for decisions for recycling, repeating, or termination decisions. The activities that the evaluator is engaged in during the course of this type of evaluation lead to explicit statements of standards, performances, comparisons, and discrepancies. Thus, the evaluator is required to identify decision points, provide the opportunity for the program personnel to formulate standards, apply explicit criteria to the standards, describe data and procedures for comparison of performance with standards, locate the cause of discrepancies, document corrective actions taken, and to be in constant communication with program personnel. The DEM is clearly an approach which requires a great deal of cooperation between the evaluator, the program director and his staff, and is an approach to evaluation which calls for constant program monitoring and modification throughout the life of the project. Problems related to the use of experimental designs are of little consequence to the evaluator until the latter phases of stage four, by which point in time the program definition and implementation are more or less set. That is, it is possible to have a good deal of confidence in the descriptions of program input and processes sans experiment. It is interesting to note that the DEM and the CIPP model both conceive of evaluation as a series of activities that are concurrent with and parallel to the activities necessary for the development, installation, and institutionalization of new programs. Steinmetz (1976:6) describes in fairly simple terms how one might apply DEM to a Teacher-Inservice program by going through a series of SPD cycles, and describes the input-output processes for some of the components and subcomponents within the program. He concludes his description as follows:

> From the daily activities of an individual teacher to educational program evaluation, the DEM can be utilized to structure the gathering of information essential for well-informed decision-making. A major feature of the DEM is its emphasis on self-evaluation and systematic program improvement.

A third approach to evaluation as a process for providing information so that alternatives can be selected by decision makers has been described by Alkin and his coworkers (Alkin, 1969; Alkin and Fitz-Gibbon, 1975). This model identifies five areas in which evaluation information is necessary for decision-making. In the earlier formulation the program areas were described as systems assessment, program planning, program implementation, program improvement, and program certification.

Systems assessment provide evaluation information to decision makers about the state of other systems in comparison to desired outcomes as described in statements of objectives. In the program planning stage, evaluation data provide the decision maker with descriptions of alternative processes, which may be introduced to meet the system's needs that had been previously determined. These two evaluation phases occur prior to the program's inception, and require the evaluator to project the attainment of goals and objectives based on needs and the probable effectiveness of alternative approaches to fulfilling those needs. Program implementation evaluation provides the decision maker with information about the extent to which the actual program corresponds to the program description developed during the planning stage. During this stage, descriptions of the treatment and its modifications from the original plan are documented and described by the evaluator. During the course of the program's implementation, modifications are introduced to maximize chances of successfully achieving program objectives. Presumably the modifications result from perceived shortcomings in the implementation to move the inputs (students) toward the desired objectives of the program. This phase of evaluation is clearly nonexperimental in nature.

The program certification phase of evaluation provides information to the decision maker about the value of a program and its potential generalizability. Within the context of program certification, the evaluator attempts to apply as rigid a set of experiments as possible. In this approach, Alkin (1969) distinguishes between evaluation of educational systems and evaluation of instructional programs. Systems assessment and program planning evaluation are seen as being useful to evaluation of educational systems, while the last three phases of evaluation are seen as necessary for evaluating instructional programs. In terms of Alkin's basic definition of evaluation, each of the five evaluation phases described above is seen in terms of four steps: (1) to define the decision areas of concern, (2) to choose information appropriate to these decision areas, (3) to collect and analyze these data, and (4) to summarize and report information to decision makers.

Alkin and Fitz-Gibbon (1975) in the later description of their evaluation model describe three evaluation stages which, with some minor modifications, basically subsume the ideas described above. Using Scriven's (1967) terminology they distinguish between preformative evaluation consisting of needs assessment and program planning evaluation, formative evaluation consisting of implementation and progress evaluation, and summative evaluation consisting of documentation and outcome evaluation. The first two major stages are interactive with the parallel program stages, whereas summative evaluation is undertaken after the program has been stabilized.

An interesting addition to summative evaluation in this model consists of the *documentation* phase of evaluation, and as these evaluation data are meant to provide information about generalizability, feedback to the program is not called for. Actual implementation of many of Alkin's ideas can be seen in the research study of bilingual education evaluations (Alkin, Kosecoff, Fitz-Gibbon and Seligman, 1974) especially the basic distinctions resulting from differences in definitions in formative and summative evaluation.

It is interesting to note that the three decision-oriented models described above (CIPP model, DEM model, and Alkin's model) conceive of evaluation as a series of activities that are concurrent with and parallel to the activities necessary for the development, installation, and institutionalization of new programs. In each phase of evaluation decisions, activities are seen as being relatively similar in that information is provided to the decision maker which enables the program to be improved, modified, or terminated within each development phase. The earlier phase of the program and its associated evaluation tend to be viewed in terms of planning. The middle phase with program installation and implementation, and the final phase with the institutionalization of the program. These three models provide for an evaluation role during the planning phase. There is some controversy as to whether or not program planning and needs assessment are conceived of as evaluation activities. Weiss (1975) maintains that these activities are basically nonevaluative in nature. Similar views are expressed by Guttentag (1973), and Guttentag and Snapper (1974) in their descriptions of Multiattribute Theory as a means of assisting planners in arriving at consensus decisions. According to this view, the first stage in the evaluation process begins with the outcomes of the planning phase.

Judgment Oriented Evaluation

Stake (1967) described an approach to evaluation which has as its major purpose a formal description of the program and a process for judging the merit, or value of the program. Both the description and judgments are examined in this model in terms of data matrices, with intent and observations comprising a description matrix, and standards and judgments making up the judgment matrix. Each of the above four major categories of data to be collected by the evaluator is described in terms of antecedents, transactions, and outcomes. Antecedents are any conditions existing prior to instruction which may affect the outcomes. Transactions consist of any and all activities which relate to the processes of education to which the recipients of the program may be exposed. Transactions are dynamic in character in that they are modified on an ongoing basis, and in effect may result in changes in intents. This can readily be seen as the teacher may modify his/her planned lesson or series of lessons as a result of student questioning, student responses, student prior knowledge, and so on, that may be different from the original expectations of the teacher. Outcomes consist of those data and measurements which describe program impact. Although in most evaluations the outcome measures are obtained after a specified amount of time in the program, some outcome measures may not be readily observed until a period of time subsequent to the student's formal termination from the program. Thus, in vocational education programs, follow-up studies would be an essential part of obtaining outcome information as an indication of program impact, and would probably include information such as income, job satisfaction, advancement, and so on.

Description of the program occurs by examining the congruence between the intents and the observations, as well as, the logical or empirical relationships or contingencies between the antecedents, transactions, and outcomes. Judgments of the value of a program are described in terms of publicly described standards. Standards may be either absolute or relative. For both types of standards, a formal evaluation would require statements of acceptable levels for antecedents, transactions, and outcomes. Prior to judgment, determination must be made whether or not each standard is being met with judgments being rendered as to importance or weighting of each set of standards. The major difference between the relative and the absolute standard is a function of whether the goals of the program and its effectiveness are to be measured in relationship to other programs. Relative standards are used when the program's outputs are to be compared with the outcomes of other programs. The evaluator determines which programs to compare to. In a subsequent paper, Stake (1970) reiterated the importance of judgments, and maintained that the purpose of judgment data is to show that the design of the program is or is not relatively effective. Without judgment data, it becomes impossible for an evaluator to show the success of a program, or lack of it. Thus, Stake's view is that the distinguishing characteristic and major purpose of evaluation is to *judge* the relative or absolute merit of programs.

In this system it is clear that the act of judging remains a rather subjective activity. As the evaluator attempts to judge the worth of a program, he/she is faced with the dilemma that arises from the different views and values of the various constituencies operating within the program. Merit or worth of a program in the eyes of students may be different from the values of the program as perceived by the teachers or administrators in the school system. Even among the teachers the standards that are used to judge worth may differ. The evaluator's responsibility in this case is to describe the definitions of merit used by the different groups who are operating within the program. Active involvement of a group obligates the evaluator to incorporate in some fashion the concerns and issues raised by the group in the conceptualization of the major properties to which attention must be given, and whose merits must ultimately be judged. Evaluation methods are selected to match the locally identified issues, as problems are best solved through direct involvement of the local people. The evaluator, therefore, has the task of gathering these subjective data through a disciplined approach to qualitative research methods. Stake (1978a) in projecting these views made the following statement at a recent debate:

> Subjective judgment is a central and essential part of the act of evaluation. Not only is the program (or whatever object) put forth to be judged as having merit or shortcoming, but also its outcomes, costs, processes, and other properties are at least sometimes subject to judg-

mental review. In addition, there is the subjective choice of properties to attend to and the choice of standards to be used. The very idea of evaluation is one of coming to know the worth of the program, partly through subjective judgment. . . . There are many problems in gathering subjective data, to be sure. But there are disciplined qualitative-research behaviors, particularly apparent in the work of a competent historian or ethnographer, but also apparent in the clinical behavior of certain teachers and other practitioners in the field. These essentially subjective efforts to understand complex phenomena can help guide our behavior in the search for understanding of the worth of educational programs.

In continuing this line of reasoning, one of the methods that has recently received attention by some evaluators is that of the case study (Stake, 1978b). Some of the issues related to generalization of findings from single case studies have been described by Kennedy (1978) who employs legal and medical models in which judgments are used to generalize from single cases. In both the legal and medical models, generalizations are designed to provide guidance to users of information rather than to those who generate the data. In Kennedy's view, therefore, generalizations from the judgments that evaluators provide are all important to educational decision makers or administrators, and from this perspective one might argue that this type of evaluation, although judgmental in nature, in essence falls under the more general rubric of decision oriented models.

Scriven (1967), in his seminal paper on the methodology of evaluation, makes a major distinction between the goals and the roles of evaluation. According to Scriven the only goal for evaluation is the determination of the worth or merit of the program or thing being evaluated. Thus, the major function of the evaluator is to provide a judgment as to the program's value. Without this judgment of value there can be no evaluation. Accordingly, the kinds of questions that an evaluator faces are of the following type: How well does this program prepare its graduates to enter the world of work? Is this particular vocational education program better than an alternative program? Is this vocational education program worth what it's costing? Therefore, in evaluation studies the values of the evaluator, which are used to determine the standards against which the merits of a program will be measured, are crucial. Scriven points out that, in most instances, the kind of decisions educators are interested in making relate to the relative merits of an alternative when compared to other programs that the educator might consider adopting. Scriven, therefore, recommends that evaluations be relative in nature and provide data and judgments about the relative outcomes of two or more programs.

Scriven makes a distinction between what he calls formative evaluation and summative evaluation. Formative evaluation is undertaken during the course of program development and serves to provide the necessary feedback to the program developer. Formative evaluation, therefore, consists of those activities whose major purpose is to improve or modify a product while it is still under development. Summative evaluation on the other hand, consists of those activities which judge the merit or worth of a completed product or program. It is aimed at providing the consumer with information as to the value of the program or product. This distinction between formative and summative evaluation has important consequences in terms of the personnel who should be doing the evaluating. Formative evaluation would probably best be carried out by evaluators working closely with the team developing the program or product. These evaluators would have a good deal of knowledge about the details of the project and the way in which the different parts operate concurrently. Because the role of the summative evaluator is to provide a report to potential consumers, it is essential that the evaluation be conducted by an independent, outside evaluator who would not be swayed in his/her judgments of the program as a result of his/her close association with the program and its personnel. In his approach to evaluation, Scriven points out that evaluation of objectives is not sufficient to constitute an evaluation of the merits or worth of a program. It is perfectly possible for a program to meet all of its objectives and yet be completely worthless. The question reduces itself to one of judging the merits of the objectives of the program.

Considering the need for judgment in evaluation and also the need for the reduction of bias in evaluation and its reporting, Scriven has developed what he calls "goal free" evaluation, and he has also described a series of organizational and social devices for controlling biases (Scriven, 1976). The basic approach to goal free evaluation is to withhold from the evaluator the statements of the program developers' prespecified objectives, goals, and intents. The evaluator is forced to look for *all* of the outcomes and effects of the program or product that he/she judges to be of merit. In this formulation it is possible for a single observer to be objective in judging the merits of a program if he/she is looking for the right thing, and if he/she is protected from numerous opportunities for bias. Scriven's 1967 paper also contains a taxonomy of possible criteria for evaluation studies. It includes the usual taxonomic classifications of cognitive, affective, and psychomotor domains. In addition, it includes a series of the variables, procedures, and effects which are of importance to evaluators.

Borich (1977:1), in describing structured hierarchical decomposition as a technique that can be used for applying systems concepts to evaluation makes the following statement:

> The purpose of program evaluation is to assess the instructional activities that comprise the global program in a manner that makes possible the rendering of a *judgment* (italics added) as to whether these activities

should be revised, deleted, modified, unchanged, or supplemented with additional instructional components.

The purpose of evaluation according to this model is to understand the components of the program so that evaluative data can be collected, which will permit the judgment of the adequacy of each component and its relationship to other program components. Evaluation thus provides the data to judge each of the parts of the program, as well as, the synthesis of the parts into more comprehensive outputs. As a tool, structured decomposition provides a graphic display of the program transactions or activities, and charts the sequence of activities to which the program participants will be exposed from the beginning to the end of the program. In the process, it also specifies some of the difficulties that may be expected in the implementation of the program activities. It forces the synthesis of the program components by simultaneously specifying the program transactions and outputs that are expected. Ultimately it fosters a common vocabulary and conception of the program by having planners, designers, and evaluators work as a team. In the earlier stages of the program the decomposition is used to examine and to arrive at agreements as to the intents of the program. Judgments are made by the evaluator as to the fidelity of or possible relationships between the specified transactions and the outcomes. This match is intended to lead to restatements of transactions and their associated outcomes.

This model may be thought of as having six stages. The first stage is the development of the decomposition model resulting from the evaluator's review of the proposal and program documents. The second stage is the actual decomposition itself. In the third stage, the evaluator arrives at top priority evaluative dimensions. Borich describes the steps that the evaluator should take as he/she moves through the decomposition model in arriving at these dimensions. The evaluative dimensions help to focus the activities undertaken by the evaluator so the data most relevant to the questions being asked can be identified. Evaluative dimensions also insure that the questions most relevant to the informational needs of the client will be answered. The fourth stage requires the evaluator to use the dimensions generated in stage three to formulate natural language questions for those groups who will use the evaluation results. In the fifth stage of the evaluation, the statistical methods that will be used to analyze the data necessary to answer the natural language questions are specified and selected. In the sixth stage, the evaluator reports his/her conclusions and results based on the statistical analyses. The final and seventh stage consists of the recommendations that the evaluator makes to the program development team. In this stage the evaluator provides judgments as to whether the program should be revised, modified, or terminated.

In examining Borich's model, it appears that there has been an amalgamation of a number of the ideas presented earlier in the decision maker and judgment approaches. On the one hand, Alkin's description of the three stages of evaluation, including a preformative stage, is incorporated in Borich's model especially in the first two stages of the evaluation, which basically consist of considering the program from the perspective of its logic and system, that is, its planning and design phase. On the other, it appears that the evaluator is called on to provide expert judgment after he/she has gained agreement by the program developers as to the important evaluative dimensions to which he/she should attend. These evaluative judgments are arrived at as a result of agreement on the intents, transactions, and outcomes built into the phases of the program. This approach is clearly in keeping with some of Stake's ideas about judgment as a central component of the evaluative process and the components that describe the program. However, Scriven's idea of "goal free" evaluation, that is, judgment based solely on the evaluator's perceptions as to what constitutes important issues are not included in this model. From Borich's perspective, the only important issues that the evaluator should attend to are those which are going to answer the questions that the program developer and/or implementors need to know.

Other Approaches to Evaluation

One of the earliest and most important approaches to evaluation is Tyler's (1942) objectives based approach to evaluation. According to this approach, the major steps in program evaluation are the establishment and classification of broadly stated goals and objectives, the definition of objectives in behavioral or operational terms, the specification of the situations appropriate to the achievement of the objectives, the selection of appropriate measures, the collection of student outcome data, and finally, the comparison of the data with the behavioral objectives.

In the system outlined above the decisions to be made are a function of the congruence between the stated objectives and the measured outcomes. As evaluation is an on-going and cyclical process in this system, feedback is used to refine and redefine the program's objectives with each phase of the cycle leading to a more sharply defined program.

Other writers have also developed evaluation models in the Tylerian tradition. For example, Metfessel and Michael (1967) developed a paradigm that presented an eight step procedure for the conduct of evaluations. The eight steps consisted of the involvement of the total school community as participants in the evaluation, the construction of broad general goals and specific hierarchical objectives, translation of the specific objectives into a form facilitating learning in the school environment that would include the process and content components, development of instrumentation that would measure program effectiveness in terms of the stated objectives, collection of data on a periodic basis that would yield information related to objectives, analysis of the data collected in the step above, interpretation of the data in terms of judgments about the desired level of performance, and finally, formulation of recommendations for implementation and revisions so that program improvements could be made. Perhaps more importantly, the Metfessel and Michael paper (1967) contains an appendix of measurement techniques and briefly describes the strengths and weaknesses of the different methods of collecting evaluation data based on the different approaches to data collection. Most evaluation models appear to include the basic notion of the congruence of objectives and outcomes as stated in Tyler's (1942) thinking. They differ in that the models described above tend to incorporate Tyler's ideas and have clarified approaches to evaluation for projects that incorporate more than curriculum development.

How does one arrive at a scheme for classifying evaluation models? Classification of evaluation models is dependent on the basic underlying assumptions and definitions that the classifier brings to bear on this task, and the perceived emphasis of the model's developer. For example, Webster and Stufflebeam (1978) classify Provus' approach to evaluation as a variation on the Tylerian approach to objectives based evaluation. Closer examination of Provus' ideas would indicate that a major thrust in the model is basically a decision management strategy and, therefore, one could classify Provus' work as a hybrid approach to evaluation. However, as it appears that his basic audience is management and its decisions, his work was classified together with the CIPP and other management models. As stated earlier, the classification of models used in this paper follows that of Worthen and Sanders (1973), who classify evaluation models in terms of judgmental, decision management, and decision objective strategies. More recently, House (1978) describes the assumptions underlying evaluation models in terms of the concepts underlying liberal democracy. In the context of liberalism he points out that the major evaluation models are all subjectivist in terms of their ethics, and similarly classifies their approach to knowledge in terms of objectivist or subjectivist epistemologies. In this scheme, managerial models and decision oriented models such as Stufflebeam's CIPP model would fit under the objectivist epistemology and imply explicit knowledge, whereas, the transactional model of Stake fits under the subjectivist approach to knowledge. Webster and Stufflebeam (1978) on the other hand approach the classification of evaluation models from the perspective of purposes for which the evaluation is being conducted. Their three major classifications are political orientation, questions orientation, and values orientation. They label those studies that promote a positive or negative view of an object irrespective of its true value as pseudo-evaluation. Studies that answer questions that may not necessarily assess the worth of an object are classified as quasi-evaluation. True evaluations are those studies that are designed to assess the value or worth of an object.

As one might expect, the classification scheme imposed on evaluation models is very much a function of the basic question that is being asked of these approaches to evaluation. Worthen and Sanders (1973) for example, approach the issue with the basic question: What are most crucial activities that are to be undertaken by the evaluator and to what use will these data be put? Webster and Stufflebeam (1978) approach the issue based on the question: What was the motivating factor that led to undertaking the evaluation in the first place? House (1978) approaches the classification issue from the perspective of the philosophical constructs underlying the sociopolitical values of the model developers.

Obviously, a number of evaluation models have been excluded from the discussion above. Exclusions are intentional and are a function of the author's view that most of the other models would not be useful to vocational educators attempting to evaluate their programs. For example, there is an adversary evaluation model in which evaluators present to decision makers the pros and cons related to particular programs, and their strengths and weaknesses. The assumption is that the best case for each side is presented and the decision maker can then make a decision on the basis of the evidence presented as to continuation, termination, or revision of the program. Popham and Carlson (1977) in their report of the implementation of this model to an educational program were very negative in their appraisal of the model's usefulness. They maintain that it is not valuable. They conclude "the adversary evaluation model brings with it not only a few real (and many imaginery) dividends, it brings also far too many deficits" (p.6). For a listing of other models, the reader may consult the taxonomies presented by House (1978), and Webster and Stufflebeam (1978).

The discussion above indicates that evaluation, to date, might be classified as being in its formative state. That is, although there is no formal agreement yet as to precisely what an evaluation model *must* contain, there does appear to be a good deal of agreement as to the concepts that a reasonably decent evaluation should contain. Areas of agreement appear to be: the need for data collection, especially if the data relate to student outcomes; statements of objectives when and where they can be obtained and/or developed; comparisons across groups with and without treatment, when and if possible; statistical analyses of data and report writing.

The work that remains is the development of a more global synthesis of some of the underlying ideas incorporated in the different models, as well as, agreement among evaluators as to some generalized statistical approaches that could be used under a number of different conditions. A number of people have recently undertaken work that is beginning to move in these directions.

For example, Dryden (1978) recently presented a model for evaluating compensatory education programs at the local level based on the ideas incorporated in the models of Alkin, Stufflebeam, Scriven, and Stake, as well as others. The interesting thing about Dryden's approach is that he attempts to state definitions and postulates based on a synthesis of the literature, that fit within the context of an evaluation model. A statistical technique that has recently received a good deal of attention in terms of its applications to evaluation studies is that of multiple linear regression (MLR) analysis. The approach has heuristic value from the perspective of research on attribute treatment interactions as an approach to evaluation, and was recently discussed in this context (Holloway and Carrier, 1978), as well as, in terms of providing insight into some difficult technical problems that have plagued many evaluation studies in the past. For example, Bridgemen (1978) describes an approach to program evaluation that takes into account the amount of treatment obtained by a control group via MLR techniques. In another study, St. Pierre and Proper (1978) investigated the attrition problem in a large scale evaluation program via such techniques. Notwithstanding these attempts, the state of the art is still in flux.

VOCATIONAL EDUCATION EVALUATION

What models or portions of models have traditionally been applied to evaluation of vocational education programs? This section presents a brief overview of some of the reviews of this literature. A decade ago, Coster and Ihnen (1968) reviewing vocational education program evaluation identified three major areas in which evaluations were conducted. They classified these three areas as goals and objectives, products (graduates) of vocational education, and accreditation studies. In the group of studies that dealt with evaluating the products or graduates of vocational education, there were a number of subgroups of studies they identified and briefly described. These were follow-up studies, explanatory studies, and cost-benefit analyses. The latter group of studies basically consisted of reports in which multiple regression analyses were used to identify independent variables that accounted for significant variance when regressed on dependent variables such as retention, placement, and income. They concluded their review as follows:

> As promising as the developments are, the financial and resource commitment does not match the magnitude of the task. Serious study is needed to define the range of variables and measures to serve as the bases for program evaluation. . . . The move toward more rigorous evaluation has only begun. The next five years not only should, but must, bring forth needed strategies and results (Coster and Ihnen, 1968:431).

Despite this call for improvement in vocational education evaluation, eight years later the Committee on Vocational Education Research and Development (CVERD, 1976), in their study of vocational education research and development, introduced their section on evaluation of vocational education programs in this negative fashion:

> The literature describing the evaluation of vocational education programs is discouraging; it yields little useful information for vocational educators. The research designs have used analytic procedures requiring simple quantitative input and have failed to encompass many important educational issues. Evaluations have used research methods that are incompatible with the complexity of the learning, teaching, and administrative situations (CVERD, 1976:107).

The criterion variables that are included in their brief review of some of the better evaluation efforts during the last ten years dealt with vocational graduates' knowledge of occupations, job readiness, job satisfaction, and earnings of vocational graduates when compared to other groups of students. In addition, a short section on the use of follow-up studies as a means of evaluating the outcomes of vocational programs was also presented. It appears that evaluation is conceived by this group and by some of those contributing to the evaluation literature basically as a function of program outcomes, that is, evaluation is perceived as summative in nature. This is precisely the problem that the CVERD group had identified earlier. It is difficult to draw conclusions about the value of vocational education to the graduates of its programs unless there is some means for understanding the relationship of the program inputs to its outputs.

Carbine's (1974) review of evaluations of vocational education suffers from the same problem in that the basic model used in examining the evaluations consists of examining the outcomes of the programs without attempting to relate these outcomes to the programs inputs. This may be a result of examining vocational education from the perspective of labor market experience. Carbine's view of evaluation requires that program outcomes be specified and quantitatively measured. These data must be collected, appropriately analyzed, and compared against a predetermined base group. He discusses the issues of vocational education in terms of earnings and employment of vocational education graduates, effects of vocational education on special target groups, socialization, further education, school retention, differences of postsecondary and secondary vocational education. His approach is based on Stromsdorfer's (1972) work and is structured in terms of cost benefit analysis. Most of the studies cited and the problems associated with the cost benefit approach to evaluation of vocational education are reviewed in the Hu and Stromsdorfer (1979) chapter in this Handbook.

Many of the shortcomings of vocational education evaluation are actually endemic to the field of vocational education statistics. Some of these shortcomings are discussed in the evaluation reports themselves. More recently, an article by Lee (1977) describes the poor status of vocational education statistics in his report of the project Base Line data.

There have been attempts to develop evaluation models or systems that are specifically geared to the needs of vocational education programs. Denton (1973) provided a plan for an evaluation system in vocational education that contained the following elements: needs assessment, development of philosophy, writing of objectives, statements of criterion questions, data collection, data analysis, formulation of recommendations, and decision-making. Although there appears to be a lack of appropriate feedback loops at various phases within this evaluation model, and some confusion of the roles of evaluator and program developer, this early attempt at synthesizing some of the general evaluation literature and making it specific to evaluation of vocational education was an important initial step. More recently Orlich, Anderson, Dodd, Baldwin and Ohrt (1978) developed a manual for vocational education evaluation. The manual emphasizes the use of planning as a method of evaluation, evaluation of short term programs, and the use of criterion referenced assessment as an approach to evaluating student outcomes and instruction. This useful pamphlet provides brief reviews of the literature in each of these areas along with charts, and examples of procedures that could be used in attempting to evaluate these types of programs. Implementation strategies are also provided for these different approaches to evaluation. One of the problems with the manual is its conceptualization of many of these issues as being separate and distinct rather than as part of overall evaluation systems. That is, while Denton's (1973) work appears to place in context the different phases of evaluation as part of an overall system, the manual by Orlich et al. (1978) treats each of these phases as unique aspects of separate evaluation systems.

Dunn (1978) in working with the New York State directors of vocational education provided a model of evaluation that incorporates many of the ideas included in earlier models. His approach incorporates formative and summative studies carried out as process, product, and goal free evaluations. The model included three phases: planning, preparation, and operation. For each phase and subphase sample forms for the design and management of an evaluation system was provided, along with a specific series of questions designed to help focus evaluation and its attendant activities. The system will become useful when it is operationalized in terms of specific variables at both the formative and summative levels, and is made specific to vocational education through the description of appropriate variables as well as replications over a series of vocational programs.

Recently, Ory, Harris, Dueitt, and Clark (1978) reported on the development and field testing of a vocational education evaluation model that incorporated six outcome variables that were arrived at through review of the literature related to vocational education objectives. Their model, which is summative in nature in that it seeks to rate existing vocational programs at the postsecondary level on a scale of strong, adequate, or weak, was based on the following outcome variables: (1) job market, (2) community support, (3) student aspirations, (4) student performance, (5) cost effectiveness, and (6) special populations. The criteria, subcriteria, and importance weightings were arrived at jointly with program personnel. The system provides planners with summative data on their programs such that, decisions for program continuation or termination could be made in the context of their programs.

If further progress is to be made in the area of vocational education evaluation, continued efforts at incorporating content variables that are specific to vocational education, with concepts drawn from general evaluation models, will have to be developed.

NOTES

1. See the chapter by Morell in this Handbook.
2. See the chapter by Abramson and Banchik in this Handbook.

REFERENCES

Abramson, T., and Banchik, G. 1979. Determinants of the evaluator's role: Political and programmatic motives. In T. Abramson, C. K. Tittle, L. Cohen, eds. *The Handbook of Vocational Education Evaluation.* Beverly Hills: Sage Publications.

Alkin, M. C. 1969. Evaluation theory development. *Evaluation Comment* 2:2-7.

Alkin, M. C., and Fitz-gibbon, C. T. 1975. Methods and theories of evaluating programs. *Journal of Research and Development in Education* 8:2-15.

Alkin, M. C., Kosecoff, J., Fitz-Gibbon, C., and Seligman, R. 1974. *Evaluation and Decision-Making: The Title IV Experience.* Monograph series in evaluation #4. Los Angeles: Center for the Study of Evaluation.

Berk, R. A., and Rossi, P. H. 1977. Doing good or worse: Evaluation research politically re-examined. In M. Guttentag, ed. *Evaluation Studies Review Annual, Vol. 2.* Beverly Hills: Sage Publications.

Borich, G. D. 1974. *Evaluating Educational Programs and Products.* Englewood Cliffs, NJ: Educational Technology Publications.

——— 1977. Program Evaluation: New concepts, new methods. *Focus on Exceptional Children* 9:1-16.

Bridgeman, B. 1978. "Experimental vs. control comparisons in program evaluation: Dichotomy or continuum." Paper presented at the annual meeting of the AERA, Toronto.

Bryant, F. B., and Wortman, P. M. 1978. Secondary analysis: The case for data archives. *American Psychologist* 33:381-387.

Campbell, D. T. 1977. The priority score allocation design. In M. Guttentag, ed. *Evaluation Studies Review Annual, Vol. 2.* Beverly Hills: Sage Publications.

Carbine, M. E. 1974. Evaluations of vocational education. In L. A. Lecht, ed. *Evaluating Vocational Education-Policies and Plans for the 1970s*. New York: Praeger.

Committee on Vocational Education Research and Development. 1976. *Assessing Vocational Education Research and Development*. Washington, D.C.: National Academy of Sciences.

Cook, T. D., and Campbell, D. T. 1976. The design and conduct of quasi-experiments and true experiments in field settings. In M. R. D. Dunnette, ed. *Handbook of Industrial and Organizational Psychology*. Chicago: Rand McNally.

Cook, T. D., and Gruder, C. L. 1978. Metaevaluation research. *Evaluation Quarterly* 2:5-52.

Coster, J. K., and Ihnen, L. A. 1968. Program evaluation. *Review of Educational Research* 38:417-433.

Cronbach, L. J. 1963. Course improvement through evaluation. *Teachers College Record* 64:672-683.

Datta, L. 1979. Better luck this time: From federal legislation to practice in evaluating vocational education. In T. Abramson, C. K. Tittle, L. Cohen, eds. *The Handbook of Vocational Education Evaluation*. Beverly Hills: Sage Publications.

Denton, W. T. 1973. *Program evaluation in vocational and technical education* Information Series No. 98. Columbus, OH: ERIC Clearinghouse on Vocational and Technical Education.

Dryden, L. J. 1978. "A model for evaluating compensatory education programs at the local level." Paper presented at the annual meeting of the AERA, Toronto.

Dunn, J. 1978. "Alternative systems of evaluation." Paper presented at the sixth annual seminar of NYS Directors of Occupational Education.

Flaherty, E. W., and Morell, J. A. 1978. Evaluation: Manifestations of a new field. *Evaluation and Program Planning* 1:1-10.

Freeman, H. E. 1977. The present status of evaluation research. In M. Guttentag, ed. *Evaluation Studies Review Annual, Vol. 2*. Beverly Hills: Sage Publications.

Glass, G. V., ed. 1976. *Evaluation Studies Review Annual Vol. 1*. Beverly Hills: Sage Publications.

Gowin, D. B., and Millman, J. 1978. "Can meta-evaluation give a direction for research on evaluation." Paper presented at the annual meeting of AERA, Toronto.

Guba, E. G. 1969. The failure of educational evaluation. *Educational Technology* 9:29-38.

Guttentag, M. 1977. Evaluation and Society. In M. Guttentag, ed. *Evaluation Studies Review Annual, Vol. 2*. Beverly Hills: Sage Publications.

––– 1977. *Evaluation Studies Review Annual, Vol. 2*. Beverly Hills: Sage Publications.

––– 1973. Subjectivity and its use in evaluation research. *Evaluation* 1:60-65.

Guttentag, M., and Snapper, K. 1974. Plans, evaluations, and decisions. *Evaluation* 2:58-64, 73-74.

Guttentag, M., and Struening, E. L., eds. 1975. *Handbook of Evaluation Research* Beverly Hills: Sage Publications.

Holloway, R. L., and Carrier, C. A. 1978. "Conceptual and operational guidelines for an aptitude X treatment interaction approach to evaluation." Paper presented at the annual meeting of AERA, Toronto.

Horst, D. P., Tallmadge, G. K., and Wood, C. T. 1975. *A Practical Guide to Measuring Project Impact on Student Achievement*. Number 1 in a series of monographs on evaluation in education. Washington, DC: Department of Health, Education, and Welfare.

House, E. R. 1978. Assumptions underlying evaluation models. *Educational Researcher* 7:4-12.

Hu, T., and Stromsdorfer, E. W. 1979. Cost-benefit analysis of vocational education. In T. Abramson, and C. K. Tittle, eds. *The Handbook of Vocational Education Evaluation*. Beverly Hills: Sage Publications.

Kennedy, M. M. 1978. "Generalization of findings from single case studies." Paper presented at the annual meeting of the AERA, Toronto.

Kromhout, O. M. 1978. "Florida's vocational curriculum system: Needs assessment and prioritization." Paper presented at the annual meeting of the AERA, Toronto.

Lee, A. M. 1977. Project Baseline: Historiographic foundations for vocational education statistics. *Educational Researcher* 67: 3-9.

Light, R. J., and Smith, P. V. 1971. Accumulating evidence: Procedures for resolving contradictions among different research studies. *Harvard Educational Review* 41: 429-471.

Linn, R. L. 1978. "The validity of inferences based on the proposed Title I evaluation models." Paper presented at the annual meeting of the AERA, Toronto.

Metfessel, N. S., and Michael, W. B. 1967. A paradigm involving multiple criterion measures for the evaluation of the effectiveness of school programs. *Educational and Psychological Measurement* 27: 931-943.

Morell, J. 1979. Follow-up Research as an evaluation strategy: Theory and methodologies. In T. Abramson, C. K. Tittle, L. Cohen, eds. *The Handbook of Vocational Education Evaluation*. Beverly Hills: Sage Publications.

Orlich, D. C., Andersen, D. G., Dodd, C. C., Baldwin, L., and Ohrt, B. A. 1978. *Evaluation Models for Vocational Educators*. Olympia, WA: Washington State Commission for Vocational Education.

Ory, J. C., Harris, Z., and Clark, D. L. 1978. *The Development and Field Testing of a Vocational Education Evaluation model*. Washington, DC: Office of Education.

Popham, W. J., and Carlson, D. 1977. Deep dark deficits of the adversary evaluation model. *Educational Researcher* 6: 3-6.

Provus, M. 1969. Evaluation of ongoing programs in the public school system. In R. W. Tyler, ed. *Educational Evaluation: New Roles, New Means, The Sixty-Eighth Yearbook of the National Society for the Study of Education, Part II*. Chicago: The National Society for the Study of Education.

Rippey, R. M. 1973. *Studies in transactional evaluation*. Berkeley, CA: McCutchan Publishing Corp.

St. Pierre, R. G., and Proper, E. C. 1978. Attrition: Identification and exploration in the national follow-through evaluation. *Evaluation Quarterly* 2: 153-166.

Salasin, S. 1977. Integrating evaluation findings—Complementary uses of decision theory and the cluster approach: An interview with Marcia Guttentag and Richard Light. *Conversational Contact Technical* 4: 178-188.

Sanders, J. R., and Nafziger, D. H. 1976. *A basis for determining the adequacy of evaluation designs*. Occasional Paper Series No. 6. Kalamazoo: Western Michigan University, The Evaluation Center.

Scriven, M. 1969. An introduction to meta-evaluation. *Educational Product Report* 2: 36-38.

——— 1967. The methodology of evaluation. Pp. 39-83 in R. E. Stake, ed. *Perspectives of Curriculum Evaluation, No. 1*. Chicago: Rand McNally.

Scriven, M. 1976. "Evaluation bias and its control." In G.V. Glass, ed. *Evaluation Studies Review Annual, Vol. 1*. Beverly Hills: Sage Publications.

Stake, R. E. 1978a. "Should educational evaluation be more objective or more subjective?" Paper presented at the annual meeting of the AERA, Toronto.

——— 1978b. The case study method of social inquiry. *Educational Researcher* 7: 5-8.

——— 1970. Objectives, priorities, and other judgment data. *Review of Educational Research* 40: 181-213.

––– 1967. The countenance of educational evaluation. *Teachers College Record* 68: 523-540.

Steinmetz, A. 1976. The discrepancy evaluation evaluation model. *Measurement in Education* 7: 1-6.

Stromsdorfer, E. W. 1972. *Review and synthesis of cost-effectiveness: Studies of vocational and technical education.* Columbus: Center for Vocational and Technical Education, Ohio State University.

Stufflebeam, D. L. 1969. Evaluation as enlightment for decision-making. In W. Beatty, ed. *Improving Educational Assessment and an Inventory of Measures of Affective Behavior.* Washington, DC: Association for Supervision and Curriculum Development, NEA.

Stufflebeam, D. L., Foley, W. J., Gephart, W. J., Guba, E. G., Hammond, R. I., Merriman, H. O., and Provus, M. M. 1971. *Educational Evaluation and Decision Making.* Itasca, IL: F. E. Peacock.

Suchman, E. A. 1967. *Evaluative research.* New York: Russell Sage Foundation.

Tyler, R. W. 1942. General statement on evaluation. *Journal of Educational Research* 35: 492-501.

Webster, W. J., and Stufflebeam, D. L. 1978. "The state of theory and practice in educational evaluation in large urban school districts." Address presented at the annual meeting of the AERA, Toronto.

Weiss, C. H. 1975. Evaluation research in the political context. In E. Struening, and M. Guttentag, eds. *Handbook of Evaluation Research, Vol. 1.* Beverly Hills: Sage Publications.

Wentling, T. L., and Lawson, T. E. 1975. *Evaluating Occupational Education and Training Programs.* Boston: Allyn and Bacon.

Wholey, J. S. 1972. What can we actually get from program effectiveness? *Policy Sciences* 3: 361-369.

Wiley, D. E. 1978. *Evaluation by Aggregation: Social and Methodological Biases.* (Contracts DHEW/OE 300-75-0332 and HEW-100-77-0104). University of Chicago and ML-GROUP for Policy Studies in Education, CEMREL, Inc.

Worthen, B. R., and Sanders, J. R. 1973. *Educational Evaluation: Theory and Practice.* Belmont, CA: Wadsworth.

METHODOLOGICAL
CONSIDERATIONS
Experimental and
Non-Experimental
Designs and
Causal Inference

chapter 6

EDGAR F. BORGATTA | *City University of New York*

In a humanistic tradition, social science has frequently been descriptive and interpretive. The distinction has been emphasized, however, between what have come to be called social philosophers and social scientists. Most scientists have some biases from their social background that guide their work and expectations. Similarly, as each person tries to understand the world, attempts are made to be objective because objectivity is presumably associated with effectiveness of operation (survival) in the society. Thus, the origins of the scientific method are ancient and pervasive, and implicitly most persons approach any research question with some model of testing reality. Intuitively, most persons have ideas about probabilities and chance, and similarly they become aware of models for rules of evidence.

At this stage of history, there is reasonable consensus in science of what is meant by *cause*. However, the scientific method is not necessarily accessible in its sophisticated forms when social scientists do evaluation research, so the procedures actually used often require more inference and provision of alternative ways for providing evidence. These latter alternatives often boil down to arguments that are based on authority, consensus, or custom rather than on the rules of evidence as mandated by the scientific method. A continuum of models for getting at causal relationships can be described as ranging from experimental to nonexperimental procedures, but to suggest this is to be misleading about what the scientific method involves. For example, one of our most exact sciences, astronomy, is nonexperimental in the sense that nothing is manipulated in an experiment. Nonexperimental procedures do not need to be unscientific, and when criticisms of nonexperimental procedures are justified, it has to be on the basis that (a) a better procedure (experimental) could have been used, or (b) that biases are involved in the observational procedures, or (c) that the observations have been insufficient for the conclusions that are to be drawn. There are other failures possible in the design of evaluation research, and some of these will become evident as experimental and nonexperimental designs for evaluation research are discussed.

Because the experimental model is one that has been formalized and is easily understood, this presentation will begin with a brief description of the experimental model. This will be followed by a discussion of the many limitations of the model when it is applied to the social and psychological sciences. This is an appropriate beginning for a discussion of causation because everything that is true when dealing with rules of evidence in the experimental model with regard to errors of interpretations is *more* true when dealing with quasi-experimental and nonexperimental models.

EXPERIMENTAL PROCEDURES

The appropriateness of an evaluation research design for gathering information on relationships among variables hinges on many things. The level of the science with regard to how variables are measured may be one of the more important considerations. A general model for attributing causal inference has long been available for science, but its explicit statement and popularization is probably most closely associated with the work of Fisher (1925).

The essence of the experimental design is the notion of two groups that are equal on relevant characteristics before some treatment (experimental manipulation, intervention, and so on) is applied to one of the groups. In order to know whether the treatment has had an effect, the groups are usually compared before and after the treatment. Thus, the most common representation of the experimental model is indicated below in Table 6.1. Groups E and C are assumed to be equal in the relevant characteristics before the experiment. Presumably, the variable that is expected to change with the treatment is measured before the experiment (T_1) and subsequently (T_2). In the ideal circumstance, effects attributable to the treatment occur and the pattern of mean scores for groups E and C might be as indicated. (Without giving the detail of how statistically significant results would be determined, numerical differences in the direction expected for particular types of interpretations are noted. The numbers are, obviously, only for purposes of illustration.)

Although the model may seem simple and straightforward, in the attempt to apply the model to research, many questions are raised. The first type of

Table 6.1: Pretest Posttest Control Group Design

Groups	Scores at Two Points in Time	
	T_1	T_2
Experimental	10	20
Control	10	10

question in examining the model obviously deals with the question of how one knows whether group E is indeed equal to group C. The particular importance of Fisher's emphasis was on the use of random assignment of subjects to samples as a method of arriving at equated groups. Representativeness of samples is dependent on sample size in random sampling; to phrase this somewhat differently, sample size affects the characteristics of the sampling distribution. If random procedures are used in selecting samples, then presumably large samples will be more likely to be representative. There are other virtues as well as liabilities associated with large samples, and the procedure of sampling needs to be understood if one wishes to carry out experiments.

A second question deals with the relation between sample size and the magnitude of change that is required in order to demonstrate statistically significant effects. Thus, it is possible to anticipate the appropriate sample sizes for an experiment before it is carried out. If one is interested in small effects rather than gross effects, large sample sizes may be necessary. For example, if serious accidents occur with a piece of machinery, but not frequently, then to test a new piece of machinery that is supposed to be safer, the design for the research will necessarily require extensive observation, whether the extension is measured in time, number of machines in use, or number of operators. Small numbers of observations simply cannot be made to be sufficient under such circumstances. On the other hand, presumably increasing the size of the samples may increase costs (money, time, use of facilities and other resources, and so on), and a simple solution in the direction of large samples is not always appropriate.

Since sample size tends to be restricted for practical reasons, it is conceivable that by mere chance there will be substantial variation in samples. The equivalence of two randomly selected samples should be examined to confirm that some chance occurrences have not led to a difference of importance. The pretesting of samples in an experiment serves the purpose of providing this type of test of equivalence, and in addition, provides what may be called the *baseline* data for the responses of the samples.

Equating samples may proceed along somewhat different lines, and traditionally there has been a concept of *matching* cases in order to arrive at equal groups. The validity of this procedure hinges on how the matching is carried out, for if there is randomization once matched pairs have been located, development of the sample then proceeds in a fashion that may be described as *stratified random samples*. That is, members from each matched pair (or matched group if more than two are found to be essentially the same) are assigned to the experimental and control groups. However, if the matching is done with presumed balance and carried out on an intuitive basis by the researcher, the principle of random allocation must be viewed as violated, and the effect on subsequent findings will be unknown. In general, there is very little to support the principle of attempting to achieve balanced groups on the basis of either intuition or expert opinion. The reason for this is that the biases in the allocations are not known, and, intrinsically, the procedure carried out is likely to be one that is highly complex. To illustrate the problem of complexity, if matching were to be carried out for purposes of selecting a stratified random sample, there would have to be a specification on which variables the matching would occur. Presumably, the relevant variables are those which are in some way related to the experimental variable, that is, the treatment or intervention which will occur. In addition, of course, variables that might be controlled are also related to the performance characteristics that will be measured before and after the experiment. Often it turns out that there are many such variables; if there are, say, ten, matching may become a very complicated thing. There simply may not be enough cases so that close matching can be carried out in order to develop much confidence in the procedure of equating the groups by this method. Stratification would appear to make sense only when there are very few, possibly only one or two important variables that are to be used. Thus, there is also an intuitive basis for the notion of random allocation in order to distribute characteristics in two samples in a way that is unbiased with regard to the experimental procedure.

The experimental method is usually considered the most powerful one for an explanatory science. That is, *demonstration* of cause and effect relationships (naively conceived) requires experimentation: the demonstration is that the manipulations are necessary and sufficient for the determination of the consequences. Some important limitations occur in the experimental procedures as applied to the social sciences. Unfortunately, in accepting experimental models from the physical sciences, social scientists have often ignored the nonparallel aspects in the sciences. It is well to point out some of these nonparallel circumstances, as they are important. The value of the experimental approaches may often be entirely vitiated because of these limitations, and it is worthwhile to consider them in some detail. In essence, these are questions that should be raised *every time* an experimental study is examined.

First, the most common design involves a manipulation of one variable and examination of the consequences on a second variable. A control in which the consequences should not occur is used, and this presumably establishes the logic for concluding that the effect is caused by the manipulation. A vital question with regard to such design has to do with the nature of the variable manipulated. In particular, is the amount of change in the manipulated variable measured in such a way that the findings are interpretable? In other words, in a physical experiment, when heat or other factors are introduced in order to cause an effect, the amount is ordinarily known and measured, and the prediction of what happens is based on a quantitative notion of the input. In much of the social and psychological experimentation that has been carried out to date, experimental manipulation involves inputs of unknown quantities. If one does not know how much input has been involved, the results of the experiment merely demonstrate that if a variable is manipulated with sufficient intensity it can cause an effect. Indeed, it really suggests that the researcher must demonstrate that the findings are more than trivial. This modest way of phrasing results of an experiment is a far cry from saying something to the effect: "The findings demonstrate that a relationship exists between variables X and Y."

Second, a problem associated with the notion of experimentation where one variable is varied (and others are held constant) and the effect on a second variable is observed is that in a highly complex system of variables there may be many interactions among the variables. That is, the relationship between the two variables involved may be affected by how they are observed within the more complex system of variables. So, for example, if one examines the effect of particular instructional materials as contrasted to a control set of usual materials, it may be that in the particular situation in which the materials are tried, they will indeed be better measured on some performance criterion. However, it may also be that in all other situations they are not better. Thus, holding the system constant by observing under particular circumstances may produce different results from observing the same two variables under other circumstances. Further, the amount of effect apparent under the circumstances where the situation is held constant may appear to be substantial, while the situation where random or general variation is permitted may lead to a diminution of the amount of observed effect. The type of criticism involved in this analysis of experimental procedures is important in making generalizations from experimentation. That is, even assuming that the first criticism above has been answered and the amount of input is measured, then the next question is whether or not a narrow experimental procedure can demonstrate a general relationship between two variables. In a system that involves many variables, examining the impact of one on the other with the remainder of the variables held constant may be an insufficient demonstration of the "true" relationship between the variables. For a more extensive discussion of these limitations see Borgatta and Bohrnstedt (1974).

INTERNAL VALIDITY

The interpretation of experiments may be limited because of the design. These limitations can be thought of as limiting internal validity, that is, the internal logic of the model, but obviously any limitations on internal validity also have ramifications for generalization (external validity). If an experiment is inappropriately interpreted, generalization will necessarily be erroneous, and thus internal validity may be seen as a limiting factor on external validity.

The situations that are associated with limitations on interpretation of experimental designs may be viewed in terms of particular designs, as is the case in the presentation by Campbell and Stanley (1966), and Cook and Campbell (1976). However, the limitations may be described generally, with emphasis placed on the circumstances under which they are most likely to arise.

The first class of limitations that should be considered deal with the problem of the classic design as suggested in Table 6.1. As noted, since there are two points in time when measurement is carried out, the amount of time between these tests may be considered as a possible relevant variable for the interpretation of the experiment. That is, time serves as an opportunity for things to occur to confound any experiment. Generally, the factor of *history* can be minimized if care is taken in the design. However, history may intervene in a number of ways to define different situations for the experimental and the control groups. For example, if, as is frequently the case, experiments are set up so that first all experimental subjects are run through the laboratory procedures and then the control group subjects are run through the procedures, history may play some part in the results found. It may be that significant events occur which alter the meaning of the experiences for subjects. Suppose for example that a new technical manual is to be tested against an existing text on the maintenance of automotive engines. If in the interim an energy crisis occurs, the students could become more interested in the topics that deal with efficiency of consumption. To attribute differences to the manual under such circumstances would be inappropriate and the failings of such a design are fairly obvious. A somewhat complicated possibility is that an historical event may interact with a treatment, as for example, by making subjects more responsive or less responsive because of the saliency of the treatment.

Having an experimental design which in some way unbalances the randomization of subjects is a violation of the classical experiment, as noted in Table 6.1. Thus, the confounding of an experiment by history should be anticipated in the original design. Randomization refers not only to the selection of subjects, but also to the order of presentation of treatment or nontreatment. If the procedure involved is a laboratory procedure, there should be either systematic variation in the presentation of the testing situations to experimental and control subjects, or the presentation should be governed by random selection of presentations. Systematic presentation is ordinarily described as a balanced design where external factors may be equated. For example, if experiments are carried on at different times of days, by different experimenters, by different use of laboratory rooms, and so forth, allocation of these should be planned to give equal presentation to the experimental and control subjects. Because there is often a restriction on the number of experimental observations, such planning is not usually a difficult task.

If the classical experimental design is not utilized, for example, by not having a control group, then history as a factor can become an obvious and potentially more important problem in interpretation. Indeed, the entire objective of utilizing control groups is to eliminate potential rival explanations, and so it is appropriate to give emphasis to other factors that could influence events and lead to inappropriate interpretation if there is no control group present. In addition to history, which may intervene between a pretest and posttest (in the absence of a control group), an important additional factor that may be considered if there is any extended period of time between pretest and posttest is the *change in subjects* which occurs during the time period. Subjects age, grow, learn, and mature in various ways, particularly if they are young persons. Thus, if one is studying characteristics of the subjects over a long time span, the changes in subjects may easily be confused with changes due to the experimental treatment unless there is a control group. Similarly, subjects may change over a shorter span in other types of experimentation in significant ways. For example, students who participate in a laboratory experiment may become fatigued, lose interest, need access to a bathroom, and so on, in the process, and it is conceivable that if there is no control group, such changes in subjects may be confused with responses to the experimental treatment.

A third type of problem, that may be due to time between the pretest and the posttest, can arise if subjects of a particular type are selected. For example, in many researches there is concern with persons who are poor performers. Or, as another example, there might be interest in persons who are highly skilled in a particular area, such as mechanics. In still another example, people may be selected because they have special problems, are in special categories of deviant behavior or behavior that is classed as clinically interesting for one reason or another. With this type of situation, *regression effects* may easily be confused with changes presumed to be due to experimental treatment unless control groups are used. For those who arrive in acute conditions with regard to some disorder, there may be a proportion who have an amelioration which occurs without any kind of intervention. This is known in medical terminology as spontaneous remission, and is associated with the idea that given time there is a presumed natural healing process. Acute psychotic periods may terminate without intervention of medicine, just as colds, coughs, pimples, and other things may go away if left alone. Such things are the regression effects associated with changes in states in individuals.

Additionally, regression effects may occur as a function of the initial measurement involved. In particular, when unreliable measures are utilized if extreme groups are chosen, a subsequent retest or test with an equivalent form inevitably results in a mean score for the group that is closer to the mean for all persons. Unlike the regression of persons toward a mean state or normal state noted above that would require an interval of time, the regression effects associated with the statistical artifact of selection of extreme groups do not require a time lapse. Again, such regression effects would be noticeable immediately if a control group is used, but they may also be demonstrated as a function of imperfect correlation that is built into the system whenever extreme groups are utilized. The strength of the regression effects depends on how extreme the selected groups are and the unreliability of the variable utilized for the selection. Regretfully, in education and social science more generally measures are relatively unreliable, and so great care must always be taken to assure that the design of research does not potentially involve regression effects.

In this examination of pretest and posttest effects that are involved through the selection of extreme groups, it has been noted that groups selected as "bright" will show an average movement toward the mean (less bright) in this same statistical artifactual sense. In addition, however, an often neglected point is that if persons are selected having characteristics close to the mean, say in an attempt to select a group of typical people, then the artifactual result of this selection will be that, at the retest, the characteristics of the subjects will show greater dispersion. One might mistake this artifact and misinterpret the result to mean that the experimental treatment has changed individuals so that more would be high and low than was the case initially. Sometimes this is erroneously described as the effect of polarizing persons, or in an attitude study, crystallizing opinions.

A fourth factor which is associated with the time span between pretest and posttest may be thought of as *instrument decay,* or the change in the measuring instruments that are utilized in the experimental procedures. That is, during the time when an experiment takes place, the instruments themselves may change for various reasons. For example, if observers are used, it is likely that they will be more experienced at the point of posttest than at the point of pretest. This is likely to be the case if a panel of observers are utilized, and the normal process of allocation of responsibilities occurs which corresponds to the time sequence of pre and posttesting. During the interim, observers who are more experienced may learn more about the processes of observation, may become more skilled, but equally may become more bored, or more arbitrary. Being an observer is not always a stimulating type of enterprise, and what might have been an exciting experience in research at the beginning of a semester may be boring as time passes. It is quite conceivable that the observers make judgmental reactions that are quite different at the beginning of an experiment than at the end, and since there is the natural staging of time from pretest to posttest, some significant alterations in the instruments may occur. In addition, instruments change with the changes of meaning in language, culture, and other aspects of society.

We have noted earlier the importance of selection in the problem of getting equivalent experimental and control groups. Selection, however, may occur even after an experiment has been designed, and the experimental group with which one starts may not be the same as the one which completes the experiment if the work is conducted over a period of time. That is, there is *attrition* of subjects over the experimental time span, and the factors involved in this attrition may not be random. For example, if subjects are drawn from a student population, notwithstanding the comments and instructions that are given to students with regard to a requirement to participate in at least two observations, subjects will differ in how they accept this as a commitment and a responsibility. Some subjects may not appear for a second session because they have lost interest, but others may also not appear for other reasons. For example, there is an attrition in all educational processes, and students may be dropping out during a semester for many reasons. Again, it is ordinarily expected that this type of selection can be controlled for in an experimental design. However, this is the case only if the issue involved is simply one of selection, independent of the experimental procedures involved.

When the factors that may interfere with the experiment are associated with the presentation of the treatment or experimental procedure itself, generally this is classified as a problem of *reactivity*. That is, the student may react to the presentation of a treatment, a set of instructions, to the experimenter, or other aspects of the presentation that are not the intended variables. Thus, for example, if subjects respond to the instructor rather than some subject matter that is presumed to be the basis of the experiment, this would be seen to interfere directly with examining the actual effects of the subject matter.

EXTERNAL VALIDITY

Internal validity issues described above focus on the internal structure and design of the experiment, and a substantial number of possible factors can arise to invalidate or limit the external validity of an experiment. If internal validity does not exist, then there is no chance that the findings can be appropriately generalized to other circumstances. Generalization to other circumstances or external validity, may be limited for all the foregoing reasons, but it is also possible to organize ways in which failings occur in attempting to generalize. This is commonly noted as the limitation of induction, which is well recognized. Intrinsically, one cannot generalize from one experiment to other situations because the effects of differences in situations are not known. Attempts at generalization should always be thought of as tentative, and this is why there is emphasis on design of research with replications. Replications permit a direct test of generalization, and in this way provide some information about the stability of findings.

To deal with problems of external validity it is necessary to ask such questions as: Is there something special about the experimental setting that might lead to the consequences observed? Is there some special reason why the subjects would be responsive? Is the sampling of the subjects appropriate to the kinds of populations to which the findings are to be generalized? Are there ways in which selection bias of participants may interact with other aspects of the design of the experiment that might lead to the results? In short, to be generalizable, findings have to arise in a situation that is representative of the situations to which they will be generalized. This last statement, of course, refers to all evaluation research and not just to experimental procedures. What requires emphasis is that not only must one guard against the types of effects that have been outlined, but there are still more subtle effects possible through the interaction of the many sources of error. These are the interactions among the possible sources, so that there can be unique effects caused by a particular setting at a particular point in time, or a particular setting for a treatment, and so forth. What becomes clear is that making the design explicit and anticipating all the possible sources of error is not a simple matter, and satisfying the ideal experimental conditions may be very difficult.

QUASI-EXPERIMENTAL AND NONEXPERIMENTAL DESIGNS

When designs of experiments are less than ideal, they are frequently called quasi-experimental (Campbell and Stanley, 1966), and when the traces of the experimental designs are even more remote, they are called nonexperimental. At this point attention will be given to the development of the quasi-experimental and the nonexperimental evaluation researches. There is a relatively short history for the current interest in these approaches that is associated with the concept of evaluation research. The interest in evaluation per se has a long history so it is easy to locate comparisons of instructional styles at the turn of the century. But the massive involvement stems from a more general applied interest, stimulated in part by programs at Russell Sage Foundation during the 1950s, and the subsequent interests of government in attempting to evaluate the impact of programs. It is easy to lose sight of how things were, but not too long ago in many areas there simply was no interest in carrying out researches to demonstrate effectiveness of programs of social science applications.

When interest developed in evaluation research, sometimes the researches were seen as threats to the professional integrity of those involved in social programs. For example, in social work in the 1950s, there was much resistance to the idea that social work effects could be measured. In fact, some of the early studies suggested that in terms of criteria of impact on the behaviors of clients, effects were not detectable. This brought a response that may seem peculiar today, but it was a justification then: "How can you measure the effects of social work if we can not tell you what social work is supposed to do?" The point here is simple. Questions about program effects lead to the issues of development of criteria and the variables that are to be important in the research, whether it is experimental, quasi-experimental, or nonexperimental. A definition in terms of what a program is supposed to do becomes necessary, and the more attention such general questions get about intentions, the more specific the outlining of expectations. "To do good," is not enough of an answer. Good intentions as the basis for a program in this context become insufficient justification.

While biases in research may produce uninterpretable or erroneous results, failings in measurement and many other aspects of design may also lead to *conservative* errors, that is, to not finding effects that actually exist. If the measurements used are insensitive or inappropriate, results cannot be detected unless they are massive. In this sense, defensiveness on the part of those who are being evaluated is reasonable, and should lead to care and interaction to make sure that the appropriate variables are included and measured fairly. It is common sense that any researcher will become familiar with the social situation and culture in which research is to be carried out. Still, there are unfortunately many examples of the design of experimental procedures, particularly questionnaires, where the researchers seem to have by-passed learning the language of the persons who were the objects of the research. Language difficulty, for example, is something that highly educated verbal people do not appreciate, whether the difficulty stems from a deprived environment or from cultural language differences. Most researchers do not know how to express themselves in a "basic" English.

Additionally, if contact with those who are being researched is not adequate, the researcher may simply be guessing about whole areas of behavior. It is easy to miss information about the way things operate if one does not have access to the ideas people have about how they operate. Thus, one may not know what practice theories are or theories about what works that exist among professionals. If one wanted to write a manual on instruction in automotive repair and design, it is not only important to know how the engine is put together, but many other questions. How do students approach learning? How do they integrate verbal instructions with sequence operations in dismantling parts? Do they follow written instructions or do they skip these and study pictures? On the basis of experience, instructors will have practice theories, and if the researcher is not going to have the experience of instructing, the least that can be done is to make sure one knows the experiences others have had.

The distinction may now be introduced between several types of validity. One type is called content validity, and refers primarily to whether the measure being used corresponds to the concept the research wants to measure. So, for example, in a test of numerical ability, one would want to make sure that the questions deal with the handling of numbers, including arithmetic and other aspects of mathematics. A second type of validity is called criterion validity, and this refers primarily to the correspondence of a measure to other measures that are supposed to measure the same thing. So, for example, one measure of scholastic ability might be correlated with another preexisting measure of scholastic ability. More often criterion validity is directed to comparison of two measures that have greater conceptual independence, such as the correlation between the measure of scholastic ability and the actual academic performance. When this type of correlation involves time duration, projection of one measure into the future, it is called predictive validity. Thus, the prediction of eighth grade performance on the basis of the sixth term scholastic ability test is more accurately identified as predictive validity. The third type of validity is called construct validity, and it relates more directly to the problems of interpretation of findings. Construct validity refers to how well findings can be accounted for by variables in a theory that is designed to explain the findings. But, construct validity may be absent for two reasons. The theory may be bad, or bad measure may limit the possibility of finding relationships. This double concern with the appropriateness of theory and of the quality of measures underlies many of the concerns with the interpretation of evaluation research. In complex evaluation designs, anticipation of what is to be found can only be drawn from familiarity with the situation. This involves not only knowledge of social and psychological theory in the abstract, but also insight into the specific information, applied theories, and the cultural reflections of the people as to what is going on.

At a more rudimentary level, familiarity with the situation is necessary to develop reasonable expectations. It must be emphasized that familiarity does not mean that the research becomes part of the culture, goes native, becomes co-opted, or otherwise loses objectivity. But familiarity is necessary in order to become aware of the multiplicity of variables that may be appropriate to consider as goals or objectives in a program, the intended results. These goals may be sequenced in when they occur.

In a program using a new approach to vocational education, for example, the series of questions of the intended consequences range from some early ones of the feasibility of getting the program into an operating system to the actual impact on the students. It has been the finding of many researches to evaluate programs that it was not possible to move to a stage of drawing up a design for an experimental or quasi-experimental comparison between a "new" and "old" program because the new program never was put in place. Therefore, evaluation appropriately begins with relatively rudimentary questions and then moves on to those which deal with impact. Early questions may focus on such things as the number of students enrolled in a program, attendance, and other matters that are frequently seen as "accounting" for the process. Subsequently, attention can be given to such questions as how well the students learned in comparison to others, their potential for employment, their actual employment, longer range consequences, and so on. These latter questions imply comparison and controls for which knowledge of the experimental method and its potential failings is important.

If a study of a new program of vocational education is carried out, routinely a series of questions will be suggested that are part of the accumulated experience in evaluation research. How will the students be selected for admission into the program? Is it a random assignment, or are students selected because it is presumed that it will be especially appropriate to certain types of people? If there is selection of this type, obviously the residual group cannot be thought of as a control group in the sense of the design of an experimental model. Where there is enthusiasm for the new program, establishing a "favored" status is possible. This is accompanied by a phenomenon, often called the "pioneer effect" or the "Hawthorne Effect," where the favored group getting attention is stimulated into productivity through self-awareness of participation in a special process. New programs under these circumstance are often initially successful. The enthusiasm of the committed instructors, the support of the administration, and so on, may all contribute to the pioneer effect. But, in these circumstances what would be evaluated is the circumstance of instituting a new program, *not necessarily the program itself.* After a short period, the program effectiveness might be no different from the prior program or any other program.

Similarly, it must be recognized that frequently when a program is instituted in one school and not another, the sample sizes that should be compared are not the number of students who participate in each of the schools, but the number of schools. The unit of analysis is an issue that becomes important for data interpretation, and it does not take much reflection to see how interpretation may be affected by what the program's supporters wish to demonstrate.

The codification of interest in interpretation of experiments was paralleled by the burgeoning interest in evaluation research, and an important book reviewing problems of such research by Suchman (1967) marks the transition from occasional researches to more systematic emphasis. Without ambiguity, the literature of doing research on situations that are applied, policy oriented, or simply defined as less than ideal from the point of view of experimental design, has grown exponentially (Guttentag and Struening, 1975; Riecken and Boruch, 1974).

The designs for research that have been suggested, and in many cases that have been implemented, have involved a great deal of ingenuity. One approach has been through the sensitizing of evaluators to variables popularized by a book titled *Unobtrusive Measures* (Webb, Campbell, Schwartz, and Sechrest, 1966). Attention is brought to the fact that often as a consequence of particular types of behavior some indirect effects may exist that can be used to confirm or assess other findings. The concept of construct validity noted earlier, suggests how such variables may be located in a system or particular situation. There are many examples of such measures, many of which come under the heading of "trace" measures. That is, traces are left that "record" the behavior. These measures are further subdivided into measures of accretion or accumulation, and measures of erosion or wear. The ideas involved are not new, but they received considerable attention, and make sense in the category of checking and providing for supporting evidence. For example, in machine shops it may be important to examine the condition of tools, not only count them but to see if they have been used or abused. Which tools are used may be observed by wear. While some of this information can be assessed by observation or interview, the traces of wear provide an important form of evidence.

CAUSAL INFERENCE MODELS

In the development of procedures to deal with the less than perfect experimental situations, one approach that has had great impact has been the development of inference models that are not experimental. These have existed implicitly in approaches such as the use of partial correlation coeffients, with successive partials, each taking another variable into account, or in multiple regression, when variables have been added sequentially to examine the effect on an observed relationship between two variables. These approaches have been familiar to economics (econometrics) and some fields outside the social sciences. In a more rudimentary way, tabular analyses that progressed from two variable to three variable tables, and possibly even to four variable tables, have been discussed in terms of techniques of teasing out causal relationships, the technique sometimes being called "elaboration." In any event, parallel to much of the development of interest in the design of research there has been considerable development of models of causal inference based on regression analysis or to use the jargon structural equation models.

Causal inference models (Blalock, 1961; Heise, 1975; Asher, 1977) move the researcher to the descriptive level where experimental models are not required. Basically, the procedure requires the development of a theory in which presumably all the relevant variables are specified, and then the paths of influence (causality) are outlined among the variables. If the model is correct, empirical observation will confirm the existence of relationships corresponding to the paths. In a dialectic process, models can be restructured if rejected, and presumably with new data can be tested again. The models permit the development of paths of direct and indirect effects, and although they are more complex, feedback loops and other structures can be built into the models. The approach is powerful, but suffers when applied to the social sciences. Experience shows that when forced to develop models of causation, the first difficulty researchers encounter is that they discover that many of the variables they use are poorly defined and measured. For example, are there really sixty possible goals in the program? Also, they discover that until they are forced to put the variables into a system, they can juggle many variables without having to face the questions of dependencies of measurement, redundancies, and so on. Therefore, this emphasis on causal inference models has had a humbling effect on many, but also has led to some rejection of scientific research. That is, there has sometimes been the judgment that if scientific studies cannot be designed that are predictive and that have external validity, then moving to other methods (usually intuitive and informal) presumably is the thing to do. Regretfully, this is analogous to the argument that maybe magic is better. By contrast, for many it means going back to the drawing boards to develop better measures, to become more systematic, more precise, and so forth. A second conclusion that comes from the two decases or so of causal inference models is the realization that what is to be predicted (or explained) can only be so done in part. Multiple regression coefficients (which involve complete "explanation" when they have a magnitude of 1.00) are found in empirical studies to actually be relatively small. This limitation on preduction gives clues to what the processes are realistically and raises questions of measurement, of theory, and subsequently of applicability of findings.

The ideal of causal models and path diagrams can be stimulating and productive, even before the models are tested. The requirement of deciding what the relevant variables are and how the paths are ordered, and whether there should both be direct and indirect effects, forces the researcher to face questions about the theory involved. The path diagrams quickly show one that vague ideas are no more than that, and that the relationships among variables have been left unspecified. Quickly, one learns the limitations of having fifteen independent variables simply by trying to fit them into a diagram. Then, when diagrams have been simplified as variables have been dropped or redeveloped in a theoretical manner, the diagram can be examined for completeness of the system in the logic of the theory. Errors of omission that are hard to perceive in the confusion of redundant variables are easier to see in a diagram representing a theory that has had careful attention.

The applicability of regression analysis and causal inference models to most experimental procedures has important ramifications for the full analysis of data. The emphasis is sometimes described as "decomposing" or unscrambling the effects. For example, suppose that a program is instituted that is especially designed to attract girls into a program involving development of skills for mechanical and technical trades. When the program itself is tested, it may be compared to other programs in a formal design, but there may be many subsidiary questions that are raised in addition to testing the program itself. What are the factors in self-selection into the program? How do peers affect entry? How does self-image affect entry? How do parental, ethnic, and other background factors affect entry? Some of the variables will become of particular interest if they can be changed, and if they can influence the entry of girls into the program, assuming the policy is to increase access and

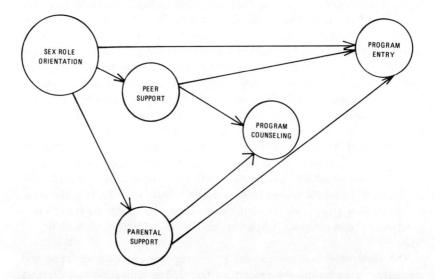

FIGURE 6.1: Preliminary diagram of possible selective factors in technical program entry for girls

participation for girls in the mechanical and technical trades. Using a few obvious variables, a preliminary diagram might be suggested as in Figure 6.1. From this preliminary outline one would proceed to ask questions as follows: Are all the relevant important variables included? Which factors will have the most direct effects? Which factors can be changed? These and additional questions are a part of any well-designed research, but it can quickly be seen how trying to organize the variables into such a diagram helps to systematize and facilitate asking appropriate questions.

CONCLUDING REMARKS

Practically speaking, what does this development of quasi-experimental approaches mean to research on vocational education programs? First, it is clear that institution of programs should be anticipated by considerations of how the intended effects will be measured, which means specification of what the intended effects are. Second, the scope of the new program has to be assessed in terms of feasibility of research findings being able to demonstrate anything at all. If the program is a pilot, often there are few cases, selected personnel and students, awareness among administrators, and other biases that may become too salient to permit any model equating of groups and making comparisons. Thus, under some circumstances it may not be wise, either on the basis of cost or the potential for finding interpretable results, to do evaluation research. This is not a criticism of the research models; rather this is a statement that the trial program that is proposed is not sufficient to be evaluated. Evaluation will always be a relative matter, and in this sense awareness of the requirements for good design suggest the difference between the initiation of new programs with or without a serious intent of knowing whether they are effective or not.

REFERENCES

Asher, H. B. 1977. *Causal Modeling.* Beverly Hills: Sage Publications.

Blalock, H. M. Jr. 1961. *Causal Inference in Nonexperimental Research.* Chapel Hill: University of North Carolina Press.

Borgatta, E. F., and Bohrnstedt, G. W. 1974. Some limitations on generalizability from social-psychological experiments. *Sociological Methods and Research* 3:11-20.

Campbell, D. T., and Stanley J. C. 1966. *Experimental and Quasi-Experimental Designs for Research.* Chicago: Rand McNally.

Cook, T. D., and Campbell, D. T. 1976. The design and conduct of quasi-experiments and true experiments in field settings. In M. D. Dunnette, ed. *Handbook of Industrial and Organizational Psychology,* Chicago: Rand McNally.

Fisher, R. A. 1925. *Statistical Methods for Research Workers.* London: Oliver and Boyd.

Guttentag, M., and Struening, E. L., eds. 1975. *Handbook of Evaluation Research.* Beverly Hills: Sage Publications.

Heise, D. R. 1975. *Causal Analysis.* New York: Wiley.

Riecken, H. W., and Boruch, R. F., eds. 1974. *Social Experimentation.* New York: Academic Press.

Suchman, E. A. 1967. *Evaluative Research.* New York: Russell Sage Foundation.

Webb, E. J., Campbell, D. T., Schwartz, R. E., and Sechrest, L. 1966. *Unobtrusive Measures.* Chicago: Rand McNally.

DOCUMENTATION OF PROGRAM IMPLEMENTATION

chapter 7

ELIZABETH C. PROPER | *Abt Associates, Inc.*

INTRODUCTION

Documentation of program implementation is important for several reasons. For example, program developers need to know what parts of their new programs seem to be functioning well and what parts are proving to be difficult to implement; evaluators need to know that the innovation effectiveness being assessed is actually in place; and policy makers need to know that the innovation which is being funded is actually reaching the targeted population. Each of these groups of people requires a different type of information. The program developers may need detailed information on the process of program components; the evaluators may need an overall measure of the degree to which a program has been implemented; and the policy makers may need to know that the program funds have been expended on program related materials and services.

Several types of instruments to assess program implementation are reviewed below; each instrument was designed to fill the developer's or evaluator's specific needs. While it is unlikely that a single all-purpose instrument will be developed which will address everyone's information needs for all types of innovations, some of the instruments discussed show promise. With minor modification they can be used in a variety of situations in which the documentation of program implementation is required. The instruments reviewed have been designed for and applied in nonvocational evaluation settings. Yet the discussion is relevant to evaluation in vocational education, because this is a developing area of methodology in evaluation. It is predictable that these instruments and procedures will be adopted or form the basis of new developments in many fields of educational evaluation including vocational education.

NATURE OF INNOVATION

The concept of trying out innovative ideas in the classroom is not new. Since the beginning of instruction, individual teachers have experimented with alternative approaches for assisting the learning process of pupils. Different approaches to teaching have also been tried on a larger scale across the years. For example, diverse methods of teaching reading have been tried not only by the individual teacher, but also by schools, school systems, and the federal government. This has been especially true over the past two decades. Prompted by the launching of Sputnik in the 1950s and fueled by the growing concern for compensatory education in the 1960s, many different federally funded programs have sprung up and have been implemented rapidly in many different locations.

The implementation of an innovation on a massive scale differs radically from the implementation of an approach by an individual teacher in an individual classroom. When individual teachers decide to try a new approach they assume responsibility for all of its aspects, beginning with the generation of the idea. They look at the idea to figure out what parts of it are going to be easy or difficult to implement, and what parts are at odds or in sympathy with the general philosophy of the school system. As they implement the approach, they try to assess what parts or components seem to be working or not working, and how they might modify the approach based both on their experience to date with the innovation and on past experience. Finally, they decide whether to make the innovation a regular part of their teaching strategy, to retain parts of it while dropping other parts, or to discontinue the entire innovation. Obviously, this does not mean that no one else is involved in the individual teacher's innovation. The original idea may have come from a colleague or an article. Assistance may have been sought in developing and applying the idea. Others may have been involved in observing the outcomes and assisting in the modifications. But, finally, the innovation is an activity for which the individual teacher assumes both the authority and the final responsibility.

This single center of control does not exist when innovations are introduced on a large scale into multiple classroom settings. Such innovations may have been developed by the curriculum committee within the school system, within another school system, or a university. Teachers may participate because they volunteer or because they have been volunteered by their superiors. They receive sets of materials and in-service training designed to enable them to apply the new approach. At the individual classroom level, the teacher still retains concern for assessing the outcomes of the innovation and may still make modifications in the approach; however, the final determination of effectiveness and the decision to continue or discontinue the innovation are made at a different level. If the innovation has been funded locally, the decision to continue or discontinue will still be made at the local, although not at the teacher, level. If the innovation has been funded extensively at the federal level, the local school system still makes local decisions regarding adoption, but decisions about further funding and/or replications are made at the federal level.

Both at the local and federal levels, decisions are based on a number of factors, including, hopefully, information about the program's effectiveness. Unfortunately, program effectiveness is often ascertained by looking primarily, and sometimes exclusively, at outcome information. For example, if a mathematics curriculum innovation is introduced at the elementary level, its effectiveness may be based solely upon posttest mathematics achievement test scores. If a new work-study approach is developed at the high school level, its effectiveness may be based solely on the number of students who both complete high school and are gainfully employed after completing the program.

The national evaluation of Follow Through is a specific example of the dependence of an assessment of program effectiveness on outcome information. Follow through is a large-scale experimental program in compensating education. It was implemented through an approach known as "planned variation" which included the systematic introduction of a variety of programs into the kindergarten through third grade years of public education by educational specialists (sponsors) from research institutions and universities, who have implemented their own educational models in groups of school districts. Individual sponsors, in some cases, developed methods of determining the degree to which their programs were being implemented; they also modified their approaches as they decided that some components were working or not working. But the almost exclusive concern of the national evaluation was to assess child outcomes, and to determine if children who participated in Follow Through performed at higher levels than comparison group children who were not in Follow Through classrooms.

This type of an evaluation which looks only at outcomes assumes, implicitly or explicitly, that implementation is a binary variable, that is, that an innovation is implemented in the treatment classrooms and is not implemented in the comparison classrooms. It also assumes either that the innovation is static or that it goes through the same developmental process wherever it is implemented. Thus, such evaluations which look only at outcomes define implementation implicitly or explicitly as an intrinsic and undifferentiated aspect of treatment.

Extensive financial and human resources have been expended in the development, implementation, and assessment of a given innovation. At the individual teacher level much has probably been learned from the experience. Teachers and others close to the innovation may know a great deal about the extent to which various components of the innovation have been implemented within specific classrooms; they may also have fairly accurate perceptions of the extent to which they have succeeded using the various components with different children. Unfortunately, in an evaluation which does not examine implementation and its relationship to outcome, this information is lost. The final report of such an evaluation is not able to describe the innovation as it really existed in the classroom; it cannot provide the decision maker with information about the problems involved in implementing the innovation. It cannot even report that the innovation was actually implemented. At best, all it can say is that the formal adoption of the program produced certain results.

This type of exclusive dependence on outcome information is lessening. As the instruments described in this chapter illustrate, there is a growing concern not only to ascertain that a program which is being evaluated has actually been implemented, but also to examine the different ways in which the program has been implemented. Furthermore, different types of instruments are being developed to address the needs not only of the evaluator, but also the policy maker, the administrator, and the program developer.

TYPES OF INFORMATION NEEDED

Policy makers, administrators, program developers, teachers, and evaluators all need information about program implementation. Each group, however, needs a somewhat different type of information. Policy makers who are considering program adoption, for example, need assurance that the proposed innovation will be effective when it is in place in their schools. They may also need to know that the innovation as implemented is compatible with the educational philosophy of the community, and with other educational programs within the system. On the other hand, those policy makers who have a program in place may want to know if the program is being implemented according to plan, and reaching the targeted population.

Administrators need to know what components will be the easiest and most difficult to implement. They also want to know what problems are likely to arise in implementation of the innovation, what aspects of the innovation are likely to receive the most and least resistance from teachers and other concerned groups, and how long it will take before one can expect to obtain impact.

Few programs remain static and most program developers and/or teachers make modifications. Teachers may base their modifications on their day-today observations within the classroom; those program developers who are not involved in the day-to-day teaching still need information about program operations and effectiveness in order to make the needed modifications. They need to know, for example, which program components teachers are finding difficult to implement, which components are making too many demands on the overall system, and which components, when implemented, are not producing the expected results.

Evaluators or researchers need to be able to attribute the results they observe to the innovation. When they attempt to measure the effectiveness of a program they need to know that the program is actually in place. Or, if the entire program is not in place, they need to know what components of the program are in place. This need to know becomes more complicated if the research or evaluation design includes a comparison group. It then becomes necessary to ascertain whether the comparison group is receiving a competing treatment or components of the treatment (innovation) under study. For example, as teachers of the innovation talk about it with their colleagues, the colleagues may begin to adopt selected components. The innovation may thus eventually get diffused into the comparison classrooms. Sometimes, one will find that the program is being diffused not only in this non-random, collegial, informal fashion, but that teachers of comparison classrooms are being invited to participate in the in-service programs, or are being provided with copies of the materials or with similar materials to those being used in the innovation classrooms. Thus, if comparisons are being made between treatment and nontreatment groups, it becomes essential to know both whether or not the treatment is implemented in the treatment classroom, and whether the treatment, some portion of it, or a close facsimile of it is implemented in the comparison classroom.

Because different groups do have different needs, implementation instruments have to be designed to address the specific concerns. Therefore, there probably can never be an all-purpose implementation scale. Most of the instruments described below were developed to assess needs of specific programs.

REVIEW OF SELECTED INSTRUMENTS

Each of the instruments was developed for a different purpose; each also uses a different method. For example, a structured interview which assessed the degree of implementation has been developed as part of an ongoing concern with assessing program implementation. Another instrument, an observation form, was designed to assess the extent to which an in-service training program resulted in different teacher behaviors. Still another instrument, an open-ended interview, was developed in order that a cost-effectiveness study might include data only from classrooms in which the innovation was well implemented. Each of these and other instruments discussed below were developed to address specific concerns. While some of them have been more successful than others, none can be considered to be an instrument capable of addressing all concerns we might have with implementation. This variety of instruments has been chosen to demonstrate that there are many different methods and reasons for exploring implementation.

The first two instruments are observation forms. The Classroom Observation Rating Form described by Ashley and Butts (1971) was developed to assess the effectiveness of an in-service training program. The Classroom Observation Schedule described by Rayder et al. (1975) was developed to aid in program monitoring.

Ashley and Butts (1971) described an observation approach to determining the effectiveness of an in-service teacher training program by assessing the extent to which teachers implemented in their classrooms the techniques they were taught in the program. The purpose of the in-service program was to enhance teaching behavior in a specific curriculum component: Science—A Process Approach. The observation instrument, The Classroom Observation Rating Form (CORF), was designed to sample teaching strategies which were identified as integral parts of the curriculum sequence. The CORF consists of four different categories of teaching strategy: (1) Teacher-Student Interaction and Student Behavior (7 items); (2) Teacher Responses and Actions (27 items); (3) Teacher Traits (7 items); and (4) Physical Classroom Environment (3 items). Each item consists of two different types of teaching strategies or behaviors. For example, within Category 2, Teacher Responses and Actions, one item deals with the way a teacher responds to a student explanation. Under behavior type A the teacher responds to explanations with questions; under behavior type B, the teacher agrees or disagrees with explanations. The items in Categories 1 and 2 were identified by teachers experienced with the specific curriculum approach; items in Category 3 were mainly derived from works by Ryans (1960 and 1963).

Twenty-three teachers who participated in the in-service program were observed on four different occasions in their own classrooms. The first observation was made of either a math or a language arts lesson, and was made prior to the start of the in-service program. The last three observations were made of science lessons, with the last observation occurring at the conclusion of the in-service program.

Two observers independently rated each session. They first observed for two minutes and then spent the next thirty seconds recording those behaviors related to Category 1. During the next two-and-a-half minute period, they repeated the process for Category 3. They then alternated these two-and-a-half minute segments until the thirty minute observation period was complete. At the end of the thirty minutes, all Category 2 behaviors which had been observed were recorded. Information for Category 4 was also recorded at the end of the observation period. This method of recording permitted counts of behaviors in Categories 1 and 3; for Categories 2 and 4, only the presence or absence of specified behaviors could be noted.

Reliabilities were computed for each category and the total score for each of the four sessions. The averaged intraclass correlation was .95 for Category 1, .96 for Category 2, .95 for Category 3, .90 for Category 4, and .97 for total score. The pooled reliabilities were .97, .98, .97, .95, and .99 respectively.

Scores were obtained by assigning positive weights to type A behaviors, negative weights to type B behaviors, and obtaining algebraic sums. A variety of scores may be obtained using this technique, ranging from a total score, through scores for each type of behavior, to counts of the number of times a given strategy was observed.

As might be expected of an instrument designed to measure the effectiveness of an in-service program on teacher behavior, this observation form focuses on the classroom behavior of the teacher and the student. The next instrument described has many diverse content areas.

Since 1968, staff involved with the Responsive Environment Program for Early Childhood Education have been developing and refining instruments to measure responsiveness. The Classroom Observation Form (COF), described by Rayder et al. (1975), was developed to provide diagnostic and evaluation information about the program as it was implemented in the individual teachers' classrooms.

The instrument provides a profile of the responsive teaching environment in nine areas. The first two areas focus on physical space: presence of specific areas (6 items), and learning center (7 items). The next three areas focus on materials in the room: language materials (8 items), children's work (7 items), and materials on family, home, and culture (5 items). Areas six and seven focus on observation of learning experiences: language/prereading (15 items), and math/premath (15 items). Area eight is concerned with classroom management. Occurrences of three types of teacher behavior (demeaning, redirecting, and ignoring) are tallied during two separate five minute time periods. The ninth and last area provides for an overall impression of the teacher's behavior both on three dimensions (organization, warmth, and imagination), and on the teacher's responsiveness to the needs and differences of the children.

While both the CORF and the COF observe teacher behavior, the COF is much more concerned with also assessing the classroom environment. This is hardly surprising given that the CORF was designed for a program concerned with helping teachers develop a process approach to teaching science, while the COF was designed for a program concerned with helping teachers with all aspects of the teaching environment. However, it does illustrate the development of program-specific tools for assessing implementation.

While observation forms can provide detail about both student and teacher behaviors, and the physical environment, they can be very expensive and time consuming. One alternative to an observation form is the interview. The next two instruments illustrate very different forms of the interview technique— the first uses an open-ended approach; the second uses a formal structured approach.

Fortune and Forbes (1976) in a study of cost effectiveness of several reading programs needed program implementation information. They pointed out that cost effectiveness is a meaningful concept only if one knows that a program is highly implemented. Their concern with implementation, therefore, was to be able to categorize sites as being at a high, moderate, or low level of implementation. They first attempted to study implementation using an open-ended interview approach in which teachers and staff trainers were asked how they had taught reading to an individual student during a specified period of time. Teachers were then asked to read a short description of the program being implemented, and to estimate the percentage of time that their reading activities agreed with those specified by the program description. Fortune and Forbes found that while this open-ended approach provided some information that could be used in an exploration of the relationship of degree of implementation to outcomes, the information was not sufficient for them to categorize the classrooms as having high, moderate, or low levels of implementation.

Hall and Loucks (1977) described a rating scale which is based on a structured interview. This rating scale was developed to assess whether or not innovations being tried out in classrooms are actually being implemented.

The Levels of Use Scale consists of eight levels (Loucks, 1977): (0) Non-use; (1) Orientation (user is seeking information); (2) Preparation; (3) Mechanical Use (user is using the innovation in a poorly coordinated manner and is making user-oriented changes); (4a) Routine (user is making few or no changes, and has an established pattern of use); (4b) Refinement (user is making changes to increase outcomes); (5) Integration (user is making deliberate efforts to coordinate with others in using the innovation); and (6) Renewal (user is seeking more effective alternatives to the established use of the innovation).

A level of use is defined for each of seven general categories: knowledge, acquiring information, sharing, assessing, planning, status reporting, and performing. This measurement of general categories which cut across specific types of innovations makes it possible for the instrument to be used to measure degree of implementation in many different programs.

To assist the interviewer in making the rating, there are descriptions of each of the seven categories at each level, and a decision point between each level. For example, the descriptive paragraph about acquiring information for Level 2 (Preparation) reads: "Seeks information and resources specifically related to preparation for use of the innovation in own setting." The descriptive paragraph for Level 3 reads: "Solicits management information about such things as logistics, scheduling techniques, and ideas for reducing amount of time and work required of use" (Loucks, 1977:5). Between Level 2 and Level 3 the decision point is, "Begins first use of the innovation."

The twenty minute focused interview, which is the basis of these ratings, uses a branching technique which is based on the between-level decision points; the interviewer probes for behaviors within each of the seven categories. The interview is taped, and the level of use of the innovation is rated by the interviewer according to each of the seven categories and overall. The taped interview permits the rater to review the interview. More than one rater can rate the interview, thus permitting the determination of indices of inter-rater agreement.

This scale has been used for program components such as individualized teaching of mathematics or reading. In cases where an innovative approach consists of more than one component, such as an innovation which includes team-teaching, multiage groups, and individualized instruction, each innovative component would be rated separately.

Both the observation approach and the interview approach demand that the evaluator have face-to-face contact with the teacher. In many evaluations this is not possible. The following types of implementation tools—one a questionnaire, the other a checklist—do not require personal contact between the evaluator and the teacher.

Butt and Wideen (1974) needed a measure which would indicate degree of implementation in an ex post facto evaluation of a junior high school science curriculum. It was not possible for the evaluators to visit the numerous schools which participated in the evaluation, so they developed their Arbitrary Implementation Scale (AIS) from a previously developed teacher questionnaire. The scale was broken into five categories: (1) The opportunity and extent of in-service education (2 items); (2) The knowledge of, acceptance, and agreement with the philosophy, aims, and objectives of the curriculum (6 items); (3) The self-perception of teaching ability for the curriculum (5 items); (4) The extent to which certain factors helped or hindered in implementation (10 items); and (5) Specific practices in teaching and evaluation (4 items). Although Butt and Wideen reported a total score, it would perhaps be more appropriate in this case to, at minimum, report a subscore for categories 1 and 4, and categories 2, 3, and 5, because the first group examines precursors of implementation and the latter implementation itself.

Owens and Haenn (1977) described a checklist approach developed both to measure degree of implementation and to provide a profile of the program as implemented. The innovation studied is an Experience-Based Career Education (EBCE) program developed at Northwest Regional Educational Laboratory (NWREL). The first instrument, the Essential Characteristics Checklist, was developed to measure the five program components which the program developers felt were essential: EBCE (1) is an individualized program; (2) is community-based; (3) is experience-based; (4) has its own identity, and is comprehensive and integrated; and (5) places major emphasis on students' career development. Each of these five components is measured on four to six characteristics with each characteristic being rated on a scale of 1 to 5, where a rating below 4 represents "failure to implement an essential characteristic consistent with the NWREL-developed EBCE program" (Owens and Haenn, 1977:10). An example of an item included on this checklist would be a question asking whether or not there was a community advisory board, and, if there was, how often it met.

The second instrument, the Process Checklist, consists of four sections: EBCE objectives, management and organization processes, curriculum and instruction processes, and student service processes. It is designed to identify variations in procedures used to operate the EBCE programs, and thus, to describe the procedures being used in each particular site. For example, an item might deal with a specific skill which may or may not be taught at a given site. The site would be asked to check if the skill was required of all students, optional, or not offered. The checklists must be filled out by someone familiar with the implemented program, such as the site director. The first list takes about twenty minutes to complete, and the second about twenty-five minutes.

Owens and Haenn have found that the instruments are useful for a variety of purposes. The instruments were used to assess program fidelity; i.e., the match of a local program to the original program specifications. The instruments have also been found to be useful as technical assistance devices; for example, to acquaint people with the characteristics and processes of the program, and to serve as tools for program planning. They have also been used to stimulate discussion among staff regarding program strengths and weaknesses. Sites often cannot implement all of a program at once, and these checklists also serve as a guide to focus efforts on specific areas to be implemented. Owens and Haenn expected that the instruments will also be useful in assessing program change across time.

The last implementation tool to be presented is one which assesses the delivery system component of the implemented program. Behr and Hanson (1977) were concerned not with issues relating to the quality of the program, but rather with the delivery of instruction. For example, they reported a study in which the delay in a reading program startup ranged from zero to twelve or more weeks. They reported data from another study of reading programs which suggested that faulty initial placement may also be a problem. Behr and Hanson were concerned with four specific implementation variables: time of the receipt of program materials; time of the start-up of program instruction; initial placement for instruction; and program pacing and completion.

They have developed a continuous data collection system in order to monitor these specific implementation concerns. Teachers were given four different preaddressed, prepaid postcards and asked to mail the first card when they received the postcard packet, thus enrolling themselves and their class in the system's service. A copy of the second card, a placement card (4 copies provided), was mailed by the teacher whenever a group of students began instruction. The placement card thus provided the start-up date for instruction for a set of students and their entry point into the program. The third type of card, the block assessment score card (6 copies provided), was returned by the teacher when a group of students completed a block of instruction. This card included proficiency data and length of time spent on the block of instruction; it also signaled that the instruction had been completed. The fourth card was returned at the end of the school year. It gave the number of students who were taught that year in each block within the applicable program.

This type of information helps solve Behr and Hanson's four concerns. First, by knowing where the students are in the scheduled sequence, one is able to provide the necessary instructional materials in a timely fashion; second, at any given time one can determine which students have not begun instruction; third, faulty placement can be checked in two different ways: (1) based on prior and concurrent experience, it is expected that a certain number of students will be placed in each block; if the number reported placed in a block deviates widely from this expected, the monitor can check to see if underplacement is occurring, (2) underplaced pupils will complete blocks more rapidly than correctly placed pupils. Finally, the program proficiency information being sent will indicate that the class is progressing or not progressing as planned.

DISCUSSION OF INSTRUMENTS

The observation approaches described above focused on the roles of the teachers and students, and the physical classroom environment. The CORF, developed to assess behavioral changes in the teachers' behavior,[1] focused primarily on those behaviors while the COF which was developed to assess the implementation of a comprehensive teaching system, focused not only on teacher behavior but also on physical manifestations in the room to determine that the concepts espoused by the system were in place. The COF thus provides a multidimensional profile of many indicators of program implementation.

Through the observation approach, the evaluator is able to be in the classroom and actually see what is going on rather than having to depend on self-reported behaviors. In that sense observation is the ideal technique for ascertaining whether or not a program is implemented. Observation does have several drawbacks, however. First of all, it is very expensive; second, only a limited number of observations can occur; and third, during the observation period, the clasroom practices may be altered somewhat by the intrusion of the observer. The first problem is the most difficult. If it can be resolved, adequate solutions can usually be found for the other two problems. However, because funds are not usually available for the necessary extensive observation, other methods of studying implementation are needed. Furthermore, it is not clear that observational techniques can address all implementation questions.

While Fortune and Forbes (1976), and Hall and Loucks (1977) each present interview approaches, their approaches are different both in purpose and in style. Fortune and Forbes tried a very open ended interview, while Hall and Loucks reported on one which is very structured. The interviews themselves had different purposes; Fortune and Forbes needed to develop a method by which they could define a program as either implemented or not implemented, while Hall and Loucks wanted to develop a method to report degree of implementation. The Hall and Loucks' structured interview seems to offer much in terms of assessing degree of implementation. Furthermore, one could arbitrarily divide the scale into implemented/not implemented segments to meet the need of studies such as that by Fortune and Forbes. The interview, like the checklist approach, is dependent upon the respondents' knowledge, memory, and willingness to communicate. Although the instrument depends on the interviewer being capable of recording and rating accurately, Loucks indicated that interrater reliability is quite high, and thus need not be a problem. This type of rating scale will tell us the degree to which a given component is implemented on several dimensions; it does not, however, readily provide the descriptive and diagnostic type of information given by process checklists such as that developed by Owens and Haenn.

The checklists developed by Owens and Haenn examined a variety of specific concerns, ranging from determining if an advisory board exists and meets regularly to determining whether and how specific skills are taught. Checklists such as this may be used with different groups, such as directors, teachers, students, advisory board members, and parents. Congruence or lack of congruence of response among groups will help program directors and evaluators know the extent to which various aspects of the program are familiar to the different groups. While an approach such as the checklist offers much information, it does not provide direct observation of individual behaviors, and thus information about process and interaction may be lost.

The questionnaire approach, such as that illustrated by the instrument developed by Butt and Wideen, provides an opportunity to obtain information on reported behavior. Although the substance of the Butt and Wideen instrument differs from the substance of the Owens and Haenn checklist, the approaches are quite similar.

The instruments developed by Behr and Hanson are tools to assure implementation and to measure implementation. They are both very obtrusive tools within a delivery system and very unobtrusive measures of implementation. Such instrumentation may be very appropriate for programs which lend themselves to an external delivery support system, while it may be not at all appropriate for other types of programs. While instrumentation of this type can provide the diagnostician with information about what appears to be happening or not happening within the delivery system, it tells nothing about the role of the teachers in the classroom such as can be obtained by an observation approach.

Some of the instruments discussed above have focused primarily on trying to measure the degree to which the program as defined by the developer is actually implemented; in other words, the fidelity of the implementation. While these methods look within the classroom to see what is happening, the technique suggests that the programs should be implemented exactly as described, perhaps even that the programs should be "teacher proof." As Owens, Rayder, and Hall and Loucks all suggest, it may be that the program which produces the best outcomes is not the one which is most faithfully installed. First, individual needs vary and thus a program which is appropriate under one set of circumstances needs to be modified for use under another set of circumstances. Second, a packaged program is not likely to be perfect; intelligent modifications are likely to improve it. In fact, the Levels of Use Scale incorporates that assumption by rating modification above mechanical use. A study reported by Hall and Loucks (1977), however, did not show that modification led to greater effectiveness. This could have happened for a number of reasons. The measuring instrument might be faulty or the program being measured may produce its best results when it is mechanically implemented. Also, it could be that some types of program modification produce more effective results, and other types of program modification produce less effective results.

CONCLUSION

At the beginning of this chapter several different types of needs for program implementation data were identified. For example, before adopting an innovation the policy maker needs to know if the innovation has worked in other places it has been tried. For that person, two types of information are needed, and a third type would be helpful. In order to say that a program has been effective where it has been implemented, one must have both a measure of effectiveness and a measure of degree of implementation. The third type of information which would be helpful would describe the way in which the implemented program differs from the prototype.This minimal level of information is also needed by researchers or evaluators. Of course, they will also need similar information for any comparison group which is being used. If the evaluators or researchers are only to determine if a given approach is effective or not, then this minimal information may suffice. However, if the evaluators or researchers are to begin to probe, for example, to determine which program components are effective or not effective, then they need have much more extensive implementation information such as that needed by the program developer or administrator.

Program developers and administrators (and often evaluators and researchers) not only need to know about the effectiveness of a given program component, they also need to know which components are being implemented in which ways, and which components are the easiest and most difficult to implement. This type of information cannot be provided by scales which measure degree of implementation. Checklists such as those described by Owens and Haenn, measures of program delivery such as described by Behr and Hanson, or multidimensional profiles such as described by Rayder et al. begin to provide component level program-specific data, thus enabling one to ascertain how individual components of the innovation are implemented differently in each location. These techniques also begin to provide the administrator with information about which components appear to be the most difficult or easy to implement.

Evaluators need to consider reliability and content/construct validity in their development of measures of program implementation. Standard approaches to reliability will be appropriate for many interview and observation instruments. Other instruments such as the one by Behr and Hanson, described above, need to be assessed for accuracy across teachers. Still others, such as the Hall and Loucks' Level of Use Scale, are construct or theory based and need studies of construct validity.

This chapter began by pointing out that in small scale innovations individual teachers are present and accountable for all aspects of the mini innovations they introduce into their classrooms, but when innovations are introduced on a larger scale the responsibilities for the various concerns become distributed across a number of people who are not present in the classroom each day. Each of these people, the policy maker, the administrator, the developer, the evaluator, needs a somewhat different type and level of implementation information. The issue is one of recognizing the types of information which are likely to be needed for any given situation, and of developing the type of instrument which can provide the necessary implementation information.

NOTE

1. The CORF, as primarily an observation of teacher behavior, is one representative of a number of teacher/group observation instruments. These instruments are reviewed by Medley and Mitzel (1963), and Rosenshine and Furst (1973). Descriptions of a wide variety of observation instruments are given in Simon and Boyer (1970), and earlier volumes of the anthology are referenced there.

REFERENCES

Ashley, J., and Butts, D. 1971. A study of the impact of an in-service education program on teacher behavior. In D. Butts, ed. *Research and Curriculum Development in Science Education.* (curriculum implementation). Austin: University of Texas.

Behr, G., and Hanson, R. 1977. "Supporting program implementation." Paper presented at the meeting of the American Educational Research Association, New York, April.

Butt, R. L., and Wideen, M. F. 1974. "The development, validation, and use of an arbitrary implementation scale (AIS) as a basis for ex post facto curriculum evaluation." Paper presented at the meting of the American Educational Research Association, Chicago.

Fortune, J. C., and Forbes, R. 1976. "The measurement of program implementation in reading instruction." Paper presented at the meeting of the American Educational Research Association, San Francisco, April.

Hall, G., and Loucks, S. 1977. A developmental model for determining whether the treatment is actually implemented. *American Educational Research Journal* 14, 3:263-276.

Loucks, S. F. 1977. "Levels of use of the innovation: the conceptualization and measurement of a variable useful for assessing innovation implementation by individuals." Paper presented at the annual meeting of the American Educational Research Association, New York City, April.

Medley, D. M., and Mitzel, H. E. 1963. Measuring classroom behavior by systematic observation. In N. L. Gage, ed. *Handbook of Research on Teaching.* Chicago: Rand McNally.

Owens, T. R., and Haenn, J. F. 1977. "Assessing the level of implementation of new programs." Paper presented at the meeting of the American Educational Research Association, New York City, April.

Rayder, N. F. et al. 1975. *The Responsive Classroom Observation Schedule—Background and Development.* San Francisco: Far West Laboratory for Educational Research and Development, March.

Rosenshine, B., and Furst, N. 1973. The use of direct observation to study teaching. In R. M. W. Travers, ed. *Second Handbook of Research on Teaching.* Chicago: Rand McNally.

Ryans, D. F. 1963. Assessment of teacher behavior and instruction. *Review of Educational Research.* 33, 4:415-441.

——— 1960. *Characteristics of teachers.* Washington: American Council of Education.

Simon, A., and Boyer, E. G., eds. 1970. *Mirrors for Behavior: An Anthology of Classroom Observation Instruments.* Supplementary Vols. A and B. Philadelphia: Research for Better Schools. (ED 042 937)

chapter 8

TEH-WEI HU   *Pennsylvania State University*
ERNST W. STROMSDORFER   *Indiana University*

I. INTRODUCTION

In order for the public to make rational decisions concerning investment in various educational programs, comprehensive information about the costs and benefits of these programs is required. Vocational education is a major component of our secondary educational system, and one which has received special attention from both educators and policy makers.

It is often argued by the program detractors that vocational education costs are too high, while program advocates see these same costs as evidence of "high quality." Neither assertion is accurate unless costs are related to benefits, and net, rather than gross benefits are measured. No valid policy statement can be made from analyses that do not include these components, yet policy statements are made on the basis of incomplete information.

There are essentially three types of evaluation in educational programs. The first is concerned primarily with *inputs*. This type of evaluation is usually conducted by a visiting team of experts and considers such matters as administration, instructional programs, physical facilities, and instructional staff. It is not, however, concerned with the specific content of programs.

The second type of evaluation, which directs its attention primarily to *process*, is usually conducted by observers over a period of time. It is concerned with the nature in which services of a school are delivered such as the grouping of children, the staffing pattern, administrative guidelines, leadership and expertise, teacher quality, and teacher attitudes toward the program. In effect, the school is observed as a total social system in which interactions take place among administrators, teachers, students, parents, and physical inputs.

A third type of evaluation can be described as *cost-benefit* or *cost-effectiveness,* and deals with *outputs* or outcomes, in relation to the inputs or costs involved. This type of evaluation is based on the theory that one cannot make a judgment about the costs of any activity unless they are related to the benefits and, conversely, one cannot make a judgment about the benefits of any activity unless they are related to the costs.

Actually, this process views the problems of decision-making as those of constrained maximization or minimization. Restated, this means that the problem is to choose among feasible alternatives so as to: (1) achieve the *most* of what is desired with *given quantities* of resources used, or (2) achieve *given quantities* of what is desired with the *least* resources used. To illustrate: Although *added costs* may be associated with vocational education, consideration should also be given to the *added benefits* which it may confer in order to determine whether the latter exceed the former and, therefore, whether further investment in vocational education is desirable.

Thus, in the field of education (as in other areas), given its limited resources, the problem is one of choice and consists of the following components: "specification of the objective function, determination of constraints, elaboration of feasible alternatives, measurement of costs and benefits of feasible alternatives, the evaluation and choice" (Judy, 1970:16).

It must be emphasized that cost analysis of vocational education is only *one* aspect of a total analysis which is essential to rational decision-making in the allocation of resources to vocational education. To illustrate the importance of linking costs to benefits, the problems of cost-benefit analysis are discussed, and previous empirical costs estimates are related to their respective benefits estimates. The limitations of cost-benefit analysis will also be presented.

II. FRAMEWORK OF COST-BENEFIT ANALYSIS

Cost-benefit analysis is a technique which concerns itself with the optimum allocation of resources. It is a tool of analysis which assesses the alternative courses of action in order to help decision makers in maximizing the net benefit to society. The essence of such an analysis lies in its ability to evaluate the total value of benefits against the total costs.

Cost-benefit analysis normally consists of several steps. The first, and most important step, is the *identification* of costs and benefits of a given program. This procedure may appear to be obvious, but in practice it raises a number of fundamental issues of methodology and economic theory. For instance, should the tax exemption to a public school system be considered as a cost or not? If considered as a cost, to whom is it a cost? Or, should the reduction of government transfer payment due to education be considered as a benefit and if so, to whom is it a benefit? And especially, how far is one to go in attempting to enumerate and evaluate external benefits and external costs of a program? These problems will be discussed in the next section. Table 8.1 illustrates some important elements of costs and benefits of education. The elements of costs and benefits of both vocational education and academic education of high schools are similar but vary in degree.

Second, the list of benefits and costs, both private or social, must be expressed as *monetary values* in order to arrive at an estimate of the current net benefits, if any, of a program. The benefits and costs are usually reflected via the price mechanism through the working of the market forces of supply and demand. In certain circumstances, however, market forces may fail to reflect all costs and benefits. This is the fundamental distinction between private and social costs and benefits. Therefore, the quantification of all costs and benefits of a program is difficult, if not at times virtually impossible. Assuming that these difficulties have been surmounted, the analyst is left with an estimate of net benefits of the project.

Finally, a *comparison* must be made of the benefits and costs of the program. The basic criterion for choosing the most desirable program from among a set of alternatives is to select the one with the maximum net present value of benefits (total present value of benefits minus total present value of costs). The comparison is in terms of the present value of benefits (or costs) and also the future benefits (or costs) which have been discounted into present values to take account of the time factor. Mathematically, present value of benefits can be expressed as $\sum_{t=1}^{n} \frac{B_t}{(1+i)^t}$, while the present value of costs is $\sum_{t=1}^{n} \frac{C_t}{(1+i)^t}$ where i is the rate of interest used for discounting and t is the time period.

There are three alternative investment criteria to evaluate a program: the benefit-cost ratio, the internal rate of return, and the present value of net benefits. The benefit-cost ratio uses present value of benefits as the numerator and present value of costs as the denominator. A program should have a benefit-cost ratio larger or equal to one in order to be worthwhile. The higher the ratio, the greater the payoff.

The internal rate of return is the rate of return which makes the discounted value of costs equal to the discounted value of benefits. The formula is as follows:

$$\sum_{t=1}^{n} \frac{C_t}{(1+r)^t} = \sum_{t=1}^{n} \frac{B_t}{(1+r)^t}$$

Table 8.1: The Definitions and Elements of Costs and Benefits of Education

Society	Private
Costs	*Costs*
Definition: opportunity costs to the society at large (welfare foregone by society as a result of expending resources on education rather than on other goods and services).	Definition: opportunity costs to the individual (welfare foregone by the individual as a result of expending resources on education rather than on other goods or services).
Elements:	Elements:
1. Schools' expenses incurred due to providing educational services (e.g., operating expenses and capital expenses).	1. Students' expenses incurred due to attending school (e.g., tuition, books, transportation).
2. Opportunity costs of non-school system inputs (e.g., PTA donations to school, foregone earnings of students).	2. Foregone earnings of students.
Benefits	*Benefits*
Definition: Welfare gained by the society at large as a result of education.	Definition: Welfare gained by the individual as a result of education.
Elements:	Elements:
1. A greater rate of economic growth (i.e., increased productivity of associated workers).	1. Students additional earnings due to education.
2. Good citizenship and reduction of crime.	2. A broader appreciation of our environment.
3. Continuation and exploration of knowledge and culture.	3. The acquisition of knowledge for its own sake.

where r is the internal rate of return and is the unknown in the equation. This solution of r will be used to compare against the interest rate representing the rate of social or private investment. If the rate of return for the program is higher than the interest rate for social or private investment, then the investment in this program would be worthwhile. If all the alternative programs have higher rates of return than the interest rate, one should choose the program with the highest rate of return.

The present value of net benefits is the difference between the discounted value of the benefits streams and the costs streams. One chooses, of course, the program with the largest net present value.

Given real world constraints, the results of each criterion may not be consistent with the other two. Therefore, the choice of the criterion is crucial, depending upon the specific circumstances of the study. Moreover, in order to apply these criteria, cost-benefit analysis has to make assumptions as to the size of the rate of interest which is to be used in discounting.

III. PROBLEMS IN COST ANALYSIS

Any complete analysis of costs should measure both social and private costs and, in some cases, the costs incurred by governmental units. Social costs are the value of resources incurred for a program by the entire society as a whole, while private costs are the value of resources incurred for the participation of the program by an individual.

Under social costs, the following should be considered:

(1) Current costs are also called operating costs and include such factors as teachers' salaries, heat, light, and other variable costs.
(2) Capital costs of sites, building, and equipment.
(3) Cost correction factors such as sales tax and property tax.
(4) Costs from nonschool system support.
(5) Earnings foregone while students are undergoing education.
(6) Incidental costs to students associated with school attendance.
(7) Job search costs.
(8) On-the-job training costs.

Under private costs, the following should be considered:

(1) Earnings foregone while students are undergoing education.
(2) Incidental costs associated with school attendence.
(3) Job search costs.
(4) On-the-job training costs.

These costs are listed separately only because each has measurement problems peculiar to it. These measurement problems include the concept of costs versus expenditures, the allocation of joint costs, and the treatment of *current costs* and *capital costs*.

EXPENDITURE VERSUS COSTS

It is common to think of the terms costs and expenditures as interchangeable. From the economist's point of view, these terms are not the same. Costs are related to a specific output. Expenditures, on the other hand, are often stated without relation to the output-time dimension. Some inputs in the vocational education program are not used up within the accounting period during which they were purchased (e.g., building, equipment, or books). Assets of this type provide a stream of services over a number of accounting periods before they are exhausted. In order to convert expenditures into costs in such cases, it is necessary to employ depreciation allowance estimates.

Further differences between expenditures and costs arise from inputs which are owned outright and involve no current outlay. Some imputed value must be attributed to these inputs for a correct accounting of economic costs. A good example of this is land rent.

Finally, a third party (nonschool system) may pay for a basic service or incur expenses on behalf of the vocational education program. These expenditures should be treated as costs of the program. Full and accurate estimation of costs (not merely expenditures) is an essential step in estimating the costs or added costs of vocational education.

JOINT COSTS

Joint costs occur within two contexts. First, at a given point in time, a specific educational input or facility may produce two or more distinct educational outputs. Second, a facility or input may be consumed over time during the investment or training process by successive cohorts of students representing either the same or a different type of output.

In actual practice costs which are joint are frequently allocated among different programs. Not only is such allocation always arbitrary in nature, it is unnecessary. When joint costs occur, the total cost of the set of programs or outputs combined can be measured. Their combined benefits must equal their combined total costs. But total *average* costs of the programs simply cannot be measured accurately in any economic sense (Hirshliefer et al., 1960:93-94; McKean, 1958:44-46).

Consider the following: Both vocational and nonvocational training occur in a comprehensive senior high school. In this school, certain costs are directly attributable to a given program in vocational education, such as the extra cost of electricity to run the power tools of the machine shop or the cost of extra wiring in the shop room. However, the building itself needs a basic electrical system to feed electricity to all of the various classrooms and shops. This cost outlay serves both the vocational and nonvocational students. Given a decision to install a machine shop in that school, no part of the *common* cost of constructing the basic school building should be included as a cost offset to the benefits flowing from the machine shop. The correct allocation of these common costs to the machine shop operation and, by extension, the costs of training students as machinists, is simply zero. This is so because, within the limits of the range of output in the school, the use of the common facilities by students taking machinist training does not reduce the ability of the other students in the school to use the same facilities. Thus, users of this joint input can consume as much as they wish without reducing the consumption of the good by others.

The above example suggests that the occurrence of joint costs does not affect the determination of marginal costs. Marginal costs are defined as the additional costs incurred as a result of additional units of output (or enrollment). Because efficient investment decisions between two (or more) alternative programs are made on the basis of marginal costs, joint costs present no basic problem to cost-benefit analysis.

CURRENT COSTS

Some current costs are specific and some are joint. Given a comprehensive school which produces more than one type of product or which provides different types of specialized training, typical joint costs could involve the items listed above. Even if, as with the school lunch programs, students are charged a fee which reflects the cost of providing lunch to each of them, differences in marginal cost between different students are not necessarily affected, if, as is often the case, each student is charged a flat fee. Of course, one would attribute as a cost of education only those costs involved in food preparation and serving, which are over and above what the student would incur if the student were not in school.

Controversy exists over whether or not such in-school programs as attendance, health, and community services represent aspects of the educational process. In some respects, these programs are similar to other public health and social services, and an argument could be made for including such expenditures in the respective community-wide programs. However, interaction effects take place between one's state of health, nutrition, quality of life, and the educational and learning processes. Thus, total exclusion of such expenditures in an accounting of the costs of education may not be warranted because these programs do facilitate the educational process. A case could be made, however, for attributing the increased effectiveness of the educational process that is brought about by such things as health expenditures as a benefit accruing from the health program. Our judgment would be to exclude these expenditures whenever possible and to recognize that in their presence, the benefits accruing to the educational process per se are overestimated.

Specific costs include such items as the cost of the shop or classroom teacher, the cost of supplies and books associated with a given educational curriculum, or maintenance or janitorial services associated with each curriculum. Clearly, the cost accounting problems associated with maintaining a separation of the joint and specific cost aspects of a given input are severe. Therefore, a clarification with school administrators or school accountants is recommended during a cost study.

CAPITAL COSTS

Social (and private) capital costs are fundamentally no different in nature than social (and private) current costs. These costs are discussed separately only because each type presents different measurement problems. Capital costs can be broken down into four different elements:

(a) Site acquisition costs
(b) Capital improvements to the site
(c) Physical plant and building costs
(d) Equipment costs

Serious measurement problems stem from several physical and institutional factors. Two of the most important factors are: (1) The physical plant of the school usually has an economic life longer than the period of training provided for any given educational cohort; and (2) the services of this capital stock are not easily valued in market terms.

Four possible treatments for valuing this capital exist. First, one can argue that once the capital stock exists, especially the physical plant and buildings, it becomes specific to the educational process and has no alternative use in the short run. This is a tenuous assumption, however, because it is easy to discover alternative uses for such capital stock. The value of the educational physical plant is not zero, but because it is not a perfect substitute for competing uses, the value of the competing uses, such as the rent of a hospital, does not reflect the exact opportunity cost of using the physical plant for educational purposes.

Second, historical costs of building construction and site acquisition can be used, but they are irrelevant because they have no necessary bearing on the present opportunity costs involved in using any capital stock.

Third, replacement costs can be used as a measure of capital costs. It is obvious, however, that to replace a building would often cost more than the current economic value of the building. Replacement costs tend to over-value the capital resource, given a rising price level and assuming no compensating technological change in construction techniques.

Fourth, an estimate of current assessed valuation could be used to arrive at a measure of capital costs. However, the valuation standard used is critical. In actual practice, the valuation standard reflects historical costs adjusted by a price index of replacement cost, so that this measure is no better than the replacement cost measure. Among these four alternative estimations, the second and third are the approaches most often adopted in program evaluation.

Once the economic value of the capital in use has been measured, the rate at which the given capital stock is consumed over the course of the investment process must be measured. This may be done in one of two ways. One is to attempt to measure an imputed rent and depreciation to the capital stock by comparison with the amount of rent that the capital item would yield if it were being used in the private sector of the economy, including interest and depreciation. This procedure is arbitrary and uncertain, however, and a great deal of judgment is involved in adjusting the estimated shadow prices to more closely reflect the true opportunity costs (McKean, 1968).

An alternative technique for estimating the rate of capital use employs the "capital recovery factor" (CRF). The application of this technique automatically accounts for both interest and depreciation. The capital recovery factor is that factor which "when multiplied by the present value of capital costs, is the level [average] end-of-year annual amount over the life of the project necessary to pay interest on and recover the capital costs in full" (Hirshliefer et al., 1960:93-94).

This technique is not without problems. First of all, the CRF does not necessarily indicate the amount of capital used in any given year. It only states the level annual amount needed to recoup the principal and social opportunity cost, that is, interest, given the project life. Second, more than one cohort of students may utilize a given capital item during the life of that item. Here again is the familiar joint cost problem. In short, reliable estimates of the costs of capital are difficult to obtain for any given program. Therefore, care should be taken to compare a number of empirical estimates of vocational costs.

IV. PREVIOUS STUDIES OF THE COSTS OF VOCATIONAL EDUCATION

Relatively few studies have contained adequate information on the costs of vocational education. Most studies have been conducted on a city, state, or regional basis rather than at the national level. It is generally known that costs of vocational education are higher than those for nonvocational programs, but uncertainty exists over the magnitude of the differences, the so-called added costs of vocational education. This section reviews past studies on costs of vocational education.

Cohn, Hu, and Kaufman (1972:93) estimated added costs of vocational education in Michigan secondary schools, based on 108 questionnaires returned from a sample of 251 schools offering vocational and/or nonvocational secondary curricula. Data generated by the questionnaires revealed average costs per student hour for vocational and nonvocational programs were $278 and $183, respectively. Average added costs were then calculated by subtracting the average cost per student hour for all nonvocational programs from that of each vocational program. Added costs per student hour ranged from a low of—$15 for home economics to $365 for welding. The—$15 figure indicates that individual vocational curricula are not necessarily more expensive than nonvocational educational programs.

Cohn, Hu, and Kaufman (1972) estimated added costs of vocational education on the basis of marginal cost. Marginal costs measure the *additional* cost incurred in a specific program when one student (or more specifically, one student enrollment hour) is added. The estimated marginal costs ranged from $157 to $187 per student hour for nonvocational programs. For vocational programs, the range was from $24 to $648. As with average costs, marginal costs of vocational programs are not categorically higher than those of nonvocational programs, but they are considerably higher on the average. Added costs on a marginal basis were $115 overall, with a range of—$126 to $498 for specific programs.

Another study on the costs of secondary education was undertaken by Hu, Lee, and Stromsdorfer (1969:123-124). Cost data were collected for Baltimore, Detroit, and Philadelphia for the period 1956 through 1960. Of these three cities, Baltimore did not have enough cost information. Total educational costs were computed on the basis of estimates of both current and capital costs. Added costs of vocational education were obtained by subtracting average costs for secondary comprehensive schools from their vocational school counterparts. The estimated average added costs for vocational education were $156 in Detroit and $116 in Philadelphia.

An additional study of the costs (and benefits) of secondary education was conducted in Worcester, Massachusetts, by Corazzini (1968). He compared per pupil costs for vocational programs with costs for pupils in basic high school programs in 1963-1964. A substantial difference was found in per pupil cost between basic high school programs and vocational programs. Specifically, costs for students in basic programs averaged $452, compared to $964 for boys' vocational school programs and $793 for girls' vocational school programs. Differences in costs were attributed principally to differences in teachers' salaries per pupil in basic and vocational education programs. It was shown that this difference was due to both higher average teachers' salaries and lower pupil-teacher ratios for vocational educational programs.

Corazzini (1968) reestimated costs by including adjustments for "public implicit costs," that is, capital costs and property tax costs. Capital costs include an implicit rent charge, estimated at 5.1 percent of total assets, and depreciation charges of 2 percent on buildings, and 10 percent on equipment. The addition of public implicit costs raised the cost estimates by $80 per pupil for basic high school education, and $246 per pupil for the boys' vocational school programs, increasing further the difference between vocational and basic high school costs. Although the Corazzini (1968) study is limited in that only average costs are estimated, the large cost differences should be noted.

Taussig (1968) generated cost data for the vocational and academic high school programs in New York City for the 1964-1965 period. He estimated combined current and capital annual costs per pupil and, from these data, average added costs of vocational education. His analysis indicated that per pupil costs were $1,188 for academic schools and $1,697 for vocational schools. Therefore, the cost differential between the two programs is $519. These added cost estimates are interesting in that the per pupil academic program costs are calculated to include students currently taking vocational programs. Taussig (1968) argued that the added costs of vocational education should reflect the most realistic alternative—an expanded system of academic high schools including the present vocational students. Although this expanded cost concept helps make it notable, the Taussig study has several shortcomings. First, capital costs were estimated by taking 22 percent of current costs, a rather simplistic assumption at best. Second, although reference to marginal cost analysis is made, there is no real attempt to estimate marginal costs.

Several other studies have estimated the costs of vocational education at the secondary, postsecondary, and junior college levels. The estimated average vocational costs for high schools range from about $430 to $615 per year based on current costs information, and $520 to $740 based on total resources costs, which include opportunity costs and capital costs (Fernback and Somers, 1970; Eninger, 1967; Kaufman and Lewis, 1968). The estimated average vocational costs for postsecondary and junior colleges range from $2500 to $2840 per year based on current costs information, and $3084 to $3874 per year based on total resources costs (Fernback and Somers, 1970; Carroll and Ihnen, 1967). The variation among these costs figures is related to the studied time period, the components of the costs estimates, and the location of schools.

V. PROBLEMS IN BENEFIT ANALYSIS

A benefit can be defined as any result of the vocational education process that increases individual or social welfare. This increase in welfare can be either economic or noneconomic. With respect to economic welfare, benefits occur either directly by increasing productivity or indirectly by freeing resources for alternative uses. Increasing productivity, as a result of education, implies more output per unit of input than before. The increase of productivity will in turn increase the wage rate of vocational graduates. In this sense, vocational education can be considered as an investment program.

With respect to noneconomic welfare, the educational process may result in an increased level of satisfaction for those participating in the educational process. The possible reduction of undesirable social behaviors or crimes as a result of education, the improvement of citizenship, and the increase in job satisfaction are also considered as noneconomic benefits. The latter type of benefit is more particular to vocational education, while the other benefits are applicable to all types of educational programs but they may vary in degree. These values may not be quantifiable in dollar value. However, to ignore these noneconomic benefits and concentrate on economic benefits will underestimate the total benefit of vocational education.

There are measurement problems for both economic and noneconomic benefits. These measurement problems include the concept of wages versus earnings, the noneconomic benefits, and transfer payment.

WAGES VERSUS EARNINGS

Wages, usually in terms of per hour or per week, are used to measure the productivity of a worker, and reflect both the demand and supply of a given type of labor requirement. Earnings are the product of wages and the time period of employment, and may also include incomes earned from one type of wages or jobs. One may have a relatively high wage and work only a short period of time, or a relatively low wage and work during the entire year. Therefore, these two measurements have two different implications. If one is to evaluate the productivity of vocational graduates, then the wage rate should be used. If one is to evaluate the earning ability, including the ability to be employed, then earnings should be used. Most studies used earnings as measurements of the economic benefits of vocational education.

NONECONOMIC BENEFITS

Economic benefits are only one of the elements which comprise one's well-being. One of the elements of satisfaction gained besides earnings are direct consumption benefits during the educational process itself, as well as improved possibility for the enhancement of consumption after education. If persons are rational in their pursuit of utility or welfare maximization, they will gravitate to those kinds of education and occupations which give them direct consumption benefits along with increased earnings. This is the crux of the matter when educators, economists, and others seek to evaluate the degree of "job satisfaction" involved in career choice.

Job satisfaction are measures of psychic well-being. If different kinds of persons gravitate to different programs, there remains the difficult task of establishing unambiguous scales to measure these direct consumption and psychic benefits. Different elements may compromise the consumption and receipt of psychic benefits by different groups. Thus, even if one asks the same kind of question of these different groups, seemingly uniform and consistent responses may have entirely different meanings and be incommensurable (Stromsdorfer, 1972). Researchers should continue to improve the instruments of job satisfaction measurement and be careful in interpreting the findings.

In addition to the measurement of job satisfaction, the possible reduction of crime and improvement of citizenship also belongs to noneconomic benefits. Some of the property crimes may be evaluated by their dollar value, while others are difficult to estimate in terms of dollar value. Citizenship can be measured in terms of political participation (such as voting), volunteering for community work, and nonavoidance of military or other national service. Again, citizenship is difficult to value in dollar terms. Therefore, one should evaluate these measures as indices and compare the relative magnitude of these indices among vocational graduates and nonvocational graduates.

TRANSFER PAYMENT

Transfer payment is defined as the amount of payment paid from one party to another without receiving the services or contributions of productivity from the other party. The simplest form of transfer payment among a family is the weekly allowance given by the parents to their children. In the public sector, it is the welfare payment paid by the government to low income families. One may argue that vocational education may increase a graduate's employment and earning power and, as a result, government may pay less welfare allowance than otherwise. This reduction of welfare payments may be a benefit to government itself, but may not reduce social benefits because the loss of government money resources is the gain to the low income families. From the entire society's point of view, the total payment still remains unchanged. If we do not compare the interpersonal utility of money, the inference on social benefits in relation to transfer payment is not necessary. It is known that interpersonal utility comparison is difficult to measure and that these measurements are rather subjective. Transfer payment should be considered when it is used to measure the impact of vocational education on the benefits of government programs.

In summary, the task of measuring benefits is at least as difficult, if not more so, than the problems of measuring costs. The next section provides a brief review of the previous studies on the benefits of vocational education and the comparison of costs to benefits.

VI. PREVIOUS STUDIES OF THE BENEFITS AND BENEFIT/COST COMPARISON OF VOCATIONAL EDUCATION

Previous benefit-cost analyses of vocational education compared different control groups with the experiences of vocational graduates. The first control group was the group of students in the combined curricula of the comprehensive high school, including students in the academic or college preparatory curriculum, and the general vocational-comprehensive curriculum. However, none of the vocational skills of these students were intensive enough to give them special marketable skills. The second control group consisted of only the students in the academic or college preparatory curriculum. All these graduates joined the labor market after high school graduation.

Most previous studies on the benefits of vocational education placed emphasis on the economic benefits and basically excluded the noneconomic benefits (Stromsdorfer, 1972). In Table 8.2 benefits of vocational education are measured in terms of posttraining earnings for vocational graduates, from six year to ten year periods. It may be argued that the vocational graduates, as compared to the academic graduates, may place a greater value on earnings than on the nonmonetary gratification to be had from a job. Thus, the benefits to vocational graduates may be overstated, because having immediate money income may be less important to the academic graduate than to the vocational graduate.

Table 8.2 provides the estimated rate of return and net present values of costs and benefits of vocational education by previous studies. These calculations are based on both operating costs and total resources costs (including operating costs, capital costs, and opportunity costs), respectively. Discussion in this chapter will focus on the comparison between benefit to total resource cost. The Hu et al., (1969) study indicated that vocational graduates earned an average of $343 and $643 more per year than do comprehensive graduates in the two respective cities. Considering the total costs of vocational education, the average rate of return to vocational education was approximately 8.2 percent for Philadelphia, and 31.8 percent for Detroit. When the benefits and costs were discounted at 10 percent of rate, the net present value of benefits were negative and $1,102 for the two cities, respectively. Similarly, the Fernback and Somers (1970) study indicated that vocational graduates earned an average of $667 more per year than did secondary academic graduates. Total social costs of vocational education amounted to an average of about $720 per year. Therefore, the average rate of return to vocational education was about 21.4 percent. If the rate of discount was at 10 percent, the net present value of benefits for vocational education was $2,484 per vocational graduate.

The study by Eninger (1967), based on 1953-1965 Project Talent data, found that vocational graduates earned $375 more per year than their college preparatory counterparts. Given the total resources costs per vocational student, about $570 per year, the rate of return to vocational education was 13.8 percent, and the net benefits (discounted at the 10 percent rate) was $307 per student.

Table 8.2: Comparative Analysis of Cost and Benefit Estimations of Selected Studies of Secondary Vocational-Technical Education[9]

Name of Study	Time Period of Study[1]	Locus of Study	Experimental Group	Control Group	Average Cost/Year[5]	Average Benefit/Year[6]	Duration of Training in Years	Duration of Benefits in Years[4]	Rate of Return (percent)	Present Value in Dollars 5%	Present Value in Dollars 10%
1. Hu, Lee, and Stromsdorfer	1959-66	Baltimore Phila. Detroit	Vocational[7]/ Technical	Compre-hensive[7]							
a. 2/1. 1.		Phila.			464	343	3	6	9.3	240	Neg
2.		Detroit			386	643	3	6	33.6	1776	1152
b. 2/1. 1.		Phila.			485	343	3	6	8.2	183	Neg
2.		Detroit			403	643	3	6	31.8	1772	1102
2. Fernbach and Somers	1964-69	Nation-wide	Vocational-Technical	Secondary Academic							
a.					592; 596; 615[3]/	667	3	10	25.9	2811	1583
b.					711; 715; 738	667	3	10	21.4	2484	1283
3. Project TALENT (Males only)	1953-65	Nation-wide	Vocational-Technical	College Prepara-tory							
a.					465; 483; 483[3]/	375	3	10	17.7	1200	542
b.					560; 574; 585	375	3	10	13.8	943	307

Table 8.2: (Continued)

Name of Study	Time Period of Study[1]	Locus of Study	Experimental Group	Control Group	Average Cost/Year[5,1]	Average Benefit/Year[6]	Duration of Training in Years	Duration of Benefits in Years[4]	Rate of Return (percent)	Present Value in Dollars 5%	Present Value in Dollars 10%
4. Corazzini (Males only)	1963-64	Worchester, Massachusetts	Vocational-Technical	Comprehensive							
a. 1.					964	312	2	10	23.1	1059	596
2.							2	10	7.4	219	Neg
b. 1.					1129	312	2	10	17.9	862	412
2.							2	10	4.1	Neg	Neg
5. Eninger (Males only) 1956-65:	1950-64	Nation-wide	Vocational-Technical	Academic							
a.					435; 447; 4653/	412	3	10	21.2	1624	763
b.					522; 547; 569	412	3	10	18.3	1358	631
1960-64											
a.					485; 491; 4963/	577	3	10	27.4	2512	1443
b.					582; 589; 595	577	3	10	22.8	2245	1199

Table 8.2: (Continued)

Name of Study	Time Period of Study[1]	Locus of Study	Experimental Group	Control Group	Average Cost/ Year[5]	Average Benefit/ Year[6]	Duration of Training in Years	Duration of Benefits in Years[4]	Rate of Return (percent)	Present Value in Dollars 5%	10%
6. Kaufman and Lewis	1959-65	Three cities in Pennsylvania	Vocational-Technical	Combined Academic and General							
1960					548; 553; 562[3],[8]	837	3	10	34.5	4278	2735
1962					562; 567; 576[3],[8]	611	3	10	25.2	2655	1549
7. Taussig.	1962-65	New York City	Vocational-Technical	Combined Academic and General							
a.					389; 412; 417[11]	240[9] / 0[10]	3	10	6.8 / –	255 / Neg	Neg / Neg
b.					484; 509; 519[11]	240[9] / 0[10]	3	10	4.6 / –	Neg / Neg	Neg / Neg

Notes to Table 2:

1/Time period of study includes the training period as well as the available time for follow-up at the time the data were gathered.

2/(a) Signifies current operating costs; (b) signifies total resource costs to society including current operating costs, capital costs and opportunity costs where applicable.

3/Each cost figure applies to a different year in the relevant 3-year training period.

4/The 6-year benefit for Hu et al., is based on the estimated length of time benefits persisted in the three-city study. The 10-year benefit period is based on Eninger, *Process and Product . . . : The Product, op. cit.*

5/Costs per year are relatively low since opportunity costs (foregone wages) are assumed to be the same between secondary vocational students and comprehensive students. Also, to the extent that they exist, these opportunity costs to society are assumed to be quite low since the influx of all high school students into the labor market at once would depress considerably an already low level of earnings for this age group.

6/All benefits are before-tax earnings and represent a social benefit, that is, an increase in value added to the gross national product.

7/Neither of these two groups had any post-secondary or junior college or college education in the 6-year follow-up period.

8/Exact components of these cost figures are not known. They include at least current operating costs. Note that they are generally consistent with the other figures on the table. These figures are deflated, assuming costs were $553/annum in 1959, the base year.

9/For males only, in training-related jobs, assuming a 12 cent per hour gain and a 2,000 hour working year. Unadjusted for any sociodemographic differences except sex.

10/Females only, in training-related jobs, unadjusted for any sociodemographic differences except sex.

11/Each cost figure is for a separate year, deflated from the 1964-65 base year. Costs are for males and females combined. Costs are difference between two averages.

Sources for Table 2:

1. Teh-wei Hu, et al., *A Cost Effectiveness Study of Vocational Education: A Comparison of Vocational and Nonvocational Education in Secondary Schools*, University Park, Pennsylvania, March 1969.

2. Benefit data are from Susan Fernbach and Gerald G. Somers, *An Analysis of the Economic Benefits of Vocational Education at the Secondary, Post Secondary, and Junior College Levels*, Preliminary Report, Madison, Wisconsin, May 1970. Cost data are from: American Institutes for Research, *An Analysis of Cost and Performance Factors for the Operation and Administration of Vocational Schools for Secondary Programs*, Pittsburgh, Pennsylvania, May 1967.

3. Benefit data are from: U.S. Office of Education, Office of Program Planning and Evaluation, unpublished *Project TALENT* data, 5-year follow-up information on high school graduates of 1960, cited in Howard Vincent, "An Analysis of Vocational Education in Our Secondary Schools," July 1969 (revised), mimeo. Cost data are from: American Insitutes for Research, *An Analysis of Cost . . . , op. cit.*, May 1967.

4. Arthur J. Corazzini, "The Decision to Invest in Vocational Education: An Analysis of Benefits," in *The Journal of Human Resources*, Supplement: *Vocational Education*, Vol. III, 1968.

5. Benefit data are from: Max U. Eninger, *The Process and Product of T and I High School Level Vocational Education in the United States, The Product*, American Institutes for Research, Pittsburgh, Pennsylvania, September 1965. Cost data are from: American Institutes for Research, *An Analysis of Cost . . . , op. cit.*, May 1967.

6. Cost and benefit data are from Jacob J. Kaufman and Morgan V. Lewis, *The Potential of Vocational Education: Observations and Conclusions*, University Park, Pennsylvania, May 1968.

7. Cost and benefit data are from: Michael K. Taussig, "An Economic Analysis of Vocational Education in New York City," *Journal of Human Resources*, Supplement, *Vocational Education*, Vol. III, 1968.

Corazzini (1968) studied samples of male students from the 1963-1964 period in Worchester, Massachusetts. He found that vocational graduates earned $312 more per year than the comprehensive graduate. With cost of training differences, vocational education received about 17.9 percent of rate of return or $412 net present value.

Studies by Eninger (1967), as well as Kaufman and Lewis (1968), found rather large payoff to vocational education. They showed at least 20 percent of rate of return and net benefits of about one thousand dollars. On the other hand, Taussig (1968) used the New York City vocational graduate data and found that vocational education had a rate of return of only 5 to 7 percent, with almost negative present value of benefits. The variations in empirical estimates are due to different methods of computing costs and benefits, and different study samples.

With a similar approach of benefit-cost estimation, Fernback and Somers (1970) found a postsecondary vocational graduate earned about $996 per year more than secondary academic graduates. The average total costs per postsecondary vocational graduate were $3,000 per year. The calculated rate of return to postsecondary vocational education was 6.8 percent, and a negative net benefit at 10 percent rate of discount. On the other hand, Carroll and Ihnen (1967) found a 16.5 percent of the rate of return to postsecondary vocational graduates, and $5,157 net present benefits.

It should be noted that there are other nonmonetary and noneconomic benefits of vocational education, which are not included in many previous studies. Only a few studies have provided detailed analysis of nonmonetary benefits. The study by Hu et al., (1969) investigated citizenship in terms of political voting participation and job relatedness to one's educational program of vocational and comprehensive graduates. The study found that vocational education is generally more immediately relevant to the job the vocational graduate has than it is to the job of the academic graduate. However, there was no significant difference between vocational and academic graduates in terms of voting participation. Kaufman and Lewis (1968) studied the job satisfaction of vocational graduates, but no statistical tests were performed to examine the significance of the difference between vocational and nonvocational graduates.

In view of the broad range of cost-benefit estimates and the lack of sufficient measurements of noneconomic benefits, it would be inaccurate to use the straightforward benefit-costs comparison for decision-making. The several weaknesses of a straightforward economic benefit-costs analysis are described below.

First, the type of cost and benefit measures used often leads to the omission of important considerations. It must be recognized that these economic costs and benefits are merely partial or proxy measures for the total costs and benefits. As discussed in earlier sections of this chapter, there are nonmonetary benefits and costs which are difficult to quantify and to place their relative weights in benefits and costs comparison. The investment criteria provide only measurable information. The use of these investment criteria will be valid only if the other nonmeasurable benefits and costs are the same for an alternative program.

Second, in estimating the benefits and costs for a program based on actual data, economists often make several strong assumptions in order to adopt these data for the purpose of evaluation. Therefore, it is important for the decision maker to examine these assumptions, and to question the judgments before making use of benefit-cost ratios.

Finally, the benefit-cost ratio may be very misleading if it is calculated for the program as a whole. Policy makers are interested in the effectiveness of resources at the margin. The ratio for the program as a whole may provide misleading guidance for incremental decisions.

Therefore, one should not accept these cost-benefit evaluations without question. They are not final answers and they do not tell us everything. It is only if one can recognize the limitations of cost-benefit analysis, that one can be discriminating and not fall prey to total skepticism or complete acceptance.

VII. CONCLUDING REMARKS

This chapter has outlined the conceptual issues of measuring the costs and benefits of vocational education, and some empirical studies of vocational education have been reviewed. Cost information alone is not sufficient for meaningful program evaluation and must be related to program benefits. Except for Taussig's study, cost-benefit studies of vocational education have tended to conclude that vocational education pays off economically. Magnitudes of benefit/cost differences vary depending on study samples and methodologies.

All previous studies have suffered from the inadequacy of cost and benefit data available for vocational education. If the federal government, and, by extension, the society wish to pursue a more rational course with respect to investment in education, adequate data must be collected based on sound cost accounting principles, and guided by agreed-upon objectives and definitions of output to measure these objectives. Future studies of vocational education should be focused not only on the economic data but also on the noneconomic benefits and costs of vocational education. In this respect, economists, educators, and psychologists should work together to improve the techniques of benefit-cost analysis of vocational education.

REFERENCES

Carroll, A. B., and Ihnen, L. A. 1967. Costs and returns for two years of post secondary technical schooling: pilot study. *Journal of Political Economy* 75:862-873.

Cohn, E., Hu, T., and Kaufman, J. 1972. *The costs of vocational and nonvocational programs.* University Park: Institute for Research on Human Resources, Pennsylvania State University.

Corazzini, A. 1968. The decision to invest in vocational education: An analysis of costs and benefits. *Journal of Human Resources* 3:88-120.

Eninger, M. U. 1967. *An Analysis of Costs and Performance Factors for the Operation and Administration of Vocational Schools for Secondary Programs.* Pittsburgh, PA: American Institutes for Research. May. (ED 066 554)

Fernback, S., and Somers, G. 1970. *An analysis of economic benefits of vocational education at the secondary, post secondary, and junior college levels.* Madison: University of Wisconsin. May.

Hirshliefer, J., Shreiffer, J., and Milliman, J. 1960. *Water supply: Economics, Technology and Policy.* Chicago: University of Chicago Press.

Hu, T., Stromsdorfer, E. W., and Lee, M. L. 1969. *A cost-effectiveness study of vocational education.* University Park: Institute for Research on Human Resources, Pennsylvania State University.

Judy, R. 1970. Costs: Theoretical and methodological issues. In G. G. Sommers, and W. D. Ward, eds. *Cost-Benefit Analysis of Manpower Policies.* Kingston, Ontario, Canada: Queens University.

Kaufman, J., and Lewis, M. 1968. *The potential of vocational education: Observations and conclusions.* University Park: Institute for Research on Human Resources, Pennsylvania State University.

McKean, R. 1968. The use of shadow prices. In S. B. Chase, Jr., ed. *Problems in Public Expenditure Analysis: Studies of Government Finance.* Washington, DC: The Brookings Institution.

——— 1958. *Efficiency in Government Through Systems Analysis.* New York: Wiley.

Stromsdorfer, E. W. 1972. *Review and synthesis of cost-effectiveness studies of vocational and technical education.* Columbus: Center for Vocational and Technical Education, Ohio State University.

Tausig, M. K. 1968. The economic analysis of vocational education in New York high schools. *Journal of Human Resources* 3:59-87.

FOLLOW-UP RESEARCH AS
AN EVALUATION STRATEGY
Theory and
Methodologies

chapter 9

JONATHAN MORELL | *Hahnemann Medical College*

If follow-up techniques are to be used to their fullest potential as a method of evaluation, it is necessary to consider the unique nature of evaluation as a form of social research (Flaherty and Morell, 1978), and to integrate that understanding with a knowledge of the advantages and disadvantages of follow-up design. It is also necessary to clearly identify those aspects of social research which are most relevant to the design of follow-up studies, and to show how each of those areas contributes to the construction of appropriate and powerful follow-up strategies. The present chapter is an attempt to meet these objectives. Although the focus of the chapter is on follow-up in vocational education programs, the issues presented will have general applicability to a wide range of evaluation settings. In order to meet these objectives the discussion will be presented in six major sections: the uses of follow-up evaluation, inference from follow-up data, attrition, statistical issues, the costs of follow-up, and the choice of relevant variables.

THE USE OF FOLLOW-UP EVALUATION

LONG RANGE CONSEQUENCES

One way to conceptualize the importance of follow-up is to consider the fluctuation of program effects over time. It seems reasonable to assume that the amount of benefit (or harm) which accrues to a person as a result of participation in a program will vary with the length of time since a person's departure from the program. Further it is likely that the magnitude of a program's influence will follow a pattern of "attenuation" or of "snowballing". Attenuation refers to the notion that the majority of influences on people will tend to lead them back to the life style they had before their exposure to a program or treatment. Change is hard, especially when the force for change is brief (as in a training program), and a person's basic life style remains essentially intact.

How much vocational education and job seeking skill must a person have before he or she can bring about long term changes in career and life style? Snowballing refers to the idea that a threshold exists past which a change continues to increase rather than attenuate. Any amount less than the threshold will result in gradual reversion to whatever living context a person had before entry into a vocational training program. Amounts over the critical level will result in relatively long term changes.

Another reasonable assumption is that many efforts at social or individual change will have unintended consequences, both positive and negative, and that the occurrence of these effects may not be immediately or readily apparent.

Because of the possibility of attenuation and snowballing, and because of the problem of unintended consequences, it is almost impossible to judge the true value of a program without the extended time perspective which is available only through the strategy of follow-up evaluation.

TYPES OF USEFULNESS OF EVALUATION INFORMATION

Evaluation is a form of social research in which considerations of usefulness take on an importance equal to that of validity. The credibility, value, and worth of an evaluation study is enormously decreased if its usefulness cannot be demonstrated. Hence the need to conceptualize the notion of usefulness in a manner which will allow evaluators and planners to systematically consider issues of usefulnes in the process of developing evaluation plans.

There are four general categories of evaluation usefulness, and the design of a study must be specifically tailored to the particular blend of uses which are intended in any given situation. Evaluation can serve to provide realistic expectations concerning what a program can and cannot do; it can provide information to a program's administrators and employees concerning ways to improve their services; it can aid policy makers in determining basic changes in program structure or funding; and finally, it can be used as political ammunition to attack or defend a program. Follow-up studies can play an important part in each of these uses for evaluation only if the most probable use of evaluation information is clearly spelled out before a study is begun. If specific uses are not clearly articulated, variables may be inappropriate for their intended realm of action and the time frame for reporting may be inappropriate. These factors have an important bearing on the usefulness of evaluation, and they are very difficult to change once a study has been implemented.

In sum, the importance of follow-up evaluation must be understood in terms of the advantages of extended time frame research, and also in terms of the unique aspects of evaluation as a form of social research. Extended time frames are necessary to provide information on unintended consequences of program action and on changes in program effects over time. Evaluation perspectives are needed to make sure that the information is useful to its audience.

DRAWING INFERENCES FROM FOLLOW-UP DATA

General Principles

Two basic issues must guide one's planning in the design of research. First, the further removed a study is from true experimental design, the greater the importance and role of data analysis in making decisions about the trustworthiness of research results. Data can be regarded as serving two purposes. The primary purpose is to yield information about some basic question (or questions) of interest. The second purpose is to act as a quality control on itself by providing information on the reliability and validity of the entire corpus of data which has been collected during a study. The second purpose is served by special analyses to check for the occurrence of bias, to test the reliability of measurements and scales, to see if actual research procedures conformed to intended research procedures, and the like. All such questions have direct bearing on the general value of the data for use in its intended manner. Although such questions do not relate directly to tests of major hypotheses of interest, they do form the basis of judgements about the adequacy of the data base for its intended purpose. Threats to validity will be present in any design and quality control tests must always be conducted. Any researcher who does not conduct such tests is derelict in his or her duty. On the other hand, the extent to which such tests are *crucial* is very much a function of the research design within which the data were collected. Any study with randomized allocation of subjects to conditions, for example, automatically has credibility which other designs do not have. Similarly, research credibility is increased by the use of multiple measures of the same phenomenon, the adequate use of control groups, an efficient mechanism for checking the accuracy of data as it is collected, and numerous other elements of sound research practice. Some research is inherently valid by virtue of the research design. In the language of Campbell and Stanley (1966) the issue becomes the manner in which plausible rival hypotheses are ruled out.[1] In some cases they are ruled out by the design of the research, while in other cases they are ruled out by additional data analyses. Although there is *always* an imperative to use research data to help with validity checks, there is wide variation among different studies with respect to the centrality of such checks in making decisions about the value of a corpus of data. As the logic of a research design admits more and more plausible alternate hypotheses, there must be increased reliance on the research data for decisions about validity. Further, as the opportunity to implement structurally sound designs decreases, the need increases for the collection of extra data for the express purpose of making judgements about validity.

Most follow-up studies in vocational education are not conducted according to the dictates of sound research design, and consequently, it is very important to collect as much data as possible to help with decisions concerning the value of such work.

The second basic issue which must guide thinking about follow-up design is that the analysis of any specific body of data is difficult (some might say meaningless) in the absence of a well developed "knowledge context" concerning the phenomenon under study. On one level this is true because of the inaccuracy and variability of statistical data which can be collected from any single study or sample. Samples may be atypical of the population from which they are drawn, and with only one sample in hand it is very difficult to know whether the data can be trusted. To complicate matters, human beings have a nasty habit of intuitively underestimating the size of samples that are needed to detect effects or phenomena which may actually exist (Tversky and Kahnemann, 1971). Consequently, estimates drawn from a limited number of samples, or from small samples, must be treated with the greatest suspicion. Statistical data become far more meaningful if one has several estimates of a single phenomenon, if a particular investigation has been replicated, or most important, if one has enough understanding of a phenomenon to know whether a particular set of results are plausible. Without such extra information, meaningful interpretation of a set of data is problematical at best.

Full exploitation of data emerges from continual attempts at finding better explanations of data than were previously available. Such attempts hinge on the development of competing interpretations and on debates among the avocates of those interpretations. These debates invariably involve an understanding of the problem under study, a knowledge of related phenomena, and a knowledge of other explanations which have been proposed to interpret similar findings. All of this knowledge represents information which extends considerably beyond the narrowly defined boundaries of specific studies. The knowledge needed is both qualitative and quantitative in character, and must be "extended across time and settings" in order to be most effective in helping to understand research evidence (Campbell, 1974:25).

The need for a "knowledge context" in the interpretation of evaluation data also arises because hypotheses are not generated randomly. The search for knowledge is guided by an elaborate set of expectations and "implicit theories" (Bunge, 1967: Ch. 12; Campbell, 1974). Although it is impossible to specify all of the expectations which guide one's research, it is desirable to specify those which have the closest intellectual proximity to our work. Basic assumptions do help determine what we find, and an understanding of those findings may be sterile without a sense of how they are constrained, directed, and influenced. In a sense, this is an argument for a need for theory as a guide for evaluation activity. (Arguments in support of this position can be found in: Riecken, 1972; Suchman, 1971; Weiss, 1972).

In sum, follow-up studies must be guided by two principles. First, the data bear a heavy responsibility for generating information on the value and validity of what has been found. Although data in all studies have such a role, the importance of that role increases as the design of a study diverges from structures which a priori can be trusted to yield valid information. For better or worse, most follow-up studies are not "structurally valid". This situation does not seem likely to change in the near future. Second, follow-up studies cannot be interpreted in isolation from knowledge which is gained from a multiplicity of sources that are external to the research itself. This is due to the variability of estimates gained through statistical analysis, and from philosophical considerations concerning the ways in which studies are conceptualized, interpreted, and judged.

With these considerations providing a basic framework for thinking about the problem of inference in follow-up studies, I will now proceed to specific recommendations for improving the quality of inferences which can be drawn from follow-up studies.

Post Hoc Follow-Up

There are many occasions where evaluation is not planned at the beginning of a program, or where evaluation procedures are not implemented until a program is in progress or has actually terminated. The general problems of post hoc evaluation are well known and will not be repeated here. On the other hand, there are problems of post hoc research which are particularly salient to the case of follow-up evaluation. The occurrence of these difficulties does not preclude the use of post hoc evaluation. If information is needed, if post hoc follow-up is the only available method of obtaining the information, and if sufficient care is taken to deal with difficulties, post hoc follow-up should most certainly be carried out. People involved in such work must realize, however, that specific issues must be dealt with, that certain problems cannot be fully solved, and that the "absolute value" of the information is likely to be less than in the case of preplanned evaluation.

The likelihood of missing data is bound to increase with delays in the initiation of data collection efforts. As delays increase there is an attendant increase in the cost of obtaining data, the difficulty of locating respondents, the probability that records will become irretrievable, and the likelihood that respondents will forget important information. Although the complete elimination of missing data is an impossibility, it is an excellent ideal guideline for all researchers. One never knows what the responses of missing respondents "would have been", or how those data might have affected group means, statistical hypothesis tests, or trends which might influence data interpretation.

The bias due to missing data is likely to become more complex and less understandable as the time increases between people's receipt of a treatment and the decision to obtain information from them. This is an untested but very reasonable assumption. People who cannot be located or fail to agree to participate a short time after a treatment has been given may very well differ from those who fail to cooperate only after a longer time interval. As the time lag of initial contact increases so does the likelihood of mixing different reasons for failure to cooperate. What direction would the bias take? Is it the more successful people who will be impossible to locate or fail to cooperate in the study, or is the problem greater with the less successful participants? Justification might be given for both points of view, but without hard data that problem must remain in the realm of speculation.

A related problem deals with the accuracy of data which can be obtained in post hoc follow-up evaluation studies. In this regard, hypotheses dealing with respondents' thoughts, feelings, or attitudes are particularly suspect. Researchers must always worry about accuracy and unbiased measurement when dealing with such variables and the further back a person must remember, the more suspect becomes the information which is obtained. Although other types of data might be somewhat more reliable when obtained in a post hoc evaluation, problems still abound. It is always good practice to collect cross validating information on factors such as education, employment, earning power, former places of residence, and other similar variables. Unfortunately time may diminish the researchers ability to locate people who could supply such information, or their willingness to do so. Further, an individual's consent is often needed to gain access to many types of records, and it seems likely that people's willingness to give that consent will decrease as time goes on.

Although a later section of this chapter will be devoted exclusively to methods of dealing with attrition, the matter is mentioned here because of its fundamental importance in conceptualizing the "why and how" of follow-up evaluation.

Another very important problem in post hoc follow-up relates to the use of follow-up to study attenuation and snowballing effects. Of necessity, much post hoc follow-up evaluation involves sampling people at only one time point after they have left a program. Unfortunately, data on a single point in time give no sense of the shape of the curve which describes changes in program effects. A single sampling does not even allow an estimate of the slope of a straight line. If a more complex curve is needed to describe fluctuations in program effects, even two sampling points are inadequate. To make matters worse, it is likely that due to attenuation effects, the greatest impact of a program will peak relatively soon after its termination. Thus, evaluation which is started too late may miss the point of maximum program effect and underestimate the value of the program which is being investigated.

A case can be made in favor of post hoc evaluation as a legitimate and, perhaps even preferred, mode of evaluation (Strasser and Denniston, 1978). Further, there is a well developed literature on the use of available data for the purposes of social research, and such data are a major element in post hoc evaluation (Cook, 1972; Hyman, 1972). Thus all is not lost, from an evaluation point of view, when evaluation plans are not built into a program from the start. On the other hand, post hoc evaluation does limit the quality of data which will be available, the types of questions which might be asked, and the value of the enterprise as a tool for studying fluctuations in program effects.

Determining Program Effects

There is considerable reason to believe that changes observed in people who have undergone employment training may be attributable to numerous factors other than the effects of the training itself (National Council on Employment Policy, 1977). Consequently, interpretation of data from follow-up evaluation must incorporate both the use of comparison groups and the collection of as much information as possible, which will help make judgements about the reasonableness and plausibility of inferences which may be drawn. Unfortunately, the aphorism "more easily said than done" was never more true than it is when the use of control groups is recommended. One solution to the difficulty is to seek out as many "naturally occurring" comparison groups as possible. These are groups which are similar to the group being studied, which are likely to be affected by similar influences, and which have not received the specific training which is being evaluated. As Campbell and Stanley (1966) so aptly point out, this strategy leaves much to be desired, as there are a host of threats to validity which cannot be solved by this approach. On the other hand, the "natural control group" strategy can be a great help if several such groups are used simultaneously, and if there is reliable knowledge about how the factors of major interest "should" behave in the absence of extraordinary events.

An important special case of the natural comparison group strategy is the comparison of program members with their own past performance. This strategy can add considerable strength to an evaluation if it is used in conjunction with other comparison groups, and if there is enough knowledge to predict or guess "what would have been" in the absence of the program which is being evaluated.

Another powerful strategy for determining program effects is the use of replication; i.e., the comparison of evaluation results from several similar evaluations.[2] As explained earlier, estimates from any single study should be viewed with grave suspicion because of statistical variability from sample to sample, and because of threats to validity when evaluation designs are not structurally sound. Confidence in evaluation results increases greatly when data from several similar programs lead to similar conclusions. It becomes difficult to argue that several sets of findings about similar programs are idiosyncratic in such a way as to produce findings which agree.

The question of "where did a change come from" can be approached with strategies other than the observation of comparision groups. (Although there is always an imperative to employ such groups if at all possible.) One might also study the dynamics of a program in order to determine precisely what the program did, and what changes in the participants can be expected from those programatic actions. (Some might call this "process evaluation.") Similar studies might be conducted on the lives of program participants, or on other groups which may help explain why changes might have taken place. Here the focus is not on attributing causality but on understanding the dynamics of change, and using that understanding to make statements about the most probable relationship between the actions of a program and change in participants during a follow-up period. If no such reasonable dynamic can be found, it may be wrong to attribute change to program action no matter what the results of comparisons between various treatment and nontreatment groups. In the case of follow-up evaluation which is often a highly imperfect inference generating system, one should not be too quick to advertise one's inferences unless there is very strong evidence of the accuracy of the conclusions.

As an example of the diversity of avenues which are open for the gathering of evaluation information, consider the following sampling of strategies. (Examples of the application of these techniques can be found in reference Note 3). Qualitative knowledge as manifest by the informed opinion of program participants and other relevant parties can be used as a check on the plausibility of results which emerge from quantitative analysis (Campbell 1974). Techniques based on the judicial adversary system have been developed for use as program evaluation techniques (Levine, Brown, Fitzgerald, Goplerud, Gordon, Jayne-Lazarus, Rosenberg, and Slater, 1978). Anthropological, ethological, and social ecological approaches have been brought to bear on various aspects of program evaluation (Lehmann, 1975; Parlett and Hamilton, 1976). It has even been suggested that the *modus operandi* method can be used for purposes of program evaluation (Scriven, 1976). This technique is useful for making causal statements about unique events for which there is much information but little in the way of comparison groups. It has been used by, among others, historians and coroners. (With such areas of application the method might be more appropriate to evaluation than we might otherwise wish.)

All of these techniques can be used (singly or in combination) to investigate numerous aspects of social or educational programs. They are by no means limited to the case of follow-up evaluation. They are particularly useful in the follow-up case because of the great importance of accurate follow-up information, and the poor research design which so often accompanies follow-up studies. Whenever information is both very important and highly suspect, special efforts must be made to support conclusions with as wide a variety of information as possible.

These nontraditional methods have still another advantage. One of the most important aspects of follow-up evaluation is to check on the occurrence of unintended consequences. It is entirely possible that these occurrences are closely intertwined with a person's general life style and may not be directly or easily attributable to the program which is being evaluated, even though a connection may exist. Given such a state of affairs, methods are called for which are able to explain the complex and subtle forces, influences, and factors which determine people's life styles. Many of the techniques cited here were developed to study the behavior of people in complex social settings, and this can be invaluable to the long range study of unintended consequences of social or educational programs.

Hypothesis Testing

Most follow-up data are correlational. By virtue of the research design (lack of randomization, control groups, and so on) conclusions must be expressed in terms of association among variables rather than in terms of causal relationships. On the other hand, the use of correlational data does not preclude the testing of specific hypotheses. On the contrary, unless it is used to test specific hypotheses the interpretation of data becomes problematical at best. Unless an explicit theory or at least a set of expectations guide data interpretation, no sense can be made of research results. Almost any result might occur by chance. Without a sense of what "should" be, there is little opportunity to decide whether results reflect real, systematic, and relevant occurrences. Thus, it becomes necessary to specify beforehand which associations are expected and which are not expected, which will be high and which will be low, which will be positive and which will be inverse. Although post hoc hypothesizing can certainly be useful, it cannot be the sole approach to data analysis.

To the extent that evaluators have a duty to explain rather than merely to report, to the extent that follow-up evaluation is more than a description of where people are and what they are doing—to that degree must hypotheses be explicitly stated and tested through the use of follow-up evaluation.

The specification of expectations prior to data analysis can serve as a validity check in addition to its use as a guide to data interpretation. If many expected associations are not found, an entire study might be suspect on the grounds that although the data may reflect some phenomenon, it is not the phenomenon which the researchers thought they were studying.

Summary—Drawing Inference from Follow-Up Data

Although follow-up evaluation entails numerous details and technical issues, the planning of follow-up evaluation studies must be guided by general principles. First, the unique advantages of follow-up evaluation are that it can be used to detect unanticipated consequences of a program, and to estimate fluctuations in a program's influences over time. Second, statistical evidence in isolation from an explanatory context or other supporting information is not to be trusted. Third, the longer one waits to implement follow-up evaluation, the greater the possibility of bias. Fourth, there are many ways to obtain required information, not all of which follow traditional designs of quantitative social science research. Finally, measures of association can and should be used to test specific hypotheses about a program. With these principals in mind, the discussion will now turn to some of the various aspects of technical expertise which must be invoked if valid and appropriate follow-up evaluation is to be conducted.

ATTRITION

Because it is impossible to know how analyses and conclusions would have been affected by information which is lost, "the only complete solution to the problem of missing data is not to have any" (Cochran and Cox, 1957, as quoted in Applebaum and Cramer, 1974). Except for obtaining the missing data (or conducting a new experiment) there is no completely acceptable solution to this problem.

If a researcher can convince himself or herself that the reason for missing data is due only to a random attrition process, all is well, as there is no reason to believe that a random process would introduce bias into the data. Unfortunately, there are very few cases where one can be reasonably certain that an attrition process has occurred on a random basis. On the contrary. In the case of follow-up research in educational settings there is a good deal of evidence to show that attrition processes are not random. (A survey of this evidence can be found in Marcus et al., 1972:196.) The present section will deal first with methods of avoiding attrition, and second, with the imperfect strategies which must be used once the inevitable occurs.

PREVENTING ATTRITION

Marcus et al. (1972) cite empirical evidence to the effect that attrition may be decreased by use of any one of four tactics. First, the form and type of delivery of letters to respondents will affect return rate. As an example, mimeographed letters and non-first class mail tends to decrease response rate (Astin and Panos, 1969). Second, efforts at explaining the objectives of the study to the participants have a positive effect on return rate. Third, repeated reminders to nonrespondents have a beneficial effect. Finally, it may be worthwhile to construct a short form of a longer questionnaire which contains only the most crucial questions, and to mail the short form to hard core nonrespondents. Many of the shorter version questionnaires will be returned, especially if it is in a convenient format such as a post card.

Still another tactic for increasing response rate is to pay people for their participation. Those who supply data might well be considered experts whose specialized knowledge is in demand. Viewed in this perspective, payment for cooperation becomes a legitimate tactic. Of course, there is always the problem of bias introduced by such payment, and one might well speculate on the effect of payment on the number and type of responses which are received. Luckily checks on such bias can be performed by randomly choosing a subsection of respondents and not offering them payment, or perhaps not telling them about the possibility of payment until after an initial request for participation has been made. Such a procedure would allow analyses on the effect of payment on willingness to cooperate, and on the effect of such knowledge on the type of responses which are obtained.

A general strategy for reducing problems due to attrition is given by Morell (in press). The plan is to restrict a follow-up study to as narrow and/or as homogeneous a subsection of a population as possible. The basis for this advice is the assumption that highly valid information on a restricted population will lead to more understanding than will less valid information on a more diverse group of people. Limiting the scope of a follow-up study in this way has several advantages. First, the more homogeneous a sample, the greater the probability of detecting differences which do exist, i.e., there is less "noise" or "error variance" in the data. Second, greater efforts can be put into encouraging responses when fewer people are the subjects of follow-up efforts. Finally, it is reasonable to assume that attrition dynamics are dissimilar for different types of respondents and that the greater the diversity of respondents, the harder it is to develop a sense of the effects that drop outs have on data interpretation.

To the extent that attrition is due to respondents simply becoming bothered by constantly having to fill out questionnaires or be interviewed, the problem can be solved by randomly splitting the respondent group into subgroups. By means of this tactic, it becomes unnecessary to interview each group at each follow-up period. Prefollow-up information can be used as a check on the randomization procedure. As long as there are a reasonably large number of respondents, the information obtained at each testing period will be generalizable to the entire group. Further, by varying the schedule of testing, all types of interesting information can be gained. As an example, consider a program designed to retrain unemployed veterans. (There is in fact, considerable activity in this area, as evidenced by the recent establishment of an "Office of Veteran's Affairs" within the Department of Labor.) If 400 veterans have been trained, they could be randomly assigned to one of four groups, each with 100 members. One of the subgroups could be interviewed in *each* of three follow-up testing periods, while the remaining groups would be contacted at only one of the three testing periods. The first group would provide information on the effects of repeated testing. The remaining groups would provide data on treatment effects at various time periods, and that data would be unconfounded with test–retest effects.

ITEM NONRESPONSE

Marcus et al. (1972) also deal with the problem of item nonresponse, i.e., respondents' failure to answer particular items on an otherwise complete questionnaire. In this regard, they remind us of a seemingly simple but apparently often ignored problem. One should not ask questions to which respondents may not have the answer. One must be especially careful if such questions are to be used as an important element of an analysis, and if different groups may have differential abilities to answer the question correctly. (There may be times when the intent of an investigation is to find out if such a differential ability exists, in which case it becomes perfectly legitimate to include such questions.) Although such advice may seem obvious, Marcus et al. cite an example from the Coleman report in which just such a problem occurred.[4]

LOCATING RESPONDENTS

Still another aspect of the attrition problem is the matter of locating respondents. People who cannot be found easily may represent a strong biasing factor because as a group they might be different from those who could be found. Fortunately, locating almost all potential respondents is not nearly as difficult a task as it might at first appear. There is a large literature on the problem of finding potential respondents, and the general conclusion of this literature is that if an investigator considers the matter important enough, a surprisingly large percentage of respondents can indeed be found (Crider, Willits, and Bealer, 1971; Eckland, 1968; McAllister, Butler, and Goe, 1973; McAllister, Goe, and Butler, 1973; Willits, Crider, and Bealer, 1969). The procedures available for tracking people include the use of the mail, telephone directories, public records, personal visits, and communication media such as specialized newspapers, alumni associations, and the like. In one example, 99.9 percent of a sample were located on the basis of ten year old data (Crider, Willits, and Bealer, 1971).

All writers on the topic of locating respondents agree that the best tactic is not to lose track of people in the first place. The only way to meet this objective is to obtain as much information as possible which will help maintain contact, prepare people to expect follow-up, to report changes of address, and endeavor to keep people's interest in a project at a high level. Since vocational education programs usually take more than a short period of time, ample opportunity exists to meet this objective. A good deal of information can be collected during registration periods and during the course of training itself. More important, the training program can include as part of its curriculum, discussion of the importance of follow-up and instructions as to what information should be submitted when people move, change jobs, or otherwise become more difficult to locate. All precautions notwithstanding, attrition will inevitably occur.

Dealing with the Inevitable

Numerous techniques exist to help researchers understand the types of bias which may exist because of attrition. Although all of these techniques have some value, none of them are any good if they are employed in isolation from an intimate understanding of the phenomenon which is under study. No "bias correction" techniques will be perfect, and there will always be uncertainty as to whether a bias correction technique will help or will simply lead to different types of data interpretation errors. An informed guess must be made, based on as much understanding as possible concerning the dynamics of data, programs, and bias.[5]

COMPARISON OF EARLY AND LATE RESPONDERS

One of the most powerful techniques for understanding attrition bias is to analyze data separately for those who supplied data after various amounts of prodding (Eckland, 1965). First request returns would be analyzed separately from second request returns, and so on. Such a procedure can yield information on systematic changes in the types of people who do not readily cooperate, and perhaps, allow the researcher to extrapolate these estimates to those who did not yield any information at all.

If this procedure is to be beneficial several conditions must be met. First, the pattern of differences between groups of earlier and later respondents must be clear. It is by no means obvious that this should be the case because even if systematic differences do exist, many people in the later response groups will be there for reasons unrelated to those systematic differences. Some people may simply have forgotten, some may have not seen their mail, some may have been particularly busy when the initial request arrived, and so on. Only some of the earlier respondents will differ from later respondents in important ways. Thus, it may be difficult to detect crucial differences between early and late responders even if such differences do exist, and even if the measurement of relevant variables is accurate, reliable, and valid. Second, the researcher must be convinced that there is no important and fundamental difference between later respondents, and those who do not respond at all. Finally, the researcher must know what to look for when searching for differences between early and late responders. Any follow-up evaluation is bound to generate a tremendous amount of data on each individual, not all of which are equally important in detecting bias due to the drop out phenomenon. A nondirected search for any and all statistically significant differences is bound to be fruitless.

COMPARISON OF RESPONDERS AND NONRESPONDERS

Another useful technique for detecting attrition bias is a comparison of respondents and nonrespondents on measures which are available for both. This may include information which was collected while people were still participating in a program, information from earlier follow-up attempts in which all people did participate, or any other information which may be available. Such analyses allow researchers to determine whether respondents and nonrespondents differ on variables which might introduce bias into later analyses. Here, too, the researcher must know what to look for. There is no guarantee that any observed difference will be important. Further, initial differences cannot be assumed to remain constant. Are initial differences important? Can they be expected to remain constant or change in a predictable direction? Is it possible to obtain information on such changes? All of these issues must be confronted before observed differences between respondents and nonrespondents can be used for meaningful explanations of bias due to nonresponse.

PARTIALLY COMPLETE DATA SETS

The attrition phenomenon is often manifest not as complete sets of missing data but as a few incomplete items on otherwise acceptable questionnaires. As always, this phenomenon presents little difficulty if the data are missing randomly, i.e., if the reasons for the missing data have no systematic relation to the questions which have been asked. How tenable is the assertion that a purely random process governs the occurrence of missing items? One way to find out is to search for obvious patterns in the missing data. Were the same questions left unanswered by a relatively large proportion of respondents? Were the missing items of a sensitive nature where one might expect a hesitancy to supply data? Did the same individual leave out a particular question on several follow-up questionnaires? Do people tend to omit answers to all items on a questionnaire which touch on the same issue? Do people who omit certain answers differ from the rest of the respondents in terms of the information which they did supply? These are the types of questions which must be answered in order to obtain a meaningful understanding of the implication of missing items.

STATISTICAL CORRECTION FOR MISSING DATA

In addition to the suggestions listed here, many other types of procedures are available for dealing with missing data, whether in the form of individual items or entire data sets. Among the suggestions discussed by Marcus et al. (1972) are: choosing appropriate alternate sample lists to "fill in" new respondents; weighing responses by the proportion of people responding; and matching nonrespondents to respondents with similar characteristics, and using the mean of the matched group as a value for the missing data. Although this is by no means an exhaustive list of strategies, it does convey a sense of the type of actions that can be taken to get around the missing data problem. All of these methods have serious problems in terms of new bias which may result from the statistical or logical procedures involved, and all may serve only to make an already difficult situation more problematical. Still they do have advantages in that they do represent a directed effort at solving the problem. As a general rule, they should not be used unless potential pitfalls have been carefully considered and the conclusion is reached that some effort is better than no effort. At such times several techniques should be employed in the hope that all will point to the same conclusion.

If one has a relatively large amount of missing data it might be helpful to draw a random sample of that data, and thus enable the evaluator to invest intensive effort in collecting a sample which can be assumed to be representative of the entire set of missing data.

USE OF EMPIRICAL DATA ABOUT DROP OUTS

As a final comment, it is important to realize that the drop out phenomenon has been the object of extensive investigation in a large number of settings (Baekeland and Lundwall, 1975). A great deal has been learned about the characteristics of drop outs, and efforts have been made to formulate general rules about the drop out phenomenon. This literature does not guarantee that general conclusions about drop outs will help interpret any given follow-up attrition problem, but it does hold out the possibility that opinions about attrition can be founded on something more than conjecture or speculation.

CONCLUSION

This section has not been an attempt to supply an exhaustive list of strategies for dealing with attrition in follow-up evaluation. It has been an attempt to supply a large enough sampling of strategies so that the general drift of reasoning about the problem can be understood. An infinite number of strategies are available and the correct choice is highly situation specific. There is, however, an underlying logic to solving the problem of bias due to attrition. This section has been an attempt to convey a sense of that logic.

Summary—The Attrition Problem

From a logical point of view missing data presents very difficult problems of data interpretation because it is impossible to know how trends in data would have been changed as a result of missing information. Various methods exist for estimating the size and direction of bias which may result from attrition. No method is perfect and each introduces its own uncertainties into the data analysis. Still, the correction methods can be used to good advantage if their limits are clearly understood, if they are used in conjunction with in depth understanding of the phenomenon under study, and if conclusions are based on agreement among various techniques.

The best solution to attrition is to exert all efforts at avoiding the problem. Research shows that surprisingly large numbers of respondents can be located, that various techniques for eliciting cooperation do work, and that the missing data problem can in fact be greatly diminished.

STATISTICS

It is beyond the scope of this chapter to explain the details of statistical analyses which may be performed on follow-up data. On the other hand, there are certain crucial statistical issues that researchers must be aware of when designing follow-up studies, which are not usually drawn together in statistical texts. This section will identify those issues, briefly explain why they are important, and point out references where further information might be obtained.

CHANGE SCORES

In a classic article on the use of difference scores in statistical analysis Cronbach and Furby (1970:80) conclude: "It appears that investigators who ask questions regarding gain scores would ordinarily be better advised to frame their questions in other ways." This conclusion is problematical because the use of gain scores seems so intuitively reasonable, especially when an investigator is interested in studying the amount of change over time. People start at level X and end up at level Y. What more sensible approach is there than measuring the amount of change for each individual, average over all individuals, and testing for statistical significance? The reasons why gain scores are problematical are not intuitively easy to understand as they are rooted in elements of measurement theory, which are far removed from every day common sense. Goulet (1975) summarizes the problem as follows: first, difference scores tend to have negative correlations with pretests. The lower a person's initial score, the greater the likelihood that he or she will manifest large changes. This is a consequence of the nature of measurement, and has nothing to do with different systematic "change dynamics" for people with high and low scores. Second, change scores have inherently low reliability. One measure of a person's change is not a particularly good estimator of other measures of that person's change. Here too, the problem is based on the nature of measurement and not on systematic elements of people's behavior. Goulet (1975) also points out that the meaning of scales or measures may change from one testing period to another. He cites the example of a test of problem solving which may become a test of memory upon second administration to the same individual.

Of the numerous suggestions which are made to the change score problem, two principles emerge. First, the problem can be avoided if research is carried out in accordance with true experimental design. When initial equality of groups can be assumed (because of the randomization process) valid statistical tests may be carried out to test for differences between the post test means of experimental and control groups. Further, random assignment opens the door to the appropriate use of pretest scores as covariates in an analysis of covariance, and this will increase the power of statistical tests (Elashoff, 1969). Second, if a study necessitates prediction of scores, the prediction should be based on as much information as possible and not just on a single predictor variable. Viewed in this perspective, multiple regression techniques can be employed which open the door to prediction based on a large amount of information.

NONEQUIVALENT CONTROL GROUPS

Because randomization is so difficult in so many evaluation situations, a good deal of effort has been put into the study of how nonrandomized comparison groups may be used in lieu of randomized controls. On the surface the problem seems relatively simple. Find a group who did not receive a treatment but who, in all other relevant respects, is similar to those who did receive the treatment. Unfortunately, randomization is the only known method to guarantee that two groups will be, on the average, equal. All other equalizing attempts are weak and uncertain in comparison with the process of randomization. The difficulty with nonrandomized comparisons hinges on the concept of "regression artifact" (Campbell and Erlebacher, 1970). The term refers to the tendency of extreme scores, upon retesting, to change in the direction of the mean of the population from which the score was drawn. Regression artifacts come about because part of any observed score is made up of random error which, by definition, will not remain stable from testing to testing. The more extreme an observed value, the more likely it is that upon retesting that observation will move in the direction of the mean rather than away from the mean. This phenomenon occurs because the random component of the score has more "room for movement" in the direction of the mean. On the basis of probability alone there is a larger pool of possible movement in the direction of the mean than in an extreme direction away from the mean. (The more extreme an original score, the greater the possibilities for regression.) The crux of the problem is that in the absence of randomized groups there can be no guarantee that two sets of scores will regress to the *same* mean. As a consequence of differential regression the possibility of observing "pseudo effects" cannot be ruled out. No method of statistical correction can remove all elements of regression artifact. Short of the random allocation of subjects to conditions there is no perfectly acceptable solution to the problem. Fortunately, statisticians have given considerable thought to the problem and have come up with various solutions, all with their unique strengths and weaknesses. Careful application of several of these methods simultaneously can result in meaningful data interpretation. The matter is aptly summed up by Cook and Reichardt (1976:138) in their annotated bibliography of statistical techniques for dealing with nonrandomized comparisons.

Our hope is that anyone concerned with experiments on non-equivalent groups will conduct multiple analyses of the data, trying (a) to rule out different threats with different analyses and (b) to bracket estimates of important parameters that are not known. We encourage the analyst to think of himself as an open minded detective who sifts through considerable messy evidence in numerous analyses and is prepared to draw honestly tentative conclusions in the normal case where one or more alternative interpretations cannot be confidently ruled out. When this happens, conclusions should be qualified and tentative; the analyst should look for replication in others' designs and analyses that do not have the same weaknesses as his own.

COVARIANCE

The analysis of covariance is often employed either to correct for nonrandomized control groups (a problem which has already been discussed), or simply to increase the power of statistical hypothesis tests. The extra power stems from the ability of covariance to remove variation due to extraneous factors. The technique has an elegance and a logic which makes it extremely appealing. Unfortunately, the appeal of covariance analysis is matched by its delicacy and its susceptibility to distortion, as a result of a violation of the assumptions of its underlying statistical model (Elashoff, 1969). It is likely that people are often misled because of the common knowledge that the analysis of variance and regression analysis are fairly robust against violations of their underlying statistical models. If analysis of variance and regression are robust against violations of assumptions, why not also a technique which combines the two? The problem lies with the type of risk that an investigator takes when he or she uses statistical procedures whose assumptions are not upheld. In the case of analysis of variance and regression, the risk is an altered probability of accepting or rejecting null hypotheses, and incorrect estimates of various parameters of interest. Covariance, however, is a technique which "corrects" observed scores, something which other techniques do not do. These corrections are useful only if the same amount and type of correction is applied to all groups which are being compared. Violations of assumptions in analysis of covariance can lead to a situation in which different corrective changes are applied in unknown amounts to different groups. As a result, the interpretation of data becomes highly problematical because there is no way to be sure that one is observing anything but artifacts of the differential correction.

SIZE OF EFFECTS

In scientific research relatively small effects may have very important theoretical implications, and consequently may be worthy of considerable attention (Keppel, 1973:25). The situation is quite different in evaluation, where the primary objective is to help people judge the social utility of a particular program or treatment. Given the major objectives of evaluation, we must attempt to determine not only if our observations are statistically significant, but also if the effects we observe are large enough to be considered in the process of program planning. One approach to the problem is intuitive; given what one knows about a program and the circumstances surrounding its operation, is a particular statistically significant effect important? As an example, does one care about "satisfaction with a program" when evaluating vocational training? Perhaps not, as the only important measures might relate to job finding potential or increases in earnings. A second approach is statistical. One can determine the amount of variation in scores which are accounted for by some other variable, or one can study the power of a statistical test, or in the case of factor analytic type studies, one can determine the variation explained by particular factors (Cohen, 1977; Gorsuch, 1974). In all of these cases the evaluator can study the amount of variation accounted for by particular elements in his or her research, and on the basis of that information decide whether particular elements of a program have practical significance for program planning.

MULTIVARIATE STATISTICS

Although it is common to do statistical analyses which attempt to summarize the effects of many dependent variables, it is far less common to find analyses which deal with multiple independent variables, or with the simultaneous operation of several independent and dependent variables.[6] This is unfortunate as many evaluation situations lend themselves to such analysis. This is particularly true in the case of follow-up evaluation, where people are sampled at several times and where a very large amount of information is collected on each individual. It may well be that many of the most meaningful questions that can be asked about follow-up data involve the simultaneous effects of many variables. In such cases it may be most appropriate (or most meaningful) to employ multivariate techniques. One obvious advantage of such techniques is the need to carry out fewer hypothesis tests, and consequently to reduce the probability of type 1 statistical errors. More important, multivariate analyses greatly expand the number and form of hypotheses about program effects which can be formulated and tested.

NONPARAMETRIC TESTS

It is very tempting to employ parametric tests on many occasions when, strictly speaking, to do so may not be appropriate. The temptation stems from a desire to capture all the information which is contained in interval scales, and a general belief in the robustness of many parametric tests against violations of assumptions. Although these arguments do carry a lot of weight, several factors weigh heavily in favor of giving much more serious consideration to the use of nonparametric tests. First, the power of many nonparametric tests is often surprisingly high, especially if the underlying distribution of scores is not normal (Marascuilo and McSweeney, 1977). Second, depending on the shape of the underlying distribution, the power of nonparametric tests can *exceed* the power of its parametric counterpart. Finally, there is often good reason to believe that the data are, in fact, not normal. As an example, consider a variable which measures the amount of time from graduation until obtaining employment. In any such situation there are bound to be some people who will wait an inordinately long time until first employment, and the shape of the waiting time distribution will almost certainly have a long tail. In such cases parametric methods might well be inappropriate.

Summary—Statistics

This section was designed to identify various statistical issues which are particularly important in the conduct of follow-up evaluation. These issues can be thought of as dealing with three areas: problematical issues in the use of parametric tests, the need to measure effect size in the conduct of evaluation, and the use of multivariate and nonparametric tests. The first category (problematical issues) encompasses the use of change scores, problems in comparisons between nonrandomized groups, and the delicacy of covariance analysis. Studying the magnitude of effects is important because evaluators cannot be concerned only with statistical significance. Their work relates to the practical matter of whether a program should be modified. Consequently, evaluators must deal not only with the existence of systematic differences, but with their practical importance as well. Finally, it was pointed out that nonparametric methods are often more appropriate and more powerful than parametric techniques, despite the robustness of parametric tests with respect to violations of their assumptions. The point was also made that multivariate analysis is often particularly approriate for many questions which are asked during follow-up evaluation.

COST OF FOLLOW-UP EVALUATION

Although relatively little has been written about the cost of follow-up, the information which is available makes it clear that several aspects of cost are especially important (Backstrom and Hursh, 1963; Orr and Neyman, 1965).

The first consideration is the considerable cost of personal interviews with respondents. According to Backstrom and Hursh (1963), survey researchers should employ either professional interviewers or amateurs who are very well trained by those in charge of the study. (The first alternative is preferable.) Insufficiently trained interviewers are bound to make mistakes, to transmit complex expectancy cues to respondents, and in general, to introduce numerous elements of error and bias into the data collection process.

Orr and Neyman (1965) point out that even when mailed questionnaires are the dominant method of data collection, there are times when expert interviewing help might be necessary. Assume that a mailed questionnaire has been sent out, that many have been returned, and that the researcher is faced with the task of obtaining information from nonrespondents. Such information is extremely important because nonrespondents may well have opinions that differ considerably from the opinions held by those who did respond, and it is necessary to check on any bias that nonresponse might introduce into the data analysis. In such a case it becomes vital to obtain a *representative sample* of the nonrespondents for analysis. One solution to the problem is to employ personal interviewers, who by virtue of hard work and face to face contact, are likely to obtain information from a relatively high percentage of those who did not initially respond to the mailed questionnaire. Although Orr and Neyman do not provide any practical advice on the point at which it becomes cost effective to invoke the personal visit strategy, they do make the point that the matter of cost in such research is intimately tied to the problem of nonresponse bias.

There is little published information on the actual cost of conducting follow-up research. Orr and Neyman (1965) calculate that in a follow-up study of 88,000 participants in Project Talent, the overall cost per respondent sought (for costs directly related to producing and mailing questionnaires) was 17.5 cents, and that the cost per questionnaire received came to 58.6 cents. (This cost included the mailing of four waves of questionnaires which resulted in a total of 61,300 returns.) It is difficult to know exactly what the Project Talent study cost because they (by their own admission) do not provide a complete breakdown of all costs for the entire study. Presumably, these costs are not insignificant.

One more general point must be noted. Costs of follow-up are bound to rise sharply as it becomes increasingly difficult to locate respondents. Even if a study does not involve personal visits to a community, time and effort must be put into searching necessary records, and into following the inevitable false leads that go along with the task of locating people. Therefore, from a cost point of view, it is essential to do everything possible before people leave a program to insure their availability and cooperation in future data collection efforts. Vocational education programs often have good opportunities to do this through long-term contact with students in one-two year programs.

RELEVANT VARIABLES AND THE USE OF DATA

MULTIPLE MEASURES OF SUCCESS

If evaluation is to be useful it must provide data on at least several of the intermediate outcomes which play a part in the complex process that leads to major changes in people's life styles. Without such data it is impossible to know precisely where a program has failed, where it has succeeded, and where efforts at program improvement should be directed. (A more detailed analysis of this issue can be found in: Morell, 1977.) Even though employment might be the most important outcome of a vocational training program, evaluators must not limit their efforts exclusively to the measurement of employment, Presumably, there is a complex process of social and psychological change which contributes to a person's ability to seek, find, and maintain employment. Data on employment alone cannot tell program planners precisely where a program is failing and how it should be improved. Essentially the same point is made by Levine (1966) in the course of a cost benefit analysis of a work experience and training program. He argues that many aspects of a person's life affect his or her ability to seek and maintain employment, and that cost benefit analysis should not ignore these issues. As examples, he cites problems of individual and family functioning which are not directly related to the issue of work skills, but which most certainly affect work related activities.

A related problem is the fact that the quality of a vocational training program may be only marginally related to whether its graduates find employment due to the numerous and powerful economic and social forces which influence employment. One might argue that the raison d'être of a vocational program is to help its graduates find employment, and that failure on that criterion implies failure of the program. This might be a valid point of view, but the slightest retreat from such an extreme position makes it necessary to consider the importance of many variables other than employment or earnings.

Another vital issue in determining appropriate measures in the evaluation of vocational programs is that such programs are known to have important secondary effects, which are not directly related to employment per se (National Council on Employment Policy, 1977). These include effects which might influence the labor market, poverty policy, and efforts at equalizing opportunity. Although the council's assessment does not dwell on social and psychological benefits to individuals and their families, it is not unreasonable to assume that such effects also exist. In light of the likelihood of "non-employment" benefits of employment programs, it is clear that an exclusive focus on employment may give an incomplete picture of what such programs accomplish.

PSYCHOLOGICAL VARIABLES

As soon as one adopts the position that psychological outcomes are important for vocational programs, one enters a murky world of ill defined variables, poor measurement, and serious questions as to which variables are really important. In this world one fact stands out. The task of evaluation is to provide data which will be useful for judging the value of a program, and pointing the way to possible improvement. Psychological variables which do not have a relatively direct bearing on this process must not be included. If the object of an investigation is research on the rehabilitation process, then there are few restrictions on which variables might be justifiably included in a study. Evaluators, however, have an ethical imperative to deal with issues that have a high potential to be immediately useful. If there is no such potential, perhaps the best alternative is to do no evaluation at all. In such cases, there is probably a vital need for good research on the topic, but that is not the same as using program related funds for evaluation.

Although there can be no precise method of guaranteeing the relevancy of psychological variables which might be measured, evaluators will be on fairly safe ground if they keep two principles in mind. First, there is at best a complex, diffuse, and indirect relationship between a person's internal psychological state (attitudes, feelings, opinions, and so on) and his or her behavior (Bem and Allen, 1974; Hogan, DeSoto, and Solano, 1977; Kelman 1974; Mischel, 1977). Relationships do exist but they are by no means easy to use in an analysis of behavior. Consequently, if evaluators are interested in people's behavior as a function of a program they should attempt to measure that behavior directly, rather than indirectly, by means of studying psychological states. This advice is not meant to preclude the use of attitudes, feelings, or traits, but such variables should not be used in evaluation without considerable thought and justification. There are times when evaluators might wish to know the relationship between specific attitudes and specific behaviors. Likewise, there are times when knowledge about people's psychological states might be important in and of itself for purposes of evaluation. But the most prudent approach is that such information is not useful for evaluation unless a strong contrary argument can be advanced.

DETERMINING THE USE OF EVALUATION INFORMATION

Morell (in press) has proposed a typology in which "usefulness of evaluation information" can be divided into four general types. First, evaluation can be used to help set realistic expectations for what a program can and cannot accomplish. Second, information can be used by program personnel to improve the quality of a treatment or a service. Third, the information can be used by those who determine policy and funding in order to effect long term changes in a treatment. Finally, information can be used for the political process of defending or attacking a program. Each of these uses of evaluation is legitimate and each demands a different type of data. If evaluation is to be optimally useful evaluators must carefully determine who their clients are, what types of actions those clients might be able to take, and how evaluation information is likely to be used.

EFFECTS OF LENGTH OF FOLLOW-UP

The longer a follow-up study continues the less it resembles program evaluation, and the more it resembles research on the life styles of particular groups of people. As time goes by, so many factors intrude to influence people's behavior and life styles, that it becomes very difficult to sort out the relationship between people's lives and the effects of a single, identifiable program. To the extent that program evaluation objectives can still be met by relatively long term follow-up, the evaluation design must incorporate techniques which are especially designed to study how the complex factors of living affect people's behavior. Fortunately, such techniques have been developed and efforts have been made to use these methods as program evaluation techniques. (These methods have already been introduced in the section "Determining Program Effects.") Another strategy is to combine follow-up studies with ongoing evaluations of similar programs (Grotberg and Searcy, 1972). Such a technique (often used by developmental psychologists) will allow continual comparison between the effects of similar programs at various times and at various lengths of follow-up, and will thus allow an accurate assessment of the complex relationship between program effectiveness and people's life styles.

Finally, evaluators must remember that the need for evaluation data may change over time. Data that were collected to test one set of hypotheses might well be used to test a different set of hypotheses, as the need for information changes with the times. Evaluators must plan for these eventualities by building maximum flexibility into their data files. Flexibility in the use of data is directly related to the manner in which the information is collected, catalogued, managed, and stored. Suggestions as to how these tasks can best be accomplished derive from two sources. First, there is a body of social science research literature which deals with methods of documentation in large scale social research. This literature deals with problems such as the appropriate use of identifiers, setting up a data base that can be easily used by other researchers, keeping track of research procedures, and the like (Rogson, 1975). A second helpful body of literature can be found in the area of management information systems, where the concept of "data structure" has been developed (Burch and Strater, 1974: Ch. 9). The manner in which data are collected and stored in a computer can have profound implications for the types of uses possible with the set of data. People engaged in follow-up evaluation must balance the need to test specific hypotheses with the requirements of developing a data base which might be put to unforseen uses, and this issue is intimately involved with concepts of "data structure".

Summary—Relevant Variables and the Use of Data

Employment is not the only legitimate outcome variable for the evaluation of vocational programs. There is a psychosocial process to vocational training/ rehabilitation, and evaluation information must be obtained on several relevant aspects of that process. Without such information one can not know if a person's employment potential has been changed, or if the training has had significant secondary effects.

Although the selection of relevant variables might involve the measurement of psychological functioning, such measurements should be chosen only with great care, as it is likely that only a few such variables can be justified in an evaluation study.

As a general rule, usefulness of evaluation information can be conceived as falling into four categories: helping to set realistic expectations, aiding program personnel, aiding policy makers, and as input into the political process. Different types of information are most appropriate in each category, and evaluators must give careful thought to the priority order of these four types of uses in the evaluation they are conducting.

As follow-up time increases, it becomes increasingly difficult to clearly relate people's actions to program activities. The passage of time and the effects of participation in a given program become ever more intertwined with numerous and continually evolving factors which influence people's lives. Ultimately, follow-up evaluation loses its link with identifiable programs, and becomes, in essence, a study of the life styles of a particular group of people. Several solutions exist to this problem. One method is to combine follow-up evaluation with the evaluation of similar ongoing programs. Another solution lies in the use of research techniques which are specifically designed to study the complexities of people's behavior in natural settings.

As a final consideration, one must consider the possibility that the uses of a data base will change with time, often in unexpected directions. Therefore, it is important to structure the data base of a follow-up evaluation in as flexible a manner as possible.

CONCLUDING REMARKS

This chapter has attempted to establish follow-up evaluation as a distinct type of social research, and to identify various topics which must be taken into consideration if worthwhile follow-up evaluation is to be carried out. The topics discussed were: general problems of inference, attrition, statistics, costs, and the choice of relevant variables. Although much has been written about all of these subjects in other sources, there is no readily available compendium of information which will show how each area relates to follow-up evaluation. The aim of this chapter has been to bring this information together. Although a single chapter cannot possibly provide all the "how to" information which may be necessary to implement evaluation, it can identify issues, point out pitfalls, and convey a sense of how problems might be solved.

Two very important issues have been omitted, sampling and questionnaire construction. Obviously these subjects are vital to the conduct of any sort of follow-up survey. Fortunately, many excellent books exist on these topics, and the instructions they supply are easily applied to follow-up evaluation studies.[7]

Another important issue which was not discussed is the matter of preserving confidentiality in social research. This omission was due to space considerations, and also because follow-up evaluation of vocational programs does not seem likely to necessitate collection of a great deal of sensitive information. On the other hand, it cannot be said that the preserving of confidentiality is a trivial or an unimportant matter. Evaluators must recognize that problems may exist and that there are effective methods of dealing with many of those problems. The integrity of computerized data files can be insured, or at the very least improved (Bank and Laska, 1978). There are ways to match existing data files to specific questionnaire responses, without anyone knowing the identity of any individual file-questionnaire link (Riecken and Boruch, 1974; Ch. 8). There are ways to let people lie on questionnaire responses without biasing the data, and thereby insure both the validity of the data and the inability of questionnaire data to be used against any individual (Fidler and Kleinknecht, 1977). If an evaluator believes that confidentiality may be a problem this literature must be consulted.

It is also important for evaluators to be aware of other sources which attempt to show how social research techniques can be specifically applied to the follow-up situation. In this regard two works are especially important, *Investigation of Methodological Problems in Educational Research: Longitudinal Methodology* (Goulet et al., 1975), and *An Analytical Review of Longitudinal and Related Studies as they Apply to the Educational Process* (Marcus et al., 1972). A sense of the importance of follow-up for vocational education can be found in: *The Use of follow-up Studies in The Evaluation of Vocational Education* (Sharp and Krasnegor, 1966). This report includes a summary of relevant work and an annotated bibliography.

No single follow-up study could possibly incorporate all of the advice given here, and it is difficult to determine what priorities should be followed.

Elsewhere, I have tried to deal with these issues by presenting a system which may help determine whether a proposed evaluation will be sufficiently valid or sufficiently useful for any given situation (Morell, in press). These issues are too lengthy to be dealt with here in detail. As a general rule, I believe that all efforts should be made at increasing the internal validity of data even at the expense of decreased generalizability. I also believe that evaluation and research are different. Unless a study can be justified by its ability to help improve programs, the study cannot be justified as evaluation. (Although it may, of course, be justifiable on numerous other grounds.) Also, I think that it is worthwhile to break "evaluation usefulness" into four categories; evaluation as a guide to setting realistic expectations, evaluation as a tool for program improvement by those who administer programs, evaluation as a guide to policy, and evaluation for the sake of the political value of its information. The specific content and focus of a study will change depending on the importance of each of these uses, and evaluation plans must be developed with these distinctions in mind.

Finally, when designing a follow-up evaluation it is important to remember that the follow-up strategy has distinct advantages which cannot be supplied by any other approach. It can yield information on the staying power of a treatment or a program, it can provide a picture of the fluctuations of effects over time, and it can tell us a great deal about unintended consequences. These are the unique advantages of follow-up evaluation, and all efforts must be made to exploit those advantages to the fullest.

NOTES

1. The Campbell and Stanley (1966) typology of threats to validity has been expanded and made considerably more relevant to those engaged in various forms of applied social research. Details of the new version can be found in: Cook and Campbell, 1976.

2. Although the use of replication is an extremely useful tool in data analysis, its most powerful application is not as obvious or easy as one might think. Excellent discussions of the issues involved in the analysis of replicated research can be found in: Keppel, 1973: Ch. 24, and in Rosenthal, 1978.

3. Campbell's (1974) main point is that quantitative data are inextricably embedded within a background of untested assumptions and qualitative understanding. By making some of that background structure explicit, we increase our understanding of the validity, meaning, and utility of our quantitative data. As examples, Campbell cites qualitative sociological analysis of interview dynamics, a topic which is ignored by quantitative social scientists who employ census data, monetary records, crime rates, and numerous similar records. All such archival data involve a collection process in which people made judgements concerning what should be recorded, how responses should be categorized, and the like. Further, complex social interactions often take place at the point of collection, and any number of expectations, pressures, and biases might be operative in such situations. Imagine the follow-up evaluation of a vocational training program in which people are asked about their social, vocational, and educational success

during a five or ten year period. It is likely that such inquiries might be quite threatening to respondents, that the amount of threat might cause incorrect responses, and that the structure of a questionnaire or an interview might very well influence the amount of threat or tension which is generated. Unless these issues are understood, quantitative analysis of questionnaire data might be misleading.

Levine et al. (1978) have used the adversary method of evaluation as an evaluative tool for a graduate psychology program. Their example makes it clear that the technique has utility for a wide variety of educational and training contexts, and that it can be relatively easily adapted to numerous organizational settings.

Parlett and Hamilton (1976) claim that educational evaluation should be carried out within a framework of "illuminative evaluation." In this system, evaluators must study the instructional system as it is actually implemented and the "learning milieu," which is defined as "the social-psychological and material environment in which students and teachers work together." In order to perform such evaluations, data are gathered from observation, interviews, questionnaires and tests, and documentary and background sources. The emphasis is not on a technological determination of whether specific objectives have been met, but on an overall asessment of the impact of the program on those who are involved with it.

The idea that entire systems must be studied is echoed by Lehmann (1975), who discusses various traditions in the study of human organizations and settings. These include the studies of psychology, ecology, community, innovation, and evaluation. Each of these contribute in a different way to our understanding of systems, and Lehmann shows how each has something to contribute to the task of program evaluation.

Scriven (1976) has proposed the modus operandi method of logical inference to deal with those situations where only one example of an innovative program is available for study, and where neither control groups nor rigorous pretest data are available. As an example, consider a program such as the Life Long Learning Center of the Free Library of Philadelphia (Pacer, 1978). This program is set up to counsel adults about career choices, career changes, and educational opportunities. Little pretest data are available, intact comparison groups would be very difficult to obtain, waiting lists are short, and resources for long term follow-up are minimal. On the other hand, the program is innovative, it provides a needed service, and it is important to obtain a sense of the value of the program for its participants. In such cases, the modus operandi technique might be useful. The system attempts to detail the logic by which coroners arrive at causal conclusions. Their problem is similar to that of the Life Long Learning Center. There is no comparison group, data are available for only a single "unit", "pretest" information is minimal, and replication is most unlikely. In general, the modus operandi method might be invoked whenever small scale innovative programs need to be evaluated.

4. For those interested in the problem, the original source for this criticism is: Bowles and Levin (1968).

5. Much of the discussion in the following section is based on the work of Marcus et al. (1972). They provide much more detail than can be reported in the present chapter.

6. Some works which might be consulted by those who must deal with such matters are: Gorden, 1977; and Sudman, 1976.

7. See note 6.

REFERENCES

Appelbaum, M. I., and Cramer, E. M. 1978. Some problems in the nonorthogonal analysis of variance. *Psychological Bulletin* 81, 6: 335-343.

Astin, A., and Panos, R. J. 1969. *The Educational and Vocational Development of College Students.* Washington, DC: American Council on Education.

Backstrom, C. H., and Hursh, G. D. 1963. *Survey Research.* Evanston: Northwestern University Press.

Baekeland, F., and Lundwall, L. 1975. Dropping out of treatment: A critical review. *Psychological Bulletin.* 82, 5: 738-783.

Bank, R., and Laska, E. M. 1978. Protecting privacy and confidentiality in a multiple-use multiple-user mental health information system. *Evaluation and Program Planning* 1, 2:151-157.

Bem, D. J., and Allen, A. 1974. On predicting some of the people some of the time: The search for cross situational consistencies in behavior. *Psychological Review* 81, 6: 506-520.

Bowles, S., and Levin, H. M. 1968. The determinants of scholastic achievement—an appraisal of some recent evidence. *Journal of Human Resources* 3: 3-29.

Bunge, M. 1967. *Scientific Research 2: The Search for Truth.* New York: Springer-Verlag.

Burch, J. G., Jr., and Strater, F. R., Jr. 1974. *Information Systems: Theory and Practice.* New York: Wiley.

Campbell, D. T. 1974. "Qualitative knowing in action research." Kurt Lewin Memorial Address, Society for the Psychological Study of Social Issues. Read at the meeting of the American Psychological Association, New Orleans. September.

Campbell, D. T., and Erlebacher, A. 1975. How regression artifacts in quasi-experimental evaluations can mistakenly make compensatory education look harmful. Ch. 19 in E. L. Struening, and M. Guttentag, eds. *Handbook of Evaluation Research.* Beverly Hills: Sage Publications.

Campbell, D. T., and Stanley, J. C. 1966. *Experimental and Quasi-Experimental Designs for Research.* Chicago: Rand McNally.

Cochran, W. G., and Cox, B. M. 1957. *Experimental Designs.* New York: Wiley.

Cohen, J. 1977. *Statistical Power Analysis for the Behavioral Sciences* New York: Academic Press.

Cook, T. D. 1972. *"Secondary Evaluations."* Paper presented at the annual meeting of the American Psychological Association, Honolulu.

Cook, T. D., and Campbell, D. T. 1976. The design and conduct of quasi-experiments and true experiments in field settings. Ch. 7 in M. D. Dunnette, ed. *Handbook of Industrial and Organizational Psychology* Chicago: Rand McNally.

Cook, T. D., and Reichardt, C. S. 1976. GUIDELINES: Statistical analysis of non-equivalent control group designs: A guide to some current literature. *Evaluation* 3, 1-2: 136-138.

Crider, D. M., Willits, F. K., and Bealer, R. C. 1971. Tracking respondents in longitudinal surveys. *Public Opinion Quarterly* 35: 613-620.

Cronbach, L. J., and Furby, L. 1970. How we should measure "change"—or should we? *Psychological Bulletin* 74, 1: 68-80.

Eckland, B. K. 1968. Retrieving mobile cases in longitudinal surveys. *Public Opinion Quarterly* 32: 51-64.

——— 1965. Effects of prodding to increase mailback returns. *Journal of Applied Psychology* 49: 165-169.

Elashoff, J. D. 1969. Analysis of covariance: A delicate instrument. *American Educational Research Journal* 6, 3: 383-401.

Fidler, D. S., and Kleinknecht, R. E. 1977. Randomized response versus direct questioning: Two data collection methods for sensitive information. *Psychological Bulletin* 84, 5: 1045-1049.

Flaherty, E. W., and Morell, J. A. 1978. Evaluation: Manifestations of a new field. *Evaluation and Program Planning* 1: 1-10.

Gorden, R. L. 1977. *Unidimensional Scaling.* New York: Free Press.

Gorsuch, R. L. 1974. *Factor analysis.* Philadelphia: Saunders.

Goulet, L. R. et al. 1975. *Investigation of Methodological Problems in Educational Research:* Longitudinal Methodology. Final Report. Washington, DC: National Institute of Education (DHEW). (ED124541)

Grotberg, E., and Searcy, E. 1972. A statement and working paper on longitudinal/ intervention research. Washington, DC: George Washington University Social Research Group. (ED091056)

Hogan, R., DeSoto, C. B., and Solano, C. 1977. Traits, tests and personality research. *American Psychologist* 32, 4: 255-264.

Hyman, H. H. 1972. *Secondary Analysis of Sample Surveyys.* New York: Wiley.

Kelman, H. C. 1974. Attitudes are alive and well and gainfully employed in the sphere of action. *American Psychologist* 29, 5 310-324.

Keppel, G. 1973. *Design and Analysis: A Researcher's Handbook.* Englewood Cliffs, NJ: Prentice Hall.

Lehmann, S. 1975. Psychology, ecology and community: A setting for evaluative research. Ch. 13 in E. L. Struening, and M. Guttentag, eds. *Handbook of Evaluation Research.* Beverly Hills: Sage Publications.

Levine, A. S. 1966. Cost-benefit analysis of the work experience program: Research strategy. *Welfare in Review.* 4: 1-11.

Levine, M., Brown, E., Fitzgerald, C., Goplerud, E., Gordon, M. E., Jayne-Lazarus, C., Rosenberg, N., and Slater, J. 1978. Adapting the jury trial for program evaluation: A report of an experience. *Evaluation and Program Planning* 1, 2.

Marcus, A. C. et al. 1972. An analytical review of longitudinal and related studies as they apply to the educational process. In *Methodological Foundations for the Study of School Effects,* Vol. 3. Washington, DC: National Center for Educational Statistics (DHEW/OE).

Marascuilo, L. A., and McSweeney, M. 1977. *Nonparametric and Distribution-Free Methods for the social Sciences.* Monterey, CA: Brooks Cole.

McAllister, R. J., Butler, E. W., and Goe, S. J. 1973. Evolution of a strategy for the retrieval of cases in longitudinal survey research. *Sociology and Social Research* 58, 1: 37-47.

McAllister, R. J., Goe, S. J., and Butler, E. W. 1973. Tracking respondents in longitudinal surveys: Some preliminary considerations. *Public Opinion Quarterly* 37, 3: 413-416.

Mischel, W. 1977. On the future of personality measurement. *American Psychologist* 32, 4: 246-254.

Morell, J. A. 1977. Evaluating outcomes in correctional drug abuse rehabilitation programs. Ch. 4 in J. J. Platt, C. Labate, and R. J. Wicks, eds. *Evaluative Research in Correctional Drug Abuse Treatment.* Lexington, MA: Lexington Books.

Morell, J. A. *The Use of Research Techniques for Program Evaluation: An Integration of Established Techniques for New Purposes.* Elmsford, NY: Pergamon Press, (in press).

National Council on Employment Policy. 1977. The impact of employment and training programs. Ch. 20 in M. Guttentag, ed. *Evaluation Studies Review Annual, Vol. 2.* Beverly Hills: Sage Publications.

Orr, D. B., and Neyman, C. A., Jr. 1965. Considerations, costs, and returns in a large scale follow-up study. *Journal of Educational Research* 58, 8: 373-378.

Pacer, M. 1978. "Adult education and community relations." Proceedings of the 13th Annual Conference on Adult Education, Hershey, PA. February.

Parlett, H., and Hamilton, D. 1976. Evaluation as illumination: A new approach to the study of innovatory programs. Ch. 6 in G. V. Glass, ed. *Evaluation Studies Review Annual.* Beverly Hills: Sage Publications.

Riecken, H. 1972. Memorandum on program evaluation. In C. Weiss, ed. *Evaluating Action Programs: Readings in Social Action Research.* Boston: Allyn Bacon.

Riecken, H. W., and Boruch, R. F. 1974. *Social Experimentation: A Method for Planning and Evaluating Social Intervention.* New York: Academic Press.

Rogson, M. M. 1975. "Documentation in massive social science experiments." Paper presented to the 83rd meeting of the American Psychological Association, Chicago.

Rosenthal, R. 1978. Combining results in independent studies. *Psychological Bulletin* 85, 1: 185-193.

Scriven, M. 1976. Maximizing the power of causal investigations: The modus operandi method. Ch. 5 in G. V. Glass, ed. *Evaluation Studies Review Annual.* Beverly Hills: Sage Publications.

Sharp, L. M., and Krasnegor, R. 1966. *The Use of Follow-up in the Evaluation of Vocational Education.* Washington, DC: Bureau of Research, Division of Adult and Vocational Research, Office of Education.

Strasser. S., and Denniston, O. L. 1978. Pre and post planned evaluation: Which is preferable? *Evaluation and Program Planning* 1, 3:195-202.

Suchman, E. A. 1971. Evaluating action programs. In F. G. Caro, ed. *Readings in Evaluation Research.* New York: Russell Sage Foundation.

Sudman, S. 1976. *Applied sampling.* New York: Academic Press.

Tversky, A., and Kahnemann, D. 1971. Belief in the law of small numbers. *Psychological Bulletin* 76, 2: 105-110.

Weiss, C. 1972. The politicization of evaluation research. In C. Weiss, ed. *Evaluating Action Programs: Readings in Social Action Research.* Boston: Allyn Bacon.

Willits, F. K., Crider, D. M., and Bealer, R. C. 1969. *A Design and Assessment of Techniques for locating Respondents in Longitudinal Sociological Studies.* Washington, DC: Center for Epidemiologic Studies, DHEW.

PART III

A major issue for vocational education is the relationship between the requirements of the world of work and the knowledges, skills, and attitudes obtained by the students as they progress through their programs. Are the students being taught what they need to know to successfully perform the job expected of an entry level employee, or is the student being asked to master skills and knowledges that are beyond the level of an entry level employee? Again, is the student being asked to master skills and knowledges that are no longer current, but may have ceased to be of importance fifteen years ago? At the administrative level, is it necessary to continue to offer a program with a particular sequence of courses that are no longer necessary for employment in the real world? Obsolescence of curriculum and instruction, as well as, laboratory and shop facilities are of more immediate concern to the vocational education program than they are in the general and academic programs of the school. For example, although new topics may be added to the basic chemistry course, no one seriously questions the need for continuing to offer the course at the high school level to students in the college preparation track. However, if a large scale program in vocational education was geared to prepare students for the labor force of a particular employer in a certain region and the plant has closed, continuation of the program must be reconsidered. Similarly, the skills required of entry level employees for work in a plant which recently has been modernized and automated would probably be different from those skills required of their counterparts who graduated from the program five and ten years earlier.

Part Three of the Handbook deals with many of these issues by providing discussions of job and task analyses, and the assessment of performance within these tasks and jobs. These approaches to evaluation have frequently been used to assess program objectives of vocational education, instruction, and curriculum. In addition, there is a discussion of the validity of objectives derived by using these procedures. Finally, a major issue of concern is the relationship between statements of objectives and the assessment of student outcomes, in terms of the implementation of these objectives in the classroom by the teachers. This latter issue is of great concern because frequently curriculum development, based on job and task analyses that are valid in the world of work, lose their isomorphic relationship to the expectations of the employers for the graduates of the programs, when implemented in the classroom.

This section of the Handbook, therefore, is concerned with the linkage between employability and vocational education, and describes in detail the evaluation and assessment procedures that have been used to determine the requirements of different jobs, the tasks of which jobs are comprised, the procedures used in assessing performance of employees and student trainees, the validity of objectives so derived, and the problems associated with attempting to develop a system of instruction based on student objectives and criterion referenced assessments.

Charles J. Teryek in his chapter, *An Overview of Job Analysis: Methods, Procedures and Uses in Vocational Education,* describes the definitions of job analysis that have been developed, the data gathering procedures that have been used, the task statements that are subsumed under job analyses, methods for carrying out job analyses, and the uses of job analysis data. At its simplest level, job analysis is meant to document the duties and tasks performed by job incumbents, and to identify the knowledges and skills that are required of them as they perform their jobs. This information is of great importance in developing vocational education curriculum, and in evaluating vocational education in terms of the information provided to students in a particular vocational education program. These procedures make it possible to examine the objectives of vocational education programs in terms of the knowledges, skills, and attitudes required of job incumbents. It is also possible to evaluate the outputs of vocational education programs in terms of the skills, knowledges and attitudes of the graduates as they relate or compare with those of actual job incumbents.

Teryek's chapter describes the more common job analysis methods, including the procedures used by the Department of Labor and their relationship to the *Dictionary of Occupational Titles,* as well as, the definitions used within their system and the instruments used to collect data. Another system described is that of the U.S. Employment Service and its approach to job analysis. A third system that he describes is functional job analysis which establishes a data base that reflects present job realities as well as future job tasks that may be inferred. The fourth approach is the job element method, developed for the U.S. Civil Service Commission, in which job qualification standards are developed along with related measurement devices. The dimensional approaches to job analyses are included, as are the successful data gathering procedures that have been developed and applied to accurately describe jobs as they exist in the real world of work.

As pointed out by Teryek, the major or primary piece of information obtained from the job analysis is the task statement. Analysis of tasks would differ depending on the purposes for which the data are being gathered, and the decisions that have to be made based on these data. Results of task analysis for training programs may very well be different from task analysis for hiring or promotional purposes.

The chapter by B. Michael Berger and Helmut H. Hawkins, *Occupational Analysis: An Automated Approach.* describes the system currently in use by the U.S. Department of Defense, one of the largest training programs in the world. The chapter presents an historical overview of the growth of the system, and the introduction of the Comprehensive Occupational Data Analysis Programs (CODAP) to develop and analyze responses to task list questionnaires. It also describes the task list development procedures, the relative time spent in using scales, the reporting system that CODAP provides, and gives examples in each instance of the input and output provided by the system to the job analyst. The system and its data are not only of importance to the military. The Vocational Technical Education Consortion of States (VTECS) has made extensive use of the army-civilian associated task lists in developing its competency based programs.

A major issue for vocational education and evaluation, even if one has job and task analyses which provide information about the required knowledges, abilities, skills, and attitudes, is the rating of the performance of employees or trainees. The chapter by Dale F. Campbell and Henry C. Lindsey, *Air Force Performance Ratings: Assessment Methods for Occupational Education and Evaluation,* describes the procedures used by the Air Force in rating performance and in using performance ratings as the basic building block on which to plan and develop instructional procedures. The Instructional System Development Approach (ISD) is described as containing five major steps. The first step is the determination of the job requirements through a detailed task analysis, followed by determination of type of instruction to meet the needs of the students, development of objectives, the planning and development of instructional methods, procedures, and equipment, and the evaluation of instruction. The chapter provides a detailed description of the system analysis requirements including the training requirements, and an example of the way in which task performance related to the required standard is developed and assessed.

Examples are given of two types of performance ratings: performance ratings in school while the student is undergoing training, and performance ratings on the job. These latter ratings assess performance after the student has graduated from a technical training program and is actually employed in the job. The chapter also describes the problems of subjectivity in assessing performance, and the procedures that have been used in the Air Force to overcome these difficulties by rating performance according to specified standards. The chapter concludes by briefly describing some instances in which civilian adaptations of the Air Force courses have been implemented.

Assuming: (1) a list describing a job and its associated task analysis, (2) behavioral objectives derived from such a listing, (3) and student outcome measures for these objectives, how does one describe the validity of the system? Paul T. Whitmore, in his chapter, *Content Validity of Behavioral Objectives,* argues that in order to appropriately assess the outputs of a program, it is necessary for the evaluator to be a fully integrated member of the team that is responsible for the development, implementation, and follow-up of the program and its graduates. He states that it is necessary to examine the rationale, procedures, and processes by which the product was derived, and that it is not possible to fully develop the content validity of the package unless the evaluator was involved from the beginning of the process. The problem thus reverts to one of insuring the content validity of the task lists upon which the performance objectives within the system have been based. Whitmore describes the five characteristics of valid task listing procedures, and uses these five characteristics in evaluating the content validity of three different approaches to the development of task lists. He points out that the approaches and procedures used in designing evaluation instruments to examine the task listing procedures can also be used to design instruction. Whitmore includes a brief discussion of the evaluation of program outcomes, in terms of the achievement of the stated program objectives, by indicating that there are two points in time when these objectives can be evaluated. The first measures student performances in the skills specified by the objectives immediately following the instruction, and the second measures performance on the job subsequent to the student's graduation from the program. He also points out that the fact that instructors have developed behavioral objectives does not necessarily mean that these objectives are worth measuring. It is the job of the evaluator to *judge the worth* of measuring the stated objectives. The evaluator arrives at this judgment based on the processes through which the objectives were derived. During this process, it is the function of the evaluator to insist that the objectives be derived from anticipated future instances in which the program graduates will be called on to perform.

Despite a thorough job analysis, task analysis, performance ratings and other student outcomes measures, and an examination of the content validity of the behavioral objectives incorporated into a curriculum, a major issue that remains is the fidelity of the instruction provided by the teacher to the statements of objectives in the curriculum. The chapter by Proper in Part Two of this Handbook indicates the need for documenting the amount of the innovation that is being implemented. In terms of vocational education curriculum, it is necessary to be certain that the teachers are in fact implementing the curriculum and teaching it according to the included tasks and behavioral objectives and using performance ratings or other scales for assessing student performance.

The last chapter in this section by Theodore Abramson and Adrienne Vogrin, *Instructional Support Systems: Curriculum Development and Evaluation by Occupational Education Teachers,* describes an attempt at curriculum development based on tasks, behavioral objectives, and performance ratings. The problem of teacher implementation of curriculum has been dealt with by making the *teachers* responsible for the development, piloting, and evaluation of the curriculum. The project proceeds on the assumption that teachers will in fact implement what they have developed. The definitions of curriculum and evaluation used in this project are shown to be grounded in the literature. The chapter also presents a brief discussion of the growth of and procedures used to implement the system, and gives examples of the objectives and assessments that were worked on by the teachers. Many teachers find it very difficult to write curriculum in behavioral objective terms, and to write assessments of the curriculum modules that simulate the tasks that the students will ultimately be asked to perform on the job. These difficulties are described and examples are given of the types of measures that the teachers did devise and use. The chapter concludes by describing some of the research, evaluation, and development work that remains to be done.

In summary, this section of the Handbook is a description of the assessment procedures that are available to bring the curriculum taught in the schools closer to the actual job requirements of the program graduates. The job analysis, task analysis, behavioral performance ratings and their validity are described in this section. The section concludes by describing a program in which vocational education teachers write and implement a curriculum based on behavioral objectives and criterion referenced assessments. A major issue that remains, even with a curriculum that is closely linked to real job functioning, is the assessment of the student outcomes that result from exposure to vocational education. The next section of the Handbook deals specifically with evaluation measures and testing issues in evaluation of vocational education programs.

AN OVERVIEW OF
JOB ANALYSIS
Methods, Procedures
and Uses in
Vocational Education

chapter 10

CHARLES J. TERYEK   *Educational Testing Service*

The purpose of this chapter is to provide vocational educators with an overview of job analysis. Job analysis is fundamental to the development of job related vocational programs and evaluation techniques. The overview is organized as follows: job analysis definitions, data gathering procedures, task statements, common job analysis methods, and job analysis uses. Advantages and disadvantages of the various job analysis data gathering procedures and common methods are also included.

JOB ANALYSIS DEFINITION

Job analysis has been defined in very general terms as a method used by management to acquire accurate knowledge concerning individual jobs (Bellows, 1954), and as a "fundamental prerequisite for an intelligent attack upon all personnel problems in any organization, whether large or small, public, or private," (Ghiselli & Brown, 1955:17). Because there are many commonly accepted definitions and procedures, job analysis has also been defined by the courts. For example, in *Kirkland v. N.Y. State Department of Correctional Services (1974),* the District Court defined job analysis as "the coming together of subject-matter experts who provide content input and psychometric experts who construct an examination using that input." The court then proceeded to list what it considered to be an acceptable job analysis procedure.

Job analysis in its broadest sense is a systematic procedure for collecting, processing, analyzing, and interpreting information about a job (Sproule,

1974). Job analysis involves the identification of job components and making judgments about their relative importance. The process of job analysis documents duties or tasks performed by job incumbents, and identifies the knowledges, skills, abilities, and personal characteristics required to perform the job. Typically, the job analyst attempts to identify what the worker does; how the worker does it; why the worker does it; and the skills required of the worker to do it (Training and Reference Manual for Job Analysis, 1946:1).

According to Wright (1974:13), a properly executed job analysis should include the following:

- A general description of the work to be done.
- The organizational setting and relationships in which the work is accomplished.
- The specific tasks which are to be carried out by the worker.
- The equipment, tools, and materials to be used.
- The working conditions, including special hazards.
- The qualifications required to learn or to perform these tasks stated in terms of knowledges, skills, abilities and personal characteristics (including physical).
- The expected manner or quality of performance.
- The process and expected outcomes of the performance.

Job analysis data can provide the necessary information to make more job related decisions about recruitment, selection, and training of personnel. Job analysis can also provide the basis for making sound management decisions for classification and advancement of individuals.

The purposes of a job analysis will determine the level of complexity of the analysis. Once the level of complexity is determined, it is important to insure that standardized data gathering techniques are used. One way to prevent individuals from providing different input for the same information is to either borrow or develop standardized definitions for terms used in the job analysis. The literature is abundant with terminology and definitions. It is not important that the definitions may be different across studies. What is important is that the terms are identified and adhered to during a particular study. The U.S. Department of Labor uses the following definitions when conducting a job analysis:

(1) *Element* is the smallest step into which it is practicable to subdivide any work activity without analyzing separate motions, movements, and mental processes involved.

(2) *Task* is one or more elements and is one of the distinct activities that constitute logical and necessary steps in the performance of work by the worker. A task is created whenever human effort, physical or mental, is exerted to accomplish a specific purpose.

(3) *Position* is a collection of tasks constituting the total work assignment of a single worker. There are as many positions as there are workers in the country.

(4) *Job* is a group of positions which are identical with respect to their major or significant tasks and sufficiently alike to justify their being covered by a single analysis. There may be one or many persons employed in the same job (Handbook for Analyzing Jobs, 1973:3).

A common procedure for conducting job analysis is to describe a job in terms of task statements, and to then identify the knowledges, skills, abilities (KSAs), and personal characteristics required to perform the tasks. *Knowledge* is usually defined for job analysis purposes as:

information about facts and concepts and includes how or why things function or what to do to have them function. Knowledge may be acquired by formal didactic means such as in a classroom, or by less formal means such as self-study, personalized instruction, by watching others, or performing tasks of a job (Wilson, 1973:130).

A *skill* is most often considered to be a description of the ability to carry out a specific task by using special competences based upon particular kinds of training and experience. Most studies emphasize that skills are based upon specific training or job experience. Skills are sometimes thought of as being either adaptive, functional, or specific content skills. Adaptive skills are those which a worker has learned early in life, and they are used to cope with the demands of the environment or interpersonal relations. Functional skills are considered as the abilities to carry out tasks dealing with things, data and people, and they are learned from specific training and experience. Specific content skills are the competence necessary to carry out a very specific job that requires extensive training or experience (Wright, 1974:22). A more elaborate scheme that also appears frequently in the job analysis literature identifies the following major skill areas: (1) manual, (2) interpersonal, (3) language, (4) general intellectual, (5) decision-making, and (6) responsibility and the consequence of error (Wilson, 1973:119).

Abilities or attributes are often general descriptions of the characteristics of human beings. One job analysis method, the Position Analysis Questionnaire (McCormick, Jeanert, and Mechum, 1969:3), identifies sixty-seven different human attributes. Wright reported another system which considers only aptitudes that "facilitate the learning of some task or job duty." These kinds of aptitudes are: (1) intelligence, (2) verbal, (3) numerical, (4) spatial, (5) form perception, (6) clerical perception, (7) motor coordination, (8) finger dexterity, (9) manual dexterity, (10) eye-hand-foot coordination, and (11) color discrimination (Wright, 1974:23).

The term *personal characteristics* is used in job analysis to cover a wide variety of physical capacities and concepts. Personality characteristics are also considered in this category. One study (Rosenfeld and Thornton, 1976:166) included items such as open-mindedness, self-confidence, thoughtfulness, tolerance of human nature, general activity, calmness, individualism, and emotional maturity under this term.

DATA GATHERING PROCEDURES

Information about a job can be gathered by a variety of methods. The method selected by a job analyst is determined by the particular job being analyzed and the purpose for analyzing the job. A study whose objective is to develop information for manpower planning in the health professions, would use different data gathering techniques and rating scales than a study that is being used for developing an x-ray technician training program. Each study would emphasize different task data and the analysis of the data could have either a broad or a narrow focus. In the manpower example, the study might focus on the analysis of entire occupations across different organizations for the purpose of developing model job descriptions. In the training example, work procedures, knowledges, skills, abilities and personal characteristics for a job in a specific organization might be studied to develop behavioral objectives for trainees.

Henderson (1976) offered an inclusive list of methods to gather information about a job: (1) interviews with workers or groups of workers performing the job or with managers supervising them; (2) observation of the jobs being performed; (3) completion of a questionnaire by the worker performing a job or by the manager supervising the worker; (4) completion of logs or diaries by employees on each task as it is done over a period of time; (5) any combination of these. The literature or document review technique should be added to this list. A brief description of each data gathering method follows.

THE INTERVIEW

When using this method, job incumbents (individually or in groups) or job incumbent supervisors are questioned to gather the necessary information. Generally, the interview should occur at the work place if conditions permit. In the event of extreme noise, safety problems, or other unfavorable conditions, a location convenient for the worker should be chosen.

The interviewer should attempt to lead the discussion so that it focuses on what the job holder does, and if appropriate, what materials and machines are used, as well as what is produced. Verification of data and clarification of terms, phrases, and so on, can be obtained through supplemental interviews of workers with the same job, or by discussion with the job holder's immediate supervisor.

In addition to being properly introduced to the worker and well prepared, Henderson suggests the job analyst consider the following in the interest of achieving a successful interview:

- Ask the superior responsible for the job to select as an interviewee the employee who knows the most about the job. (He should be careful not to select a "bootlicker." There is also the danger that the worker singled out by the manager may feel that his social interactions with the work group are jeopardized. If this is a problem, the best solution may be to let the group make the selection.)
- Establish immediate rapport with the jobholder, know his name, speak in language he understands, briefly review the purpose of the interview, and explain why he was selected and that he will have the opportunity to review the final job analysis report for accuracy and validity. It's important not to show impatience if the jobholder is nervous or ill at ease.
- Use structured outlines to obtain information wherever possible. When duties are not performed in a regular manner, he should ask the jobholder to describe them in order of importance and frequency of occurrence. He should make sure to give the jobholder enough time to answer and also ask additional questions to stimulate thought about infrequently occurring assignments. At this point, the analyst might well give the jobholder an opportunity to complain about any dissatisfactions.
- The discussion should be focused on what the jobholder does and the materials, devices, tools, machines, and so forth that he uses in performing the job. Distinction should be made between what the jobholder does and what the machinery produces. If the jobholder's comments begin to stray from the confines of the interview, the analyst should summarize the data collected so far and return to the subject. The interview should end on a friendly note with appreciation for the jobholder's time and effort (Henderson, 1976:14).

The interview method has the disadvantages of being relatively costly and time consuming. Its advantages are the opportunity to receive first-hand information and to immediately clarify any questions that may arise.

QUESTIONNAIRES

Questionnaires are usually thought to be useful only when soliciting information from highly verbal workers. However, if properly designed, the questionnaire can be used to solicit information about jobs that are routine, or about jobs that are filled by workers with limited ability to express themselves. This is perhaps the least expensive and most efficient method for collecting information about a job. A properly designed questionnaire can provide a wide variety of information in a minimum amount of time. The major disadvantages are that many workers have to be surveyed to obtain an acceptable number of returns containing the appropriate information, and unless proper preparation of the worker occurs, accurate and complete data will not be submitted.

Some general guidelines to follow when developing a questionnaire are to: (1) ask only absolutely necessary questions, (2) ask brief questions that require brief answers, (3) use a reading level for the questions that roughly approximates the reading level of the workers being surveyed, (4) provide space for additional comments, (5) ask questions in a logically grouped sequence, (6) pay considerable attention to the appearance of the questionnaire.

OBSERVATION

A common method for gathering data about a job is to observe the worker's performance and to record the observations. General categories of information about the job can be identified before the actual observation, and a checklist can be developed. An alternative approach is to simply take notes during the observation while documenting job behaviors, the environment, and the equipment being used. Whichever procedure is used, the job analyst must be careful to observe the entire work cycle. Otherwise, parts of the job that occur infrequently could be omitted. Job analysts suggest that the observation be supplemented with some other method to avoid omission of important job information which could result from inadequate observation.

The observation method is relatively costly and time consuming. It has the added disadvantage of sometimes requiring a backup data gathering method. However, an advantage of the observation is that clarification of unclear behavior can occur immediately if the worker or supervisor is properly prepared.

DIARY OR LOG

This method for gathering data about a job requires that workers keep a record of their activities. Since this is the least structured method, considerable effort and discipline is demanded of the worker. The log can be given structure by requiring that information be recorded at specific intervals. The record can be constructed to include tasks that occur on an hourly, daily, weekly, or monthly basis. Questions for the worker to use as the entries are made can provide additional structure and insure that important data are not omitted.

This method requires that workers have the skill to communicate in writing. They must be able to synthesize their thoughts and record them in clear concise terms. The log, therefore, could present a problem when gathering data about some jobs. The job analyst can overcome this disadvantage, however, by asking the workers to supplement the transcription with tape recordings.

Advantages of this method are its usefulness in gathering data about activities which occur infrequently, and its suitability for use in analyzing professional and highly technical occupations where subtle tasks may tend to be overlooked by the untrained eye.

LITERATURE AND OTHER DOCUMENT REVIEW

When jobs are not subject to rapid change, have remained fairly stable for a period of time, and there is little disruption in organizational continuity, a review of the literature and other documents may be sufficient to provide the necessary job descriptive data. Budgetary reports, organizational charts, existing job descriptions, forms, and other paperwork used by job incumbents are examples of documents that could prove useful for this purpose. The major limitation of this procedure is that complete, appropriate documentation seldom exists and, therefore, data obtained should always be verified by an interview or another procedure.

The interview, observation, questionnaire, literature and document review, and diary or log, can be used singularly or in any combination to gather the necessary data about a job. Generally, the analyst can get the maximum amount of information by combining the observation method with any of the other techniques. Time and budget constraints, availability of professional staff, and the number of workers in each job are but a few of the factors for consideration when selecting a method to gather job data. For all methods, information is usually categorized and recorded on some type of form, as attempts are made to determine the relevance and importance of tasks prior to determining the KSAs and personal characteristics.

TASK STATEMENTS

The primary piece of information obtained from a job analysis is the basic task statement. Task statements contain information about an action by someone to produce an expected output. Task statements must be specific enough to derive KSAs and personal characteristics.

Analysts examine tasks in terms of the decisions that are to be made about the tasks. Collecting and gathering large amounts of data about individual tasks does not indicate the completion of a good task analysis. As stated earlier, analysis of tasks for training purposes differs from analysis of tasks for hiring or promotional purposes. Successful task analysis is, therefore, the process of collecting specific kinds of information which are relevant to the decisions that are to be made.

Folley reports that:

> Describing a task is like describing a person. You can say many things about either. The choice of information to be mentioned depends on what you want to do with the description. For example, if you want to describe a man to his tailor, you would use a standard set of body measurements expressed in the form of clothing sizes. The size of the person is the information relevant to the tailor's purpose of making a suit. In describing the same person to a personnel manager, you would be much more likely to say something about his aptitudes, intelligence and personality characteristics. These are the kinds of information the personnel man needs to know about the person in order to decide whether to hire him. Clothing sizes do not help (Folley, 1964:2).

Task statements generally consist of an action verb, an object, an expected output, and whatever procedures, tools, equipment, or aids that are needed to perform the task.

The Mid Altantic Personnel Assessment Consortium (Job Analysis and Test Development Workshop, 1977), suggested the use of the following four-column chart when developing task statements. (The sample task was provided by the author.)

Verb	Object	Expected output	Equipment, work aids, processes
describes sanitation legal require- ments	to training session participants	to participants to give infor- mation necessary for working within the law	using transparencies instructors' notes, and 1976 Pennsylvania Cosmetology Law Bulletin

The action verb describes observed behavior. Examples of common action verbs are: speaking, handling, copying, jumping, touching, pushing, and lifting.

The object part of a task statement describes the receiver of the action. It is the easiest part of the task statement to define and examples are:

- journeyman level—mechanic
- entry level—cosmetologist
- pretraining candidates

Expected output describes the immediate output expected in relation to the action verb. Expected output usually begins with the word "to" or the phrase "in order to." Examples of acceptable expected outputs are:

- to give job incumbents information needed for decision-making
- in order to provide background for learner to evaluate training

Procedures, tools, equipment, and work aids provide a tangible and meaningful reference associated with the work being analyzed. The items in this category must be clearly and specifically defined so that the task reader can obtain the item referred to. Specific examples in this part of an acceptable task statement are:

- New Jersey State Board of Barbering Law, 301, 1976
- Johnson model 401—liquid scintillation counter (LSC)

In order for task statements to be useful, they must contain all of the information in each of the areas described above. The language in a task statement should be brief and simple, and expressed in a manner that can be easily interpreted by people who have not studied the job. Task statements should be sufficiently well stated so that performance of the task by different individuals produces the same results. They should also provide sufficient information for developing the knowledge, skills, abilities, and personal characteristics for a given job. Another format and example of task statements and supporting data are given below:

Condition: Given information which is circulated at or before the beginning of a tour or shift

Standard: Must comprehend and remember (with the aid of his notebook) all significant timely information needed in the performance of his duties

Task: T 2:   Reads a written description of the major incidents that have occurred within his assignment to identify situations to which he should be attentive

T 3:   Listens to announcements and takes notes on items of concern

T 4:   At the beginning of each tour of duty, picks up a copy of a "hot sheet" listing the license plate numbers of reported stolen vehicles

> T 5: Reads a posted list of known drug addicts, burglars, con-men, places of suspected criminal activities, etc.

(Rosenfeld and Thornton, 1976:64)

COMMON JOB ANALYSIS METHODS

Although there are currently a number of methods available for conducting a job analysis, many of the methods use parts of the Department of Labor model or variations of it. This may be a result of the thoroughness of the model and the ability to tailor it to a particular job or situation. Some of the more widely recognized approaches and variations are discussed below.

DEPARTMENT OF LABOR METHODOLOGY

This is perhaps the most widely used and researched method for conducting job analysis. The history of this method can be traced to the U.S. Employment Service Technique, which resulted from the need to register all working individuals in the population according to their occupational characteristics.

The original classification and analysis schemes reflected the Depression years and the job market of the times (surplus of workers, shortage of jobs), and the methodology consequently emphasized job characteristics. Subsequent variations of the methodology were developed during the war years, and reflected that job market (surplus jobs, shortages of workers). As a result, worker physical demands and personal traits were included.

In 1949, significant resources were allotted to conduct additional research to develop a scheme that reflected what the worker does in a job, and the requirements of the worker to do the job. This research effort became known as the Functional Occupational Classification Project (FOCP). Job analysts sampled over 4,000 jobs to develop a standardized "work performance," "worker traits," classification methodology.

During the late 1950s, FOCP provided the data for developing additional job analysis methodologies that were used experimentally by the State Employment Securities agencies (currently the State Employment Service), and the data were also used in the research and development phase for the third edition of the *Dictionary of Occupational Titles*.

The Department of Labor methodology involves:

> determining what the worker does in relation to Data, People and Things; the methodologies and techniques employed; the materials, products, subject matter, and services involved; machines, tools, equip-

ment, and work aids used; and the traits required of the worker for satisfactory performance (Job Analysis for Human Resource Management, 1974:26).

A brief description of each part of the methodology follows:

Worker Functions: The relationship of all jobs to Data, People, and Things is expressed by the following twenty-three worker functions:

Data	*People*	*Things*
0 synthesizing	0 mentoring	0 setting up
1 coordinating	1 negotiating	1 precision working
2 analyzing	2 instructing	2 operating-controlling
3 compiling	3 supervising	3 driving-operating
4 computing	4 diverting	4 manipulating
5 copying	5 persuading	5 tending
6 comparing	6 speaking-signaling	6 feeding-offbearing
	7 serving	7 handling

(Job Analysis, 1974:58)

Worker functions are listed in order of complexity and the complexity of a job is expressed in terms of this relationship (described below).

Work Fields: There are ninety-nine work fields in which all jobs can be classified. The work fields have been grouped by technological or socioeconomical objectives which are similar and fall within the categories of getting materials and making products, processing information, and providing services.

Machine, Tools, Equipment, and Work Aids: These are instruments and devices which are necessary to perform the specific tasks. The Department of Labor defines each of the separate parts of this category and gives examples of each.

Materials, Products, Subject Matter, and Services: These are basic materials such as fabric, metal, or wood; final products such as automobiles or baskets; knowledge such as physics or insurance; and type of services such as barbering or dental.

Worker Traits: These are the requirements made of the worker. They consist of the following components: (1) training time, (2) aptitudes, (3) temperaments, (4) interests, and (5) physical demands. This information provides the analyst with the trait demands made of the worker, and it helps focus on the type of work involved.

The foregoing summary is intended to familiarize the reader with the basic Department of Labor approach to job analysis. Additional detail can be obtained from the Department's *Handbook for Analyzing Jobs* (1972). The Handbook is an absolute essential for anyone planning to use the method.

POSITION ANALYSIS QUESTIONNAIRE (PAQ)

The PAQ was developed in 1972 by McCormick, Jeaneret, and Mechum at the Purdue University's Occupational Research Center. It consists of 189 job elements which are organized into the following six groups: (1) information input, (2) mediation processes, (3) work situation and job content, (4) interpersonal activities, (5) work output, and (6) miscellaneous job characteristics. Job elements are defined as a "general class of behaviorally related activities," which are human attributes required by a job. The elements do not refer to specific worker activities in a given technological context and as such cannot be considered to be tasks. They represent "generalized human behaviors involved in work" (Job Analysis, 1974:11).

The PAQ is administered in machine scorable form and requires that each element is rated on a scale. Some elements require a simple rating of applicability to a given job, some require a judgment as to "importance," "extent of use," or "time," while others require their own unique scales.

The PAQ also contains a list of seventy-six human traits or attributes which are rated in terms of their relevance to each job element. The result is an attribute profile for each element. The attribute list contains items adapted from the Department of Labor worker traits, and parts of the Structure of Intellect as described by J. P. Guilford (Guilford, 1971).

U.S. EMPLOYMENT SERVICE TECHNIQUE

This method of job analysis evolved over a ten year period from research, reports, and the experience of many job analysts. It was formally accepted as the recommended method for the U.S. Employment Service in 1946, when the procedure was documented in detail (Training and Reference Manual for Job Analysis, 1946). Essentially, seven parts of the job analysis schedule are used to identify the job, accurately describe the job tasks, and indicate the requirements for successful job performance. A brief description of each of the seven job analysis parts follows:

Identification Data: This part of the job analysis is to identify the job title, type of establishment in which the job occurs, the number of job holders, and other similar information.

Work Performed: This part of the job analysis is used to describe the tasks performed by the worker. The scope of the job is clearly defined in terms of what the worker does, how he or she does it, and why she or he does it. Generally, the job duties are tersely described in the present tense with statements that begin with a functional verb.

Source of Workers: This part of the job analysis provides information about job experience and training not necessarily associated with experience. The information indicates to the placement officer or vocational counselor where workers can be recruited and the qualifications workers must have.

Performance requirements: This part of the job analysis provides information that allows detailed analysis of the "basic minimum skills, knowledges, abilities, and responsibilities required of the worker for successful performance of the job" (Training and Reference Manual for Job Analysis, 1946:24). The level of difficulty of the work tasks is determined in light of responsibility, job knowledge, mental application, dexterity, and accuracy.

Comments: This part of the job analysis provides the job analysis user with background information about the job that does not readily fit into any other category. Equipment, materials and supplies, and definitions of terms are included in this section.

Physical Demands: This part of the job analysis describes the physical abilities of the person filling the job, and the working conditions under which the job occurs. Twenty-seven of the most common physical activities are identified, as are twenty-eight working conditions.

Characteristics Required of the Worker: This part of the job analysis provides information about the basic abilities and personal traits necessary to perform the job. Forty-seven worker characteristics have been identified and are evaluated on a four point scale.

The Job Analysis Schedule forms are designed to gather data in the above categories. They vary in detail from completion of a simple checklist for worker characteristics, to blank spaces for a narrative of performance requirements.

FUNCTIONAL JOB ANALYSIS (FJA)

This technique for analyzing jobs was developed in 1955 by Dr. Sidney Fine of the W. E. Upjohn Institute for Employment Research (Prien and Ronan, 1971:371). FJA is concerned with establishing a data base that reflects present job realities, as well as job tasks that may occur in the future. FJA uses modified Department of Labor worker function scales (people, data, things) to categorize job tasks. A job analyst observes and interviews workers to rate both the work performed and the level of instruction required to perform the work.

Functional job analysis uses an eight level scale of worker instructions to indicate the level of discretion a worker has in the performance of a task. Level one of the scale covers situations in which inputs, outputs, tools, equipment, and procedures are all specified. Level eight represents the other extreme of the scale in which information and/or directions comes to the worker in terms of tactical, organizational, strategic, or financial needs.

The worker function scales are used to determine the level of complexity of each task, and the tasks' orientation to data, people and things. Orientation is expressed as a percentage and allows the measurement of a worker's involvement in each of the three worker functions when performing a given task. An example of a task rating is as follows:

> A task which involves analyzing (Data level 4), negotiating (People level 6), and handling (Things level 1) might have the following orientation: Data, 40 percent; People, 55 percent; and Things, 5 percent. Since, according to FJA, every task calls for the worker to function in relation to data, people, *and* things, the minimum orientation for each primitive factor is 5 percent. Thus, for example, no task can be oriented completely to data and people, to the exclusion of things (Job Analysis, 1974:9).

JOB ELEMENT METHOD

The Job Element approach to job analysis was developed by E. S. Primoff of the Personnel Research and Development Center of the U.S. Civil Service Commission. Job elements are defined as fundamental units that describe worker characteristics. A job may be a knowledge, skill, ability, willingness, interest, or personal characteristic that is necessary for successful job performance (Primoff, 1975:2). The method was designed to identify and develop job qualification standards, and related measurement devices. It consists of five basic steps.

The first step requires the selection of a panel of raters (approximately six) who know the requirements of the job. The raters should have actual experience in the job or should have job supervisory responsibility.

The second step requires the panel to meet and develop a set of item contents for each of approximately fifteen job elements.

The third step requires each of the raters to rate each item in the following categories: (1) barely acceptable workers, (2) superior workers, (3) trouble likely, and (4) practicality. A three point scale is used for each category.

The fourth step consists of summarizing the data obtained from the raters. The analyst determines total values for each item across all raters. A total value is derived for each element. A FORTRAN computer program for calculations is available, or hand calculations by clerical staff can be used for this part of the job analysis.

The fifth step involves the interpretation of results. An item index is computed by multiplying the number of Superior ratings (S) for an element times the number of Practical ratings (P), plus a Weight (W) which is derived from the extent to which there will be trouble if the element is ignored. Generally, elements which have the highest item index percentage are considered most useful, and elements with percentages of less than 50 percent are not used. Ideally, the panel participates in the interpretation process.

COMBINATION (MULTIDIMENSIONAL) APPROACH

Rosenfeld and Thornton (1976) suggest a checklist, combination data gathering approach to job analysis. This approach has the advantage of allowing sophisticated factor analysis or a less complicated level of analysis, such as rational judgment by a committee of experts.

The procedure begins with a review of existing job descriptions to develop a draft checklist of tasks. Generally, a review of the literature and a committee of experts will produce sufficient task descriptions. These are supplemented and altered by interviews and observations of a small sample of job incumbents. The checklist is then refined by job analysts, and reviewed with a larger sample of job incumbents and supervisors. The draft checklist is revised and developed into a form that can be self-administered. After a series of pilot tests, the final version of the checklist is administered to a carefully selected sample of workers and various analyses are conducted. The tasks in the Rosenfeld and Thornton study were analyzed in two ways:

(1) By task to identify the more important, complex, etc. tasks in each job and to investigate differences in time spent on individual tasks by race, sex, and other biodata variables.
(2) By statistically grouping tasks (factor analysis) to identify or verify the major dimensions of each job and by statistically grouping people (hierarchical cluster analysis) to identify groups of job incumbents who reported spending their time in similar fashion. (Rosenfeld and Thornton 1976:3).

Other multidimensional methods which incorporate several data gathering techniques and job analysis procedures are the "Domain Sampling" approach (Drauden and Peterson, 1974), and an approach by Dumas and Muthard (1971) which combines a work sampling strategy with Fine's functional job analysis approach.

The domain sampling approach uses an advisory committee to identify the entire domain of worker characteristics for a particular job. A survey of job incumbents is then conducted to determine a "composite average job." A matrix of worker performance requirements and characteristics is then developed by job analysts.

The Dumas and Muthard approach uses a rating form structured according to the people, data, or things categories. Trained observers record a sample of worker behaviors which are analyzed, and performance requirements are inferred.

JOB ANALYSIS USES

In an early article, Zerga (1943) provided the following list of twenty different uses for job analysis information:

(1) Job grading and classification
(2) Wage setting and standardization
(3) Provision of hiring specifications
(4) Clarification of job duties and responsibilities
(5) Transfers and promotions
(6) Adjustment of grievances
(7) Establishment of a common understanding between various levels of workers and management
(8) Defining and outlining promotional steps
(9) Investigating accidents
(10) Indicating faulty work procedures or duplication of effort
(11) Maintaining, operating and adjusting machinery
(12) Time and motion studies
(13) Defining limits of authority
(14) Indicating cases of individual merit
(15) Indicating causes of personal failure
(16) Education and training
(17) Facilitating job placement
(18) Studies of health and fatigue
(19) Scientific guidance
(20) Determining jobs suitable for occupational therapy (Zerga, 1943:251)

The next sections provide a brief description of several major uses of job analysis that appear in the current literature.

Test Development: Recent court decisions have pointed out the necessity for employee selection and promotional tests to be job related. Unless specific relationships can be shown between the work performed and test content, test validity is considered to be questionable. In Griggs v. Duke Power Company, the Court struck down the power company's testing practices which required successful completion of an intelligence test for hiring and promotion. The court stated that:

Neither the high school completion requirement nor the general intelligence test is shown to bear a demonstrable relationship to successful performance of the jobs for which they are used (401 U.S., 1971).

Task data which accurately reflect current job content and requirements provide the single most valuable source for constructing job-related tests.

While this use of job analysis is considered by many to be of value only to major standardized testing producers and users, it is an important use for consideration by the vocational educator. Properly constructed end-of-course or end-of-training written examinations that are derived from existing job requirements could be a valuable tool for providing the employer with the most capable student for filling a job.

Performance Evaluation: As important as performance evaluation is to management, it is often conducted in a superficial manner that yields results of questionable value. The reason for this can probably be traced to the lack of relevant job-related criteria. Vaguely developed performance standards and qualities such as "attitude" and "commitment," which can be and usually are defined differently by various supervisors, make it impossible for an organization to reward its most productive workers. Job analysis can identify the appropriate performance and develop standardized definitions to improve evaluation.

The vocational educator can use job analysis data to develop the criteria for student performance evaluation. A previous section of this chapter discusses the test-development uses of job analysis where the concern was mainly the development of cognitive paper and pencil instruments. Here the emphasis is on the "practical" aspects of a job, and the goal of the vocational educator is to determine if students can perform job-related tasks at a job entry level. By using a properly conducted and current job analysis, the vocational educator can be assured of selecting the most relevant tasks and requiring student performance at the appropriate level.

Training Program Development: The content of private training programs and public vocational schools is frequently based on tradition, misconceptions, or personal whims. Many times this is true of the manner in which school shop equipment and related instructional materials are selected.

In a changing society where technology rapidly creates new jobs and alters existing ones, there is no reason to assume that employees have the same training needs they always had. An up-to-date job analysis can provide the necessary information to design courses or individual lesson plans. Properly written and validated task statements can serve as the basis for behavioral objectives, related evaluation, and assessment needs.

Job Grading and Classification: The grouping of jobs into families for grading and classification purposes begins with the proper analysis of each job. A core of common elements for each job can be identified, and job families, grades, and classes established. Equally important for this purpose is the identification of uncommon job elements. Job groupings which result from this process can provide information that enables an organization to rank jobs across families as well as within families. Comparison within and across organizations can also be made.

Vocational education administrators can find this information helpful in planning the curriculum needs for a school. Data establishing the need for courses which are common across job families, such as mathematics, English, and science, as well as data substantiating the need for specialized courses can be obtained.

Employee and Vocational Counseling: To provide appropriate counseling, the employer and the vocational educator must have specific information about the possibility of vertical progression within an occupation and lateral movement between occupations. Comprehensive career counseling for prospective and senior employees concerning job compensation, training, and so on, can be made available so that career alternatives can be determined.

Recruitment and Selection: The goal of the recruitment officer in an organization and the placement counselor in a vocational school is to place the right person in the right job. Human beings have different attitudes, attributes, temperaments, and abilities. Organizations and jobs within an organization are equally as variable. Job analysis can be used to determine job requirements and the specific qualities required of workers to do the job.

Without properly gathered and validated job information, interviewing for selection is little more than a subjective process, and appropriate placement a matter of chance. Detailed information about jobs gives the recruitment officer and placement counselor a clear picture of job content, and provides the basis for objective decisions.

In summary, various job analysis techniques have been used over the years to describe job requirements and worker qualifications. For test validity purposes, the recently promulgated *Uniform Guidelines on Employee Selection* (1977) state that "any method of job analysis may be used if it provides the information required" (p. 65546). A Detroit study in the emergency medical field, *A Job Analysis Study of Emergency Medical Service Classes* (1974), suggested that any of the professional methods gave essentially identical results even though the costs to use each of the methods varied considerably.

A key point to consider when selecting or modifying a job analysis method is to carefully consider the need for documentation. From the professional standpoint, proper documentation is highly desirable; from the legal standpoint, proper documentation is absolutely essential.

Job analysis will continue to play an important role in selection, classification, education, and assessment. Currently, because each of these purposes require different data and analysis, analysts usually conduct several job analysis of the same job. Research is needed to show if a single job analysis can most efficiently provide the necessary data for all purposes.

Refinement of the job analysis procedure, and the use of computers to store and analyze task data will allow job analysis to become more accessible to people who have a need for it. There is a need to identify procedures to more efficiently computerize, store, and access the data. There is little justification for independent job analysts to repeatedly develop the same task statements.

Finally, research is needed to identify methods to more positively link task statements to relevant knowledges, skills, abilities, and personal characteristics. This task is by far the most difficult, but it is perhaps the most essential.

REFERENCES

A Job Analysis Study of Emergency Medical Service Classes. 1974. Detroit, MI: U.S. Civil Service Commission and the City of Detroit.

Bellows, R. M. 1954. *Psychology of Personnel in Business and Industry.* New York: Prentice-Hall.

Drauden, G. M., and Peterson, N. G. 1974. *A Domain Sampling Approach to Job Analysis.* St. Paul, MN: Department of Personnel, Test Validation Center.

Dumas, N. S., and Muthard, J. E. 1971. Job analysis method for health-related professions: A pilot study of physical therapists. *Journal of Applied Psychology* 55: 453-465.

Folley, J. 1964. *Guidelines for Task Analysis.* Valencia, PA: Applied Science Associates, Inc.

Ghiselli, E., and Brown, C. 1955. *Personnel and Industrial Psychology.* New York: McGraw Hill.

Guilford, J. P. 1971. *The Nature of Human Intelligence.* New York: McGraw-Hill.

Handbook for Analyzing Jobs. 1972. Washington, DC: U.S. Department of Labor, Manpower Administration.

Griggs v. Duke Power Company, 401 United States 424 (1971).

Henderson, R. I. 1976. *Job Descriptions.* AMACOM Division of American Management Association.

Job Analysis and Test Development Workshop. 1977. Harrisburg, PA: Mid Atlantic Personnel Assessment Consortium, May.

Job Analysis for Human Resource Management: A Review of Selected Research and Development. Manpower Research Monograph No. 36. Washington, DC: U.S. Department of Labor, Manpower Administration. 1974.

Kirkland v. New York State Department of Correctional Services, District Court. (1974)

McCormick, E. J., Jeaneret, P. R., and Mechum, R. W. 1969. *The Development and Background of the Position Analysis Questionnaire (PAQ).* Lafayette, IN: Occupational Research Center, Purdue University.

Prien, E., and Ronan, W. 1971. Job analysis: A review of research findings. *Personnel Psychology* 24: 371-396.

Primoff, E. S. 1975. *How to Prepare and Conduct Job Element Examinations.* Washington, DC: U.S. Civil Service Commission, Personnel Research and Development Center.

Rosenfeld, M., and Thornton, R. 1976. *The Development and Validation of a Multi-Jurisdictional Police Examination.* Princeton, NJ: Educational Testing Service.

Sproule, C. F. 1974. *Pennsylvania State Civil Service Commission Examiner's Manual.* Harrisburg: Pennsylvania State Civil Service Commission.

Training and Reference Manual for Job Analysis.1976. Washington, DC: Department of Labor, Employment Service.

Uniform Guidelines on Employee Selection Procedures. 1977. Washington, DC: Federal Register. Vol. 42, No. 251, Dec. 30.

Wilson, M. 1973. *Job Analysis for Human Resource Management.* Washington, DC: Manpower Management Institute. (draft).

Wright, G. H. 1974. *Public Sector Employment Selection.* Chicago: International Personnel Management Association.

Zerga, J. E. 1943. Job analysis: A resume and bibliography. *The Journal of Applied Psychology* 27: 249-267.

OCCUPATIONAL ANALYSIS
An Automated Approach

chapter 11

B. MICHAEL BERGER
HELMUT H. HAWKINS

U.S. Army Military
Personnel Center

INTRODUCTION

This chapter provides an historical overview of the U.S. Army's system for job analysis and a description of its data analysis programs. The Comprehensive Occupational Data Analysis Programs (CODAP), developed by the U.S. Air Force and in use by the U.S. armed forces, several federal and nonfederal agencies, and several foreign military services, will also be discussed in terms of applications to management systems. Finally, the chapter will consider the application of occupational data in the Instructional Systems Development cycle.

HISTORICAL OVERVIEW

In order to define, evaluate and modify the interface between people and machines in large scale organizations, one must gather and analyze job-specific information (Gagne, 1962). As early as World War I (WWI), Army managers recognized this requirement and searched for methods of matching persons to jobs and jobs to persons. In retrospect, these early matching efforts were cumbersome if not crude. Jobs were not rigidly defined and soldiers were simply assigned to perform a series of related tasks. If successful, a person remained in the job. If unsuccessful, the person was transferred. Because promotions were rare and systematic training, if available, was rudimentary at best, workers learned on the job through interaction with skilled supervisors and other soldiers. Eventually a soldier-job match was achieved. Unfortunately, since commanders structured work to meet local needs rather than to match a predetermined standard of performance, a soldier transferred to another job with the same title might be unable to perform the work because former training did not match new requirements (History of the Army Job Analysis System, 1946).

By the end of WWI, however, analysts had identified and classified more than 1000 Army occupations based on cursory observation of worker performance (History of the Army Job Analysis System, 1946). Approximately 560 of these occupations were accompanied by some form of job description, and were thus the official standard for employment of troops. Interestingly, no specifications were developed for pure military occupations (such as infantryman).

The process of identifying occupations and developing specifications on the basis of simple observations continued, more or less unchanged, until the outbreak of hostilities in Europe. The prospects of mobilization and a mammoth increase in the size of the force highlighted the inadequacy of the 1918 procedures. An approach for effecting standardized job requirements based upon comprehensive observation and interview of workers to determine skills, knowledge, and other factors inherent in work, was introduced in 1936 with the assistance of the U.S. Employment Service (Task Analysis, CODAP Executives' Overview Guide, 1973).

The expansion of the 1940s provided a wealth of experience in developing job standards based on information about worker performance gathered from on-site interviews. By the end of the war, observation-interview techniques had been "debugged," and became the standard method for occupational analysis and evaluation.

Unfortunately, the procedure suffered from a number of constraints—it was time-consuming, labor-intensive, and perhaps most importantly, subject to considerable error in accounting for the variation in work performed within a job or occupational grouping. Moreover, due to the variegated number of occupations within the Army structure and the lack of a sufficient number of trained observation-interviewers, job descriptions once developed, tended to remain unchanged despite significant changes in the actual work performed (Holt, 1971).

The advent of high speed computers presented the opportunity for investigation of automated data collection and analysis. In 1966 (Archer, 1966), the Army contracted for a computer based occupational analysis system capable of gathering, storing, retrieving, and summarizing occupational data. The system concept envisioned large scale administration of task inventories to replace individual observation-interviews. In addition, a key-word concept would permit retrieval of data across surveys by focusing on task action verbs such as "manage" or "repair." Finally, the use of task matrices and groups of common tasks would permit comparison of jobs in different fields. In short, the system would permit comparison of job structures, training requirements, and use of personnel at any level.

The first questionnaires consisted of several hundred task statements and equipment items compiled primarily by trainers at Army schools. Task statements were edited and formatted for publication by a small staff who operated the Occupational Data Bank.

Questionnaires were divided into five sections. An Organization Information section provided demographics on the unit in which the individual was employed; a Biographical Data section provided information about the respondent (such as pay level, length of military service, source of training, and civilian education); the Task section contained the job tasks; and an Equipment section listed job related items which the respondent marked as being used or maintained. A Special Requirements section permitted collection of skill and knowledge information pertinent to the job. In these early questionnaires, the demographic information was handwritten, and transferred to the computer via keypunching. This was later redesigned to a response format compatible to the remainder of the questionnaire, which had been designed for optical scanning. The change traded flexibility of open-ended responses regarding job titles and organizational framework, for speed and convenience in the processing of more than 60,000 questionnaires per year.

Respondents rated each task using the following four part "frequency of performance" scale:

NO—if a task had not been performed in the past year,

SELDOM—if a task was performed once per month or less,

OCCASIONALLY—if a task was performed more than once per month, but less than twice a week, and

FREQUENTLY—if done twice a week or more.

It should be noted that the scale modeled ratings made with observation-interview techniques (Army Job Analysis Manual I, 1960), and generally reflected traditional work measurement procedures.

By 1968, computer reports for several enlisted occupations had been prepared for personnel managers and trainers. Flexible formats provided information by specialty, pay level, level of skill (apprentice, fully qualified worker, first line supervisor, and so on), and other variables in terms of the percent of respondents marking each rating scale point. Similar reports were generated for the equipment items, and the skill and knowledge options in the Special Requirements section. A Biographic Summary provided demographic data about respondents and their units.

The computerized system was favorably received in that it overcame the disadvantages of the traditional system of observations and interviews. It was more economical because it provided substantially broader coverage, and hence, greater representativeness of job incumbents and job types. In addition, the data were quantitative and in a standardized format, could be stored, manipulated, and restored for future analyses. Finally, extensive statistical analyses for summarizing the data could be accomplished.

As the system matured, modifications were introduced. For example, the key-word and common task concepts discussed above were found to be difficult, if not impossible, to manage as the number of surveys increased. The purpose for using key words and common tasks was to improve career opportunities for all soldiers. The aim had been to regroup the more than 9000 identified Army duty positions into more manageable patterns. However, to achieve this goal required soldiers to respond to more common rather than job specific tasks, and increased questionnaire length considerably. Moreover, research showed, and continues to show (Army Occupational Survey Program, 1976), that workers rarely perform more than 25 percent of the tasks covered by their occupational specialty. The requirement that every task be rated led to frustrations, which caused respondents to abandon questionnaires entirely or deviate from instructions by making random or incorrect marks as they struggled to find tasks they performed.

In addition, each new task necessitated comparison with every task in the data bank which, by 1971, had grown to more than 450,000 items. Aside from the enormity of this process, the key word concept required identical wording of tasks, even if wording differed from common usage on the job.

The key word and common task concepts were discontinued in 1971, and replaced by job specific questionnaires written in the "language of the job" being surveyed. With this change in procedures, the capability of conducting interoccupation analyses, an original catalyst for automation, had to be changed to a manual operation and was ultimately dropped. Wherever possible, for example in areas of administration, supply, vehicle operations, and other routine topics, standardized task items were used. The task section was modified to include duty or functional headings such as PERFORM VEHICLE MAINTENANCE DUTIES, which grouped related tasks. Headings made it easier for respondents to identify tasks associated with their job, and decreased the respondent and administrative burdens considerably (Proceedings, Military Occupational Data Bank 1971 Users Conference, 1971). A task section page from a 1972 questionnaire is shown in Figure 11.1. In addition to the analytical shortcomings discussed above, the system did not meet the quantitative requirements originally projected. That is, all officer

SECTION 3: TASK STATEMENTS

Fill in the answer space in the:

No column, if task not performed at all in past year.
Seldom column, if task performed once per month or less.
Occasionally column, if done more than once a month, but less than twice a week.
Frequently column, if done twice a week or more.

TASK STATEMENTS		NO	SELDOM	OCCASIONALLY	FREQUENTLY
C. Operate card punch (keypunch) (continued)					
11. Replace print ribbon on card punch machine	11	□	□	□	□
12. Perform routine operator maintenance on card punch	12	□	□	□	□
13. Diagnose/correct machine malfunctions	13	□	□	□	□
D. Operate card verifier	D	□	□	□	□
1. Operate card verifier using a program card	1	□	□	□	□
2. Operate card verifier without using a program card	2	□	□	□	□
3. Clear card jams on card verifier machine	3	□	□	□	□
4. Perform routine operator maintenance on card verifier	4	□	□	□	□
E. Operate sorter	E	□	□	□	□
1. Sort card in minor, intermediate and major sequence	1	□	□	□	□
2. Operate sorter to block sort cards	2	□	□	□	□
3. Sort cards in alphabetical/numerical sequence	3	□	□	□	□
4. Operate sorter to select cards with predetermined data	4	□	□	□	□
5. Operate sorter to select cards by rejection	5	□	□	□	□
6. Operate sorter to count cards	6	□	□	□	□
7. Change, adjust and test sorting brush	7	□	□	□	□
8. Clear card jams on sorter	8	□	□	□	□
9. Perform routine operator maintenance on sorter	9	□	□	□	□
10. Diagnose/correct machine malfunctions	10	□	□	□	□
F. Operate interpreter and wire control panel	F	□	□	□	□
1. Operate interpreter, to print data on cards	1	□	□	□	□
2. Wire interpreter control panel to straight print	2	□	□	□	□
3. Wire interpreter control panel to selective print	3	□	□	□	□
4. Wire interpreter control panel to print repetitively	4	□	□	□	□
5. Wire interpreter control panel for X elimination	5	□	□	□	□

E/741/3/05/27/25/

2665

FIGURE 11.1: Task section page from 1972 U.S. Army occupational survey questionnaire

and enlisted specialties could not be surveyed on a three-year cycle as had been planned. Army units simply could not process or administer the volume of questionnaires such a plan required. More important, however, it had been found that selection, assignment, training, and utilization processes associated with enlisted jobs were far more task dependent and, hence, more amenable to automated analysis, than the management and executive skills associated with officer duties. High dollar payoffs made it prudent to concentrate survey activities in the enlisted area. This policy has continued.

By 1972, surveys of 300 enlisted specialties had been completed. To increase flexibility of output and make it more responsive to user needs, major changes in task rating methods were proposed. Two scales, "relative time spent performing tasks," and "relative task importance," were to be added. In addition, respondents were to report how they learned each task (formal schooling, on the job, and so on) and provide judgments as to how tasks should be learned.

While this planning was in progress, the Army was instructed to review and consider the advantages of a "common system [to be used by all of the services] . . . generally agreed to be useful for minimizing manpower needs such as numbers, quality, training required, etc." (Phillips, 1972).

Analysis revealed that a family of standardized computer programs (collectively known as CODAP–The Comprehensive Occupational Data Analysis Programs), developed by the U.S. Air Force Human Resources Laboratory to support the Air Force occupational analysis program, could replace the Army system and preclude the need for underwriting a major system redesign. While changes would be necessary, virtually all goals for the new Army system would be realized, conversion would be rapid and cost effective, and a basis for interservice research and development in the field of occupational analysis would be established. The latter would be accomplished because each of the other military services was already using the CODAP methodology (CODAP Implication Study, 1972).

Coincident with the system conversion, the staff of the occupational survey element was reorganized along functional lines into three elements— inventory development, survey administration and control, and data analysis. This functional division has recently been supplemented by a small methods and management element.

THE CODAP METHODOLOGY

Conceptually, CODAP is to occupational analysis what BIOMED is to medical research, and SPSS is to the social science researcher. Comprised of a set of interactive computer programs which organize, analyze, and report occupational information, CODAP provides the job analyst or researcher with

TASK SECTION

IF YOU DON'T DO IT – – DON'T MARK IT!

Time Spent on Your Job

Column headers (left to right): VERY LITTLE | BELOW AVERAGE | SLIGHTLY BELOW AVERAGE | AVERAGE | SLIGHTLY ABOVE AVERAGE | ABOVE AVERAGE | VERY MUCH

I DO

		Time Spent on Your Job						

B. Perform lens surfacing calculations/inspection duties (cont) — B

( )								
( ) 21. Record amount and base direction of prescribed prism	21	□	□	□	□	□	□	□
( ) 22. Record identification data	22	□	□	□	□	□	□	□
( ) 23. Record special procedures	23	□	□	□	□	□	□	□
( ) 24. Verify segment inset	24	□	□	□	□	□	□	□
( ) 25. Record segment inset	25	□	□	□	□	□	□	□
( ) 26. Inspect lenses for surface defects using inspection lamp	26	□	□	□	□	□	□	□
( ) 27. Place sphere laps in appropriate storage rack	27	□	□	□	□	□	□	□
( ) 28. Place cylinder laps in appropriate storage racks	28	□	□	□	□	□	□	□
( ) 29. Insp surfaced lenses for power accuracy using lensometer	29	□	□	□	□	□	□	□
( ) 30. Prepare surface worksheet for plastic lens blanks	30	□	□	□	□	□	□	□

C. Perform lens surfacing duties — C

( )								
( ) 1. Layout semi-finished lens blanks for surfacing	1	□	□	□	□	□	□	□
( ) 2. Apply lens coating for blocking	2	□	□	□	□	□	□	□
( ) 3. Block glass/plastic lens blanks using alloy blocking unit	3	□	□	□	□	□	□	□
( ) 4. Reclaim alloy from blocking bodies using reclaim tank	4	□	□	□	□	□	□	□
( ) 5. Clean blocking bodies	5	□	□	□	□	□	□	□
( ) 6. Reduce diameter using chipping pliers	6	□	□	□	□	□	□	□
( ) 7. Reduce diameter using lens cribber	7	□	□	□	□	□	□	□
( ) 8. Select appropriate sphere lap	8	□	□	□	□	□	□	□
( ) 9. Select appropriate cylinder lap	9	□	□	□	□	□	□	□
( ) 10. Clean sphere laps	10	□	□	□	□	□	□	□
( ) 11. Clean cylinder laps	11	□	□	□	□	□	□	□
( ) 12. Check sphere laps for accuracy using gauge set	12	□	□	□	□	□	□	□
( ) 13. Check cylinder laps for accuracy using gauge set	13	□	□	□	□	□	□	□
( ) 14. True sphere laps using truing disc and hand pan	14	□	□	□	□	□	□	□

(right margin: 42E0/3/12/42/25/ ... 0191)

FIGURE 11.2: Task section page from U.S. Army CODAP style occupational survey questionnaire

tremendous flexibility in conducting studies or research in the field of work. While similar in concept to the original Army system described above, CODAP enjoys greater mathematical flexibility by virtue of a different scaling procedure and a more sophisticated task list construction process (Morsh and Archer, 1967; Carpenter, 1974).

The task list is the key element in CODAP because there is a direct relationship between the quality of the list and credibility of scaled output. A task section page from CODAP questionnaire is shown at Figure 11.2. Note that tasks continue to be grouped under functional (duty) categories to minimize a respondent's search for tasks comprising the job he or she performs.

TASK LIST DEVELOPMENT

Task list development begins with a list of suggested task statements from an Army school. An Inventory Development specialist in the Occupational Survey element adds to, or modifies the list by conducting a literature search, limited observation-interviews, and discussions with experienced job incumbents. Items are added or modified to insure complete coverage of worker tasks at all levels of the occupation being surveyed. Throughout the process, attention is given to the construction of task statements on a comparable level of specificity. This is important because tasks are rated on a "relative time spent performing" scale, and all ratings are ultimately converted to percent of total job time in order to account for 100 percent of a worker's time. Therefore, failure to control the level and quality of task statements can significantly erode the quality of the final job description for individuals or groups.

Figure 11.3 illustrates the hierarchial relationship between duties, tasks, and elements. Because job analysis is generally conducted at the task level, the task must be carefully defined. Falling midway between a duty and an element, a task is a statement of a highly specific action. It has a definite beginning and end, is performed in relatively short periods of time, must be observable (in that a definite determination can be made that the task has been performed), must be measurable (in the sense that an observer may conclude that the task has or has not been properly performed), and is independent of other actions. Thus, a task describes a finite and independent part of the job (Analyzing Training Effectiveness, 1976). This definition suggests that a listing of duties in a questionnaire would be too broad and vague, whereas, a list of items written at the element level would be excessively long and detailed. In short, the task appears to be a workable compromise between collecting overly general and overly specific information about the things people do. In the Army, approximately 600 tasks seem

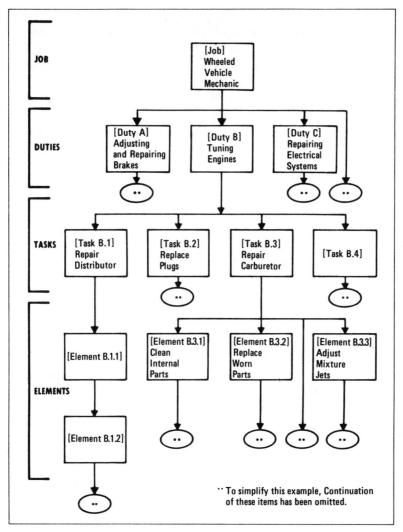

FIGURE 11.3: The hierarchical relationship between duties, tasks and elements. (From "Analyzing Training Effectiveness," Pamphlet 71-8, U.S. Army Training and Doctrine Command, 1976)

sufficient to account for the content of most occupations regardless of pay level, level of skill, type of training, or job location.

In addition to the task section, Army CODAP questionnaires contain five sections designed to address other aspects of work. These are biographical, equipment, special requirements, job satisfaction, and a write-in personal comment section. The number of equipment and special requirement items vary according to the occupation under investigation, in terms of the quantity of equipment and complexity of the job. Biographical, job satisfaction, and personal comment sections are standardized for all questionnaires, and are frequently used for cross-occupational comparisons.

Prior to publication, the questionnaire draft is returned to the school for comments; distributed to a selected group of highly skilled supervisors in the occupation; and discussed with occupational and management analysts who will ultimately use the survey results. Once finalized, the questionnaire is published and distributed worldwide through a network of Survey Project Officers located at major military installations. Experience dictates a census for all jobs with a total population of less than 1000. This generally exceeds requirements for statistical reliability. However, stratification requirements necessary to address some issues, coupled with respondent losses due to travel, training, illness, and occasional unwillingness to respond, make it prudent to collect data from as many job incumbents as possible. Interestingly, by establishing the cutoff at 1000, complete or census coverage is obtainable for more than 70 percent of all Army jobs. In the larger occupations respondents are selected using stratified random sampling procedures, with pay level and location as the primary stratification criteria. Equally broad job incumbent coverage is recommended for nonmilitary applications of CODAP.

THE CODAP RATING SCALE

Traditional occupational analysis relied almost exclusively on Frequency of Performance and similar categorical scales. The CODAP procedure depends almost entirely upon the worker's perceptions of the time spent performing a particular task in relation to another task, i.e., Relative Time. As reported by Christal (1974), the time spent scale has statistical characteristics founded on "a clearly defined range with a base value of zero." Since the sum of individual or group values across rated tasks equals 100 percent, the time spent values for an individual or group of workers can be transformed into the percentage of individual or group time spent on a task. This property renders the relative time spent scale very useful for occupational studies seeking to understand the interrelationship of tasks in a job or series of jobs. Values derived from the relative time spent scale provide the basis for computation of the overlap between individual jobs, individual jobs with a group job description, or one job with another.

In a comparative study (Carpenter, Giorgia, and McFarland, 1975), it was found that the relative time spent scale produced more reliable job information than frequency of performance, or exact percent time spent scales. Moreover, ratings on the relative time spent scale tended to maintain stability and consistency over time—characteristics not readily obtainable with the other scales. Although each of the military services has adjusted the length of the time spent scale to meet its unique requirements (Navy—five point; Air Force—nine point; Army and Marine Corps—seven point), the premise for use of the scale is the same—to account for variations in work on a temporal rather than frequency continuum, so that more powerful statistical manipulation of the data can be performed. The Army's seven point scale is verbally anchored as follows:

(1) very much below average time spent performing
(2) below average time spent performing
(3) slightly below average time spent performing
(4) average time spent performing
(5) slightly above average time spent performing
(6) above average time spent performing
(7) very much above average time spent performing.

Theoretically, a respondent makes a comparative judgment about the relative time spent on each task in relation to other tasks performed as part of the job. In making these judgments, respondents are urged to ignore what might be considered "ideal" amounts of time or what other workers do. Respondents are also instructed to scan the entire task list prior to making their ratings, checking only the tasks they perform. This scanning procedure generally narrows a 600 item task list down to about 150 tasks, which are then rated using the time spent scale. Thus, the ratings deal with work actually performed (including work associated with practice and training), and reveal what workers actually do rather than what they should do.

CODAP DATA APPLICATIONS

The CODAP system offers a convenient, systematic, and flexible procedure for job analysis. A wide variety of computations summarizing what people do are possible using one or more of the programs. Special job descriptions can be ordered to define work performed by any group of individuals possessing personal or situational characteristics captured in the background, equipment, special requirement, or job satisfaction sections of the questionnaire. Such reports might reflect work performed in support of a particular piece of equipment, i.e., tractors or X-ray machines; work performed by men versus women in the same job series (an important issue in contemporary society); work performed by persons possessing different levels of skill or education; work performed by satisfied or dissatisfied job holders; work performed by persons in a particular department, organization or location; work performed as a variation in pay, and so on.

Three of the more commonly used programs and their output reports will be discussed in detail. Brief descriptions of other CODAP programs are included in the Appendix. A hypothetical job, "Widget Repairer" (Information Guide to the Army Occupational Survey Program and Selected CODAP Programs, 1977), will be used in the discussion for ease of illustrating the reports generated by the Job Special, the Group Summary, and the Group Difference programs.

JOB SPECIAL

The Job Special program produces a composite description of the work performed by any group of individuals possessing characteristics of interest, such as:

- Work performed by persons with common job titles.
- Work performed in a .specified department (shipping, maintenance, accounting, and so on).
- Work performed by apprentice, fully qualified, or supervisory personnel in the same occupational field.

Job Special reports provide five items of information for the group selected.

(1) The percent of group members who perform each task.
(2) The average percent time spent on each task by members who perform it.
(3) The percent time spent on each task by all members of the group.
(4) The cumulative percent time spent.
(5) The number of tasks performed.

It should be noted that a task is included in Job Special only if some member of the group performed the task. If not performed it will not appear even though it was included in the questionnaire.

Figure 11.4 depicts a Job Special report prepared at the task level for a group of fifty Widget Repairers selected from a total sample of one hundred. The number of cases (100) are shown at the top of the report, as are the number of duties and tasks in the questionnaire, and the number of members in the group.

In this example the report is keyed to tasks performed at the apprentice level of skill, which forms the basis for the percent of members performing computations. The report shows that 90 percent of this group repairs widgets (task A1), and that this task consumes 50 percent of their total work time. By way of contrast, only 4 percent of the group performs task A5 (Evaluate Subordinate Work Performance), and collectively spend only 5 percent of their work time on this task. Moreover, task A5 represents less than one-fourth of one percent of the total work time for the entire worker sample. Therefore, the task would be considered insignificant for both job identification and training.

The cumulative sum column keeps a running total of the average percent time spent by all members in the group. The information provided in this column is particularly useful if the job tasks have been costed for training resource requirements, in that the training analyst can determine how many tasks can be trained given the total number of training dollars available. For example, if "cost to train" is twenty dollars per task, it will cost one hundred dollars to train all five tasks. However, if resources are limited and training trade-offs must be made, the analyst can report with confidence that training covering approximately 50 percent of the Apprentice Widget Repairers work can be provided for forty dollars. Similar comparisons can be made with respect to costs associated with formal as opposed to on the job training for various tasks.

GROUP SUMMARY

The Group Summary program produces reports based on either the percent of members performing each task, or the average percent time spent by

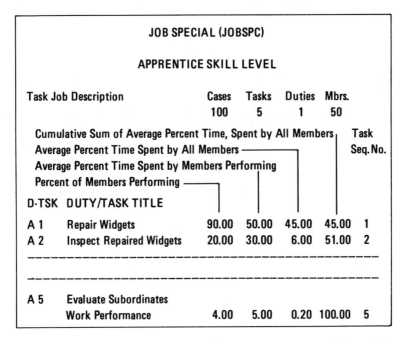

FIGURE 11.4: Example of a CODAP Job Special Report. (Adapted from "CODAP Information Guide," U.S. Army Military Personnel Center, 1977)

```
┌─────────────────────────────────────────────────────────────────────┐
│                      GROUP SUMMARY (GRPSUM)                           │
│                                                                       │
│  Task Group Summary                                                   │
│                                                                       │
│  Percent Members Performing    All      Apprentice   Fully    First-Line │
│                             Respondents            Qualified  Supervisor │
│                                                     Worker            │
│                                                                       │
│  A 1  Repair Widgets          62.00       90.00      40.00     20.00  │
│  A 2  Inspect Repaired Widgets 37.00      20.00      60.00     40.00  │
│  ─────────────────────────────────────────────────────────────────  │
│                                                                       │
│  ─────────────────────────────────────────────────────────────────  │
│                                                                       │
│  A 5  Evaluate Subordinates                                           │
│       Work Performance        31.00        4.00      40.00    100.00  │
└─────────────────────────────────────────────────────────────────────┘
```

FIGURE 11.5: Example of a CODAP Group Summary Report. (Adapted from "CODAP Information Guide," U.S. Army Military Personnel Center, 1977)

all workers in a previously defined group. The information is displayed in duty-task order (the same order in which the tasks appeared in the questionnaire). Group Summary is particularly useful for comparing groups of workers who have different titles but perform similar work, comparing workers at different pay or skill levels, comparing workers having varying levels of job satisfaction, comparing workers at different geographical locations, and so on.

Figure 11.5 depicts a Group Summary report for four groups: the entire Widget Repairer sample, and three progressively more experienced worker levels (apprentice, fully qualified worker, first line supervisor) within the larger sample. The report is keyed to the percent of members performing each task. The report clearly shows that 62 percent of the entire worker sample repair widgets. It also shows that 20 percent of the first line supervisors perform this task. Unfortunately, only further analysis could determine whether the supervisors actually do the work, simply supervise it, or try to maintain proficiency in a skill which they supervise others in performing. A "supervise" task could answer this question. However, supervise tasks should only be included under unusual data requirement situations because they substantially lengthen the questionnaire.

An analyst interpreting this particular Group Summary report could offer convincing evidence to management that a proposal to provide apprentice workers with supervisory development training would be inappropriate, because few if any apprentices would use the training. Moreover, an analysis of background information pertaining to time between promotions might point out that complete retraining could be in order prior to use of these skills.

An analyst comparing Group Summary reports prepared with both the time spent and percent performing options could determine if workers were employed in the manner specified in their job descriptions, or if workers were using their training as management intended.

GROUP DIFFERENCE

The Group Difference program permits the study of differences in task performance between any two previously defined groups. Data may be displayed in either the percent performing or percent time spent formats. Calculations may appear in the same order as the original questionnaire, or may be displayed to highlight the degree of difference between the groups. In the latter form, the least difference (or greatest similarity) appears toward the middle of the printout, while the greatest difference appears at the beginning and end of the report. The report may be shortened by requesting display of only those tasks in which differences exceeds a given value, for example, the analyst may wish only to see tasks with a time spent difference exceeding 30 percent.

Figure 11.6 depicts a Group Difference report comparing apprentice and fully qualified workers, based upon percent of group members performing each task. The report reveals that 90 percent of the apprentice workers are repairing widgets (task A1) but only 40 percent of the fully qualified workers perform this task. The amount of difference (in this example 50 percent) is

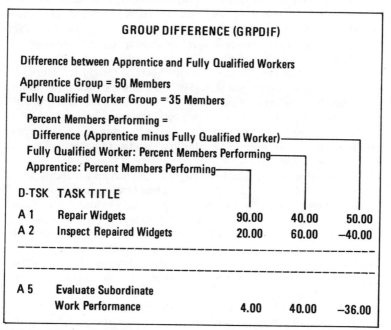

FIGURE 11.6: Example of a CODAP Group Difference Report. (Adapted from "CODAP Information Guide," U.S. Army Military Personnel Center, 1977)

shown in the third column of the report. A negative sign (−), as in tasks A2 and A5, indicates a shift in "direction" of the difference value—in this case from apprentices to fully qualified workers.

The analyst examining this report might conclude that too many fully qualified workers were being assigned from the repair line to the inspection department, with the bulk of the repair function being turned over to less qualified workers. In addition, it might be determined that far too many of the less qualified workers were performing inspections. Policy changes would swiftly correct both situations.

A variety of additional programs are available, for example:

(1) An extremely important process for the experienced CODAP analyst is the grouping process (programs OVRLAP and GROUP) which can "cluster" respondents into groups that permit identification of workers who perform similar tasks. Time spent or percent performing tasks may be used as the basis for the clustering routine (Archer, 1966). Clusters are formed through a staging process. First, all responses are scanned to locate two individuals (or small groups) who have the highest degree of task similarity. This "similarity" cluster is then compared to all other individuals or groups until the next highest degree of similarity (or overlap) is found. The process continues until all respondents form a final similarity cluster, containing the union of all tasks performed by all respondents. A graphic display program (DIAGRM) depicts the clusters much like a branching tree diagram, and indicates the average percent of overlap among members of each cluster. The degree of similarity can then be examined by producing other CODAP reports about the members of the cluster. Examination of a cluster might reveal highly similar work being performed in allegedly unrelated departments. On the other hand, workers believed to be performing similar work might fragment into several clusters. Reports might support a reorganization, revision of operating instructions or job descriptions, or additional studies to determine the causes of these findings.

(2) CODAP has a stepwise multiple linear regression capability to relate background items and task data. Reports can be generated to produce actual data values for background variables provided by each respondent, which can then be used for case by case examination of members of a group. Background data for an entire group can be printed and compared with similar data for other groups.

(3) CODAP programs can provide statistical data on "secondary" factor responses in addition to the "primary" time spent, and percent performing factors. Secondary items are generally questions requiring subjective responses on matters such as the adequacy of training provided in school or on the job, or supervisory opinions of the abilities of their subordinates.

(4) The CODAP system includes a wide range of "maintenance" programs which edit and prepare data for selected output. Certain programs extract and reprint any CODAP reports saved on a master file. This report depository precludes the need to regenerate reports from raw data files each time a copy of a report is needed.

CODAP AND INSTRUCTIONAL SYSTEMS DEVELOPMENT

The continuing need for trained personnel, especially in the military departments, attests to the importance of accurate and reliable occupational information. In the Army alone, more than 150,000 recruits are trained each

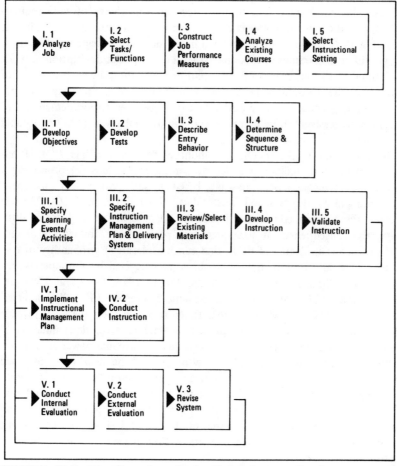

FIGURE 11.7: The five phase Instructional Systems Development model. (From "Instructional Systems Development Executive Summary and Model," Pamphlet 350-30, U.S. Army Training and Doctrine Command, 1975)

year. In addition, new equipment systems result in termination of some jobs and establishment of others. To meet these requirements, the military services have developed training programs based upon systematic analyses of job demands, the behavioral components of work, and the need for most effective methods conveying skills and knowledges to assure job competency.

An approach for training design, the Interservice Procedures for Instructional Systems Development (IPISD) has been developed (Instructional Systems Development Executive Summary and Model, 1975). IPISD provides a "how to do it" manual for instructional design based upon systematic determination of training needs and priorities.

The five phase IPISD model is shown in Figure 11.7. Each phase in the process is a unique function in the design of a training program. As the model suggests, the most important input is accurate knowledge of work requirements, and the priorities associated with various job components. It is in this area that the CODAP system has been most successfully tested and applied. By providing the trainer or task analyst with a composite description of work performed at various levels of an occupational structure, the analyst is able to determine what to train, when to train, and the level of competency required. Thus, training becomes more cost effective, is tailored to job demands, and becomes progessively more complex as the individual advances in the occupational hierarchy.

In recognition of the training communities demand for data, CODAP has been expanded to include a series of computer routines for processing a special set of secondary factors (data based on scales other than time spent performing tasks) (Christal and Weissmuller, 1976). For example, CODAP can provide the training community with task specific indices of learning difficulty, the consequences of inadequate task performance, immediacy of task performance (i.e., degree of delay that can be tolerated), probability of task performance, and type of training required as perceived by the supervisor or the trainer (Christal, 1970; Sellman and Fugill, 1974; Goody and Watson, 1975; Mead, 1975; Stacy, Thompson and Thomson, 1977; Waldkoetter, Gilbert, Raney, and Hawkins, 1976). Taken together, these measures provide the training analyst with a comprehensive data base for determination of training priorities for given qualitative and quantitative manpower allocations. Figure 11.8 represents a simplified flow diagram of the decision process used by the Army Aviation School incorporating the factors used to select tasks for training at the school, training at the unit level, or not at all (IERW/ RWIPC Task Validation and Selection, 1976). With exception of the percent performing factor, all data is ordered on a scale of 1 (low) to 7 (high), and represents the pooled relative judgments of first line supervisors on the three factors.

The left column of Figure 11.8 depicts the initial selection of tasks to be trained at the school—they must be flight associated, difficult to learn, have a

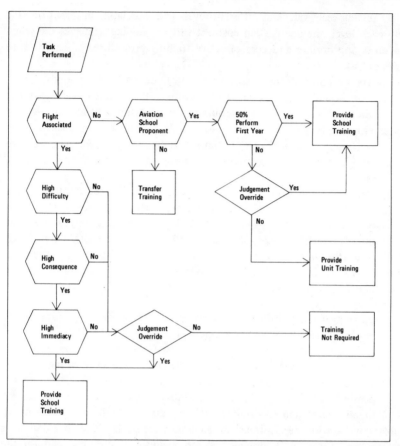

FIGURE 11.8: A "decision-tree" for determining type of training for Army helicopter pilots. (From "IERW/RWIPC Task Validation and Selection, U.S. Army Rotary Wing Aviator Training," U.S. Army Aviation Center and School, 1976)

high consequence if performed inadequately, and must be performed immediately without recourse to information on how they are to be performed. Conversely, tasks with low mean values on each of the factors would not be trained at the school unless policy considerations (judgment override) would dictate otherwise. The decision as to what constitutes high and low values on each factor for determining type of training is flexible, and can be adjusted upward or downward to reflect availability of training resources.

Task rating values between the extremes, and tasks which are performed by a given percentage of workers under specified conditions (in this case by 50 percent or more of the aviators within their first year on the job), are also considered for school training. The remaining tasks are trained at the unit level or not at all, depending on judgments by school or doctrine experts.

By setting scale values at different levels and associating different training with each level, the analyst can cost-out various training strategies and select the most appropriate and cost effective training procedure for each task or series of tasks.

Efforts are currently underway to develop "bench mark" (Goody, 1976) or "task-anchored" (Stacy et al., 1977) rating scales, permitting comparative task training analyses across job groupings. By providing respondents with a set of empirically derived representative tasks or bench mark tasks at each scale level against which they can compare their own job tasks, comparisons within and between job categories can be made to assist in cross-occupational analyses.

In addition, work is underway to apply the CODAP methodology to the more complex and unstructured officer or executive level positions (Ulrich, Barucky, and Tauscher, 1977); to relate task performance criteria to aptitude requirements (Christal, 1974; Stacy et al., 1977); to apply CODAP based task analysis in the new equipment development cycle (Baran, Czuchry, and Dieterly, 1977; Hawkins, 1978); and to isolate differential utilization of men and women in the same job series (Waldkoetter, Gilbert, Hawkins, and Wethy, 1976).

Discussion of the validity and reliability of the CODAP/task inventory job analysis procedure is beyond the scope of this chapter. The reader is referred to Cragun and McCormick (1967) for a study on the relative validity of various time rating scales; to Carpenter (1974) for an analysis of inaccuracies in individual job descriptions and their relationship to the overall group job description; to Christal (1971) on the stability of group job descriptions; and to Madden, Hazel and Christal (1964) on supervisor-worker agreement regarding worker job descriptions. In general, these studies lend strong support to the use of the methodology for job analysis, job typing, and for the making of training decisions.

SUMMARY

An automated occupational analysis system is an effective management tool, which can be applied to solving problems associated with manpower structures, training, effective utilization of personnel, and motivation (job satisfaction, morale, quality of life, and so on). A system such as CODAP provides an orderly way to collect and process data collected from workers, and provides a variety of useful and easily understood report formats which are based upon proven analytical and statistical techniques.

The system does not, however, solve problems for the analyst or manager. Rather, it provides necessary information upon which to base sound judgments which are themselves fully supportable with empirical data.

Introduction of an automated system such as CODAP requires a substantial investment in people, time, and money. Further, there is the inevitable problem of gaining acceptance from managers and trainers who have operated for years with systems reminiscent of the Army's systems of WWI and WWII, and who are perhaps apprehensive, if not suspicious of innovation.

For several years agencies involved in the Vocational-Technical Education Consortium of States (V-TECS) training development programs have made extensive use of Army-civilian associated task lists for their vocational education development efforts. As the next step, real data collected from workers in civilian occupations should serve as the bases for continued vocational education program development at the high school and postsecondary levels.

REFERENCES

Analyzing Training Effectiveness. 1976. Fort Monroe, VA: U.S. Army Training and Doctrine Command. February. (Pamphlet No. 71-8)

Archer, W. B. 1966. *Computation of Group Job Descriptions From Occupational Survey Data.* Lackland Air Force Base, TX: Personnel Research Laboratory, Aerospace Medical Division. December. (PRL-TR-66-12)

Army Job Analysis Manual I. 1960. Washington, DC: Department of the Army, Office of the Adjutant General, Research and Development Division, Systems Development Branch. (SDB 1-60-OR)

Army Occupational Survey Program Survey Series III and IV Summary Statistics. 1976. Alexandria, VA: U.S. Army Military Personnel Center.

Baran, H. A., Czuchry, A. J., and Dieterly, D. L. 1977. "Analyzing the Training Impact of New Weapon Systems." Paper presented at the 19th annual conference of the Military Testing Association, San Antonio, TX. October.

Carpenter, J. B. 1974. *Sensitivity of Group Job Descriptions to Possible Inaccuracies in Individual Job Descriptions.* Lackland Air Force Base, TX: Human Resources Laboratory. March. (AFHRL-TR-74-6)

Carpenter, J. B., Giorgia, M. J., and McFarland, B. P. *Comparative Analysis of the Relative Validity for Subjective Time Rating Scales.* 1975. Lackland Air Force Base, TX: Human Resources Laboratory. December (AFHRL-TR-75-63)

Christal, R. E. 1974. *The U.S. Air Force occupational research project.* Lackland Air Force Base, TX: Human Resources Laboratory. (AFHRL-TR-73-75)

——— 1971. *Stability of Consolidated Job Descriptions Based on Task Inventory Survey Information.* Lackland Air Force Base, TX: Human Resources Laboratory. August. (AFHRL-TR-71-48)

——— 1970. Implications of Air Force occupational research for curriculum design. In B. B. Smith, and J. Mos, Jr., eds. *Report of a Seminar: Process and Techniques of Vocational Curriculum Development.* Minneapolis: Minnesota Research Coordinating Unit for Vocational Education, University of Minnesota. April.

Christal, R. E., and Weissmuller, J. J. 1976. *New CODAP Programs for Analyzing Task Factor Information.* Lackland Air Force Base, TX: Human Resources Laboratory, Occupational and Manpower Research Division. May. (AFHRL-TR-76-3)

CODAP Implication Study. 1972. Washington, DC: Department of the Army, Office of the Deputy Chief of Staff for Personnel. September.

Cragun, J. R., and McCormick, E. J. 1967. *Job Inventory Information: Task and Scale Reliabilities and Scale Interrelationships.* Lackland Air Force Base, TX: Personnel Research Laboratory, Aerospace Medical Division. November. (PRL-TR-67-15)

Gagne, R. M., ed. 1962. *Psychological Priniciples of System Development.* New York: Holt, Rinehart, and Winston.

Goody, K. 1976. *Task Factor Benchmark Scales for Training Priority Analysis.* Lackland Air Force Base, TX: Human Resources Laboratory, Occupational and Manpower Research Division. June. (AFHRL-TR-76-15)

Goody, K., and Watson, W. J. 1975. "Task factor benchmark scales for use in determining task training priorities." Paper presented at the 17th annual conference of the Military Testing Association, Indianapolis, IN, September.

Hawkins, H. H. 1978. "Use of occupational data in determination of qualitative and quantitative personnel requirements." Unpublished working paper. Alexandria, VA: U.S. Army Military Personnel Center. January.

"History of the Army Job Analysis System." 1946. Unpublished manuscript. Washington, DC: Department of the Army, Office of the Adjutant General.

Holt, P. E. 1971. In Proceedings, Military Occupational Data Bank 1971 Users Conference. *Opening address.* Washington, DC: Department of the Army.

IERW/RWIPC Task Validation and Selection, U.S. Army Rotary Wing Aviator Training. 1976. Summary report. Fort Rucker, AL: U.S. Army Aviation Center and School. June.

Information Guide to the Army Occupational Survey Program and Selected CODAP Programs. 1977. Alexandria, VA: U.S. Army Military Personnel Center.

Instructional Systems Development Executive Summary and Model. 1975. Fort Monroe, VA: U.S. Army Training and Doctrine Command. (Pamphlet No. 350-30)

Madden, J. M., Hazel, J. T., and Christal, R. E. *Worker and Supervisor Agreement Concerning the Worker's Job Description.* 1964. Lackland Air Force Base, TX: 6570th Personnel Research Laboratory, Aerospace Medical Division. April. (PRL-TDR-64-10)

Mead, D. F. 1975. "Determining training priorities for job tasks." Paper presented at the annual conference of the Military Testing Association, Indianapolis, IN, September.

Morsh, J. F., and Archer, W. B. 1967. *Procedural Guide for Conducting Occupational Surveys in the United States Air Force.* Lackland Air Force Base, TX: Personnel Research Laboratory, Aerospace Medical Division. September. (PRL-TR-67-11)

Phillips, P. 1972. *Consideration of Army Use of CODAP.* Memorandum. Washington, DC: Office of the Assistant Secretary of the Army (Manpower & Reserve Affairs). February.

Proceedings, Military Occupational Data Bank 1971 Users Conference. 1971. Washington, DC: Department of the Army, Office of Personnel Operations.

Sellman, W. S. and Fugill, J. W. K. 1974. "The Royal Australian Air Force occupational measurement program." Paper presented at the 16th annual conference of the Military Testing Association, Oklahoma City, OK, October.

Stacy, W., Thompson, N., and Thomson, D. 1977. "Occupational task factors for instructional system development." Paper presented at the 19th annual conference of the Military Testing Association, San Antonio, TX, October.

Task Analysis, CODAP Executives' Overview Guide. 1973. Washington, DC: Department of Defense, November. (DoD 1125.6-M-I)

Ulrich, T. E., Barucky, J. M., and Tauscher, L. J. 1977. "Current status of occupational analysis." Paper presented at the convention of the American Psychological Association, San Francisco, CA, August.

Waldkoetter, R. O., Gilbert, A. C. F., Hawkins, H. H., and Wethy, R. B. 1976. "Organizational effectiveness related to non-MOS task performance of a critical sub-group." Paper presented at the annual conference of the Military Testing Association, Gulf Shores, AL, October.

Waldkoetter, R. O., Gilbert, A. C. F., Raney, J. L., and Hawkins, H. H. 1976. "Establishing training priorities in an Army supply military occupational specialty." Paper presented at the annual conference of the Military Testing Association, Gulf Shores, AL, October.

APPENDIX
Description of
CODAP Programs

AUTOJT: Automated Job Type Selection. Calculates, evaluates, and reports between-group differences for specified pairs of groups. Up to 850 pairs can be compared in a single run.

AVALUE: Average Value. Calculates mean and standard deviation of a selected background or computed variable using all valid responses for each task in the inventory.

AVGPCT: Average by Percent Performing. A version of AVALUE—computes an average level based on percent of members in each level performing each task.

CORREG: Correlation and Regression. Computes the correlation matrix, number of valid and invalid cases in the sample, and means and standard deviations of variables.

DIAGRM: Graphical Presentation of Hierarchical Grouping Actions. Generates a treeline diagram visually displaying the order in which groups merge in the grouping process.

DIST2X: Computing a Two-Way Distribution. Distributes a group of individuals on a row and a column variable. Frequencies, percentages, means and standard deviations may be computed.

DUVARS: Computing a Duty Variable for Each Case. Used as an aid in selecting meaningfully different job-type groups based upon time spent or tasks performed.

EXTRCT: Reordering and Extracting Reports from the Report File. All CODAP reports can be placed on the Report file for recall. EXTRCT generates desired output.

FACSUM: Task Factor Summary. User may print any vectors on the Job Description File. FACSUM can calculate differences between vectors, maximums or minimums of sets, cumulative percentages, and categories of tasks.

GRMBRS: Reporting Group Membership. Identifies the two groups combining at each stage of the hierarchical grouping process. A wide variety of information about the groups is provided.

GROUP: Clustering Individuals and Groups of Individuals. The similarity matrix computed in OVRLAP is used to form clusters of cases. Several formulae for combining groups are available.

GRPDIF: Difference Comparison Between Job Descriptions. Calculates difference between two job descriptions in terms of percent performing each task or average percent time spent.

GRPSUM: Summarizing Job Descriptions. Calculates percent performing each task or average percent time spent on each task for any group which can be computed by JOBGRP or JOBSPC.

INPSTD: Raw Data Editing and Input. Receives all collected raw data. Converts task responses to percentages, reorganizes data to standard format, constructs data vectors, and writes formatted data for HISTORY file used in other programs. Will accept 1700 background variables, 1700 task variables, 26 duty variables, and 200,000 cases.

JOBGRP: Calculating Composite Job Descriptions. Calculates job descriptions for groups formed in hierarchical grouping process. Limited to 7000 cases (maximum allowed by OVRLAP/ GROUP).

JOBIND: Calculating Individual Job Descriptions. Calculates job descriptions for individual cases. Selected background information may be included.

JOBINV: Printing of Duty and Task Titles. Prints a list of duty and task titles included in an inventory.

JOBSPC: Calculating Composite Job Descriptions. Calculates job descriptions for "special" groups whose membership is defined in terms of some combination of background or computed variables.

KPATH: Ordering a History File. Assigns continuous sequence numbers to individual cases merged during OVRLAP/GROUP.

MTXPRT: Printing an Overlapped Matrix. Calls for OVRLAP to overlap all possible pairings of a set of composite job descriptions, then prints between-group values in matrix form. Maximum input is 100 groups.

OVRLAP: Relating Responses to Each Other. Generates an overlap or similarity matrix of all possible paired comparisons between individual cases, in terms of percentage of common tasks performed or percentage of time spent on tasks. The time spent option is generally preferred. Input is limited to 7000 cases.

PRDICT: Printing Dictionary of Variable Titles. Identifies all codes and descriptive titles of all background or computed variables used in a study. Codes are then used to call for data in other CODAP programs.

PRIJOB: Calculating Primary Job Identifiers. Calculates tasks which are determined to be "primary identifiers" of job types (the top x-number of tasks or tasks performed by a specified minimum percentage of group members).

PROGEN: Program Generation Program. Allows a CODAP expert to add, extract, or manipulate data in ways not encompassed by standard programs, and do so with a minimum amount of additional programming.

PRTVAR: Printing Variables. Enables user to select variables and printout formats to produce a report of the case data values for selected background and computed variables.

REXALL: Computing Interrater Reliability. For a group of raters, computes the average interrater reliability coefficient of a single rater and the stepped up reliability coefficient for the total group. Computes distribution, mean, and standard deviation.

SETCHK: Editing Raw Data. This program makes certain checks to raw data to insure valid input to the CODAP system.

TSETUP: Initialize the Job Description and Report Files. Writes information at the head of these files to prepare them for accumulation of reports and statistical information which will occur throughout the system.

TSKFAC: Task Factor Values. Creates new records on the Job Description file representing values for task factors. "Decks" may be generated by AVALUE, AVGPCT, or REXALL and reported by AUTOJT, FACSUM, MTXPRT and PRIJOB.

VARMEN: Variable Means and Standard Deviations. Extracts up to 100 computed and background variables from a KPATH or History file and computes means and standard deviations. Also computes number of valid and invalid cases in the sample.

VARSUM: Summarizing Background and Computed Variables. Computes frequency distributions within specified intervals, makes total frequency counts, and calculates means and standard deviations on selected variables for any group identified through JOBGRP or JOBSPC.

AIR FORCE
PERFORMANCE RATINGS
Assessment Methods
for Occupational
Education
and Evaluation

chapter 12

DALE F. CAMPBELL   *Vernon Regional Junior College*
HENRY C. LINDSEY   *Community College*
                          of the Air Force

Why all the emphasis on performance? Employers from across the country continue to complain that their workers cannot adequately perform. Unfortunately, many workers still emerge from educational institutions filled with the "what," but woefully short in the "how to" category. With the reverse transfer phenomenon, many baccalaureate-degreed students are returning to community colleges and technical institutes to receive occupational education for employment entry. In 1974, two-year colleges were receiving as many transfer students from four-year institutions as they were sending to them (Lee, 1976). Students are well aware that while most employers think theory is nice, it has to be harnessed to something. Employers simply do not have time to educate their employes all over again in the "how to" category.

The Instructional System Development (ISD) process assists the Air Force in satisfying its job requirements by providing both the "what" and "how to." The ISD model prescribes an approach to the planning and development of instruction that can be adapted to both civilian and military educational programs. Many civilian institutions are designing their own performance-based curricula with the current emphasis on accountability.

ISD provides the framework for the Air Force's vast technical education system. A basic knowledge of ISD's components is essential to understand Air Force performance ratings in the classroom and on the job. These components can be adapted to almost any comprehensively designed occupational technical program.

INSTRUCTIONAL SYSTEMS DEVELOPMENT (ISD)

ISD is a systematic approach for curriculum development and revision which applies educational technology, instructional psychology, and programmed learning principles to educational programs to insure that graduates possess the knowledge, skills, and attitudes essential for successful job performance.

This scientific method insures an effective integrated functioning system of students, instructors, materials, equipment, procedures, techniques, and facilities in achieving behaviorally stated educational objectives. A brief overview of the five-step model, depicted in Figure 12.1, will provide the necessary foundation to understand the Air Force's complex technical education system.

Step 1: Determine job requirements through detailed analysis of tasks performed.

Step 2: Determine the type of instruction (formal classroom, on-the-job, and so on) required to best meet the needs of the student population.

Step 3: Develop objectives which specify the behaviors desired as an end product of the instruction, the conditions under which those behaviors are to be demonstrated, and an acceptable standard of performance. Develop a parallel testing program based on achievement of the standards expressed in the objectives.

Step 4: Plan and develop instructional methods, media, and equipment. All elements are developed and integrated to effectively support the objectives. Lessons and study materials are validated so that the designed instruction will be appropriate for the target population.

Step 5: Conduct and evaluate instruction. Evaluation of instruction and its relevancy to job requirements is conducted continuously to insure the viability of the ISD process. Feedback from this step regenerates the ISD cycle for later iterations.

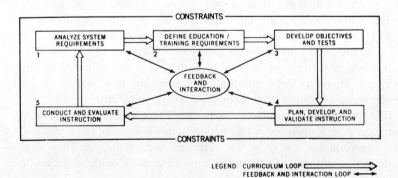

FIGURE 12.1: Model for instructional system development

All technical education courses are structured to enhance student accomplishment of the behavioral objectives. The measurement program is designed to insure that all graduates achieve a minimum performance standard which prepares them for their initial job assignment.[1] Before focusing on the performance aspects of instruction and on-the-job, a more detailed knowledge of Steps 1 and 2 of the ISD process is required.

Step 1: Analyze System Requirements

The application of the first step of the ISD model to technical instruction begins with a general description of the system, and concludes with the documentation of specific job tasks and related data. In this context, system is defined as the composite of equipment, skills, and techniques (including all related facilities, equipment, materials, services, and personnel) that is capable of performing and/or supporting an operational role. The entire analysis is directed toward determining the worker's role in the system—a role described in terms of duties and tasks necessary to perform system functions such as control, operate, and maintain. The process of identifying and organizing these duties and tasks requires the accomplishment of the following activities.

(1) Identify system factors such as mission, policies and procedures, major components or items of equipment, and functions.
(2) Identify job performance requirements of the system.
(3) Develop an inventory of valid job duties and tasks and supporting data.

The identification of job performance requirements is one of the most critical activities in the ISD process, because the tasks and related data form the basis for the remaining actions.

Typically, the identification, organization, and analysis of job performance requirements information is accomplished from the general to the specific in an order similar to that shown in Figure 12.2.

As the major job duties and tasks are identified, there is a need to determine who should perform them. This involves matching the duties with career field summaries, and then the duties and tasks with an occupational specialty. Air Force personnel make the decision when to create new occupational specialties in any emerging technologies where existing specialties do not suffice. In order to maintain consistency, examples throughout the chapter will be in the occupational specialty—Aircraft Maintenance Specialist, Air Force Specialty Code (AFSC) 43151, shown in Table 12.1.

One of the most comprehensive sources of job data for an existing Air Force specialty is the Occupational Survey Report, produced by the Air Force Occupational Measurement Center at Lackland Air Force Base, Texas.

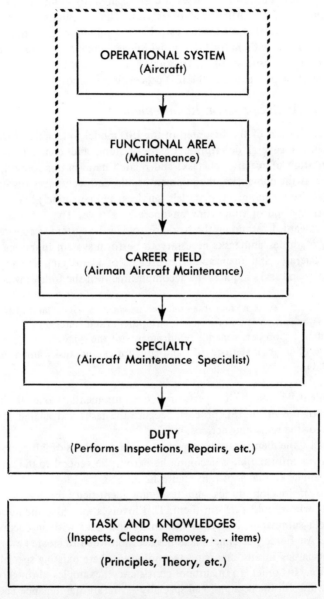

FIGURE 12.2: Sequence of identification and analysis

Table 12.1: An Airman Air Force Specialty Description

Aircraft Maintenance Specialist

Semiskilled AFSC 43151*

1. Specialty Summary

. Inspects, repairs, maintains, troubleshoots, services, and modifies aircraft and aircraft installed equipment; and performs crew chief and maintenance staff functions.

2. Duties and Responsibilities

a. Performs *inspections,* functional checks, and preventive maintenance on aircraft and aircraft installed equipment: Performs preflight, post-flight, and periodic/phase inspections of aircraft including structures, landing gear, engines, instruments, cockpits, cabins, flight surfaces, and controls. Inspects and performs functional checks of aircraft systems such as hydrualic, electrical, pressurization, lubrication, anti-icing, vacuum, induction and exhaust, and installed equipment such as external tanks, tow reels, hoists, and APUs. Inspects aircraft components for cleanliness, alignment, proper clearance and operation, evidence of wear, cracks, and looseness in accordance with applicable technical orders. Launches and recovers aircraft. Inspects and inventories 780 equipment.

b. Repairs, maintains and *services* aircraft and aircraft installed equipment: Removes, installs, or adjusts aircraft and aircraft system components such as control surfaces, wheels, brakes, tires, cowling, enclosures, hose, and tubing. Determines and accomplishes maintenance actions required to correct malfunctions indicated in aircraft forms and clears forms upon completion of maintenance. Cleans aircraft and engines. Identifies corrosion and applies protective measures. Troubleshoots malfunctions pertaining to aircraft structures, landing gear, control surfaces, induction, exhaust, ventilation and heating systems. *Services oil, de-icing, fuel, hydraulic and oxygen (gaseous and liquid) systems.* Tows and parks aircraft and performs engine run-up. Obtains engine oil samples (SOAP). Operates ground power equipment. Operates and maintains non-powered ground equipment. Performs operator maintenance on aircraft installed auxiliary power unit. Interprets diagrams and applicable publications and initiates technical order deficiency reports (AFTO Form 22). Completes maintenance data forms.

c. Performs aircraft allied functions: Inspects and loads tow targets aboard aircraft; assembles and disassembles glider type targets. Preflights target towing equipment and performs in-flight operator duties associated with launch and recovery of targets. Performs assigned maintenance in repair and reclamation of aircraft and the removal, repair, and installation of aircraft wheel and tire assemblies.

d. Supervises aircraft maintenance personnel: Assigns work and reviews completed work to insure compliance with applicable technical publications and local procedures. Instructs subordinates in maintenance of aircraft and aircraft installed equipment. Insures compliance with appropriate procedures prescribed by USAF management directives. Conducts on-the-job training.

3. Specialty Qualifications

a. Knowledge:

(1) Knowledge of electrical, hydraulic, and mechanical principles as applied to aircraft; concepts and application of AFM 66−1. Maintenance Management System; maintenance and data reporting; and use of diagrams and technical publications is mandatory. Possession of mandatory knowledge will be determined in accordance with AFM 35−1.

Table 12.1: An Airman Air Force Specialty Description (Cont.)

(2) Knowledge of supply procedures is desirable.

b. Education: Completion of high school with courses in physics, hydraulics, and electronics is desirable.

c. Experience:
(1) Experience in functions such as repair and maintenance of aircraft and related installed and ground support equipment is mandatory.

(2) Experience in functions such as performing or supervising aircraft inspections is desirable.

d. Training: Completion of a basic aircraft maintenance course is desirable.

e. Other:
(1) Normal color vision as defined in AFM 160–1 is mandatory.

(2) A minimum aptitude level of Mechanical 50 is mandatory.

4. **Specialty Data**
   a. Grade Spread:
   Sergeant and staff sergeant. 43151
   Airman first class 43131
   b. Related D.O.T. Jobs:
   Airplane Mechanic 621.281
   Tire and Tube Repairman 915.884
   The Repairman 915-884
   c. Related DOD Occupational Subgroup:600

5. ***Specialty Shredouts**
Suffix   Portion of AFS to Which Related
   A . . . .Reciprocating Engine Aircraft
   C . . . .Jet Aircraft One and Two Engines
   E . . . .Jet Aircraft Over Two Engines
   F . . . .Turbo-Prop Aircraft

An occupational survey report is published after inventories have been collected from job incumbents and the data have been analyzed. A single comprehensive report is prepared for the entire survey sample. However, separate reports can be made available for describing particular job types, specialties, or organizational units.

Table 12.2 illustrates entries extracted from an actual occupational survey report compiled for the 431X1 career ladder. These extracts show the percent of time spent and the percent of members performing several tasks. The task "1 8" is included five times to show differences based on Air Force Specialty (AFS) skill level. Airman specialties are divided into four levels: 3- (semi-skilled), 5- (skilled), 7- (advanced), and 9- (superintendent) levels. In Table 12.2, a comparison of the 3-skill level (circled) personnel shows that only

Table 12.2: Extracts from Occupational Survey Report

Description of current job in aircraft maintenance career ladder based on background variables. Shows percent members performing and percent time spent on tasks. Tasks are sorted high to low percent time spent by group menbers.

Task job description, Cases=9233, Tasks=362, Duties=14, MBRS= 9232
All airmen in Crr Field DAFSC 431X1X/91 TOTAL SAMPLE

    Cumulative sum of average percent time spent by all members . . . .
    Average percent time spent by all members . . . .
    Average percent time spent by members performing . . . .
    Percent of members performing. . . . .

D-Tsk	Duty/Task Title	:	:	:	:
F 16	Inspect Aircraft for Structural Damage	72.89	1.60	1.17	1.17
F 17	Inspect Airframe and Components	70.82	1.60	1.13	2.30
M 2	Defuel or Refuel Aircraft	68.08	1.64	1.12	3.41
G 9	Launch and Recover Aircraft	62.31	1.66	1.03	.769
1 8	Inspect and Service Liquid Oxygen Systems	42.67	1.25	0.53	42.78

Task job description, Cases= 9233, Tasks=362, Duties= 14, MBRS=174
DAFSC 43131A App Reciprocating Engine Aircraft

1 8	Inspect and Service Liquid Oxygen Systems	6.32	2.24	0.14	91.91

Task job description, Cases=9233, Tasks=362, Duties=14, MBRS=174
DAFSC 43131E App Reciprocating Engine Aircraft

1 8	Inspect and Service Liquid Oxygen Systems	37.58	1.87	0.70	55.98

Task job description, Cases=9233, Tasks=362, Duties=14, MBRS=1607
DAFSC 43151E Jet Aircraft Over Two Engines Specialist

1 8	Inspect and Service Liquid Oxygen Systems	47.92	1.22	0.59	47.44

Task job description, Cases=9233, Tasks=362, Duties=14, MBRS=672
DAFSC 43171E Jet Aircraft Over Two Engines Technician

1 8	Inspect and Service Liquid Oxygen Systems	54.17	0.85	0.46	51.79

3-, 5-, and 7-skill levels

37.58 percent of the apprentice aircraft maintenance specialists perform it. The skill level is indicated in the duty AFSC (DAFSC). When a 3-skill level airman is upgraded to a 5-skill level, the airman's duty AFSC is recorded 43151E. The table also shows that the percent of members performing this task increases as they advance from the 3- to the 5- to the 7-skill level (37.58 percent, 47.92 percent, 54.17 percent), but the average percent of the members' time spent on this task decreases as they move from the 3- to the 5- to the 7-skill level (1.87 percent, 1.22 percent, .85 percent). This step of the ISD process helps to establish at what skill level, in the airman's career, instruction is required for this task.

A study of the entire report reveals that a large number of advanced aircraft maintenance personnel perform this task. In this case, the data substantiate the inclusion of the task in the specialty description (see marked task in Table 12.1). Tasks are normally included where at least 30 percent of the personnel are performing them. Critical tasks that might only rarely be performed are also included, despite the percentage performing the task. These tasks might be in the area of an operational emergency requiring immediate response (AFM 50-2, 1975).

Step 2: Define Instructional Requirements

Step 2 of the ISD model identifies specific educational requirements and selects methods for providing instruction. One of the first actions in this step is to determine if instruction is required. When a decision is made to provide instruction, the next action is to select the most cost-effective method or methods.

When instructional requirements have been determined, they are normally documented in an educational standard. Educational standards accomplish exactly what the title implies. They establish the standard for student performance—a standard in terms of job tasks, knowledges, and proficiency levels. Also, the educational standards are a type of Air Force contract. They specify that graduates will have the capability of performing specific duties and tasks required to perform on the job. Educational standards currently in use by the Air Force are the Specialty Training Standard (STS) and the Course Training Standard (CTS).

SPECIALTY TRAINING STANDARDS

The Specialty Training Standard (STS) is an Air Force publication used to standardize and control the quality of individual instruction required to achieve the skills within an entire Air Force specialty. These skills are based on job performance requirements and are documented in terms of tasks, knowledges, and proficiency codes. The tasks and knowledges listed in STSs correlate with, or elaborate on the .specialty description for the Air Force specialty. When the duties, responsibilities, and specialty qualifications used by the Air Force are found inadequate (partially obsolete, incomplete, not clear, and son on), a tentative STS is prepared to include tasks and knowledges which are essential.

A sample page from the Aircraft Maintenance Specialty, STS 431X1E, is shown in Table 12.3. The proficiency code key values for the standard are defined in a separate code key page shown as Table 12.4. Code levels assigned to tasks and knowledges constitute firm commitments on the content and level of performance the student must achieve. So it is most important that these code levels reflect the educational requirements that were established in

Table 12.3: Sample Page from a Specialty Training Standard (STS)

STS 431X1E

PROFICIENCY LEVEL, PROGRESS RECORD AND CERTIFICATION

1. Tasks, Knowledges and Study References	2. 3 Skill Level			3. 5 Skill Level			4. 7 Skill Level		
	A	B	C	A	B	C	A	B	C
	AFSC/Crs	Date OJT Started	Date Completed and Trainee's Supervisor's Initials	AFSC/Crs	Date OJT Started	Date Completed and Trainee's Supervisor's Initials	AFSC/Crs	Date OJT Started	Date Completed and Trainee's Supervisor's Initials
22c. Inspect and service system and components	2b			3c			4c		
23. ANTI-ICING/ DEICING SYSTEM									
SR: See index for applicable TO covering specific systems									
a. Function and operation	B			B			C		
b. Perform operational check	1b			2c			4c		
c. Inspect and service system and components	2b			3c			4c		

Table 12.3: (Continued)

			NO ADVANCED COURSE
24. OXYGEN SYSTEM			
SR: See index for applicable TO covering specific systems and TO15X-1-1			
a. Function and operation	B	B	C
b. Perform operational check	1b	2c	4c
c. Inspect and service system and components	2b	3c	4c
25. DRAG CHUTE			
SR: See index for applicable TO covering specific systems			
a. Function and operation	B	B	C
b. Perform operational check	1b	2c	4c
c. Inspect and service system and components	2b	3c	4c

Table 12.3: (Continued)

26. ENGINE AIRBLEED SYSTEM			
SR: See index for applicable TO covering specific systems			
a. Function and operation	B	B	C
b. Perform operational check	b	2b	3c
c. Inspect and service system and components	2b	3c	4c
27. EGRESS SYSTEM			
SR: See index for applicable TO covering specific systems			
a. Function and operation	B	B	C
b. Inspect components	2b	3c	4c

313

Table 12.4: Defined Proficiency Code Key Scale Values

Qualitative Requirements

	Scale Value	Definition: The Individual
TASK PERFORMANCE LEVELS	1	Can do simple parts of the task. Needs to be told or shown how to do most of the task. (EXTREMELY LIMITED)
	2	Can do most parts of the task. Needs help only on hardest parts. May not meet local demands for speed or accuracy. (PARTIALLY PROFICIENT)
	3	Can do all parts of the task. Needs only a spot check of completed work. Meets minimum local demands for speed and accuracy (COMPETENT)
	4	Can do the complete task quickly and accurately. Can tell or show others how to do the task (HIGHLY PROFICIENT)
*TASK KNOWLEDGE LEVELS	a	Can name parts, tools, and simple facts about the task. (NOMENCLATURE)
	b	Can name the steps in doing the task and tell how each is done. (PROCEDURES)
	c	Can explain why and when the task must be done and why each step is needed. (OPERATING PRINCIPLES)
	d	Can predict, identify, and resolve problems about the task. (COMPLETE THEORY)
**SUBJECT KNOWLEDGE LEVELS	A	Can identify basic facts and terms about the subject (FACTS)
	B	Can explain relationship of basic facts and state general principles about the subject. (PRINCIPLES)
	C	Can analyze facts and principles and draw conclusions about the subject. (ANALYSIS)
	D	Can evaluate conditions and make proper decisions about the subject. (EVALUATION)

EXPLANATIONS

* A task knowledge scale value may be used along or with a task performance scale value to define a level of knowledge for a specific task (Examples: b and 1b)

**A subject knowledge scale value is used alone to define a level of knowledge for a subject not directly related to any specific task, or for a subject common to several tasks.

—. This mark is used alone instead of a scale value to show that no proficiency training is provided in the ATC course, or that no proficiency is required at this skill level.

X This mark is used alone in ATC course columns to show that training is not given due to limitations,in ATC resources.

Step 2 of the ISD process. The phrasing of the task and knowledge statements, as well as the code levels used, are carefully selected.

The coding in columns 2A, 3A, and 4A of the STS indicates the minimum proficiency recommended for each task or knowledge for qualification at the 3-, 5-, or 7-skill levels of the Air Force specialty. Column 2A also shows the proficiency to be attained at an apprentice-level course. Proficiency code is the minimum proficiency recommended for the 3-skill level AFSC, and the proficiency attained in the course is the same except when dual codes are entered. The proficiency code key values are shown in Table 12.4. When dual codes are entered, the second code shows the proficiency attained in the course. The task performance scale value (code 1, 2, 3, or 4) defines the performance level for a specific task statement. The task knowledge scale value (code a, b, c, or d) defines the level of knowledge for a specific task. Accordingly, code a, b, c, or d may be used alone or with a numerical value for a specific task statement. The subject knowledge scale value (code A, B, C, or D) defines the level of knowledge for subject matter not directly related to any specific task, or for subject matter common to several tasks. Accordingly, this scale (A, B, C, D) is used alone rather than with a numerical scale value.

COURSE TRAINING STANDARD

Course Training Standards (CTS) are used to document the educational requirements for a specific course of instruction. Typically, the tasks and knowledges contained in a CTS reflect unique educational requirements for a specific system, such as the White Diesel Engine rather than a specialty such as knowledge and maintenance of diesel engines. Table 12.5 shows a sample page from a CTS for technical instruction which uses the same key as the STS shown in Table 12.3.

PERFORMANCE RATINGS IN SCHOOL

The Air Force uses criterion-referenced testing in rating the effectiveness of student learning. Criterion-referenced instruction tests the student's ability to accomplish the objectives—to perform the behavior called for under the conditions specified, and to the desired standard.

This is different from the norm-referenced test in which the student is tested on his or her performance in relation to other students, rather than in relation to the objectives. It should be apparent that when well-designed behavioral objectives exist, criterion test items are relatively easy to develop (Campbell, 1975).

Table 12.5:   Sample Page from a Course Training Standard (CTS) for Technical Training

Task, Knowledge and Proficiency Level	
1. CONSTRUCTION FEATURES AND OPERATING PRINCIPLES OF WHITE DIESEL ENGINE	
a. The design features of model 40 SX-6 engine	B
b. Operating principles of diesel engines	B
c. Importance of optimum engine performance, and factors affecting engine power output	C
d. Locate and identify engine and system components	4c
e. Arrangement and operating of engine system components	B
2. ENGINE LUBRICATION SYSTEM COMPONENTS	
a. Clean and replace oil filters and strainers	3c
b. Check oil for dilution, cleanliness, and proper grade	3c
c. Inspect system for leakage	3c
d. Adjust oil pressure regulating valves	3c
e. Service engine oil system	3c
3. ENGINE AIR INTAKE AND EXHAUST SYSTEMS	
a. Cleaning and servicing of air cleaners, filters, breathers, and strainers	B
b. Inspect turbochargers for operating condition and oil seals for leakage	3c
c. Inspect and maintain intake and exhaust silencers and ducts	3c
d. Inspect system for leakage and general condition	3c
4. ENGINE AIR STARTING SYSTEMS	
a. Inspect and service air compressor systems	3c
b. Inspect, clean, and adjust engine air starting components	3c

The development of performance-based objectives and tests is the third step in the ISD model. From a careful analysis of the job requirements that were established in Step 2 of the process, a criterion objective is constructed as shown below:

Sample Criterion Objective

JOB REQUIREMENT: Perform power supply output voltage checks of an operational R-278/GRC27 radio receiver, using technical orders and necessary test equipment

CRITERION OBJECTIVE: Using necessary test equipment, and Technical Order 31R2-GRC27-12, perform power supply output voltage checks of an operational R-278/GRC27 radio receiver. Measurements must be within = 10% of actual voltages determined by the instructor

Success or failure of the objective would be based upon the student's ability to perform the power supply output voltage checks within the required tolerances. Success or failure would not depend on how well the other students were able to perform.

For instruction involving the operation and maintenance of equipment, it is comparatively easy to develop behaviorally stated objectives. For other kinds of instruction, it may be more difficult to do this, but the analysis of behaviors should be just as precise as for the behaviors involving equipment. Traditionally, most education courses whether conducted in high schools, in civilian or military colleges have had a fixed length, and often there has been no clear-cut instructional criterion for successfully completing the course. In part, this is because such courses entail the learning of knowledges, skills, and attitudes which are very general in application. Because the instruction has general application, it is difficult to establish realistic standards of proficiency for the instructional objectives. Yet, more and more educational institutions are finding ways to resolve these problems. Fixed length of instruction is being replaced by fixed achievement requirements. Since the amount of time to attain fixed achievement is not uniform for all students, course length is now variable. In many cases, individualized instruction has replaced group instruction, thereby facilitating fixed achievement requirements and variable course length. A content analysis approach is used to establish a basis for the definition of objectives, so that criteria for successful completion of the course can be established (AFM 50-2, 1975). Even attitude and motivation objectives, which usually are considered the most difficult to pin down, are now being specified. Consider this objective indicative of students exercising the responsibilities of citizenship: The student, if eligible, will voluntarily register to vote within six months following the course. Registering to vote is an action suggesting an attitude (Cohen, 1973).

The idea of designing the criterion tests with the objectives prior to developing the instruction is important. In conventional instruction, objectives are developed, then the instruction, and the tests are usually developed from the instruction. This means the tests may test the instruction and not the objectives, with the result that students might perform well on the tests but poorly on the job. Under the ISD process, the objectives are based on job requirements, the tests developed are based on the objectives, and then the instruction is developed. After instruction, the tests serve as a check to see whether the instruction has been effective. Can the student accomplish the objectives? If he or she can not, the instruction is modified (Campbell, 1975).

PERFORMANCE RATINGS ON THE JOB

As a part of the unified instructional system of the Air Force, instruction and performance ratings continue after the students graduate from the

Table 12.6: Extract of Specialty Training Standard

STS 431X1E

	PROFICIENCY LEVEL, PROGRESS RECORD AND CERTIFICATION								
1. Tasks, Knowledges and Study References	2. 3 Skill Level			3. 5 Skill Level			4. 7 Skill Level		
	A	B	C	A	B	C	A	B	C
	AFSC/Crs	Date OJT Started	Date Completed and Trainee's Supervisor's Initials	AFSC	Date OJT Started	Date Completed and Trainee's Supervisor's Initials	AFSC/Crs	Date OJT Started	Date Completed and Trainee's Supervisor's Initials
22c. Inspect and service system and components	2b			3c			4c		
23. ANTI-ICING/ DEICING SYSTEM									
SR: See index for applicable TO covering specific systems									
a. Function and operation	B			B			C		
b. Perform operational check	1b			2c			4c		
c. Inspect and service system and components	2b			3c			4c		

various Air Force technical and professional schools.

When students leave an Air Force technical or professional school, they go directly to work using their acquired skills on a job in their occupational specialty. While this seems elementary, it is of course a beneficial by-product of a user-oriented system that prepares the number of qualified technicians the Air Force needs. Instruction is not wasted through delay and misplaced employment.

Once on the job, Air Force apprentices are assigned to experienced craftsmen or technicians who act as their on-the-job supervisors.[2] The documentation previously developed in support of an ISD curriculum now provides a direct relationship between the classroom curriculum, and also functions to meet the stated educational requirements for the job.

Table 12.6 is an extract of the Specialty Training Standard (STS) referenced earlier in Table 12.3. Note that for each skill level, the supervisor annotates the date on-job-training (OJT) starts (Column B) and the date instruction is completed (Column C), which is certified by the supervisor's initials. The supervisor documents completion of each step as it is accomplished.

Simultaneously with assignment to a job and a supervisor, apprentices are also enrolled in Career Development Courses (CDC) related to their Air Force specialties, which are taken by correspondence. These courses are developed and updated by the Air Force technical schools through the same rigorous process of ISD previously described.

Apprentices are periodically tested on the performance aspects of their job by their respective supervisors. A closed-book proctored examination is also administered to the apprentices on the knowledge skill area and/or management requirements of their Career Development Courses. When they have the required amount of experience and the supervisor believes they are ready, each apprentice takes a test for the next level of his or her specialty, 3- (semiskilled), 5- (skilled), 7- (advanced), or 9- (superintendent) level. This test is tied to the airman's and noncommissioned officer's promotion which helps to motivate them positively.

The Community College of the Air Force (CCAF) awards four semester hours of credit for successful attainment of each of the skill levels through its Air Force Specialty Internship Program. Typically, the average time of experience in a particular specialty area before reaching the 7- (advanced) level is six years. Most noncommissioned officers have eighteen years of experience in their Air Force specialty before attaining the 9- (superintendent) level. CCAF associate degree programs are designed for the career enlisted members of the Air Force, relevant to the role and specialty of each noncommissioned officer (CCAF, 1977-1978).

COMMON PROBLEMS IN RATING PERFORMANCE

Performance ratings in the classroom and on the job directly measure the products of an objective, and are inherently more valid than written tests. But performance ratings usually require judgment by the examiner and tend to be

Objective No. ___9___

Input to Student	Given: T-37 aircraft in flight and set up at proper altitude in practice area for performance of a Cuban Eight.
• Instructions • Questions • Item Stem Including Alternatives • Problem • Aids	Verbal Instruction: "Demonstrate correct procedures for setup of Cuban Eight maneuver."
Correct Output	A rating of 3 or better. No instructor assistance.
• Answer • Product • Performance (including rating scales)	

SEGMENT ELEMENT — PILOT PERFORMANCE RATING

Segment	Element	1	2	3	4	5	6	7
Set Up for Cuban Eight	A/S Control	over +15kts		within +11 to 15kts		within +4 to 10kts		within +3kts
	Procedure/Checks	U		F		G		E
	Pitch (att) Control	U		F		G		E
	Directional Control	U		F		G		E

FIGURE 12.3: Scale for rating pilot performance

less reliable than written tests. An examiner should rate performances or products under controlled conditions. This means that students should be tested under conditions that give them the best possible chance to display the skill or product. And, test conditions should not change from one student to another.

The observer must rate student performance according to a fixed standard. For example, an observer might use the Pilot Performance Rating scale shown in Figure 12.3 to rate the pilot's execution of the setup procedures of a Cuban Eight maneuver. A rating of 3 for air speed (A/S) is specified as the standard acceptable for achieving the criterion objective, where a 7 rating would be the highest rating attainable on the scale.

At the start of instruction, this scale might be used to assess entry-level behavior. The scale could then be used to provide feedback to the students on their progress. For example, if students are assessed after each week of instruction, they can keep track of their progress and pace themselves accordingly.

A rating scale can help flag a need for revising the course materials. If students fail to achieve the criterion rating, the course may need revision. How far below criterion performance students fall indicates the scope of needed revision. The lower the performance rating, the more revision is required. When students equal or surpass criterion performance, they need no further instruction.

The problem is that when scales are used to judge quality, observers may differ in their judgments. These differences are called rating errors. Rating errors can be classified into three broad groups: (1) error of standards, (2) error of halo, and (3) logical error.

ERROR OF STANDARDS

Some observers tend to overrate or underrate because of the difference in their standards. Standards of physical measurement are fixed units—inches, centimeters, ounces, grams. The categories for knots of air speed in Figure 12.3 are examples of standards of physical measurement. The scale between U (unsatisfactory) and E (excellent) in this figure is also an example of mental standards, where there may be as many different standards as there are observers.

ERROR OF HALO

Observers sometimes allow their rating of performance to be influenced by their general impression of the individual. Such an impression is usually formed on the basis of observations or knowledge extraneous to the rating. If allowed to influence judgment, the impression would result in a shift of the rating. This shift is called an error of halo. If the observer is favorably impressed, the shift is toward the high end of the scale. Note that halo error can be either favorable or unfavorable, and that it affects only certain persons rated.

Halo error results from the likes, dislikes, opinions, prejudices, and moods of people. When considering friends or close acquaintances, observers tend to give undeservedly high ratings in all favorable traits. Such a halo error is often called "error of leniency."

Some people believe that close-set eyes show dishonesty. An observer holding this belief would likely be affected by it when rating a person with close-set eyes. Similarly for racial, sexual, or national stereotypes held by raters. All these preconceptions influence observers. When halo error is traced to such sources, it is sometimes called "error of stereotype."

LOGICAL ERROR

A logical error may occur when two or more traits are being rated. It is present if an observer tends to give similar ratings to traits which do not necessarily go together. For example, some observers may think that an industrious person is also efficient. Industrious persons may often be efficient, but not necessarily so.

The term, logical error, means that the traits are related in the mind of the person making the error. The relationship may not appear to be logical to someone else. As a matter of fact, the person who exhibits an error of this sort is probably not fully aware of it.

WAYS TO AVOID RATING ERRORS

Checklists, numerical scales, descriptive scales, and graphic scales are a few of the ways to avoid rating errors.

CHECKLIST

A checklist is a useful and simple method of rating students' ability to perform certain minimum level set procedures. The observer uses the checklist shown in Figure 12.4 to indicate whether the student performed satisfactorily or unsatisfactorily on instrument flying proficiency. Breaking a performance into many observable elements reduces the error of standards. Because of its broad differentiations, the checklist is usually high in reliability.

NUMERICAL SCALE

A numerical scale divides performance into a fixed number of points. The number of points on the scale depends on the number of differentiations

---

— CHECKLIST —

INSTRUCTIONS: If the performance is satisfactory, place a + sign in the space provided. If the performance is unsatisfactory, place a — sign in the space.

1. Maintains constant heading . . . . ☐
   (within 5° of course)

2. Maintains constant altitude . . . . ☐
   (within 50 feet)

3. Can make a timed turn (gyros caged) . . . ☐
   (within 10° of a new heading)

4. Can make a steep turn . . . . ☐
   (within 50 feet of altitude)

FIGURE 12.4: Checklist for rating proficiency in instrument flying

required, and on the ability of observers to differentiate. For example, a squadron engineering officer must find out which aircraft maintenance personnel are below criterion performance, so they can be given on-the-job training. The officer may elect to use a rating scale, but how many points should the scale have?

How many points are needed will depend, in part, upon how well observers can differentiate. Most people are able to make at least five differentiations. Few trained observers can reliably make more than nine differentiations. It is not surprising that most rating scales contain five to nine points.

DESCRIPTIVE SCALE

The descriptive scale uses phrases to indicate levels of ability. The example in Figure 12.5 shows a descriptive scale for rating pilot ability. Five levels of ability are described. Such a scale is more versatile than the numerical scale, because the degrees of excellence can be varied to suit the occasion. For example, suppose an operations officer wants to evaluate the flying ability of some pilots, all of whom satisfy criterion performance. The question is the degree to which each is better than satisfactory. A numerical scale might be useful, except for the common feeling that the lowest numbers on the scale indicate inferior performance. By using a descriptive scale, the operations

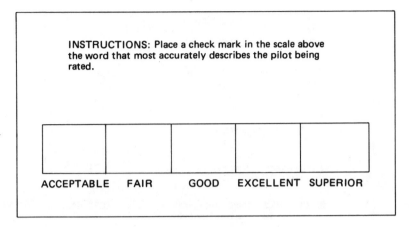

FIGURE 12.5: Descriptive scale for rating pilot ability

officer gives the observers a frame of reference. Here the lowest rating possible is labeled "acceptable." Had a numerical scale been used in this instance, observers would have tended to shift ratings toward the high end of the scale.

The major disadvantage in using descriptive scales is a semantic one. An "excellent pilot" does not mean the same thing to all observers. Another disadvantage: It is hard to select phrases which describe degrees of performance that are equally spaced. When the scale shown in the example is used, most people feel that there is less distance between "excellent" and "superior," than between "fair" and "good."

GRAPHIC SCALE

The graphic scale is a combination of the numerical and descriptive scales. Besides a numerical scale, various adjectives or phrases are set below a continuous horizontal line representing the range of the ability or trait being measured. Here, the observer must consider not only the numerical range of the scale but also the phrases that describe the various positions on the scale.

Three typical forms of the graphic scale are shown in Table 12.7. In Example A, the observer is given instructions for judging the trait of industry. The observer is told to mark the scale after considering energy and application to duties, day in and day out. These instructions help reduce error of halo, and improve objectivity and reliability. They also encourage observers to consider the same things about each person.

The descriptive phrases below the scale, however, allow errors of standards to affect the rating. Phrases that describe observable behavior would help

Table 12.7: Typical Forms of a Graphic Scale

Example A

Industry: Consider energy and application to duties day in and day out	1	2	3	4	5
	Lazy	Indifferent	Diligent	Energetic	Untiring

Example B

Cooperation: Demonstration of willingness to work with others	1	2	3	4	5
	Creates friction	Indifferent to others	Gets along with most people	A harmonious team worker	Actively promotes harmony in working with others

Example C

Initiative: Action taken on own responsibility	1	2	3	4	5
	Slow to act, even when a decision is much needed. Waits for others. Lets opportunities pass. Does not volunteer. Reticent.		Takes needed action without delay. Volunteers for some tasks. Undertakes all routine jobs without supervision. Dependable.		Anticipates needs. Works ahead and prepares for possibilities. Actively seeks opportunities. Eager.

reduce error of standards. They would probably reduce error of halo to an even greater degree.

Example B shows a graphic scale with certain types of behavior represented by each point on the scale. With most scales, observers must not only observe, they must also evaluate their observations in the form of a rating. People can more accurately observe than they can evaluate, and the difficulty of evaluation increases rating errors. The scale in Example B requires the observers only to record, not to evaluate, the actions of the person being rated. Hence, this type of graphic scale allows for much objectivity. If trained users of this scale observe accurately and record honestly, all rating errors except that of halo should be eliminated. The halo error itself should be considerably reduced because of the objectivity built into the scale. In preparing this type of scale, the instructor must make sure that the behavior described for each point is actually an improvement over the point just below it. In each case, distances between the points should appear to the observers to be about equal.

The scale in Example C is similar to that in B, except descriptive phrases are not provided for all points. In some respects this is an improvement. Many times observers feel that the rating should fall somewhere between two points. The fuller descriptions of Example C increase the likelihood that observed behavior can be pinpointed on the scale. Generally, the more detailed descriptions should contribute to better rating results.

PRODUCT RATING

Since the product, unlike the performance, is usually a tangible thing, product rating is more reliable than process rating. The example in Figure 12.6 shows a product scale for rating the ability to fly a link trainer. The pilots being tested are required to fly a pattern that corresponds with the pattern shown at A. On completion of the exercise, the pattern produced is compared with the patterns on the scale. From the comparison of the product with the scale, a rating is produced. If followed carefully, this

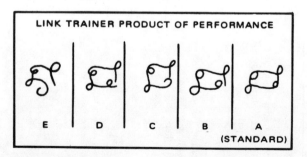

FIGURE 12.6

procedure can eliminate nearly all rating errors. The scale provides a tangible standard that a rater can use to measure the product.

The above examples provide a broad sample of the types of rating methods and their respective strengths and weaknesses. Through the training of observers and careful design of a rating scale, common rating errors can be avoided (AFP 50-58, 1973).

CIVILIAN ADAPTATION TO INSTRUCTIONAL SYSTEMS DEVELOPMENT

What is the potential for adapting the various aspects of the comprehensive technical education system of the United States Air Force? With current pressures for instructional accountability, civilian institutions are developing their own systems of performance-based instruction and evaluation, or are adapting other systems. The Instructional System Development which has been so effective for the Air Force has been widely discussed and considered by civilian educators, and many have adopted and/or adapted the ISD.

FEASIBILITY STUDY

In the late 1960s, the U.S. Office of Education (USOE) awarded a contract to the Aerospace Education Foundation (AEF) to obtain, field test, and evaluate certain Air Force courses in a civilian educational environment (Straubel, 1969). As part of this contract, the AEF conducted an exhaustive survey in which eighty-two Air Force courses in twenty-seven career areas were identified as having direct applicability to the civilian sector. This also included a study to determine empirically the civilian effectiveness of three Air Force instructional units by comparing them with their counterparts in selected educational institutions in Utah. The three courses selected and the Utah schools which participated are listed as follows:

(1) A 90-hour segment from the Air Force Standardized Electronic Principles Course: At Weber State College, Ogden; Dixie College, St. George; Utah Technical College, Salt Lake City; Utah Technical College, Provo; and Jordan High School, Salt Lake City.
(2) A 60-hour segment of the Air Force Aircraft Pneudraulic Course: At Utah State University, Logan.
(3) A 20-hour segment from the Air Force Medical Service Specialist Course: At Utah Technical College, Salt Lake City.

The results, confirmed by the USOE, AEF, and by Utah educators participating in this important experiment, showed that student performance measured in these studies was as good or better than student performance resulting from the use of conventional techniques and material (Straubel, 1970).

CURRENT APPLICATIONS

The Vocational Technical Education Consortium of States (V-TECS) of the Southern Association of Colleges and Schools has adopted a modified form of the Air Force's first three steps of the ISD model. The sixteen member states are currently developing task booklets and performance objectives for ninety-seven occupational areas. V-TECS is now in the dissemination phase to the member states (Lee et al., 1977).

Appalachian State University has adopted the Air Force's Technical Instructor Course to provide the basic educational skills for local community college occupational instructors. Appalachian State University revised the course, omitting only those portions pertaining solely to the military. Sixteen modules of the performance-based instructional materials were, for all practical purposes, adopted in their entirety. Currently, the material is being utilized in a graduate level course: Teaching in the Occupational Programs (Campbell, 1977).

While all courses of instruction are designed to meet the needs of the Air Force, some courses of instruction are adaptive to civilian college needs. The latest copy of the Community College of the Air Force General Catalog (1977-1978) can be consulted for course descriptions in particular areas of interest.

PERFORMANCE RATINGS ON THE JOB

Numerous aspects of the comprehensive, dual channel, on-the-job training system have obvious application in institutions with occupational programs. There are, however, some serious limitations in adapting portions of the system that might not first come to mind. How does one insure that the student has (or has access to) the required tools necessary for successful completion of an occupational course by correspondence? Are the performance standards of the supervisor in private industry the same as required by the institution? Is the supervisor familiar with the performance standards and rating instruments? Admittedly, the Air Force has a special, controlled environment which can compensate for the above limitations. There are, however, some useful insights for civilian educators to be derived from the Air Force system and its past use. The Community College of the Air Force has provided 250 civilian institutions over 650 courses as of October 1977 through its curricular materials exchange program.[3]

The United States Air Force places great value on learning how to perform—whether in the classroom or on-the-job. Conducting most of its own instruction, and then employing the products of that instruction, the system has been tested and shaped by the criteria for efficiency and accountability.[4] These same two tests are now in the forefront of educational discussion. Instruction in and evaluations of secondary and postsecondary vocational programs should be able to adopt many of the Air Force methods of assessing performance.

NOTES

1. ATC. 1976. *Instructional System Development.* Fact Sheet. Randolph AFB: Headquarters Air Training Command. February.
2. Phipps, J. L. 1973. "Postsecondary Institutions and the Air Force: A Partnership in Career Education." Paper presented at the meeting of the American Association for Higher Education, Denver, Colorado. November.
3. See note 2.
4. See note 2.

REFERENCES

AFM 50-2. 1975. *Instructional System Development.* Washington, DC: Department of the Air Force.

AFP 50-58. 1973. *Handbook for Designers of Instructional Systems, Vol. 2.* Washington, DC: Department of the Air Force.

Campbell, D. F. 1977. The easily adaptable instructor training course of the USAF. *American Vocational Journal* 52, 3: 24-26.

——— 1975. "Developing performance-based objectives and criterion measures for industrial arts education." Proceedings of the 37th Annual Conference of the American Industrial Arts Association. 416-421.

Cohen, A. M. 1973. Defining instructional objectives. In J. E. Roueche, and B. R. Herrscher, eds. *Toward Instructional Accountability.* Palo Alto, CA: Westinghouse Learning Press.

Community College of the Air Force. General Catalog, 1977-78, No. 5, Lackland Air Force Base, TX.

Lee, C. W., Hirst, B. A., Hinson, T. M., Koscheski, B. J., and Netrick, L. M. 1977. *Fourth Progress and Information Report of the Vocational-Technical Education Consortium of States.* Atlanta: Commission on Occupational Education Institutions, Southern Association of Colleges and Schools.

Lee, R. 1976. Reverse transfer students. *Community College Review* 4, 2: 64-70.

Straubel, J. H. 1970. A supplement to the final report, Project no. 8-0301.

———. 1969. *The Evaluation of Three U.S. Air Force Instructional Systems within Civilian Education.* Final Report, Project no. 8-0301. Washington, DC: Aerospace Education Foundation.

chapter 13

PAUL G. WHITMORE | *Applied Science Associates, Inc.*

Programs of most any kind, but instructional programs in particular, are made up of inputs, processes, and outputs. Approaches to the formal evaluation of programs can be divided into two classes: those that emphasize inputs and those that emphasize outputs (Caro, 1971). The interest in this chapter is with the latter—outputs.

The principal outputs of an instructional program are the performances learned by the students. It is the intent of the program to improve each student's ability to function in some particular set of situations which the student may encounter at some future time (Whitmore, 1966). It is easy to see this intent in most vocational instruction. *All* instruction worthy of the name ought to have this intent. If it does not, then it more properly should be viewed as recreation or entertainment.

The outputs of an instructional program are specified by the terminal performance objectives of the program. Evaluation of the program's outputs consists of more than just comparing the job performance specified in the terminal objectives. Before such a comparison can be interpreted meaningfully, it is necessary to make a judgment concerning the sources and processes used in deriving the terminal performance objectives. This chapter will focus principally on this aspect of evaluation.

All of us can recall instructional programs that do not appear to have been designed with such an intent. This does not mean that they could not be so designed. Traditional maintenance training programs, for instance, often include a portion dealing with the theory underlying the operation of the

331

equipment to be maintained. This theory portion does not teach students to perform tasks. Rather, it teaches them to describe equipment functions and to trace energy flow through these functions. Most often, energy flow is traced through some logical sequence, such as input to output. The level of detail in these theory courses differs from one program to another. In some cases, students are required to learn intricate details about the equipment's construction and manufacture. These theory courses are most often justified on the grounds that the technicians will require this kind of information in order to *troubleshoot* the equipment. Students will often practice tracing energy flow from malfunction to symptoms. This theory course is often the most difficult in the program. Student attrition is usually higher in theory courses than in other parts of the program. Thus, students are often washed out of the program for failing that part of the program for which job performance was least clearly established.

The proper design of a course dealing with troubleshooting begins with a listing of the job situations in which troubleshooting ought to be performed. The behavioral objectives of such a course should specify the appropriate *skills* to be applied in these situations. This approach to course design begins with an analysis of the future job situations in which graduates of the course will perform: It is a performance analysis approach.

One common objection to the performance analysis approach to instructional design is the belief that it destroys innovation and flexibility in subsequent job performance—it casts all workers in the same mold. And, indeed, this approach is sometimes applied in such a manner as to make this objection valid. This objection is valid when the instruction requires students to learn long sequences of specific actions for specific situations, rather than learn when and how to apply skills. The objectives should not specify the detailed actions to be made in response to a particular situation, but rather the skills to be applied in arriving at the proper sequence of detailed actions. Different technicians may well apply the *same* skills to arrive at somewhat *different* sequences of actions to find a particular equipment malfunction.

Instructions should focus on skills. Skills are identified from sequences of actions. The analysis proceeds by listing the job situations, the sequence of actions for each situation, the skills for each sequence of actions, and finally, arranging the skills into learning hierarchies.

How are actions and skills different? An action is the selection of a specific checkpoint during a troubleshooting sequence. A skill is the recall and application of a rule or set of rules for selecting the next checkpoint in many troubleshooting sequences. A sequence of actions is the steps required to set up a multimeter to measure a range of resistance between 10 and 100 ohms. Skills are the recall and application of instructions for setting up a multimeter to make resistance measurements in any given range. The application skill may include the following subordinate skills: Location of all controls and displays involved in resistance measurements, manipulation of resistance controls, selection of the proper resistance range for any given measurement situation, and the reading of a meter set at any given resistance range to within one-half a graduation on the meter face. A step is reading the value of a particular resistor: The skill is reading the value of any given resistor. Subordinate skills include giving the integer value for each color in the resistor color code, and recalling and applying the rules for interpreting the placement of color bands on resistors. The skills that are derived from the sequences of actions are arranged in learning hierarchies (Gagné, 1965) to show which skills must be learned before other skills can be learned. Subordinate skills should be added to the hierarchy where necessary until they connect to the entering skills of the student population (Mager and Pipe, 1974).

Troubleshooting courses designed by means of the analytical approach will possess the following characteristics: (1) functional relationships are introduced as needed in learning the skills for isolating malfunctions from symptom patterns, (2) tracing energy flow through the equipment is done only to facilitate the logic for isolating malfunctions, and proceeds from symptom to source (rather than source to symptom), and (3) the level of detail of equipment information is fixed by the analysis (rather than varying from time to time according to instructor opinions or student capability).

The adequacy of the specific judgments made during the application of the analytic approach cannot always be assessed simply by examining the product of the analysis; that is, by examining the objectives of the course of instruction. It is possible for a course to appear to have been derived from an exhaustive inventory of job situations and actions, without actually having been so derived. Hence, it is necessary to examine the rational processes by which the product was derived. For this reason, the evaluation of the content validity of the objectives is, in fact, an evaluation of the process by which the objectives were derived. Except in the simplest of cases, this evaluation cannot be done after the objectives have been developed. The evaluator must observe the process and inquire into it at the time choices and decisions are made. The evaluator should enter the process at the very beginning and continue with it in a collaborative role through the development, implementation, and followup evaluation of the program. It may be difficult for the evaluator to maintain objectivity and encourage innovation in this kind of relationship. This difficulty might be solved by using an evaluation team made up of internal and external evaluators, in the same way that organizational development efforts often use internal and external change agents.

ESTABLISHING THE CONTENT VALIDITY
OF THE OBJECTIVES

Characteristics of Content Validity

Before data are gathered about the achievement of stated objectives, it is first necessary to examine how those objectives were derived. An assessment of the content validity of the stated objectives not only should be a part of the evaluation, it should be the first part. There may be no point in continuing with the evaluation if the content validity of the objectives cannot be established.

The content validity of a set of performance objectives is established by the analytical processes through which the set of objectives was derived. The objectives are based on skills derived from a list of tasks. The content validity of this list of tasks must be established. Then, objectives are derived from these validated task lists. There is no index for expressing the degree of content validity. It is a judgment. The evaluator critically examines the process, looking for flaws, omissions, or weak logical connections. If a flaw is found, additional analytical processes are sought. Sometimes several processes are used that supplement each other.

There are five characteristics of a valid task listing procedure.

First, all relevant tasks must be included. A procedure is required that is comprehensive in designating likely tasks.

Second, the procedure must also exclude irrelevant tasks. People should not be evaluated on things they don't need to do.

Third, a chain of tight logical links should be established from the requirements imposed on the job by the larger system of which it is a part to the tasks which make up the job. Jobs do not exist in isolation. There should be a clear connection between the system's demands and the tasks that make up the job.

Fourth, tasks must be identified that are realistic with regard to the characteristics of the available workers and to the characteristics of the job environment. It is useless to define a job that can not be done by real people in real conditions.

Fifth, needless changes in established job practices and traditions should be avoided. Traditional job language should be maintained, insofar as possible, to facilitate communication with workers already in the field. Changing the language or the structuring of the activities can make it difficult to gather information about a job or to communicate test requirements to examiners.

Task Listing Procedures

There are three different kinds of approaches for developing task lists: (1) empirical approaches, (2) relational approaches, and (3) functional approaches. The procedures in each of these categories will be evaluated against the five characteristics of a valid task list described in the preceding section. It should be noted that the task listing procedures used for designing evaluation instruments can also be used for designing instructional programs. It makes sense to combine this activity for both efforts.

1. EMPIRICAL APPROACHES

Existing Task Lists: The simplest and one of the most common ways of developing a task list is to survey and combine existing task lists for a given job. These lists can usually be found in or inferred from the job manuals. However, there are severe limitations to this procedure as a sole source for the task list. It assumes that the current job manuals define the job completely and accurately. This is not likely to be entirely true unless the manuals were themselves based on a recent, comprehensive, and accurate task listing effort. In most cases, existing task lists are likely to have errors of inclusion, errors of exclusion, and are not likely to be based on a tight logical chain leading from system requirements to individual tasks.

If the job documents have been around for some time and have been regularly updated, they *may* (1) reflect current job practices, (2) be realistic with regard to the characteristics of workers and of the job environment, and (3) reflect current job language and task structuring. However, if the updating did not involve some kind of feedback from actual job practice, the job documents themselves may not meet these requirements. It is not uncommon for technical writers to write for an audience of technical writers rather than for workers.

Task Lists Obtained from Job Practices: Another common way of developing a task list is to survey current job practices. Workers' activities over some fixed period of time may be recorded by the workers themselves (job diary), by observers, or by recollection by the workers in response to an interview or questionnaire. This source of information describes current practices and the realities of the job environment. However, current practices are not necessarily optimum or even correct practices. Management conditions on the job may have allowed improper practices to develop and spread, and some system goals may have been neglected. The skills for attaining them may have eroded. As a result, task lists obtained from current job practices may contain errors of both inclusion and exclusion, and may omit some system requirements. But, they will reflect the actual job environment, real workers, current job practices, current job language, and task structuring.

Many job analysts *validate* a task list, obtained by compiling existing task lists, by comparing it to actual job practices. Most often, a tentative task list made up from document sources will be sent to workers in the field who check which tasks they actually do and add tasks not on the list. Actual job practice does not define a criterion against which to validate a task list because actual job practices are not necessarily proper practices. Job practices may be wrong and the initial task list may be right. Differences between different sources of information simply indicate a problem that needs to be investigated. One source of information about job tasks is not necessarily the right source. In some instances, existing task lists and actual job practices may both be wrong.

2. RELATIONAL APPROACHES

Frequently an initial task list is developed from the relations among the actions and the objects found in a job. In this usage, a task is defined as a combination of an action and an object-acted-upon.

Relational analysis is performed by listing a set of action words along one dimension of a matrix, and a set of object words along the other dimension. Expert judges (experienced workers) are asked to check those cells in the matrix that represent proper or actual combinations of an action with an object.

Relational analysis is often used to list tasks for equipment maintenance positions. A restricted set of action words is prepared, such as check, align, service, repair, replace, adjust, and so forth. These words are listed along one dimension of a matrix and the names of all the assemblies in the equipment are listed along the other dimension. Experienced maintenance personnel or engineers, check all combinations of action words with assemblies which define real tasks.

Some form of relational analysis is usually appropriate for those task listing efforts which deal with a restricted set of actions and an extensive set of objects, many of which may require several actions. Often the objects are clustered into equipment subsystems. In such cases, the work can be made more manageable by developing a separate matrix for each subsystem.

Relational analysis can and has been used to develop task lists for other than equipment oriented jobs. For instance, Powers and De Luca (1972) used relational analysis to develop a task list for each of the four staff positions in the headquarters of combat maneuver battalions. Objects were selected from the general job environment. As an example, one object was designated as "replacements." The actions included such terms as "brief" (meaning to inform), "determine priorities," "welcome," "confer with BnCO" (battalion commander), and "confer with Unit CO" (company commander). Respondents indicated how often they performed each action/object combination, how much time they spent doing it, the difficulty of each, and the importance of each. However, some of Powers and De Luca's objects strained the meaning of the word "objects": examples are state of discipline, social events, local civilians. Some of these terms are less than adequate with regard to their operational rigor. It remains an interesting approach, but not nearly as appropriate to this kind of job as are the task listing approaches looked at next.

3. FUNCTIONAL APPROACHES

The functional approaches differ from the empirical and relational approaches principally in that they derive tasks from job outcomes. There are four procedures that are examined:

(1) Troubleshooting analyses
(2) Job models
(3) Mission analysis
(4) Systems analysis

Troubleshooting Analyses: Troubleshooting analyses have most often been used to develop printed job aids, which present procedures for specific troubleshooting strategies to guide technicians on the job (Shriver and Trexler, 1966). Troubleshooting analysis is an analysis of the equipment functions in order to identify symptom patterns, and to determine optimum procedures for isolating malfunctions. It is frequently used in conjunction with relational analysis to develop task lists for equipment maintenance jobs.

The analysis begins with a listing of the replaceable components or assemblies in the equipment, and the authorized adjustments and alignments. All discrete malfunctions are identified for each entry in the list. The symptoms and indicators[1] of each malfunction are then listed by tracing the effect of the malfunction on the signal or information flow through the equipment. Troubleshooting strategies are developed by sorting symptoms and indicators to develop logic trees leading to the isolation of the malfunction. These logic trees define the troubleshooting tasks. (This description of troubleshooting analyses has been grossly oversimplified for clarity.)

In evaluating performance in a maintenance job for which job aids have been developed from a thorough troubleshooting analysis, it makes sense to design a performance test that exercises the worker's ability to use the job aid. The separate characteristics of the job aid are listed, and malfunctions are selected that require the worker to use all the different characteristics at some point or other. However, if one is evaluating the effectiveness of a printed job aid itself or a job for which no such aid exists, then performance items are selected on the basis of their frequency of occurrence, isolation time, and criticality of the malfunctions. In the latter case, the task list is supplemented with actual or predicted malfunction data for the given type of equipment.

Clearly, troubleshooting analysis is a specialized technique applicable to only a few kinds of jobs. However, it illustrates the application of rational analysis, which is common to all the functional approaches.

Job Models: The job model was introduced by Ammerman (1965) to deal with task listing for man-ascendant jobs.[2] It provides a basis for structuring job activities, for applying behavioral science theory and data to the definition of job functions, and for deriving job functions from system characteristics. Task lists for jobs in machine-ascendant systems are based upon an initial identification of tangible objects (machine components) with which the worker must interact. In such contexts, the functions and subfunctions of the equipment and its components have already been derived by the hardware designer before the job analyst arrives on the scene. These are the "givens." The job analyst may have to ferret out tasks from the equipment functions and configurations, but task listing will not have to begin with a description of the system environment to determine overall system functions.

In a man-ascendant system, however, this functional analysis will not have been accomplished prior to the arrival of the job analyst. Brown and Jacobs (1970:4) comment:

> It is significant to note that the training objectives for members of a *machine-ascendant system* may be ascertained largely from an analysis of the functions of the machine; also, a criterion of satisfactory performance is readily available—the machine either works or does not work. To achieve the same ends for the members of the . . . *man-ascendant system* is clearly more complex.

In the man-ascendant system, the job analyst may have to: (1) structure the environment and identify its elements, (2) make value judgments regarding the system's objectives, (3) "invent" the functions or missions of the system, and (4) engineer the accomplishment of system missions by integrating behavior components in much the same manner as equipment engineers integrate machine components. There are behavioral principles that determine the design and arrangement of behavioral components just as surely as there are engineering principles that determine the design and arrangement of hardware components to achieve the system's missions. These behavioral principles may be less certain and less clearly defined and agreed upon than engineering principles, but they are there.

In dealing with a machine operator job, the analyst first determines what specific function the machine ought to perform in a given situation. What a person must do to the machine to have it perform the specified function is then deduced from the theory of the machine's operation and its displays and controls. In a similar manner, in dealing with a supervisory, administrative, or job counseling function, the analyst first determines what function the subordinate ought to perform in the situation. How the supervisor, administrator, or counselor must treat the subordinate in order to facilitate the performance of the specified function is then deduced from a theory of operation for human beings. Such considerations form a significant part of the job model.

A job model has three major sections (Whitmore, 1973):

(1) A specification of broad job functions derived from appropriate system characteristics.
(2) A specification of general behavioral considerations appropriate to the analysis of each broad job function.
(3) A specification of the information categories required to explicate each broad job function, the appropriate sources of such information, and procedures for gathering the information.

The job model records the reasons for making choices and the choices themselves, so they can be available for examination at a later time by other people.

If a system analysis has been conducted beforehand, the first section should summarize the findings of this analysis, specify those system characteristics most pertinent to the derivation of broad job functions, and state the broad job functions themselves. If a complete, formal, and validated systems analysis has not been conducted, then this section should at least specify the assumptions that were made about the system in order to derive the broad job functions. A flowchart may be helpful in conceptualizing the job, and can be included in this section to relate job inputs and outputs to other parts of the system. In this section, the various job environments are identified and those characteristics, both physical and social, that impose special requirements on job performance are specified.

The second section of the job model describes the behavioral processes pertinent to the performance of each job function. As Miller (1962) points out, it indicates what should and what should not be identified and described in detail. It will specify the types of job aids to be used to support job performance, if they are used.

The third section of the job model lists the categories of information required to complete the job description, the appropriate sources for each category of information, and the appropriate procedures for obtaining the information. Different categories of information may have to be obtained from different sources. As discussed earlier, it should not be assumed that existing documentation and present job incumbents are appropriate and valid sources for all information. If the job function has not been performed adequately in the past, with regard to some job effectiveness criterion, then it may be necessary to develop different ways for performing the function, rather than merely describing old processes. There may not even be adequate criteria for some job functions, such as leadership, supervision, and peer motivation. In such cases, it may first be necessary to invent the criteria.

Job incumbents will generally be the most appropriate sources for information about the frequency of various job situations, but they may be very poor sources for information about the criticality of tasks. In many instances, criticality may be more validly established by means of an analysis of missions and mission requirements (discussed in next section).

Different analysts may construct different models for the same job. Where vast differences occur, emphasis should be placed on merging the two models, rather than on picking one over the other because each analyst may have selected a different aspect of the system or job for major emphasis. Multiple analysts working independently may provide the best means of arriving at a comprehensive and efficient job model. The development of an effective job model may be viewed as a creative process, and should not be viewed as wasteful duplication. In this context, work by several analysts increases the probability of evolving a comprehensive model.

In sketching out a job model for Army officers, Whitmore (1973) equated leadership to the behavior management of subordinates: "defining, eliciting, and maintaining the occurrence of productive or appropriate behaviors and . . . identifying and minimizing the occurrence of inappropriate behaviors among . . . subordinates."

The second part of the model analyzed the behavior management function from a contingency management point of view. This analysis contained these parts:

(A) Behavioral Analysis and Basic Principles. Reviews basic principles of contingency management.
(B) Productive Behavior and Objectives. Relates organizational objectives to contingency management practices.
(C) Inappropriate Behavior. Identifies general contingency management practices for dealing with inappropriate behaviors among subordinates.
(D) Group Interactions. Identifies the nucleus of most management and decision systems as a small group of individuals who interact on a face-to-face basis. Lists general interpersonal behaviors within the group required for effective group problem solving.

(E) Typical Conceptions Held by Students. Lists misconceptions common in the target population regarding behavior management practices.

(F) Functional Model. Presents the beginning of a hierarchic fractionation of the function into subfunctions and subsubfunctions.

The functional model was presented in part as follows:

> The primary function of a manager as regards guiding, directing, and motivating his people can be stated in this manner:
>> Designs and implements management practices that strengthen productive behaviors and weaken counter-productive behaviors emitted by his people.
>
> This primary function can be fractionated into three first-order subordinate functions on the basis of contingency management considerations, as follows:
>> 01 Designs and implements practices for reinforcing productive behavior.
>>
>> 02 Designs and implements practices for minimizing the inadvertent reinforcement of counterproductive or disruptive behavior.
>>
>> 03 Designs and implements practices for minimizing the occurrence of aversive stimuli in the environment.
>
> In order to design and implement practices for reinforcing productive behavior, the contingency manager must accomplish the following second-order functions:
>> 01 01 Identifies and defines productive behaviors.
>>
>> 01 02 Specifies and implements techniques for monitoring the occurrence of productive behaviors.
>>
>> 01 03 Identifies potentially effective and feasible positive reinforcers.
>>
>> 01 04 Designs and implements techniques for the contingent administration of positive reinforcers on an appropriate schedule.
>>
>> 01 05 Modifies reinforcement program if desired changes fail to occur.
>
> To accomplish the first of three second-order functions, the contingency manager must be able to identify valid organizational objectives, analyze organizational objectives into individual objectives, and analyze individual objectives into behavior sequences. To accomplish the second, he must have a catalog of monitoring techniques appropriate to the kinds of people and to the organizational situations with which he is concerned. To perform the third, he must have information regarding potentially effective reinforcers for the kinds of people he manages. Also, to accomplish the fourth second-order function, he needs a catalog of appropriate techniques.

The second and third first-order functions were broken down in a similar manner.

The third part of the job model identified specific information required to complete the hierarchic fractionation to a task level. Examples of questions listed in the third part of the job model are as follows:

(1) What kinds of counterproductive behaviors occur in various job environments?
(2) What kinds of inadvertent reinforcers typically maintain various counterproductive behaviors?
(3) What kinds of changes are typically effective in stopping the inadvertent reinforcement of counter productive behaviors?
(4) What kinds of events or conditions do workers generally consider aversive in various job environments?
(5) What kinds of changes are typically effective in minimizing aversive events and conditions?

The adequacy of a job model clearly depends upon the skill and sophistication of the analyst. The job model offers the potential for developing a comprehensive task list that excludes irrelevant tasks. The logic underlying the task list is available for examination. The linkages from system considerations to individual tasks are specified by the model. The third part of a job model, when complete, should tie the model to real characteristics of the target population. However, it does not guard against making needless changes in established job practices, job language, and job traditions.

The job model approach is a useful task listing procedure for those jobs or parts of jobs that have not been well structured in the past, and that are not determined by clearly identified characteristics of the job environment; that is, it is more appropriate for the man-ascendant aspects of systems than for the machine-ascendant aspects. The evaluation of a job model should inquire into the model's specific assumptions, examine each logical link, and suggest alternatives wherever possible.

Mission Analysis: Major objectives which are to be attained by a team or organization are called missions. The analysis of missions must include tasks that are concerned with the interactions among team members and the cues that trigger them. Mission analysis is essentially a flowcharting technique for identifying the actions of successively smaller groups of people. Typically, the flowchart shows the sequence of actions and decisions. A preferred method is to flowchart the actions of each member or subgroup in separate, parallel strips, as shown in Figure 13.1. The primary interest of a mission analysis may be in all or in only one member of the team.

The first step in conducting a mission analysis is to define the mission. A mission is an effect produced by a system on some part of its environment. For instance, if the system is an automotive repair shop, then one of its

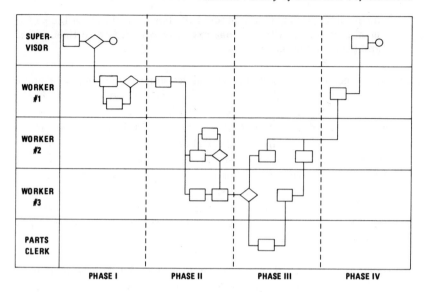

FIGURE 13.1: Mission analysis flowcharts arranged in parallel strips

primary missions is to return clients' automobiles to operating condition. This mission will include the intake and initial diagnosis procedures by the service manager, the final diagnosis by a senior mechanic, the repair by a journeyman mechanic, interactions with the parts clerk, road test by the senior mechanic or service manager, billing by the cashier, and pickup by the customer. The interchanges between individuals are shown as arrows that cross from one strip to another.

There are several steps in the conduct of a mission analysis:

(1) Define the mission objective in operational terms. Remember, a mission objective describes an effect on some part of the environment produced by the actions of the system.

(2) List the major time sequenced phases of the mission. This way it is not necessary to keep the whole thing in mind simultaneously.

(3) List the components of the system. The components may all be individuals or they may be a mixture—individuals and subgroups.

(4) Develop a tentative list of actions and decisions performed by each component in each phase of mission performance.

(5) Flowchart the actions and decisions of each component in parallel strips, showing the interchanges between components. (See Figure 13.1)

(6) State the initiating cues for each action and decision shown in the flowchart.

(7) State the standard of performance for each action and the decision rules for each decision. Be sure that standards are related to subse-

quent actions; that is, the product of step 1 should allow the performance of step 2 without being excessive with regard to time, effort, and personnel resources.

The actions, decisions, cues, standards, and decision rules provide the content for a list of tasks that can be readily converted into full behavioral objectives. The procedure produces a comprehensive list of relevant tasks free of irrelevant entries, and with all logical links clearly established. However, it can introduce needless changes from traditional practices and language.

Most mission analyses consist of several different levels. The first level may use subgroups as its components. Next, selected subgroup actions are flowcharted using subsubgroups as components. And, finally, subsubgroup actions are flowcharted using individuals as components. In this way, mission analyses can relate individual actions to organizational goals with a clearly defined chain of logical links.

Systems Analysis: Another way to develop a task list is to begin with the purposes of the job, and the situations in which the job is to be performed; that is, to perform an analysis of the job system. Two kinds of systems analyses will be described:

(1) Analysis of a single job which occurs in a larger system.

(2) Analysis of one or more jobs in a multijob organization.

(1) Analysis of a single job. McKnight and Adams (1972) conducted an outstanding analysis of the job of driving a private automobile. Many activities can be analyzed into stages that occur in the same order every time they are done, such as changing a tire. Driving a car does *not* fit this pattern. There are a countless number of things that can happen differently from one trip to the next. Driving is more usefully seen as responding to a series of situations, which may occur in any of an infinite number of sequences on any given trip. Action within any given situation, however, can be described along a time line, but the situations themselves are not ordered along a time line. McKnight and Adams started their analysis by identifying all the situations which can occur while driving a car. In their words:

> The first step in the process was to identify those aspects of the (highway transportation) system that were capable of creating situations to which the driver must respond—for example, curves in the road, traffic control devices, cars ahead, snow, rain, and driver fatigue. Over 1,000 specific behaviorally relevant system characteristics were identified. These system charactericstics were then taken singly and in combination with each other to identify potential critical situations with which a driver may have to cope.

In order to identify the specific purposes and situations which constitute a given job, one begins by analyzing the system in which that job occurs. The initial steps in the systems analysis process are concerned with ensuring the comprehensiveness and validity of the task list. With regard to the identification of system characteristics, McKnight and Adams note:

> Inasmuch as this activity formed the foundation for latter analyses, particular pains were taken to see that the analysis was very broad, since to overlook any relevant system characteristics could result in the omission of potentially critical . . . behaviors (p. 7).

They began both the situation analysis and the purpose analysis by identifying a restricted number of broadly defined classes of characteristics "which shape the responses the individual must make as a driver; that is, that might impose behavioral requirements upon the driver." The broad classes of characteristics from which the situation analysis commenced consisted of driver characteristics, vehicle characteristics, roadway characteristics, traffic characteristics, and characteristics of the external environment. These general characteristics guided the identification of specific characteristics gleaned from various sources of information. They started with a few general classes of characteristics. Then they identified subclasses within each general class. And, finally, they identified specific characteristics within each subclass. They used brainstorming and an extensive review of the literature in each step of the process.

The initial list of characteristics was arranged into a logical hierarchy or tree-structure. This hierarchy was examined for logical gaps at each level. The gaps were filled in, and in this manner, the hierarchy was extended so as to be as comprehensive as possible. Parts of the final hierarchy had as many as seven levels. These situation characteristics were then taken singly and in combination, to define the situations with which the subsequent analysis would be concerned.

McKnight and Adams also conducted an analysis of the system's purposes or goals. It was not nearly as elegant as the situation analysis, but it was equally important. As they defined it, the purpose or goal of the highway transportation system is to assure "the movement of passengers and material from one place to another with safety, efficiency, comfort, and responsibility." The characteristics of the goal impose general behavioral requirements on drivers:

Safety requires that drivers behave in a way that will minimize the chances of injury or property damage.

Efficiency requires that drivers avoid interfering with the rapid and economical flow of traffic.

Comfort requires that drivers operate in ways that will not cause discomfort to passengers, other drivers, or pedestrians.

Responsibility means that drivers should be morally and financially responsible for the consequences of their acts.

These general goal characteristics were used to identify specific goals or purposes in each situation defined by the situation analysis. These specific goals defined what the effects of the driver's behavior ought to be in the situation. Then the analysis proceeded backward from the necessary effects of the behavior to the identification of the behavior itself. This analysis was based on the operational characteristics and principles of automobiles. This resulted in the list of tasks.

Tasks were divided into on-road behaviors and off-road behaviors. They identified six classes of on-road tasks and three classes of off-road tasks.

Many of these tasks contain major subtasks. *Task 36 Reacting to Traffic* contains three subtasks:

36-1	Reacting to Other Vehicles
36-2	Responding to Pedestrians and Other Road Users
36-3	Reacting to Collisions and Emergencies

Each of these subtasks was analyzed into actions. *Subtask 36-2 Responding to Pedestrians and Other Road Users* was analyzed in part as follows:

36-2	RESPONDING TO PEDESTRIANS AND OTHER ROAD USERS
36-21	Observes Pedestrians
36-211	Watches for pedestrians near intersections, crosswalks, and school crossings
36-212	Yields right-of-way to pedestrians at all times
36-213	Watches pedestrians for indication of entry onto roadway
36-2131	Pedestrians walking toward roadway
36-2132	Children
36-2132-1	Walking
36-2132-2	At Play
36-2133	Pedestrians apparently under the influence of alcohol
36-2134	Pedestrians who are running
36-2135	Pedestrians who are distracted (e.g., reading)
36-214	Watches pedestrians standing on roadway for sudden movements to avoid traffic
36-22	Passes pedestrians carefully
36-221	Provides maximum possible clearance when passing pedestrians, using passing lane if possible

36-222   Does not pass vehicle ahead when pedestrians reduce
                lane clearance

These actions provide the basis for preparing a checklist for evaluating performance of each subtask.

Single-job system analysis produces a comprehensive list of relevant tasks free of irrelevant entries, with all logical links clearly established. It can introduce needless changes from traditional practices and language, although the extensive literature review as conducted by McKnight and Adams would tend to guard against such changes. This procedure is probably preferable to an object/action matrix, in some instances, in which the latter has been typically used. For instance, the task lists developed by Powers and De Luca (1972) for battalion staff positions would have been more comprehensive had they used a single-job systems analysis rather than an action/object matrix.

(2) Analysis of multiple jobs. The procedure to be described in this section is not a tried and tested procedure for preparing a task list, but the need and logic are sufficiently compelling to warrant its inclusion. Similar techniques have been used in educational planning (Kaufman, 1972).

Organizations consist of individuals formed into one or more levels of subsystems operating to attain individual, subsystem, and organizational purposes. The multijob systems analysis process moves in three phases, from the organization to its subsystems to the individuals who make up the organization. If we conceive of the system as being a triangle with organizational characteristics at the apex and individual characteristics at the base, then the analysis proceeds from apex to base.

Phase I—The Apex Analysis At this level, the analysis is concerned with defining the system as a single entity—its gross capabilities and purposes, its relationships to other systems, and the environment in which it operates. The product is an identification of the missions required of the system, that is, the situations in which its various purposes are to be attained.

Phase II—Middle Analysis At this level, the analysis is concerned with identifying the functional (duties) and structual components within the system required for accomplishing each mission, the relationships among these components, and the relationships between these components and elements outside the system.

Phase III—The Base Analysis This analysis proceeds in two stages. In the first stage, the analysis is concerned with identifying the activities required to perform each duty in each situation in which it might reasonably occur—that is, within the context of each system mission. These activities are the tasks required of each position incumbent or job holder. They are specified at the least detailed level at which adequate reliability or precision of meaning can be obtained from job holders and instructors.

In the second stage, the analysis is concerned with describing the performance of each task in adequate detail to elicit rudimentary or unpracticed task performance from individuals representative of those who will be trained to perform the task.

The Apex Analysis identifies the missions required of the organization. The Middle Analysis breaks these missions into duties and allocates the duties to positions. The Base Analysis breaks the duties into tasks and then describes the tasks in sufficient detail to allow untrained individuals to perform them in a rudimentary manner.

The Apex Analysis ends with the development of a list of missions for the system. The Middle and Base Analysis proceed from this point using mission analyses, job models, and single job system analyses as appropriate. The Base Analysis may even use action/object matrices and troubleshooting analyses for developing task lists for maintenance jobs. Multijob system analysis is a combination of all the other methods plus an initial mission listing procedure. It combines and extends mission analysis, job models, and single job systems analysis to a more complex problem. Hence, it should produce a comprehensive list of tasks free of irrelevant entries in each position, with all logical links clearly established. However, it may introduce needless changes from traditional practices and language.

Skill Identification

Gagné (1966) described a procedure for identifying skills which proceeds by asking what prerequisite behaviors must be in an individual's repertory in order for the desired terminal task to be performed. The same question is then asked about the behaviors identified in the first cycle. This procedure is continued until behaviors already in the repertory of the target population are reached. The outcome of this procedure is a learning hierarchy consisting of the requisite skills arranged in successive levels of learning subordination.

Mager and Pipe (1974) have substantially improved the workability of this procedure by breaking it into several separate operations. First, they do an analysis of each task and the steps required to perform it. Second, they list the skills that must be learned by members of the target population in order to perform each step. And, third, they arrange these skills into a learning hierarchy consisting of the requisite skills arranged in successive levels of learning subordination (Pipe, 1975). These skills form the basis for preparing the objectives of the instructional program, and the learning hierarchy establishes the basic sequence for learning these skills.

Taxonomies of Objectives

Some investigators during recent decades have sought to apply some form of taxonomy to the selection or development of objectives for vocational curricula (Bloom, 1956; Yagi et al., 1971). The claim is made that there should be some kind of numerical balance or rational numerical pattern among objectives in different categories, and that this pattern should guide the selection and development of objectives. The view taken here is that instructional objectives are selected or developed solely for the purpose of insuring that proper performances be made by members of the target population, in some specified set of future situations. Thus, the process of preparing such objectives must begin with the identification of the situations and the performances which are proper in those situations. This frequently means that we need some systematic approach for comprehensive identification of criterion situations, rather than for the identification of performances or skills. It does not seem likely at this point that a taxonomic schema can be developed that is universally applicable to all types of jobs. Rather, it seems more likely that process schemata, such as the previously described task listing procedures, are more useful. Once the situations have been identified, one needs to identify the proper performances in each situation. Miller (1962) notes that the selection of relevant cues and actions needs to be based on a theory of task performance. The job model task listing procedure requires the analyst to specify a theory of task performance, so that it can be available for examination rather than be left implicit.

Taxonomies of objectives, of tasks, of stimuli, or of responses are primarily useful as sources of words to use in preparing objectives. All too often, taxonomies are expected to serve as easy substitutes for comprehensive task listing procedures and for adequate theories of task performance. There are no easy substitutes.

ESTABLISHING THE ACHIEVEMENT OF THE OBJECTIVES

There are two major aspects to the evaluation of instructional outcomes; i.e., outcome evaluation. The first aspect measures students' performance of the skills specified by the objectives immediately following instruction. This measurement provides a basis for making inferences about the adequacy of the instructional procedures for the target population from which the students were drawn. It answers the question, "Did the students learn the skills they were supposed to learn?" If a substantial number of students failed the test for a particular objective, then either the instructional procedures for that objective were faulty or the derivation of subordinate skills was not adequate for the target population; i.e., students were not provided with instruction in necessary subordinate skills.

The second aspect of instructional evaluation measures performance on the job tasks of graduates who *mastered* all the skills specified by the objectives. It answers the question, "Are these the right skills for learning these tasks?" If a substantial number of students fail a particular task or set of tasks, then that task was not properly analyzed into skills; i.e., one or more critical skills were omitted from the list of skills.

Basically, a test is a procedure for gathering data about performances in order to make a decision about those performances. The first step in constructing an achievement test for evaluating the effectiveness of the instruction is to determine the kinds of decisions or actions that are to be based upon the outcome of the test. Thus, the tests or data gathering procedures should be tailored to the decisions that will be made on the basis of these data. If one is constructing a test for an instructional module, the primary concern will be with determining which students have or have not learned the specified performance. The fact that some passing students learn more than other passing students is of little concern, unless some action will be based on this difference. There is little point in differentiating between students unless they are to be treated differently (Whitmore, 1970).

The first aspect of outcome evaluation should be conducted in the form of developn.ental trials during the latter stages of preparing the instructional programs. The instruction, when applied to members of the target population, should produce the performances (emphasis on skills) specified by the objectives. The instruction should be modified until it has the effect on student performance specified by the objectives. These same objectives and tests derived from them are used to control student progress during the routine administration of the instructional program. If the developmental trials have been properly conducted leading to the preparation of effective instruction, then later difficulties in student achievement would suggest problems in program management and/or incentives, or a shift in the target population.

The second major aspect of outcome evaluation (i.e., evaluating the effectiveness of skills selected for the students to learn for producing adequate job performance) is accomplished, basically, by determining the adequacy of job performance of students who have successfully completed the instructional program. Such evaluation may be accomplished by means of job-sample proficiency tests, observations of on-the-job performance, supervisory evaluations, follow-up questionnaires to graduates, self check lists, and so on. These instruments should be designed to gather information about the performances of the graduates (emphasis on tasks) specified by the objectives of the instructional program. Of course, it is necessary to find out whether the graduates do other things than those specified in the objectives.

In some instances, the evaluator's responsibility may include evaluating the *efficiency* of the instructional delivery system as well as its effectiveness. Does it achieve its objectives with minimum resources—such as student input, facilities and equipment, faculty and staff, and so on? Or, if it fails to meet some objectives, what needs to be done to insure objectives will be achieved? To conduct this evaluation, the evaluator can use task listing procedures to develop performance objectives for the operation of part or all the instructional program. For instance, an evaluator could use a job model of instructors, such as the one developed by Melching and Whitmore (1973), as a basis for evaluating the performance of instructor personnel. Or, the evaluator might do a systems analysis of the instructional and motivational situations likely to be encountered by students, to determine how other components of the delivery system should operate to achieve the systems purposes for students. Or, one could do a mission analysis of student learning in the instructional environment. The task lists and objectives generated by these efforts would suggest the kind of information to be collected about the system, and the judgments to be based on such information.

A FINAL NOTE

The fact that instructors have developed behavioral objectives, even well stated ones, does not mean that those objectives are worth measuring. The first task of the evaluator is to assess the worth of measuring the stated objectives. This is done by examining and judging the process by which these objectives are derived. The evaluator must insist that such objectives be derived from anticipated future situations in which graduates of the program are likely to have to perform. Instructors must not be allowed to avoid this requirement by protesting that it does not fit their situation. The evaluator must be prepared to provide them with imaginative and feasible examples for their subject matter. If anticipated future situations cannot be defined for a program, the need for the program must be challenged. Students should not be required to invest substantial portions of their lives preparing for nothing.

NOTES

1. Symptoms are defined as readily accessible indications of improper operation of the equipment available on its "skin" or surface. Indicators are less readily available indications of improper operation that require removing a panel or using a test instrument.

2. Folletie (1960) distinguishes between man-ascendant, and hardware or machine-ascendant systems as the two ends of a continuum dealing with the relative amount of hardware that is critical to the functioning of a system. An automotive repair shop is an example of a machine-ascendant system, and a counseling center is an example of a man-ascendant system.

REFERENCES

Ammerman, H. L. 1965. *A Model of Junior Officer Jobs for use in Developing Task Inventories.* HumRRO Tech. Rep. 65-10. Alexandria, VA: Human Resources Research Organization. (NTIS No. AD-624 048)

Bloom, B. S., 1956. ed. *Taxonomy of Educational Objectives: The Classification of Educational Goals. Handbook 1, Cognitive Domain.* New York: McKay.

Brown, F. L., and Jacobs, T. O. 1970. *Developing the Critical Combat Performance Required of the Infantry Rifle Platoon Leader.* HumRRO Tech. Rep. 70-5. Alexandria, VA: Human Resources Research Organization. (NTIS No. AD-704 946)

Caro, F. G. 1971. Issues in the evaluation of social programs. *Review of Educational Research* 41:87-114.

Folletie, J. F. 1960. *A Performance Requirement for Basic Land Navigation.* Research Report 4. Alexandria, VA: Human Resources Research Organization. (NTIS No. AD-237 952)

Gagne, R. M. 1965. *Conditions of Learning.* New York: Holt, Rinehart & Winston.

Kaufman, R. A. 1972. *Educational System Planning.* Englewood Cliffs, NJ: Prentice-Hall.

Mager, R. F., and Pipe, P. 1974. *Criterion-Referenced Instruction: Analysis, Design, and Implementation.* Los Altos Hills, CA: Mager Associates.

McKnight, J. A., and Adams, B. B. 1972. *Driver Education Task Analysis, Volume II: Task Analysis Methods.* Tech Rep. HS 800 368. Washington, DC: U.S. Dept. of Transportation.

Melching, W. H., and Whitmore, P. G. 1973. *A Model of the Functions of a Master Instructor.* HumRRO Tech. Rep. 73-23. Alexandria, VA: Human Resources Research Organization.

Miller, R. B. 1962. Task description and analysis. In R. M. Gagne, ed. *Psychological Principles in System Development.* New York: Holt, Rinehart, and Winston.

Pipe, P. 1975. *Objectives– Tool for Change.* Belmont, CA: Fearon Publishers.

Powers, T. R., and DeLuca, A. J. 1972. *Knowledge, Skills and Thought Processing of the Battalion Commander and Principal Staff Officers.* HumRRO Tech. Rep. 72-20. Alexandria, VA: Human Resources Research Organization.

Shriver, E. L., and Trexler, R. C. 1966. *A Description and Analytic Discussion of Ten New Concepts for Electronics Maintenance.* HumRRO Tech. Rep. 66-23. Alexandria, VA: Human Resources Research Organization. (NTIS No. AD 647 229)

Whitmore, P. G. 1973. *Use of the Job Model Concept to Guide Job Description Procedures for Army Officers.* HumRRO Tech. Rep. 73-26. Alexandria, VA: Human Resources Research Organization.

——— 1970. *"A rational analysis of the process of instruction in collected papers prepared under work unit TEXTRUCT: Methods of instruction in technical training."* Professional Paper 34-70, Human Resources Research Organization.

——— 1966. *"The content validity of instructional objectives."* Paper presented at the 13th annual convention of the Southwestern Psychological Association, Arlington, TX.

Yagi, K., Bialek, H., Taylor, J., and Garman, M. 1971. *The Design and Evaluation of Vocational Technical Education Curricula through Functional Job Analysis.* HumRRO Tech. Rep. 71-15. Alexandria, VA: Human Resources Research Organization. (ED 023 913)

INSTRUCTIONAL
SUPPORT SYSTEMS
Curriculum Development
and Evaluation
by Occupational
Education Teachers

chapter 14

THEODORE ABRAMSON

ADRIENNE VOGRIN

*Queens College,
City University of New York
Woodcliff Lake Public Schools*

This chapter describes the New York State effort to involve occupational education teachers, and university and state education department personnel in the development of an Instructional Support System for Occupational Education (ISSOE).

The purpose of ISSOE is to develop, implement, continuously monitor, and evaluate a modularized curriculum based on *behavioral objectives* and *criterion referenced measures,* which will ultimately be developed and used by occupational educators throughout New York State. ISSOE is based on the premises that: teachers will more readily utilize that which they have developed themselves; that university teacher trainers through in-service type workshops can help teachers write these materials, especially performance ratings and assessments; and that personnel from the state education department, with curriculum expertise can serve as resources for this effort.

In this chapter the need for direct teacher involvement is followed by a brief description of some of the major definitions and concepts of curriculum development and a similar discussion of evaluation, because the concepts underlying ISSOE are drawn from this literature. A synthesis of these elements leads to the operational methods employed by ISSOE.

AUTHORS' NOTE: *The authors acknowledge the helpful critiques of earlier versions of this chapter by Carol Kerr Tittle. The opinions and shortcomings are those of the authors.*

Teacher Involvement

Past efforts at major curriculum revisions have generally been failures at the implementation stage, unless massive efforts at teacher training and retraining have been undertaken. The changes in the mathematics and science curriculums in the post-Sputnik era serve as examples of costly curriculum revision efforts that were developed and managed by subject matter specialists without the involvement of educators. Schwab (1969) characterized the field of curriculum as moribund, and described the contributions of educators and curriculum developers to the "new" major high school science curriculums as "small" and "at the vanishing point." Even today the ubiquitousness of these curricula is questionable, and their implementation by teachers may be a factor in the recent rise of the "back to basics" movement. Seven years later the field of curriculum was all but interred after being pronounced dead (Huebner, 1976). Straumanis (1976), in replying to Huebner, felt that the curriculum field should once again limit itself to descriptions of *what* is to be taught through the specification of the desired learning and development *outcomes*. More recently, Harmer (1977) in describing curriculum as moribund observed that, the teacher is the *critical* factor in the development of curriculum, and attributed the sterility of curriculum development at the high school level to teachers' alienation from and resistance to external curriculum development activities, and their conscious acceptance of the status quo.

Among the reasons that are frequently cited for the difficulties in revising and implementing new curriculum are lack of agreement as to course content, and the unwillingness of teachers to change what they have been doing or to learn the knowledge and skills necessary to implement new curriculum.

Occupational educators at the secondary and postsecondary levels emphasize the preparation of young people for direct entry into the work force, and frequently resist curriculum change to a greater degree than their colleagues who teach the academic subjects. Often, this is so because many of the occupational educators have lost contact with the new equipment, and lack the knowledge and skills necessary to impart new skills to their students. Additionally, curriculum revisions in occupational education are implemented differently in different geographic areas to accommodate local job needs. Finally, the procedures for examining student outcomes are frequently so diverse as to make evaluative judgments and decisions about the value of the program difficult, if not impossible.

Despite these problems, there has recently been an increased emphasis on revising occupational education curriculum areas, so they will more accurately reflect the needs of the labor market. The state of Florida, as a member of the Vocational-Technical Education Consortium of States (V-TECS) since its formation in 1973 (State of Florida, 1976), has been a leader in this movement. Richardson (1977) in describing the very elaborate Florida State competency-based automotive mechanics curriculum, justified the system in terms of industry's needs as follows: "The process requires a great amount of time and effort, but the effort is justified because the materials bring automotive repair training much closer to the *needs of* industry" (italics added). The success of attempting to impose this external curriculum development effort on schools and teachers will probably not be any more successful than other such efforts, perhaps because too little emphasis is placed on what actually happens in the classrooms where curriculum is implemented (Goodlad, 1977; Beane, 1975; Schwab, 1969).

It appears that a crucial ingredient in effecting curriculum change is the involvement, at all stages of the process, of the instructional personnel who ultimately bear responsibility for curriculum implementation.

Exclusion of teachers can only lead to sterile curriculum, that is, curriculum that does not reach its target audience, the students. While teacher involvement may be seen as a necessary condition for successful curriculum revision, it is not a sufficient one in the absence of materials that specify expected learner outcomes, and procedures for examining student progress.

To understand ISSOE beyond its insistence on teacher involvement from the very start of the curriculum development process, a brief discussion is required of the meaning of *curriculum* and *evaluation* in the context of the ISSOE project.

Definition of Curriculum

In the United States, a basic responsibility of the local school has been curriculum. Traditionally, control of the local school curriculum has been exercised by local school boards with some regulation by the state governments (Schick and Pfister, 1974). Even though school districts have traditionally planned their own curricula and although scholars have studied curriculum as a scholarly field of study for more than a half-century (Caswell, 1966), Taba (1962) reported a general "lack of rigorous, systematic thinking about curriculum planning." Specifically, the curriculum planning literature was seen as eclectic in its quality and lacking a conceptual framework, thereby, providing little guidance for the local school district.

Johnson (1967) identified two basic types of definitions of the term *curriculum.* The first defines curriculum as "a plan for what is to be learned, developed prior to instruction," and the second defines curriculum as "an activity of the learner." Curriculum defined as a plan for what is to be learned is the product of the curriculum development process, whereas, curriculum as an activity of the learner, is itself a process—an aspect of instruction.

Curriculum as a product of the curriculum development or planning process may be seen in the three following definitions: (1) "is a written plan for subsequent action" (Beauchamp, 1972); (2) "a structured series of intended learning outcomes" (Johnson, 1967); (3) "a set of intended learnings" (Goodlad and Richter, 1966). On the other hand, the definitions provided by Tyler (1950), and Neagley and Evans (1967) are more in keeping with the notion of curriculum as a learner activity: (1) "planned learning

Table 14.1: **Definitions of Major Terms in The ISSOE System Developed by Teachers**

Course:
A state-approved course of study. The course consists of modules of instruction essential to the acquisiton of competencies expected by the world of work.

Unit:
A portion of the course which consists of a logical clustering of modules of instruction.

Module:
A portion of the course which addresses related tasks drawn from occupational analysis expressed in performance terms. Each module contains one or more tasks and major objectives, suggested instructional content and criterion referenced assessment.

Task:
An activity which has a definite beginning and ending, and is performed within a limited period of time by an indivdiual. One or more tasks are included in each module.

Major Objective:
A statement of what the student should be able to do, the conditions under which the task will be performed, and the standards for evaluating the performance. The achievement of a major objective will be reported as a component of the student's employability profile.

Enabling Objective:
A subordinate objective which describes in performance terms a cognitive, affective, and/or psychomotor skill which the student will need to accomplish the major objective. Achievement of an enabling objective is not reported; performance of and recording of this achievement is left to the discretion of the instructor.

Suggested Instructional Content:
A brief listing of suggested demonstrations and points of information which the instructor may wish to employ to assist the student in meeting the major objective.

Criterion Referenced Assessment:
Criterion referenced assessment is derived form the performance objectives and directly measures the individual student's ability to successfully complete the tasks identified in the module. The test items are performance-based and replicate as closely as possible the tasks as they would be evaluated in the world of work.

---

experiences" (Tyler, 1950), (2) "all of the planned learning experiences provided by the school to assist pupils in attaining the designated learning outcomes to the best of their abilities" (Neagley and Evans, 1967).

If the local districts employ these definitions interchangeably, then the products of their curriculum planning process are likely to vary from district to district. Inconsistencies in the literature may explain why MacDonald (1965) suggested that local school district curriculum planning tasks should include the complex process of the selection of "curricula language."

The teachers working in the ISSOE system operationalized their concept of curriculum through the definitions shown in Table 14.1.

The basic curriculum idea is embodied in the terms Unit, Module, and Task. Examination of the definitions of these terms indicate that the modules, which singly or in groups comprise the units, state intended learning outcomes (in the form of a task and major objectives in each module) with a series of subordinate learning outcomes stated as enabling objectives. Although stated in terms of student outcomes, curriculum is defined as a product of the curriculum development process, and curriculum planning takes place prior to the planning of instruction. Instruction per se is at most only suggested.

The curriculum premises underlying ISSOE may be summarized as follows:

(1) Teachers should have input into the development of curriculum.
(2) A statewide comprehensive curriculum should be developed although it is clearly understood that not all regions will use all modules due to employment needs.
(3) Curriculum should be such that students can experience success with it, and that all students will emerge from the course with various levels of skill abilities.

Definition of Evaluation

Evaluation is a major part of the ISSOE system. As with the term curriculum, the concept of evaluation is not easily defined. Guba (1969), and Stufflebeam et al. (1971) described three major categories of definitions. Evaluation is: (1) equated with the term *measurement,* (2) identical to the congruence between performance and objectives, and (3) professional judgment. The problems with each of these definitions described by Guba (1969) are briefly sketched below. The first definition of evaluation developed out of the educational achievement testing movement of the 1920s and 1930s and leads to a narrow mechanistic approach to evaluation which is devoid of value judgments, limited to instrument development and interpretation, and possible only in terms of variables for which measurement instruments exist. The congruence definition, although certainly broader than the measurement definition of evaluation, also presents some difficulties. This type of evaluation is possible only to the degree that the evaluator's ingenuity can operationalize the program objectives. Furthermore, the objectives of the program had to be stated in terms of student outcomes, even where the program did not directly involve students or instruction. Finally, congruence between objectives and student outcomes, turns evaluation into a process that yields information after the fact. Evaluation as expert judgment does violence to our notions of objectivity, reliability, validity, and generalizability.

More recently, in speeches before groups of administrators and managers, Wholey (1976) defined evaluation "as systematic measures and comparisons to provide specific information on program results for use in policy or management decisions." This definition appears to combine the congruence and measurement definitions, but appears to be post facto in that policy decisions are to be based on *program results.* A more fruitful approach would be to expand the congruence definition so that feedback data would be collected on a periodic basis. These data permit process evaluation to be implemented through modification and adjustment of the *product* at different points in time prior to the project's final stages. Thus the probability of attaining the program's terminal objectives would be maximized.

ISSOE's approach to evaluation is eclectic. It incorporates the above expanded congruence notion, which includes feedback and process evaluation, measurement of performance and achievement, and professional judgment. The development process begins during the summer and consists of the following steps. A self-selected group of teachers: (1) identifies the major units in their occupational course, (2) divides the units into modules, (3) identifies the tasks, major and enabling objectives for each module, (4) writes behavioral objectives, and (5) develops criterion-referenced assessment devices for each unit. As a rule, the behaviorally stated tasks were perceived by the teachers as entry level job skills. These written packages are then evaluated and revised by other teachers in the same content areas throughout the Occupational Planning Regions of New York State during the first year of the process. The occupational teachers themselves serve as professional expert evaluators in the development process.

Each module contains a criterion referenced assessment designed to directly measure the individual student's ability to successfully complete the task identified in the module. This approach serves as an evaluation of the individual teacher's instructional planning process. The occupational teachers in the subject field then meet to evaluate the student data, and decide whether it is the curriculum or the instructional planning that is in need of revision.

In effect, there are two stages at which evaluation is carried out in the ISSOE system—the classroom level and the system level. Within each teacher's classroom or shop, the congruence definition serves as the basic procedure for assessing whether or not the students' performance matches the criterion performance called for in the major objective. Student outcome performance for each major objective is assessed through the criterion measures developed during the teachers' curriculum planning and writing work. Student performance serves as feedback to the teacher who may then work with the student on some of the enabling objectives, modify the instructional process, or do both before retesting the student's performance on the major objective. At the system level, the teachers serve as expert judges in determining where additions to, deletions from, and changes in the materials are needed. Each teacher's classroom data serve as the bases for discussion related to system changes which are approved by obtaining the consensus of the other experts, the teacher's colleagues in the ISSOE system. In addition, local employers were asked to rate the ISSOE tasks with respect to their entry level job needs. Such an approach to system evaluation via large-scale expert judgments tends to increase objectivity, validity, and generalizability.[1]

SYSTEM IMPLEMENTATION

The first step for the teachers in the ISSOE system was the analysis of each of the subject areas into units and modules. Much of this work was based on task analyses, curriculum guides, bulletins, and lesson plans that the teachers brought with them as well as their teaching and working experience. Group participants, with the help of the available trainers and consultants, wrote and refined major objectives for these modules. Major objectives were then broken down into enabling objectives, and in some cases, learning and instructional activities were suggested. Finally, group participants worked on developing criterion referenced measures for the major objectives.

Examination of the ISSOE definitions indicates, that the major objectives were meant to break down the goals or broad objectives incorporated in the modules into all of the knowledges and performances that the student *must* master to attain entry level job skills. Enabling or subordinate objectives describe some of the underlying abilities that the students need to complete the tasks included in the major objective, and along with the suggested instructional content are meant as guidelines for the teachers. Use of enabling objectives and suggested instructional content are left to the instructor's discretion.

The teachers attempt to design major objectives and criterion referenced assessments that replicate the tasks that the students would face in the world of work. There are two reasons why the criterion referenced assessment is done simultaneously with the development of the major objectives. First, by considering the tasks and their assessments, the teachers are forced to do three things more rigorously than if the major objectives were separately

Table 14.2: Teachers Participating in ISSOE In-service Training by Region and Content Area, 1977-78[1]

					Region Name and Number							
Content Area	Broome Tioga BOCES 8	Cortland-Madison BOCES 95	Erie #1 BOCES 12	Fonda-Fultonville Cent. Sch. 4	Jefferson, Lewis, Ham., Herk., Oneida BOCES 6	Mid-Hudson BOCES 3N	Nassau BOCES 1W	Oswego Onondaga BOCES 9N	Rochester City School 10	Suffolk County BOCES 1E	Yonkers Public Schools 3S	Total
Automotive Mechanics	12	6	19	18	8	15	21	4	24	8	13	148
Building Industries		4	4			5			9		7	29
Carpentry		1		9	6	9	5	9	11	7	7	64
Conservation	5	1		7	2	3			7		4	29
Business: General Merchandise/ Retailing					31			8		11	4	54
Foods	4	3	10	14	3	14	3		11	5	4	71
Health Assisting	5	4	11	6	2	8	1	12		3	14	66
Office Practices	22	1		5		19	15	16	30	16	8	132
Distributive Education					4	7						11
Total	48	20	44	59	56	80	45	49	92	50	61	604

[1]More regions and teachers were to be added as of March 1978

Table 14.3: Modifications and Development of ISSOE Food Trades Curriculum from July 1976 to June 1977

	Units		Modules		Major Objectives		CRM		Nature of Change
	Final 6/77	Summer 1976	Final 6/77	Summer 1976	Final 6/77	Summer 1976	Final 6/77	Summer 1976	
Orientation	1	1	2	3	12	12	1	1	1 module deleted
Tools and Utensils	1	1	5	5	5	5	1	0	1 CRM developed
Equipment	1	1	4	4	4	4	1	0	1 module title change, 1 CRM developed
Standards	1	1	7	4	8	4	1	0	3 modules added, 4 M. objective added, 1 CRM developed
Menu	1	1	2	0	2	0	2	0	Beyond unit title, beyond unit developed during year
Product Handling	1	1	1	1	1	1	0	1	Unit reorganized during year
Food Preparation	1	1	8	8	32	8	10	8	1 module title change, added 24 M.O., CRM made more specific, 2 added
Career Development	1	1	6	0	6	0	0	0	Changed from "employment", newly developed unit
Beverages	1	1	3	1	3	1	1	0	Divided into separate modules with M.O.s, 1 CRM developed
Dining Room Service	1	1	5	0	5	0	1	0	Newly developed unit
Nutrition	1	1	5	0	5	0	1	0	Nutrition unit completely developed Fall-Spring 1976-77
Baking	1	1	1	0	2	0	0	0	Newly developed unit
Total	12	12	49	26	85	35	19	10	

Table 14.4: Modifications and Development of ISSOE Building Industries Occupations Curriculum from July 1976 to June 1977

	Units		Modules		Major Objectives		CRM		Nature of Change		
	Final 6/77	Summer 1976	Final 6/77	Summer 1976	Final 6/77	Summer 1976	Final 6/77	Summer 1976	MOD	M.O.	CRM
Carpentry	1	1	10	10	55	56	26	10	Same	Phrase changes 1 deletion	Added 16 specific assessments
Electrical	1	1	6	7	19	16	17	8	Combined 2 to 1	Phrase changes Added 3	Added 9 specific assessments
Masonry	1	1	7	7	27	29	6	5	Same	Deleted 2 M.O.	Added 1 CRM Original CRM's Reorganized
Environmental Control	1	0	3	0	5	0	5	0	Creation of Environmental Control Unit began in March 1977. Minor editorial changes were completed for final product.		
Total	4	3	26	24	106	101	54	23			

developed: (1) They must state the major objectives in behavioral terms that are *in fact* measurable; (2) They must assure themselves that the tasks really are representative of the entry level world of work; (3) They must be reasonably certain that the assessments of student performance are isomorphic to the tasks stated in the major objectives. Second, by developing assessments prior to instruction, the teachers avoid the possibility that they are evaluating their instruction rather than student performance. By agreeing in advance on acceptable student performance and its assessment, regardless of instruction (instruction may vary from teacher to teacher), the probability is increased that one is assessing the ability of the student to perform. Incidentally, the aggregate student performance for a particular teacher may serve as an indication of that teacher's instructional effectiveness.

Rapid expansion of the number of districts and teachers involved in the ISSOE effort necessitated the continuation of the involvement of university personnel in helping the teachers to write objectives and assessments. As of March 1978 (see Table 14.2), the total number of teachers involved in ISSOE had increased to 604 from fewer than 100 during the previous year.

The final products of the summer workshops, the modules, major objectives, and criterion referenced measures served as the bases for the curriculum revisions developed in the following year. Although some of the material from the summer were retained, many of the objectives were refined and changed. In addition, where some modules and objectives were dropped new ones were often added. The evaluation feedback system which resulted in the above changes and modifications is indicative of the operation of the evaluation component that was built into the ISSOE system. Tables 14.3 and 14.4 show the numbers and types of changes that occurred in a one-year period.

DEVELOPMENT OF OBJECTIVES AND ASSESSMENTS

The ISSOE definitions and premises have been presented earlier. Table 14.5 shows the basic ISSOE format used in developing each major objective within each module. Each major objective is entered on its own format sheet which contains information that identifies the major objective in terms of its course, unit, and module titles. The task incorporated in the major objective statement is listed at the top of each sheet to simplify and speed up the process of selecting the module and major objective being sought from among all the objectives contained within the particular module. A code number is included so that computerized storage and retrieval will eventually be possible. In addition to these basic identifying data and the major objective itself, each sheet contains space for enabling objectives and suggested instructional content. The specific example shown in Table 14.5 is drawn from the first module in the Cashiering unit of the General Merchandise/Retailing course.

Table 14.5: Basic ISSOE Format

COURSE:	General Merchandise/Retailing	MODULE:	Machine Operations
UNIT:	Cashiering	TASK:	Open Cash Register
CODE:			

MAJOR OBJECTIVE:

Given an operational cash register and necessary forms, material and money, the student will perform all opening functions between shifts or at the beginning of day, according to store standards.

ENABLING OBJECTIVES

The student will:
1. Identify, select various register forms.
2. Review functional opening checklist: power, ink, tapes, date.
3. Appropriately obtain opening information from the cash register by reading or reset.
4. Enter pertinent information on register form.
5. File opening form.
6. Obtain cash fund.
7. Count and place cash in register drawer.

SUGGESTED INSTRUCTIONAL CONTENT

The teachers had a great deal of difficulty specifying the modules, tasks, and objectives. The first major task required of the teacher was to specify units, break the units into modules, specify the tasks to be included in each module, and finally to state the objective and develop the assessment. Part of the problem involved in the initial decision regarding units, modules, and tasks arose from a shift in definitions. Vocational teachers, in their courses for certification, are asked to develop task analyses which arise from various "jobs" (i.e., change a tire). Therefore, often the tendency was to state a subpart of a job as a major objective. For example, in the early development of the Foods curriculum one task was defined as "How to use French Knife properly". Later the task was redefined. While, how to use a French knife could be a task, the next step of writing a major objective about the use of the French knife is a problem. If major objectives were written for all such tasks, the number of major objectives and associated assessments would be astronomical.

The teachers struggled with their belief that objectives could be stated without a condition that says "after the students have received the instruction," thereby, implying that only after instruction could the student have learned a skill. For example, consider the following objective: MAJOR

OBJECTIVE: "After the student has received the instruction and information in this module the student will be able to interpret, extend, and properly use all types of formulas." Major problems were encountered as the teacher in each curriculum area attempted to include a unit called orientation. Arguments raged regarding the modules and tasks to be included. Confusion reigned as teachers insisted that they must teach safety rules, tools, and so forth before they could do anything else. It was difficult for them to state behavioral objectives and develop assessments for the modules. For example, one objective from the course entitled Building Industry Occupations was: In order to function effectively in the carpentry shop the student will know *all* general rules and procedures used in the shop. Is knowing the same as behaving in a safe manner; or in the following example, is listing the same as behaving? Given instruction and information, student will be able to list specified number of safety and shop behavior rules, with 90 percent accuracy. Distinguishing enabling objectives from the major objective was a further problem. Consider the following example:

MAJOR OBJECTIVE

Given the necessary tools, materials, and instruction the student will be able to draw a schematic, wiring diagram, cable layout, and safely install at least two different doorbell and two different alarm circuits in accordance with the N.E. & local codes in a time period determined by the instructor.

ENABLING OBJECTIVES

Given the symbols for each of the following electrical devices and the device itself, the student will identify each by drawing the symbol and pictorial diagram for each to include labeling of the component parts, in a time period specified by the instructor: (1) Transformer, (2) Doorbell (3) Normally open push buttons, (4) Relay, (5) Normally open contact, (6) Normally closed contact, (7) Magnetic switch, (8) Thermostat. Given five multiconductor cables, the student will identify each to include conductor size and number of conductors in not more than five minutes total. Given the following desired electrical outcomes and a floor plan for each instance, the student will draw a schematic, wiring, and cable layout for each so that the circuit works electrically, the connections are properly shown, and a minimum amount of material is wasted, in a time period specified by the instructor: (1) Doorbell controlled from two places, (2) Two chimes in parallel controlled from two places, (3) Open circuit—six window—a door burglar alarm, (4) Closed circuit—six window—two door burglar alarm, (5) one electric heater, thermostatically controlled. (There was another enabling objective comparable in length to the three already shown—we have spared the reader.) Another problem that arose was the mismatch between the objective and its assessment. Consider the following example:

MAJOR OBJECTIVE

The student will be able to state, recognize or select a standard menu, a flyer or stationary menu to the satisfaction of the instructor.

ASSESSMENT

A group of true questions to be included in a true or false written test.

(1) The menu states what is available for the cus-   1   T   F
tomer.

(2) A standard menu is a printed or written list on   2.
the table or the counter, or is presented to the
customer.

(3) A flyer states specials for the day and is generally   3.
attached to the standard menu.

(4) A stationary menu is placed in a conspicuous   4.
place, on the wall in some restaurants or cafe-
teria.

Teachers were encouraged to develop paper pencil tests or other simulations not requiring performance testing to assess student outcomes, so that tests of student performance could be easily administered, to groups if necessary, and objectively scored. At the same time, teachers attempted to keep the paper pencil measures as simple as possible, so that reading problems would not interfere with the student's ability to show what was learned. To assist the teachers with this task, a series of models and examples based on their work were developed for the teachers to consider as they reviewed, revised, and wrote the materials. For instance, in the electrical unit of the Building Industries Occupations the following example was developed:

MODEL:

Given —

(select
one)   a list of terms or materials, set of pictures of tools or materials, a
floor plan, a set of diagrams,

the student will —

(select   list, label, match, select, define, draw,
one)

(select   symbols, code specifications, materials, cable layout, tools, com-
one)   mon trade terms, tools,

            used/required for —

(select
one)   installation of fuse boxes, residential wiring,

        to —

(select
one)   specifications, codes, standards.

Example: Given a set of diagrams of tools, the student will circle all of
the tools used for the installation of an overhead service entrance cable.

The assessment for this major objective consists of a set of diagrams of
tools containing more items (perhaps twice as many) than are required for the
task described, from which the student must select all the appropriate tools
by drawing a circle around the "right" tools. This type of assessment may be
individually or group administered in written form or orally. If the instructions are given orally, no reading is required of the students. Another example
of a similar nature is:

Example: The student will locate all the outlet boxes in a residence by
marking an "X" in all appropriate places on a given floor plan.

Here too, once given the floor plan, assessment is possible without requiring
reading skill beyond that necessary to read a blueprint (an enabling
objective).

An example taken from the masonry unit, which will require some student
reading skill if the assessment is group administered is:

Example: Given a set of numbered tools, the student will identify and
specify the use of all tools needed to blend a one-bag mix of practice
mortar by hand.

This assessment consists of two columns as shown below to be completed
by the student.

Next to each number, list the tool name and write the use of each.

	Tool Name	*Tool Use*
1.	_____	_____
2.	_____	_____
3.	_____	_____

Table 14.6: Assessment for "Opening Cash Register"

CRITERION-REFERENCED MEASUREMENT

GENERAL MERCHANDISE/RETAILING

Name _____   UNIT: Cashiering
                                          MODULE: Machine Operations
Date _____   Teacher: _____

Check one only: Completed Objective ☐   Incomplete ☐

MAJOR OBJECTIVE:
Given an operational cash register and necessary forms, material and money, the student
will perform all opening functions between shifts or at the beginning of day, according
to store standards.

Did student according to store standards:	YES	NO
1. Match appropriate form to cash register being used?	___	___
2. Review functional opening checklust:		
a) power?	___	___
b) ink?	___	___
c) tapes?	___	___
d) dates?	___	___
3. Obtain all opening information from cash register?	___	___
4. Enter all information on register form?	___	___
5. File all information?	___	___
6. Obtain open cash fund?	___	___
7. Count and place cash in register drawer?	___	___

STUDENT MUST OBTAIN YES FOR EVERY FUNCTION

REMARKS: _____

_____

_____

_____

_____

Performance objectives were treated the same way. A series of model
major objectives were prepared such as this Food trades example:

> Given (# of hand tools, # of cooking utensils, pieces of service
> equipment) the student will use safely, clean and store properly within
> the time frame set by the instructor.

The assessment consists of a checklist of all the equipment and all the
performances required of the students. The assessment shown in Table 14.6

for the task described in Table 14.5 is an example of such a checklist. The examples of the work presented above must be viewed in the context of a system which is continuously updated, especially since not all of the materials are of comparable quality. The unevenness in the materials reflect differences in teacher ability to master the basic concepts, and write within the given ISSOE framework. Also, some of the content is inherently more difficult to specify behaviorally and measure objectively. In this regard, ISSOE's insistence that each major objective be accompanied by an assessment helped to clarify for the teachers the distinction between student skill or *process* objectives and *product* objectives. The teachers felt that students should be assessed just as they would be judged on the job—in terms of the things they do and the products they produce. To the teachers, the skills exhibited by the students as they progressed through their tasks defined the necessary process which led to the product that was to be made, prepared, developed, designed, or presented. This thinking led to the development of models for process rating scales and product rating scales. The issue of a three point scale, e.g., poor, fair, good versus a five point scale, e.g., poor, inadequate, fair, good, excellent has not yet been resolved, and may ultimately vary from course to course or even from module to module within any given unit depending on what the teachers find most useful.

The major problem in developing the process rating scales stems from the difficulty in defining the crucial steps in the process, and the skills that the student must master to successfully carry through the task specified in the major objective, from its beginning to its completion. The main quandry in generating product scales is the dilemma of defining characteristics that adequately describe the qualities that the finished product must possess. Furthermore, adjectives that describe either extreme of each characteristic must also be developed. Two examples of the five point process rating scales that the teachers were considering in the deck framing module (carpentry unit) and breakfast cookery module (food-preparation unit), respectively were:

Table 14.7: Sample Process Rating Scales

Process Scale	1 Poor	2 Inadequate	3 Fair	4 Good	5 Excellent
Carpentry					
TASK: Layout and install floor joist and boxheader					
Select tools, materials, equipment					
Layout floor joist and boxheader using 50' tape					

Read and interpret plans,
Place joist
Select nails and nail joist and boxheaders
Install boxheader
Install joist
Straighten boxheader

Food Preparation

TASK: Select equipment, prepare plate for service and clean up

Makes personal preparations (ties back hair, washes hands, puts
  on apron)
Selects correct equipment
Prepares sink and preparation area
Measures and handles ingredients
Plates food items
Cleans sink and preparation area
Returns equipment to storage area

The product scales for these two tasks considered as three point scales were:

Table 14.8: Sample Product Rating Scales

CARPENTRY TASK: Layout and install floor joist and boxheader	1–Poor	2–Fair	3–Good	FOOD PREPARATION TASK: [1] Prepare breakfast foods: eggs, pancakes, waffles, bacon	1–Poor	2–Fair	3–Good
Product Scale				**Product Scale**			
cuts sloppy . . . . .clean				appearance dull . . . . shiny			
measurements inexact . . . . .precise				appearance fine pieces . . . . . . large pieces			
durability/installation shaky . . . . strong (not secure) (secure)				consistency dry or watery . . .slightly moist			
straightness not straight . . . . . . straight				texture soggy . . . . .crisp			
hardware placement inappropriate . . . appropriate				lightness white & yolk. . . . white & yolk not well blended . well blended			
fit unacceptable. . . . acceptable				lightness compact & heavy . . fairly light			

				taste stale, flat, salty . .well seasoned			
				flavor raw or burned . . . .well cooked			
				tenderness rubbery or tough . . . . . tender			

[1]not all product qualities apply
to all breakfast foods

Many other tasks within the same units can be described in terms of these scales. For example, most of the assessments within the Food Preparation Unit of the Food Trades course can be described in terms of some of these adjectives, as they are descriptive of many properly prepared foods. A major issue that the teachers have yet to resolve in using these scales is the specification of the criterion score that must be attained for the student to pass. Are there items which are absolutely crucial to successful performance, such as "makes personal preparation" in the food preparation unit? Must a minimum score of "fair" (e.g., 3 on a 5 point scale) be attained on each item of the rating scale, or is an overall rating to be the criterion regardless of the individual item ratings? The teachers will have to decide the answers to these and similar questions as they develop such scales for the remaining modules.

In the curriculum areas that the teachers worked on during the year, they developed a good deal of facility in writing objectives and assessments. Note that the task in Table 14.9 encompasses a number of underlying skills and knowledges that are in fact subsumed in this assessment. Another example of a teacher developed assessment is shown in Table 14.10. Although this assessment may be adequate for this major objective, the teachers used the same basic assessment for *all* the automotive modules—a questionable practice.

It is precisely in this area of measurement of student outcomes that some of the other currently available vocational curriculum materials appears to be weakest. That is, although students outcomes may be behaviorally stated, the specific assessments related to each student objective are not specified.

In the ISSOE system, the student certified as being capable of performing a particular task or set of tasks, as shown by completion of certain modules, will have been assessed on each and every accompanying criterion referenced measure shown within the system. Thus, his performance level and ability is completely specified within any region of the state unless regional differences have been incorporated in the major objective statement, such as differences in local building codes in urban, suburban, and rural areas.

Table 14.9: Criterion Measure for Payroll Calculations Developed/Adapted by Teachers during One Year of Work in ISSOE Project

CRITERION-REFERENCED MEASUREMENT

MODULE: Payroll Procedures
TASK(S): 01 Calculate a payroll

Listed below are five employees of MPG Corporation and payroll information. Using the applicable tax tables and related information, calculate the gross income, total deductions and net income for each employee.

Timothy Gilbert and Ruth Widger have reached maximum Social Security deduction prior to this payroll period.

Employees receive time and one-half for any hours or portion of hours over 40.

Employee	Total Hours	Hourly Rate	Overtime Rate	Gross Income	Marital Status	Exemptions	Medical Insurance	Group Life Insurance	Union Dues	Federal Income Tax	State Income Tax	City Income Tax	Social Security	Total Deductions	Net Income
							Deductions Required by Law								
Sandra Rodgers	45	2.30			S	0	0	0	1.00						
Mark Vallely	45	3.00			M	2	4.46	0	0						
Eunice Spada	42	3.50			M	4	4.46	1.36	0						
Timothy Gilbert	40	12.50			M	3	4.46	1.64	0						
Ruth Widger	43	13.60			M	7	4.46	0	0						

Did the student calculate gross income, deductions, and net income for five employees within _____ minutes with 85% accuracy? ☐ Yes ☐ No

Comments: _____

Table 14.10: **Criterion Measure for Work on Automatic Transmission Developed/Adapted by Teachers during One Year of Work in ISSOE Project**

Name _____
Date _____
Teacher_____
Class _____

Check one *only:*
Met Major Objective ☐
Needs Further Instruction ☐

MODULE: AUTOMATIC TRANSMISSION 17320505

REMARKS:

MAJOR OBJECTIVE: 01

Given a car with an automatic transmission and the necessary tools and equipment, the student will:
• R & R transmission assembly
• Make necessary adjustments
• Complete the task according to manufacturers specifications, in twice the flate rate time.

Did student, when applicable:	YES	NO
1. Observe safety standards?	___	___
2. Use trade acceptable standards?	___	___
3. Meet manufacturer's specs?	___	___
4. Use proper procedure?	___	___
5. Use proper tools?	___	___
6. Observe good housekeeping practices?	___	___
7. Complete necessary paper work?	___	___
8. Complete the job in an acceptable time period based on flat rate time?	___	___

PROPOSED FUTURE WORK

In a curriculum development effort of this magnitude, many things happen before data are collected which would help in making decisions about whether or not the direction being taken is consonant with the project's ultimate goals. In a sense, ISSOE was designed to foster such an atmosphere with the proviso that as the project evolved, planning, research, evaluation, and development needs would be identified by the teachers and administrators in the field who were attempting to implement and live in the schools with ISSOE. The teachers and regional coordinators identified three areas of immediate concern: validation, test development, and management of assessments. Other evaluation activities that will have to be considered in the future are follow-up and cost effectiveness studies.

In validating a curriculum that provides students with entry level job skills, it is imperative that the content of the curriculum match as closely as possible industry's expectations for the program graduates. Evidence for this match must result from the work of the teachers developing the major objectives and from the job setting. Therefore, it is necessary to examine the skills required of entry level job holders as they *exist* on the job, and to compare these skills and knowledges with those being taught to the students in the occupational training program.[2]

Is it possible to develop a model from which a more manageable set of items can be generated so that the testing phase of ISSOE may be more easily managed by the teachers? Unless such a model and procedure can be developed, the need for testing each student as each major objective is completed will in fact make this system unmanageable. For example, if during the course of a school year, a teacher were to work with forty students and fifty major objectives, and if the students were to complete the fifty objectives, the teacher would be required to administer 2000 assessments—a situation which would require more than ten assessments per day for each school day. Thus, while it is necessary to continue to develop assessments to insure the integrity of each major objective, the procedure for selecting test items is equally crucial to the implementation of ISSOE.

A second issue related to the ISSOE assessments has recently developed as a result of ISSOE expansion. As the number of teachers in the system has grown, problems related to item and test construction have become apparent. The teachers seem to have difficulty in generalizing from the measures currently available within the ISSOE system to other major objectives that they are attempting to implement in their classrooms. It appears to be necessary to develop a pamphlet or set of guidelines for the teachers that describes, in fairly simple language, the general approaches to measurement and assessment incorporated in ISSOE with specific examples showing how the general ideas can be applied to the major objectives as they are implemented in the classroom situation. Among the references that should be consulted in this effort are Erickson and Wentling (1976), especially chapters 5-7; Boyd and Shimberg (1977); and chapter three in the manual by Orlich, Anderson, Dodd, Baldwin, and Ohrt (1978).

SUMMARY

The Instructional Support System for Occupational Education (ISSOE) described in this chapter is unique, in that it is a curriculum development effort based in large measure on the involvement and work of teachers in all phases of the program. The underlying theoretical and practical concepts are grounded in the curriculum and evaluation literature. Some of the problems in attempting to implement such a large scale system, and some examples of the work that has been accomplished to date were briefly described in the latter half of this chapter. Insistence on teacher involvement at the grassroots level may well make ISSOE one of the few occupational education curriculum projects that really works. Measured in terms of teacher output and enthusiasm, the project would have to be classified as a success.

NOTES

1. For a discussion of these issues, see the chapter by Whitmore in this Handbook.
2. For a fuller discussion of these validation issues, see Whitmore's chapter in this Handbook.

REFERENCES

Beane, J. A. 1975. Curriculum trends and practices in high schools. *Educational Leadership* (November) 129-138.

Beauchamp, G. A. 1972. Basic components of a curriculum theory. *Curriculum Theory Network* 10: 16-22.

Boyd, J. L., and Shimberg, B. 1971. *Handbook of Performance Testing.* Princeton, NJ: Educational Testing Service.

Caswell, H. L. 1966. Emergence of the curriculum as a field of professional work and study. In Helen F. Robinson, ed. *Presidence and Prominence in the Curriculum Field.* New York: Teachers College Press.

Erickson, R. C., and Wentling, T. L. 1976. *Measuring Student Growth, Techniques and Procedures for Occupational Education.* Boston: Allyn and Bacon.

Goodlad, J. I. 1977. What goes on in our schools? *Educational Researcher* 6: 3.

Goodlad, J. I., and Richter, M. 1966. *The Development of a Conceptual System for Dealing with Problems of Curriculum and Instruction.* Los Angeles: University of California, Cooperative Research Project, No. 454.

Guba, E. G. 1969. The failure of educational evaluation. *Educational Technology* 9: 29-38.

Harmer, E. A. 1977. Veteran teachers and curriculum development. *Phi Delta Kappan* 58: 751-752.

Huebner, D. 1976. The moribund curriculum field: Its wake and our work. *Curriculum Inquiry* 6: 153-167.

Johnson, M., Jr. 1967. Definitions and models in curriculum theory. *Educational Theory* 17: 127-140.

MacDonald, J. B. 1965. Educational models for instruction-introduction. In J. B. Macdonald, and R. R. Leeper, eds. *Theory of Instruction.* Washington, DC: Association for Supervision and Curriculum Development.

Neagley, R. L., and Evans, N. D. 1967. *Handbook for Effective Curriculum Development.* Englewod Cliffs, NJ: Prentice Hall.

Orlich, D. C., Andersen, D. G., Dodd, C. C., Baldwin, L., and Ohrt, B. A. *Evaluation Models for Vocational Education.* Olympia, WA: Washington State Commission for Vocational Education.

Richardson, R. L. 1977. Designing competency-based materials for the automotive mechanics curriculum. *Technical Education News* (October-November) 7-23.

Schick, R., and Pfister, A. 1974. *American Government, Continuity and Change.* Boston:

Houghton Mifflin.

Schwab, J. J. 1969. The practical: A language for curriculum. *School Review* 78: 1-23.

State of Florida. 1975. *Individualizing Instruction for Competency-Based Education.* Tallahassee: Department of Education, Division of Vocational Education.

Straumanis, E. 1976. The scope of our work. Reply to Dwayne Huebner. *Curriculum Inquiry* 6: 170-173.

Stufflebeam, D. L., Foley, W. J., Gephart, W. J., Guba, E. G., Hammond, R. I. Merriman, H. O., and Provus, M. M. 1971. *Educational Evaluation and Decision Making in Education.* Itasca, IL: Peacock.

Taba, H. 1962. *Curriculum Development, Theory and Practice.* New York: Harcourt Brace.

Tyler, R. W. 1950. *Basic Principles of Curriculum and Instruction.* Chicago: University of Chicago Press.

Wholey, J. S. 1976. The role of evaluation and the evaluator in improving public programs: The bad news, the good news, and a bicentennial challenge. *Public Administration Review* 36: 679-683.

PART IV

The chapters in this section have been selected with a view toward describing measurement techniques that are specific to evaluation in vocational education, and to raising current measurement issues that are likely to have an influence in vocational education evaluation. In this part of the Handbook, then, the chapters *add to* existing resources for evaluation, rather than duplicating them, with the exception of the first chapter on attitude measurement. This chapter was included because many educational measurement texts do not provide a summary of the main ideas in attitude measurement. Special attention is given here to the basic concepts and available instruments in the measurement of job satisfaction, outcomes for manpower evaluations, and assessment in career education programs, all topics of special interest to the evaluator and administrator of vocational education programs. The current issues in measurement focus on topics that are of concern to evaluators and administrators under several current federal regulations: the Education Amendments of 1976 (PL 94-482), and Title IX of the Education Amendments of 1972.

In the first chapter, *Attitude Measurement,* Edgar F. Borgatta has provided a discussion of the concept of attitude, and describes several of the classic approaches to attitude measurement. These approaches include Thurstone Scaling, Guttman Scaling and the simple additive score approach. Borgatta emphasizes, as Quinn does in the following chapter, the importance of starting from a conceptual or theoretical definition of the attitude to be measured. As he notes, the emphasis on theory and research in the building of scales and involvement of expert and judgmental screening of items continues to be important in the building of attitude measures. The Guttman Scaling approach is intuitively appealing because the idea of scaling is based upon response patterns—individuals who respond in a particular way have all responded in the same way in prior items. Borgotta states that a limitation to the use of Guttman-type scaling is the logical necessity that people proceed through the same set of items with the same response patterns. Most attitudes probably cannot be scaled in this manner. The most frequently used procedure, which Borgotta labels the additive score approach, is that of asking a number of questions and adding up the scores on the items. The limitations of this procedure are the relative ease with which anyone can proceed to develop an attitude measure, and the resulting lack of research and theory for most attitude measures. The following chapter illustrates the necessary search for theoretical and research bases for the measurement of attitudes that are important in vocational education.

The usefulness of examining the concept upon which an attitude measure is to be constructed is stressed by Robert P. Quinn and Thomas A. Gonzales in their chapter, *A Consumer's Guide to Job Satisfaction Measures*. These authors describe the uses of job satisfaction in vocational education program evaluation, and provide a review of the literature describing alternative definitions of job satisfaction. They list sources available to evaluators to locate the measures of job satisfaction they describe, as well as discussing the criteria evaluators can follow in selecting measures of job satisfaction. These criteria include a consideration of what they call facet-free and facet-specific measures, the occupational specificity that may be required in job satisfaction measures, and the measurement considerations of reliability and validity. They provide a helpful discussion of the problems of administering and scoring job satisfaction measures, the availability of norms, as well as a consideration of efficiency in measurement in evaluation. The very consideration of measures of job satisfaction in vocational education evaluation provides a more individual focus on the outcomes of vocational education, as opposed to a societal outcome of providing a skilled labor force. While these job satisfaction measures have not been traditional in vocational education evaluation nor in employment (manpower) training program evaluations, as described by Bresnick, they nevertheless relate to earlier issues discussed for evaluators—the nature of the outcomes to be measured, and the tension unique to vocational education in serving the specific needs of an industrial/ technological society versus serving the individual. The addition of measures of job satisfaction to evaluation of vocational education would provide a different form of linking education to work settings, and would emphasize the counseling or guidance of individuals for occupational and career choices, as suggested in Bonnet's paper on career education.

The historical relationship between vocational education and employment training programs is reviewed by David Bresnick in his chapter, *CETA's Challenge to the Evaluation of Vocational Education.* The separation of job training into the Department of Labor, and the vocational education programs into the Office of Education has had implications for the outcome measures used in these two settings. Vocational education programs, as housed within the Office of Education, have been viewed as skill development programs, and a small part of the larger educational effort carried out in schools. To the Department of Labor, the primary focus of training and employment programs has been jobs. Individuals were brought into programs because they needed jobs, and training was merely a means to that end. In the Comprehensive Employment and Training Act of 1973 (CETA) the focus has been on increasing access to the job market, particularly for disadvantaged individuals. The outcome measure taken as a priority for evaluation has been increases in earnings. The problems in assessing increases in individual earnings are described by Bresnick. There is a need for longitudinal data since there is some evidence that earnings differentials drop off sharply after the first year of employment. Another problem is that of differentiating varying degrees of effectiveness among CETA programs, particularly the effectiveness of placement efforts. Also, as Bresnick points out, the focus on placement and earnings are compromises in the attempt to measure the impact of jobs on the lives of individuals. The efforts to develop career education programs point to another area of concern for evaluators and administrators of vocational education programs.

Deborah G. Bonnet provides a review and discussion of outcomes of career education in her chapter, *Measuring Student Learning in Career Education.* Career education programs may be funded or conducted in conjunction with vocational education. A frequently cited problem in evaluating career education is a lack of student outcome measurement instruments. Many of the measures currently used were developed for purposes other than evaluating career education. As Shoemaker (1978) presented the federal perspective on measuring career education outcomes, there are few if any instruments currently available which meet good measurement standards. Shoemaker noted that the Center for Vocational Education at Ohio State University has developed guidelines for the selection of instruments to assess career education outcomes, and that there are evaluation handbooks for practitioners developed by the Center. Among the handbooks is one, *Career Education Measures: A Compendium of Evaluation Instruments,* that includes abstracts of about 200 measures. Bonnet's chapter in the Handbook provides a detailed analysis of instruments currently available for each. of the USOE career education goals, and makes suggestions for further development of measurement approaches to the evaluation of career education outcomes.

Problems in evaluating career education, in addition to developing outcome measures, included the manner in which career education may be interwoven into the curriculum, and taught through both the academic and vocational courses. Also, career education can be considered a developmental concept, with resulting implications for a developmental perspective on student outcomes. While developing and testing new measures for career education evaluation are high priorities, Bonnet points out that another important area is that of collecting the data needed for establishing standards of acceptable performance at high school or postsecondary graduation. Bonnet helpfully points out the evolving nature of the concept of career education with its accompanying goals and definitions of objectives. She also makes a strong plea that career educators concern themselves with better defining the goals of career education, rather than leaving it to evaluators to develop the goals through the measures that they use.

In a closely related area, that of the use of interest measures and career guidance, Carol Kehr Tittle has examined a measurement-related issue for evaluators and administrators. As mentioned earlier, the Education Amendments of 1976 and Title IX of the Educational Amendments of 1972 have brought the issue of sex discrimination to the attention of evaluators. Title IX mandates that tests and other materials used by counselors and teachers in guidance must be nondiscriminatory. The implications for evaluators of career activities in vocational programs is that the sex fairness of interest measures and guidance activities must be documented. Under the VEA of 1976, the policy of equal access for minorities and women to programs funded under the legislation is required. In addition, the states are required to set forth specific actions taken to overcome sex discrimination, and to specify incentives adopted to encourage enrollment of both women and men in nontraditional courses of studies. Thus federally funded programs, as well as local education agencies programs, must be concerned with eliminating discrimination based on sex in vocational education, and with providing sex fair counseling and guidance activities and materials.

In the chapter, *Interest Measures, Career Guidance, and Sex Bias: Issues for Program Evaluation,* a summary of the National Institute of Education *Guidelines for Assessment of Sex Bias and Sex Fairness in Career Interest Inventories* is provided. The guidelines give evaluators a checklist to use as the basis for documenting sex fairness in these instruments. Recent research studies that have implications for evaluators of career guidance activities are also described. The research developments include new interest measures, an activities checklist, and studies of the impact of career interest inventories on career choice. In this latter area, evaluators may find the concept of *exploration validity* useful in examining the extent to which career interest inventories, or other locally developed measures, result in stimulating the student to undertake exploration activities—to seek information about occupations new to the student, and to try new experiences that may be related to career choice. The chapter concludes with a broader consideration of the evaluation of sex fairness in career guidance. Here criteria are considered for examining sex bias in career guidance activities. Recommendations for evaluation criteria are developed in two areas, process measures and outcome or impact measures. As state plans develop and federally mandated evaluations of sex discrimination in vocational education (Harrison, 1978) are carried out, evaluators will have access to more standardized measurement procedures for determining equal access in sex bias. Bias is considered in a somewhat different context in the following chapter.

The last chapter in this section is *Test Bias: Current Methodology and Implications for Evaluators* by Carol Kehr Tittle. Evaluators who have used standardized achievement tests as measures for program evaluation are aware of charges of test bias. As the link between education and work is increased by a stronger emphasis in vocational education on job placement and follow-up studies, evaluators in vocational education will also become aware of the criticisms of standardized tests as biased against minorities, and as having an adverse impact on minorities. Greater attention to performance testing in vocational education, a situation similar to achievement testing where there is no external criterion readily available as a criterion for test validity, also increases the need for evaluators to be aware of issues of test bias. These issues are of concern also in conjunction with the assessment requirements of PL 94-142, the Education of the Handicapped Act, and the VEA concern with special populations.

Although the test bias work to date has been carried out on paper and pencil, multiple choice tests, mainly nationally-standardized instruments, many of the procedures and recommendations are adaptable or are of concern in performance testing and rating. The discussion in Tittle's chapter should provide the sensitivity necessary to adapt the existing test bias framework as necessary for vocational education program evaluation. The discussion focuses on content validity, empirical analyses of item bias, test and item format and test directions, and equating, scaling, and norms groups. The chapter concludes with a series of recommendations to evaluators. The recommendations describe the documentation and data evaluators should look for in test manuals or which they should provide in the development of new assessment procedures in vocational education.

This section of the Handbook has focused on measures specific to vocational education outcomes, and tried to assist the evaluator to recognize the social setting in which vocational education and evaluation both occur. Diversity in students and a focus on special populations requires a responsiveness and change from what may be called a traditional psychometric perspective. The last two chapters in this section have tried to suggest how educators and evaluators can meet some of the challenges, and to suggest where responsiveness may occur. While this section has focused on particular measures and testing issues, the annotated bibliography of the Handbook provides further resources in the area of measurement. Technical references concerned with reliability and validity are annotated, as well as references in other handbooks to summaries of measurement standards and procedures.

REFERENCES

Federal Register. *Uniform Guidelines on Employer Selection Procedures.* December 20, 1977 and August 25, 1978.

Harrison, L. R. 1978. "A national study of sex stereotyping and discrimination in vocational education." Paper presented at the annual meeting of the American Educational Research Association, Toronto.

Shoemaker, J. S. 1978. "Measuring career education outcomes: A federal perspective." Paper presented at the annual meeting of the American Educational Research Association, Toronto.

ATTITUDE MEASUREMENT | # chapter 15

EDGAR F. BORGATTA | *City University of New York*

The measurement of attitudes has become a part of many social sciences, and applications of attitude inventories have become important to the applied fields related to the social sciences. Intrinsically, an individual may be described in terms of physical characteristics, behavior, and then internalized qualities. These latter qualities are called sentiments, to include the broad range of characteristics of the person from very general dispositions, sometimes called basic personality traits, to very specific reactions, sometimes called opinions. Somewhere in between, organizing the way a person responds to the environment are *attitudes,* less specific than opinions but not as general as personality traits.

The concept of attitude is usually defined as the individual's general response to a topic. Definitions may become more detailed than this, and particular aspects of interest may be identified, such as the fact that attitudes are viewed as learned, or that they are evaluative in nature, or that the context affects the definition, and so forth. Ultimately, however, what people mean by the word attitude depends upon how they end up measuring the attitude. For this reason, understanding aspects of how attitudes have been and are measured is most important.

Evaluation of vocational education programs is frequently concerned with the measurement of variables in the affective domain, such as attitudes of program graduates and their employers. This is particularly true in the case of follow-up studies in which the attitude of program graduates toward work continues to be a major area of concern. For example, Chern and Pettibone

(1973) in their two-year follow-up study of public vocational school graduates found that the graduates' major area of concern dealt with the affective and social variables in the work situation. More recently the importance of the affective domain can be seen in the Vocational Education Amendments of 1976 (PL 94-485), which included employer satisfaction as a variable to be included in evaluation and accountability studies. It would appear that attitude measurement is an area of concern not only in measurement in general, but in evaluation per se, and in evaluation of vocational education in particular.

This chapter will focus on the central approaches to measurement of attitudes. The ideas about how attitudes should be measured now have a long history, and not too much that is "new" is really to be found in the literature of the last decade. What has happened that has been important is that the advent of computers has made it possible to reduce what looked like complicated procedures to rather routine applications, and thus it has been possible to put the history of attitude measurement in perspective. There have been many approaches to the measurement of attitudes, but the classic approaches, those of Thurstone Scaling, of Guttman Scaling, and of simple additive scores encompass most of the principles, and include most of the questions of assumptions about the nature of attitudes. Some specialized approaches have been productive for particular applications, but, in general, the history of attitude measurement suggests that some rather simple approaches to measurement may be the most efficient and also the most justifiable.

Thurstone Scaling

It is appropriate to review some of the work of L. L. Thurstone at the beginning of this examination of approaches to attitude measurement because Thurstone has been an important influence and stimulus to the field of measurement. In a pivotal work presented in a sociological journal, Thurstone (1928) presented a set of procedures under the title: "Attitudes can be measured." The title is itself revealing, as at the time the question of whether or not such things as attitudes could be measured was a matter of serious debate. This article was subsequently incorporated into a classic monograph, and it is essentially from this point that the debate shifted from a question of whether attitudes could be measured to one of how they should be measured (Thurstone and Chave, 1929).

Thurstone's procedure may be described as focusing on the organization of content rather than on the ordering and distributing of individuals. Thus, the initial ingredients of a Thurstone Scale are the specification of a content and the identification of items that are presumed to measure it. So, for example, one content could be called *work orientation,* and the description of the content could be specified as ranging from *extremely not work-oriented* to *extremely work-oriented*. Here we encounter the first ambiguity of the procedure, but one that recurs in the development of some other types of scales. In particular, how does one know what the extremes of a variable (attitude) are? So, for example, in an early presentation of the method, Thurstone specified a variable as Pacifism-Militarism. Theoretically, is this the same variable as say, Antimilitarism-Militarism? One cannot answer the question except as a matter of opinion, unless one carries out an empirical study to find out if the two content specifications coincide. We may note as an aside, that much subsequent evidence suggests that placing concepts that are presumed to be opposites at the extremes of scales may not be justifiable, and that often presumed opposites simply are not. So, in more modern applications it is frequently a more conservative and possibly more justifiable approach to describe content areas in terms of the extremes of *absence* of something, and at the other end of the scale the *most* of it that can exist. For instance, in the Thurstone example, while a bit awkward, the extremes might be defined from absolute absence of militarism to extreme militarism. Note that we have already introduced three possible concepts at the presumed opposite extremity of militarism, and more could be suggested.

Having specified the content extremes, one can conceptually postulate a continuum that can be divided into equal size intervals, say for example, eleven steps. The question of whether the steps are conceptualized as equal or not has some bearing on the way instructions are given, and possibly also on the distribution of responses. Usually, however, the procedure is carried out without much fuss about the equality of intervals, and the instructions might be to rate an array of statements presented to involve the content of the attitude from one to eleven. The statements would be rated on an implied continuum going from one extreme to the other, without naming the intervals they were intended to represent. Or, if statements are each separately typed on cards, the instructions would be to place the items in eleven ordered piles.

The statements used are assumed to have something to do with the content, and they should be drawn on the basis of familiarity with the theoretical and research literature. So, for example, if one is dealing with work orientations, one might draw many items from the literature on work motivation and job satisfaction, and from the literature on the place of work in society. The statements are usually presented in the form of assertions, and it is a special characteristic of the Thurstone scaling model that the statements are supposed to locate someone on the continuum through an indication of agreement or disagreement. Thus, for example, the following statement is of an appropriate type for the scaling: It is good to work about eight hours each workday. This locates the response on the continuum in the sense that one can disagree with the statement because one thinks eight hours is too much or too little. This type of statement can be contrasted to the type that divides the content, as for example: It is good to work eight hours or more each workday. Only those who feel that eight hours or more is too much will disagree.

Thurstone scaling proceeds by gathering a large number of statements that are presumed to be relevant, and then by having "judges," possibly as many as 100 of them, rate the statements in the eleven intervals. Good items would be those on which judges agree, which is to say those that tend to get the same ratings from many judges, and where the spread of the ratings for an item is narrow. Statements on which judges did not agree, would be spread broadly among the eleven intervals. From the statements on which the judges agreed, and which could thus be considered as discrimination statements, a scale could be built. It might have a substantial number of statements, but twenty statements typically would produce a scale with attractive properties of discrimination.

Having devised a scale, it could now be administered and used to assess attitudes of students about work orientations. Scoring of responses and following the logic of the system becomes relatively simple. Each statement has an average value on the eleven point scale originally used, and so if a student agrees with a given item, it becomes part of the student's score. For example, a student might agree to only three items, and the expectation on the basis of the logic of the scaling is that they would be in about the same range of the content. They might have values for the three statements of say, 2.5, 3.0, and 3.5, and it then follows that the student would have a sum for the three statement of 9.0 and an average score of 3.0. Another person might have agreed with five statements, with scores of 5.0, 5.0, 5.5, 6.5, 7.0, and 7.0, and such a person would have an average for the five items of 6.0.

In summary, with the Thurstone Scaling procedure the attitude scale is built in advance based on judgments, and then it is applied to respondents. The procedure can be cumbersome, but it has virtues. For example, the emphasis on building a broad array of statements that are theoretically related to the content suggests the importance of exploring competing theories, and alternate definitions and uses of concepts, and *not* proceeding in a naive operationalist manner to simply state: I am going to measure concept X this way. This emphasis on search of theory and research in the building of scales, and of involving expert and judgmental screening of items, persists in more sophisticated concerns of building measures, although interest in the Thurstone Scaling procedures as such have receded.

The limitations of Thurstone Scaling stem in large part from the assumptions about the way items should be chosen. Most statements simply are not of the type that identify a person on a scale in the sense we have outlined.

Table 15.1: Response Patterns for A Perfect Guttman Four-item Scale

Pattern Name	Items			
	D	C	B	A
Type I	+	+	+	+
Type II	+	+	+	−
Type III	+	+	−	−
Type IV	+	−	−	−

Alternative Presentation of Response Patterns

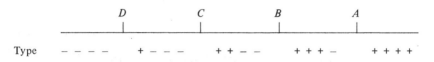

Most statements tend to separate persons as being above or below the point where the statement intersects a continuum of content, and thus are usually described as cumulative or monotonic in nature. (Recall the earlier example: It is good to work 8 hours or more each work day.) This limitation has resulted in the historical fact that very few Thurstone Scales have been developed. Additionally, there is good evidence that using alternative ways of creating scales and collecting data may be more efficient.

Guttman Scaling

An appealing model of attitude scaling stems from the work of Guttman (1944), who proposed a "cumulative" type of scale which is simple to understand. The model depends on the assumption that someone who is strongly in favor of something is at least mildly in favor of it. So, having a strong position can be expected logically to be inclusive of weaker positions. Guttman's suggestion quickly leads to a "perfect" or "errorless" type of scale that corresponds to the logic. To give an example, note the following items.

(A) Have you completed 12th grade?
(B) Have you completed 11th grade?
(C) Have you completed 10th grade?
(D) Have you completed 9th grade?

If one has answered item A with a yes, logically each successive question should be answered yes. If one answers questions B with a yes, each successive question should be answered with a yes, and so forth. The responses to these questions lead to patterns of responses, or types of responses. Assume

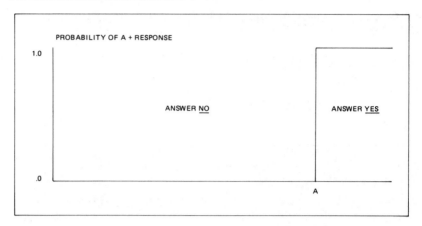

FIGURE 15.1: Trace line of a "perfect" Guttman type item

we use the symbol + to mean a yes and − to mean a no. Then the types of response patterns generated from the four questions (items) would be as shown in Table 15.1.

Conceptually the Guttman type scaling is easy to understand, and specifications for scaling under ideal conditions can be outlined. There should be a reasonably large number of items selected from a universe of discourse or content areas, and they should be spread in the continuum to give good discrimination. That is, each type should have a proportional number of cases. This latter comment leads to an alternate presentation of the continuum, as described in Table 15.1. Here it is seen that the continuum is divided by each of the questions, and so the questions actually form classes, with which each type can be associated.

The line, as shown in Table 15.1, is then divided by the proportion of positive responses for each question or item and this may be thought of as a continuum of content. Question A may be thought of as the most difficult, and thus the least likely to be answered yes. Question B is the second most difficult, and so forth.

Each item, further, can be represented as dividing a probability space, so that to the left of the item location persons answer no, and to the right they answer yes. This leads to the representation of the item or question in the form of a "traceline," as shown in Figure 15.1 for item A. Here only the traceline for item A is shown, and there would be one such line for each item.

The problem with Guttman Scaling is that questions are not answered without error, and perfect scales are nonexistent. Dealing with error introduces complications in the model that make it both difficult to handle and obviously deficient or inefficient in several ways. When scales have been constructed, errors in the responses lead to what have been called "error types" or non-scale types. So for example, if one answered item A with a yes and the other items with a no, the resulting type (- - - +) would not fit the logical patterns, and one would ask why. It could be that the instructions were not interpreted correctly by the respondent, that the response to item A was an error, or that the respondent in a perverse manner was simply not cooperating. There may be many sources of errors, but whatever the source, there are enough errors so that even using a variety of techniques to handle the errors, Guttman scales with more than a few items are hard to find.

Assuming that scales could be composed having a large number of questions or items, Guttman proposed that the acceptability of a scale could be judged on the basis of a Coefficient of Reproducibility, defined as the proportion of actual cases of perfect types for a scale corresponding to a perfect scale of similar characteristics. The formula for this coefficient is noted below, after error types have been considered in more detail. Guttman suggested that a Coefficient of Reproducibility of 85 percent would be a reasonable basis for considering the scale acceptable. This sounds reasonable but, as will be seen, has led to some serious problems for inexperienced users of Guttman Scaling.

The problems with Guttman Scaling in handling error types led to a literature of alternate treatments but the conclusion appears to be relatively simple. So-called errors can be of two types. If one encounters an error type such as the one noted about (- - - +), and if one uses a logic based on the number of errors that could be involved, it is clear that at least two possibilities may be contrasted. If the most difficult item (A) was answered in error, then only one error occurred. But, it could be that there were three errors, and questions B, C, and D all should have been answered yes. The argument, which is quite reasonable in general, is that the alternative that involves the *minimum* number of errors is most likely. In extreme cases, the reasonableness is more obvious, so for a scale with many items, encountering a type such as + + + - + + + + + + suggests that the - (minus) must have been an error. These errors have been called minimum-error classifications, or unambiguous classifications.

The second type of error, however, has proven more troublesome and has pointed to the limitations of Guttman Scaling. These are the so-called ambiguous errors which, for four items, are represented by the types - + - -, + - + -, and + + - +, each of which could have been recruited from two perfect types with only one error. So, - + - - could have been recruited from - - - - or + + - - with only one error. Similarly + - + - could have been recruited from + - - - and + + + -, and + + - + could have been recruited from + + - - or + + + +. When such an ambiguous error occurs, where should it be placed? An early analysis by Hays and Borgatta (1952) suggested that

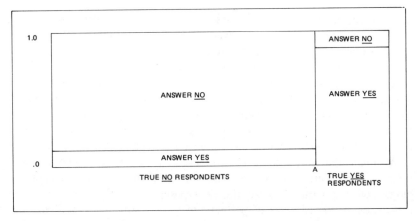

FIGURE 15.2: Trace line of a Guttman type item with error

the ambiguous error type be placed with neither of its logical recruitment locations *but* between them. Thus, for example, the type – + – – should be placed with the perfect type + – – –. The principle that underlies this solution requires reference to the traceline of an item that has error, such as is illustrated in Figure 15.2. Note that the assumption is that the errors are distributed uniformly, and we may say that an error should be defined more accurately as the probability that a person who is really a yes respondent will say no, and a person who is really a no respondent will say yes to a given question. The empirical fact is that this type of traceline does not correspond

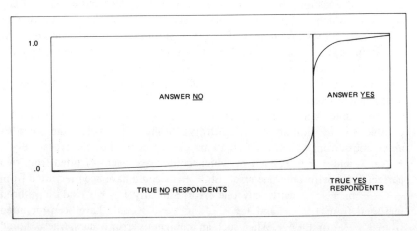

FIGURE 15.3: Traceline of an item where the error of response is greater the closer one is to the decision point

to experience, and the probability of making an error is associated with how close a respondent is to the decision point, the point that divides the yes and the no respondents. Experientially, tracelines appear to be more in the character shown in Figure 15.3 than in the simpler model of the Guttman type item. Experientially, also, the ambiguous types of errors occur in the apparent association of errors with items that are close to each other. Therefore, if there are two items U and V that are close to each other, persons close to the decision points are those most likely to be involved in errors in answering those items. Table 15.2 illustrates the difficulty and introduces some numbers to show the relationship of the distribution of respondents to the characteristics of a scale. Table 15.2 shows a set of four items (W, X, Y, and Z) that have been associated with data collection in three fictitious examples, and assumes a sample size of 1,000 respondents for each instance in which samples were drawn. The numbers on the right indicate the number of respondents with the response/pattern or type shown on the left, and there are three columns to represent the three samples. Below the types or patterns are the number of respondents in each sample that answer the item with a + (a yes).

It should be noted from the first line below the types, Sample Time 1, that the number who answer + to items W, X, Y, and Z respectively, decrease, and this corresponds to the idea of increasing difficulty in responding to the items. This must happen if the scale is properly ordered, and for this reason in presenting Guttman scales, the ordering of items is expected to correspond to the number of + responses. However, in the example the order of the

Table 15.2: Example of Three Samples Answering the Same Four Items, with A Hypothetical Difference Only for Items X and Y of A Small Number of Responses

Types	Items				Sample Time 1	Sample Time 2	Sample Time 3
	W	X	Y	Z			
Type I	+	+	+	+	210	210	210
Type II	+	+	+	−	200	200	200
Type III	+	+	−	−	100	90	95
Type AE	+	−	+	−	90	100	95
Type IV	+	−	−	−	200	200	200
Type V	−	−	−	−	200	200	200
Sample:							
Time 1	800	510	500	210			
Time 2	800	500	510	210			
Time 3	800	505	505	210			

responses was fixed on the basis of the Sample Time 1, and it is seen that the number of respondents to items X and Y, 510 and 500 + responses respectively, is close. The two items, thus, would be judged as being close in difficulty, and one should not be surprised to see them involved in error. The error is the ambiguous type (Type AE), and this is characteristic of how such errors are found for items adjacent to each other. Comparison of Sample Time 1 with Sample Time 2 shows that they are very close, with a shift of only ten responses. This is seen in the row for Sample Time 2 with the order of the items X and Y reversed, with Y now 510 and X 500 + responses.

The reader may want to play with these arrangements, but if the items for X and Y are shifted in order for Sample Time 2, the scale will look exactly like the one for Sample Time 1. What happens may not be clear, however. Only the Type III and Type AE are involved in the shift, and they are reversed so that the Type III becomes Type AE and the Type AE becomes Type III. In other words, in a case where the two items are very close, it is shown that with a slight change in distributions the ambiguous error types become associated with the type that falls between the two perfect types, Type II and Type IV, which would involve only one error each. This principle can also be further emphasized by pointing to the fact that in the case of the third hypothetical sample, Time 3, when the number of + responses for items X and Y are the same, there is really no way to order the scale.

Some of the practical problems of Guttman Scaling *appear* easy to handle. For example, with regard to the illustration given in Table 15.2, removal of one of the items, X or Y, results in a perfect scale. In practice, this is what tends to happen. A researcher will ambitiously gather data for a large number of items, expecting to build an acceptable Guttman type scale, only to discover that the data simply do not go together that well, and may possibly end up with a Guttman type scale of only a few items. Unfortunately, this is a serious problem, as data are hard to come by, and throwing any away is wasteful. A procedure for retaining data and improving the Guttman type scales when there are surplus items has been described (Stouffer, Borgatta, Hays, and Henry, 1952). Making things better does not necessarily remove the basic problems, and the discussion now turns to an evaluation of Guttman Scaling.

A basic shortcoming of Guttman Scaling is that the model does not correspond to reality as we know it. First, it assumes random distribution of error, when all experience points to the fact that errors are more frequently made as one approaches the point where one could be on either side of the issue. Second, Guttman Scaling implies classes in which people are equal in characteristics, but the fact is that the classes can be subdivided and ordered, being limited only by locating further good items. Third, and this has not yet been noted, the solution of the ambiguous type placement turns out to be exactly the same as adding the number of positive responses, which conceptually is a lot easier than going through the elaborate model of creating types. Fourth, and this will now be shown, it is difficult to evaluate the "goodness" of a Guttman type scale.

The Coefficient of Reproducibility is defined as:

$$CR = 1 - \frac{\text{Number of errors}}{\text{Number of items times Number of cases}}$$

For the Sample Time 1 in Table 15.2, there were ninety errors. Therefore, 90/4x1,000 equals .0225, which subtracted from 1 yields .9775, a respectable looking number. However, how does one interpret such a number? Is it like a correlation coefficient which ranges from zero relationship to a perfect relationship of 1.00? If so, the number is impressive. To judge the CR it is necessary to compare what one finds to a scale with "chance" distribution, to see how much better than chance one is doing. For example, if we took a three item Guttman type scale with percentage of + responses of 20 percent, 50 percent, and 80 percent, if there is no association between the items, that is, they are totally independent of each other, the CR equals .9333! And, if one is dealing with a four item scale, similar to the one in Table 15.2, say with percentage of + responses of 20 percent, 50 percent, 50 percent, and 80 percent, the CR when there is no relationship among the items is equal to .8850. What is obvious is that the lowest value of the CR is not zero, and every different distribution will have a different CR which is its minimum, that is, that would occur by chance alone. For this reason, a number of alternative indices for interpretation have been suggested (Borgatta, 1955), but there is no simple solution. At best, one ends up stating that one found a Guttman type scale with a given ratio of found errors to those which would be expected by chance.

Finally, Guttman type scales also suffer from the fact that they require getting information in a dichotomous form. Using items that have more than two categories leaves the researcher either with the problem of throwing away information or building in what are known as logical dependencies. That is, in one question one can only be—by definition—consistent, so that if an item in a scale is used to provide two pieces of information, these data do not involve independent pieces of information. The two pieces of information are said to have correlated errors.

Overall, Guttman type scaling is hard to defend as a procedure in attitude measurement, but there are occasions when it may be the appropriate model. For example, if a content is seen as being genuinely cumulative, as for example when people proceed through a growth or learning process that seems to be in a necessary order, then the idea of a model like the Guttman

Scaling makes sense. Additionally, it should be stated that if items can be ordered in the sense of Guttman Scaling, those errors that are distant from the decision point may be correctable as illogical in the model, and potentially this has some virtue. But, with all the problems noted, one should be especially careful in the use of Guttman type scaling.

Additive Scores

The idea of asking a number of questions and then adding up the scores of the items after they have been aligned according to content is possibly the easiest way to conceive of creating an index, and with some qualification perhaps this turns out to be the best way. That is, if one deals with gathering information following some relatively simple rules, the additive scores provide measures that have desirable measurement characteristics.

As a simple example, if one has screened items in a preliminary judgmental way, say procedures adapted from the logic of Thurstone Scaling, and one uses dichotomies and aligns the content, then several things can be expected. If the items divide the population in half, roughly speaking, between the yeses and the nos, the agrees and disagrees, the likes and dislikes, and so forth, and if the items are indeed measures of the same content and have some reasonable reliability, then adding the scores together will result in a curve that will approximate a normal curve, assuming a substantial number of items, say twenty, are used. But, the situation is more favorable than this, and in the case of items that are distributed in the population with regard to dividing points, the good distributional characteristics of the resulting curve will not be altered. For some purposes, this will help in the definition of a measure, increasing the variance or spread.

This common sense approach corresponds to the major models of test development in the area of testing, and as a familiar example, so-called IQ tests are usually constructed as multi-item tests in which scores are simply the addition of the responses. This idea about how indices should be formed, therefore, has a nebulous and relatively ancient history. In the area of attitude measurement when reference is made to additive scores, sometimes the name Likert Technique is used to identify the procedure, since Likert (1932) presented a specific set of suggestions for a format and presentation of items for additive scoring.

How does one go about developing an additive score? The answer, it is hoped, will always emphasize the question of theoretical relevance on the one hand, and knowledge of the bases of "test development" in general. What this means is that one should know the subject matter in which one is doing research very well, and the awareness that most of our knowledge is tentative or provisional should keep one cautious. The idea that one knows how to measure something in advance of seeing what actually happens seems a little presumptuous in the development of measures, and this will be discussed a little later with regard to the concept of validity. The basic assumption here is that the least that one will do is what Thurstone suggests, namely to explore the possible alternate definitions of a concept, circumstantial factors in definitions, possible components of a concept, and so on, and then build the score from the distillate. The distillation process will be examined in the context of dealing with the score construction.

Assume that one has constructed the usual haphazard type of questionnaire. Then, how does one build a score? It is assumed that items that belong in the same score should be related to each other. On the one hand, the concept may be unitary, but it is also possible that the concept of interest is related to a typology, and the typology may be based on several component variables. A basic first rule for the construction of scores is that the several component variables should be developed separately into measures. So, there is an implicit mandate drawn from the long history of measurement that suggests, that concepts should be selected and defined in the sense of being composed of just one thing, just one content. Therefore, this suggests that the items in the score should be related to each other. The word "align" with regard to content, should be noted. The content must all be scored in the same direction, i.e., an item that is scored high on a concept, like work orientation, must be added to another item in which the high score also means high work orientation, and not the opposite. This may be a trivial point, but frequently in order to avoid problems of nonattention, random marking, test direction biases, and other possible format and response tendencies, the content alignment is often varied in a questionnaire.

Then, how does one know that items are related to each other? The intuitive and theoretical exercises that precede the formation of the questions or items represent a partial answer, and previous experience by others may be extensive in some areas of measurement. However, ultimately in development of new measures and in checking the operation of measures borrowed from others, it is necessary to examine how the items are actually related. The procedures for this vary, but it is common to examine the intercorrelations among the component items, and it is also appropriate to see how well each item correlates with the score to which it contributes. This procedure, while varied in the techniques of different researchers, is generally known as "item analysis." There is no simple way of describing item analysis in terms of standards of test development because item reliability and how well the content can be measured may be a function of the content itself. The process, however, consists of correlating the items to the total score (omitting the item being examined) to determine whether adding the item to the provisional score will or will not improve the score. Sometimes this is described as a process of purification, and items that do not fit the score are dropped. It is a way of reducing the number of items from the original more inclusive panel. It should be noted that this idea of a reduction to an acceptable set of items is a part of each of the scaling procedures discussed above.

Now, if one has planned in advance, the response categories of the items may all be the same length. It may be that all questions have response categories of say, agree, probably agree, probably disagree, and disagree. In this case, if the aligned items are scored 1, 2, 3, and 4, respectively, they may be added together, and the effect is that, more or less, each item will have about the same weight in the final score. This occurs because with a fixed format of this type the variance or spread of the responses is restricted, and by experience it is seen that the variances fall within a rather narrow range. So, assuming that the items are roughly about as good, they are given about equal weight. Note by contrast that if the items have different response categories, so that one item may be answered with a dichotomy of yes or no, and another item by seven categories ranging from always to never, then something may need to be done so that one gets about the same weight as the other. This is a problem that should be anticipated when one is designing the measuring instrument. How important such an issue is in the development of the score depends, also, on how many items there will be in the final score. If there will be few items, then weighting is extremely important, but if there are many, say twenty or more, then the question of how much difference weighting makes may be less important. In fact, general experience is that with scores that involve many items, weighting has very little effect on the ability of the score to correlate with (predict) another variable.

Reliability and Validity

The question of how good a score is for measuring an attitude requires attention to several aspects of measurement. The first aspect cannot be answered in any statistical sense, but requires reference to the whole scientific context in which the measurement takes place. This is the question of how valid a measure is, which means: How well does the measurement carried out correspond to the concept in the theory? This may be phrased more directly by asking: Does the measure that has been devised actually measure what it is supposed to measure? There are a number of concepts of validity. However, before one goes to the question of validity, the second aspect of interest, reliability, should be examined. Reliability usually is thought of as the consistency with which an instrument measures, or in a common sense way, the ability of a measure to provide the same results in different applications. There are a number of ways for assessing reliability, and these will be considered briefly.

A common sense approach to the idea of reliability is the successive use of a measure on two (or more) occasions with the same subjects, and then examining how well the sets of scores correlate. If the correlation is high, the measure is judged reliable, and if low, relatively unreliable. There is no absolute standard, and some classes of variables have very high reliabilities, such as measures of verbal abilities, while by contrast attitude measures (and values) very often have low reliability levels. In the attitude area, reliabilities in the range of test-retest correlations of from .3 to .8 appear to be the reasonable expectations, but reliabilities on the high side of the range indicated are not frequent. This is important to know because the reliability of a score is automatically a *ceiling* on the predictive validity of the score. In this sense there is no way that a measure can be more valid than it is reliable.

If a measure has a given level of reliability (or unreliability), it is appropriate to ask what the sources of unreliability are. This focuses on a concept like test-retest reliability, on the method of assessing reliability itself. Is the unreliability due to the fact that the test is not consistent or stable, or can something have changed between the testings? These two things are different, and it may be that a score is quite reliable, but a test-retest assessment of the reliability could turn out to be very low. This could happen because the subjects have changed during the test period; as for example, when they have differential experiences that are related to the attitude variable that is being measured. It becomes extremely important to distinguish between the reliability of a score and the stability of subject performance. The latter may be important to study, but it is a separate issue.

This leads to clarification of the concept of reliability, and in particular, the idea of consistency becomes more focal. One way of eliminating the confusion in a test-retest situation resulting from subjects changing over time is to develop some split-half measure of reliability. What should be the way to split the halves of the score? This is not clear, but some procedures, such as comparing the odd with the even numbered items in a score at least eliminate the most gross effects possible, such as the learning that may go on between the first half and the second half of a set of questions. But, even so, one cannot be sure that the even and odd numbered items in a score will give a balanced set of halves.

The concept that is recommended for measuring reliability is known as Coefficient Alpha, which is a measure of the internal consistency of a set of items. In essence, Coefficient Alpha measures how strongly items are related to each other. The Coefficient Alpha turns out to be the upper limit of reliability because it deals only with how the items relate to each other; pragmatically, it turns out to operate as a very good measure of reliability because the types of errors that actually get involved in the collection of data go beyond the basic problem of the sampling of the content in the score.

This, then, turns out to be the acceptable way of reporting reliability information, but it is so only because most things we do are not necessarily the ideal things. For example, a more adequate concept of reliability would be the intercorrelation between tests that are defined to be exactly equivalent. But how would one use this concept when it is already a difficult task to find a set of items that will form a reasonable basis for constructing one score? There are many ways of dealing with the problems of reliability that permit one to become more knowledgeable about the data and the information it can yield. For example, having an estimate of reliability, in considering the relationship of an attitude variable to another variable one can ask: What difference it would make if one had a more reliable measure? Or, one can ask the specific question: Suppose I could double the number of items in the score I am using to measure an attitude, and the items were as good as the one I already have, what difference would this make for the reliability of the score?

It will be recalled, that in discussing how additive scores are composed, the model initially used was of dichotomous items. It is clear that if one asks questions that are answered only yes or no, an opportunity to get more information efficiently may be lost. It may be that without using much more time, respondents could have made the distinction between definitely yes, probably yes, probably no, and definitely no. In other words, it may be possible to get more information by increasing the number of response categories. This is analogous to getting more information by several dichotomous items that divide the population at different points in the continuum, but in the latter case this approach has the virtue of getting the information in adequate measures, but using more time and effort. Efficiency issues have to be balanced in collecting data designed to be reliable, and so, historically, there has been interest in the effect of increasing the number of response categories, but much more attention has been given to the effect of increasing the number of items in a score.

Assuming items of equal reliability, increasing the number of items can be described by an efficiency curve, so that each additional increment gets smaller when an additional item is added. Practically speaking, a "law of diminishing returns" operates so that one has to see if adding an additional item, which takes additional time, interest, and so forth on the part of the respondent, is worth it in terms of the increment in reliability. So, for example, an item that has a reliability of .5 when put in combination with three items of the same characteristics will give a score that has a reliability of .8, but adding an additional four items (doubling the length of the score in terms of number of items) will *not* bring the reliability up to .9. This, then, leads to "rule of thumb" suggestions. For example, if items are carefully selected, have four or five response categories, and are in the reliability range of about .5, then four or five such items will form a score that is satisfactory in the attitude area. It must be noted, immediately, that this sounds easier to do than it actually is. Without repeating items, that is, without having items that sound alike, it is often extremely difficult to find as many as five items that fit together and form a reasonable score.

A suggested model for reliability is presented through a simplified hypothetical situation. Suppose one has measured two different attitude concepts with two items each. What should the matrix of relationships look like for the items, for attitudes A and B, and items 1 and 2? This matrix is shown in Table 15.3, and here it is noted that what one would expect boils down to (a) high relationship among the items in a score and (b) low relationships (or none) to items not in the score. Suppose further that the notion of alternative forms is reintroduced, so we have attitudes AA and BB, each with two items. This is also show in Table 15.3, and it is seen from the model that items should correlate as well with those in the alternate form as they do within their own score. As a result, this is the condition of noting the difference between scores that are thought to be independent, and the way items are clustered within scores. To show the integrity of an attitude measure, it must be viewed along with other measures in its content domain, that is, along with other attitude measures.

We may now return to the concept of validity. The model matrix in Table 15.3 can be related to the concept of validity in the following way. How does one know that one is measuring what is supposed to be measured? The

Table 15.3: Intercorrelation Matrix for Items in Two Attitude Scores, A and B, and The Alternate Forms AA and BB. Correlation Values Shown are Hypothetical for Illustration Only

		A Items		B Items		AA Items		BB Items	
Attitudes		1	2	1	2	1	2	1	2
A	1	---	.50	---	---	.50	.50	---	---
	2		---	---	---	.50	.50	---	---
B	1			---	.50	---	---	.50	.50
	2				---	---	---	.50	.50
AA	1					---	.50	---	---
	2						---	---	---
BB	1							---	.50
	2								---

answer comes by logic of association of the measure to the theory, or most immediately, by finding two independent ways of measuring the same things. That is, if there is good reason to believe that attitudes are expressed in two quite different ways, then the parallel attitudes should correlate when they are appropriately measured. This is the model shown in Table 15.3, except that instead of having alternate forms we should think of having alternate methods of measurement of the attitudes A and B. For example, A could be a person's attitude toward work by self report, and AA could be an observer's rating of the attitude toward work as expressed in the person's behavior. This is known as the multitrait and multimethod approach to validation (Campbell and Fiske, 1959), and for demonstration of validity there is a requirement that there be discrimination between the methods and convergence for each trait (intercorrelation in the sense as suggested by Table 15.2).

Interest in measuring attitudes is found in all of the social and psychological sciences, and they have all contributed to the development of methods and techniques of measurement. Projective techniques that are related to personality analysis have ranged from the very abstract to fairly direct and easily rationalized procedures. Among the more successful attempts to measure attitudes with projective techniques have been the approaches dealing with distortion and error, on the assumption that people lean in the direction of their prejudices and tend to see what they want to see. Many such studies were popular during the post-World War II period, but they are of less interest now, largely because among many of the interesting things that can be done, not many have a great deal of efficiency. In general, this is the experience—indirect measurement of attitudes is not efficient.

Much of the more recent attention on the measurement of attitudes has focused on developing more complex measures that can be inclusive of many of the attitudes a person has. This has been approached in many ways, but the most general approach has been through *factor analysis*. The origins of factor analysis are related to those of scaling, and in the early work the name of Thurstone was very prominent. Factor analysis permits the handling of complex sets of data, where there are many variables, and leads to the reduction in the number of variables that are needed to summarize the original complex set of data. For example, if there have been a hundred attitude items in a questionnaire, it may be that only a half dozen or so attitudes will actually summarize all the information that is gathered. This is the idea of having underlying themes or content, and the factor analysis "transformation procedures" locate these underlying contents, essentially without loss of information. Factor analysis is a very powerful procedure when applied to research on attitudes, and it is used in two ways. First, it is used to explore a domain of content when there is little known about the particular area and one wants to get an idea of the types of basic variables that exist. For example, one might want to find out how many different types of orientations there are to work. (This is quite different as an approach from assuming that people only fall into one dimension of liking work or not liking it.) Then, assuming a variety of content is located, the second task for factor analysis is the refinement and location of that structure of content in replicating studies. This second task is closely related to the development of additive scores, because one consequence of factor analysis usually is to develop scores corresponding to the factors. There are many models of factor analysis, and the procedures should not be utilized without familiarization with the limitations and consequences of selecting a particular model of factor analysis (Harman, 1967).

Another direction in terms of complexity has been in the development of procedures for dealing simultaneously with the classification of persons on the basis of a number of attributes. The general approach is called multidimensional scaling (MDS), and highly sophisticated models have been developed for such scaling (Kruskal and Wish, 1978). The procedures involved, however, are frequently unsatisfactory to those who apply them because there are many ambiguities of interpretation about what the complex classifications mean.

Many specialized approaches have been developed for attitude measurement. Some of these, such as the semantic differential originated by Charles Osgood, have enjoyed extensive use. The use of the semantic differential in attitude research is described and elaborated by Heise (1970). For special purposes, special approaches may be appropriate. Intrinsically, however, the semantic differential was not developed for attitude research, and thus it has serious limitations in application, most common of which are that its utility for semantic analysis interferes with the potential for measurement of attitudes as more commonly defined. Similar experience can be noted with other procedures, and with the history of attitude measurement well into a second generation of sophisticated attention, the variety and ingenuity of approaches should not be underestimated. Before exploring more exotic approaches to attitude measurement, however, the student should be well versed in what the mainline approaches can do. There are many excellent general works that bear on the topic of attitude measurement and measurement more generally (e.g., Nunnally, 1978).

REFERENCES

Borgatta, E. F. 1955. An error ratio for scalogram analysis. *Public Opinion Quarterly* 19: 96-100.

Campbell, D. T., and Fiske, D. W. 1959. Convergent and discriminant validation by the multitrait-multimethod matrix. *Psychological Bulletin* 56: 81-105.

Chern, H. I., and Pettibone, T. J. 1973. A two year follow-up study of public vocational school graduates. *Journal of Vocational Behavior* 3: 99-101.

Guttman, L. 1944. A basis for scaling qualitative data. *American Sociological Review* 9: 139-150.

Harman, H. H. 1967. *Modern Factor Analysis.* Chicago: University of Chicago Press.

Hays, D. G., and Borgatta, E. F. 1952. Some limitations on the arbitrary classification of non-scale response patterns in a Guttman scale. *Public Opinion Quarterly* 16: 410-416.

Heise, D. R. 1970. The semantic differential and attitude research. In Gene F. Summers, ed. *Attitude Measurement.* Chicago: Rand McNally.

Kruskal, J. B., and Wish, M. 1978. *Multidimensional Scaling.* Beverly Hills: Sage Publications.

Likert, R. 1932. A technique for the measurement of attitudes. *Archives of Psychology* No. 140.

Nunnally, J. 1978. *Psychometric Theory* New York: McGraw-Hill.

Stouffer, S. A., Borgatta, E. F., Hays, D. G., and Henry, A. F. 1952. A technique for improving cumulative scales. *Public Opinion Quarterly* 16: 273-291.

Thurstone, L. L. 1928. Attitudes can be measured. *American Journal of Sociology* 33: 529-554.

Thurstone, L. L., and Chave E. J. 1929. *The Measurement of Attitudes.* Chicago: University of Chicago Press.

| A CONSUMER'S GUIDE TO JOB SATISFACTION MEASURES | **chapter 16** |

ROBERT P. QUINN   *University of Michigan*
THOMAS A. GONZALES   *University of Michigan*

USES OF JOB SATISFACTION IN VOCATIONAL EDUCATION PROGRAM EVALUATION

Two overall goals are evident in research on and discussions of vocational education. Perhaps simply stated, those two goals appear to be (1) a societal outcome—providing a skilled labor force that meets the needs of the economy, and (2) an individual outcome—providing individuals with skills and training that lead to satisfactory employment. Evaluation being a matter of accountability, the relative importance of societal and individual outcomes determines "to whom" and "for what" vocational education will be accountable.

Vocational education must, of course, be accountable to society for providing a skilled labor force, considering the mandates responsible for bringing it to its present state. According to this emphasis, questions of program evaluation are expressed in the language of economics and manpower policy-making. It is no coincidence that successful application of the techniques of cost-benefit analysis to program accountability has continued to grow, considering the compatible forms of the questions and answers. It is also no coincidence that the growing criticism of the use of cost-benefit analysis that has accompanied its growth is predominantly from those who urge the recognition of noneconomic factors in evaluation and planning of programs. Somers and Wood (1969) commented in their editors' foreward to a collection of articles on the developments and applications of cost-benefit analysis:

The arguments of the critics . . . assume special force when applied to manpower policies. They feel that evaluation of programs to aid the disadvantaged in terms of society's monetary benefits and costs alone is inappropriate: non-monetary considerations should also be taken into account. Although it is generally recognized that nonpecuniary factors affect social welfare, such factors are seldom incorporated into cost-benefit models. The critics feel that cost-benefit analysis concentrates on the quantitative to the exclusion of the qualitative, thereby sacrificing worthy programs on a "cross of gold" (1969, p. vii).

Somers and Wood are receptive to these critics and note that cost-benefit analysis cannot and should not purport to establish the goals of manpower policy, goals which are likely to be determined by noneconomic as well as economic factors. Preeminent among noneconomic factors are social-psychological dimensions such as job satisfaction. The use of job satisfaction measures in program evaluation and the level of sophistication of measures of job satisfaction are likely to vary, therefore, as a function of the relative importance of economic and noneconomic goals, of societal and individual outcomes.

Young, Clive, and Miles (1971) cite job satisfaction as a potentially useful criterion for the priority determination phase of vocational education program planning. They feel that measures of the degree of job satisfaction of graduates of various curricula would add a useful dimension to program appraisal. They note, however, that while many follow-up studies and reviews recognize the importance of job satisfaction, the significance and interpretation of the results has been questioned. They seem to concur with Little (1970) on the "fragmentary and sporadic" nature of the information presently available on job satisfaction within the context of vocational education. Moreover, researchers in the field of vocational education who emphasize accountability in terms of economic factors tend to recognize job satisfaction by the inclusion of only one or two overall job satisfaction questions, feeling confident that they have tapped its potential. Grasso (1975), in a study comparing vocational education and standard curricula at the secondary school level, describes just such a situation:

> Job satisfaction, at best an elusive criterion, is explored in dummy variable form; its mean is the proportion who reported being highly satisfied. . . . While this very limited measure may be an oversimplistic representation of satisfaction, prior experience has justified its continued use and generates confidence that it captures the quality intended surprisingly well (p. 62).

Such treatments are typical where the focus is on societal outcomes, and extensive use is made of economic factors.

The growth of consumer advocacy and the concern for the "quality of working life" are but two indications that in recent years the focus of accountability has begun to shift in the direction of individual outcomes. According to this emphasis, program evaluation should include measures of how well education and/or skills training satisfy the employability, job competency, and other work-related needs of individuals. Moreover, the assessment should incorporate social-psychological dimensions of job attitudes for the assessment to be relevant to the individual's perceived satisfaction of needs.

Efforts are being made in this direction. Smith, Passmore, Copa, and Moss (1971) used the Minnesota Satisfaction Questionnaire and the Minnesota Satisfaction Scales in developing a state-wide program evaluation system. For these researchers, accountability was also recognized as a main concern. However, the goal of vocational education as seen by them was the mutual satisfaction of the individual and society—improvement of the individual's work adjustment, and the maintenance of an appropriate distribution of skilled workers. The Theory of Work Adjustment (Dawis, England, and Lofquist, 1968; Lofquist and Dawis, 1969), from which the Minnesota measures came, was developed in the field of vocational rehabilitation but has found wide acceptance as a general theory of work behavior. The program evaluation of Smith et al. is unique in its extensive measurement and use of job satisfaction data as a way of dealing with the needs of individual workers. While the utility of these instruments in a state-wide program evaluation was inconclusive, this and other related research has demonstrated that more sophisticated methodology and theoretical frameworks exist than are generally being used to tap the potential of relevant social-psychological dimensions.

The recent research literature in vocational education reveals widely differing conceptions of the place of job satisfaction in program evaluation. While many writers and researchers in vocational education recognize job satisfaction to be of some importance, limited use of and research into its potential are the rule. Given that evaluations of appropriateness and adequacy should be based on the overall design and purposes of a study, one notes differing levels of job satisfaction measurement within vocational education program evaluation studies. In a national follow-up study, Noeth and Hansen (1975) used a one-question index of job satisfaction as a criterion—"How satisfied with your current job are you?" Todd (1972), in examining the effect of different occupational experience patterns, opted for an established measure of job satisfaction, the Hoppock Job Satisfaction Blank. This four-question measure is a facet-free or general job satisfaction measure no longer widely used. While attitudes toward preparation for the world of work were of primary concern in Todd's (1972) study, the hypothesized nature of job satisfaction was inadequately explained.

A study by Opacinch (1974) included a short measure of job satisfaction that incorporated a general or facet-free question with facets generally considered important in work. The facets were salary, opportunity for advancement, opportunity for salary increase, fringe benefits, job overall, opportunity for friendship with co-workers, communication with supervisor, status of job, and opportunity to do things that one was trained to do. Except for the heavy emphasis on contextual or extrinsic factors at the expense of work content facets, Opacinch's measure represents a step in the right direction. A similar measure was developed by Worth, Hietala, Spurlin, and de Mik (1973) in a follow-up evaluation study of a manpower development program. Job satisfaction was considered an important component of posttraining success, and was measured through six facets cast into a format of "on this job how do (did) you like your _____." In addition, expression of dissatisfaction with five of these same facets was invited by the open-ended stem of "The thing I dislike most about _____ was." Considerable practical information may be gained by this concise measurement approach.

One final example, by Gillie and Mann (1973), represents a commendable effort to tap the multidimensionality of job satisfaction, but a failure to take advantage of the information generated by the measurement. Data on six direct job satisfaction characteristics and nine indirect characteristics represent a potential wealth of information on the job satisfaction of a large sample of graduates of associate degree programs. An extensive literature review was cited in support of the selection of variables, but an overall formulation or model was not described. The analysis seemed to follow a systematic process of examining all possible bivariate or trivariate relationships for any of significance, rather than testing predetermined hypotheses. It appeared that some of the potential information and its implications may have slipped through the net. Nevertheless, this represents one of the better efforts at tapping job satisfaction for program evaluation.

To summarize, vocational education may be viewed as having to meet two separate and not necessarily compatible goals: (1) a societal outcome—an appropriate distribution in the skilled labor force, and (2) an individual outcome—skills and training that lead to satisfactory employment. The accountability of vocational education to society is appropriately and successfully assessed using cost-benefit and resource utilization techniques which emphasize economic factors. While this approach is predominant, recent years have seen a shift in emphasis toward individual outcomes, and the need for incorporating social-psychological dimensions such as job satisfaction into evaluation models is increasingly being recognized. In general, the level of sophistication of use and measurement of job satisfaction in evaluating vocational education programs correlates with the relative importance of the individual outcome goal expressed or implied by the investigator.

DEFINING JOB SATISFACTION:
INCLUSIONS AND EXCLUSIONS

Although several widely accepted theories of job satisfaction exist, few, if any, can justifiably claim to be a well-developed, powerful theory of job satisfaction. Various formulations of job satisfaction have definitions that allow measurement constructs to be developed, but a precise theoretical framework of causal relationships has yet to be developed. As a consequence, we know a great deal about variables that correlate with job satisfaction, but little about the exact antecedent or consequent nature of their relationships with job satisfaction.

Many current formulations of job satisfaction draw upon Maslow's (1954) theory of need fulfillment. Basically, a need-fulfillment theory of job satisfaction assumes some structure of human needs and the degree of fulfillment that some job affords. According to Maslow (1954, 1970), five need categories (from physiological, up through safety, belonging and love, esteem, and self-actualization) exist in a hierarchy of prepotency. The strength or importance of a need depends on its position in the hierarchy and the degree of satisfaction of all lower needs. Job satisfaction is a function of the degree to which aspects or facets of the work environment fulfill the needs at and below the worker's level of prepotency within the hierarchy. Various conceptualizations of the process of assessing fulfillment produce different theoretical formulations of job satisfaction.

What has been called discrepancy theory maintains that satisfaction is determined by the differences between the actual rewards a person receives and some other reward level, with various theorists making distinctions of what "some other reward level" should be. Locke's (1969) discrepancy formulation emphasizes *perceived* (not actual) discrepancy between what one *wants* from the job and what one perceives it as offering. Lawler (1973) indicates that although Porter (1961) has never presented an actual theory of job satisfaction, the latter's manner of measuring need satisfaction implies a discrepancy theory. Porter's approach, probably the most widely used discrepancy approach, considers the discrepancy between the person's reports of how much of a given reward there *should be* and how much he or she actually receives. An indication of overall job satisfaction would, accordingly, be given by the addition of the discrepancies for each aspect, or facet of a job.

Equity theorists like Adams (1963) argue that satisfaction is determined by a person's perceived input-outcome balance—a ratio of what he or she receives from the job relative to what he or she puts into it. Equity or inequity is evaluated by comparison to relevant others. Equity is said to lead to satisfaction; inequity of over-reward or under-reward leads to dissatisfaction in the form of guilt or feelings of unfair treatment, respectively. Clearly the "should be" of discrepancy theory and the "perceived input-outcome balance relative to others" are similar.

A theory that has received considerable attention because of its unique conceptualization of job satisfaction is called two-factor theory in the literature, and motivation-hygiene theory by its author (Herzberg, 1966, 1968; Herzberg, Mausner, Peterson, and Capwell, 1957; Herzberg, Mausner, and Snyderman, 1959). This theory differs from previous concepts of job satisfaction in that satisfaction and dissatisfaction are said to operate on separate continua, and factors that contribute to satisfaction are distinct from those that reduce dissatisfaction. The fulfillment of two sets of human needs, psychological growth and pain avoidance, is brought about by the provision of motivator and hygiene factors respectively. According to Herzberg, satisfaction in work will result to the extent that the factors of achievement, recognition for achievement, advancement, possibility for growth, interesting, challenging work, and responsibility are present. The absence of certain other factors will result in dissatisfaction; these are supervision, relations with coworkers, company policy and administration, status, good working conditions, and security. The correspondence with Maslow's needs can readily be seen. Herzberg's definition of job satisfaction, then, does not allow for a construct of what is traditionally called "overall job satisfaction." Measures based on Herzberg's construct (Borgatta, Ford, Holobovitch, and Walters, 1971; Ford and Borgatta, 1970) focus on the reactions to the work itself as the most powerful motivating (satisfying) factor.

Job satisfaction, we have seen, is typically defined in terms of perceived need fulfillment. It is not, however, the fact of perceived need fulfillment that interests job satisfaction researchers, but the person's affective response to it. As Seashore (1974) puts it:

> Job satisfaction is better regarded as an attitude arising from two concurrent evaluative activities of a continuing nature in which the individual assesses his job and work environment as he perceives them in terms of his assessment of whether they are likely to aid or undermine the realization of his basic values (relatively constant for an adult) and their associated experienced needs (changing in priority with life experiences) and their associated concrete life goals (mainly short-run and changeable as subgoals are achieved, abandoned, or substituted). Job satisfaction is thus a dynamic process although at any given time of measurement it can be treated as a static attitudinal state; the fluctuation of satisfactions and dissatisfactions is emphasized as an expected condition to be taken into account in the explanation of the behavior of individuals in relation to their jobs (pp. 155-156).

Locke (1976), in a recent extensive treatment of job satisfaction, provides a definition which illustrates this same conceptual core of an affective response to perceived need fulfillment:

Job satisfaction results from the appraisal of one's job as attaining or allowing the attainment of one's important job values, providing these values are congruent with or help to fulfill one's basic needs. These needs are of two separable but interdependent types: bodily or physical needs and psychological needs, especially the need for growth. Growth is made possible mainly by the nature of the work itself (p. 1319).

WHAT JOB SATISFACTION IS NOT

While psychologists may disagree about a definition of job satisfaction, they agree considerably as to what job satisfaction is *not*. The latter agreement is not, however, always shared by those in other disciplines. As a result, interdisciplinary discussion about job satisfaction frequently flounders upon an unrecognized misunderstanding of what the concept conventionally excludes.

First of all, job satisfaction is not just any psychological reaction in an employment setting. For example, it is sometimes confused with involvement with the work role, alienation, identification with the organization, or motivation to perform—to name but a few such concepts. Each of these can be defined theoretically so as to be independent of job satisfaction, and measures of each are available. Further confusion arises from the growing use of two concepts that subsume a variety of psychological matters in ways sufficiently unclear as virtually to defy operationalization: the "meaning of work" and "subscription to the work ethic." Certainly involvement, (lack of) alienation, identification, motivation, and the like are under certain conditions positively correlated with job satisfaction. Nevertheless, to *equate* the former concepts with satisfaction not only does a disservice to the unique characteristics of these concepts themselves, but stretches the definition of job satisfaction to the point where available theories of work behavior can no longer deal with it.

We urge, therefore, that job satisfaction not be used as a psychological catch-all. If a program evaluation employs an existing measure of job satisfaction like those presented by Robinson, Athanasiou, and Head (1969), there is little danger of doing so, since the measures in their volume hew closely to the narrow, affective reaction definition of job satisfaction. The danger is considerably greater if one develops a "home grown" measure of job satisfaction for evaluation purposes.

A second misunderstanding of job satisfaction defines it in terms even broader than those described above. This residual definition equates job satisfaction with all job-related attitudes, as well as all attributes of jobs other than those considered by labor economists. For example, representatives of organized labor sometimes treat job satisfaction as all those aspects of work that have not traditionally been subject to collective bargaining. Likewise, many labor economists use job satisfaction as an umbrella term that covers all work-related matters beyond their more conventional domain of wages, hours and such. At times job satisfaction is even used to refer to all information about jobs that is based on workers' self reports—not only their attitudes, but their descriptions of their working environments as well.

A final misunderstanding about job satisfaction lies not in its definition so much as in the extent to which it is a teachable attitude. Most psychological theories of job satisfaction would grant that education may affect job satisfaction through either of two mechanisms. First, increasing education is assumed to increase one's value on the labor market which in turn increases one's chances of securing a job with greater occupational rewards, both economic and otherwise. A second mechanism postulates that education influences the values that individuals seek to realize through work, their expectations about their work, and the standards by which they judge their jobs. To the extent that education may influence either of these environmental or personal factors, it may in turn affect job satisfaction. The linkage between the educational process and job satisfaction is thus usually regarded as an indirect one, quite unlike that between education and many other attitudes. While one may refer to education as imparting to its recipients certain socially acceptable attitudes—attitudes toward racial minorities, for example—one seldom hears of satisfaction with work as being "taught" in the same sense. The legitimate role of education in influencing work-relevant values, expectations, and standards is a matter of some debate. Trying to teach workers to like their job pushes education even further into the realm of brainwashing.

In summary, if job satisfaction is defined as an attitude, it is as a consequence an affective reaction to an object—namely, one's job. There is considerable agreement that this reaction is a function of the extent to which the job either fulfills one's needs or facilitates the realization of one's values. Major theories of job satisfaction differ principally in how they conceptualize these processes of fulfillment or realization. These theories concur, however, in *not* treating job satisfaction as: (1) a concept covering all psychological reactions in work environments; (2) a residual category encompassing everything about jobs that has not traditionally been the concern of labor economists or union negotiations; or (3) a teachable attitude.

SECONDARY SOURCES

In 1976 Locke estimated that by 1972 a minimum of 3,350 articles or dissertations dealing with job satisfaction had already been published. This staggering amount of published material should not, however, discourage first-time users of job satisfaction measures from becoming acquainted with the relevant concepts and instruments. Fortunately, there are available several more approachable secondary sources of information. The most ambitious and recent of these is Locke's (1976) review chapter, which deals with conceptual definitions of job satisfaction, causal models of job satisfaction, and some of the antecedents and consequences of job satisfaction. While Seashore and Taber (1975) treat similar matters, the emphasis of their review is more upon measurement concerns than theoretical ones. Although job satisfaction has traditionally been the province of those investigating employing organizations, the social indicators movement has also begun to pay increasing attention to job satisfaction. Reviews of job satisfaction theory and research from a social indicators perspective have been prepared for the Organization for Economic Co-operation and Development by Barbash (1976), and Portigal (1976). A useful and sobering complement to all these secondary sources is Nord's (1977) questioning of several latent assumptions that he attributes to job satisfaction research.

For securing actual measures of job satisfaction, two compendia are especially helpful. Robinson, Athanasiou, and Head (1969) present thirteen general job satisfaction measures—five job satisfaction measures for particular occupations, and eight measures of satisfaction with particular job facets. They include either a copy of the actual measure or a selection of representative items. Scoring instructions for each of the instruments are also included. Accompanying each instrument is a cursory report of estimates of its reliabilities and validities, and an occasional caveat to users. Lest the convenience of the Robinson et al. volume lull the potential user of a job satisfaction measure into a state of comfortable, but premature closure, the volume's date, 1969, should be kept in mind. For many of the measures in the volume, considerable information on reliability and validity has accrued during the intervening decade. Questions in some of the measures have been modified, dropped, or amended, and scoring methods have sometimes been altered. But since each measure's original citation is presented in the volume, its post-1969 history is fairly readily traceable through the *Social Sciences Citation Index*— if not by direct contact with the measure's developers. In spite of all this, the choice of measures in the Robinson et al. (1969) volume is surprisingly up-to-date. Reviewing the last two years of the *Journal of Applied Psychology,* we tallied the measures used in studies of job satisfaction, and the frequency with which each was used. Single-question measures aside, the vast majority of such uses were for measures provided by Robinson et al. (1969). Part of this correspondence was, however, due to the frequent use of the Job Descriptive Index which happens to be in the Robinson et al. volume.

A second, and more recent source of measures is Chun, Cobb, and French's (1976) *Measures for Psychological Assessment.* This volume does not present actual measures. Instead, it cites the original source of each measure as well as a few references to applications of the measure. Using the Chun, Cobb, and French volume it is possible to identify the variety of settings in which a particular satisfaction measure has been employed, as well as the analytic use that has been made of it. Such information is presented only scantily by Robinson et al. (1969).

CRITERIA FOR SELECTING MEASURES

The remainder of this chapter reviews several criteria that might be considered in selecting a job satisfaction measure for use in educational program assessment. No attempt is made to recommend particular measures, as a recommendation is impossible without taking into account the needs of a specific investigator. The measures cited below are mentioned for illustrative purposes only. Moreover, as we will argue later, some of the measures that are psychometrically the most sound may be inefficient ones for use in program evaluation. These reservations aside, the two instruments in most common use in the fields of industrial and organizational psychology represent two measurement extremes. The first of these is the meticulously developed and amply documented Job Descriptive Index (Smith, Kendall, and Hulin, 1969). Second are the all-too-frequent "home grown" measures of job satisfaction wherein investigators pull together questions—often only a single question—from unspecified sources.

Facet-Free and Facet-Specific Measures

Facet-free and facet-specific measures of job satisfaction are distinguished as follows by Seashore and Taber.

> Facet-free ... data are obtained when the respondent is asked to indicate his global satisfaction with his job and job environment without specifying in advance the facets to be considered or how they are to be combined. In effect, each respondent provides a net response derived from his own set of facets, weighted or otherwise combined in his own unique fashion, with unstated and unique assumptions not only about the context for evaluation, but also about his own "fit" to the job and its environment, and with the environmental "reality" defined by his own perceptions and cognitions. Normative, cognitive, and unconscious elements in the evaluation are invited. The stimulus questions are usually phrased (or non-verbally displayed) with an intent to impose the fewest possible constraints upon his perceptual, cognitive, and evaluative processes. ...
>
> Facet-specific ... data are obtained when the respondent is asked to represent his satisfaction with respect to some specified facet of his job or job environment. Since the facet specification is never exhaustive or definitive, the difference between a facet-free and a facet-specific in-

quiry is only one of degree. For example, the query "How satisfied are you with your pay?" elicits a net response that includes consideration of unspecified subfacets (amount of pay, certainty of pay, rate of increase, adequacy to need, and so forth), unspecified "reality" (last week's pay, pay after deductions, pay confidently expected next year, and the like), and unknown perceptual, cognitive, and evaluative processes. Nevertheless, facet-specific methods allow the inquirer some control over the range of facets to be included in his data, an added degree of comparability among different respondents, and closer and more confident linkage between the response obtained and the "reality" of the job environment or of the person under investigation (1975, p. 335-336).

Most of the job satisfaction measures that are presented by Robinson, Athanasiou, and Head (1969) or that are widely used in organizational research are facet-specific ones. One reason for this is the higher internal-consistency reliabilities of facet-specific measures. Doubling the length of a test quadruples its true score variance (Guilford, 1954). It is, therefore, not surprising that many facet-specific measures have internal consistency reliabilities greater than .80 when these measures use dozens of questions. The number of questions possible in a facet-free measure is, on the other hand, very limited. Facet-free questions are all variations of a single question, the venerable: All in all, how satisfied are you with your job? It is difficult to rephrase this question in many ways without either (a) irritating respondents by repetitiousness, or (b) inadvertently introducing references to specific job facets. In spite of this limitation, the reliability of a brief, facet-free measure can be quite respectable. The three Quality of Employment Surveys have used a five-question facet-free measure with an internal consistency reliability of .77 (Quinn and Staines, 1978).

Which type of measure should be used—facet-free or facet specific? If one is able to devote considerable questionnaire or interview time to measuring job satisfaction, the answer is both.[1] The two types of measures correlate only .55 (Quinn and Staines, 1978), indicating that the measures are not interchangeable and that each may capture a unique portion of job satisfaction variance. If one cannot spend much time measuring job satisfaction, a facet-free measure would be the better choice. While five job facets can hardly be an adequate sample of job facets, a five-question facet-free measure can be quite reliable, and has been demonstrated to meet many standards of test validity (Mangione, 1973).

Coverage of Facets

If one chooses to adopt a facet-specific measure of job satisfaction, either in addition to or instead of a facet-free one, there remains the task of insuring that the facets measured are an adequate sample of all such possible facets. The results obtained through any facet-specific measure will reflect the mix of facets characterizing the measure. A satisfaction measure heavily laden with facets describing the *content* of one's job will have different correlates than a measure in which *contextual* facets (pay, physical working conditions, and so on) predominate.

The more widely used facet-specific measures all include a considerable variety of job facets. Table 16.1 shows some of the different types of facets included in five facet-specific measures—four of the measures nominated by Robinson, Athanasiou, and Head (1969) as the "best" they reviewed, plus the more recent one used in the national Quality of Employment Surveys. Generally speaking, each measure contains an extensive complement of facets, touching upon content and contextual facets, motivators and satisfiers (Herzberg, Mausner, Peterson, and Capwell, 1957), and the several levels of Maslow's (1970) need hierarchy.

The facets described in Table 16.1 are on an intermediate level of generality. They are not as specific as individual questions. It may, for example, take several questions to measure satisfaction with achievement, each question representing a slightly different nuance of the achievement concept. On the other hand, the list in Table 16.1 is not sufficiently general that it could be said to represent any definitive set of basic dimensions or factors underlying all job facets.

Can such basic dimensions be identified empirically? If so, they would provide a useful standard for evaluating how well a particular facet-specific measure has sampled from the universe of all facets. The best measure in terms of facet selection would be that which encompassed the greatest number of such dimensions. Another benefit of the identification of these dimensions is the guidance the dimensions would provide in generating job satisfaction subscores. The occupational payoffs of educational experiences may not be across-the-board ones. They may be confined instead to particular aspects of jobs—pay, for example, rather than relations with one's co-workers. It would be useful, therefore, to have a satisfaction measure that, in addition to measuring overall satisfaction, provided subscales for more limited sets of job facets. For example, in addition to providing a summary score indicating overall job satisfaction, the Job Descriptive Index (Smith, Kendall, and Hulin, 1965) provides subscale scores indicating satisfaction with work, supervision, people, pay, and promotions. The world of work is cut up somewhat differently in the instrument used in the national Quality of Employment surveys (Quinn and Staines, 1978; Quinn and Shepard, 1974). Its subscales assess satisfaction with challenge, comfort, relations with co-workers, financial rewards, resource adequacy, and promotions.

Several investigations have attempted to identify basic dimensions of job satisfaction through factor analytic or similarly intended statistical pro-

Table 16.1: Comparison of Content Areas Covered in Five Job Satisfaction Measures[a]

	Satisfaction Measure				
Content Area	Job Satisfaction and Dissatisfaction[b]	SRA Attitude Survey[c]	Job Descriptive Index[d]	IRC Employee Attitude Scales[e]	Overall Job Satisfaction[f]
Wages	X	X	X	X	X
The work itself, task content	X	X	X	X	X
Relations with co-workers	X	X	X	X	X
Technical aspects of supervision	X	X	X	X	X
Advancement, promotions	X	X	X		X
Physical working conditions	X				X
Relations with supervisor	X		X	X	X
Achievement	X		X	X	X
Job security	X	X			
Recognition	X	X			
Responsibility	X				
Possibility of growth		X	X		X
Relations with subordinates		X	X		X
Company policy and administration	X				
Resource adequacy				X	
Occupational status					X

[a] Adopted from Mangione (1973)
[b] Dunnette, Campbell, and Hakel (1967)
[c] Burns, Thurstone, Moore, and Baehr (1952)
[d] Smith, Kendall, and Hulin (1969)
[e] Carlson, Dawis, England, and Lofquist (1962)
[f] Quinn and Staines (1978)

cedures. Because each job satisfaction measure has a somewhat different sample of facets, complete agreement among factor analytic studies of facet-specific measures could hardly be expected. Nevertheless, Kahn's recent (in press) review of "the accessible universe of job measures" indicates that there is at least "a core of agreement." According to Kahn,

> A limited number of underlying properties appear recurrently in studies of work. The specific measures used to get at those properties vary a good deal, but the concepts appear repeatedly. The different purposes for which studies are undertaken are expressed more in terms of the relative weight given to these different job components than by the choice of the components themselves.

Eight dimensions of jobs constitute this set:

(1) *task content*—what the worker actually does on the job;
(2) *autonomy and control* by the worker over the worker's job;
(3) *supervision and resources* necessary for task performance;
(4) *relations with co-workers;*
(5) *wages* and other financial rewards;
(6) *promotions;*
(7) *physical working conditions;*
(8) *organizational context.*

These dimensions were inferred principally from factor analyses of workers' reports of their *satisfaction* with job facets. An alternative set of dimensions is provided by cluster or factor analyses of the *importance* that workers assign to job facets: challenge, comfort, relations with co-workers, financial rewards, resource adequacy (including supervision) and promotions (Quinn and Shepard, 1974).

Occupational Specificity

The measures of job satisfaction mentioned above were presumably intended to be applicable to all occupations. Additional measures, some of which are presented in full by Robinson, Athanasiou, and Head (1969), are custom-tailored to specific occupations or classes of occupations. There are, for example, measures specifically designed to assess the satisfaction of primary and secondary school teachers, school administrators, scientists, managers, salespeople, and blue-collar workers. It has been argued that such occupationally specific measures provide more useful information for action programs of job modification than do generalized measures, since the details of the specific occupations are more extensively assessed. Whether the reliabilities and validities of occupationally specific measures are superior to those of generalized ones is not known.

The issue of whether to use an occupationally specific or a generalized measure is a recurrent one for industrial and organizational psychologists who often study single occupations—even single occupations in single employing establishments. In vocational education program evaluation the issue may often be moot. Unless the educational program is designed to prepare individuals for a specific occupation, the investigator has little choice but to adopt a measure that is applicable to as many occupations as possible.

But there is a problem with the generality of even the alleged generalized measures. Most of these measures were developed and evaluated in the customary habitat of industrial and organizational psychologists—in a study of employees in a particular employing establishment, usually an establishment large and prosperous enough to pay for the study. Our own use of job satisfaction measures has, on the other hand, been principally in household surveys of employed people. Job satisfaction questions that are harmless enough in single-firm employee surveys often create unanticipated problems in occupationally heterogeneous surveys of the general population. Many questions in facet-specific measures are totally inapplicable to the ten percent or so of American workers who are self-employed. Another difficulty of unknown magnitude is created by job facets that refer to an employee's "organization," the organization's "policy," or "supervision." While such abstractions are possible within large, highly differentiated organizations, they are difficult for employees at the corner delicatessen where the owner is simultaneously organization, policy, and supervisor. A quarter of all American workers are employed by establishments that have less than ten workers; half of American workers are in establishments that have less than 50 employees. If a program evaluator anticipates that a substantial number of the program's recipients may subsequently be employed by smaller, less organizationally tidy establishments, particular care should be taken to insure that all the facet-specific job satisfaction questions used make sense in such an employment setting.

Weighted and Discrepancy Measures: The Lorelei

The presentation and scoring of most facet-specific measures is straightforward. Workers indicate how satisfied[2] they are with a variety of facets, and each individual's total score is the average over all facets of his or her reported satisfaction. Each facet contributes equally to the resultant average.[3] There are ways of treating the facets differentially that are far more conceptually elegant than this. The two major types of such treatment are based on the assumption that job satisfaction is a function of an individual's work-related needs, and the extent to which the work environment meets those needs.

A *weighted score* is based upon two types of information: a worker's reported satisfaction with a facet, and the worker's rating of how important that facet is to him or her. The resultant satisfaction score for the facet is obtained by multiplying these two values. A *difference score* for a facet is obtained by subtracting the reported degree of fulfillment ("is now") from the individual's report of how much of the facet he or she would like to have ("would like"), or how much he or she thinks there should be ("should be"), or even his or her rating of its importance. Both weighted and discrepancy scores attempt to embody the psychological calculation that produces a person's assessment of his or her job satisfaction, while unweighted scores reflect only the result of the calculation.

The logic of weighting is sound, it is intuitively captivating, and the scoring procedures are simple. But weighting procedures are the Lorelei of job satisfaction measurement, because there is no evidence that weighting provides a significant gain in either reliability or predictive power.[4] Systematic attempts to test the hypothesis that the use of importance ratings as weights will increase the validity of satisfaction ratings have without exception failed to confirm the hypothesis (Decker, 1955; Ewen, 1967; Larsen and Owens, 1965; Locke, 1961; Mikes and Hulin, 1968; Quinn and Mangione, 1973; Schaffer, 1953), and several plausible explanations for this failure have been proposed (Ewen, 1967; Ghiselli and Brown, 1955; Quinn and Mangione, 1973). There is even some evidence that importance weighting may actually reduce the validity of satisfaction ratings (Quinn and Mangione, 1973). The evidence against discrepancy scores is less damning. They have proved to be adequate measures of satisfaction in hypothesis testing and predictive schemes (Locke, 1969; Porter and Lawler, 1968), and occasionally are found to work better than nondiscrepancy scores (Wanous and Lawler, 1972).

Whether a weighted or discrepancy score is simply adequate or even marginally better than simple averaging of satisfaction ratings is not sufficient grounds for using such scores. Facet-specific measures are rather long to begin with. Weighting or discrepancy scores require that this length be doubled because each facet is assessed twice—once in terms of satisfaction, and again in terms of either importance or "would like" ratings. Marginal improvements that might be obtained by using discrepancy scores do not seem justified in terms of the expense entailed in doubling a measure's length. It is literally a waste of time.

Reliabilities

Among the important psychometric properties one may consider in comparing job satisfaction measures, and other attitude measures as well, is reliability. While a general knowledge of the properties of reliability is an advantage, an overemphasis on having high reliability coefficients often produces misguided judgments no better than those of the completely uninitiated. In addition to the size of a reliability coefficient, proper interpretation requires knowledge of: the type of reliability (internal consistency or temporal stability) assessed; the design used to assess it and the corresponding sources of score variation it accounts for; and the uses to be made of the measure. Further, reliability information is best considered in light of logical and statistical factors that potentially affect it.

The purpose of having a highly reliable measure is to insure that measurement results are repeatable, and that error in measurement is kept to a minimum. Each measure of some attitude, ability, and so on as represented by a score is theoretically composed of each person's true value of the intended construct (e.g., job satisfaction), called his or her "true score," plus a component of measurement error. Because these errors are assumed to be independent of each other and of the true score components, the variance of observed scores (V_x) is equal to the variance of the true scores (V_t) plus the variance of the errors (V_e). In other words, $V_x = V_t + V_e$.

Since the objective of measurement is to estimate an individual's true score as closely as possible, it is desirable to reduce V_e relative to V_x in any way one can. Why, then, not merely calculate the error variance and arrive at true score variance by subtraction: $V_t = V_x - V_e$?

Unfortunately, the composition of an observed score as true score plus some separate error component is strictly theoretical. Since there is no accurate way of actually separating the true score and error components of any observed score, one cannot compute error variance. But by considering reliability as an evaluation of the relationship of a measure to itself, one may derive estimates of the degree to which the measure is reliable. One does so by evaluating *consistency* both in the relationship among the components, usually questions, in the measure (i.e., internal consistency) or between successive measurements separated by some time interval (i.e., temporal stability).

Assessment of reliability typically involves a correlation coefficient, usually a product-moment correlation. If one is interested in the *internal consistency* of a measure, one can correlate parts of the measure with other parts or with the total score. One may also correlate parallel or equivalent forms of the measure administered at the same time. These may literally be separately constructed forms that use different—but parallel or equivalent—questions; or they may involve the postmeasurement random division of questions into assumed equivalent forms (split-half procedures). Determination of high reliability by these designs attests to the internal consistency or homogeneity of the questions in the measure. If the reliability as estimated by an internal consistency design is low, the only way that it can be increased is by improved content sampling or by adding questions. In a facet-specific job satisfaction measure, this means a better or larger selection of job facets.

Alternatively, one may require that results using a particular instrument be reproducible over successive administrations, separated by a substantial time interval. In other words, the measure must be consistent over time or have *temporal stability.* In this case the correlations that estimate reliability are among administrations that use *parallel or equivalent* forms of a measure, separated by some time interval. Or the correlation could be based on a test-retest design wherein two administrations of the *same* instrument are separated by a time interval. Reliability estimates based upon designs that administer and then readminister parallel or equivalent forms include most of the same sources of error as do designs tapping internal consistency. They are also sensitive to some sources of influence that are considered external to the instrument itself and that intervene between the two administrations. Nunnally (1967) suggests that errors that occur within a test and a testing situation randomly influence the average correlation among the questions— which is the mathematical basis of reliability estimates. He postulates three major sources of error intervening between successive administrations of a test. The first involves systematic differences in the content of alternative forms of a test. This would apply to parallel or equivalent forms, and would result in the correlation between the two measures being less than that predicted from the average correlation among questions in each measure. The second might be subjectivity of scoring as a result of differences between scorers or differences in a single scorer—a matter of only occasional concern with job satisfaction measures. Third, and most significant, is the variation in scores from one occasion to another because the respondent does in fact change with regard to the measured attributes. The effects of fluctuations in attitude, ability, and many psychological and environmental factors will not be included in a reliability estimate based on internal consistency determined at a single administration.

Some sources of score variation can be seen as functioning as consistent or systematic variance in some reliability assessment designs and as inconsistent or error variance in others. Table 16.2 summarizes the work of Nunnally (1967), and Thorndike (1976), and presents the various designs and their treatment of several sources of score variance as either systematic (S) or error (E). The magnitude of reliability coefficients obtained for a particular measure will be positively related to the number of sources of variation that can be considered to yield consistent or systematic differences among people.

The interpretation of reliability data is affected as well by three logical considerations. First is the intended coverage of the measure and the homogeneity of its questions. If a narrowly defined, simple construct were the object of measurement, one may require high internal consistency. If, however, one is attempting to measure a complex composite of several dimensions, assessing and requiring high internal consistency would be inappropriate. Job satisfaction falls between these two extremes, because one may speak

Table 16.2: Treatment of Sources of Score Variance of Reliability Assessment Designs[a]

Source	Parallel forms, Interval	Parallel forms, No Interval	Test-retest, Interval	Split-half	Inter-item Internal Consistency
General and specific characteristics of the person (i.e., favorableness of the attitude that operates over various measures; test-taking skills; comprehension of instructions)	S	S	S	S	S
Specific person-item characteristics (i.e., chance correspondence of the sampling of items and the person's knowledge of the area)	E	E	S	E	E (?)
Temporary physiological or environmental factors of test situation (i.e., fatigue; motivation; physical conditions)	E	S	E	S	S
Temporary and specific person-test characteristics:					
1. Test as a whole (i.e., comprehending test-taking task; "tricks" of test-taking)	E	S	E	S	S
2. Specific questions or parts of measure (i.e., fluctuations in memory)	E	E	E	E (?)	E (?)
External to person's attitude, ability or test properties:					
1. Administration and scoring	E	E	E	–	–
2. Chance guessing	E	E	E	E	E

[a] S = Systematic Sources of Variance; E = Error Sources of Variance; ? = Exact treatment is questionable; – = Illogical conjunction.

both of an overall feeling of satisfaction and of satisfaction with narrower aspects of jobs, some of which were enumerated above. A fairly low internal consistency reliability coupled with a substantial temporal stability in a test-retest design would indicate the presence of such a complex composite. A second consideration is the nature of the measured attitude with regard to its change over time within a person. If the attitude is assumed to be relatively stable over time, it is appropriate to evaluate its temporal stability. If the attitude does fluctuate over time but is consistent within one time period, temporal stability estimates would be inappropriate. Here one must ask oneself how much job satisfaction should reasonably be expected to change within the period of measurement. Too much stability would be suspicious, suggesting that the satisfaction being measured is a stable personality trait rather than a true evaluation of a job—and jobs should be expected to change somewhat even during relatively brief periods. A final logical consideration in interpreting reliability estimates is the use to be made of the measure's results. If used as a predictor, temporal stability is essential. If used as a measure of a current state, as would be the case in most program evaluation, temporal stability is less important.

Two interesting relationships between statistical factors and reliability estimates also deserve consideration. The prospective user of a job satisfaction measure should take into account the samples upon which its reliability estimates are based, because the size of reliability coefficients is directly related to the dispersion of observed satisfaction scores of these samples. With error variance assumed to be independent of observed score variance and remaining relatively constant, increases in observed score variance will raise the reliability coefficient, and decreases will lower it. Resultant problems can occur in several ways. If a reliability coefficient were determined on a sample with a greater observed score variance than the sample in which the program evaluator is interested, the reliability would be overestimated. This would be the case where reliability estimates are based on national probability samples of workers, or on samples that are occupationally and demographically very heterogeneous. If the sample of interest to the program evaluator were selected on the basis of another related variable (e.g., occupation, age, or race), or drawn from those exceptionally high or low in average level of job satisfaction, reliability coefficients based on national probability samples of the general population would overestimate the reliabilities obtainable in the evaluator's more restricted sample. Ideally, reliability estimates should be based on a sample as similar as possible to the sample one plans to study. Fortunately, in the likely absence of such information, methods are available to estimate reliability coefficients for a sample differing in variance from the sample on which reliabilities were originally assessed.

The number of questions in a job satisfaction measure also influences its reliability coefficients. More questions increase the reliability estimates, assuming the added questions are comparable to the original ones in their contribution to measurement. One may consider adding questions to a measure to raise its reliability coefficients, or the consequences for reliability estimates of shortening a measure. Since most of the widely used measures of job satisfaction are quite long, we anticipate that most users of these measures in vocational education program evaluation will want to make them shorter. Formulae are available for re-estimating the new reliabilities of such newly created "short forms" (Nunnally, 1967:223). Along the same lines this chapter concludes with a discussion of the much neglected topic of the *efficiency* of available job satisfaction measures.

Validities

Validity is a psychometric concern at least as important as reliability. Whereas reliability may be viewed as a relationship of a measure to itself, validity may correspondingly be viewed as the relationship of a measure to things other than itself. A measure is designed to represent some construct or hypothetical formulation of some attitude, ability, trait, and so on. The central concern of validity is how accurately a measure operationalizes the construct it is intended to represent. Fine distinctions in the meaning of the word "represent" produce the three currently accepted types of validity plus a fourth which is less widely used. The types of validity are only conceptually independent. They are, in fact, found to be interdependent. Considering the uses to be made of a measure, different validities are required and different evidence may be used to support them.

The American Psychological Association (1966, 1974) has formalized standards for three forms of validity: *content* validity, *criterion-related* validity, and *construct* validity. If the measure is intended to determine how an individual reacts at present in a universe of situations that the instrument is meant to represent, content validity is needed. If the measure is to be used to predict or estimate the score on a different measure (or itself at a future time), criterion-related validity is needed. If a measure of the degree or amount of some hypothetical attitude, trait, or quality of a person is desired, construct validity is needed. Obviously, both content and criterion-related validity contribute to construct validity.

A less widely used concept is *face* validity. It cannot be considered a true type of validity for which evidence can be presented because it concerns only the appearance of validity, the degree to which an instrument "looks like" it measures what it is intended to measure. Face validity is important when it is necessary to convey the appropriateness of the instrument to potential readers of the program evaluator's assessment who are unfamiliar with psychometric methods and procedures (e.g., administrators, legislators, teachers). Each of the first three types of validities will be illustrated by the procedures used by Mangione (1973) to validate an early version of the job satisfaction measures used in the 1969, 1973, and 1977 Quality of Employment Surveys.

The *content validity* of a measure is demonstrated by evidence that the sample of questions contained in the measure is representative of the class or universe of tasks, conditions or processes about which conclusions are to be drawn. A measure of a trait, for example, should contain items that sample representatively from behaviors or experiences related to that trait. An achievement or ability measure should sample adequately the universe of subject matter. A measure of facet-specific job satisfaction should contain questions that represent the domain of relevant aspects of work. The determination of "representativeness," however, is largely value-laden and subjective. Conclusions about content validity are based on logic, and any empirical evidence is secondary. Evidence is of three kinds. Using the subjective judgments of experts as to the appropriateness of questions, one may obtain a measure of inter-judge agreement as one estimate of content validity. This procedure is greatly enhanced if the developer of an instrument has specified in advance the domain or universe of attitudes, behaviors, and so on that is of interest, and the methods by which the corresponding questions have been selected or written.

A second form of evidence is high internal consistency reliability, or homogeneity of the questions. Questions in such a valid measure correlate highly with one another and with the measure's total score, indicating that they all reflect the same attitudinal or behavioral domain. While this indicates that a single domain or content has been adequately sampled, it does not indicate how well this sampling represents what was intended. It can be seen that reliability of an internal consistency type is in this way tied to validity. Reliability is a necessary, but not sufficient, condition for validity.

A third form of evidence for content validity is the analysis of a measure's factor composition. Like internal consistency, factor analysis (and several similarly intended statistical procedures) is based on correlations among questions and indicates content validity in a similar manner. If the questions in a measure designed to tap one attitude adequately sample the domain of affective responses related to that attitude, factor analysis should yield one large, general factor as evidence supporting the measure's content validity. Finding several potent factors would indicate that more than one attitude is being tapped by the measure. As with internal consistency reliability evidence, however, the factors are only indirect evidence and still must be established as representative of the relevant construct.

For example, evidence of content validity of the Quality of Employment Surveys' job satisfaction measures was presented by Mangione (1973) in several forms, predominently factor analytic. Item selection for the surveys' facet-specific measure drew heavily from extensive review of previous major factor analytic studies, and from the item analysis of responses to open-ended questions asked of a national population about an "ideal job." The thirty-four selected facets were reduced to twenty-three following factor analysis of the importance ratings given them by a national sample of workers. These twenty-three facets loaded (at least .40) on five factors, which became the subscales of Challenge, Comfort, Relations with Coworkers, Financial Rewards, and Resource Adequacy. Content validity was also examined indirectly by evaluating internal consistency reliability using alpha coefficients. Following Nunnally's (1967) suggestion that "sensible" item construction is at least as important as adequate sampling of the domain for content validity, issues of item wording, administration, and social desirability of responses were also examined.

Criterion-related validity is important when prediction or estimation is the intended use of the measure. Criterion validity as a general term includes functional relationships between an instrument and some independent criterion occurring before (postdictive validity), during (concurrent validity), or after (predictive validity) the instrument is applied. The association between the variable of interest and some other variable is based on the theoretical formulation of the construct, and in this way criterion-related validity contributes to construct validity. The measure, or operationalized construct, is predicted to be related to certain variables in specified ways; it is also predicted to be unrelated to certain other variables. Empirical evidence of association (or lack of it) between the predictor and the criterion measures is the sole basis of criterion-related validity.

Empirical evidence of association is of two kinds: score differences among groups, and correlational data. Statistical differences between means on the criterion variable in the direction hypothesized is evidence of criterion validity. It indicates that the predictor measure can differentiate groups in the manner theorized. Correlational data are a second form of evidence for criterion-related validity. The mathematical basis of correlation and mean differences are closely related, and associations between variables can be hypothesized and tested for statistical significance in a similar manner using appropriate techniques. The American Psychological Association's (1966) standards regarding the conduct of criterion-related validity studies may be summarized as follows: (1) The sample used to generate the functional association between predictor and criterion should be independent of the sample used to construct the predictor and/or criterion measures. (2) Properties of the validating sample that might affect the association between predictor and criterion should be clearly identified and explained. (3) Evidence should be reported clearly and allow the user to make determinations of efficiency of the predictor. (4) When the predictor is combined with

426 EVALUATION MEASURES AND TESTING ISSUES

others, the gain in predictive validity it affords should be indicated separately.

For example, the measure of overall job satisfaction ultimately used in the national Quality of Employment Surveys was composed of a facet-specific measure and a facet-free, five question measure. Mangione (1973) used eight criterion measures to examine the criterion-related validity of the overall measure and its two components. Evidence was primarily correlational, with consideration given to the limiting effects that reliabilities have on the maximum correlation possible between two measures. In a *postdictive* scheme, prior experiences of work related illness or injury were assumed associated with current job satisfaction, but the evidence did not support this hypothesis. *Concurrent* validity was examined by testing the extent to which current job satisfaction covaried with other current attitudinal responses—job tension, life satisfaction, depression, somatic complaints, performance impairment, zest, and intention to turnover. In general, high criterion-related validity was indicated, the highest being with respect to job-related tension, intention to turnover, life satisfaction, and depression. The measures that included facet-free questions had higher concurrent validities with respect to attitudes than did facet-specific measures. *Predictive* validity was assessed with respect to the relationship between job satisfaction and later turnover. The satisfaction of a sample of 295 workers was correlated with turnover information gathered two years later by follow-up study. All measures save one subscale of the facet-specific measure correlated significantly with actual turnover.

Construct validity is a concern when one's interest is to increase her or his understanding of the psychological qualities being measured. The process involves specifying the domain of observables, the extent of correlation among the observables, and whether a measure or measures consisting of such observables act as though they measure the intended construct. Again, the ways in which content-validity and criterion-related validity contribute to construct validity can be seen. Construct validity is a combined logical and empirical process which incorporates validity evidence from both of these previous approaches.

Mangione (1973) explored the construct validity of the Quality of Employment Surveys' job satisfaction measures using this combination of approaches. He reiterated the evidence of content validity and its implications for adequate representativeness of the items. He then analyzed the relationships among thirty-three job characteristics and their antecedence, and consequence to job satisfaction. His results tended to indicate moderate construct validity of a convergent-discriminant type.

As indicated previously, face validity concerns not true validity, but rather the appearance of validity. It contributes to the acceptance of a measure by potential users. While content validity asks whether the items reflect an adequate sampling of relevant behaviors while the instrument is being constructed, face validity asks whether the items "look like" the object of measurement *after* measurement construction. A test may have content validity but not face validity, and vice versa. Face validity is also irrelevant to criterion-related validity, because it is useless to know that a measure looks like it should correlate with another measure. Since evidence that bears on face validity is intuitive and not empirical, face validity contributes nothing to construct validity and no example will be given here. While it makes a measure more understandable to users not acquainted with statistical and measurement procedures, high face validity may reduce the efficiency of measures affected because of transparency.

Potential Problems in Administration and Scoring

The completion of a job satisfaction measure, like any attitude assessment, represents a particular kind of task for the respondent. The revealing of information about oneself is often accompanied by apprehension if not suspicion, particularly when personal attitudes are revealed. The respondent needs the reassurance of knowing how and for what purposes the information will be used. Some measures are more transparent than others, and the object of measurement becomes apparent to the respondent. Cooperation, and not acquiescence, can be enhanced by the proper preparation of the respondent. In selecting a measure this matching of preparation and transparency of the measure should be kept in mind.

It is also vital that respondents be able to understand the task as given to them by the instructions in the instrument. The investigator should consider potential language problems of the sample of interest and possible problems of comprehension. The measure should be evaluated in terms of its general language complexity and its use of occupationally specific jargon or terminology.

It was noted above that adding more questions to a well constructed measure generally adds to its reliability, a psychometric plus. However, a trade-off is involved in that longer measures represent a more difficult task for the respondent and instrument efficiency may suffer. The user must judge carefully the capacity of his or her respondents to tolerate a long measure without becoming careless, insincere, unthinking, or even hostile to it. The more complex the task the more likely is measurement error. Fortunately, most of the widely used job satisfaction measures are simple, pencil and paper questionnaires.

From the investigator's viewpoint there are two˙ additional problems involving the scoring of measures. Deriving a score from questions that are scaled is usually a straightforward procedure. However, a few job satisfaction measures ask open-ended questions and probe for more detailed information. Such questions allow respondents more direct input and allows them the benefit of freer participation. This information is particularly useful when changes—such as changes in training programs or in employing organizations—are to be based on workers' reports of their satisfaction with their work environments. The disadvantage of open-ended questions is that they are difficult and time consuming to score. Another scoring problem results from rather intricate score derivations required by some measures. In addition to the extra computational effort and cost, the meaning of such scores is not always intuitively understandable to users who do not have a working knowledge of such statistical procedures.

Availability of Norms

Sometimes circumstances require that an educational program evaluation be conducted without a control group. Some research strategies that might be used in this situation are discussed by Borgatta in this volume.[5] In the absence of a control group it is especially important that one use a job satisfaction measure for which adequate norms are available.[6] It is meaningless to know, for example, that men who participated in a program and who subsequently secured jobs have a mean job satisfaction score of 42 on the Job Descriptive Index's measure of satisfaction with pay. Reference points are clearly needed to make the number meaningful. Fortunately, the developers of the Job Descriptive Index maintain statistical norms for their instrument. Comparison statistics are available not only for the whole normative sample, but for subsamples differentiated according to sex, age, income, and other demographic characteristics. By this reckoning a score of 42 would be a high one—at the 80th percentile for men in the normative sample, for example. The Job Descriptive Index's normative sample shares a limitation with the normative samples of most other job satisfaction measures. They are all samples of convenience that have accrued as various firms have used each instrument and reported descriptive statistics to the instrument's developers. The normative samples for the job satisfaction measures from the Quality of Employment Surveys are an exception because they are national probability samples of all people employed in 1969, 1973, and 1977.

Efficiency

Given two measures with equal reliabilities and validities, the more efficient measure is the one requiring less time to administer. Usually this amounts to its being the one with the fewer questions. Efficiency is seldom considered in test development. Two major textbooks on psychometric theory devote eighty-nine and thirty-seven pages to reliability but say nothing about efficiency. Nor do Robinson, Athanasiou, and Head (1969) consider efficiency in their evaluation of job satisfaction measures. Some of this failure to consider efficiency may stem from the context in which much job satisfaction research is conducted. Most commonly, job satisfaction is measured in a single firm, through pencil and paper questionnaires administered to groups of employees who volunteer to participate in the study under varying degrees of subtle coercion. The time set aside for this data collection is often not even an issue if the firm is particularly interested in the results of the study. Added to these conditions is the fact that, since job satisfaction is a *major* variable in the study, high reliabilities and validities for the job satisfaction measure used may be extremely important. All these conditions have combined to produce several job satisfaction measures that are good, but long. While the five job satisfaction measures in Table 16.1 have some impressive psychometric credentials, their average length is sixty questions and the *shortest* contains thirty-six questions.

Thirty-six questions may not seem like much in a study where job satisfaction is a central concern. But it is a lot in a program evaluation where job satisfaction may be but one of a large number of criteria. Depending upon his or her priorities, the program evaluator may reasonably decide to use a briefer measure and settle for whatever reduction in reliability or validity may result. The next step would be for the evaluator to obtain a short form of one of the better established, but long measures. Unfortunately, such short forms are so rare as to be nearly nonexistant. An attitude prevails of "use my measure at its 80-question best, or don't use it at all." Small wonder, then, that so many investigators are led in frustration to develop their "home grown" job satisfaction measures.

Industrial and organizational psychologists could, therefore, be of considerable service to those in other disciplines by developing variable length versions of their job satisfaction measures. The potential user could then select a measure the length of which (and the reliabilities and validities as well) was appropriate to the priority the user assigned to job satisfaction in his or her program evaluation. It may in many cases even be discovered that the loss in reliability or validity that results from shortening a measure is not all that great. For example, the job satisfaction measure used in the 1977 Quality of Employment Survey contained thirty-eight questions—five facet-free ones and thirty-three facet-specific ones. The internal consistency reliability of the measure was .85. An item analysis designed to reduce the number of questions produced two short forms of twenty-one and nine items respectively, both having very respectable internal consistency reliabilities (Quinn and Staines, 1978).

PROGNOSIS

If past ways of using job satisfaction measures in vocational education program evaluation persist, the choice of job satisfaction measures in future program evaluations will be highly variable, subject principally to the theoretical emphasis of the evaluator. At the beginning of this chapter a distinction was made between societal and individual outcomes and between economic and noneconomic goals. The program evaluator's choice of either goal or outcome—for theoretical, disciplinary, pragmatic, or other reasons—is likely to determine how central job satisfaction will be to the evaluation. This in turn will determine how much time and/or expense will be devoted to its measurement—in other words, whether the program evaluator will be a "light" or an "intensive" user of job satisfaction measures. Unfortunately, both types of consumers will face problems in selecting job satisfaction measures, albeit quite different types of problems.

The intensive user of job satisfaction measures is likely to be a program evaluator who emphasizes individual outcomes and noneconomic goals, and who as a result is willing to incorporate a fairly long measure of job satisfaction in the evaluation. This evaluator's problem is selecting one job satisfaction measure from the many available. To aid in the selection, this chapter has suggested some secondary sources for accessing job satisfaction measures and commentaries upon them; it has also suggested several criteria that should be used in comparing such measures.

For the intensive user of job satisfaction measures in vocational education program evaluation, we urge mainly two things. First, use a measure that, in addition to providing an overall job satisfaction score, has subscales that assess satisfaction with regard to more limited aspects of jobs. Vocational education in general, and more narrowly constructed training programs in particular, may have occupational payoffs that are discernable but that are confined only to certain aspects of jobs. These payoffs may go undetected when the program evaluation measures only overall job satisfaction, be it through facet-free or even a facet-specific measure. Second, in considering the psychometric information used in selecting a measure, take into account the extent to which this information has been based upon samples of people whose demographic and occupational characteristics are compatible with those participating in the educational program. Some job satisfaction measures have obtained apparently impressive psychometric credentials through their use with only a few samples that were very limited both demographically and occupationally.

The light user of job satisfaction measures is likely to be a program evaluator who emphasizes societal outcomes and economic goals, and who as a result wants to devote at most only a few questions to measure job satisfaction. This consumer does not have the luxurious problem of selecting one job satisfaction measure, because there is very little from which to select. If one is restricted to only a few questions, the best bet seems to be a set of facet-free questions, although such questions would obviously mask any occupational payoffs to education that are limited to particular aspects of jobs. Although industrial and organizational psychologists have on many occasions used short forms of job satisfaction measures (or developed their own "home grown" versions of longer measures), the use of such measures has seldom been advocated except as an act of desperation. The psychometric credentials of any short form of a measure seldom live up to those of the parent measure, although the short form's credentials may be quite adequate for many of its users. In recent years, increasing numbers of investigators outside the disciplines of industrial and organizational psychology have required measures of job satisfaction that are psychometrically respectable and, above all, short. They have not customarily required that any such measure be the *sine qua non* of job satisfaction assessment. Developers and refiners of job satisfaction measures within the disciplines of industrial and organizational psychology have for the most part been insensitive to such requirements. Perhaps the next few years may see refinements in job satisfaction measures that are better attuned to consumers' needs.

NOTES

1. The Quality of Employment Surveys carry this double measurement to an extreme. The surveys' facet-free and facet-specific measures are converted to z-scores, and the two measures are combined with equal weights into a measure of overall job satisfaction.

2. The Job Descriptive Index (Smith, Kendall, and Hulin, 1969), and the Quality of Employment Surveys' measures (Quinn and Staines, 1978) do not actually use the word "satisfaction." Instead, the worker is asked to describe his or her job using terms or statements that are evaluatively phrased.

3. More precisely, each facet's contribution to the average depends upon its variance and correlation with other facets.

4. This is also true of life satisfaction (Campbell, Converse, and Rodgers, 1976).

5. Other discussions of evaluation strategies in the absence of control groups are given by Campbell (1975) and Nunnally (1975).

6. Even *with* a control group norms are useful in giving the investigator a "feeling" for the magnitude of experimental-control differences.

REFERENCES

Adams, J. 1963. Toward an understanding of inequity. *Journal of Abnormal and Social Psychology* 67:422-436.

American Psychological Association. 1974. *Standards for Educational and Psychological Tests.* Washington, DC: American Psychological Association.

Barbash, J. 1976. *Job Satisfaction Attitude Surveys.* Paris: Organisation for Economic Co-operation and Development.

Borgatta, E., Ford, R., Holobovitch, J., and Walters, R. 1971. *Reactions to Your Job Questionnaire.* Ridgewood, NJ: Roy W. Walters & Associates, Inc.

Burns, R., Thurstone, L., Moore, D., and Baehr, M. 1952. *General Manual for the SRA Employee Inventory.* Chicago: Science Research Associates.

Campbell, D. T., 1975. Reforms as experiments. In E. L. Struening, and M. Guttentag, eds. *Handbook of Evaluation Research, Volume 1.* Beverly Hills: Sage Publications.

Campbell, A., Converse, P., and Rodgers, W. 1976. *The Quality of American Life.* New York: Russell Sage Foundation.

Carlson, R., Dawis, R., England, G., and Lofquist, L. 1962. *The Measurement of Employee Satisfaction.* Minneapolis: University of Minnesota.

Chun, K., Cobb, S., and French, J. 1975. *Measures for Psychological Assessment: A Guide to 3,000 Original Sources and Their Applications.* Ann Arbor: Survey Research Center, University of Michigan.

Dawis, R., England, G., and Lofquist, L. 1968. A theory of work adjustment. In *Minnesota Studies in Vocational Rehabilitation.* Minneapolis: Industrial Relations Center, University of Minnesota.

Decker, R. 1955. A study of three specific problems in the measurement and interpretation of employee attitudes. *Psychological Monographs* 69, Whole No. 401.

Dunnette, M., Campbell, J., and Hakel, M. 1967. Factors contributing to job satisfaction and job dissatisfaction in six occupational groups. *Organizational Behavior and Human Performance* 2:143-174.

Ewen, R. 1967. Weighting components of job satisfaction. *Journal of Applied Psychology* 51:68-73.

Ford, R., and Borgatta, E. 1970. Satisfaction with the work itself. *Journal of Applied Psychology* 54:128-134.

Ghiselli, E., and Brown, C. 1955. *Personnel and Industrial Psychology.* New York: McGraw-Hill.

Gillie, A., and Mann, E. 1973. *Job Satisfaction Characteristics of Selected Associate Degree Graduates.* Vocational-Technical Education Research Report. University Park: Department of Vocational Education, University of Pennsylvania.

Grasso, J. 1975. *The Contributions of Vocational Education, Training, and Work Experience to the Early Career Achievements of Young Men.* Columbus: Center for Human Resources Research, Ohio State University.

Guilford, J. 1954. *Psychometric Methods.* New York: McGraw-Hill.

Herzberg, F. 1968. One more time: How do you motivate employees? *Harvard Business Review* (Jan.-Feb.):53-62.

––– 1966. *Work and the Nature of Man.* Cleveland: World Publishing.

Herzberg, F., Mausner, B., Peterson, R., and Capwell, D. 1957. *Job Attitudes: Review of Research and Opinion.* Pittsburgh: Psychological Services of Pittsburgh.

Herzberg, F., Mausner, B., and Snyderman, B. 1959. *The Motivation to Work.* New York: Wiley.

Kahn, R. *Work and Health.* Rockville, MD: National Institute of Mental Health. In press.

Larsen, J., and Owens, W. 1965. The assignment of job attitude items to subscales. *Journal of Applied Psychology* 49:172-181.

Lawler, E. 1973. *Motivation in Work Organizations.* Monterey, CA: Brooks/Cole.

Little, J. 1970. *Review and Synthesis of Research on the Placement and Follow-Up of Vocational Education Students.* Columbus: Center for Vocational and Technical Education, Ohio State University.

Locke, E. 1976. The nature and causes of job satisfaction. In M. Dunnette, *Handbook of Industrial and Organizational Psychology.* Chicago: Rand McNally.

——— 1969. What is job satisfaction? *Organizational Behavior and Human Performance* 4:309-336.

——— 1961. "Importance and satisfaction in several job areas." Paper read at the annual meeting of the American Psychological Association, New York.

Lofquist, L., and Dawis, R. 1969. *Adjustment to Work: A Psychological View of Man's Problems in a Work-Oriented Society.* New York: Appleton-Century-Crofts.

Mangione, T. 1973. "The validity of job satisfaction." Doctoral dissertation, University of Michigan.

Maslow, A. 1970. *Motivation and Personality.* New York: Harper and Row.

Mikes, P., and Hulin, C. 1968. Use of importance as a weighting component of job satisfaction. *Journal of Applied Psychology* 52:394-398.

Noeth, R., and Hanson, G. 1975. *A Five-Year Follow-Up of Students Enrolled in Post-secondary Vocational-Technical Transfer Programs.* Iowa City: American College Testing Program.

Nord, W. 1977. Job satisfaction reconsidered. *American Psychologist* 32:1026-1035.

Nunnally, J. C. 1975. The study of change in evaluation research: Principles concerning measurement, experimental design, and analysis. In E. L. Struening, and M. Guttentag eds. *Handbook of Evaluation Research, Volume 1.* Beverly Hills: Sage Publications.

Opacinch, C. 1974. *Extending the Model of Program Evaluation: Career Graduates and Their Employers.* Catonsville, MD: Catonsville Community College.

Porter, L., 1961. A study of perceived need satisfactions in bottom and middle management jobs. *Journal of Applied Psychology* 45:1-10.

Porter, L., and Lawler, E. 1968. *Managerial Attitudes and Performance.* Homewood, IL: Richard D. Irwin.

Portigal, A. 1976. *Towards the Measurement of Work Satisfaction.* Paris: Organisation for Economic Co-operation and Development.

Quinn, R., and Mangione, T. 1973. Evaluating weighted models of measuring job satisfaction: A Cinderella story. *Organizational Behavior and Human Performance* 10:1-23.

Quinn, R., and Shepard, L. 1974. *The 1972-73 Quality of Employment Survey: Descriptive Statistics, with Comparison Data from the 1969-70 Survey of Working Conditions.* Ann Arbor: Survey Research Center, University of Michigan.

Quinn, R., and Staines, G. 1978. *The 1977 Quality of Employment Survey: Descriptive Statistics with Comparison Data from the 1972-73 and 1969-70 Quality of Employment Surveys.* Ann Arbor: Survey Research Center, University of Michigan.

Robinson, J., Athanasiou, R., and Head, K. 1969. *Measures of Occupational Attitudes and Occupational Characteristics.* Ann Arbor: Survey Research Center, University of Michigan.

Schaffer, R. 1953. Job satisfaction as related to need satisfaction at work. *Psychological Monographs* 67, (14) Whole No. 364.

Seashore, S. 1974. Job satisfaction as an indicator of the quality of employment. *Social Indicators Research* 1:135-168.

Seashore, S., and Taber, T. 1975. Job satisfaction indicators and their correlates. *American Behavioral Scientist* 18:333-368.

Smith, B., Passmore, D., Copa, G., and Moss, J. 1971. *Project IMPROVE: Developing and Testing a Statewide System for Evaluation of Vocational Education Programs.* Minneapolis: Minnesota Research Coordinating Unit in Vocational Education.

Smith, P., Kendall, L., and Hulin, C. 1969. *The Measurement of Satisfaction in Work and Retirement.* Chicago: Rand McNally.

Somers, G., and Wood, W., eds. 1969. *Cost-Benefit Analysis of Manpower Policies.* Kingston, Ontario: Industrial Relations Center, Queens University.

Thorndike, R. 1976. Reliability. In B. Bolton, ed. *Handbook of Measurement and Evaluation in Rehabilitation.* Baltimore: University Park Press.

Todd, J. 1972. *Relationships among Selected Occupational Experience Programs in Secondary Schools. A Mini-Grant Research Project Presented to the Tennessee Research Coordinating Unit: 1972-73.* Knoxville, TN: Occupational Research and Development Coordinating Unit.

Wanous, J., and Lawler, E. 1972. Measurement and meaning of job satisfaction. *Journal of Applied Psychology* 56:95-105.

Worth, C., Hietala, R., Spurlin, O., and de Mik, G. 1973. *Survey of Post-Placement Experiences of TAT Graduates.* Oak Ridge, TN: Oak Ridge Associated Universities Training and Technology Project.

Young, R., Clive, W., and Miles B. 1971. *Vocational Education Planning: Manpower Priorities and Dollars.* Columbus: Center for Vocational and Technical Education, Ohio State University.

chapter 17

DAVID BRESNICK | *City University of New York*

THE SEPARATION OF VOCATIONAL EDUCATION AND EMPLOYMENT AND TRAINING

An Historical Overview

Until World War II, the intervention of the national government in training for employment was minimal. The first governmental intervention was the Morrill Act of 1862, which established the land grant colleges and prescribed that they establish programs for training and research in the field of agriculture. The second intervention was the Smith-Hughes Act of 1917, which established one of the original programs of matching grants for state efforts. The Smith-Hughes Act provided for programs in the area of vocational education—defined as agriculture, home economics, and trades and industry.

However it was not until the post World War II period that the idea of a national commitment to minimize unemployment gave impetus to a federal manpower policy, as embodied in the Full Employment Act of 1946. The Full Employment Act of 1946 was a response to the widespread unemployment of the depression and a new concept of the power of the Federal Government, fostered by the mobilization of the World War II years. This melding of ideas is captured in a 1944 campaign speech of Franklin Delano Roosevelt:

> To assure the full realization of the right to a useful and remunerative employment, an adequate program must, and if I have anything to do about it, will, provide America with close to 60 million jobs.

> If anyone feels that my faith in our ability to provide sixty million
> peacetime jobs is fantastic, let him remember that some people said the
> same thing about my demand in 1940 for fifty thousand airplanes
> (cited in Bailey, 1950: 43).[1]

The raising of the unemployment issue during the campaign, and the
agreement of Roosevelt and Dewey about the need for a policy are credited
with stimulating Congress to move toward the adoption of the Full Employment Act of 1946. While the Full Employment Act of 1946 set admirable
goals it did little to move the country toward a manpower policy. The World
War II GI Bill was of far greater impact on people's lives, and the legitimation
of national efforts to provide job training. The GI Bill spent some $14.5
billion on training benefits, and led to an additional $4.5 billion for training
post-World War II veterans. In the 1950s efforts at a national manpower
policy lagged because employment was generally high. During the 1960
presidential election campaign rising unemployment, from 5.1 percent in May
to 6.2 percent in November, gave impetus to Senator Paul Douglas' efforts to
enact the Area Redevelopment Act of 1961, which provided low interest
loans and grants for community facilities to stimulate economic development
and job creation in depressed areas. A small portion of the act, providing
$14.5 million for job training in the first year, became the model for the
Manpower Development and Training Act (MDTA) of 1962. (See Mangum,
1968, for a discussion of the origins of manpower policy.)

MDTA attracted widespread, bipartisan support in part because of its
ability to encompass contradictory aspirations and views of the American
economy. For Senator Joseph Clark, it's chief senate sponsor, it was an
opportunity to train residents of depressed communities for new jobs, mirror-
ing a program in Pennsylvania with which he was familiar. For Congressman
Elmer Holland, the chief house sponsor, it was a defense against the automation that he saw as a threat to his own constituents working in Pennsylvania
steel mills. To some like William McChesney Martin, Chairman of the Federal
Reserve Board and Arthur Burns, ex-Chairman of the Council of Economic
Advisers, it was a reaffirmation of their belief that no shortage of jobs existed
for individuals possessing the proper skills.

Yet amidst the agreement, fundamental disagreements existed. There was
the question of the extent to which unemployment could be attributed to
technological and structural changes in the American economy, versus the
belief that unemployment reflected the lack of growth in an increasingly
productive economy facing an expanding labor force.

MDTA, with its emphasis on job training, was thought by its congressional
sponsors to belong most naturally in the Bureau of Vocational Education of
the Department of Health, Education and Welfare (HEW). But at that time

the Vocational Education Bureau of the Office of Education was small and unresponsive to the congressional initiatives. If MDTA had come several years later (after the expanded program of the Vocational Educational Act of 1963), it might well have been lodged in the expanded Bureau of Vocational Education. Instead a dichotomy was produced which juxtaposed the Department of Labor (DOL) and manpower, with HEW and vocational education.

As Congress began developing MDTA, it was the DOL which responded with considerable interest and enthusiasm, realizing that manpower programs deserved a higher priority on the national agenda. Within the Labor Department the Bureau of Labor Statistics (BLS) understood the need for a broader research agenda. The Employment Service of DOL also saw the opportunity for an expanded role. Once involved in MDTA and serving as the vehicle for congressional appropriations, DOL and its newly created Manpower Division aggressively sought expansion of these programs. Before long the Manpower Division accounted for over 80 percent of its budget. Manpower achieved a predominant influence in DOL, while vocational education, even after its strengthening during the 1960s, was just one among many programs of the Office of Education within the Department of Health, Education and Welfare.

DOL found the job of dominating MDTA an easy one, given the vast disparity between its institutional commitment and that of HEW. This domination of MDTA and later the Comprehensive Employment Training Act (CETA) by the DOL had an important impact on the program. Vocational education programs, housed within the Office of Education, had always been viewed as skills development programs. They were a small part of a larger educational effort being carried out in schools across the country, to provide knowledge and skills to young people before they entered the world of work. To the DOL the primary focus of training and employment programs has been jobs. Individuals were being brought into the programs because they needed jobs, and training was merely a means to that end. This basic difference in orientation has had profound importance for the development of employment and training programs. It has shifted the grounds for conceptualization and evaluation.

At its inception MDTA emphasized locally-based programs. MDTA's approach was administered by two existing public agencies: the public schools and the Employment Service (ES).[2] The ES was able to identify eligible people and suitable occupational goals while the schools could provide skills training. Competing with programs lodged in the schools (the institutional component of MDTA), was On-The-Job Training (OJT), a program to reimburse local employers for the costs of training. In subsequent years, as the War Against Poverty gained prominence, MDTA programs became oriented toward a disadvantaged clientele through administrative, rather than congressional action. Skills centers were created within the institutional programs to serve the poor. By 1966, the DOL had declared the objective of spending at least 65 percent of its monies for training the disadvantaged. In 1968, reinforcing this targeting approach, the disadvantaged were specifically defined as those who were both poor and without satisfactory employment plus either (1) under 21 or over 44 years of age; (2) without a high school degree; (3) a member of a minority group; or (4) physically or mentally handicapped. The poverty orientation led DOL to seek a job-oriented alternative to institutional training. Almost from the outset, the number of specific programs that came within the manpower umbrella began to proliferate. After the creation of the Office of Economic Opportunity (OEO), the DOL was delegated responsibility for the Neighborhood Youth Corps (NYC) work experience program. By the late 1960s a dozen separate categorical programs, each with its own appropriation account, had come within the purview of the Manpower Administration. OEO-funded projects were granted directly to program operations, including community action agencies, schools, voluntary agencies, and businesses. A major alternative called skill centers was developed jointly by OEO and DOL under the institutional aid component. These skill centers were independent of the local school systems, creating a separate group of independent contractors.

As the proliferation of program sponsors and program monitors within the federal government continued, problems in coordination arose. A series of DOL-HEW-OEO teams which visited thirty cities in 1966 spurred the impetus for reform. One response was the Concentrated Employment Program (CEP) modeled after a Chicago program known as Jobs Now. CEP called for the establishment of comprehensive service centers in poverty areas which could perform outreach and intake, work orientation, referral to job training or job placement, and supportive services including basic education and health services. Another effort to achieve coordination was the Cooperative Area Manpower Planning System (CAMPS), which sought to establish coordinating committees at the area, state, regional, and national levels. But the problems of coordination that were set loose by the proliferation of categorical programs finally led to the adoption of special revenue sharing, as embodied in the Comprehensive Employment and Training Act of 1973 (CETA).

Evaluation of Employment and Training Programs

Although the expectations placed upon MDTA were legion, it is probably correct to say that its major purpose was to increase access to the job market of individuals who were displaced by automation and otherwise disadvantaged. Thus, the measure of these programs was taken as the increased earnings of those who entered the program. Employment and training programs, it would appear, are here to stay. They have made explicit the connection between training and work, and have focused attention on the need to judge impact on the basis of increased earnings for the individual. To what extent, though, have they demonstrated that training programs can increase individual earnings? To what extent have they increased our knowledge of the type of training programs that are most effective, and our knowledge of the relative impacts of general knowledge, skills and attitude change in altering the income potential of individuals? Finally, what have they told us of the relative impact of training programs when compared to other strategies for raising individual earnings?

First, consider the question of increased earnings: to what extent do individuals who have participated in MDTA and CETA programs make more money than they would have without those programs? The most frequently used design to assess program effectiveness is the simple before/after assessment, where an individual's annual earnings before receiving the training are compared to earnings after completion of the program. These studies on the whole indicate a rise in annual income.

The majority of MDTA and CETA evaluations have in fact used such a design, although a few studies have introduced control groups of varying types. Magnum and Walsh (1973) in their summary of the progress of MDTA written in anticipation of the passage of CETA, argued that a substantial gain in earnings resulted from participation in MDTA. While recognizing that problems of control exist, they stated that comparing all pre and posttraining experiences of all terminees for whom records were available in the fiscal years 1971 and 1972, resulted in 15.5 percent and 14.6 percent gains in average hourly wages during fiscal 1971, respectively, for institutional and OJT enrollees. For fiscal 1972, gains of 8.7 percent for institutional and 6.3 percent for OJT enrollees were recorded. Magnum and Walsh then corrected for the average hourly earnings gains of all production workers (5.9 percent in 1971 and 4.1 percent in 1972), and concluded that MDTA was indeed effective. They then calculated earnings gains of $1,621 for institutional and $1,336 for OJT enrollees. A more recent policy statement by the National Council on Employment Policy (1977) cited some of the same studies relied upon by Magnum and Walsh, and concluded that institutional training results in earnings increases of from $1100 to $1900 and OJT results in slightly higher earnings. This general perspective of indicating substantial earnings gains is followed by Perry, Anderson, Rowan, and Northrup (1975) in their recent analysis of employment and training programs.

However, a basic and often recognized limitation of these studies is inadequate controls. Is it accurate to attribute the rise in individual income to the program's effect? While it appears incontrovertible that individuals earn more after they have gone through the training program than they did before taking the training, it is unclear to what extent this income differential is the result of the program treatment.

Failure to use controlled experiments leaves open the possibility that factors other than the program treatment are causing the earnings differential. The effects of *history,* both in terms of rising wage scales and the maturation of individuals, undoubtedly are important in the employment field. Even without any training, an individual entering the labor market after a lapse of time might anticipate earning more money due to the rises in wages, increased age, and experience.

The effects of maturation in particular are pointed to by the fact that most of the earnings increases tend to result from more sustained employment, rather than rises in actual wages. As individuals grow older it may be that they will be employed more continuously in any event.

Indeed, each of the major commentators listed above recognized the need for controlled experimentation, and the lack of it in the employment and training field. Yet Magnum and Walsh (1973) are able to cite only one major study using controls, selected retrospectively, relying upon participants, friends and relatives, and in part, canvassing their neighborhoods. The more recent statement by the National Council on Employment Policy (1977) cited a number of studies using controls, but none are identified as true experimental designs. These studies indicated a tremendous variability in earnings gains over control groups. For example, earnings gains for non-white females ranged from $200 to $1600, and for white males from $48 to $557.

The technical problems relating to proper controls have led to such dubious techniques as comparing actual earnings differentials to average changes in earnings of large populations, projecting earnings increases of single years over long periods of time, and selecting control groups retrospectively. One of the hazards of such techniques is indicated by studies which show that earnings differentials drop off sharply after the first year (National Council on Employment Policy, 1977).

Another major shortcoming of the evaluations is the failure to differentiate among programs to assess varying degrees of effectiveness. Most programs contain elements of knowledge, skill, and attitudinal change in addition to placement efforts. In fact, as the problem of locating jobs in a high unemployment economy has persisted, and as placement has become a major focus of evaluation, efforts directed at placement have increased. These new directions highlight another question about employment and training programs: To what extent has their success been the result of efforts directed toward placement rather than the effect of training? This is a particularly important question when raising the issue of the value of these programs to society in general.

Aside from any benefit which might accrue to an individual from participation in employment and training programs, does the society at large benefit? Posing this question from a human capital perspective, is the investment being made in increased skills going to bring a reasonable return, given possible alternative uses of society's resources? Such an analysis requires longitudinal data and rigorous control procedures. The lifetime earning streams of participants in training and employment programs must be compared to similar individuals lacking such program benefits. Then the return on the investment of society's resources must be compared to alternative possibilities, for example in job creation, direct payments, or differently-organized training programs. The effects of such programs on the labor market must be considered. Is the government merely paying to displace another individual equally as competent from the same job, in effect choosing one individual over another, or is it genuinely filling jobs that would otherwise go begging or be filled with less qualified personnel? Of major importance here is labor market conditions, which have shifted dramatically since the inception of MDTA, a time of relatively full employment, to today's robust unemployment.

A major shortcoming of the evaluations of employment and training programs is the failure to have available longitudinal data. In part this results from the relative newness of programs. But it also reflects the orientation of administrators toward the everyday job of administering programs, and the difficulties of maintaining records and follow-ups on individuals once they have left the program. Such difficulties have long been associated with vocational education programs, which also suffer from the lack of longitudinal data. In both areas the costs and difficulties of maintaining such records combine with a fear on the part of program administrators that evaluations may show small effects at best, and also will not strengthen their own hands in seeking more institutional support. Such a phenomenon, of course, is not unique to training programs and can be applied to most operating organizations.

Despite the difficulties of proving that MDTA and CETA programs are providing individual and social benefits, their success in turning the attention of program administrators away from concerns with skills and knowledge to earnings and placements can be clearly demonstrated. This development is a distinct contribution of the Labor Department and its orientation and mentality. Confirmation of this attitude is demonstrated by a survey of research conducted by the U.S. Department of Labor (1975). A survey of all dissertation research supported and reported indicated that of 121 projects for which summaries were provided (out of a total of 194 projects), approximately twenty concerned knowledge, twenty concerned skills, forty concerned placement on a job, forty concerned earnings, and fifty concerned labor market conditions.[3] Other aspects of the research program, while more difficult to deal with in a quantitative fashion, also emphasized the importance of placement and earning over skills and knowledge.

442 EVALUATION MEASURES AND TESTING ISSUES

Under CETA, this concern with placements and earnings has continued. Since CETA called for the delegation of considerable responsibility to local prime sponsors, guidelines and manuals were produced to help these local groups with the multitude of problems they would face. The program assessment guides of the U.S. Department of Labor (1974, 1976) are examples of such manuals, and contain detailed suggestions of factors to be considered in evaluation of employment and training programs. Since the publication of the initial handbooks, the performance indicators have been revised and new suggestions made for their use. In August 1977, a subset of these indicators were selected for nationwide application in a new attempt to apply performance indicators systematically.

In cautionary language and carefully restating the right of sponsors to select appropriate measures of performance, the manual lists several participant effectiveness measures which have proved useful in the past: the *positive completion ratio*, the percentage of participants who have been placed in jobs or otherwise terminated the training successfully; *the placement ratio,* the percentage of employees who entered unsubsidized employment; and *the job entry completion rate,* a measure of the quality of the program which stresses retention on the job for some period of time. The CETA manual (U.S. Department of Labor, 1976) also strongly recommends that these measures be used to compare programs, but warns that only comparable programs should be used. Similar objectives and clientele groups are stressed. Additional measures that may be useful in such comparisons are the training related employment ratio, which focuses on job related placements and the placement wage index which estimates the average wage of those individuals placed after participating in the program.

These measures are obvious compromises in an attempt to measure the impact of jobs on the lives of individuals. They make do with information which may be easier to come by because of lack of specificity and longitudinal capability. Despite their shortcomings, they do demonstrate how the new emphasis on the effect of programs on the lifetime earnings of individuals has come to dominate employment and training programs.

These measures may indeed be helpful, particularly as methods of comparison among differing programs. While they do not address the ultimate effectiveness of the CETA program, they should provide valuable information about the relative effectiveness of specific programs in a particular prime sponsor's jurisdiction. Whether such information will be available when program decisions are being made is a separate question, and the extent to which performance matters in a highly charged political atmosphere, where contract renewal may be based upon other factors is, of course, an important and additional question.[4]

The CETA manual also suggests measures of effectiveness related to the specific tasks of CETA in addition to the measures of placement and earnings.

The percent of individuals removed from the ranks of poverty, the extent to which minority groups are placed, the percent of employers who alter personnel practices to help the disadvantaged, and the improvement of job quality are all additional measures of effectiveness. The manual also suggests a number of measures which are more traditionally associated with educational evaluations, focusing on the skills, attitudes and motivational factors of the participants. These measures include increased educational or vocational skill level, percent of participants who report the program was helpful, changes in participant work habits, motivation, self-esteem, family stability, and participation in school or community activities.

The diversity of programs funded under CETA provides a fertile environment for the use of comparative indicators of the success of programs in placing individuals in new jobs, and imparting new knowledge and attitudes. Certainly knowledge developed about which programs are most effective in producing placements can be used in revising funding approaches. Another area in which comparative data are useful is the ultimate question of the benefit/cost ratio of CETA programs.

The costs of administration in relationship to the training or stipend portion of the program may be useful in determining which programs get the most money to individuals who need the money. Some programs may spend considerable resources on hiring trainers or administrators. Total average costs per participant or costs for training, administration, or stipends may also be calculated. Other relevant comparisons include cost per placement, positive termination, or positive completion.

A more difficult measure to calculate is the benefit/cost ratio of particular programs. If an average benefit per participant could be calculated, that figure divided by the average cost per participant would provide a benefit/cost ratio. The annual benefit divided by the annual cost would provide a measure of the return on the investment. Calculation of future benefits, however, may be highly speculative as will benefit/cost ratios. A decision as to the discount rate for calculating opportunity costs may be decisive in determining the magnitude and direction of the benefit/cost ratio.

While such results would be rather complete in the case of individuals, the social benefit of the program would require further calculations. To what extent are the benefits realized by individuals in the program derived by depriving nonparticipants of benefits they would ordinarily obtain? The answer to that question requires considerable additional analysis and data.

Perhaps one of the greatest disappointments of the national effort in employment and training is the failure to develop reliable longitudinal data on the effects of these programs. Longitudinal data would allow better understanding of the long run implications of the programs for their participants and the rest of society. Part of the problem is that since their inception, employment training programs have not been directed at long-term job creation, bur rather at helping a few workers affected by changing job markets or otherwise disadvantaged. As the employment and training problem has mushroomed due to rising unemployment rates, job displacement effects are becoming an increasing probability. Furthermore, a shift to job creation strategies makes an assessment of the social benefits of employment and training more important than ever. The perspectives developed by the analysts of human capital will need to be applied to full-scale employment and training programs more carefully. They will present exacting tests and perhaps some discouraging results, but they will mark the maturation of the employment and training debate to refocus on the new issues confronting American society.

For the meantime, however, employment and training programs have moved the concerns of evaluators dramatically from knowledge and skill acquisition, to the bread and butter issues of jobs and earnings. This challenge to vocational education has already been reflected in the vocational education community and promises to shape future evaluations.

NOTES

1. Bailey's treatment of the origins of the full employment legislation is a classic.

2. This discussion of the development of MDTA is based largely on two invaluable sources: Garth L. Mangum and John Walsh, *A Decade of Manpower Development and Training* (Salt Lake City: Olympus Publishing Company, 1973); and Joseph Ball, "CETA Planning and implementation: Pouring New Federalism into Old Battles?" Presentation at the 1975 Annual Conference of the American Society for Public Administration.

3. The author acknowledges the assistance of Susan Flaschenberg in carrying out this analysis of the report.

4. These issues were raised poignantly for the author while serving as a member of the Dutchess County Manpower Planning Council.

REFERENCES

Bailey, S. K. 1950. *Congress Makes A Law.* New York: Vintage Books.

Ball, J. 1975. "CETA planning and implementation: Pouring New Federalism into old battles?" Paper presented at the 1975 annual conference of the American Society for Public Administration.

Mangum, G. L. 1968. *MDTA, Foundations of Federal Manpower Policy.* Baltimore: Johns Hopkins Press.

Mangum, G. L., and Walsh, J. 1973. *A Decade of Manpower Development and Training.* Salt Lake City: Olympus Publishing.

National Council on Employment Policy. 1977. The impact of employment and training programs. In M. Guttentag, ed. *Evaluation Studies Review Annual, Volume 2.* Beverly Hills: Sage Publications.

Perry, C., Anderson, B., Rowan, R., and Northrop, H. R. 1975. *The Impact of Government Manpower Programs, in General, and on Minorities and Women.* Philadelphia: Industrial Research Unit, The Wharton School.

U.S. Department of Labor. 1976. *Planning and Evaluation under CETA: A Guide for Prime Sponsors.* Washington, DC: Office of Policy, Evaluation and Research, Employment and Training Administration.

–––. 1975. *Manpower Research and Development Projects, 1975 Edition.* Washington, DC.

–––. 1974. *Program Assessment Guide for Prime Sponsors under the Comprehensive Employment and Training Act of 1973.* Washington, DC: Manpower Administration.

MEASURING STUDENT LEARNING IN CAREER EDUCATION	**chapter 18**

DEBORAH G. BONNET	*New Educational Directions, Inc.*

INTRODUCTION

The most frequently cited obstacle to evaluating the success of career education programs is a scarcity of student outcome measurement instruments. The recency of the career education movement and the intangible nature of many of its goals are among the factors contributing to this problem. However, career education outcome measurement is not an insurmountable problem. This chapter demonstrates that there exist within the state of the art methods of measuring most, if not all, of the facets of student learning which career education seeks to promote. Currently used tests and other evaluation criteria are examined and promising, though untested, measurement approaches are proposed.

The framework for the analysis which follows is the list of nine learner outcome goals set forth by the Office of Career Education (OCE) of the U.S. Office of Education (USOE) (Hoyt, 1977). These outcome goals are shown in Table 18.1.

Other sets of outcome goals based upon different views of the career education concept could have been chosen. As demonstrated by Hansen (1977), there is at this time no single definition of career education which enjoys unanimous support within the career education community. Working defini-

---

AUTHOR'S NOTE: *The writer wishes to acknowledge reviews and suggestions of Lois-ellin Datta, Terry Newall, Diane Richards and Fred Gannon.*

Table 18.1: USOE Learner Outcome Goals for Career Education[*]

It is important to note that these learner goals are intended to apply to persons leaving the formal educational *system* for the world of work. They are *not* intended to be applicable whenever the person leaves a particular *school.* For some persons, then, these goals become applicable when they leave the secondary school. For others, it will be when they have left post-high school occupational educational programs. For still others, these goals need not be applied, *in toto,* until they have left a college or university setting. Thus, the applicability of these learner outcome goals will vary from individual to individual as well as from one level of education to another. This is consistent with the developmental nature, and the basic assumption of individual differences inherent in the concept of career education.

Career education seeks to produce individuals who, when they leave school (at any age or at any level) are:

1. Competent in the basic academic skills required for adaptability in our rapidly changing society.

2. Equipped with good work habits.

3. Equipped with a personally meaningful set of work values that foster in them a desire to work.

4. Equipped with career decision-making skills, job-hunting skills, and job-getting skills.

5. Equipped with a degree of self-understanding and understanding of educational-vocational opportunities sufficient for making sound career decisions.

6. Aware of means available to them for continuing and recurrent education.

7. Either placed or actively seeking placement in a paid occupation, in further education, or in a vocation consistent with their current career decisions.

8. Actively seeking to find meaning and meaningfulness through work in productive use of leisure time.

9. Aware of means available to themselves for changing career options—of societal and personal constraints impinging on career alternatives.

*Hoyt, 1977

tions of career education and other pertinent concepts as used in this chapter are given in Table 18.2. The OCE view of career education revolves around the concept of work as productive activity, and thus extends beyond career education definitions concerned only with preparation for paid employment. At the same time, the OCE view excludes some concepts from the domain of career education which are included by those who view one's career as one's life and career education as all education. The OCE learner outcome goals were chosen because they seem to encompass the student objectives of most operational career education programs, yet they are specific enough to be discussed in measurement terms. The goals themselves are not dependent on the program's implementation strategies, and apply to such diverse settings as alternative high school programs for experience-based career education and

Table 18.2:   **Definitions in Career Education**

Work:	Conscious effort aimed at producing benefits for oneself and/or for oneself and others. (Includes unpaid as well as paid work.)
Career:	The totality of work one does in her or his lifetime. (One has only one career.)
Vocation:	One's primary work role at any given point in time. (Includes work of students, homemakers, and volunteer workers.)
Occupation:	Refers to paid employment.
Leisure:	Consists of activities, other than sleeping, in which one engages while not performing in his or her vocation. (Includes both "work" and "play.")
Career education:	An effort aimed at refocusing American education and the actions of the broader community in ways that will help individuals acquire and utilize the knowledge, skills, and attitudes necessary for each to make work a meaningful, productive, and satisfying part of her or his way of living.

traditional classrooms, where career education is incorporated into academic or vocational instruction.

Career Education and the 1976 Vocational Amendments

Long before career education became a popular movement in the early 1970s, many of career education's goals were evident in vocational education philosophy and practices. Congress restated the commonality of the purposes of vocational and career education through several provisions of the Vocational Amendments of 1976. Vocational education is defined as "organized educational programs which are directly related to the preparation of individuals for paid or unpaid employment, or for additional preparation for a career requiring other than a baccalaureate or advanced degree" (PL 94-482 Title II). Nothing in the act indicates that this emphasis on education as preparation for work is limited to technical skills training; preparation for employment may include the development of positive work attitudes, effective work habits, and basic skills. Other provisions of the amendments establish goals and specify methods with clear relationships to the goals and methods of career education.

The Amendments' emphasis on expanding educational opportunities and aspirations for the disadvantaged, the handicapped, and for all persons irrespective of their sex is shared by career education as expressed in goals 4, 5, and 9, and elsewhere in *A Primer for Career Education* (Hoyt, 1977). Section 131 of the Amendment allows vocational education monies to be used for research and development programs to overcome sex bias and sex stereotyping; Section 133 allows the development of sex-fair curriculum, including guidance and testing materials; and Section 136 supports activities for overcoming sex bias and sex stereotyping without restricting the nature of these efforts. Assistance in career decision-making and job and educational placement services are supported through Section 134, which requires 20 percent of Part A-Subpart 3 funds to be devoted to vocational guidance and counseling for children, youth, and adults. This section gives special priority to vocational guidance activities involving community-school collaboration, also a priority of career education. Section 135 encourages joint efforts in inservice training, including exchanges of personnel between schools and businesses and industries. Section 132 allows the support of elementary and secondary programs designed to familiarize students with "the broad range of careers for which special skills are required, and the requisites for careers in such occupations." Section 150 recognizes homemaking as work and encourages the participation of both males and females in consumer and homemaking education programs to prepare them for homemaking, and for combining the roles of homemaker and wage earner. These are only examples of parallels between the philosophy, goals, and methods of vocational education (as expressed by Congress) and those of career education (as expressed by OCE), but these examples demonstrate that federal vocational education monies may be used to support substantial portions of what OCE considers a comprehensive career education program. It follows that vocational education evaluations may include evaluations of programs' effectiveness in achieving their career education outcomes.

Career Education Evaluation Design

Measuring students' skills, knowledge, attitudes, or behavior is only one task of evaluating a program's success in achieving its outcome goals. The following discussion of measurement techniques assumes that the measures are used with evaluation designs meeting the following standards: (1) The evaluation is designed to allow reasonable inferences that the program caused the measured effects. *A Practical Guide to Measuring Project Impact on Student Achievement* (RMC Research Corporation, 1975) presents five such designs. (2) Statistically reliable results are considered necessary for predicting that a program will continue to be effective or that it will be effective if implemented elsewhere. However, statistical reliability is not taken as sufficient evidence that a program is worth maintaining, expanding, or replicating. (3) If inferential analyses reveal reliable program effects, the *amount* of difference the program makes is evaluated against program costs and educational priorities in deciding whether to maintain, expand, replicate, revise, or discontinue the program. (4) In deciding whether program goals have been met (as opposed to whether progress has been made toward them), program students' terminal performance is evaluated against performance levels required for career success. Adequate performance levels vary according to the individual's career goals. Establishing rational standards of adequacy for students with given career plans requires current job analysis data showing the relationships between workers' "career education" skills, knowledge, attitudes, and behavior and their "career success," where the definitions of success should include measures of work satisfaction. Ideally, standards of adequate performance should also be based on predictions of future career requisites. Since the capacity for establishing rational standards of adequate student performance is limited, this fourth standard for evaluations is a goal for evaluators rather than a requirement for acceptable evaluation practices.

There are several unique characteristics of career education with important implications for evaluation design:

- Career education is often infused into the curriculum and taught through academic and vocational courses. As individual teachers usually have a good deal of latitude in the planning and implementation of career education activities, identifying the amount and type of career education their students experience is a challenging evaluation task in itself. At the secondary level, where each student has several teachers, the problem is compounded. Distinguishing career education from other learning activities can also present difficulties.
- As career education is a developmental concept, so also are most of its student outcomes. That is, young people can be expected to make some progress toward many career education goals without special career education intervention. Simple pre-post evaluation designs, therefore, are inadequate for most of the outcomes, necessitating either a local comparison group or pre-post data on norm-referenced measures used in regression designs.
- The first outcome goal, competence in basic academic skills, is what Datta (1977) calls a bipolar assertion. Proponents claim that career education facilitates basic skills development while opponents assert that career education impedes it. Even if local career education objectives for basic skills suggest otherwise, it may be desirable to apply two-tailed statistical tests to basic skills results in recognition of the concerns of the opponents. The experience-based career education stance on the basic skills issue is that the program is equally as effective as traditional programs. This presents an interesting challenge to evaluators who recognize that there is no technique for substantiating a research hypothesis of no differences.[1]
- Students' skills, knowledge, attitudes, and behavior do not constitute the only appropriate focus of career education program evaluation.

From the OCE perspective, career education is an educational reform movement, seeking to change educational attitudes, practices, and policies including the establishment of collaborative relationships between educational systems and the community. The extent to which these changes occur is worth systematic evaluation, and in some cases may assume even higher priority than investigations of student learning.

Measuring the USOE Learner Outcome Goals

The demand for career education evaluation results preceded the development of career education measures. As a result, many instruments originally designed for other purposes came into common use as career education evaluation tools. Now that alternatives to these instruments are available it is appropriate to re-examine their use in evaluating career education programs. The following analysis suggests that while some are valid indicators of career education program impact, the use of others should be discontinued. Criticisms of the use of instruments in career education evaluation are just that—they do not reflect the tests' quality or utility for their intended purposes.

Even tests developed specifically for career education were not necessarily designed within the context of the USOE goals. The result is that the items comprising a single test scale often address student attributes which, in the context of the USOE goals, are distinctively different even though the attributes may be closely related under the construct from which the scale was developed. For evaluation results to reveal the program's specific strengths and weaknesses, independent measures are needed for each objective. Thus, where program objectives distinguish among career education concepts in the same manner as the OCE goals, it becomes necessary either to extract subscales from existing test scales, to develop new measures dealing exclusively with the set of student attributes defined by each objective, or to use existing instruments as they stand and evaluate the achievement of multiple objectives simultaneously. The latter is the simplest solution and is sometimes adequate, but the first two alternatives are preferable.

The USOE goals define broad categories of learner outcomes rather than specific behaviors. This is appropriate for national goals, but local programs must develop more specific objectives to define operationally what the goals mean to them. These local objectives provide the framework for curriculum development and evaluation. As an example, the second goal, "Equipped with good work habits," is useful for neither instructional nor evaluation purposes until the program defines work habits and decides which work habits to promote. The following discussion analyzes measures for various objectives associated with each of the goals. However, the alternative interpretations are not exhaustive—each of the goals holds possibilities for yet other meanings.

Although much of the following discussion is relevant to all levels of education, the focus is on the secondary student. The learner outcome goals refer to the individual's status at the point when he or she leaves the formal educational system and, therefore, require that secondary students meet them fully only if they do not intend to pursue postsecondary training (see Table 18.1). The discussion is also concerned almost exclusively with content validity, that is, with apparent congruity of measures with the intent of career education goals. Where the data are available, other criteria for measurement such as internal consistency, stability, and construct and predictive validity, should enter into instrument selection decisions even though they are not examined here.[2] The USOE learner outcome goals are discussed in the order in which they appear in Table 18.1.

1. Competent in the Basic Academic Skills Required for Adaptability in Our Rapidly Changing Society: Basic academic skills are usually defined as reading, writing, and mathematics. By tying goal 1 to the "back to basics" movement OCE appears to endorse this definition (Hoyt, 1977).

Career education evaluations have rarely addressed reading, writing, and mathematical skills even though this is the only goal for which there are widely-accepted and readily-available instruments. Any of the well-established norm-referenced achievement batteries should suffice here. As a general rule, the best one to use is the one used in the local testing program, as it is most likely to be accepted locally and because existing data often can be utilized, reducing or even eliminating the need to administer tests specifically for career education program evaluation.

There is some consensus that criterion-referenced minimal competency tests are more appropriate than norm-referenced tests for evaluations of this outcome at the secondary level (Hoyt, 1976). This is worth considering, particularly if there is local acceptance of minimal competency measures as valid indicators of basic skills achievement.

On the other hand, the phrase "required for adaptability in our rapidly-changing society" suggests higher-level skills than are typically measured by tests of minimum competencies required for functioning in today's society. The phrase may even suggest that this goal goes beyond the basic academic skills of reading, writing, and mathematics. However, interpreting the goal to include other basic academic skills requires defining which adaptations individuals should be able to make, then identifying the skills required to make them. Only after these tasks are accomplished will it be appropriate to examine methods of measuring these skills.

2. Equipped with Good Work Habits: Since the OE definition of work extends beyond paid employment to all productive activity, good work habits refer to volunteer, household and school work as well as to paid work. This discussion, however, will concentrate on school and employment settings. Direct behavioral measures appropriate to both settings will be considered, and measures of school and work-related attitudes underlying work habits also will be discussed.

Within the school context, good work habits include prompt arrival to class, regular school attendance, and timely completion of work assignments. These three behaviors are not only measurable and relevant to educational concerns; they are also recorded routinely in most schools.

Each student's attendance or tardiness rate, or the proportion of work assignments completed on time can be treated statistically in the same manner as a test score and used in conventional research designs. One special advantage of these measures is that they can often be retrieved from past years, which means that a comparison group can be constructed after the fact. For example, a school just beginning a career education program can compare the attendance records of current sophomores to those of the previous year's sophomore class.

All three of these behaviors are influenced by factors beyond the student's control. This does not necessarily mean that the reason for each absence, tardiness, or missing assignment need be investigated, because in the work setting the behaviors themselves are likely to be important regardless of the reasons for them. However, circumstances may result in a systematic bias favoring one of the groups being compared or one of the data collection periods. In the case of the evaluation design comparing attendance records from different years, for example, the evaluation could be rendered invalid by a flu epidemic resulting in unusually high absenteeism during one of the years.

Other indicators of students' work habits may be found in classroom behavior. Carefully designed and executed evaluations of work habits ex-hibited in the classroom can yield useful results, although they have the disadvantage of requiring considerable investments in data collection. The measurement of classroom behavior begins with specific lists of desirable and/or undesirable behaviors. This should be done even if an available instrument is used so that an appropriate one can be chosen—otherwise, a class where spontaneous discussion is encouraged may be rated low because students do not consistently raise their hands before speaking. Data collection may involve counting the number of incidents of each behavior or subjec-tively rating the desirability of behavior along several dimensions. Data may be collected for each student or for the classroom as a group. When the classroom teacher acts as the observer, data may be collected less obtrusively, for longer periods of time, and for lower costs than if collected by an independent observer. However, observation may be a full-time task in itself and the more subjective the observation task, the more necessary it becomes to use objective observers. Unless the particular work habits of interest can be assessed by classroom teachers on a daily basis without undue burden, time sampling becomes an important issue. That is, decisions must be made concerning the day, the time of day, and the duration of each data collection session. Some systems also require predetermining the points in time during the session when particular observations will be made.

The design of classroom behavior evaluations must take into account an unusually large number of factors influencing the measures besides the possible effects of career education, including the reliability of judges or observers, teachers' classroom management styles, class size, the nature of classroom activities, room arrangements, and even weather. Conclusive classroom behavior evaluation results would be valuable evidence of career education's impact, but the decision to undertake this task should probably be made only where there is good reason to expect positive findings (or where unlimited evaluation resources are available.)

A behavioral measurement technique which introduces control over many of the variables affecting general classroom behavior is the simulation exercise, where all students involved in the evaluation are assigned the same task to perform. To the extent possible, the task is designed to elicit the work habits being evaluated without introducing contaminating skills requirements. If, for example, students' persistence in pursuing a difficult task is of interest, the task should be difficult, and preferably novel, for all of the students involved. On the other hand, if efficiency in the performance of manual tasks involving the use of tools and materials is to be evaluated, the task should be familiar to all of the students. Behaviors such as assembling all necessary tools and materials beforehand will indicate foresightedness, rather than knowledge of which tools and materials are required.

For career education programs involving work experience, such as experience-based career education (EBCE) and co-op programs, the site resource person or employer may be asked to evaluate students' work habits within the work setting. In this situation it may be impossible to construct a group of comparison students in a similar program. Comparisons of program students' work habits at the beginning and end of the program are likely to be contaminated by developing technical skills and increasing familiarity with the site's personnel and setting. However, employers' ratings can be used as program evaluation data, particularly if the program is willing to be held accountable for producing workers whose work habits compare favorably to those of the average employee (as opposed to the average student). It is common practice to ask site resource persons to rate students in work experience programs on dimensions such as punctuality, appearance, and work pace, using scales such as unacceptable-acceptable-outstanding. In the absence of instructions to the contrary, employers probably tend to weigh the student's youth and inexperience and, perhaps even the temporary nature of the employer's commitment to the student-worker in making these judgments. But if the program is intended to equip students with work habits which make them competitive with older workers in permanent employment settings, the employer can be asked to compare the student to his or her entry-level employees. For example, one interview or questionnaire item might read:

> In comparison to other workers in similar positions, how often does this student take it upon him/herself to accomplish necessary tasks without being specifically asked to do so?
> a. I would not want a worker in this job to do this
> b. Less often than other workers
> c. About as often as other workers
> d. More often than other workers

If more students are rated "d" and "b," the program can be considered successful in producing individuals capable of competing with currently employed workers. This approach fails to address the actual level of student performance and leaves open the possibilities of being simultaneously above average and unacceptable, or average and nearly-perfect. Similarly worded follow-up questions asking the employer to rate student performance according to an absolute scale (e.g., unacceptable-acceptable-outstanding) would serve as a check for these possibilities. Once asked to make comparative judgments, employers may be more inclined to judge students against the same expectations they hold for their regular employees. Questions should specify the work habits the employer is asked to rate. Questions such as, "How do you rate this student's attitude?" are open to diverse interpretations and should be replaced with several questions focusing on more narrowly-defined qualities, such as apparent interest in the work, concern for quality work, and responsiveness to superiors' instructions.

Employers should only be asked to rate behaviors which students have had the opportunity to demonstrate. For programs which are not intended to involve students in job tasks at the site or where students spend only a short period of time at any one site, the range of work habits which can be evaluated by employers is limited.

Work habits are often described as incorporating attitudes, as well as the more overt behaviors described above. Young and Schuh's list of student objectives defining good work habits (1975) is:

(a) Students will plan work effectively.
(b) Students will adapt to varied work conditions.

(c) Students will endorse a positive attitude toward the concept of quality in relation to a work task.

(d) Students will endorse a positive attitude toward conservation.

(e) Students will endorse a positive attitude toward responsibility for their own behavior and accomplishment of self-imposed tasks.

(f) Students will demonstrate a desire for continuous learning, both in school and out.

Paper and pencil attitudinal measures usually involve asking students to respond to each of a series of statements using a two to seven point scale of disagreement to agreement. Typical test items designed to tap attitudes which presumably correspond to good work habits are: "Time passes more quickly for people who keep busy on the job," and "If your supervisor is not polite about telling you what to do, you should not do it."

There are several available instruments of this type, including the Employment Readiness Scale, The Survey of Work Values, and Viewpoints on Work.[3] However, none of these instruments deals exclusively with attitudes which correspond directly to specific work habits—they all include items concerning general desire to work (If I had my choice, I would never work at all)[4], and work values (A good job is a well paying job).[5] Although work values and desire to work are closely associated with work habits, their appearance in a separate OE goal statement indicates that there is some consensus that they should be evaluated separately. Also, the measurement of work values raises several philosophical issues which will be discussed later.

The improvement of attitudes toward school and learning is a common objective of career education programs. Although none of the OE goals concerns this objective directly, it is considered one mechanism for achieving goal 1 (basic skills), and is closely related to goal 6 (the concept of learning as a lifelong process) as well as to goal 2 (work habits) as defined by Young and Schuh.

Attitudes toward school often have been measured with the school scales of self-concept tests such as the Coopersmith Self-Esteem Inventory and the Self-Appraisal Inventory. Instruments of this type are designed to assess the student's general affect for school (I enjoy school), and self-confidence in the student role (I find it hard to talk in front of class).[6] Little success has been demonstrated by career education in affecting these dimensions (New Educational Directions, 1977a). One reason may be that career education programs' efforts to improve attitudes toward school usually focus on instilling an appreciation for the relevance of education to the student's present and future needs. Greater enjoyment of school may result as a side effect of this appreciation or of changes in the curriculum associated with the career education program, but few if any career education activities have the primary purpose of making students like school. Thus, it may be appropriate to evaluate students' general affect for school, but greater attention should be given to the question of career education's impact on the student's recognition of the value of education through items such as, "Most of what I learn in school will help me later in life."

Although the present version of OE's goals does not specify interpersonal skills as a career education outcome, their development is a common career education objective and interpersonal skills associated with work roles can be considered a subset of work habits.

The National Institute for Education evaluation model for Experience Based Career Education includes the following objectives which clarify the meaning of employment-related interpersonal skills (Young and Schuh 1975):

> The student can effectively participate in peer and adult interactions based on appropriate role relationships and obligations, acceptance of the validity of individual rights and perceptions, and ability to contribute to the resolutions of conflicts resulting from personal needs and values.

> The student will demonstrate the ability to cooperate with others as a means of attaining goals.

> The student will demonstrate the ability to conduct conversations with an adult that reveals the student's self-confidence, ability to discuss a fixed topic for a reasonable amount of time, and an understanding of the other person's message and feelings.

> The student will demonstrate an increase in behaviors that reveal a tolerance for people who are different in ideas or background than himself/herself, an openness to change and a willingness to trust others when circumstances warrant.

Employment-related interpersonal skills may be categorized according to the individual's role with respect to: (1) peers, (2) superiors, (3) subordinates within the organizational structure, and (4) customers, clients, patients, or business associates from outside of the organization. It may be desirable to evaluate interpersonal skills associated with each of these roles separately. Also, the career plans of the program's students may be taken into consideration in deciding which categories should be given greatest emphasis in evaluation. Employer ratings of interpersonal skills are appropriate for evaluating programs involving work experience. Classroom behavior ratings may hold promise, particularly for classes which include team projects. Simulation techniques involving role playing of either routine or particularly sensitive work situations are worth considering.

Behavioral measures are intuitively preferable to paper and pencil tests but some aspects of interpersonal skills can probably be tapped adequately by the latter. Most self-concept tests, such as the Coopersmith Self-Esteem Inventory and the Self-Appraisal Inventory, contain scales addressing the individual's extroversion, leadership, and self-confidence in interpersonal relationships. The Employment Readiness Scale, the Survey of Work Values, Viewpoints on Work, and similar tests of work-related attitudes contain items concerning attitudinal and personality characteristics which are likely to be reflected in interpersonal relationships at work, such as: "I usually try to get along with people even if I do not like them," and "I resent being told what to do."[7] A full-length test along these lines should not be difficult to construct, and may be a good alternative to the more expensive behavioral measures for programs that wish to evaluate interpersonal skills in isolation from other work habits.

The Work Behavior Scale of the Career Orientation Battery takes another approach to measuring interpersonal skills by presenting sensitive work situations, and asking students to choose among several alternative ways of dealing with them. The National Assessment of Educational Progress (NAEP) Career and Occupational Development exercise R305010 measures students' ability to recognize desirable and undesirable supervisory behaviors. Students view a short film portraying interactions among the members and leader of a team, and list the best and worst things the leader did as a boss. Scoring criteria are given in the exercise volume.

In conclusion, success in equipping students with good work habits may be measured either behaviorally or attitudinally and in relation to either school or employment settings. This should not be construed to mean that the various assessment approaches discussed here are alternative means to measuring the same thing. Attitudes are related to behavior, but the relationship is not a perfect one and when the unavoidable errors of measurement are introduced the relationship becomes even less perfect. Similarly, work habits in the school setting are worthy of evaluation if their improvement is among the program's objectives, but where work habits are evaluated in the school setting because it is impossible to evaluate them in the employment setting, it should not be assumed that the transfer is complete—that the individual will behave on the job just as he or she does at school.

3. Equipped with a Personally Meaningful Set of Work Values that Foster in Them a Desire to Work: This outcome goal goes beyond stating the goal itself (producing individuals who desire to work) by also specifying the mechanism through which the goal should be achieved (via personally meaningful work values). The term work values is sometimes used to refer to the values which result in preferences for some types of work or working conditions over others, but in the context of this goal, work values are the individual's reasons for engaging in productive activity. A person's set of reasons for working and his or her set of valued work characteristics are certainly related, but failure to distinguish between the two has on occasion resulted in attempts to evaluate goal 3 by measuring such things as the importance the student places on a climate-controlled workplace.

Desire to work is most appropriately measured by student report, through either paper and pencil measures or interview data. It may at first appear adequate to measure whether students engage in work, but if this were the case there would be no need to mention desire to work in goal 3 because working behavior is addressed in goal 7. Attitudinal tests which address desire to work include the Employment Readiness Scale, The Survey of Work Values, and Viewpoints on Work. As discussed under goal 2, however, all of these instruments also contain items addressing attitudes other than the desire to work. The Attitude Scale of the Career Maturity Inventory has the same problem, although its items which address attitudes other than desire to work concern a different set of dimensions than the instruments listed above.

One difficulty in constructing scales dealing exclusively with desire to work is that there are only so many ways to ask the question, "Do you want to work?" without the tests' items becoming excessively redundant. One concept which may aid in the construction of a pure desire to work scale is the career education definition of work, encompassing productive activity associated with all life roles rather than solely the work accomplished in conjunction with the individual's primary vocation on which existing instruments tend to concentrate. Another alternative to measuring desire to work is to administer an existing instrument and to analyze separately the responses to selected items.

It could be argued that achievement of goal 3 can be evaluated adequately by measuring desire to work alone, under the assumption that people who desire to work have a good reason for it. On the other hand, positive desire to work evaluation results are made more compelling when reinforced with evidence that the measured desire is founded on enduring values and not simply on temporary circumstance. Furthermore, it is significant that this goal is worded to convey career education's recognition that there are many reasons for working, and the conviction that no single set of reasons (such as those commonly referred to as the Protestant Work Ethic) should be imposed on the individual by the educational system. Rather, the student should be exposed to a broad range of work values and encouraged to make personal decisions concerning values which are meaningful to him or her. Although evaluative judgments should not be placed on these decisions, the sum of the individual's work values should constitute sufficient motivation to engage in productive activity.

Thus, from a career education point of view it is legitimate to measure desire to work through questions with "right" and "wrong" answers, but measuring the work values underlying the desire to work is not so simple—

implying that one value or set of values is more valid than another is contrary to career education philosophy. This poses a problem with many popular instruments used in measuring work-related attitudes because they often address work values, at least to the extent of asking whether financial reward is the *only* reason to work, and whether personal satisfaction and service to others are *good* reasons. Keying such questions as having right and wrong answers is philosophically incongruent with career education, even though the problem is probably not so serious as to invalidate these instruments as desire to work measures so long as values-related items are keyed to conform with the work values held by all or most factions of the community. For example, students' rejection of the attitude that making money is the only good reason for working appears to be valid evidence of their desire to engage in work, especially in unpaid work. On the other hand, measures of desire to work should avoid more controversial values, such as "hard work builds character," not only because career education philosophy proposes no desirable response to that statement, but also because many highly motivated individuals would disagree with it.

The first step in equipping students with personally meaningful sets of work values is usually an exposure to the diverse values held by various cultures and individuals. The effectiveness of this exposure has been evaluated by asking students to list all of the reasons people work. This could be extended to tap the personal meaningfulness to individuals' work values by asking students to check those reasons which they themselves consider important. If we assume that choosing personal values always involves the conscious rejection of other values, the scoring of this question could be dichotomous (0 or 1), with the desirable result being that some, *but not all,* of the values of which the student is aware are reported as personally meaningful.

Another approach to evaluating the personal meaningfulness of work values is based upon the assumption that career education should result in greater diversity in the values held by the individuals comprising a group. Each student is asked to report his or her work values either through structured inventories or open-ended questions, and the appropriate measure of heterogeneity is used to determine whether career education increases the diversity among the sets of work values held by individual students in the group.

There is intuitive appeal in the practice of counting the number of work values students report and assuming that the more values held the better, but this indicator is difficult to defend within the framework of the goals of career education. One problem is that a person with a single compelling reason to work achieves the intent of the goal to the same degree as a person with a larger number of reasons. Another problem is that the value-counting approach skirts the personally meaningful issue altogether; indeed, the students who report possessing the largest number of values may have blindly (though perhaps temporarily) accepted every value to which they were exposed. The same logical inconsistencies are evident in the evaluation criterion of total work value strength when calculated by summing the reported importance of each of several values, and it is difficult to imagine how a direct measure of total work value strength would differ from desire to work measures.

Although the USOE has chosen to avoid the implication that some work values are more valid than others, local career education efforts need not be constrained by this policy. Changes in the strength of particular work values may be appropriately evaluated with existing work values inventories if local objectives specify the values which should increase and those which should decrease. However, there are dangers in establishing such objectives. On one level, value-related objectives could easily conflict with the values of one or more factions of the community. Research reveals other dangers; relationships between employment success and work values vary not only from occupation to occupation but also as a function of a number of cultural and individual variables (New Educational Directions, 1977b). Judgments of the maturity or immaturity of work values can lead to puzzling conclusions, if interactions among work values and other variables are overlooked. For example, based upon the premise that maturity by definition increases with age, the scoring key of the Attitude Scale of the Career Maturity Inventory was empirically derived so that the proportion of correct responses increased monotonically with age, and the majority of twelfth-graders answered "correctly." The scoring key indicates that, "The most important part of work is the pleasure which comes from doing it," is a mature work value, whereas, "I want to really accomplish something of my work—to make a great discovery or earn a lot of money or help a great number of people," is an immature one. There is evidence that possession of the latter value is counterproductive, at least to employment success, if it represents an unrealistic goal for the individual, but the exact opposite is true for those who are capable of attaining it (Hubbard, 1974). It is difficult to conceive of any work value which would be productive for all people in all situations.

Still, it seems that reasonable criteria could be established for judging some work values as more desirable than others—for assigning a higher score to the person who reports "development of my talents" as an important reason for working than to the person whose main reason for working is "to impress my girlfriend." One criterion which would discriminate between those two values is their probability of enduring throughout a lifetime. Evaluations of work values based upon concise and well-conceived standards for judging values along a temporary-permanent dimension would provide validations of "desire to work" data while remaining in harmony with career education's concern for preserving individual choice. Whether such standards could be constructed is another question.

In summary, measuring desire to work poses no serious problems beyond those inherent in any effort to measure the affective domain. Although there is no direct way to measure the personal meaningfulness of work values, several indirect strategies hold promise. There is no apparent rationale for using the number of work values possessed by students as an evaluation criterion. The strength of particular values is a useful criterion only if decisions are made a priori concerning which values are and are not valid, which the USOE has wisely avoided. The only obvious criterion for judging the validity of a value is its likely endurance, but operationalizing this criterion appears to be a difficult task. It seems best at this point to limit evaluations of work values to investigations of increases in group diversity and whether valuing decisions have been made.

4. Equipped with Career Decision-Making Skills, Job-Hunting Skills, and Job-Getting Skills: Career decision-making refers not only to the choice of a career goal, but also to decisions regarding how the goal will be pursued. As used here, career planning means the same thing.

It is congruent with career education philosophy to evaluate secondary programs according to whether students approaching graduation have career plans. However, having a career plan is not sufficient, as career decision-making is viewed as a lifelong developmental process rather than a once-in-a-lifetime ordeal. Since it is both likely and acceptable for today's eighteen year olds to change their career directions a number of times during their lifetimes, competence in the decision-making process itself is a vital skill if these career changes are to be purposeful.

The general career decision-making model is a system, with inputs, processes, and outputs. The inputs are personal information (aptitudes, skills, interests, and values) and career information (knowledge of a variety of career options), and the output is a career plan (not only a career goal, but also plans for achieving it). Thus, decision-making skills could be defined as those associated with the process of integrating personal information with career information in arriving at career plans. More often, though, they are defined more broadly to include the skills of "gathering the inputs into the system"— of becoming self aware and career knowledgeable. Engaging in the decision-making process repeatedly during one's lifetime would make little sense without updating the inputs, which include feedback in the form of outcomes of previous career plans. Also, defining career decision-making skills to include the seeking of personal and career information, as well as the process of sorting and integrating it, has the advantage of recognizing that these steps are far less independent than a systems diagram might suggest.

As they are taught and measured, decision-making skills also include attitudes and beliefs associated with decisions to make career decisions, such as appreciation of the importance of planning ahead, willingness to make one's own decisions rather than to succumb to external pressures, belief in control over one's own destiny, and willingness to reassess prior decisions and to reverse them when the situation warrants. Like several other OE outcome goals, decision-making skills constitute a multidimensional domain, making it especially important to define the goal locally before choosing evaluation instruments in order to avoid mis-matches between measures and programs' efforts. The following discussion will deal primarily with seven scales of two popular instruments which are representative of the most common approaches to measuring the various facets of decision-making skills and associated attitudes. Neither of these instruments was designed specifically for career education evaluation, and thus criticisms of their use for this purpose do not reflect on the instruments themselves.

Four of the Career Maturity Inventory's (CMI) six scales tap elements of career planning skills. The Attitude scale, which has been described as a measure of attitudes toward work, is defined more precisely by its author as including involvement in and conceptions of the career choice process, independence in decision-making, orientation toward work, and work values. It was designed to measure, "the maturity of attitudes that are critical in realistic career decision-making." These attitudes include desire to work and maturity of work values, which relate more specifically to goal 3, but the majority of the scale's fifty items are quite pertinent to career decision-making as defined within the context of the USOE learner outcome goals. Examples of true-false items are: "Your parents probably know better than anybody else which job you should enter"; You should choose an occupation, then plan how to enter it." One caution in using the Attitude scale is that it should not be chosen without first examining the scoring key as well as the items because, as discussed under goal 2, the method of deriving the key resulted in some items whose "correct" responses may conflict with local career education objectives. The scale appears to be a useful tool as it stands but its appropriateness as a career decision-making measure would be enhanced by discarding about 20 percent of the items at the scoring stage.

The CMI's Goal Selection Scale requires the student to select from among several alternatives the occupation best suited to an individual whose interests, experiences, aptitudes, and/or skills are described. For example:

Peter has little interest in school. He would rather be on the move and has had some summer jobs that allowed him to travel. His last one took him across the country as a helper on a moving truck. Before that, he worked for the Department of Public Works, poisoning weeds along the roadside.

As soon as he finishes school, he wants to get a job that he can do right away.
Which one of the following occupations would be the best for him?

a. carpenter
b. animal keeper
c. tree surgeon
d. truck driver
e. don't know

In terms of the general decision-making model, the personal information is given, the career information (the nature of the alternative occupational choices) is assumed, and the task is to process the two in identifying the best career choice. Although the occupational titles are fairly common ones, the contaminating factor of career knowledge puts this scale in question as a measure of decision-making skills per se.

The CMI's Planning Scale, designed to measure foresightedness in career planning, is even more contaminated by career knowledge than the Goal Selection scale. A sample item demonstrates this problem:

Nanette has decided to be an interior decorator. Three steps she can take to become one are:

1. graduate from a school of design
2. finish apprenticeship in a decorating studio
3. attend college for a few years and take courses in interior decoration and related subjects

What is the correct order of these steps?

a. 1 2 3
b. 2 1 3
c. 2 3 1
d. 3 1 2
e. don't know

The scale could be a valid measure of career knowledge, but its common use in evaluating career decision-making skills needs re-examination.

The Problem Solving Scale uses an interesting approach to assessing effectiveness in coping with problems which arise in the course of career development. A sample item is:

Art's friends are going to college after high school, which is what he would like to do. *But,* his girl wants to get married.

What should he do?

a. Move away
b. Talk it over with his girl
c. Go to college; postpone marriage
d. Get married; go to college later
e. Don't know

Many of the items, like the one above, focus on the importance of making one's own decisions rather than responding to the wishes of others. ("c" is the keyed answer.) A few of the items reveal the difficulty of constructing this type of question; insufficient information is given for making well-informed choices among the alternatives. The *best* course of action in these situations would probably be to back up from the information processing stage and collect more "system inputs." Nonetheless, the scale holds promise and the measurement strategy seems worth developing further.

As an aside, another approach which seems reasonable but is somewhat difficult to implement is seen in eleven of the items of the Career Planning Scale of the Career Orientation Battery. These items assume that multiple criteria are considered in making career decisions, and that some criteria should be given greater weight than others. The student is forced to choose the more important of two personal or occupational variables, such as your sex and your grades. The problem with this approach is that it is all too easy to enter into the realm of work values, as in the item requiring a choice between, "how much you would enjoy doing different jobs," and "how much money you would make."

The Assessment of Career Development (ACD) contains three scales often used in evaluating career decision-making skills. The Exploratory Occupational Experiences Scale consists of a list of ninety activities typical of occupations in each of six clusters (sorted mail; ran for a school or club office). The student indicates on a three point scale the number of times he or she has engaged in each activity, and cluster scores as well as total scores are reported. In the terms of the general decision-making model, the scale measures the degree to which students have applied the experiential approach to input data gathering. Although acceptable for most school-based career education programs, it would be a poor choice for experience-based career education (EBCE) or similar exploratory programs because participation in the program would guarantee the student's involvement in a sampling of the activities, thereby rendering the results useless for evaluating the program's impact.

The ACD's Career Planning Involvement Scale applies the same format as the Exploratory Occupational Experiences Scale but the list of experiences reads much like the suggested activities section of a career education curriculum guide: "watched and talked with workers in jobs related to a school subject we were studying"; "took part in an actual or a practice job interview." Although clearly inappropriate as an outcome measure for career education programs, it has promise as a treatment measure.

The forty item Career Planning Knowledge Scale is described accurately in the ACD's technical manual as a sampling of facts, concepts, and understandings useful in career planning and addressing knowledge of basic career development principles, reality factors, and the career planning process. Even though its items address concepts as diverse as the impact of work on one's life and the contents of the *Occupational Outlook Handbook,* the scale's internal consistency is respectable at about .75. Of the measures discussed here, it deserves the highest recommendation for its broad sampling of career decision-making skills and the apparent absence of contaminating variables.

Several of the released exercises used in the National Assessment of Educational Progress Career and Occupational Development (NAEP/COD) surveys concern decision-making skills. Among them are exercises R103002, R103003, and R104003 which ask students to relate their own interests, skills, and school subjects to occupational requirements. In exercise R104009 students are asked to list "ten different things that a person should think about in choosing a career," and in exercise R104011 students list five things they could do now to find out more about a job that interests them. Exercise R104015 is a series of interview questions for determining how much the student knows about the career she or he is considering most seriously. All of these exercises are open-ended; scoring criteria are provided in the NAEP/ COD exercise manual.

One final point should be made regarding decision-making skills measurement. Several years ago it was popular to attempt to evaluate the wisdom of secondary students' career plans by asking students to state their plans and applying various types of external criteria to their soundness. This was due, at least in part, to the wording of the sixth learner outcome goal set forth in the USOE career education policy paper of 1975 (Hoyt, 1975). These attempts resulted in philosophical problems in establishing criteria of "wisdom" as well as in operational difficulties in applying the criteria. Therefore, the 1976 revision of the goal statements included a change in the original goal 6 to clarify the position that it is not appropriate to evaluate whether an individuals' career decisions are reasonable. Rather, we should examine whether they are reasoned.

Job-hunting and getting skills, the other part of goal 4, are readily measurable through paper and pencil knowledge tests as well as direct tests of skills. The Job-Seeking Scale of the Career Orientation Battery consists of true-false questions about sources for finding job openings ("All job openings in a town are advertised in the local newspaper"), job application and follow-up procedures ("Once you have submitted a job application you should wait for the employer to contact you"), and interview behavior ("During an interview you should keep your answers to questions as short and to the point as possible"). Similar tests based upon the local career education curriculum should not be difficult to construct.

Public concern over young people's abilities to complete job application forms makes this skill an important focus of career education evaluations, and involving community resources in the evaluation adds an extra dimension of credibility to the results. The test itself may consist of completing the standard job application blank of a local industry or business. Criteria for scoring each item and item weightings could be established in collaboration with the company's personnel director, while keeping in mind that the object is to measure the ability to complete the form rather than to judge the individual's job qualifications. Appropriate community resource persons may also do the actual scoring.

The National Assessment of Educational Progress Career and Occupational Development exercise R306009 measures the ability to prepare letters of job application. Students respond in writing to their choice among three help wanted ads. The exercise volume describes scoring criteria for both the content and the mechanics of letters.

The PALS Program in Pontiac, Michigan (Jeter, 1976), demonstrated impressive results through a simulation technique for measuring job interview skills. Students were interviewed by local personnel managers who did not know which were in the program and which were in the comparison group. The interviewers rated each student on dimensions such as poise, use of English, personality, and also decided which students to hire.

5. Equipped with a Degree of Self-Understanding and Understanding of Educational-Vocational Opportunities Sufficient for Making Sound Career Decisions: Self-understanding and career knowledge, the inputs into the career decision-making process, will be discussed separately.

Self-understanding or self-awareness is the depth and validity of the individual's perceptions of his or her own aptitudes, skills, interests, and values. It is also the least measurable career education goal. Any direct measure of how well a person knows him/herself must presume that someone else knows him or her even better. This premise is unacceptable, at least for most people and for most of the personal traits relevant to career decision-making.

Nevertheless, self-understanding is an important career education outcome, and wide interest in this goal has generated numerous attempts to measure at least some of its dimensions. No full solution has been or is likely to be found to this measurement problem, but each of the approaches presented below has its merits.

The most popular approach is to evaluate self-esteem or self-acceptance in lieu of self-understanding. Self-esteem inventories involve various forms of self-report of personal attributes on positive-negative scales, where positive self-descriptions indicate high self-esteem. But positive self-descriptions should not be confused with accurate ones, even though there may be a degree of correlation between esteem and understanding. Evaluating self-esteem is acceptable if its improvement is a local objective. Unfortunately, statements like "Self-awareness was measured with the Coopersmith Self-Esteem Inventory" are common in career education evaluation reports.

The Self-Appraisal Scale of the Career Maturity Inventory assumes a relationship between self awareness and the ability to extrapolate from limited data about a fictitious character:

> Bucky is an Explorer Scout and takes part in most of his troop's activities. He enjoys being outdoors and is looking forward to a canoe trip that they have planned. He has learned the names and markings of most of the birds in his area and is interested in nature. He has also been active in efforts to conserve the environment and thinks he'll study ecology in college. What do you think?
>
> a. There is no doubt that he has the interest and ability to be an ecologist.
> b. He should discuss his interests with his scoutmaster and do what he suggests.
> c. His interest in nature is probably only a temporary one, and he shouldn't make plans based on it.
> d. His interest in ecology is developing, and he should follow it, but with the understanding that it may change later on.
> e. Don't know.

Another approach has been to measure the student's willingness to make definitive statements about him or herself without attempting to judge the validity of self descriptions. This type of test consists of a series of questions such as, "Do you like to work with your hands?" and the response options are yes, no, and I don't know. I don't know is scored as incorrect, and either of the other two options is correct.

The elementary and junior high levels of the Career Orientation Battery contain Self-Assessment scales designed to measure introspective behavior through self-report with items such as, "Do you often think about your personality?" Other items on the same scale are based on the belief that some common conclusions are reached by everyone who undergoes self-examination. These common conclusions include: "I am neither worthless nor perfect," and "while I share some traits with other people, I am also unique."

The correlation between self-reports and external measures of personal traits seems to be a sensible indicator of self understanding, but only if the external measure can be assumed to hold greater validity than the self-report. This condition may be met in the case of academic aptitudes and skills, where students predict their percentile rank and the correlation between predicted and actual scores serves as the evaluation criterion. On the other hand, previous feedback from similar tests may contaminate the self-report and make this criterion insensitive to career education programmatic effects. Interest and values inventories could be used in the same way but most of them are constructed so as to guarantee rather high correlations, as the external measure is nothing but a more complex form of the self-report measure. The correlational approach may nonetheless prove useful for assessing self understanding of some aptitudes, skills, interests, and values. However, it should be used only in full recognition that the evaluation involves an uneven sampling of the domain of career-relevant personal characteristics.

Understanding of educational-vocational opportunities or career knowledge, is readily measurable through objective paper and pencil tests. It is usually defined as knowledge of a variety of specific vocations in terms of the nature of the work, working conditions, and lifestyles associated with the work, training, educational requirements and opportunities, and the characteristics of individuals who are most likely to find success and satisfaction in the vocation. Generally, this outcome is evaluated through broad survey tests addressing a wide range of occupations, such as the appropriate scales of the Assessment of Career Development, the Career Development Inventory, or the Career Maturity Inventory.

Broad survey tests make sense at the elementary level, where career education programs are designed to expose students to a wide variety of careers. However, most K-12 career education models indicate that by high school, students are expected to have focused their career interests and their pursuit of career knowledge on some subset of the universe of career options. That is, investigation of career opportunities is individualized at the secondary level, at least to a degree. This makes it reasonable to limit the types of occupations sampled by the knowledge test. Programs designed around one of the many occupational clustering systems may use different tests for students investigating different clusters. For example, a career education program for the gifted and talented in Seattle, Washington (Cox, 1975), developed an occupational knowledge test limited to the two highest level occupational categories of the *Dictionary of Occupational Titles.* Local development of tests for each of the fifteen USOE occupational clusters may be out of the question, but programs with a smaller number of clusters may consider this approach. Broad survey tests of career knowledge are the best choice for programs which are not individualized or are individualized to the point where a different test would be required for virtually every student if the cluster sampling strategy were used.

Not all career knowledge is occupation-specific even though this goal seems to refer primarily to that which is. Some examples of general career information are: the differences between junior colleges and four-year universities; the significance of the Equal Employment Opportunity Act; the meaning of "union shop"; the difference between a commission and a salary. Items measuring general career knowledge are often included in tests dealing primarily with specific occupations. The General Occupational Information Scale of the Career Orientation Battery deals exclusively with concepts of this type.

6. Aware of Means Available to Them for Continuing and Recurrent Education: A review of eighty-one career education evaluation reports from 1975-1976 (New Educational Directions, 1977a) revealed no existing instruments for evaluating outcome 6, but constructing one should not be difficult. On the knowledge level, the test could focus on the various methods for keeping abreast of new developments in one's career field and for developing new skills needed for promotions or occupational changes. Since education is defined as learning rather than as schooling, it extends beyond continuing education or adult courses to include professional reading, attendance at conferences, informal learning from co-workers, formal training sessions offered by employers, and practical experience.

The essence of this goal, however, is the attitude that learning is a lifelong process, not one which terminates on graduation day. Thus, a thorough evaluation of this goal should also address appreciation of the need for continual skill upgrading, the attitude that the new graduate does not know all there is to know about his or her field, and willingness to devote time and effort to ongoing self development. In addition, the behavior of continuing one's education may be measured through follow-up surveys.

7. Either Placed or Actively Seeking Placement in a Paid Occupation, in Further Education, or in a Vocation Consistent with Their Current Career Decisions: Let us first examine who would and would not achieve this goal without the qualifying phrase "consistent with their current career decisions."

A vocation is one's primary work role at any given point in time and includes paid employment, volunteer work, homemaking, and going to school. Thus, the only circumstance under which this goal would not be met is where the school leaver is unemployed, out of school, does not devote a substantial amount of time to volunteer or homemaking work, and is making no effort to become involved in any of these endeavors. Taken literally, the goal is met by the person who is actively seeking a spouse in order to become a full-time homemaker. Allowing such extremes, few people would fail to meet the goal of being in possession or pursuit of a vocation, limiting the goal's usefulness as an evaluation criterion. However, two approaches may be taken to strengthen the criterion.

Other educational goals, such as those of a vocational education program, may impose more stringent criteria of success after leaving the program. Where this is the case, follow-up study data are appropriately evaluated according to these criteria.

Where this is not the case it may be appropriate to deal with unemployed non-students by focusing on whether they perceive themselves as having a vocation, thus avoiding the problem of deciding how much homemaking or volunteer work constitutes a vocation. Those who perceive themselves as having no vocation should then be asked whether they are seeking one.

The "consistent with current career decisions" part of the goal seems to call for follow-up data which focus not on current vocational status but on the relationship between present endeavors and career goals. One approach is to ask "What are you doing these days," "What is your career goal," and "What, if anything, does what you're doing have to do with your career goal?" If the last question is not asked and judgment of the relationship is left to the evaluator, relationships may be overlooked. For example, the recent graduate who is currently a masseuse and wants to become a ceramics engineer may be working to save money for college, but this would not be readily apparent from answers to the first two questions.

This measurement strategy—and, indeed, the goal itself—assumes that the school leaver has current career goals. Without them, the outcome goal cannot be achieved. There are, therefore, three conditions to the goal, all of which must be met by individuals acclaimed as successful career education program products: possession or active pursuit of a vocation, possession of a career goal, and a relationship between the two.

8. Actively Seeking to Find Meaning and Meaningfulness Through Work in Productive Use of Leisure Time: Work is conscious effort at producing benefits for oneself or for oneself and others. Leisure consists of activities, other than sleeping, in which one engages when not performing her or his vocation. A vocation is one's primary work role at any given point in time.

One purpose of this goal is to recognize that few people can realistically expect to satisfy through their vocation all of the needs stemming from their personal work values. In order to live in harmony with their work values most people therefore must engage in work other than that performed as part of their vocations. Under this interpretation of the goal's intent the evaluation question becomes, "Is the individual actively seeking to satisfy all of his/her needs to work through either vocational or avocational activities or a combination of the two?" This could be evaluated by asking students or former students to: (1) list their work values or to choose from a comprehensive list of work values the ones representing their own needs for work; (2) describe their vocational and avocational activities associated with each value; and (3) explain these matches. Scoring could be dichotomous—the individual either is or is not doing something about all of her or his needs for work. This approach could also be modified to account for the degree to which individuals' needs are satisfied.

Other interpretations of the goal focus more specifically on the productiveness of students' use of leisure time. This outcome could be evaluated by asking students to list their leisure time activities of the past week or so, and evaluating the productiveness of the activities according to some set of pre-established criteria. The problem is formulating the criteria. In light of the career education definition of work, which by implication defines productivity, the criteria must classify as productive those activities of benefit only to the individual performing them, as well as activities of benefit to others. Any pre-established set of criteria for "productive for oneself" assumes that we know what individuals need and that everyone needs the same things. These assumptions are difficult to defend.

However, the productiveness of reported leisure activities could be evaluated against the student's own goals. Students could be asked to list their long and short-term goals related to all of their life roles (not just their primary work role) and to describe which goals, if any, were served by each of their recent leisure activities. The evaluation criterion could be the proportion of leisure time spent in goal-oriented activities.

One other possibility for evaluating this goal is to focus on "actively seeking" rather than on productivity. That is, are students bored in their leisure time or do they engage in satisfying activities? Do they exercise conscious choice in their use of time, do they seek out new endeavors, or are they creatures of habit? It seems that behaviors such as these and/or the attitudes associated with them should be measurable by self report.

9. Aware of Means Available to Themselves for Changing Career Options— of Societal and Personal Constraints Impinging on Career Alternatives: The history of this goal helps to clarify its meaning. The 1975 USOE policy for career education set forth nine learner outcome goals. In 1976, the members of a panel convened by the Office of Career Education for reviewing the 1975 goals pointed out that something important was missing. The goals said quite a lot about helping the individual to adjust to society and to cope with reality. Yet there was nothing said specifically about developing the individual's capacity to change reality, to overcome the obstacles society may place in her or his career path, to alleviate the inequities of the status quo. This goal was added in order to fill this gap.[8] The panel did not discuss how this goal might be measured, but several measureable outcomes seem to fit the goal well.

One such outcome is the elimination of sex role stereotyping, one of the most pervasive constraints on career alternatives. Within the context of career education, the appropriate focus is the degree to which the individual allows his or her sex to limit personal career alternatives. The Sex Equity Scale of the Career Orientation Battery consists of items scattered throughout the test to measure the objective: "Students will regard gender as irrelevant in matters pertaining to career planning, preparation, and employment." An evaluation technique which demonstrated the success of the PALS program in Michigan involved asking students to indicate how much thought they had given to pursuing each of a number of occupations on a five-point scale ranging from "have not given thought" (to pursuing this career) to "have definite plans and know how to carry out" (my pursuit of this career). Separate scores were computed for male, female, and nonstereotyped jobs. Boys' and girls' scores were then compared for each category, with the result that the students' sex was unrelated to the kinds of occupations they had considered. This strategy and modifications of it hold promise for evaluating efforts to eliminate not only sex stereotyping but also stereotyping by race, ethnicity, and handicapping conditions.

Yet another set of stereotypes which career education clearly wishes to eliminate concerns age. Internalization of the concept of career development as a lifelong process should, for example, lead to the attitude that one is never too old to change the direction of her or his career path.

Internality or locus of control—the degree to which individuals perceive themselves as having control over themselves and their environments as contrasted to being controlled by external forces—is another criterion for goal 9. The Children's Nowicki-Strickland Internal-External Control Scale is probably the most appropriate one for teenagers. Locus of control measures require particularly careful review because they often include items which, indeed, are beyond the individual's control. Thus, a high external score on some locus of control measures may indicate unrealistic perceptions rather than awareness of one's potential for shaping one's own life and environment.

Finally, evaluations of this goal may focus on the first clause, "aware of means available," by testing students' knowledge of sources of career counseling for adults, sources of financial assistance and training needed for changing jobs, and sources of help for those discriminated against because of race, sex, handicaps, and age.

Future Directions for Career Education Evaluation

The preceding analysis demonstrates that a potential exists for measuring most aspects of all of the USOE learner outcome goals. A reasonable selection of instruments is already available for: reading, language, and mathematical skills (goal 1); some aspects of work-related attitudes (goals 2 and 3); some definitions of decision-making and job-seeking skills (goal 4); self-esteem (goal 5); and knowledge of a wide variety of career options (goal 5). However, saying that there are nine career education goals is inaccurate. Several of the goal statements, such as goal 4, list two or more distinctively different outcomes. Within outcomes there are alternate interpretations and multiple objectives, each requiring unique measures. A need still exists for measures for some objectives associated with goals 1-5, as well as for measures of goals 6-9.

If we are to meet these needs, we must be willing to think beyond the forced-choice test with right and wrong answers. Some facets of career education learning are best measured behaviorally, in either natural or simulated settings. Others can be measured with paper and pencil or interview data, but by evaluating student responses in new ways—for example, by evaluating the relationships between the individual's goals and actions rather than evaluating the goals and actions themselves.

Developing and testing new measures is a high priority for career education evaluation, but it is not the only one. Collecting data needed for establishing standards of acceptable performance at high school graduation is also an important task. Only when we know how good an eighteen year old's basic skills, work habits, and career knowledge must be for him or her to be reasonably assured of success in a career in agribusiness, for example, will we be able to say whether our agribusiness students have been given enough help in these areas.

Longitudinal studies of career educated individuals would be ideal for this purpose, while also fulfilling two other needs. First, they would indicate the effectiveness of career education programs in meeting the movement's overriding goal, expressed in OCE's definition of career education as, "to make work a meaningful, productive, and satisfying part of (the individual's) way of living." Appropriate criteria of long-term success include measures of job entry, career advancement, and, perhaps most important, work satisfaction (including leisure-time work). Second, longitudinal studies are needed to validate not only career education measures, but the goals themselves. For example, it seems reasonable that career decision-making skills should enhance future career success, but research results to confirm this are lacking.

Another task of advancing career education evaluation rests more on the shoulders of career education conceptualizers and practitioners than on evaluators and researchers. The OCE learner outcome goals are conceptual statements, designed to accommodate diverse operational definitions of the concepts. This is particularly true for the ninth goal, whose potential meanings are just beginning to be explored. At both national and local levels much progress has been made toward defining precisely the purposes of career education, but much work still remains. It is imperative that career educators take the initiative in setting career education objectives, and that evaluators insist that the objectives be established before choosing evaluation criteria. Like it or not, evaluators generate expectations for new educational programs through their choice of outcomes to evaluate. To avoid creating inappropriate expectations for career education, evaluators must make certain that the goals are defined first by career education programs rather than by career education evaluation.

NOTES

1. Statistically nonsignificant results mean that we have no evidence that there are generalizable differences. This does not mean that there are no differences; it may mean only that we failed to detect them.

2. Only eleven available instruments (many of them multiscaled) are referenced herein, but there are many others. Those used in forty-five evaluations performed in the 1975-1976 academic year are listed along with gross indices of their sensitivity to career education instruction in *What Does Career Education Do For Kids?: A Synthesis of 1975-76 Evaluation Results* (1977). New Educational Directions, Inc., Office of Career Education, USOE.

A series of five handbooks for career education evaluation includes the following collection of abstracts of about 200 available measures: *Career Education Measures: A Compendium of Evaluation Instruments* (1978). N. L. McCaslin, Charles J. Gross, and Jerry P. Walker. The Center for Vocational Education of the Ohio State University.

3. Complete references to the instruments follow the *References* at the end of this chapter.

4. Viewpoints on Work.

5. The Survey of Work Values.

6. Self-Appraisal Inventory.

7. Viewpoints on Work.

8. In 1977 the fifth goal of the 1976 version was dropped, leaving the present nine goals.

REFERENCES

Cox, W. W. 1976. *Final Report: Career Education for Gifted and Talented Students.* U.S.O.E. Grant No. G0075-02316, Highline Public Schools #401, 15675 Ambaum Blvd. S.W., Seattle, WA.

Datta, L. 1977. "Some observations on the status of evaluations and of evaluating career education." Presented to the Inter-institutional consortium for Career Education.

Hoyt, K. B. 1977. *A Primer for Career Education.* Monographs on Career Education. Washington, DC: Office of Education.

——— 1976. *Perspectives on the Problem of Evaluation in Career Education.* Monographs on Career Education. Washington, DC, Office of Education.

——— 1975. *An Introduction to Career Education: A Policy Paper of the U.S. Office of Education.* Washington, DC: DHEW. Publication No. (OE) 75-00504.

Hubbard, R. L. 1974. *Future Achievement Orientations: Job Training and Economic Success.* (ED 103-642)

Jeter, K. 1976. *Final Report: Pontiac Adult Student Learning System.* USOE grant No. 0-73-5287. School District of the City of Pontiac, Pontiac, MI.

McCaslin, N. L., Gross, C. J., and Walker, J. P. 1978. *Career Education Measures: A Compendium of Evaluation Instruments.* Columbus: The Center for Vocational Education, Ohio State University.

New Educational Directions 1977a. *What does Career Education do for Kids?: A Synthesis of 1975-76 Evaluation Results.* Washington, DC: Office of Education.

——— 1977b. *Work Attitudes and Employment.* The Indiana State Board of Vocational-Technical Education, Research Coordinating Unit, Grant No. 13-76-C-1.

RMC Research Corporation 1975. *A practical guide to measuring project impact on student achievement.* (ED 106 376)

Young, M. B., and Schuh, R. G. 1975. *Evaluation and Educational Decision-Making: A Functional Guide to Evaluating Career Education.* Washington, DC: Office of Education. (ED 117 185)

REFERENCED
TESTS

Assessment of Career Development
  Dale Prediger, John Roth, and Bert Westbrook
  Houghton Mifflin
  One Beacon Street
  Boston, Massachusetts 02107
  1974
Career Development Inventory
  Donald E. Super, Martin J. Bohn, Jr., David J. Forrest,
  Jean Pierre Jordaan, Richard H. Lindeman, and Albert S. Thompson
  Teachers College
  Columbia University
  New York, New York 10027
  1976
Career Maturity Inventory
  John O. Crites
  CTB McGraw Hill
  Del Monte Research Park
  Monterey, California 93940
  1973
Career Orientation Battery
  New Educational Directions
  Box 307
  Crawfordsville, Indiana 47933
  1976
Children's Nowicki-Strickland Internal-External Control Scale
  Stephen Nowicki and B. R. Strickland
  The Psychological Center
  Department of Psychology

Emory University
Atlanta, Georgia 30322
1970
Coopersmith Self-Esteem Inventory
Stanley Coopersmith
Self Esteem Institute
1736 Stockton Street
San Francisco, California 94133
Employment Readiness Scale
Anthony M. Alfano
2518 Texel Drive
Kalamazoo, Michigan 49001
1973
National Assessment of Educational Progress Career and Occupational Development Technical Report: Exercise Volume. Career and Occupational Development Report No. 05-COD-20
NAEP
Suite 700, 1860 Lincoln Street
Denver, Colorado 80295
Roy H. Forbes, Director
1977
Available from GPO
Self-Appraisal Inventory
Instructional Objectives Exchange
P.O. Box 24095
Los Angeles, California 90024
1970
Survey of Work Values, Form U
Patricia C. Smith, Stephen Wollach, James G. Goodale and Jan P. Wijting
Psychology Department
Bowling Green State University
Bowling Green, Ohio 43403
1975
Viewpoints on Work
New Educational Directions
Box 307
Crawfordsville, Indiana 47933
1977

chapter 19

CAROL KEHR TITTLE | *University of North Carolina
at Greensboro*

Evaluators of vocational education programs find that career guidance and counseling activities are often components of these programs. At both the secondary and postsecondary levels, career guidance frequently includes the use of career interest measures. Evaluators will be familiar with the standard technical requirements for these measures, such as those of reliability and validity that are described in test reviews published in Buros (1972). The recent Vocational Education Act (VEA) in the Education Amendments of 1976, and Title IX[1] of the Education Amendments of 1972 have brought another issue to the attention of evaluators. Title IX mandates that tests and materials used by counselors or teachers in guidance must be nondiscriminatory. Educational institutions at all levels need to determine whether a test or other measure is sex-biased. They need to examine whether or not the use of an interest inventory may result in occupations or interest areas being suggested to girls for exploration that are different from those suggested to boys, for example. Evaluators of career activities in vocational programs must, therefore, be concerned with documenting the sex-fairness of interest measures and guidance activities.

The VEA of 1976 sets forth the policy of equal access for minorities and women to programs funded under the legislation and, in fact, requires states to set forth the specific actions taken to overcome sex discrimination, and to specify the incentives adopted to encourage enrollment of both women and men in nontraditional courses of study. The state plan is also to include model programs developed to reduce sex bias and sex stereotyping in training

AUTHOR'S NOTE: *The author acknowledges the helpful critiques of earlier versions of this chapter by Esther E. Diamond and Ted Abramson.*

programs and placement in all occupations (Section 104.187, Federal Register, 1977). Federally funded programs, as well as Local Education Agencies' (LEAs) programs must be concerned with eliminating discrimination based on sex, and with providing sex fair counseling and guidance activities and materials.

The next section of this chapter defines sex bias in career interest measurement, and describes the National Institute of Education (NIE) guidelines that may be used to assist the evaluator in determining whether these measures are discriminatory on the basis of sex.[2] These topics are followed by a summary of recent research that has implications for evaluation, and recommendations for process and outcome measures in evaluating sex fairness in counseling and guidance activities.

THE NIE GUIDELINES

The National Institute of Education in 1974 sponsored the development of *Guidelines for Assessment of Sex Bias and Sex Fairness in Career Interest Inventories.* The guidelines were developed by the NIE Education and Work staff, a senior consultant, and a nine member planning group, and discussed in a workshop conference whose participants represented inventory users, authors, publishers, and the public. As Diamond (1975: p. xxiii) describes the process, the working definition of sex bias used in the development of the guidelines was:

> Within the context of career guidance, sex bias is defined as any factor that might influence a person to limit—or might cause others to limit— his or her consideration of a career solely on the basis of gender

This definition is consonant with the definition of sex discrimination used in the VEA of 1976 (Federal Register, 1977: 104.73[c]):

> "Sex discrimination" means any action which limits or denies a person or a group of persons opportunities, privileges, roles, or rewards on the basis of their sex.

The working definition of sex bias cited by Diamond was used to consider several aspects of interest measurement—the inventory itself, technical information, and the interpretive information that accompanies the inventory. The NIE Guidelines are summarized below.[3]

(1) The inventory itself.
  (a) The same form should be used for women and men unless it is empirically shown that separate forms minimize bias.

  (b) Scores should be given on all occupations and interest areas for both women and men.
  (c) Item pools at the inventory and scale levels should reflect experiences and activities equally familiar to each sex.
  (d) Occupational titles should be in gender-neutral terms, or both male and female titles should be present.
  (e) Use of the generic "he" should be eliminated.
(2) Technical information.
  (a) Technical manuals should describe how the inventory meets these guidelines.
  (b) The rationale for separate scales by sex or combined sex scales should be given.
  (c) The same vocational areas should be indicated for each sex even if it is empirically demonstrated that separate inventory forms are more effective in minimizing sex bias.
  (d) Sex composition of the criterion and norm groups should be described.
  (e) Criterion and norm data should be updated every five years.
  (f) The information on career options distributions suggested for each sex should be provided.
  (g) The validity of interest inventories for minority groups should be investigated.
(3) Interpretive information.
  (a) Interpretive materials should point out that vocational interests and choices of women and men are influenced by many environmental and cultural factors, including early socialization, sex-role expectations, and home-versus career conflict.
  (b) Orientation to the inventory should encourage respondents to examine stereotypic sets toward activities and occupations.
  (c) The users' manual should state that all jobs are appropriate for qualified persons of either sex and should attempt to dispel myths about women and men based on sex-role stereotypes.
  (d) Interpretive materials should encourage exploratory experiences in areas where interests have not had a chance to develop.
  (e) Case studies and examples should represent men and women equally, and include examples of each in nonstereotypic roles.[4]

Many of the guidelines apply to interest inventories and accompanying manuals regardless of whether the inventories have occupational scales or homogeneous scales. These two types of scales refer to the methods of scale construction traditionally used for interest inventories. Occupational scales are based on the empirically-determined relationship between the interests expressed by the taker of the interest inventory and those of individuals already employed in different occupations. Two examples of this type of scale are the occupational scales of the Strong-Campbell Interest Inventory (SCII), and those of the Kuder Occupational Interest Survey DD (KOIS).

Homogeneous scales, scales based on internal criteria, are developed through some form of clustering items—similar types of activities for a job or interest areas, the theory of the test constructor, or perhaps sorting by judges. The responses of the test taker are reported for scales internal to the instrument—developed by factor analysis or logical assignment. Examples of instruments with homogeneous scales are Holland's Self-Directed Search (SDS), the American College Testing Program Interest Inventory (ACT), and the Ohio Vocational Interest Survey (OVIS).

The majority of the guidelines provide direct aid to the evaluator in reviewing interest measures used in vocational education programs. For example, checking that the same inventory form is given to both girls and boys (Guideline 1a), and that each person taking the inventory receives the scores for all the scales in the inventory (Guideline 1b) are readily done. Similarly, reviewing the inventory and accompanying interpretive and technical manuals for elimination of the generic "he," for gender-neutral language (e.g., firefighter, letter carrier, and flight attendant), and case studies representing both men and women is also straightforward. More attention is required to determine the "affirmative" spirit of the interpretive material: Is there a discussion of the likely relationship between experience and interests? How is attention drawn to the effects of socialization and sex role expectations in this culture? What implications are given and what suggestions are made to encourage both girls and boys to explore and undertake activities that are traditionally viewed as appropriate only to the opposite sex?

Guideline 1b, scores should be given on all occupations for both women and men, applies to the interest inventories with occupational scales. Both the SCII and the KOIS, for example, use the same set of items for the basic inventory, yet the criterion or occupational groups are constructed separately by sex. On the SCII there is an occupational scale for physician(m) and physician(f) on the profile form for test results. These scales are constructed on the basis of responses of a group of male and female physicians, respectively. Response differences between the occupational group and the men or women-in-general groups are used to derive the scale scores. The profile reports both scores, asterisking the same sex score (i.e., an asterisk appears by the physician (f) for a girl's profile). This practice reinforces the stereotype of sex differences in occupations, and is presently justified only by item data which show sex differences in response rates for example, items such as the following show differences (Stebbins, Ames, and Rhodes, 1975): "Would you like to race automobiles?"

Response Rates

Response	Male race drivers	Female race drivers
Like	95%	95%

Indifferent	5%	5%
Dislike	0%	0%

	Men-in-general	*Women-in-general*
Like	75%	10%
Indifferent	20%	10%
Dislike	5%	80%

Occupational scales on the SCII are constructed by examining the differences in responses for members of an occupational criterion group from a sample of men-in-general or women-in-general. In the example here, the responses of male race drivers are not very different from those of a representative sample of men (men-in-general). When a male responds "like" to the item, there is little here to distinguish him from male "race drivers." However, when a woman responds positively, she has given an unusual response, one that differentiates her from women-in-general and that is similar to female "race drivers." This type of item response means that the item would appear on the female-normed scale for race driver, but the item would not be used for the male-normed scale for race driver.[5]

The KOIS does not use men-in-general and women-in-general groups in constructing occupational scales. Differences in occupational scales for men and women reflect directly the response differences between women and men in the same occupation. Scores on cross-sex scales for the KOIS (same-named occupational scales for females and males) reflect directly any sex differences in responses, therefore. On the SCII, however, with the use of the in-general groups for scale construction, the more traditional a woman's interests are, the less likely she is to respond the way the men-in-general group does, and therefore, the higher her score on male-normed scales is likely to be (for traditionally female occupations). Conversely, on the KOIS, women will often get *lower* scores on cross-sex norms than on their own (same sex) norms.[6]

The items in the item pools currently used for instruments with occupational scales were not examined for sex bias when originally constructed. That is, the items were not selected to be equally desirable by a general sample of both females and males. In the absence of this criterion for item selection, the development of new occupational scales is limited to items that are already in the item pool and which vary on this characteristic. As one example, Johansson and Harmon (1972) examined items common to the earlier Strong Vocational Interest Blank (SVIB) for females and males—two separate forms—for fourteen occupational criterion groups. They found between 15 percent to 21 percent of these items represented sex-stereotypic responses only, and hence were not valid in differentiating occupationally-related differences. As they suggested, the ultimate goal for the SVIB and the SCII is a set of scales that do not incorporate sex differences. This goal, stated in Guideline 1c, that item pools reflect experiences and activities equally familiar to each sex, is not met for the SCII. (The guideline has been met with some homogeneous scales described below.) As a result, the evaluator must carefully examine the interpretive materials and the guidance setting for steps taken to counter the sex stereotyping that remains in the instrument.

Guideline 1c, however, has been largely met with the item pool for one of the interest inventories with homogeneous scales—an experimental form of the ACT, the Unisex Interest Inventory (Uni II). Rayman (1976) examined the ACT IV items for sex differences, had sex-balanced items written (i.e., items likely to exhibit 10 percent or less difference in "like" responses between the sexes), and constructed the Uni II. This instrument was administered along with the ACT IV to 3,000 college-bound students. The results showed the average differences between males and females (percentage of "like" responses) was much smaller for the Uni II than for the ACT IV. There were no significant differences between raw score means for the sexes in the Realistic, Artistic, and Conventional Scales; statistical (but not practical) differences were found for the Investigative and Enterprising Scales. The sex balance was least well achieved for the Social Scale. Hanson and Rayman (1978) pursued this development and examined validity-related analyses. They concluded that the sex-balanced scales were generally valid, as measured against the ACT IV.

Guideline 2f is concerned with another aspect of the homogeneous scales— the distribution of career options suggested for each sex. For example, are careers in the interest areas of science suggested in the same proportion (overall frequency) to both boys and girls? Ideally, for sex-fair counseling, the proportion should be the same. Hanson and Rayman have demonstrated that the same raw score means can be achieved using sex-balanced items. However, with the usual unbalanced item pools, this equality does not occur and, therefore, raw scores are "normed" (adjusted to within-sex means and S.D.s, and placed on a scale with the same M and SD for each interest area). This procedure highlights another controversy, because unequal distributions of suggested options result for the sexes unless same-sex norms are used.

Hanson, Noeth, and Prediger (1978) also examined four ways of reporting scores: interest profiles based on (a) raw scores, (b) combined sex norms, (c) same sex norms, or (d) opposite sex norms. Their samples were tested with either the VIP or ACT (1970 or 1972) and followed up in college in 1975. They concluded that same sex-norms provided results showing criterion-related validity as high as or higher than the other procedures, and same sex norms offered the additional advantage of suggesting similar vocational options to females and males (Guideline 2f). (See also Prediger and Hanson, 1977, for similar conclusions.)

Gottfredson and Holland (1975) presented a study in which the use of the SDS raw scores appeared to be more efficient predictors of self-reported occupational choices (one to three year follow-up) than sex-specific norms. Holland (1977) has pointed out that interest inventories have multiple purposes—exploration and prediction—and that some may function better than others for each purpose, as part of the justification for using raw scores with the SDS.

Prediger and Cole (1975) argued strongly for a different criterion, and examined the relationship between sex-role socialization, employment data, and interest inventories. Although not specifically taken up as an issue in the NIE Guidelines (except in Guideline 2f), the issue may be resolved in evaluation by checking whether both types of information are reported to the student in vocational guidance. That is, if both the same-sex and opposite-sex norms (or both raw scores and normed scores) on any homogeneous scales are reported, students can question and explore whether response differences are due to sex-role socialization and limited experience, or to genuine differences in their interests as individuals. Recent recommendations of the Office of Civil Rights (OCR) and the AMEG Sex Bias Commission include providing scores on both sets of norms for everyone. This permits individuals to determine how they rank with others of their own sex exposed to similar socialization experiences, and how they rank with individuals of the opposite sex (E.E. Diamond, personal communication, February 1978).

For the SDS, which reports only raw scores for each scale, the evaluator has no easy path to a judgment of equal access to occupational programs. The distributions of suggested areas for career exploration do differ by sex (reflecting the current occupational segregation patterns). The Holland scales reflect socialization practices, and women tend to score highest on the Social and Artistic scales and very low on the Realistic scale. The pattern of sex differences does not meet definitions of sex-fairness in counseling. Without extensive supplementary interpretive materials for the student and career guidance staff, a likely conclusion is that a vocational education program should not rely on the SDS by itself in career guidance.

The other guidelines in the technical information area are more easily evaluated. The evaluator can check to see if the technical manual contains a section on how the interest inventory meets the guidelines (Guideline 2a), whether there is a rationale given for the use of separately normed scales for females and males or whether combined sex scales are used (Guideline 2b), and whether the same vocational areas are suggested to each sex (Guideline 2c). Similarly, it is easy to check whether the criterion and norm groups are identified as to composition—female, male, or combined groups—and whether the date of data collection for these groups is given and is within the last five years (2d and 2e). For example, Lunneborg and Lunneborg (n.d.) checked this guideline for occupational criterion groups on the SCII. They counted the number of SCII groups tested in 1968 or later and found 67 of the 124 criterion groups did not meet this criterion. There was a 1942 female dentist group and 1953 social work samples for both sexes. Use of the NIE guidelines by evaluators will encourage test publishers to update their samples or to periodically use small samples to check for any significant changes in responses.

The last technical guideline is one for which limited information exists: Guideline 2g recommends the investigation of the validity of interest inventories for minority groups. Gump and Rivers (1975) reviewed the literature for validity studies for black women and found little direct evidence.[7] They concluded that the validity of current inventories with occupational scales constructed on white samples predominantly, was questionable. Lamb (1979), however, studied the validity of the ACT Interest Inventory for classifying students into educational major groups, for both females and males of five ethnic groups. Lamb found the structure of interests was comparable across the white and minority samples, with the exception of native American (Indian) males. The accuracy of classification was comparable for most minority groups. Lamb's sample consisted of college seniors, however, and it is not clear to what extent these findings would generalize to the secondary level. Evaluators may again have to look to the interpretive materials and the career guidance activities to make a determination of sex fairness, because technical data to support sex fairness for minority group women are not likely to be available.

The guidelines for interpretive information should be applied to both the materials for school staff, such as a Test User's or Interpretive Manual, and to the profiles or interpretive leaflets that students receive with score reports. The evaluator needs to determine that both the student and counselor materials, for example, point out that vocational interests and choices of women and men are influenced by cultural factors such as early sex-role socialization and sex-role expectations (Guideline 3a). Does the interpretive material make clear that all jobs are appropriate for qualified persons of either sex (Guideline 3c)? Is the next step for students to identify occupational or interest areas where they have not had any experience, and to explore these areas to see whether interests may develop if the individual is given an opportunity for exploratory or compensatory experiences (Guideline 3d)? The evaluator can also check case studies and examples given in these materials to be sure that both females and males are represented equally, and that not all the mechanics are males and the secretaries all females, for example. A number of publishers have improved interpretive materials since the publication of the NIE Guidelines (AMEG, 1977).

In summary, the evaluator will find that the NIE Guidelines are valuable reminders for checking interest inventories and accompanying materials in career guidance for sex-fairness, because sex-fairness is a major step in guaranteeing equal access to programs and employment opportunities under the VEA of 1976. The next section examines recent research studies that have implications for evaluators of career guidance activities in vocational education programs.

RECENT RESEARCH IN INTEREST MEASUREMENT AND EVALUATION

Two implications of recent research on sex bias in interest measurement for evaluation are examined here: (1) the development of new or local interest measures and activities checklists; and (2) the impact of career interest inventories on career choice. In the area of interest measurement, one primary source of sex bias in the development of local measures is the use of a pool of items or activities that are stereotyped for females and males in our culture. The best way to check for such bias is to examine the "desirability" of each item for representative samples of females and males, separately, and to use items that overall appear equally preferred or liked by each sex. This caveat applies whether the scales to be developed are homogeneous or occupational (empirically keyed to occupational group members).

The work by Hanson and Rayman (1978) indicates that it is possible to construct item pools that include items which are chosen by female and male college students with approximately the same frequency. They were relatively successful in developing and selecting items for five of the six Holland-type homogeneous scale areas. The area in which they were least successful was that representing the Social area. It is likely that similar results could be obtained for check lists and local interest inventories developed for the use of students served by vocational education programs. Therefore, evaluators and local staff should be aware of the need for determining the overall equality in preferences or in liking particular activities for each sex. Unless items are examined for sex bias, interpretations of test results and evaluation of program effects will not be clear; program effects may be confounded with irrelevant sex differences.

The second area is of direct concern to evaluators also—an examination of the impact of career interest inventories on career choice. There is an extensive body of literature that examines predictive validity—the relationship between scores on an interest inventory and later occupational status—for several of the major interest inventories.[8] However, the effect to be examined here is more properly called *exploration validity* (Tittle, 1979), and is of more immediate concern in evaluation where this may be a major reason for the use of interest inventories. That is, to what extent is the career interest inventory useful in stimulating the student to explore—to seek information about occupations new to the student and to try new activities that may be related to career choice? The impact of career interest inventories here is focused on the interpretive materials provided with the inventory results and guidance activities as a stimulus to exploration.

Recent research results suggest that the evaluator should focus on these effects, and that test publishers and career guidance staff should be designing interpretive material for interest inventory results that encourage more career exploration. Holland (1975, 1977) and Holland, Takai, Gottfredson, and Hanau (1978) have summarized exploration-related validity studies (using experimental designs and the SDS) for the number and types of occupations considered by clients that support the use of the SDS for exploration. Cooper (1976) compared other materials, using a control group design. She examined the effects of the SCII, a nonsexist Vocational Card Sort (VCS, Dewey, 1974), and auxiliary materials designed to make women respondents aware of myths and realities of women in the world of work. For her sample of college women some differences were found. The VCS was more effective in broadening career options and increasing the frequency with which women students read occupational information. The differential effects of interest inventories and other materials have direct implications for evaluation. Evaluators can suggest examining such effects in formative evaluation. And the criteria of number of career options considered and pursuit of occupational information are some of the outcome variables that evaluators may use. Also, any analysis should test for differential treatment or program effects for female and male students.

Takai and Holland (1978) have also examined the effects of the VCS, the SDS, and the Vocational Exploration and Insight Kit (VEIK), a combination of the VCS, the SDS, and a plan for exploration activities. In a sample of 241 high school girls, there were no significant differences between the effects of the VCS and the SDS on the variety of occupations criterion, and the SDS was more effective than the combination treatment, the VEIK. No significant differences were obtained on a satisfaction scale criterion. Other criteria examined but not used in the MANOVA were pre-post measures on the number of occupations considered, satisfaction with choice, and the variety of information-seeking activities (self-reported). A no-treatment group was not included in the design. The study does suggest other outcome variables for evaluators. This study and the Holland et al. (1978) study also indicate that further refinement of criteria is needed. Oliver (1977) summarized research on modes of test interpretation and listed additional criteria such as accuracy of self knowledge, certainty of choice, and realism of choice. These criteria do not seem as relevant as the exploration-related criteria (also reported in Oliver's study).

Another research study with implications for evaluation of vocational education programs with career interest inventories is that by Cole (1973). Cole examined the vocational interests of women as expressed on the SVIB-W, the Vocational Preference Inventory (VPI), and the KOIS (for the KOIS only 9 scales constructed on males but scored for women were used, since the women's occupation scales were felt to be too limited in type of occupations represented). In her study, an intercorrelation matrix of occupational scale scores or VPI scale scores was analyzed, with the final analysis representing the configuration of the scores in a two-dimensional plane. The results showed a circular hexagonal configuration which orders the domain of vocational interests and occupational scales—Realistic, Investigative, Artistic, Social, Enterprising, and Conventional (using Holland's typology).

Cole suggested that by locating a woman's interests within the observed circular structure, similarities can be shown not only with the location of women's occupations but also with men's occupations at a corresponding location in the structure for men. Cole strongly recommended that the interest inventory scales be used only to locate a woman's interests on the circular structure or the primary categories of the structure. Lists of both men's and women's occupations that relate to that location should then be used. The implications for evaluators are that interpretive materials relating interest inventory scores to the broad domain of occupations are an addition to career inventories that may lessen the effect of "biased" item pools and separate criterion groups for occupations. This is one of a set of criteria that evaluators may use to collect data and reach judgments of sex bias in career guidance activities, including interest inventories. Additional criteria are discussed next.

EVALUATION AND SEX FAIRNESS IN CAREER GUIDANCE

The discussion thus far has concentrated on sex bias and interest measures. This section will consider criteria for examining sex bias in career guidance activities more generally. The recommendations for criteria are in two categories, process measures and outcome (impact) measures.

a. Process Measures: Some process measures have been described in the NIE Guidelines. Examination and evaluation of the interest inventory, the technical manual, and interpretive/profile materials are part of the process evaluation. Similar evaluation of career guidance books, workbooks for students, films, and other audiovisual materials for sex bias can be carried out by the evaluator, or groups of students and teachers using checklists or counting forms. These forms should ensure that similar materials are available for both sexes, or that different materials for one sex or the other are intended to ensure "affirmative action" rather than continued sex discrimination. The checklist should include ratings or counts on such characteristics as: language usage, illustrations, case studies, and presentation of nontraditional roles and occupations for each sex. (See Harway and Astin, 1977; Vetter, 1975; and Saario, Jacklin, and Tittle, 1973, for sample guidelines that can be adapted for evaluation.)

Other process measures should examine counselor and vocational teacher statements and career guidance/classroom documents for sex bias, as well as access to counselors and specific occupational programs. Is there equal access to guidance counselors and vocational programs? Are programs and courses recommended without regard to the sex of the student? What steps are taken to recruit females and males into nontraditional (for their sex) programs? If specific guidance or instructional materials are judged to be sex biased, what ancillary materials or services are provided to counteract the use of these materials?

Schiffer (1979) recommends that career guidance staff develop and use a checklist to ensure a regularized procedure for counseling students and countering sex bias in existing tests and materials. Students should also have this checklist. Evaluators also will find that Schiffer's checklist provides a framework for determining sex bias in career guidance. The major categories included are: limits of the tests; providing a full-range of career choices; attention to test results; and counseling back-up for students seeking to try nontraditional jobs (and vocational education programs). Cook (cited in Schiffer, 1979) also developed a set of criteria for monitoring counseling and guidance activities through a review for the U.S. Office of Education. She includes such criteria as: female and male students are referred to counselors in approximately equal numbers; men and women are equally represented on the counseling staff; and students are provided information about their rights to equal educational and employment opportunities under the law. (Cook lists nineteen criteria altogether.) Evaluators can determine whether VE and career guidance staff have attended inservice workshops on sex bias in vocational education. Evaluators should be familiar with the state plan for ensuring equal access to VE programs and any provisions for school career counseling. In summary, documents, records, checklists, observations of teacher-student and counselor-student interactions, interviews and question-naires are all possible methods for evaluators to use in conducting a process evaluation of career guidance activities to determine if equal access and sex fairness exist.

b. Outcome Measures: Outcome or impact measures of career guidance activities can occur at two times: the first is short-term, a concurrent evaluation of specific activities; and the second is long-term, the follow-up study of student choices at the conclusion of the program. In the evaluation component which focuses on equal access and sex bias, the evaluator will be analyzing data separately for females and males, as well as for the total group.

Evaluation of specific activities can include, for example, student ratings of satisfaction of inventory results, of counselor activities, and of career guidance materials. One rating form that has been used in several studies of interest inventories (e.g., Denker and Tittle, 1976) asks students to rate the reasonableness of major interests identified by the inventory (on a five point scale ranging from Strongly Agree to Strongly Disagree). Other short term effects can be placed under the heading of exploration validity, examining the pre-post activity differences on such variables as: number of occupations considered; number of nontraditional occupations considered; number of supplementary experiences sought (e.g., books on occupations, voluntary work that is occupationally related); and cooperative education and work experience placements.

The follow-up evaluation should examine differential program effects by sex on variables such as type of job placement and attendance in postsecondary institutions. Attendance in different types of postsecondary institutions should not reflect sex discrimination, nor should type of job placement. The program evaluation design needs to include this analysis.

CONCLUSIONS

Current laws have brought new issues and measurement problems to evaluators of vocational education programs. Title IX and the Vocational Education Act, in the Education Amendments of 1972 and 1976, now require equal access to educational programs and the elimination of sex discrimination. These acts and regulations mean that evaluators should be familiar with definitions of sex bias and sex fairness in interest measurement and career guidance activities, as they are a part of vocational educational programs. The NIE Guidelines were described to assist evaluators to understand the issues of sex fairness in interest measurement. Recent research studies on interest measurement were examined for their implications for the construction of local or new interest measures, and for the assessment of the impact or outcome of taking interest inventories, along with related career guidance activities.

Exploration validity is a concept with which evaluators should be familiar, with its implications for measuring short-term impact of career interest measures and career guidance. Finally, additional criteria for examining sex bias in career guidance activities more generally were proposed. These criteria were grouped into two areas—process evaluation and outcome (impact) evaluation. These criteria should assist evaluators to design and conduct evaluation studies that will include an examination of the legally-mandated areas of equal access and sex discrimination in career guidance and counseling in vocational education programs.

As state plans develop and federally mandated evaluations of sex discrimination in vocational education are carried out, the evaluator can look forward to more standardized measurement procedures for determining equal access and sex bias. In the meantime, the criteria proposed here and the resources cited will assist the evaluator to meet the challenge of evaluating sex bias in vocational education programs.

NOTES

1. See Saario (1976) for the history and analysis of policy implications of Title IX at the secondary level. Schiffer (1979) has described the legal issues related to selecting and using interest inventories under Title IX and the 14th Amendment to the Constitution (The Equal Protection Clause). Roby (1976) provides an excellent review of the evidence of inequality in vocational education.

2. The evaluator will recognize that while this discussion and analysis is carried out in the context of sex bias, many of the guidelines are relevant to the use of these measures with groups whose experiences and cultural background do not match those groups upon whom the instruments were developed and normed. Such groups include minorities, re-entry women, those for whom English is not their first language, the economically disadvantaged, and those with special handicaps.

3. Stebbins, Ames, and Rhodes (1975) provide extended comments on the rationale for each guideline and give examples of their purposes. Evaluators may find their discussions a helpful reference for school staff. The evaluator will find Diamond (1975) a useful reference for the technical and research issues, as well as the research studies in Tittle and Zytowski (1979).

4. Harway and Astin (1977) review studies of sex bias in other vocational and career counseling materials. Vetter (1975) developed guidelines for analyses of vocational materials that could be used by evaluators. Other guidelines for analyzing curriculum materials are found in Saario, Jacklin, and Tittle (1973).

5. Johansson and Harmon (1972), Webber and Harmon (1979), and Hansen (1979) provide further examples of analyzing the SCII for sex differences and the implications for occupational scale construction.

6. Johnson (1977) and Lunneborg (1975) provide further examples and discussion of the issue of cross-sex norm interpretation.

7. Picou and Campbell (1975) contains a series of papers on minority groups, but again lacks data on interest inventories.

8. A review by Tittle and Denker (1977) summarizes some of this literature, generally showing that inventoried interests are not as predictable for a broad sampling of occupation for women as are the interests of men.

REFERENCES

AMEG Commission on Sex Bias in Measurement. 1977. A case history of change: A review of responses to the challenge of sex bias in interest inventories. *Measurement and Evaluation in Guidance* 10: 148-152.

Buros, O. K. 1972. *The Seventh Mental Measurements Yearbook, Vols. I and II.* Highland Park, NJ: Gryphon Press.

Cole, N. S. 1973. On measuring the vocational interests of women. *Journal of Counseling Psychology* 20: 105-112.

Cooper, J. F. 1976. Comparative impact of the SCII and the Vocational Card Sort on career salience and career exploration of women. *Journal of Counseling Psychology* 23: 348-352.

Denker, E. R., and Tittle, C. K. 1976. "Reasonableness" of KOIS results for re-entry women: Implications for test validity. *Educational and Psychological Measurement* 36: 495-500.

Dewey, C. R. 1974. Exploring Interests: A non-sexist method. *Personnel and Guidance Journal* 52: 311-315.

Diamond, E. E., ed. 1975. *Issues of Sex Bias and Sex Fairness in Career Interest Measurement.* Washington, DC: DHEW.

Federal Register. 1977. *Vocational Education, State Programs and Commissioner's Discretionary Programs.* Washington, DC: Office of Education, DHEW.

Gottfredson, G. D., and Holland, J. L. 1975. Vocational choices of men and women: A comparison of predictors from the Self-Directed Search. *Journal of Counseling Psychology* 22: 28-34.

Gump, J. P., and Rivers, L. W. 1975. A consideration of race in efforts to end sex bias. In E. E. Diamond, ed. *Issues of Sex Bias and Sex Fairness in Career Interest Measurement.* Washington, DC: DHEW.

Hansen, J. C. 1979. Sex differences in vocational interests: Three levels of exploration. In C.K. Tittle, and D.G. Zytowski, eds. *Sex-Fair Interest Measurement: Research and Implications.* Washington, DC: DHEW.

Hanson, G. R., Noeth, R. J., and Prediger, D. J. 1978. The validity of diverse procedures for reporting interest scores: An analysis of longitudinal data. *Journal of Counseling Psychology* (in press).

Hanson, G. R., and Rayman, J. 1978. Validity of sex-balanced interest inventory scales. *Journal of Vocational Behavior* (in press).

Harway, M., and Astin, H. S. 1977. *Sex Discrimination in Career Counseling and Education.* New York: Praeger.

Holland, J. L. 1977. *Toward Definable and Beneficial Resolutions of the Interest Inventory Controversy.* Baltimore, MD: Department of Social Relations, Johns Hopkins University.

———. 1975. The use and evaluation of interest inventories and simulations. In E.E. Diamond ed. *Issues of Sex Bias and Sex Fairness in Career Interest Measurement.* Washington, DC: DHEW.

Holland, J. L., Takai, R., Gottfredson, G. D., and Hanau, C. 1978. A multivariate analysis of the effects of the Self-Directed Search on high school girls. *Journal of Counseling Psychology* (in press).

Johansson, C. B., and Harmon, L. W. 1972. Strong Vocational Interest Blank: One form or two? *Journal of Counseling Psychology* 19: 404-410.

Johnson, R. W. 1977. Relationship between female and male interest scales for the same occupation. *Journal of Vocational Behavior* 11: 239-252.

Lamb, R. R. 1979. Validity of the ACT Interest Inventory for minority group members. In C. K. Tittle, and D. G. Zytowski, eds. *Sex-Fair Interest Measurement: Research and Implications.* Washington, DC: DHEW.

Lunneborg, P. W. 1975. Interpreting other-sex scores on the Strong-Campbell Interest Inventory. *Journal of Counseling Psychology* 22: 494-499.

Lunneborg, P. W., and Lunneborg, C. E. *Assessing the Strong-Campbell Interest Inventory by the NIE Guidelines for Sex Fairness in Career Interest Measurement.* Seattle: University of Washington (no date).

Oliver, L. W. 1977. Evaluating career counseling outcome for three modes of test interpretation. *Measurement and Evaluation in Guidance* 10: 153-161.

Picou, J. S., and Campbell, R. E. 1975. *Career Behavior of Special Groups: Theory, Research and Practice.* Columbus, OH: Charles Merrill.

Prediger, D. J., and Cole, N. S. 1975. Sex-role socialization and employment realities: Implications for vocational interest measures. *Journal of Vocational Behavior* 7: 239-251.

Prediger, D. J., and Hanson, G. R. 1977. Some consequences of using raw-score reports of vocational interests. *Journal of Educational Measurement* 4: 323-333.

Rayman, J. R. 1976. Sex and the single interest inventory: The empirical validation of the sex-balanced interest inventory items. *Journal of Counseling Psychology* 23: 239-246.

Roby, P. A. 1976. Toward full equality: More job education for women. *School Review* 84: 181-211.

Saario, T. T. 1976. Title IX: Now what? In A. C. Ornstein and S. I. Miller, eds. *Policy Issues in Education.* Lexington, MA: Lexington Books, D.C. Heath.

Saario, T. N., Jacklin, C. N., and Tittle, C. K. 1973. Sex role stereotyping in the public schools. *Harvard Educational Review* 43: 386-416.

Schiffer, L. 1979. Legal issues regarding sex bias in selection and use of career interest inventories. In C. K. Tittle, and D. Z. Zytowski, eds. *Sex-Fair Interest Measurement: Research and Implications.* Washington, DC: DHEW.

Stebbins, L. B., Ames, N. L., and Rhodes, I. 1975. *Sex Fairness in Career Guidance.* Cambridge, MA: Abt Publications.

Takai, R., and Holland, J. L. 1978. *The Relative Influence of the Vocational Card Sort, The Self-Directed Search, and the Vocational Exploration and Insight Kit on High School Girls.* Baltimore, MD: Department of Social Relations, Johns Hopkins University (unpublished).

Tittle, C. K. 1979. Implications of recent developments for future research in career interest measurement. In C. K. Tittle, and D. G. Zytowski, eds. *Sex-Fair Interest Measurement: Research and Implications.* Washington, DC: DHEW.

Tittle, C. K., and Denker, E. R. 1977. Re-entry women: A selective review of the educational process, career choice, and interest measurement. *Review of Educational Research* 47: 531-584.

Tittle, C. K., and Zytowski, D. G., eds. 1979. *Sex-Fair Interest Measurement: Research and Implications.* Washington, DC: DHEW.

Vetter, L., Stockburger, D. W., and Brose, C. 1974. *Career Guidance Materials: Implications for Women's Career Development.* Columbus: Center for Vocational Education, Ohio State University.

Webber, P., and Harmon, L. W. 1979. The reliability and concurrent validity of three types of occupational scales for two occupational groups: Some evidence bearing on handling sex difference in interest scale construction. In C. K. Tittle, and D. G. Zytowski, eds. *Sex-Fair Interest Measurement: Research and Implications.* Washington, DC: DHEW.

chapter 20

CAROL KEHR TITTLE   *University of North Carolina at Greensboro*

Evaluators of training programs that use tests for selection, and evaluators of Title I programs that use standardized tests as measures of achievement are aware of the charges of test bias. As the link between education and work is increased by a stronger emphasis in vocational education on job placement and follow-up studies, evaluators in vocational education will also become aware of the criticisms of standardized tests as being biased against minorities, and as having an adverse impact on minorities. And as there is greater attention given to performance testing in vocational education, that is, to situations similar to achievement testing where there is no external criterion readily available as a criterion for test validity, evaluators also need to be aware of the issues of test bias. The methodology which is discussed below is important particularly in relation to assessments of students whose first language is not English, and those whose socio-cultural environment does not match that of the "majority" cultural group on which most tests and performance assessments are developed and standardized (Mercer, 1972).

There are a number of sources that will help vocational education evaluators to understand the minority group perspective on testing. Cronbach (1975) has provided an historical review of the controversy over mental testing, and Samuda (1975) has a wide-ranging review of the research lit-

AUTHOR'S NOTE: *The writer acknowledges the helpful comments of Esther E. Diamond and Ted Abramson, and the library work of Vivian Shulman.*

erature and writings on the psychological testing of minorities. Wargo (1976) summarized test criticisms as seen from the perspective of a federal-level evaluator of compensatory education programs. The debates over standardized tests focus not only on the difference in test scores and individual items which are identified as biased—items that may represent life styles or experiences more typical of middle socioeconomic groups in American culture—but also on the use and interpretation of the tests. As Samuda points out, there are a number of social, economic, educational, and psychological implications of testing. Testing tends to preserve the status quo and, thus, the positions of minority groups in a less-favored status are maintained, e.g., fewer minority students in major professional schools, in high level positions throughout the business and scientific worlds, hence lower social and economic status and the psychological effects of lowered status.

The antitesting arguments and feelings are strongly held by some minority group members. An example of the positions taken is cited by Williams, Mosby, and Hinson (1976), as stated by the National Association of Elementary School Principals:

NAESP views with growing concern the misuse of standardized tests. Standardized tests can be a valuable educational tool when used as a means of measuring the academic program of a school or school system.

Unfortunately, under the misguided opinion that testing is accountability, our schools have been deluged with standardized tests in which the only attempts at interpretation have been to compile the scores and pronounce judgments on the basis of statistical manipulations.

The association urges its members to resist individually and to encourage their local, state, and national associations to resist any use of standardized testing for purposes that cannot benefit the child (Williams et al., 1976:12).

This statement was presented at a conference on the use of achievement tests with disadvantaged and minority students for educational program evaluation. Title I evaluations have been criticized for using tests that are biased against minorities, both black students and those of Hispanic background, as well as other socio-cultural minorities. An earlier conference on test bias, one aspect of which focused on the methods used to study item bias, was held by the National Institute of Education (Angoff, 1975).

Another series of papers presented in a special issue of the *Journal of Educational Measurement* (1976) dealt with the statistical models that have been proposed for analyzing bias in the use of tests in selection procedures in college admission and employment settings. These models will not be described here, as the articles by Peterson and Novick, and Sawyer, Cole, and Cole provide descriptions and identify the major conflicts in assumptions in the different models. Novick and Ellis (1977) describe the models as based on a group parity concept, which they find unacceptable. They present the case for broadening the models to include measurement of individual disadvantage and individual utilities.

Understanding the statistical models will be of interest to vocational education evaluators if follow-up studies are conducted in which the placement of students in occupations has involved employer use of tests for hiring employees. If, for example, minorities or women are not hired in proportion to their numbers in qualified applicant pools, this might be an instance of adverse impact resulting from the use of tests. Follow-up studies would reflect not the effect of training but the effect of tests in differentially selecting members of minority groups from the set of qualified applicants.

Another situation in which the vocational education evaluator would be interested in the determination of adverse impact is the use of tests to select students for admission to occupational programs. Also, tests such as the Differential Aptitude Tests might be used to recommend vocational courses to students.[1] These uses of tests would, it appears, be subject to the same guidelines developed for the employer selection procedures. The use of tests in employment selection is being codified in the *Uniform Guidelines on Employee Selection Procedures* that appeared in the Federal Register, December 20, 1977. The Uniform Guidelines represent a consensus among four federal agencies: the Civil Service Commission, the Equal Employment Opportunity Commission, the Department of Justice, and the Department of Labor. Because there is now one set of guidelines being formulated, they are important to psychologists working in employment selection, and to evaluators who should understand their main requirements.

The next section describes key definitions and requirements in the Uniform Guidelines. The following section reviews the procedures and methods that have been used for examining test and item bias in the educational assessment setting—in the absence of an external criterion. The last section presents a series of recommendations to evaluators. These recommendations list the data that evaluators should find in test manuals, the data that are needed to make the determination that a test is fair for use with particular groups, and the procedures evaluators will find useful in minimizing test bias in local test development for vocational education evaluation purposes.

UNIFORM GUIDELINES ON EMPLOYEE SELECTION PROCEDURES

The Uniform Guidelines (Federal Register, 1977) are intended to represent professionally acceptable methods of the psychological profession for demonstrating whether a selection procedure validly predicts or measures performance for a particular job:

These guidelines incorporate a single set of principles which are designed to assist employers, labor organizations, employment agencies, and licensing and certification boards to comply with requirements of Federal law prohibiting employment practices which discriminate on grounds of race, color, religion, sex, and national origin (p. 65543).

Several key definitions are part of the Uniform Guidelines:

(a) *Employment decisions*—include but are not limited to hiring, promotion, demotion, membership (for example in a labor organization), referral, retention, licensing and certification. Other selection decisions, such as selection for training or transfers, may also be considered employment decisions if they lead to the decisions specified above.

(b) *Discrimination*—the use of any selection procedure which has an adverse impact on the hiring, promotion, or other employment or membership opportunities of members of any racial, ethnic, or sex group will be considered to be discriminatory and inconsistent with the Uniform Guidelines unless the procedure has been validated in accordance with the guidelines.

(c) *Adverse impact*—a selection rate for any racial, ethnic or sex group which is less than four-fifths (80 percent) of the rate for the group with the highest rate, will generally be regarded by the federal enforcement agencies as evidence of adverse impact. Smaller differences in selection rate may constitute adverse impact, where they are significant in both statistical and practical terms.

(d) *Selection procedure*—any measure, combination of measures, or procedure used as a basis for any employment decision. Selection procedures include the full range of assessment techniques from traditional paper and pencil tests, performance tests, training programs or probationary periods, and physical, educational and work experience requirements through informal or casual interviews and unscored application forms.

(e) *Selection rate*—the proportion of applicants who are hired, promoted or otherwise selected.

(f) *Unfairness of selection procedure* (differential prediction)—a condition in which members of one racial, ethnic, or sex group characteristically obtain lower scores on a selection procedure than members of another group, and the differences are not reflected in difference in measures of job performance.

(g) *Content validity*—demonstrated by data showing that a selection procedure is a representative sample of important work behaviors to be performed on the job.

(h) *Criterion-related validity*—demonstrated by empirical data showing that the selection procedure is predictive of or significantly correlated with important elements of work behavior.

(i) *Construct validity*—demonstrated by data showing that the selection procedure measures the degree to which candidates have identifiable characteristics which have been determined to be important for successful job performance.

The data which test users should maintain—whether employer or vocational school using tests in selection—are records which provide information on the applicant and selected groups by sex and racial/ethnic groups (designated as blacks, American Indian, Asian, Hispanic including persons of Mexican, Puerto Rican, Cuban, Central or South American or other Spanish origin or culture, and whites—Caucasians other than Hispanic). Evaluators should know that these classifications are also those used for developing and monitoring affirmative action programs, and could also be used for the new VEA requirements to monitor and affirm equal access to vocational education programs.

The guidelines provide General Standards for validity studies and, in Part II, Technical Standards for validity studies; Part III describes the required documentation of validity evidence. The General Standards indicate that for the purposes of satisfying the guidelines, users may present criterion related validity studies, content validity studies, or construct validity studies (see the definitions above). The General Standards also describe the conditions under which evidence presented or studies done by other users or test publishers may be substituted for local data.

A key element in the Technical Standards for validity studies is the review of information about the job for which the selection procedure is to be used. This review should generally include a job analysis, and job analysis is mentioned for all three types of validity studies. In using criterion related validity, the importance of investigating possible bias both in the selection of the criterion measures and in their application is considered. Bias in subjective evaluations, such as supervisory ratings, should be examined; evidence of racial, ethnic, or sex bias or lack of bias is of particular concern if there are significant differences in measures of job performance for different *groups*. As vocational education programs develop more elaborate systems of assessing performance, evaluators also need to determine if there are differences in rating on the part of some raters that are attributable to group membership rather than individual differences.

The definition of content validity in these guidelines is more stringent than that usually applied to educational achievement tests. Content validity must claim and demonstrate that the selection procedure is a representative sample of one or more work behaviors of the job, or a representative work sample. Measures of knowledge, skill, or ability must be representative of a job behavior, and the *level* of complexity and difficulty of the knowledge, skill, and ability must match that of the job behavior. The content validity defined here has implications for any tests used to select students for vocational programs.

Construct validity is described as the most difficult to demonstrate in the employment field. The guidelines remind the user that there needs to be a series of research studies and the level of proof required is generally, at the very least, the level required for criterion-related validity studies, and typically is greater. Part III of the guidelines provides a detailed listing of all the descriptive information and data to be provided with each of the three types of validity studies. This section can be used by evaluators in studies of the assessment procedures in vocational education programs and their relationship to job analyses (content and other validity studies), and in studies using employer ratings of entry level job performance (criterion-related validity).

The discussion of the fairness of the selection procedures (p. 65547-8) draws attention to this developing concept of "fairness." There is not consensus on the methods of preference to examine fairness or unfairness, but the guidelines provide some help to test users. Unfairness is demonstrated through showing that "members of a particular group perform better or poorer on the job than their scores on the selection procedure would indicate through comparison with how members of other groups perform" (p. 65547). This definition considers fairness as compatibility between the probability of successful job performance and the probability of being selected (or, in vocational education settings or college admission settings, compatibility between the probability of successful course performance and the probability of being selected for the vocational program or college). The 1976 issue of the *Journal of Educational Measurement* (cited earlier) has sufficient areas of disagreement in the models proposed and their underlying philosophy, that evaluators can look forward to refinements and/or changes in the concept of fairness as presented in the Uniform Guidelines.

The other problem of test fairness with which evaluators are concerned is one which has arisen in connection with educational achievement tests. Here there are no external criteria, as for criterion-related validity studies, and there are no education "jobs" or work samples on which there is national consensus. Yet there are charges of test bias in educational assessment and evaluation as described earlier for Title I (Williams et al., 1976). These charges emphasize cultural differences among subgroups taking standardized tests. As a result of this controversy, a number of methods have been proposed and studied as definitions of test bias or fairness. It is this series of procedures which are described next.

EDUCATIONAL ASSESSMENT AND TEST BIAS

The review of methods and the recommendations presented in the following section are based on a rationale developed in an earlier article (Tittle, 1975). The studies discussed below have all been carried out on paper and pencil, multiple choice tests, mainly nationally-standardized instruments, as well as some criterion or objectives-referenced tests. Some of the procedures and recommendations are, however, adaptable or of concern in performance testing and rating. They will provide the evaluator with the framework that has been developed on multiple choice tests, and a sensitivity to adapt them as necessary in vocational education program evaluation.

In an earlier article, I discussed an approach to the problem of fairness in educational achievement testing, in the absence of an external criterion (Tittle, 1975). Traditionally, attention has been paid to content validity for achievement tests, but there has been little attention given to construct validity. Both types of validities are essential to defining a set of procedures that will permit the development of a fair educational achievement test. The *Standards for Educational and Psychological Tests,* published by the American Psychological Association, discusses both content and construct validity. However, more detailed guidelines or adaptations of the Standards to meet the criticisms of achievement tests have not been developed, as they have been for employment selection procedures.[2]

The 1975 article described a set of procedures that, when carried out, permit the conclusion that a test is a "fair" measure from the standpoint of specific subgroups within a test population. The attempt to specify a set of procedures was stimulated by ideas presented by John Rawls in his 1971 book, *A Theory of Justice.* The most useful ideas were drawn from Rawls' concepts of: (1) an original agreement for the principles of justice or fairness, which is criticized from the standpoint of the least advantaged groups (those with the least authority and income, or unequal basic rights because of fixed natural characteristics, e.g., sex and ethnic groups); and (2) the various types of procedural justice and, in particular, pure procedural justice.

Rawls' description of pure procedural justice is applicable to the problem of fairness in achievement testing: "Pure procedural justice obtains when there is no independent criterion for the right result: instead there is a correct or fair procedure such that the outcome is likewise correct or fair, whatever it is, provided that the procedure has been properly followed" (1971:86). A distinctive feature of pure procedural justice is that the procedure for determining the just result must actually be carried out; where there is no independent criterion by reference to which a definite outcome can be known to be just, a "fair procedure translates its fairness to the outcome only when it is actually carried out" (1971:86). This idea translates directly to the development of tests that can be described as fair for particular groups. A test can be judged as fair if an agreed-upon set of procedures have been used in the test development and standardization processes. The set of procedures can include item and test analyses and test reviews (as described in the last part of this chapter), documenting both content and construct validity.

Rawls has been criticized by Bell (1973), among others, for shifting the liberal view of equality of fair opportunity to equality of results. However, the development of a set of procedures to define a fair test does not assume that an achievement test or assessment procedure is unfair because of differences between subgroups in average test scores. Nor would it be claimed that the procedures suggested would eliminate subgroup differences. However, it is proposed that the test user have adequate *documentation of the decisions* made in the test development process in order to determine whether, in fact, observed differences arise from sources not directly or logically related to the construct being measured. For example, if part of the source of variation in reading comprehension test scores is attributable to familiarity with the subject matter of reading passages, then this factor should be equalized across subgroups. In the assessment of bilingual students' skills in vocational programs, the score should be attributed to occupational knowledge or skills, and not differences in language skills. Evidence is needed that one group is not more subject to the effects of such variables than are other groups.

The development of a set of procedures which can be followed and reported in test development manuals provides one way to deal with the problem of test and item bias in educational testing and assessment, and permits a clearer understanding of the outcomes of vocational educational measurement. If differences attributable to fixed characteristics of the individual, such as sex, ethnic group, level of educational disadvantage, are minimized, then remaining differences may be more clearly interpreted in terms of such variables as "opportunity to learn" the content of a particular test (Anderson, 1975). The review of some of the technical procedures which have been proposed thus far in the study of item and test bias is grouped into several areas. The first area is *item content,* where two areas are examined: "face" validity, and stereotyping of various subgroups; and content validity, the match between the test and the curriculum. The second major area related to items is labeled here as *empirical analyses of item bias,* including item selection for tests. The next major area is *test/item format and directions.* A fourth area is identified as *equating, scaling, and norms groups.*

Item Content

1. Face Validity, Stereotyping, and Positive Representation: There have been earlier reviews of the stereotyping of women and minorities which appear in instructional and test materials (e.g., Tittle, McCarthy, and Steckler, 1974). Most test publishers, as with publishers of instructional materials, have developed written guidelines to assist test authors, item writers, and test editors to avoid this aspect of item bias. Another aspect of bias in item content is inclusiveness—positive representations of such groups in text and

illustrations. In addition, the experiential background of students should be taken into account. Judges have been used to examine item bias in terms of "cultural" or experiential differences for subgroups: by Spencer (1973), to identify items with bias against black students for the National Teacher Examination common examinations; by Armstrong (1972), to identify biased items against Hispanics and blacks on an intelligence test; and by Coffman (1961), to identify items in the Scholastic Aptitude Test on which females and males were likely to score differently. Some publishers may already use judges, but the procedures used and the results should be described and summarized in test manuals.

2. *Content Validity:* This is a complex issue: to define procedures to match test content for divergent groups and different curricula. As Anderson (1970) has noted, test specialists have not developed scales for describing the similarity between teaching and testing. This is a critical need, as several studies have demonstrated. Bianchini (1976) gave an example drawn from the California Miller-Unruh statewide testing program in Grade 1. For the first five years of this program the Stanford Reading Achievement Test was used; 65 percent of Grade 1 pupils were in the first quartile of the national norms, and 25 percent of the students scored in the chance range. There were questions about the representativeness of the test content and the national norms. According to Bianchini, the real problem was, What does a first grader learn to read? The answer was *words*. He estimated the congruence between tests and vocabulary in the instructional materials in use in the state at that time was about 19 percent. Later the Cooperative Primary Reading Test was adopted and the results were much closer to the national norms. This was ascribed to the norms being easier, but according to Bianchini, "55 percent of the vocabulary used in the Cooperative Primary Reading Tests was the same as the vocabulary of the first grade readers provided by the state at that time" (Bianchini, 1976:21).

Anderson (1975) presented a similar effect in a study of southern schools. Comparing the performance of black and white pupils in different schools, it was clear that part of the difference in test scores was based on a variable that Anderson called "opportunity-to-learn test bias." That is, the curricular materials in use differed for the schools, and therefore, the match with the test content also differed.

Other studies have examined standardized reading tests for the early grades and curricular materials, and have also concluded that the tests are not well matched to the curricula (see Jenkins and Pany, 1976; Armbruster et al., 1977, for analyses of reading curricula and reading tests). Porter, Schmidt, Floden, and Freeman (1977) reported an analysis of elementary school mathematics tests for a study to describe the effect of teaching behavior (and program effects). A major concern for evaluation is a clear understanding of effects, which in the present conduct of program evaluation could show the same aggregate effect through several different routes. For four tests they found differences on all three factors (mode of presentation, nature of the material, and operations). Boruch (1977) has also called attention to the effects of poor measurement as contributing to findings of no significant differences in program effects.

Rakow, Airasian, and Madaus (1975) compared the sensitivity of two item selection techniques for curriculum evaluation—to identify items which differentiated *between* groups (between curricula) as opposed to *within* groups (within a curriculum program). Cahill, Airasian, Madaus, and Pedulla (1977) reported a similar study showing the relative insensitivity of the total test score in identifying achievement differences between groups. They developed subtests of items that maximally differentiated performance *between* the groups (as opposed to within group discrimination). Their study used item data already in existence and was based on empirical analysis, rather than ratings or other item selection procedures before the study was conducted. Hanson, Schutz, and Bailey (1977) described a model for "program fair" evaluation of instructional programs in reading readiness. Although developed for kindergarten-level evaluation, the ideas go further than Rakow et al. in suggesting test development strategies and how to present outcome patterns for different programs using criterion referenced tests.

The effects of lack of matching between the test and the curriculum are shown in another study of out-of-level survey testing by Long, Schaffran, and Kellogg (1977) using the reading achievement scores of Title I ESEA students for grades two, three, and four. Students in grades two, three, and four were given grade level and instructional level (e.g., reading second grade readers although in grade three) reading tests in September and May. Grade equivalent scores from the two testings were significantly different, favoring instructional level testing at grades two and three and grade level testing at grade four. Although the authors did not have teachers examine the match between the test content and the curriculum, this study also suggests that the match between the content and the test is important.

An experimental demonstration of the effect of manipulating test specifications and item content for black and white candidates (adults) on the National Teacher Examination (NTE) was provided by Medley and Quirk (1974). Another study by McCarthy (1975) demonstrates the effects of changing item context on women's performance in mathematical problem solving items. McCarthy found systematic differences in test scores for a sample of high school students in grades ten to twelve. Items were constructed on the same mathematical content but varying the item context: context familiar to females; context familiar to males; or neutral context. She used an item-total test score criterion to select the "best" items for females, males, and total group (using the same number of items in each set). Females scored significantly higher on the test constructed of items "best" for females; males scored higher on the male test and the total group test.

These studies suggest that evaluators developing tests should include procedures designed to demonstrate consensus that test specifications and test content have been judged to be representative for the *subgroups* likely to take the test. Evaluators selecting tests and assessment procedures should look for information on these procedures in test publishers' materials. Hoepfner (1976) included teacher ratings and review of content and difficulty as part of examining item bias. Angoff (1975) has also suggested that the identification and analytic verification of a common core of items, judged by representatives of various subgroups, would be useful in developing an unbiased test for minority groups.

Empirical Analyses of Item Bias

A variety of procedures have been suggested for the empirical analyses of item bias, and examining bias in the absence of an external criterion. These procedures all provide evidence for evaluators on the construct validity of the test in a particular sense: reducing the relationship between status variables such as minority or sex classifications and item performance. Evidence on construct validity will be particularly important for vocational aptitude tests used to recommend, select, or place students in vocational courses. There may well be experience differences for minorities and women that lead to item responses that are based on the differential experiences, and not on the underlying ability the test is presumed to be measuring. Cole (1978) cites a dissertation by Carlson of an IEA test of "understanding" science that shows sex-differentiated practical experiences. Similarly Cronbach (1978) has pointed to the limitations of the Armed Forces Vocational Aptitude Battery as a measure of "aptitude" for females; some tests are better labeled as tests of trade and technical *information*. According to Cronbach, the tests are especially unsuitable for girls who might have talents along craft and technical lines.

Typically, the procedures to define item bias look for items that function differently for two groups, e.g., blacks and whites, females and males. These procedures have sought to define bias in terms other than the group means. "Outlying" items are identified according to a particular criterion and are considered for removal as "biased" items. Removing such items may not affect differences in group means if they are large in the beginning.

Among the earliest methods suggested to examine item by group interactions was one by Coffman (1961). Coffman computed item difficulty data (p, the proportion obtaining the right answer) separately for subgroups, and then used an arcsin formula to transform them for comparison. A later series of studies at ETS used an analysis of variance of item difficulties subjected to the arcsin transformation (Cardall and Coffman, 1964), and plotting item difficulties using deltas (p values converted to a normal deviate, delta = 4z + 13) for different groups. In this latter procedure, items falling away from the line of best fit are regarded as contributing to item by group interaction (Angoff and Ford, 1971). Breland et al. (1974) provided a modification of this procedure, and Echternacht (1974) gave a description of a procedure to derive significance levels for distributions generated by plotting delta differences on normal probability paper. Other procedures have included dividing subgroups into quartiles on total test scores, computing chi squares on the number right for each item (Schueneman, 1976), and a method by Fishbein (1975) for computing confidence intervals, average p values for each group, and testing D for individual pairs of items. Veale and Foreman (1976) have computed chi square and likelihood estimators across item alternatives to compare subgroups as a way of identifying biased items.

Studies by Green and his colleagues also examined the use of item selection procedures to define biased items and construct an "unbiased" test. Green (1972) compared items selected on an item-test correlation criterion, and examined the correlations and mean differences between tests formed in this manner for different subgroups, such as males and females and minority groups. Green and Draper (1972) extended this method to compare estimated item characteristic curves and the usefulness of intergroup factor analysis. A combination of these procedures was used by Ozenne, Van Gelder, and Cohen (1974).

Merz (1976) also provided a review and comparison of five item bias techniques: analysis of variance; delta values, point biserials, chi square, and multivariate, such as factor analyses and analysis of variance of factor scores. He found no clear cut method of preference among the ones he examined. Recently Fishbein (1977) looked at another definition for fairness of items: that groups of equal overall ability (statistically equated) in the subject should not perform significantly differently on an item in that subject area.

Fishbein's method calls attention to a problem with the majority of the item by group interaction methods. As Cole (1978) and others have noted, the item difficulties and item discrimination methods (r_{it}) are dependent on the ability levels of the groups being studied. If groups of differing ability are used in studies, the meaning of the item difficulty and item discrimination indices change. This problem has led a number of researchers to suggest methods based on latent trait models, models in which the measure of an individual's ability is independent of the distribution of abilities of examinees. Briefly, "A latent trait model specifies a relationship between observable examinee test performance and the unobservable traits or abilities assumed to underlie performance on the test" (Hambleton and Cook, 1977:75). Major concepts, assumptions, limitations, and examples of applications of latent trait models are given in a special issue of the *Journal of Educational Measurement* (1977).

Latent trait models assume that only a single ability (or latent trait) is measured, and that the item responses of a given examinee are statistically independent. The item characteristic curve (icc) is a mathematical function that relates the probability of success on an item to the ability measured by the item set. The number of parameters required to describe an icc depends on the particular latent trait model—the number of parameters is typically one, two, or three (Hambleton and Cook, 1977).

The one parameter model (the Rasch model) has been proposed and used to assess item bias by Durovic (1975, 1978), and Wright (1977). The Rasch model assumes that all items in a set have equal discriminating power, and thus the items vary only in terms of difficulty. As Hambleton and Cook note (1977:83), this is a very restrictive assumption and likely to be violated with most tests. On the other hand, the three parameter model requires large numbers of examinees to estimate parameters and extensive computer time (Lord, 1977).

While there are no studies on which to base consensus among experts of the extent to which the use of one or another method is preferable, it appears that the use of at least one of these procedures, with a clear specification of the decision-making rules for including items in the test, would enable the evaluator to make a judgment as to whether or not a test is fair for a particular subgroup. It may be that the absence of such a procedure, for example, is more important than the use of a particular procedure, until optimal procedures are identified.

In terms of assembling the total test, for norm-referenced measures particularly, only Diamond (1975) has suggested a decision rule for selecting items. Diamond would reduce mean differences between subgroups by examining subgroup differences when selecting items on the basis of pretest data. Differences between the percentage of upper and lower groups selecting the correct answer can be calculated separately for each subgroup. The differences between subgroups should not average over 5 percent in either direction for any given subtest. Other recommendations for dealing with this part of the test development process have not been located. The decision rules used at this particular stage of test construction can be identified as another procedure, to be considered by test developers and evaluators, to define a fair test.

If a situation arises in vocational education evaluation where large-scale educational assessments are undertaken, it will be important for evaluators to begin to define a set of procedures to deal with other aspects of construct validity. Further evidence on test fairness can be provided through the construction of experimental tests and correlations with a standard set of measures. Frederiksen (1976) has suggested several techniques to determine whether a test measures the same thing in different cultures, essentially the problem in which charges of test bias arise. Students can be asked to think aloud and to be interviewed about how they solve problems or answer questions. Practice materials or other activities to make groups similar with regard to test taking abilities can be used. The interrelationships among a variety of tests can be used to test hypotheses about construct validity. A complete set of procedures designed to assist test users to make the judgment that a test is fair may, in some cases, include these more extensive studies of construct validity.

Test and Item Format, Test Directions

Studies of test and item format to be reported to test users are another important area for evaluators to consider in defining test fairness. For example, Sherman (1976) examined the use of the "I don't know" alternative in the National Assessment of Educational Progress. For science questions, groups using the response more frequently than the national average and who were correct less often included Southeastern adults, age seventeen, adult females, black adults, and rural adults. Sherman used a regression analysis to modify the correct response data for the groups' use of the response. The modification of the correct response percent had a large impact on the sex differences in science performance. Sex differences at the three younger ages were reduced, and differences were virtually eliminated at the adult level.[3]

Equating, Scaling and Norms Groups

Other procedures that need to be examined for test bias in evaluation are those used in equating, scaling, and norms groups. Slinde and Linn (1978) conducted a study of the adequacy of the Rasch model for vertical equating (equating between more than one level of a test). They used a mathematics achievement test of the College Entrance Board. The results of their study indicated that the Rasch model did not provide a satisfactory means of vertical equating, because the sample tests they constructed (an "easy" test of eighteen items and a "hard" test of eighteen items) differed in their precision for some levels of ability. These results suggest, as does the problem of out-of-level testing (Long et al., 1977), that problems of equating and scaling are of concern, although in a particular sense they may be more accurately considered an issue in test content. Presumably the tests used in the out-of-level testing study were as well-normed and equated as are most published tests. But the change in content necessary between grades or between vocational programs is a more difficult measurement problem for test validity and comparisons across programs. Even within what is apparently the same test, as in the Slinde and Linn study, examinees of different experience or ability may not be responding to the "same" item. An item is not the same task for all students.

RECOMMENDATIONS TO EVALUATORS

Drawing on the research literature and the definition of test fairness as the documentation of carrying out a set of procedures, the following recommendations describe the documentation and data evaluators should look for in test manuals or provide for in the development of new assessment procedures.

The procedures used to characterize a fair educational achievement test are grouped into three sections: (1) Test specifications, item writing and editing; (2) Item analysis, item selection and score distributions, and (3) Experimental and correlational studies. The first two sections describe procedures that would be completed for any vocational education achievement test; the third section describes procedures appropriate where subgroup differences remain and the evaluator needs evidence that the test measures the same construct for different groups.

1. Test Specifications, Item Writing and Editing

Recommendation 1:   Test specifications should provide for and test content should include balanced representation of minorities and women.

This recommendation means that the test developer should provide documentation that positive models are included and, for example, women and minorities should be presented as participants in all occupations, the sciences, mathematics, and so on. It is not adequate to eliminate stereotyped language/examples and leave subgroups as invisible participants in the various aspects of culture. The implementation of this procedure in test specifications and test content should be described in the test manual.

There are several steps which can be taken to meet this recommendation. Test and item writing specifications must be free from stereotyping and racist or sexist language, and they must meet standards of inclusiveness—positive representation of subgroups. Stereotyping and language demeaning to minorities should be treated in special publications for test authors, item writers, and test editors. Models for sexism in language in book publications have been developed by Scott, Foresman and Company, the McGraw-Hill Book

Company, and other publishers. The American Psychological Association (1977) has a section of the *Publication Manual* that provides editorial guidance and examples of how to rephrase sexist language.

In addition to documenting the use of written guidelines, the extent to which these guidelines result in fair test specifications and item content should be judged by representative members of the subgroups with whom the test may be used. These representatives can be identified as subject matter specialists are now identified, i.e., primarily through a peer referral system. The difference would be that these reviewers would be "experts" in women's studies, black studies, or Hispanic studies, for example; perhaps also expert in the subject matter of the test. Appropriate subgroups can be identified through school census data. The judging procedures might take several forms; test plans and item pools can be judged by subgroup members rating *each* *"item"* on such characteristics as relationship to entering skills, superior levels of achievement, and appropriate weighting.

(1) Entering skill: extent to which ability to perform (pass the item, master the content, demonstrate the skill) is required for entrance to the occupational level for which the assessment procedure is intended.
(2) Superior standard: to do well on the "item" is to demonstrate in part superior overall performance in the occupation at entry level.
(3) Weighting of importance: how important is performance on the item to success at the entry level in the occupation?

In a study in an employment setting (Rosenfeld and Thornton, 1974), ratings similar to these for the occupation of police officer were made by a set of persons that included minority members. The ratings were intercorrelated and factor analyzed to define the most clustered job requirements for each rating set. In this study, the results indicated that ratings by minority and majority members were appreciably similar, and that one rating on relationship to successful performance was satisfactory (represented all four ratings) and had the greatest clarity of factor structure. Similar results might be expected in ratings for vocational assessments at the high school and postsecondary level.

In summary, the first condition of a fair test is:

Procedure 1: Test specifications should provide for and test content should include balanced representation of minorities and women. This balance can be attained procedurally by:

(1) Use of a writer's and editor's manual which provides guidelines for eliminating stereotyping, and biased presentation of women and minorities; the manual should include guidelines for inclusiveness of content—positive examples of these groups in occupational, social, and personal settings.

(2) Judgments of test plans, item pools, or other assessment procedures by representative subgroup members—on entering and superior levels of performance for the entry-level occupation for which the assessment is intended.

(3) Reports of the extent to which the above procedures were implemented, and the publication of results of judgments/ratings in test manuals and/or evaluation reports.

The procedures above deal with the perceived fairness of the test, not with empirical data on test performance. Procedures for empirically examining the fairness of a test are discussed next.

II. Item Analysis, Item Selection, and Score Distributions

Recommendation 2: Item and test analysis procedures should provide evidence that item by group interactions have been examined, and the basis for selecting items or other assessment procedures should be described.

The various techniques which may be used to implement this procedure are providing evidence on the construct validity of the test in a particular sense: that performance is not related to variables which are outside the scope of the educational process; that is, sex, race, and ethnic group membership are variables which should not be highly related to performance. The methods which have been suggested for examining item by group differences were mentioned earlier, and include computing item difficulty data separately for subgroups, then using one of a variety of methods to compare them.

Other studies have used item selection procedures to identify biased items. In these studies items selected on an item-test correlation criterion were compared between tests formed in this manner for different subgroups. Item characteristic curves of the latent trait models and intergroup factor analysis have also been used to identify biased items. A decision rule for reducing mean differences between subgroups on the basis of pretest data has also been proposed. Diamond (1975) suggests calculating the differences between percentage of upper group and percentage of lower group selecting the correct answer separately for subgroups (females and males, for example). If difficulty levels and discrimination are satisfactory for each group separately, calculate the combined group data; keep a record of the signs of the group differences; sum the subgroup differences for the upper groups and determine the average; for any given subtest, it is suggested that the differences should not average over 5 percent in either direction; if the average difference is larger, substitute more "favorable" items until the difference is reduced to desired limits.

If the items which are pretested are examined for item by group interactions or a latent trait model, and if a method has been followed that specifies the decision-making rules for including items in a test so as to minimize differences between subgroups in the final test distribution for *comparable* subgroups, these procedures and the results should be reported in the test manual to justify the claim of a fair test. Further evidence on construct validity and test fairness may be provided through construction of experimental tests and correlations with a standard set of measures, as described next.

III. Experimental and Correlational Studies

Recommendation 3: Further evidence on construct validity should be reported if there are differences in item by group performance and mean differences for comparable groups.

Counterhypotheses to account for any performance differences of women and minorities as *groups* need to be considered and evidence gathered to accept or refute such differences as based on a fair test. There are two types of studies which are particularly relevant here. The first is the experimental manipulation of item or test content, with comparisons made of the performance of comparable sets of subgroups. The second is the demonstration within subgroups of similar patterns of correlations for the test with a specified set of measures.

Medley and Quirk (1974) provide one example of experimentally modifying test content and examining differences between groups on test performance. An earlier study by Milton (1958) examined sex-role identification, and achievement in problem solving for high school students. The difference between males and females in solving problems was nonsignificant when a covariance adjustment was made for scores on a measure of sex-role identification. Because of this finding, in a second study he altered the role appropriateness of the content of the problem-solving task. The difference in problem-solving between males and females was reduced when the problems were framed in a content appropriate to the feminine role. Milton concluded that to achieve maximum results in measuring problem-solving skills in women, it seemed advisable to frame the problem-solving task in content appropriate to the sex-role. The implications from this study were tested with mathematics problem-solving items by McCarthy (1975). Her results substantiate the earlier findings by Milton of the influence of the context of the item on test performance of female and male high school students.

Correlational studies can also be used to provide evidence to justify claims that a test is fair. These studies should be based on hypotheses predicting specific patterns of relationships with other measures. For example, measures of attitudes toward mathematics might be expected to correlate with achievement in mathematics differently for males and females; partial correlations might show no difference in mathematics achievement test results for males and females when correlated with grades and years of math course experience, or between specific subskills in mathematics achievement.

Recommendation 3, then, is further concerned with the construct validity of a test. The procedures are intended to justify the claim that a test is fair by presenting evidence based on experimental studies and patterns of correlations.

In summary, fairness in educational assessment has been defined as carrying out and reporting the results of a set of procedures in three main areas:

    (1) Content validity (test plans, item specifications, item writing, item editing):
        (a) Writing, editing, and reviewing according to a manual designed to eliminate stereotyping and prejudiced language and to meet criteria of inclusiveness,
        (b) Ratings/judgments of performance as demonstrating entry level or superior standards in the occupation.
    (2) Construct validity - 1:
        (a) Analysis of item by group interactions, use of latent trait models,
        (b) Item selection procedures and test distributions (basis used for decision-making).
    (3) Construct validity - 2:
        (a) Experimental manipulation of test content or item content/types,
        (b) Within subgroup patterns of intercorrelations of the test with other measures.

While these procedures have dealt with the measurement process itself, similar recommendations can be specified for test administration directions and all manuals, forms, and other interpretive materials accompanying the assessment instrument. Further study of the procedures described here will lead to identifications of those that are most critical to test validity.

These recommendations and procedures should assist evaluators of vocational education programs. They provide guidance to the evaluator, as do the *Uniform Guidelines*. Evaluators in vocational education must recognize the social setting in which education occurs. Diversity in students requires a responsiveness and change in the traditional psychometric perspective. The issue of test bias provides a challenge and it demands a response from evaluators.

NOTES

1. Cronbach (1978) has noted another form of test bias (sex bias) in the Armed Forces Aptitude Battery (ASVAB), for example: "it is ill designed for females. Lack of

trade and technical information . . . will be scored as evidence of low trade and technical aptitude. Hence the fact that a person has not had experience with machinery may discourage later opportunities to find out if interest and ability lie in that area. Girls are more likely than boys to have this occur" (Cronbach, 1978:1).

2. Work on defining more detailed guidelines has been conducted at the Educational Testing Service, with the formulation of guidelines for testing minorities. A second effort is underway by the Association for Measurement and Evaluation in Guidance Commission on Sex Bias in Measurement, which is currently concerned with bias in achievement tests.

3. Hanson and McMorris (1978) studied the effects of item formats in evaluating program outcomes in early reading. For domain referenced testing, format effects were important. They recommend that the format be selected that was used most frequently in instruction.

REFERENCES

American Psychological Association. 1977. Guidelines for Nonsexist Language in APA Journals. Publication Manual, Change Sheet 2. Washington, DC.

Anderson, L. W. 1975. "Opportunity to learn test bias and school effects." Paper presented at the annual meeting of the National Council of Measurement in Education, Washington, DC.

Anderson, R. C. 1970. Comments on Professor Gagne's paper. In M. C. Wittrock, and D. E. Wiley, *The evaluation of Instruction*. New York: Holt, Rinehart & Winston.

Angoff, W. H. 1975. "The investigation of test bias in the absence of an outside criterion." Paper presented at the National Institute of Education Conference on Test Bias. Washington, DC.

Angoff, W. H., and Ford, S. F. 1971. *Item-race interaction on a test of scholastic aptitude.* Research Bulletin 71-59. Princeton, NJ: Educational Testing Service.

Armbruster, B. B., Steven, R. O., and Rosenshine, B. 1977. *Analyzing content coverage and emphasis: A study of three curricula and two tests.* Technical Report No. 26. Urbana Center for the Study of Reading, University of Illinois. (ED 136-238)

Armstrong, R. A. 1972. "Test bias from the non-anglo viewpoint: A critical evaluation of intelligence test items by the members of three cultural minorities." Doctoral dissertation, University of Arizona.

Bell, D. 1973. *The Coming of Post-Industrial Society.* New York: Basic Books.

Bianchini, J. C. 1976. "Achievement tests and differentiated norms." Paper presented at the U.S. Office of Education Invitational Conference, Achievement testing of disadvantaged and minority students for educational program evaluation. Reston, VA.

Boruch, R. F., and Gomez, H. 1977. Sensitivity, bias, and theory in impact evaluations. *Professional Psychology* 8:411-434.

Breland, H. M., Stocking, M., Pinchak, B. M., and Abrams, N. 1974. *The Cross-Cultural Stability of Mental Test Items: An Investigation of Response Patterns for Ten Socio-Cultural Groups.* Princeton, NJ: Educational Testing Service.

Cahill, V. M., Airasian, P. W., Madaus, G. F., and Pedulla, J. J. 1977. "Insensitivity of the total test score for identifying achievement differences between groups." Paper presented at the annual meeting of the American Educational Research Association, New York.

Cardall, C., and Coffman, W. E. 1964. *A method for comparing the performance of different groups on the items in a test.* Research Bulletin 64-61. Princeton, NJ: Educational Testing Service.

Coffman, W. E. 1961. Sex differences in responses to items in an aptitude test. Pp. 117-124 in *Eighteenth Yearbook of the National Council on Measurement in Education.* East Lansing, MI.

Cole, N. S. 1978. "Approaches to examining bias in achievement test items." Paper presented at the annual meeting of the American Personnel and Guidance Association, Washington, DC.

Cronbach, L. J. 1978. Caution urged in use of armed forces battery. *Guidepost* 20, 12:1, 10.

——— 1975. Five decades of public controversy over mental testing. *American Psychologist* 30:1-14.

Diamond, E. E. 1975. Minimizing sex bias in testing. *Measurement and Evaluation in Guidance* 9:28-34.

Durovic, J. J. 1978. "Use of the Rasch model in assessing item bias." Paper presented at the annual meeting of the Eastern Educational Research Association, Williamsburg, VA.

——— 1975a. Definitions of test bias: A taxonomy and an illustration of an alternate model. *Dissertation Abstracts International* 36, 5.

Echternacht, G. 1974. A quick method for determining item bias. *Educational and Psychological Measurement* 34:271-280.

Federal Register. 1977. *Uniform Guidelines on Employee Selection Procedures.* Proposed Rule Making. Part VIII, vol. 42, no. 251, pp. 65542-6552. Washington, DC: Office of Education, DHEW. (Final *Guidelines,* August 25, 1978.)

Fishbein, R. L. 1977. "The fairness of test items for statistically equated groups." Paper presented at the annual meeting of the American Educational Research Association, New York.

——— 1975. "An investigation of the fairness of the items in a test battery." Paper presented at the annual meeting of the National Council on Measurement in Education, Washington, DC.

Frederiksen, N. 1976. *How to tell if a test measures the same thing in different cultures.* Research Memorandum RM-76-7. Princeton, NJ: Educational Testing Service.

Green, D. R. 1972. Racial and ethnic bias in test construction. Monterey, CA: CTB/McGraw-Hill.

Green, D. R., and Draper, J. F. 1972. "Exploratory studies of bias in achievement tests." Paper presented at the annual meeting of the American Psychological Association, Honolulu.

Hambleton, R. K., and Cook, L. L. 1977. Latent trait models and their use in the analysis of educational test data. *Journal of Educational Measurement* 14:75-96.

Hanson, R. A., and McMorris, R. F. 1978. *Item formats for domain-referenced assessments.* Los Alamitos, CA: SWRL Educational Research and Development.

Hanson, R. A., Schutz, R. E., and Bailey, J. D. 1977. *Program-Fair Evaluation of Instructional Programs: Initial Results of the Kindergarten Reading Readiness Inquiry: Technical Report 57.* Los Alamitos, CA: SWRL Educational Research and Development.

Hoepfner, R. 1976. "Achievement test selection for program evaluation." Paper presented at an Office of Education Invitational Conference, Achievement testing of disadvantaged and minority students for educational program evaluation. Reston, VA.

Jenkins, J. R., and Pany, D. 1976. *Curriculum biases in reading achievement tests.* Technical Report No. 16. Urbana: Center for the Study of Reading, University of Illinois. (ED 134 938)

Journal of Educational Measurement. 1976. "On bias in selection." 13, 1.

Journal of Educational Measurement. 1977. "Applications of latent trait models." 14, 2.

Long, J. V., Schaffran, J. A., and Kellogg, T. M. 1977. Effects of out-of-level survey testing on reading achievement scores of Title I, ESEA students. *Journal of Educational Measurement* 14:203-213.

Lord, F. M. 1977. Practical applications of item characteristic curve theory. *Journal of Educational Measurement* 14:117-138.

McCarthy, K. 1975. "Sex bias in tests of mathematical aptitude." Ph.D. Dissertation, City University of New York.

Medley, D. M., and Quirk, T. J. 1974. The application of a factorial design to the study of cultural bias in general culture items on the National Teacher Examination. *Journal of Educational Measurement* 11:235-245.

Mercer, J. R. 1972. "Anticipated achievement: Computerizing the self-fulfilling prophecy." Paper presented at the meeting of the American Psychological Association, Honolulu.

Merz, W. R. 1976. "Test fairness and test bias: A review of procedures." Paper presented at an Office of Education Invitational Conference, Achievement testing of disadvantaged and minority students for educational program evaluation. Reston, VA.

Milton, G. A. 1958. *Five studies of the relation between sex-role identification and achievement in problem solving.* Technical Report 3. New Haven, CT: Yale University.

Novick, M. R., and Ellis, D. D., Jr. 1977. Equal opportunity in educational and employment selection. *American Psychologist* 32:306-320.

Ozenne, D. G., Van Gelder, N. C., and Cohen, A. J. 1974. *Achievement Test Restandardization.* Santa Monica, CA: System Development Corporation.

Porter, A. C., Schmidt, W. H., Floden, R. E., and Freeman, D. J. 1977. "Impact on what? The importance of content covered." Paper presented at the first annual meeting of the Evaluation Research Society, Washington, DC.

Rakow, E. A., Airasian, P. W., and Madaus, G. F. 1975. "A comparison of the sensitivity of two item selection techniques for program evaluation." Paper presented at the annual meeting of the National Council on Measurement in Education, Washington, DC.

Rawls, J. 1971. *A Theory of Justice.* Cambridge: Harvard University Press/Belknap.

Rosenfeld, M., and Thornton, R. F. 1974. *The Development and Validation of a Police Selection Examination for the City of Philadelphia.* Princeton, NJ: Center for Occupational and Professional Assessment, Educational Testing Service.

Samuda, R. J. 1975. *Psychological Testing of American Minorities: Issues and Consequences.* New York: Dodd Mead.

Schueneman, J. 1976. "Validating a procedure for assessing bias in items in the absence of an outside criterion." Paper presented at the annual meeting of the American Educational Research Association, San Francisco.

Sherman, S. W. 1976. "Multiple choice test bias uncovered by use of an "I don't know" alternative." Paper presented at the annual meeting of the American Educational Research Association, San Francisco.

Slinde, J. A., and Linn, R. L. 1978. An exploration of the adequacy of the Rasch model for the problem of vertical equating. *Journal of Educational Measurement* 15:23-35.

Spencer, T. L. 1973. An investigation of the National Teacher Examination for bias with respect to black candidates. *Dissertation Abstracts International* 33, 8.

Tittle, C. K. 1975. Fairness in educational achievement testing. *Education and Urban Society* 8:86-103.

Tittle, C. K., McCarthy, K., and Steckler, J. F. 1974. *Women and Educational Testing: A Selective Review of the Research Literature and Testing Practices.* Princeton, NJ: Educational Testing Service.

Veale, J., and Foreman, D. I. 1976. "Cultural variation in criterion-referenced tests: A "global" item analysis." Paper presented at the annual meeting of the National Council on Measurement in Education, San Francisco.

Wargo, M. J. 1976. "Achievement testing of disadvantaged and minority students for education program evaluation: An evaluator's perspective." Paper presented at the U.S. Office of Education Invitational Conference, Achievement testing of disadvantaged and minority students for educational program evaluation. Reston, VA.

Williams, R. L., Mosby, D., and Hinson, V. 1976. "Critical issues in achievement testing of children from diverse ethnic backgrounds." Paper presented at the U.S. Office of Education Invitational Conference, Achievement testing of disadvantaged and minority students for educational program evaluation. Reston, VA.

Wright, B. D. 1977. Solving measurement problems with the Rasch model. *Journal of Educational Measurement* 14:97-116.

PART V

Evaluation studies of vocational educational programs do not occur in a vacuum. They must take into account the context in which the program operates and the constituencies to whom the program is responsive. In effect, this means that evaluations of vocational education must be attuned to the needs of industry and labor, as well as the traditional school constituencies of students, parents, and school personnel. Therefore, it is necessary to understand how evaluation research, as a relatively new element in the social sciences fits within this political context, and the role the evaluator takes when conducting studies of vocational education programs. In addition, the political realities that face evaluators working in school districts are important to consider when reviewing evaluation reports. Finally, the views of industry in terms of the services needed by vocational education students, and the need for evaluating programs offered and/or sponsored by industry are of importance in understanding the total picture of the politics of vocational education evaluation.

The chapter by Carol H. Weiss, *Evaluation Research in the Political Context,* describes politics in three programmatic phases that give rise to areas of concern for the evaluation researcher. The first is the fact that the programs that are being evaluated are political creatures in that they are proposed, debated, and ultimately funded through political procedures and decisions. The projects' development leads to a number of problems in terms of evaluation, not least of which is the diffuseness of general goal statements that are normally not measurable but essential for political acceptance. Weiss also describes some of the political issues related to decision-making by superordinate units or agencies, as well as the politics implicit in the evaluation itself. That is, the selection of the programs to be evaluated are implicit political statements. The very structure of the evaluation research enterprise that is ultimately undertaken is also a function of the politics related to the commissioning of the evaluation.

Given the politics of social program funding and evaluation, the problem that the evaluator faces is related to the role that he/she is to play in attempting to carry out the mandate to evaluate vocational education programs. The chapter by Theodore Abramson and Gail R. Banchik, *Determinants of the Evaluator's Role: Political and Programmatic Motives,* attempts to describe the role of the evaluator along a continuum in which the role of the evaluator is completely predetermined by the total political agenda of the funding agency to the other end of the continuum, where the motives underlying the evaluation are solely determined by the need for information for program improvement. Issues such as internal versus external evaluation and the interface, administrative, and technical roles of the evaluator are described at different points along this underlying dimension.

The chapter by Anthony J. Polemeni and Michael H. Kean, *Evaluation Politics in Large City School Districts,* presents the views of directors of offices of research and evaluation in large cities. The problems that they describe, especially in relationship to the evaluation report, may be magnified by the size of the school system involved but are not uncommon regardless of the size of the district. The "we versus they" feeling is an issue to which vocational education evaluation must devote a good deal of thought and discussion. There will be more evaluation, not less, and these issues are probably as important in the long run as are the technical issues involved in conducting evaluation studies. Some of the models described in Part Three of this Handbook, in the chapter by Abramson, do devote some time to the interaction phase of evaluation in which the evaluator must work with the school and program personnel. Basically, it is up to the evaluator to use his/her ingenuity to develop alternative procedures for collecting the necessary evaluation data, and providing better "benefits" for both control and comparison groups from whom large amounts of data have to be collected.

In considering the political context in which evaluations occur, it is necessary to understand the agenda of the various constituencies that comprise the vocational education community. Recently, a new mechanism for the involvement of industry has been developed. The chapter by Gail R. Banchik, Henry H. Coords, Theodore Abramson and Dorothea Sterne, *Industry-Education Councils: A Case Study,* describes one of the more successful industry education councils in New York State. Since the evaluation dimensions that will be included in any study of a program are a function of the values held by the group commissioning the evaluation, it becomes important to understand this view of industry as it applies to vocational education. This chapter attempts to describe, through a case study, the programs undertaken by an industry education council. The work undertaken by the Niagara Frontier Industry Education Council (NFIEC) fits well within the guidelines presented by Ungerer (1978) in his description of the work and education initiative program, which is a combined effort of the Departments of Labor, Health, Education, and Welfare, and Commerce, to find ways of bringing the world of work and education more closely together. Examination of the programs undertaken by NFIEC make it clear that industry feels that the student body and the teachers currently lack information about the needs and requirements of industry. Evaluation of these types of programs must, of course, take this feeling into account, and must ultimately evaluate the outcomes of these programs by examining the relationship between increased cooperation and increased student abilities resulting from these types of programs.

REFERENCE

Ungerer, R. A. 1978. The work and education initiative: an overview. *Journal of Career Education* 4:4-14.

chapter 21

CAROL H. WEISS | *Harvard University*

Evaluation research is a rational enterprise. It examines the effects of policies and programs on their targets (individuals, groups, institutions, communities) in terms of the goals they are meant to achieve. By objective and systematic methods, evaluation research assesses the extent to which goals are realized and looks at the factors associated with successful or unsuccessful outcomes. The assumption is that by providing "the facts," evaluation assists decision makers to make wise choices among future courses of action. Careful and unbiased data on the consequences of programs should improve decision-making.

But evaluation is a rational enterprise that takes place in a political context. Political considerations intrude in three major ways, and the evaluator who fails to recognize their presence is in for a series of shocks and frustrations. First, the policies and programs with which evaluation deals are the creatures of political decisions. They were proposed, defined, debated, enacted, and funded through political processes; and in implementation they remain subject to pressures, both supportive and hostile, which arise out of the play of politics. Second, because evaluation is undertaken *in order to* feed into decision-making, its reports enter the political arena. There evaluative evidence of program outcomes has to compete for attention with other factors that carry weight in the political process. Third, and perhaps least

AUTHOR'S NOTE: *Paper presented at the annual meeting of the American Psychological Association, Montreal, August 30, 1973.*

recognized, evaluation itself has a political stance. By its very nature, it makes implicit political statements about such issues as the problematic nature of some programs and the unassailableness of others, the legitimacy of program goals, the legitimacy of program strategies, the utility of strategies of incremental reform, and even the appropriate role of the social scientist in policy and program formation.

Knowing that there are political constraints and resistances is not a reason for abandoning evaluation research; rather it is a precondition for usable evaluation research. Only when the evaluator has insight into the interests and motivations of the other actors in the system, understands the roles that he himself is consciously or inadvertently playing, realizes the obstacles and opportunities that impinge upon the evaluative effort, and the limitations and possibilities for putting the results of evaluation to work—only with sensitivity to the politics of evaluation research can the evaluator be as creative and strategically useful as he should be.

PROGRAMS ARE POLITICAL CREATURES

Evaluation research assesses the effects of social programs, which in recent years have increasingly been governmental programs and larger in scale and scope than the programs studied in earlier decades. There have been important evaluations of job training programs, compensatory education, mental health centers, community health services, Head Start and Follow Through, community action, law enforcement, corrections, and other government interventions. Most evaluation efforts have been addressed to new programs; while there have been occasional studies of long-established traditional services, it is the program into which new money is being poured that tends to raise the most immediate questions about viability and continuation.

The programs with which the evaluator deals are not neutral, antiseptic, laboratory-type entities. They emerged from the rough-and-tumble of political support, opposition, and bargaining; and attached to them are the reputations of legislative sponsors, the careers of administrators, the jobs of program staff, and the expectations of clients (who may be more concerned with hanging on to the attention, services, and resources available than with long-run consequences). The support of these groups coalesces around the program. But the counterpressures that were activated during its development remain active, and it remains vulnerable to interference from legislatures, bureaucracies, interest groups, professional guilds, the media. It is affected by interagency and intra-agency jockeying for advantage and influence.

The politics of program survival is an ancient and important art. Much of the literature on bureaucracy stresses the investment that organizations have in maintaining their existence, their influence, and their empires. As Halperin (1971) succinctly notes:

Organizational interests, then, are for many participants a dominant factor in determining the face of the issue which they see and the stand which they take. . . . Organizations with missions strive to maintain or to improve their (1) autonomy, (2) organizational morale, (3) organizational "essence," and (4) roles and missions. Organizations with high-cost capabilities are also concerned with maintaining or increasing (5) budgets.

It is not only around evaluation that social scientists bemoan the political factors that distort what they see as rational behavior. An economist recently noted:

You may go through a scientific analysis to answer the question of where the airport should be located, but an altogether different decision may finally emerge from the bureaucracy. [Margolis, 1971]

Bureaucrats, or in our terms program administrators and operators, are not irrational; they have a different model of rationality in mind. They are concerned not just with today's progress in achieving program goals, but with building long-term support for the program. This may require attention to factors and to people who can be helpful in later events and future contests. Administrators also must build and maintain the organization—recruit staff with needed qualifications, train them to the appropriate functions, arrange effective interstaff relations and communications, keep people happy and working enthusiastically, expand the influence and mission of the agency. There are budgetary interests, too, the need to maintain, increase, or maximize appropriations for agency functioning. Clients have to be attracted, a favorable public image developed, and a complex system managed and operated. Accomplishing the goals for which the program was set up is not unimportant, but it is not the only, the largest, or usually the most immediate of the concerns on the administrator's docket.

Particularly when an organization is newly formed to run new programs, its viability may be uncertain. If the organization is dealing with marginal clienteles, it can fall heir to the marginal repute of its clients, and it is likely to have relatively low public acceptance. Organizational vulnerability can become the dominant factor in determining what actions to take, and the need to build and maintain support can overwhelm the imperatives to achieve program goals.

In sum, social programs are the creatures of legislative and bureaucratic politics. The model of the system that is most salient to program managers—and the components of the system with which they are concerned—are bound to be different from the model of the social scientist/evaluator. Their view is probably no less rational. In fact, evidence suggests that programs can and do survive evaluations showing dismal failure to achieve goals. They are less likely to survive a hostile congressional committee, newspaper exposes, or withdrawal of the support of professional groups.

There have been occasional references in the evaluation literature to the need to pay attention to the achievement of organizational "system" objectives as well as to the achievement of program goals (e.g., Schulberg and Baker, 1968; Weiss, 1970), but the notion has never caught on. So evaluators continue to regard these concerns of program staff as diversions from their true mission, and give them no points on the scorecard for effectiveness in the politics of organizational survival.

The disparity in viewpoint between evaluation researchers and program managers has consequences for the kind of study that is done, how well it is done, and the reception it gets when completed. Obviously the political sensitivities of program managers can dim their receptivity to any evaluation at all, and when a study *is* undertaken, can limit their cooperation on decisive issues of research design and data collection (Weiss, 1973). Again at the completion of the study, their political perspectives will lessen the likelihood that they view the evaluative findings as conclusive or the need to act on them as imperative. Even rigorously documented evidence of outcomes may not outweigh all their other interests and concerns.

More subtly, some of the political fallout shapes the very definition of the evaluation study. As an example let us look at the specification of program goals which become the evaluator's criteria for effectiveness. Because of the political processes of persuasion and negotiation required to get a program enacted, inflated promises are made in the guise of program goals. Public housing will not only provide decent living space; it will also improve health, enhance marital stability, reduce crime, and lead to improved school performance. Because statements of goals are designed to secure support for programs, they set extravagant levels of expectation. Furthermore, the goals often lack the clarity and intellectual coherence that evaluation criteria should have. Rather than being clear, specific, and measurable, they are diffuse and sometimes inherently incompatible. Again, it is the need to develop coalition support that leaves its mark. Holders of diverse values and different interests have to be won over, and in the process a host of realistic and unrealistic goal commitments are made.

Given the consequent grandiosity and diffuseness of program goals, there tends to be little agreement, even within the program, on which goals are real, real in the sense that effort is actually going into attaining them, and which are window dressing. With this ambiguity, actors at different levels in the system perceive and interpret goals in different ways. What the Congress writes into legislation as program objectives are not necessarily what the secretary's office or the director of the program see as their mission, nor what the state or local project managers or the operating staff actually try to accomplish. The evaluator is faced with the task of sifting the real from the unreal, the important from the unimportant, perhaps even uncovering the covert goals that genuinely set the direction of the program but are unlikely to surface in open discussion, and discovering priorities among goals. Unless he is astute enough to direct his research toward authentic goals, he winds up evaluating the program against meaningless criteria. Unless he is skillful enough to devise measures that provide valid indicators of success in this complex web of expectations, he runs the risk of having his report disowned and disregarded. It is not uncommon for evaluation reports to meet the disclaimer: "But that's not what we were trying to do."

While the evaluation study is in progress, political pressures can alter or undermine it. Let us look at one final example of how organizational politics can affect the shape of evaluation research. Programs do not always keep to their original course; over time, often a short span of time, they can shift in activities and in overall strategy and even in the objectives they seek to attain. They are responding to a host of factors: budget cutting or budget expansion, changes in administration or in top officials, veering of the ideological winds, changes in congressional support, public appraisal, initiation of rival agencies and rival programs, pervasive client dissatisfaction, critical media coverage. Whereas the evaluator wants to study the effects of a stable and specifiable stimulus, program managers have much less interest in the integrity of the study than in assuring that the program makes the best possible adaptation to conditions. Which leaves the evaluator in a predicament. He is measuring outcomes of a "program" that has little coherence: What are the inputs? To what are the outcomes attributable? If the program succeeds, what activities should be replicated? If the program fails, what features were at fault? Unless programs under study are sheltered from the extremes of political turbulence, evaluation research produces outcome data that are almost impossible to interpret. On the other hand, to expect programs to remain unchanging laboratory treatments is to ignore the political imperatives. In this regard, as in others, programs have a logic and a rationality of their own.

THE POLITICS OF HIGHER ECHELON DECISION-MAKING

Much evaluation research is sponsored not by individual projects or by managers of federal programs but by superordinate levels, such as the director of the agency or the secretary or assistant secretary of the federal department, and the reports often go to cognizant officials in the Office of Management and Budget (OMB), the White House, and to members of congressional committees. If the organizations that run programs have a vested interest in their protection, these higher-level decision makers can view the conclusions of evaluation research with a more open mind. They are likely to be less concerned with issues of organizational survival or expansion, and more with ensuring that public policies are worth their money and produce the desired effects. Of course, some legislators and cabinet or subcabinet officials are members of the alliance that supports particular programs; but it is generally true that the further removed the decision maker is from direct responsibility for running the program, the more dispassionately he considers the evidence.

This of course does not mean that policy makers venerate outcome data or regard it as the decisive input for decision. They are members of a policy-making system that has its own values and its own rules. Their model of the system, its boundaries and pivotal components, goes far beyond concern with program effectiveness. Their decisions are rooted in all the complexities of the democratic decision-making process, the allocation of power and authority, the development of coalitions, the trade-offs with interest groups, professional guilds, and salient publics. How well a program is doing may be less important than the position of the congressional committee chairman, the political clout of its supporters, or the other demands on the budget. A considerable amount of ineffectiveness may be tolerated if a program fits well with the prevailing values, satisfies voters, or pays off political debts.

What evaluation research can do is clarify what the political trade-offs involve. It should show how much is being given up to satisfy political demands, and what kinds of program effects decision makers are settling for or foregoing when they adopt a position. It will not be the sole basis for a decision, and legitimately so: other information and other values inevitably enter a democratic policy process. But evidence of effectiveness should be introduced to indicate the consequences that various decisions entail.

As a matter of record, relatively few evaluation studies have had a noticeable effect on the making and remaking of public policy. There are some striking exceptions, and in any case, our time frame may be too short. Perhaps it takes five or ten years or more before decision makers respond to the accumulation of consistent evidence. There may need to be a sharp change in administration or a decisive shift in expectations. But to date, devastating evidence of program failure has left some policies and programs unscathed, and positive evidence has not shielded others from dissolution (Rossi, 1969). Clearly other factors weigh heavily in the politics of the decision process.

Perhaps one of the reasons that evaluations are so readily disregarded is that they address only official goals. If they also assessed programs on their effectiveness on political goals—such as showing that the Administration was "doing something," placating interest groups, enhancing the influence of a particular department—they might learn more about the measures of success valued by decision makers. They might show why some programs survive despite abysmal outcomes, why some that look fine on indicators of goal achievement go down the drain, and which factors have the most influence on the making and persistence of policy. Just as economic cost-benefit analysis added the vital dimension of cost to analysis of outcomes, *political-benefit* analysis might help to resolve questions about political benefits and foregone opportunities.

It is true that many public officials in the Congress and the executive branch sincerely believe that policy choices should consistently be based on what works and what does not. It is also true that, like all the other actors in the drama, policy makers respond to the imperatives of their own institutions. One seemingly peripheral but consequential factor is the time horizon of the policy process. Presidents, governors, legislators have a relatively short time perspective. They want to make a record before the next election. Appointed officials in the top positions of government agencies tend to serve for even shorter periods. Their average tenure in federal departments is a little over two years (Stanley, Mann, and Doig, 1967). The emphasis therefore tends to be on takeoffs not on landings. It is often more important to a politically astute official to launch a program with great fanfare to show how much he is doing than to worry about how effectively the program serves people's needs. The annual cycle of the budget process also has the effect of foreshortening the time perspective. When decisions on funding level have to be made within twelve months, there is little time to gather evidence (at least competent evidence) on program outcomes or to consider it.

What does it take to get the results of evaluation research a hearing? In a discussion of policy analysis (of which evaluation research is one phase), Lindblom (1968) states that differences in values and value priorities constitute an inevitable limitation on the use of objective rational analysis. As we have already noted, maximizing program effectiveness is only one of many values that enter decisions. Therefore, Lindblom (1968:34, 117) explains, the way that analysis is used is not as a substitute for politics but as a

> tactic in the play of power. . . . It does not avoid fighting over policy; it is a method of fighting. . . . And it does not run afoul of disagreement on goals or values . . . because it accepts as generally valid the values of the policy-maker to whom it is addressed.

It does appear that evaluation research is most likely to affect decisions when it accepts the values, assumptions, and objectives of the decision maker. Research evidence is pressed into service to support the preexisting values and programmatic objectives of decision makers. This means obviously that decision makers heed and use results that come out the way they want them to. But it suggests more than the rationalization of predetermined positions.

There is a further important implication that those who value the *criteria* that evaluation research uses, those who are concerned with the achievement of official program goals, will pay attention as well. The key factor is that they accept the assumptions built into the study. Whether or not the outcome results agree with their own wishes, they are likely to give the evidence a hearing. But evaluation results are not likely to be persuasive to those for whom other values have higher priority. If a decision maker thinks it is important for job trainees to get and hold on to skilled jobs, he will take negative evaluation findings seriously; but if he is satisfied that job training programs seem to keep the ghettos quiet, then job outcome data mean much less.

THE POLITICS IMPLICIT IN EVALUATION RESEARCH

The third element of politics in the evaluation context is the stance of evaluation itself. Social scientists tend to see evaluation research, like all research, as objective, unbiased, nonpolitical, a corrective for the special pleading and selfish interests of program operators and policy makers alike. Evaluation produces hard evidence of actual outcomes, but it incorporates as well a series of assumptions; and many researchers are unaware of the political nature of the assumptions they make and the role they play.

First, evaluation research asks the question: How effective is the program in meeting its goals? Thus, it accepts the desirability of achieving those goals. By testing the effectiveness of the program against the goal criteria, it not only accepts the rightness of the goals, it also tends to accept the premises underlying the program. There is an implicit assumption that this type of program strategy is a reasonable way to deal with the problem, that there is justification for the social diagnosis and prescription that the program represents. Further, it assumes that the program has a realistic chance of reaching the goals, or else the study would be a frittering away of time, energy, and talent. These are political statements with a status quo cast.

For many programs, social science knowledge and theory would suggest that the goals are not well reasoned, that the problem diagnosis and the selection of the point and type of intervention are inappropriate, and that chances of success are slight. But when the social scientist agrees to evaluate a program, he gives it an aura of legitimacy.

Furthermore, as Warren (1973) has noted, by limiting his study to the effects of the experimental variables—those few factors that the program manipulates—the evaluator conveys the message that other elements in the situation are either unimportant or are fixed and unchangeable. The intervention strategy is viewed as the key element, and all other conditions that may give rise to, sustain, or alter the problem are brushed aside. In particular, most evaluations—by accepting a program emphasis on services—tend to ignore the social and institutional structures within which the problems of the target groups are generated and sustained. The evaluation study generally focuses on identifying changes in those who receive program services compared to those who do not, and holds constant (by randomization or other techniques) critical structural variables in the lives of the people.

Warren suggests that there is an unhappy convergence between the preferred methodology of evaluation research—the controlled experiment—and the preferred method of operation of most single-focus agencies. Agencies tend to deal in piecemeal programs, addressing a single problem with a limited intervention, and

> for various reasons of practice and practicality they confine themselves to a very limited, relatively identifiable type of intervention, while other things in the life situation of the target population are . . . left unaltered. . . . The more piecemeal, the fewer the experimental variables involved, the more applicable is the [experimental] research design. [Warren, 1973:4, 9]

Methodologically, of course, experimental designs can be applied to highly complex programs (which is what factorial designs are about), but in practice there does seem to be an affinity between the experiment and the limited focus program. And if there is anything that we should have learned from the history of social reform, it is that fragmented program approaches make very little headway in solving serious social problems. An hour of counseling a week, or the introduction of paraprofessional aides, or citizen representation on the board of directors—efforts like these cannot possibly have significant consequences in alleviating major ills.

Another political statement is implicit in the selection of some programs to undergo evaluation, while others go unexamined. The unanalyzed program is safe and undisturbed, while the evaluated program is subjected to scrutiny. What criteria are used in selecting programs to evaluate? Obviously, newness is one criterion. The old established program is rarely a candidate for evaluation research. It is the new and (perhaps) innovative program that is put on trial while the hardy perennials go on, whether or not they are accomplishing their goals, through the sheer weight of tradition.

Other criteria for selecting programs for evaluations are even more overtly political. Thus in a discussion of program analysis, Schultze (1968) makes two recommendations: (1) program analysts should give more consideration to programs that do not directly affect the structure of institutional and political power than to programs that fundamentally affect income distribution or impinge on the power structure, and (2) analysts can be more useful by studying new and expanding programs than long-existing programs with well-organized constituencies (cf. Hatry, Winnie, and Fisk, 1973:110-111). There are persuasive reasons for such prescriptions. Evaluators, like all other analysts, who ignore the political constraints of special interests, institutional power, and protective layers of alliances, may confront the decision maker with troublesome information. If time after time they bring in news that calls for difficult political choices, if they too often put him in a position that is politically unviable, they may discredit evaluation research as a useful tool. Nevertheless, there are serious political implications in restricting evaluation to the unprotected program and the program marginal to the distribution of economic and political power.

The structure of the evaluation research enterprise also has political overtones. Evaluation is generally commissioned by the agency responsible for the program, not by the recipients of its efforts. This is so obvious and taken for granted that its implications are easily overlooked. Some of the consequences are that the officials' goal statements form the basis for study and if recipients have different needs or different ends in mind, these do not surface. Another probability is that the evaluator interprets his data in light of the contingencies open to the agency: the agency is the client, and he tries to gear his recommendations to accord with realistic practicalities. Furthermore, study findings are reported to decision makers and managers, and usually not to program participants; if the findings are negative, officials may not completely bury the report (although sometimes they try), but they can at least release it with their own interpretations: "We need more money," "We need more time," "The evaluation was too crude to measure the important changes that took place." (For further common defenses, see Ward and Kassebaum in Weiss, 1972:302.) To the extent that administrators' interpretations shape the understanding of the study's import, they constrain the decisions likely to be made about the program in the future and even to influence the demands of the target groups. An evaluation report showing that Program A is doing little good, if interpreted from the perspective of the participants in the program, might well lead to very different recommendations from those developed by an agency-oriented evaluator or a program official.

Most of these political implications of evaluation research have an "establishment" orientation. They accept the world as it is, as it is defined in agency structure, in official diagnoses of social problems, and in the types of ameliorative activities that are run. But the basic proclivity of evaluation research is reformist. Its whole thrust is to improve the way that society copes with social problems. While accepting program assumptions, evaluation research subjects them to scrutiny; its aim is to locate discrepancies between intent and actual outcome.

In fact, social science evaluators tend to be more liberal in orientation than many of the agencies they study (Orlans, 1973). Their perspectives inevitably affect their research. No study collects neutral "facts." All research entails value decisions and to some degree reflects the researcher's selections, assumptions, and interpretations. This liberal bias of much evaluation research can threaten its credibility to officialdom. Thus, a federal assistant secretary writes:

> The choices of conceptual frameworks, assumptions, output measures, variables, hypotheses, and data provide wide latitude for judgment, and values of the researcher often guide the decisions to at least some degree. Evaluation is much more of an art than a science, and the artist's soul may be as influential as his mind. To the extent that this is true, the evaluator becomes another special interest or advocate rather than a purveyor of objectively developed evidence and insights, and *the credibility of his work can be challenged.* [Lynn, 1973:57; italics added]

In this statement, there seems to be an assumption that such a thing as "objectively developed evidence" exists and that assumptions and values are foreign intrusions. But the message that comes through is that "objectively developed evidence" is that which develops only out of government-sanctioned assumptions and values. Certainly evaluators should be able to look at other variables and other outcomes, wanted and unwanted, in addition to those set by official policy.

The intrinsically reformist orientation of evaluation research is apparent in its product. Evaluation conclusions are the identification of some greater or lesser shortfall between goals and outcomes, and the usual recommendations will call for modifications in program operation. The assumptions here are (1) that reforms in current policies and programs will serve to improve government performance without drastic restructuring, and (2) that decision makers will heed the evidence and respond by improving programming. It is worthwhile examining both these assumptions, particularly when we take note of one major piece of intelligence: evaluation research discloses that most programs dealing with social problems fail to accomplish their goals. The finding of little impact is pervasive over a wide band of program fields and program strategies. True, much of the evaluation research has been methodologically deficient and needs upgrading (Mushkin, 1973; Campbell and Erlebacher, 1970), but there is little evidence that methodologically sounder studies find more positive outcomes. Numbers of excellent studies have been carried out, and they generally report findings at least as negative as do the poor ones. Moreover, the pattern of null results is dolefully consistent. So despite the conceptual and methodological shortcomings of many of the studies, the cumulative evidence has to be taken seriously.

What does the evaluation researcher recommend when he finds that the program is ineffective? For a time, it may be a reasonable response to call attention to possible variations that may increase success: higher levels of funding, more skilled management, better trained staff, better coordination with other services, more intensive treatment, and so on. If these recommendations are ignored, if the political response is to persist with the same low-cost low-trouble program, there is not much more that the social scientist can learn by evaluating participant outcomes. If program changes are made, then further evaluation research is in order. But there comes a time when scores or even hundreds of variants of a program have been run, for example, in compensatory education or rehabilitation of criminal offenders, and none of them has shown much success. If it was not evident before, it should be clear by then that tinkering with the same approaches in different combination is unlikely to pay off. There needs to be serious reexamination of the basic problem, how it is defined, what social phenomena nurture and sustain it, how it is related to other social conditions and social processes, and the total configuration of forces that have overwhelmed past program efforts. Fragmented, one-service-at-a-time programs, dissociated from people's total patterns of living, may have to be abandoned; and as Moynihan (1970) has suggested, integrated policies that reach deeper into the social fabric will have to be developed. What this suggests is that in fields where the whole array of past program approaches has proved bankrupt, the assumption is no longer tenable that evaluation research of one program at a time can draw useful implications for action or that piecemeal modifications will improve effectiveness (Weiss, 1970).

As for the other major premise on which the utility of evaluation research is based, that policy makers will heed research results and respond by improving programming, there is not much positive evidence either. We have noted how the politics of program survival and the politics of higher policymaking accord evaluative evidence relatively minor weight in the decisional calculus. It is when evaluation results confirm what decision makers already believe or disclose what they are predisposed to accept that evaluation is most apt to get serious attention. Thus, for example, the Nixon Administration was willing to listen to the negative findings about the Johnson Great Society programs. As Schick (1971) has pointed out, evaluation research is comfortably compatible with a government perspective of disillusionment with major program initiatives, stock-taking, and retrenchment. The fiscal year 1973 budget submitted to Congress proposed to cut out or cut back programs that were not working. The evaluation researcher—now that somebody was paying attention to findings—was cast in the role of political hatchet man. Because evaluation researchers tend to be liberal, reformist, humanitarian, and advocates of the underdog, it is exceedingly uncomfortable to have evaluation findings used to justify an end to spending on domestic social programs. On the other hand, it is extremely difficult for evaluators to advocate continuation of programs they have found had no apparent results. The political dilemma is real and painful. It has led some social scientists to justify continued spending on avowedly ineffective programs to preserve the illusion that something is being done. Others have called for continued spending, whatever the outcome, so as not to lose the momentum of social progress. Others justify the programs in ways that they used to belittle in self-serving program staff: the programs serve other purposes, the evaluations are not very good, the programs need more money, they need more time. My own bent is to find some truth in each of these justifications, but they tend to be declarations based on social ideology and faith, rather than on evidence that these factors are responsible for the poor showing or that the programs are achieving other valued ends.

What would be a responsible position for evaluation research? It seems to me that there are a few steps that can be taken. One reform in evaluation research would be to put program goals in sensible perspective. Among the many reasons for the negative pall of evaluation results is that studies have accepted bloated promises and political rhetoric as authentic program goals. Whatever eager sponsors may say, day care centers will not end welfare dependency, and neighborhood government will not create widespread feelings of citizen efficacy. Programs should have more modest expectations (helping people to cope is not an unimportant contribution), and they should be evaluated against more reasonable goals.

Another course would be to evaluate a particularly strong version of the program before, or along with, the evaluation of the ordinary levels at which it functions. This would tend to show whether the program at its best can achieve the desired results, whether accomplishments diminish as resource level or skills decline, and how intensive an effort it takes for a program to work. If the full-strength "model" program has little effect, then it is fruitless to tinker with modest, low-budget versions of it.

More fundamentally, however, it seems to me that now in some fields there is a limit to how much more evaluation research can accomplish. In areas where numbers of good studies have been done and have found negative results, there seems little point in devoting significant effort to evaluations of minor program variants. Evaluation research is not likely to tell much more. There is apparently something wrong with many of our social policies and much social programming. We do not know *how* to solve some of the major problems facing the society. We do not apply the knowledge that we have. We mount limited-focus programs to cope with broad-gauge problems. We devote limited resources to long-standing and stubborn problems. Above all, we concentrate attention on changing the attitudes and behavior of target groups without concomitant attention to the institutional structures and social arrangements that tend to keep them "target groups."

For the social scientist who wants to contribute to the improvement of social programming, there may be more effective routes at this point than through evaluation research. There may be greater potential in doing research on the processes that give rise to social problems, the institutional structures that contribute to their origin and persistence, the social arrangements that overwhelm efforts to eradicate them, and the points at which they are vulnerable to societal intervention. Pivotal contributions are needed in understanding the dynamics of such processes and in applying the knowledge, theory, and experience that exist to the formulation of policy. I suspect that in many areas, this effort will lead us to think in new categories and suggest different orders of intervention. As we gain deeper awareness of the complexities and interrelationships that maintain problem behavior, perhaps we can develop coherent, integrated, mutually supportive sets of activities, incentives, regulations, and rewards that represent a concerted attack and begin to deserve the title of "policy."

How receptive will established institutions be to new ways of looking at problems and to the new courses of action that derive from them? We suggested earlier that decision makers tend to use research only when its results match their preconceptions and its assumptions accord with their values. There will certainly be resistance to analysis that suggests changes in power relations and in institutional policy and practice; but legislatures and agencies are not monoliths, and there may well be some supporters, too. As time goes on, if confirming evidence piles up year after year on the failures of old approaches, if mounting data suggest new modes of intervention, this will percolate through the concerned publics. When the political climate veers toward the search for new initiative, or if sudden crises arise and there is a scramble for effective policy mechanisms, some empirically grounded guidelines will be available.

Of course, there remains a vital role for evaluation research. It is important to focus attention on the consequences of programs, old and new, to keep uncovering their shortcomings so that the message gets through, and to locate those programs that do have positive effects and can be extended and expanded. It is important to improve the craft of evaluation so that we have greater confidence in its results. To have immediate and direct influence on decisions, there is a vital place for "inside evaluation" that is consonant with decision makers' goals and values—and perhaps stretches their sights a bit. There is also a place for independent evaluation based on different assumptions with wider perspectives, and for the structures to sustain it. One of the more interesting roles for evaluation is as "social experimentation" on proposed new program ventures, to test controlled small-scale prototypes before major programs are launched and gain good measures of their consequences. Nevertheless, given the record of largely ineffective social programming, I think the time has come to put more of our research talents into even earlier phases of the policy process, into work that contributes to the development of schemes and prototypes. I believe that we need more research on the social processes and institutional structures that sustain the problems of the society. I have hope that this can contribute to understanding which factors have to be altered if change is to occur and, in time, to more effective program and policy formation.

REFERENCES

Campbell, D. T., and Erlebacher, A. 1970. How regression artifacts in quasi-experimental evaluations can mistakenly make compensatory education look harmful. In J. Hellmuth, ed. *Compensatory Education: A National Debate, Vol. 2.* New York: Brunner/Mazel.

Caplan, N., and Nelson, S. D. 1973. On being useful: The nature and consequences of psychological research on social problems. *American Psychologist* 28, 3:199-211.

Halperin, M. H. 1971. *Why Bureaucrats Play Games.* Reprint 199. Washington, DC: Brookings Institution.

Hatry, H. P., Winnie, R. E., and Fisk, D. M. 1973. *Practical Program Evaluation for State and Local Government Officials.* Washington, DC: The Urban Institute.

Lindblom, C. E. 1968. *The Policy-Making Process.* Englewood Cliffs, NJ: Prentice-Hall.

Lynn, L. E., Jr. 1973. A federal evaluation office? *Evaluation* 1, 2:56-59, 92, 96.

Marolis, J. 1971. Evaluative criteria in social policy. Pp. 25-31 in T. R. Dye, ed. *The Measurement of Policy Impact.* Tallahassee: Florida State University.

Moynihan, D. P. 1970. Policy vs. program in the '70's. *The Public Interest* 20:90-100.

Mushkin, S. J. 1973. Evaluations: Use with caution. *Evaluation* 1, 2:30-35.

Orlans, H. 1973. *Contracting for Knowledge.* San Francisco: Jossey-Bass.

Rossi, P. 1969. Practice, method, and theory in evaluating social-action programs. Pp. 217-234 in J. L. Sundquist, ed. *On Fighting Poverty: Perspectives from Experience.* New York: Basic Books.

Schick, A. 1971. From analysis to evaluation. *Annals of the American Academy of Political and Social Science* 394:57-71.

Schulberg, H. C., and Baker, F. 1968. Program evaluation models and the implementation of research findings. *American Journal of Public Health* 58, 7:1248-1255.

Schultze, C. L. 1968. *The Politics and Economics of Public Spending.* Washington, DC: Brookings Institution.

Stanley, D. T., Mann, D. E., and Doig, J. W. 1967. *Men Who Govern: A Biographical Profile of Federal Political Executives.* Washington, DC: Brookings Institution.

Ward, D. A., and Kassebaum, G. G. 1972. On biting the hand that feeds: Some implications of sociological evaluations of correctional effectiveness. Pp. 300-310 in C. H. Weiss, ed. *Evaluating Action Programs: Readings in Social Action and Education.* Boston: Allyn and Bacon.

Warren, R. 1973. "The Social Context of Program Evaluation Research." Paper presented at Ohio State University Symposium on Evaluation in Human Service Programs.

Weiss, C. H. 1973. The politics of impact measurement. *Policy Studies Journal* 1, 3:179-183.

——— 1972. *Evaluation Research: Methods of Assessing Program Effectiveness.* Englewood Cliffs, NJ: Prentice-Hall.

——— 1970. The politicization of evaluation research. *Journal of Social Issues* 26, 4:57-68.

chapter 22

THEODORE ABRAMSON

GAIL R. BANCHIK

*Queens College,
City University of New York*
City University of New York

The literature relating to the politics of evaluation tends to be somewhat confusing because of the merging of some of the definitions of the terms "politics" and "politicians." For example, politics may be thought of as the art or science of political government or the policies, goals, or affairs of a government or of the groups or parties within it. Still, other meanings that touch on the word politics might be the methods or tactics involved in managing a state or government, or politics may be taken to mean partisan or factional intrigue within a given group. Similarly, a politician may be described as one who is actively involved in politics, or holds or seeks a political office. The more pejorative connotation of the term politician is one who is interested in personal or partisan gain or other selfish interests. Because of the interchangeability of the meanings of the word politics and politician, a number of papers that deal with the political aspects of evaluation appear to be discussing the same issues when, in fact, their definitions of these terms are different.

In this chapter, we consider the role of the evaluator from the perspective of the motivations that give rise to the evaluation study, and consider these motivations as extending along a continuum in which one extreme is labeled purely political motives and the other extreme purely programmatic motives. In this context, politics will be used to mean partisan or factional intrigue

AUTHORS' NOTE: *Banchik is a Ph.D. candidate in the Educational Psychology Program.*

within a given group, or interests in or activities undertaken for partisan, personal, or other selfish gains and interests.

We prefer to describe many of the activities in which evaluators engage, as they work with policy and program personnel, in terms of negotiation rather than in political terms. Negotiation in this sense means to arrange for or bring about by discussion or a settlement of terms. A purely political evaluation is one which is undertaken for the sole purpose of justifying a previously arrived at position by government, administration, or program personnel, whereas the purely programmatic evaluation is undertaken solely for the purpose of determining appropriate program modifications.

It is clear that in the real world neither of these two extreme positions exist. However, they do provide useful benchmarks for conceptualization of the evaluator's role. But, the more one moves from the purely political toward the purely programmatic evaluation, the greater will be the need for the evaluator to bring to bear his/her skills as a negotiator.

In the nonpolitical evaluation, objective, systematic, and unbiased methods are employed to assess the extent to which program goals have been realized. Once provided with these "facts," the policy maker is able to make the correct decision based on the evaluation. In the political situation, the decision has been made before the evaluation is even conducted. The aim of the evaluation, then, is to collect only the data which will support the already made decision. It is important to note that political and nonpolitical evaluations are not mutually exclusive. On one hand, it is difficult to imagine an evaluation situation without some political aspects. On the other, even a political evaluation might yield some unbiased and potentially useful results. Nevertheless, the fact remains that the role of the evaluator will be heavily determined by the extent to which the underlying motive is political.

In the following sections, the evaluator's role in politically-based and programmatic evaluations will be discussed in the context of internal and external evaluations. Furthermore, various evaluator roles as set forth by Stufflebeam and other writers, will be examined as they are manifested in both a political and nonpolitical evaluation situation.

INTERNAL VS. EXTERNAL EVALUATIONS

A distinction may be made not only between evaluators concerned with program evaluations and those involved in political evaluations, but between external and internal evaluators. An external evaluator is one who has been contracted, from the outside, to evaluate a project with which he/she is not directly involved. An internal evaluator is already involved with or employed by the institutions for which he/she is doing the evaluation. Scriven (1972) has suggested that there are advantages to hiring an outside evaluator who has not been made aware of stated goals. In this way, a "goal free evaluation" can be conducted. It is his contention that the uninformed external evaluator will be looking for all of the effects of the program (in an unbiased manner) rather than being confined to checking on only certain alleged effects.

In theory, the concept of an external evaluator who has a naive but critical approach, seems sound. In practice, however, it is not often feasible. First, there is always the possibility that the evaluator in this position will miss the point of the program (Alkin and Fitz-Gibbon, 1975). In the case where financial and temporal restraints are imposed, it may be important that the evaluator focus attention only on those program effects which will directly influence the decisions in question. Even the most expert evaluator might be unable to do this if he/she is operating in a goal free setting. Second, the decision to employ an internal or external evaluator is often based on how it will appear to interested outsiders, such as agencies with legal mandates to collect evaluation data, special interest groups, and so on. For instance, an external evaluator may be contracted to carry out a politically-based evaluation in which the decisions have already been made. Because the evaluator is to collect data that will support the decisions, it can hardly be called a goal free or objective evaluation. Nevertheless, to an interested outsider, the use of an external evaluator suggests that an unbiased evaluation has indeed taken place. In fact, it is often the intent of the policy makers and program personnel to give just such an impression. That is, they employ external evaluators because they are above reproach and wish the "true value" of their program to be honestly determined.

POLITICS AND PROGRAM GOALS

When a new social or educational program is implemented, its goals are often stated in a way that is not only nonoffensive to potential adversaries of the program, but tends to enhance the program's image. Goals set forth in this manner are characteristically diffuse and ambiguous. Due to the purposeful vagueness of these statements, attainment of goals is often difficult, if not impossible, for the evaluator to measure (Weiss, 1975). Thus, even if the motives for the evaluation are "pure" in the sense that they are related to program improvement, the evaluator may be in the compromising position of having to interpret program objectives in such a way that the program will be placed in a good light. Most methodologists are unable to incorporate such relevant political issues into research designs (Sjoberg, 1975), although Bayesian decision-making may lay the basis for such a possibility (Berk and Rossi, 1976). Nevertheless, just as hard data are examined, the political implications should also be taken into consideration in judging the effectiveness of the program as a whole. Politics must be accepted as a fact of life without totally threatening the evaluator's integrity.

An extreme case of a political evaluation is that which has been termed "pseudo-evaluation" (Webster and Stufflebeam, 1978). The evaluator is used (or misused) specifically for his/her technical expertise. It is expected that he/she will collect and report only those data that will enhance the program's image by showing the successful attainment of the program's goals. Similarly, the evaluator may be expected to support an earlier established decision to terminate the program. If the data or the report do not conform to these standards, the evaluator, rather than the program, will be changed.

In a nonpolitical program evaluation, an evaluator is needed for more than his/her technical ability. Stufflebeam, Foley, Gephart, Guba, Hammond, Merriman, and Provus (1971) suggest that an evaluator, in this situation, has three roles; the interface role, the technical role, and the administrative role.

The Interface Role of the Evaluator

The interface role of the evaluation specialist has two phases (Stufflebeam et al., 1971), the identification of decision situations and the provision of relevant data in time for this decision. In order for these phases to be successfully executed, utmost cooperation is needed between the evaluator and decision makers. It is this *cooperation* which really characterizes the interface role. Without this interaction, the role is nonexistent. For this reason, many politically-based evaluations are without any interface role on the part of the evaluator. In these cases, the evaluation specialist is expected to *accommodate* policy makers rather than to cooperate with them in jointly arriving at evaluation decisions.

Other writers have discussed the interface role of the evaluator in their own terms. Borich (1977) speaks of the evaluation specialist in the program planning stage as a logician and systems analyst. In these roles, the evaluator works with administrators to identify alternatives and clarify what is needed. For example, at this early point the objectives of the program, as well as the roles of the various individuals who operate the program, may be jointly examined and agreed upon by both the evaluator and policy makers. According to a model of evaluation which uses legal and paralegal terms to describe the roles of the evaluator (Anderson, Ball, Murphy, and Associates, 1975), the evaluator acts as a detective. He/she conducts investigations, with the cooperation of decision makers, in order to discover the types of information that are needed. Relationships between the evaluator/detective and policy makers are an integral part of these investigations. In a politically-based situation, the evaluation specialist does not act as a detective, but as an attorney for the defense. The evaluator gathers only that information which will aid the case of the defendant/policy maker.

An evaluator successfully working in an interactive manner with management needs certain skills and knowledges. The specialist should be familiar with recent innovations in the fields of evaluation and vocational education (or the specific area of the evaluation). This knowledge will enable him/her to ask the right questions of the decision makers. Morell (1978) describes the role of the evaluator as an initiator of action. In this role, the main task is to ask the right questions, questions that are both relevant and answerable. In other words, just finding answers is useless unless the appropriate questions have been asked. These questions serve to focus the evaluation on the important issues so that the data collected provide the program director with relevant and timely information useful in making needed midcourse program modifications. In a discussion of the role of the evaluator in public programs (Wholey, 1976), it was suggested that a useful technique in getting at the right questions is for the evaluator to contrast the policy makers' diffusely stated program goals with the absence of measurable objectives, and then to assist in the development of plausible connections between program activities and objectives. In order for this to be done, skill at negotiating and knowledge of the factors involved in public relations are needed by the evaluator in the interface role. Understanding attitudes and philosophies of the program's personnel and ascertaining measurable goals to which they subscribe cannot be easily accomplished without a cooperative effort. For such an effort to occur, the evaluator should be as knowledgeable about human nature as about data analysis.

Most of the tasks included in the interface phase occur during formative stages of an evaluation. That is, the aim of the evaluator is to help to mold and modify the program objectives so that the probability of achieving stated goals is maximized. In a summative evaluation, on the other hand, the evaluator wants to present data which will aid decision makers in judging the attainment of the program's goals at the end of a specified period. While a formative evaluation necessitates constant cooperation between evaluators and management, a summative evaluation, occurring after program stabilization requires relatively less interaction and minimal interventions in the program. In fact, tests which are routinely administered to students as part of the program are often used in the summative evaluation. Thus, it is possible to be less obtrusive in conducting summative evaluations than it is in formative studies.

Rippey (1973) argues that the concept of "transactional evaluation" differs from Scriven's (1967) concept of formative evaluation as an attempt to guide improvement of a single program while it is underway. A transactional evaluation is that which places great emphasis on the interface role of the evaluator. Besides doing everything that he/she would normally do in a formative evaluation, the transactional evaluator also focuses on the roles of the decision makers themselves. Thus, the evaluator will take into consideration, not only prospective program modifications, but the views of the policy makers who will be adversely affected by these changes. Criticisms of the evaluation will be welcomed and utilized in a constructive manner. By attempting to deal with the conflict generated by impending change, the transactional evaluator is able to create a climate for change (Pitts, 1978). In order for transactional evaluation to successfully take place, the interface role of the evaluator must be expanded and improved. It may be argued that transactional evaluation is essentially a more complex version of formative evaluation.

Cronbach, in recent years, has stressed the importance of the interface role and of formative evaluations. In his earlier work he defined evaluation as the "collection and use of information to make decisions about an educational program" (Cronbach, 1963). As such, the measurement of outcomes was emphasized. Over a decade later, the role of the evaluator is conceptualized as not that of a short-term consultant to be brought in at the end of the program, but as an individual who works alongside management through all the phases of program development (Ross and Cronbach, 1976). The evaluator's role is not only to measure previously stated objectives, but to serve as a naturalistic observer who conducts the evaluation based on what he/she observes. The evaluator is interested in process or how people interact, as well as in product or outcomes.

Consistent with this revised conceptualization of evaluation, Cronbach and Snow (1977) suggest that "one group evaluation studies" which are case studies based on naturalistic observations, should be encouraged in psychological studies of learning and instruction. In these studies, not only should outcomes be assessed, but a "complex treatment of substantial duration" should be documented. The purpose of such a study is not to be able to generalize from one program to another in a reductionist manner, but to generalize about molar behavior in naturalistic environments. In order to achieve this, research is required "that is representative of instructional complexity and duration, and that concerns itself with what students do in typical situations" (Cronbach and Snow, 1977:390). Thus, research findings are not merely conclusions, but "updatings" of the current view of the program (Ross and Cronbach, 1976).

The Technical Role of the Evaluator

The technical role of the evaluator consists of the actual tasks involved in the production of information. Borich (1977) refers to this role as that of "quantifier of activities and outcomes," "data analyzer," and "reporter of program effects." In the legal model of evaluation, (Anderson, et al., 1975) the role would be equivalent to that of court reporter, in which data are simply collected and reported. The skills and knowledges needed to success-fully execute the technical role are many. Alkin, Kosecoff, Fitz-gibbon, and Seligman (1974) have developed a detailed checksheet of these tasks. They may be summarized as the operationalization of objectives, the development of instruments to measure attainment of objectives, sampling, data collection, the arrangement of data in a usable form, data processing, data analysis, the interpretation of data, and the reporting of results. Thus, the evaluator in the technical role should possess measurement, statistical, computer, and communication skills. Evaluators in politically-based situations and evaluators who are conducting nonpolitical program evaluations both must assume the role of the technician. In the former case, the evaluator's technical expertise is essential in the collection, arrangement, and interpretation of those data which will support the politically advantageous decision. In a nonpolitical formative or summative evaluation, the specialist's technical ability is used in the collection, arrangement, and interpretation of all relevant data which will help to determine whether the program in question should be modified, continued, or discontinued.

In his attempt to erase the formal boundaries between program planning, program development, and program evaluation, Borich (1977) has developed an evaluation model in which the evaluator enters the picture in the program planning, rather than in the program evaluation stage. In this way, he/she works alongside planners and developers. This revised model demands that the evaluator's technical expertise be expanded and applied throughout the planning, development, and evaluation process. Thus, it may be said that the technical role of the evaluator will be more prominent in a formative than in a summative evaluation.

The Administrative Role of the Evaluator

The third function of the evaluator, the administrative role, includes processes such as deciding on the need for an evaluation, and planning, coordinating and assessing the evaluation itself. Since this is not only the role of the evaluator, but of the decision maker as well, interaction is necessary. For this reason, there is a great deal of overlap between the interface and the administrative roles. Furthermore, the same skills and knowledges which are needed in the interface role, are also necessary for administration. Again Borich's (1977) roles of "logician" and "systems analyst" can be seen as administrative.

Stufflebeam et al. (1971) emphasize that the actual decision to conduct an evaluation is, in part, the responsibility of the evaluator in the administrative role. Because evaluations, whether political or nonpolitical, are often man-dated by funding-agencies, the decision to evaluate is often not up to the evaluation specialist. Nevertheless, in nonpolitical program evaluations, planning, organizing, and appraising the evaluation remains the administrative chores of the specialists. On the other hand, in politically-based evaluations, the evaluator generally does not have an administrative role. The evaluator's sole function is to provide appropriate data that have been properly analyzed and reported.

An issue which bears on the role of the evaluator is whether there is an evaluation team or an individual evaluator. According to a segmentation model (Bucher and Strauss, 1961), each subgroup within a profession should be able to perform certain tasks which other subgroups cannot. It has also been suggested that as certain tasks of a growing profession begin to be identified, a hierarchy develops in which certain tasks are delegated to individuals of varying status and education within that profession (Wilensky, 1964). Accordingly, it seems that an evaluation team where each member has expertise in a specific role or task would fare better than an individual evaluator. It is difficult to imagine one individual who can perform all the interactive, technical, and administrative tasks required of an evaluator. If an individual evaluator does undertake a program evaluation, he/she would be well advised to know how, where, and when to identify and employ others who have the skills which the evaluator lacks.

The question of who will be in charge comes to mind when an evaluation team, rather than a single individual, is conducting the evaluation. For instance, will the program director manage the team? If this is the case, will it be considered an internal evaluation, and possibly one which is biased? It seems clear that whoever heads the team should be skilled in all the tasks identified in Stufflebeam's et al. (1971) administrative role.

SUMMARY

This paper examined the role of the evaluator as it is derived from the motive for the evaluation. Motive for evaluation was looked at as a bipolar dimension, with program evaluation at one extreme and political evaluation at the other. Within the program/political dimension, the evaluator's role in terms of internal or external evaluations and formative or summative evaluations was discussed. Finally, the evaluator's interface, technical and administrative roles were described as a function of the motive for the evaluation.

Before undertaking an evaluation, it would behoove the evaluator to understand the policy maker's motives for having an evaluation conducted. In order to further legitimatize evaluation as a profession, specialists should become sensitized to the distinctions between program and political evaluations if they wish to be the ultimate arbiters of their own roles.

REFERENCES

Alkin, M. C., and Fitz-Gibbon, C. T. 1975. Methods and theories of evaluating programs. *Journal of Research and Development in Education* 8: 2-15.

Alkin, M. C., Kosecoff, J., Fitz-Gibbon, C. T., and Seligman, R. 1974. *Evaluation and Decision-Making: The Title VII Experience.* CSE Monograph Series in Evaluation, No. 4. Los Angeles: Center for the Study of Evaluation, University of California.

Anderson, S. B., Ball, S., Murphy, R. T., and Associates. 1975. *Encyclopedia of Educational Evaluation: Concepts and Techniques for Evaluating Education and Training Programs.* San Francisco: Jossey-Bass.

Berk, R. A., and Rossi, P. H. 1976. Doing good or worse: Evaluation research politically reexamined. *Social Problems* 23: 337-349.

Borich, G. D. 1977. Program evaluation: New concepts, new methods. *Focus on Exceptional Children* 9: 1-16.

Bucher, R., and Strauss, A. 1961. Professions in process. *American Journal of Sociology* 66: 325-334.

Cronbach, L. J. 1963. Course improvement through evaluation. *Teachers College Record* 64: 672-683.

Cronbach, L. J., and Snow, R. E. 1977. *Aptitude and Instructional Methods: A Handbook for Research on Interactions.* New York: Irvington Publishers.

Morell, J. A. 1978. "Developing evaluation plans for community mental health settings: A model for appropriate selection of optimally useful evaluation." Paper presented at the annual meeting of the National Council of Community Mental Health Centers, Inc.

Pitts, M. 1978. "My views on evaluation after having read the new rhetoric—by Robert Rippey. Paper presented at the annual meeting of the AERA. Toronto.

Rippey, R. M. 1973. *Studies in Transactional Evaluation.* Berkeley, CA: McCutchan Publishing Corp.

Ross, L., and Cronbach, L. J. 1976. Handbook of evaluation research. *Educational Researcher* 5: 9-19.

Scriven, M. 1972. Prose and cons about goal-free evaluation. *Evaluation Comment* 3: 1-4.

———. 1967. The methodology of evaluation. Pp. 39-83 in R. E. Stake, ed. *Perspectives of Curriculum Evaluation.* AERA Monograph Series on Curriculum Evaluation, No. 1. Chicago: Rand McNally.

Sjoberg, G. 1975. Politics, ethics, and evaluation research. In M. Guttentag, and E. L. Struening, eds. *Handbook of Evaluation Research, Vol. 2.* Beverly Hills: Sage Publications.

Stufflebeam, D. L., Foley, W. J., Gephart, W. J., Guba, E. G., Hammond, R. I., Merriman, H. O., and Provus, M. M. 1971. *Educational Evaluation and Decision-Making.* Itasca, IL: F.E. Peacock.

Webster, W. J., and Stufflebeam, D. L. 1978. "The state of theory and practice in educational evaluation in large urban school districts." Address presented at the annual meeting of the AERA, Toronto.

Weiss, C. H. 1975. Evaluation research in the political context. In E.L. Struening, and M. Guttentag, eds. *Handbook of Evaluation Research, Vol. 1.* Beverly Hills: Sage Publications.

Wholey, J. S. 1976. The role of evaluation and the evaluator in improving public programs: The bad news, the good news, and a bicentennial challenge. *Public Administration Review* (Nov.-Dec.):679-682.

Wilensky, H. L. 1964. The professionalization of everyone. *The American Journal of Sociology* 70:137-158.

EVALUATION POLITICS
IN LARGE CITY
SCHOOL DISTRICTS

chapter 23

ANTHONY J. POLEMENI

MICHAEL H. KEAN

New York City
Board of Education
School District of Philadelphia

There was a time, not long ago, when the major problems faced by an educational evaluator had to do with the best way to collect, analyze, and report data on student achievements and program outcomes. This is no longer true. In spite of the fact that major progress has been made in the field of educational evaluation, there have also developed new problems which require consideration.

The major problems today concern responses to the results in the evaluation report by school superintendents, principals, teachers, unions, and parent groups. The evaluation report has become politicized and has become the source of problems which must be faced by evaluators as they attempt to protect their findings from special interest groups. Each of these groups has a different perspective on the evaluation report. For example, there is often an unwillingness to publicize results which, though truly illustrative of the situation, might have negative political repercussions. It might be found, for instance, that grouping for a particular subject produces maximum growth in academic or social achievement. If, however, grouping would result in sex segregated or racially segregated classroom then such findings would, in many localities, be considered a political anathema. Some educational research findings may be (legitimately) unacceptable to the various groups who have an interest in the public schools.

For a variety of reasons, evaluation results are often not considered in making program or management decisions: The results may be considered politically inexpedient; the results are available too late for incorporation in the recycling design; the person in a key management position simply does not agree, philosophically, with the results. Whatever the cause, the net result is the same: The evaluation might just as well never have been conducted. This situation gives rise to a concomitant problem in that the morale of evaluation workers suffers when they become aware that their work may be in vain. As in most such situations, reduced morale results in reduced quality of output. Some of these situations also suggest that the evaluator needs to forecast or simulate alternative *evaluation outcomes,* establish policy alternatives, and determine the political or administrative feasibility of using evaluation findings.

Another situation in which evaluation data may purposely be ignored is if they adversely affect patronage possibilities (e.g., teacher aides). Education and evaluation, as they become more and more a function of community involvement, become more and more susceptible to the possibility of patronage. Where the clubhouse has built a cozy network based on nepotism and favoritism, it is obvious that any evaluation results which are considered threatening will be treated as nonexistent. This threat to the use of evaluation may be most obvious in large city systems, where school administration is bureaucratized.

Lay persons, particularly on Boards of Education, demand gross oversimplification in reports of evaluation studies. That the difference is significant at the .05 level is not enough for them. What does it mean? It means that the result could have been obtained by chance alone in only five out of a hundred samples. Yes, but what does that mean? And so the report travels back and forth, back and forth, the evaluator trying to stress the limitations of the study, lay users trying to make the findings universally applicable to satisfy their own purpose.

Frequently there is resistance to evaluation findings by supervisory personnel—including school principals—who "know in their bones" that the way they are doing it is the best way it can be done. This situation leads them to say such things as, "I know your findings prove my program is not working, but I just feel the students are getting something out of it and I am going to stick with it." Without faulting intuitive judgment completely, because there is a place for it in the educational process, the evaluator's view is that it must be tempered by a realistic appraisal of the data.

Classroom teachers frequently oppose the collection of data because they are unable to see any profit for their own students. This is almost always the case with control groups from whom vast amounts of data must be collected without any program to compensate them for their time. In large measure their reluctance is well-founded since the period between data collection and report dissemination usually runs a year or more, and the students who contribute to the data are no longer with the teacher. While future benefits may accrue, it is difficult for the teacher to defend such practice to the students or their parents.

Project managers are threatened by evaluation because, if the evaluation is negative, they might be out of a job. Such a consideration causes all sorts of things to happen: data disappear, project personnel are unavailable for interviews, students to be observed have suddenly gone on a class trip, the evaluator is incompetent, the evaluator is biased, and so on. While it is not absolutely impossible to evaluate a program without the project manager's approval, it is extremely difficult.

Personnel responsible for securing federal and state monies feel threatened by evaluation results because negative findings could result in lack of funding or lack of refunding. This fear is similar to that of the project managers (except for the political consideration which motivates the fear) although, in the final analysis, both fear the loss of their jobs if evaluation results are negative.

A Brief Historical Perspective

It is important to note that significant educational evaluation has a very short history. Evans (1974a), noted that educational evaluation as institutionalized today through federally-mandated evaluation studies, is in large part an outcome of the massive social action programs in the 1960s. Those were the times of sudden major federal support for manpower and poverty programs, and the period of the Great Society programs. Most of these funding decisions by the Congress and the Executive Branch of the federal government were made without access to "hard data" to determine the size and character of the problems which were being addressed by the new programs. Also, very few of these programs were ever subjected to any kind of objective evaluation to measure the effectiveness of these efforts.

Another significant development in American education, which has greatly affected evaluation, has been the demand for accountability in education. However, the term accountability is far from being clearly defined. According to Evans (1974a), it is hard to tell whether the accountability movement is a cause, an effect, or merely an indicator of the increased interest in evaluation.

Hoyt (1976) suggests that accountability is now a permanent part of American education. He emphasized its impact in regard to two basic questions, both of which are highly relevant to the field of educational evaluation, namely:

(1) The question of *process*: What have you done?
(2) The question of *product*: What benefits have resulted from your actions?

One of the basic premises, according to Hoyt, is that it is impossible to solve a problem unless its dimensions can be clearly defined. Therefore, we cannot determine *how good* a particular practice is until we have first clearly stated *what it is* that we are trying to accomplish.

The accountability movement has had a considerable impact on many federal and state funding agencies, which now demand more detail about the objectives of funded programs as well as anticipated outcomes. Evans (1974a) stressed the fact that, although political interests may still govern many decisions in the executive branch of the federal government and the congress, there is a significant increase in the number of persons from such agencies who are demanding more rationalized policy processes in the implementation of new programs.

The consequences of the accountability movement have, in short, become an important factor in the manner in which the educational evaluator must operate. Accountability has also affected the cost of evaluation tasks.

Evaluation Problems in Vocational Education

Vocational education is a form of education which frequently combines vocational training with the teaching of nonvocational fundamental skills. Thus, according to a study conducted by the National Planning Association (1972), vocational education serves as an umbrella for a wide variety of programs. The Association concluded that most of the programs attempted to supply students with a marketable skill while, at the same time, providing them with a basic knowledge of English, arithmetic, and social studies. The common denominator of these programs is their eligibility for federal support through the different vocational education acts and amendments. This lack of a sharp line between vocational and non-vocational education has contributed to a controversy over the role and adequacy of vocational education. The lack of a sharp line also contributes to the evaluator's problems in determining costs and resources allocated directly to vocational education, versus shared costs. Also, there are politics involved in attributing costs to the vocational education programs. Program or per pupil costs tend to be higher because of equipment for training, and tend to vary widely between vocational education programs. It is in the interests of vocational educators to see some costs allocated to the nonvocational programs.

Vocational education is one of the largest of the publicly supported training programs in the United States today. As such, it is responsive to political groups, and minority students and women are among the new target groups for vocational education. There is also the need for "adaptability" skills which are required in our rapidly changing world of business and industry, as well as the need for continued up-grading of job knowledge and job skills, as part of the emerging concept of "lifelong" education and learning. Responsiveness to these requirements. of vocational education impose new dimensions on the teaching/learning process, which need careful definition. Vocational education has a broad out-reach, including not only a great variety and levels of policy makers and educators, but members of business, industry and labor. However, there has been little correlation of these efforts, and no firm foundation of facts and verified principles to build upon. This state of flux may result in evaluators defining the important outcomes of vocational education by what is readily measurable.[1] Vocational education is a form of education which is in a flux of development rather than a well-defined discipline.

Cost of Evaluations

There is frequently a tremendous disparity between the amount of evaluation data required and the amount of funding provided for the conduct of evaluation. This happens most often where a figure such as one-half of one percent is determined to be appropriate for the evaluation of each individual program. Where the program costs run to several hundred thousand dollars or more, this base rate may be meaningful and applicable. But where the cost of a program runs to figures like thirty thousand dollars, the evaluation agency is being requested to perform its functions for something like one hundred-fifty dollars, which is absurd on the face of it. While it is often the case that programs may be placed together under an "umbrella" in larger cities, so that the evaluation funds can be shifted from larger appropriations to smaller, such a procedure of cost efficiency in evaluations does not provide a universal solution to the problem of evaluating vocational education programs, particularly in individual schools or in smaller districts.

Evaluator Qualifications and Roles

Traditionally, educational evaluators have been chosen among professionals or graduate students with academic degrees in psychology, testing, and measurement. These persons are frequently hired on a consultant basis to carry out specific evaluation assignments. There are several problems which may be created by this procedure. First, each evaluator approaches his/her assignment with more or less a preconceived notion of how such tasks should be carried out. Therefore, the evaluation of separate vocational education programs, which have received funding from the same source, are frequently treated in distinctly different manners. There are no uniform guidelines that can be applied. Second, each evaluator expresses his/her findings and observations in a more or less idiosyncratic manner, depending upon experience in reporting and style of writing. There are those who produce extensive verbal analyses of program objectives and outcomes that may take the proportions of mini-dissertations. There is also the opposite terse type of reporting limited to essential statistical data and information about levels of statistical significance of obtained achievement data. Third, most evaluation is of a summative nature which is limited to a reporting and comparison of pre and posttest data.

Evaluator qualifications are of concern because it is probable that school people will increasingly demand that evaluators not only collect and analyze data but also provide prescriptions for upgrading the program. The major question here is whether the average evaluator has sufficient subject matter knowledge to make such recommendations for program modifications. This is a serious question, deserving serious consideration. Let us assume that an evaluator has the training and experience to evaluate vocational educational programs. However, it does not follow that he/she would also be qualified to prescribe specific program modifications. The possibilities of errors in judgment are obvious. For example, suppose that an evaluator prescribes a specific program modification which is implemented. Then, the next year when he/she returns, the program administrator makes such a statement as, say, "You know, that idea you gave us last year has now ruined the program to a point that the funding agency is reconsidering the merits of refunding it."

The role of the evaluator becomes further complicated in situations where the accountability concept is applied to the long-term outcomes of a program. Hoyt (1976) puts it in these words:

> If carried to the extreme, the general call for accountability can effectively hinder the introduction of any new educational concept. That is, the expected benefits from education, almost without exception, are stated in long-term goals as well as in short-term goals. The long-term goals, typically, are stated in terms that reflect expected behaviors of pupils once they have become adults and left the formal system of education. Such goals, therefore, are ones that defy evaluation prior to the time a generation of pupils has passed through the educational system and assumed adult roles.

It is, therefore, essential that the evaluator carefully distinguish between long-term process goals and short-term product goals in an educational program. Hoyt emphasizes that there is no simple "cookbook" solution to these problems which must be left to the discretion of the practitioner.

It is evident from current trends in evaluation that we may see the approaching end of the politically appointed and, therefore, also often politically motivated evaluator, who will only grind the axe of the people who did the hiring. Future trends will probably be toward the employment of evaluators through competitive procedures to ensure objective data collection and reporting. Some legislative mandates already impose such selection and qualification requirements in evaluation. Those program administrators who do not comply may increasingly face the danger of termination of funding.

Future Trends

As indicated in the introductory part of this chapter, there are new problems in evaluation which have arisen during the past few years. Evans (1974b:12) enumerates a total of seven such new areas of concern, to which reference is being made:

(1) There is the problem of an increasing data collection burden which has created a considerable level of resistance to it. People are getting increasingly reluctant to answer long questionnaires. Many such investigations now also require prior clearance and review by concerned parties.

(2) The gathering of data on adult learners is further complicated by the fact that some interviewees demand payment for their participation.

(3) There is an increasing sensitivity about how findings can be reported, and to whom they may be disseminated. New systems for review and clearance have evolved, leading to multiple involvement procedures that can be highly unproductive and discouraging to the evaluator. Some evaluation studies are simply stopped for these reasons.

(4) There is the increase in the politicization of evaluation reports which are frequently being used as weapons either to promote or dispute educational practices.

(5) Many program people are beginning to realize that evaluation must be taken seriously and that there will be increasing demands for accountability in reporting. Some school administrators feel threatened by these demands and are, therefore, reluctant to get involved in otherwise worthwhile program efforts and developments.

(6) Some of the new legislative mandates for evaluation are unrealistic in terms of the level and amount of reporting that is required. Or, as Evans puts it, "They want to know whether or not a program is any good and they want to know it yesterday."

(7) We can expect further public debate on the validity and appropriateness of different types of evaluation methods and the manner in which results are being reported. The major problem here is that the public generally lacks the professional knowledge and perspective which permits an objective assessment of different approaches to evaluation. Therefore, we may, as Evans puts it, arrive at the ironic situation that "after a large scale formal evaluation has been put aside because of technical questions raised about its methodology, policy-makers and program officials then return to the old and familiar

methods of making the decisions of formulating the policy-methods that are highly partisan and subjective in nature."

In conclusion, there are many political problems in educational evaluation today, but there is also reason for optimism. In spite of the new problems in reporting data to diverse interest groups, as well as increasing levels of politicization of evaluation, there is emerging what appears to be a far better operational definition of evaluation methods and techniques, including information about potential benefits or shortcomings. There is also a certain measure of soundness and vitality in these conflicts which should prompt us to continue our efforts to establish mutually agreeable procedures for the evaluation and reporting of educational programs. It is an open arena for debate and discussion in which the evaluator must be prepared to stand accountable for his or her actions, with the awareness that there will never be a comfortable panacea of total agreement. But, clearly, there is an important task which must be performed.

NOTE

1. See Bonnet's chapter in this Handbook for another expression of concern over the role of evaluators in defining the outcomes of career education programs.

REFERENCES

Evans, J. W. 1974. "Evaluating educational programs—are we getting anywhere?" Paper presented at the annual meeting of the American Educational Research Association, Chicago.

Evans, J. W. 1974b. Evaluating educational programs—are we getting anywhere? *Educational Researcher* 3,8:7-12.

Hoyt, K. B. 1976. *Perspective on the Problem of Evaluation in Career Education.* Monograph on Career Education. Washington, DC: Office of Career Education (DHEW/OE).

National Planning Association, 1972. *Policy Issues and Analytical Problems in Evaluating Vocational Education.* Washington, DC: Center for Priority Analysis.

INDUSTRY-EDUCATION
COUNCILS
A Case Study

chapter 24

GAIL R. BANCHIK
HENRY H. COORDS
THEODORE ABRAMSON

DOROTHEA STERNE

City University of New York
Fisher-Price Toy Company
Queens College,
City University of New York
The Niagara Frontier
Industry Education Council

Three major groups that have a great deal at stake in terms of the skills, knowledges, and attitudes of graduates of vocational education programs are the schools, organized labor, and industry. Each of these groups has their own agenda of concerns, and are thus part of the political context in which vocational education and its evaluation take place. One's perspectives and values are crucial factors in determining which variables will define the evaluation dimensions in looking at any program.

Secondary and postsecondary education institutions, which administer most vocation and occupational education programs, include general educational goals that go far beyond the specific skills and knowledges of a particular vocational program in which the student is enrolled. These general goals, at the very least, typically consist of basic communication, mathematics, and citizenship skills. Organized labor has a stake in vocational education because the graduates of these programs enter the labor force and are frequently prime candidates for joining the unions. One of the concerns of labor is that these graduates do not displace people who are already employed by providing sources of cheap labor that will reduce wages and other benefits currently enjoyed by the workers represented by organized labor. Industry which is interested in maximizing efficiency so that the cost of production can be minimized, is generally interested in obtaining the best and most capable work force at the least cost to itself.

AUTHORS' NOTE: *Banchik is a Ph.D. candidate in the Educational Psychology Program.*

It is important for vocational educators and evaluators of vocational education programs to be aware of these three distinct groups and the political context within which they operate. This chapter focuses on the perspective of industry through a case study description of the specific programs undertaken by a successful industry-education council.

In recent years, there has been a growing concern over the lack of communication and cooperation between industry and occupational education programs. Since one of the major goals of vocational education is to provide a labor force that is capable of meeting the needs of the economy, the worlds of business and of occupational education should be intimately linked; that is, vocational education should produce a skilled and adaptable group of workers who are able to supply the manpower needed to run the nation's industries. In enacting the Vocational Education Act of 1963 (PL 88-210), and subsequent amendments in 1968 and 1976 (PL 94-482), the federal government has recognized the importance of this relationship between occupational education and industry. For instance, the 1976 evaluation-related amendments require that annual follow-up studies of vocational education programs judge effectiveness in terms of graduates' employment in training-related occupations, employer satisfaction with graduates, or graduates' continuation in education.

Potential barriers to increased industry-education cooperation are multifaceted (Hensley, 1978). The participation of industry is frequently not sought during the time that vocational education programs are being developed. It is unlikely that individuals in business can be strongly committed to a program if their participation has not been encouraged through all phases of policy development. Security considerations in certain industries impose another barrier. That is, a number of companies require that restrictions be placed on the visits and observations of outside persons, including school personnel and students. Time and money, appropriately allocated, are needed to effect communications between industry and education. Both schools and industries often reserve time and space for only those activities yielding immediate payoffs (Hensley, 1978). Finally, a barrier to cooperation results when competencies perceived by business for a working life are unclear to members of the education community.

Communication is a major component for an efficient vocational educational system that provides students with up-to-date descriptions of and training for jobs that are not only current, but that are likely to exist in the foreseeable future. Thus, vocational educators should be familiar with the skills that must be mastered by students who are about to enter the job market. Similarly, business people should specify not only job openings, but employer preferences for the types and level of training desired for employees in entry-level jobs. For this familiarity with the needs of industry by school personnel and vice versa, open, regular, and timely communication is needed. One approach to these issues has been through the establishment of advisory councils for occupational education.

This chapter will briefly mention recent research which shows a need for a liaison and improved communication between industry and education, followed by a description of Advisory Councils for Occupational Education in New York State. Finally, Industry-Education Councils, as a concept, and an apparently successful attempt at bridging the gap between business and vocational education will be discussed in some detail.

Extent of Cooperation Between Industry and Education

There is some evidence to attest to the lack of cooperation and communication between business and education. For example, in a recent survey, 1,267 Illinois employers were asked about their hiring practices (Niss and Pledge, 1977). It was found that there is often not a good match between training in vocational programs and demand in related occupations. In another study, a survey of bookkeeping occupations indicated substantial discrepancies between school curriculum and employment requirements (Cohen and West, 1978). These findings were so compelling that the New York State Education Department has recently altered the statewide syllabi for high school instruction in bookkeeping in the direction of the survey's results.

Lack of regular and timely communication between occupational educators and industry is not universal. There are a number of reported instances of formalized cooperative efforts as well as many informal examples of communication between business and education. The state of Louisiana has implemented a two-phase training program which custom-tailors its courses to the specific requirements of companies involved in beginning or expanding manufacturing operations (Borseau, 1978). These courses are being offered in more than thirty-five vocational-technical schools throughout the state. The two phases of this course consist of a preliminary pre-employment course, and on-the-job training. This program has been cited as a contributing factor to Louisiana's increased labor productivity.

New York State Advisory Councils for Occupational Education

New York State has recognized the need for maintaining an ongoing informational flow between industry and vocational education, and has attempted to institutionalize this link through the formation of advisory councils. In the foreword to *A Handbook for Members of Advisory Councils for Occupational Education* (New York State Education Department, undated) it is stated that, "advisory councils exist to help guide occupational education for people seeking preparation for realistic employment opportunities" (p. 3). Every board of education in New York State which maintains a state approved occupational education program is required to appoint an advisory council for occupational education. The actual administration of vocational education, as is true of all elementary and secondary programs, is in the hands of the local board of education. For this reason, whether an advisory council exists as an active, innovative, policy-making body or merely as a superfluous, mandated, nonfunctional adjunct organization varies from district to district.

Despite interdistrict differences, the Handbook suggests that local advisory council members become familiar with the activities of the State Advisory Council, and that they transmit recommendations to the state council, particularly when their concerns extend beyond the geographical boundaries of their districts. Examples of such concerns include a need for regional planning, an impending change in the employment market, and descriptions of particularly successful local programs and procedures that should be considered for regional or statewide adoption.

The duties of local advisory councils are not specified in sufficient detail to provide a clear picture of what it is they are supposed to do. According to the Handbook, the council is required to "advise the board of education on the development of and policy matters arising in the administration of occupational education, including the preparation of long range and annual program plans" (p. 4). Furthermore, it states that it is the duty of the council "to assist with an annual evaluation of occupational education programs, services, and activities provided by the school district" (p. 9). Terms such as "advise" and "assist" lend themselves to differences in interpretation. This may be a strength as well as a weakness of the system. On the one hand, lack of specificity may leave room for local initiatives and necessary interdistrict differences. On the other, these same interdistrict differences may be so disparate as to preclude the possibility for any meaningful functional summary across districts. In practice, the system falls somewhere in between these two extremes. Ultimately, the more effective, innovative, and influential councils serve as models for the less successful ones.

Additionally, it is suggested that advisory councils appoint consultant committees in each of the specific occupational fields for which the district provides an instructional program. *A Handbook for Members of Consultant Committees for Occupations* (New York State Education Department, undated) states that the purpose of such committees is to assist in planning, to develop new programs, and to evaluate and revise existing programs. The consultant committees for occupations (CCO) should consist of at least five individuals from labor and management, representing the occupation under consideration. The rationale for the existence of these committees is based on the need of the educational institution for access to intra and interdistrict, and regional information concerning particular occupations so that it may identify potential job and labor market needs. In addition, CCOs help the schools develop viable job descriptions, skill requirements, educational materials, equipment lists, and facilities layouts. The basic source of this knowledge is the employee and employer involved in the occupation. Providing these types of data to vocational educators is the primary function of the CCOs.

Advisory councils and their consultant committees have some serious limitations. As mentioned before, at best they have only advisory functions without the actual power to implement recommended changes. In a comprehensive report on the status of school councils (Davies, Stanton, Clasby, Zerchykov, and Powers, 1977) it was found that there is an absence of data concerning the quantity and quality of advice given by advisory councils, and the extent to which the advice influences those with authority to act. Similarly, the relationship of school boards to school councils is not well documented. For the most part, boards of education appear not to see councils as very high priorities (Davies et al., 1978). This may be a result of the school board's fears that councils may, if unchecked, usurp the board's prerogatives and responsibilities. There is also the familiar skepticism that councils are no more than political stepping stones for citizens, and in the case of advisory councils for occupational education, for industrialists. Therefore, the effectiveness of advisory councils is often determined by their ability to persuade school administrators and boards of education to institute changes that frequently require increased expenditures, to update equipment, modifications in plant and personnel allocations, or other changes that are not generally perceived by school boards as politically and/or practically feasible "at this time."

An additional problem is that local councils are sometimes too narrow in focus. For instance, consultant committees may consist of local employers who want the schools to serve local needs or sometimes even the particular interests of individual council members (Cohen and West, 1978). A more useful approach should be more global and should take into consideration the needs of an entire region, be more future-oriented, and be less political.

Local Industry-Education Councils

Recently, another attempt has been made to bridge the gap between industry and vocational education. The National Manpower Institute in Washington has provided funding for and has implemented twenty-one regional industry-education councils across the nation. Simply stated, the purpose of these councils is to serve as liaisons between business and education. There are no guidelines for either the councils or for their co-ordinators. Thus, each council functions independently of the others.

Industry-Education Councils differ from Advisory Councils in a number of important ways. The most notable distinction is that the former function independently of rather than as adjuncts to the educational establishment. This autonomy is a result of their federal source of funding and of their creation being independent of any local educational agency. For this reason, they have more than an "advisory" function. They not only develop and implement their own agendas external to the local school districts, but they are also able to directly affect the implementation and modification of vocational education programs, and policies in their school systems. Notwithstanding this independence, and possibly because of it, council membership usually includes representatives from the highest administrative and decision-making levels of education, such as superintendents and district directors of vocational education. Another difference resulting from the very extensive executive talent involved, is that industry-education councils consist of top echelon business and labor executives. Furthermore, these councils never concern themselves with specific occupations, as do advisory councils. Generally, the activities they work on are of a more global nature. In short, industry-education councils can be characterized as autonomous organizations whose members are drawn from leading positions in industry and education, and whose purpose is to effect the cooperation of industry and education.

A pamphlet entitled *Work Education Councils: Profiles of Twenty-one Collaborative Efforts* (National Manpower Institute, 1977) describes the activities of these councils and their different stages of development. The remainder of the present chapter, however, is devoted to a description of one of the oldest and apparently most effective of the councils, (National Manpower Institute, 1977) the Niagara Frontier Industry-Education Council.

The Niagara Frontier Industry-Education Council

The Niagara Frontier Industry-Education Council (NFIEC) was organized by the Buffalo Chamber of Commerce and the Erie County Board of Cooperative Educational Services (BOCES) in 1973. Broadly, its goal is to link policy makers from both education and industry so that they will best be able to prepare young people to be productive, working members of society. More specifically, the aims of NFIEC are to (1) provide direction and resources for teachers of career education in all grades, (2) establish a "Center for Career Information," (3) promote an awareness of career education among students and parents, (4) promote a better understanding in the community of the needs and problems of education, and (5) provide opportunities for business people and government and labor leaders to meet with educational personnel.

Surveys reported in the New York State Regional Plan for the Buffalo-Erie county region indicated that for a large number of students the formal guidance programs provided in the schools were not functioning as significant sources of occupational information. Over half of the students surveyed responded that they had not received any counseling regarding the job opportunities associated with the occupations listed on the questionnaire. All schools in the Niagara Frontier area, including BOCES, vocational high schools, and public and private high schools, provide prospective workers for the local labor market. Clearly, an innovative effort was needed which would inform this large student and staff population of local job opportunities, and of changes in the character and procedures of industrial practices and commercial efforts.

In addition to the informational needs that educational agencies had concerning industry, a flow of information was needed from the schools to industrial and commercial agencies which included descriptions of school programs that prepared students for entry into industry. Employers needed to know the entry level skills and knowledges of their prospective employees who were graduates of the school's occupational education courses. Communications of these kinds were minimal, were usually informal and irregularly scheduled, and were basically the responsibility of school personnel who had many other duties to perform. Frequently, school-industry communication consisted of the industry contact that the teacher had or made when attempting to place a program's graduate(s).

In sum, the need to improve the vocational education graduate's knowledge of the expectations that industry has of him/her, and his/her ability to perform within the context of current employment situations, required program updating and improvement by the schools, as well as availability and usage by the students of all available community resources. The first step leading toward this improved and expanded school/community program was improved communications. NFIEC was developed to fill this need and to act as the liaison agency between educational institutions and industrial/commercial concerns. NFIEC was to serve as the vehicle for improvement not only in communication, but in school instruction and administration of occupational education through the use of community resources. Such resources included personnel with specialized knowledge and skills, and a wide variety of materials, specialized equipment, and facilities. Special emphasis is placed on employing those resources which are current, which are normally not accessible through other channels, and which are made available to schools on a volunteer basis. Communication being a two-way channel, it is equally important that industry be informed of what is occurring in the educational community. Much of the expertise already developed by educators in the training of prospective employees can be used to benefit industry.

From this brief explanation emerge some additional overall objectives of NFIEC. One goal was to change the attitude of the community toward vocational education from negative or neutral, to supportive and positive. A second goal was to persuade educators to abandon some traditional and obsolete approaches to occupational education in favor of more up-to-date relevant, and needed methods. Third, NFIEC was to encourage more parental and community involvement in the goal setting activities of vocational education programs. Finally, NFIEC would assist educational agencies to employ commercial and industrial resources for the improvement of the occupational education curriculum.

NFIEC Programs

The NFIEC is currently offering a variety of programs. Students, school personnel, and industrialists all may benefit from getting involved in one or more of these activities. Although each NFIEC sponsored program has something unique to offer its participants, they all share a common underlying goal: to promote cooperation between the worlds of business and education. Program offerings include: a Special Workshop on Occupational Awareness for educators, a Resource Bank containing the names of potential speakers, a Center for Occupational Information, Economics Training for Teachers, Teacher Exchange Days during which teachers work in area companies, Executive Exchange Days during which school superintendents and business executives team up for a typical working day, Community Breakfast Meetings, an Energy Symposium for students, and a Shadow Program in which students are offered realistic work experience. The subsequent paragraphs describe some of these programs in more detail.

The *Special Workshop on Occupational Awareness* is essentially a graduate course organized by the NFIEC under the auspices of the State University at Buffalo. The course offers educators first-hand exposure to the industrial, labor, and economic institutions of the community. Teachers, counselors, and administrators attend weekly on-site sessions as the guests of area industry, government, and labor organizations. Of the educators who have been enrolled in the course thus far, only 12 percent had jobs directly involving occupational education. The remainder were teachers concerned with a variety of subject areas, guidance counselors, and administrators. Seemingly, interest in increasing one's occupational awareness is not only the domain of the vocational educator, but of other school personnel as well.

So far, there has been no formal evaluation of the *Occupational Awareness Course,* although an ever increasing enrollment can attest to its popularity.

Initially, the workshop consisted of one section of twenty-five educators and twelve cooperating businesses per semester. Presently, there are three sections of seventy-eight educators and forty-six industrial/commercial institutions involved in the program. An indirect measure of the effects of these workshops is the second-hand benefits that students are obtaining from the exposure their teachers have had to various business organizations. For instance, at least fifty participating teachers have followed up their sessions at a particular business with a class project in which students learn about various functions connected with running the company. These projects involved aspects of industry such as product design, engineering, production, quality control, marketing, accounting, finance, and personnel.

In another effort to expose teachers to the world of business, NFIEC recently created a *Teacher Exchange Program*. In this program, a sponsoring business provides a work program, in consultation with the teacher, which allows the teacher's active participation in the work of the company for one day a week. In this way, the teacher gains knowledge of the business, the way it operates, the goods and services it provides, the skills required of its labor force, its current labor needs and hiring practices, and exposure to the work climate and values of the particular company with which he/she is involved. Additionally, the sponsoring institution is encouraged to send one of its members to the teacher's school in order to talk to the students and faculty about the company's goals and employment opportunities, as well as its services to the community.

It is the goal of the Teacher Exchange Program to provide realistic, on-the-job experience in business settings for teachers who, in turn, will discuss career opportunities with their students in a knowledgeable manner. Again, it is hoped that this program will result in a heightened sense of mutual awareness and cooperation between private sector organizations and the educational community.

As is the case with all of these programs, NFIEC not only sponsors but organizes the Teacher Exchange Programs. First, it sends material about this program to local businesses, industries, and nonprofit organizations. Then it contacts member school districts to gather support for the program from superintendents, principals, and teachers. Additionally, it provides guidelines to businesses, industries and nonprofit organizations to help in setting up work programs. Finally, it supplies contacts for interested teachers.

The NFIEC *Resource Bank* was developed in 1974. It consists of a catalogue of local business and industry volunteers who are willing to take time from their day to talk to classes about their particular professions. At this time, the bank includes over 1,200 volunteers, indexed by occupation. Over 700 of these books have been distributed to area schools. Contacts between teachers and potential speakers are handled individually, not through the NFIEC office. For this reason, it is difficult to evaluate the effectiveness of the bank. Generally, the catalog is underemployed and its use is, for the most part, limited to "Career Days" in the schools. An analysis of the number and subjects of the teachers who actually utilize the bank might result in a more efficient use of this resource.

Based on a survey which found that over 250 secondary students per week, of their own volition and on their own time, visited the public library specifically to seek information about careers, NFIEC recently implemented the *Center for Occupational Information.* This center, housed at the Erie County Public Library, is accessible to all students who seek information about various careers. Additionally, a mobile van belonging to the local BOCES has been loaned to NFIEC so that all schools and shopping plazas can be visited with career information.

The Center for Occupational Information tells students not only what kinds of careers might be available to them, but the source of training for these careers as well. Although the center is not yet fully operational, considerable progress has been made in cataloging the various types of work that are available in the Niagara Frontier region through extensive staff work and cooperation with industrial organizations throughout the area. In addition, the catalogue provides some idea of the future job market within each occupational classification. This is not a global listing, but one limited to the specific jobs and industries existing within a geographical radius to which the student might aspire without severe geographical dislocation. Finally, the center also offers a comprehensive list of all the local educational institutions which provide special training in preparation for the occupations that are catalogued. With constant monitoring of its operations and timely up-dating of its data, along with the cooperation of industry, the center will make available to students much of the basic information necessary for informed decision-making and appropriate selection of a career.

Initiated by the NFIEC in 1977-1978, the *Shadow Program* offers students the opportunity to spend a full forty-hour week on the job "shadowing" a regular employee and getting both a broad and specific appreciation for the world of work. Students involved in these short internships come from the junior or senior classes of vocational schools. Thus, they are already trained with a particular career path in mind. These students are selected by a coordinator who checks with their teachers in order to ascertain whether they have the skills to be expected of a potential employee.

Evaluation Concerns

Now that NFIEC is five years old, where does it go from here? Needless to say, new programs may be implemented and more industrialists, educators, and students may become involved. This increase in the number of people involved in NFIEC programs would undoubtedly enhance the apparent success of the council. Of equal importance, however, is the development and implementation of a formative and summative evaluation program, which would serve to assess on a more formal basis the effectiveness of NFIEC or other councils with similar programs.

Before the actual evaluation begins, it is necessary to determine which evaluation issues are important to involved industrialists, representatives of labor, and school district personnel. For instance, evaluative data that would enhance industry's image at the expense of the educational community or vice versa, might prove destructive to the effectiveness of the industry-education council. Thus, the first step taken by the evaluator should be to ascertain which evaluation procedures are acceptable to the groups represented on the council. At the same time these activities must minimize the inherent differences in perspectives and expectations between educators and business people. For this reason, evaluators of new programs of this type would do well to develop their skills as negotiators. Past evaluations of vocational education programs have studied specification of objectives, description of management procedures, assessment of major student outcomes, and have used unobtrusive measures when possible. These are facets of evaluation which should continue to be acceptable to business, labor, and education groups.

Generally, an important step in evaluation procedure is the specification of objectives. Once the objectives are clearly stated and operationalized, it is possible to determine the type of data that should be collected, stored, and retrieved to assess whether or not the goals have been realized. When the effectiveness of NFIEC and each of its programs has been assessed by measuring goal attainment, it will be possible to modify the council activities accordingly.

Management procedures, student outcomes and school-industry labor relationships are among the general areas in which evaluations could be undertaken. Since the individuals who are currently directing NFIEC and the involved business people and educators seem to be instrumental in the apparent success of the council, it is important to understand what it is they do that is making NFIEC work so well. Thus, any evaluation design should allow for the assessment and full description of the personnel involved in NFIEC, the constituencies they represent, and the administrative procedures that have been successful. Data should be collected on the effects that NFIEC participation has on students. Each program should be evaluated on an individual basis using unobtrusive measures where possible. For instance, it would be useful to know how many of the students who participated in the Shadow Program actually pursued the occupation in which they had "interned" after their graduation. This is one of the ways in which the effectiveness of this program on future career decisions may be measured. As a process variable example, the resource bank materials could be used more efficiently if records of the number of teachers who have actually used this bank and the subjects that they teach were accurately described along with the categories of business/professional/trades-people who have visited the classrooms. Still another example would be the determination of the number of students per week who visited the Center for Occupational Information.

An evaluation of NFIEC would serve not only to assess its effectiveness resulting in its modification and improvement, but would also make possible a comparison between NFIEC and other industry-education councils. This way there may be a meaningful description across councils as well as an exchange of ideas and resources. This type of communication could be more easily established if there were general uniform guidelines for all industry-education councils. The lack of such guidelines, however, should not preclude a productive communication system between councils.

Summary

In order to have an effective vocational education system, there is an obvious need for communication and cooperation between business and education. This need has been evidenced in the legislation and in the research literature, as well as in the real life experiences of program graduates and their employers. Attempts have been made to bridge the gap between industry and vocational education programs in New York State and elsewhere, through the creation of advisory councils. The effectiveness of these councils in serving as a vehicle for bridging the gap between the schools and the world of work is generally perceived as inadequate to the challenge.

A relatively new supplementary approach, industry-education councils, has been established and funded by the federal government in order to further promote communication and cooperation between business and vocational education. One of these councils, NFIEC, was described in the present chapter. In examining the activities, programs, and projects undertaken by NFIEC it becomes clear that the basic approach consists of sharply focusing or refocusing existing structures so that their programs more directly meet the needs that industry feels will benefit it by helping its prospective labor force become more knowledgeable about what industry expects of them and what industry can provide for them. Some of these programs operate directly with the students and some of them indirectly through school personnel. This approach is clearly in keeping with the concept of minimizing direct costs to industry, while maximizing direct benefits to industry. Only one of the eight programs that NFIEC has developed provides students with direct work experience, perhaps because this type of program requires cooperation not only of the schools and industry but also of organized labor. The other seven programs call for school-industry cooperation in refocusing existing structures or modifying schedules to permit involvement of students and/or school personnel.

To date the effectiveness of the activities of this council have not been evaluated. Some ideas for basic evaluation activities were briefly sketched in this chapter. Notwithstanding the lack of formal evaluation data, a brief description of NFIEC indicates that progress is being made toward the improvement of occupational training through better industry-education communication.

REFERENCES

Borseau, S. 1978. Public-private combo pays off in Louisiana. *Career Education News* 7:3-4.

Cohen, L., and West, L. J. 1978. Occupational curricula: The school/job match. *New York University Education Quarterly* 9:16-21.

Davies, D., Stanton, J., Clasby, M., Zerchykov, R., and Powers, B. 1977. *Sharing the Power? A Report on the Status of School Councils in the 1970's.* Boston, MA: Institute for Responsive Education.

Hensley, G. 1978. Problems and possibilities of increased interaction among business, industry, and education. *Journal of Career Education* 4:24-33.

National Manpower Institute. 1977. *Work Education Councils: Profiles of Twenty-One Collaborative Efforts.* Washington, DC.

New York State Education Department. *A Handbook for Members of Advisory Councils for Occupational Education.* Albany: Office of Occupational Education. (undated)

———. *A Handbook for Members of Consultant Committees for Occupations.* Albany: Office of Occupational and Continuing Education. (undated)

Niss, J., and Pledge, M. T. 1977. Illinois employer preferences for vocationally trained personnel. *The Vocational Guidance Quarterly* 25:204-210.

CONCLUSION

The concluding remarks provide a fitting place for the editors of this volume to identify themes that seem important in the development and conduct of vocational education evaluation. The issues or themes that can be identified revolve primarily around the conceptualization of evaluation itself. Evaluation in vocational education typically occurs now in conjunction with federally mandated evaluations or grant-related requirements for evaluation. Offices of research and evaluation in large cities may not even have responsibility for the evaluation of vocational education in conjunction with the federally mandated requirements. Evaluation is often a separate function that is carried out within the office responsible for occupational education. This form of organizational relationship may have limitations for the independence and usefulness of the evaluation.

Federal attempts to insure program change and improvement through external mechanisms, such as the VEA of 1976 evaluation requirements, and through data collection systems such as the Vocational Education Data System (VEDS) under pilot development, are not necessarily geared to assist local education authorities to improve or change programs. The evaluation requirements in the VEA are not accompanied by money to assist states with this function, although there is a contract to develop models for state use in evaluating vocational education (Smith, Regal, and Holt, 1978). The VEDS system focuses on collecting, through the National Center for Education Statistics, enrollment, and financial, and follow-up data on vocational education programs and students. The VEDS system will take considerable cooperation and patience to evolve into a usable data base. Aside from many of the problems cited by Datta in her chapter, there are additional problems. Most of the accounting systems in use in schools are not program oriented. Some LEAs will have trouble distinguishing between state and local dollars that are funding programs, and will also have problems in ascribing proportional costs of shared facilities in buildings and administration, for example. These are in addition to the basic definitional problems, such as defining what is a program in vocational education, and defining the various disadvantaged or special populations.

However, what is of concern here is the accumulating data that seems to indicate a need for a more flexible view of evaluation. The VEDS system and the NIE (1978) studies of state use of evaluation data may help to inform policy for the targeted groups that are included as priorities in the federal legislation. On the other hand, although they may provide some level of evaluation useful to the states, the models for the second level of evaluation— that required of the states to evaluate every vocational education program within a five year cycle—are not specified. Although site visitation teams and questionnaires are often used, these methods are not well validated and have not been evaluated for their effectiveness in program change and improvement. It is interesting that one of the more recent efforts to assess the impact of federal legislation at the local level (Berman, 1977) summarized the findings of a Rand study as follows:

> Our overall findings can be stated quite simply. Federal change agent policies had a major effect in stimulating local districts to undertake projects that were generally consistent with federal categorical guidelines. This local response resulted from the availability of federal funds and, in some programs, from guidelines that encouraged specific educational practices. But the adoption of projects did not insure successful implementation; moreover, successful implementation did not guarantee long-run continuation. Neither those policies unique to each federal program nor those policies common to all of them strongly influenced the fate of the innovations that had been adopted by the districts. In sum, the net return to the federal investment was the adoption of many innovations, the successful implementation of few, and the long-run continuation of still fewer (with the exception of the special case of bilingual projects, where federal and state funding continues to be available).
>
> All the federal programs funded projects that were implemented successfully, as well as projects that were dismal failures and many projects in between. The difference between success and failure depended primarily on how school districts implemented their projects, not on the type of federal sponsorship. The guidelines and management

strategies of the federal change agent programs were simply over-shadowed by local concerns and characteristics.

The findings for use of federal monies in vocational education will be more positive than these findings for innovative programs at the elementary level because subpart 2 monies in the VEA provide for maintaining and improving current programs, not just developing new programs. However, one of the main recommendations was that the states should be allocating no less than 10 percent of the funds to leadership training and staff development activities of local school districts. And in fact, the discussion further emphasized regional arrangements where less competitive districts in an area could draw on skills of stronger districts and secondly, that peers could be used to help their counterparts in other districts (e.g., principals, teachers, middle management, and superintendents). These recommendations provide a different orientation toward influencing program change and improvement. But it also suggests that the current emphasis in evaluation focuses on descriptive and outcome measures which are often unrelated to the diagnostic purpose of program improvement. Effort may need to be put into integrating the ideas of program improvement, change, and evaluation at the local level. This is similar to the emphasis that some organizational theorists (e.g., Pondy, 1977) have used to contrast evaluation that may be useful for smaller organizational units than the state and federal levels.

If this is accurate, then effort needs to go into the development of local evaluation models, taking into account that a variety of approaches are probably needed according to the problems with which individual local organizations may be concerned. This focus would shift some of the evaluation effort from assessing variables connected with individuals to identifying organizational variables and evaluation approaches that are more matched to the problems identified internally to the organization. What we are saying here is that different contexts or problems will require different evaluation approaches; important next steps are for teaching staff, administrators, and evaluators to undertake the task of defining and testing various approaches to evaluation. It also suggests the importance of substantive knowledge of areas within vocational education. In order to understand why some outcomes occur, organizational, instructional and learner variables that are directly related to assisting local program development and improvement should be part of evaluation studies. For example, the variable "opportunity to learn" is an important construct in program evaluation in the early school years (Cooley and Leinhardt, 1978). We have not found examples of this type of directly diagnostic variable applied in vocational education program evaluation.

To summarize these themes and issues, we see needed developments in research on evaluation at the different levels at which evaluation occurs in vocational education. In particular, we place as a high priority the development and assessment of evaluation methods available to local agencies. We would also argue that a heavy reliance on outcome measures that are student defined, and on status variables that describe the vocational education program will be of only partial assistance in improving local programs, assuming that improvement is needed.

At the federal level of evaluation, there is a concern as to whether the approaches being used will bring to the surface issues important in providing a focus for funding, such as has happened with the Case Studies in Science Education (Stake, 1978). This set of case studies conducted for the National Science Foundation appears to be useful in identifying, for example, teacher support systems as a priority area for definition and improvement in science education. It is not clear that this type of variable will surface under the current evaluation systems proposed and being carried out in vocational education. Thus, it may be useful to try to specify the criteria of "effective" evaluations to determine whether they can provide guidance for the next stage of development in evaluation concepts.

We turn now to a consideration of developments that have or are likely to impinge on the conduct of evaluation by evaluators and administrators. We refer here to the current efforts to improve the ethical standards that are found in applied educational and social research. In particular, the need for informed consent, rules of data gathering, and confidentiality have caused changes in the way evaluators and administrators conduct evaluations. Most evaluators, particularly those conducting large scale evaluation for government organizations or in university-based research, know that informed consent of subjects must be obtained and that adequate provisions are required to maintain confidentiality of individual data. However, another development is in process and may be part of the evaluation literature by the time this book is in print. This development is the project on educational evaluation standards. The history of the project to develop evaluation guidelines and standards (Joint Committee, 1977) began with the process that resulted in the 1974 revision of the *Standards for Educational and Psychological Tests*. The Joint Committee on Test Standards recommended a companion volume to the test standards. This recommendation was taken up by the major organizations concerned with the test standards: the American Educational Research Association, the American Psychological Association, and the National Council on Measurement in Education. The new project on evaluation standards has been conducted at the Evaluation Center, Western Michigan University.

We can judge the impact that such standards might have by Shepard's (1977) list of the functions that might be served by the evaluation standards.

She identified the following functions: expanding the definition of evaluation; disseminating definitions and methodology with authority; encouraging promising new practices; discouraging bad practices; aiding in negotiating contracts with clients; making trade-offs among standards explicit; serving as a checklist for evaluating evaluations; and focusing research in needed areas of evaluation methodology. As she noted, there are also risks in premature codification of a developing field. At this stage, the evaluation standards have been submitted and reviewed by a National Review Panel, and further revision is being undertaken. It would be inappropriate to identify the individual guidelines because they are not finalized, but we can alert evaluators and administrators to the major areas with which the standards for educational evaluation are likely to be concerned.

The first category of the standards, in their early version, was entitled *accuracy*. This area was concerned with the technical adequacy of the evaluation findings. This area may be concerned with the validity and reliability of the instruments and evidence collected, and the appropriateness of the conclusions drawn from the data analysis. The second area was *utility*. The utility of evaluation findings is concerned with serving the practical information needs of different audiences.

The third category was entitled *propriety*. This category may be more accurately called ethics, in the sense that the standards in this area are concerned with such ideas as a conflict of interest for evaluators, the public's right to know, the rights of human subjects, and the fiscal responsibility of evaluators. The fourth category was *feasibility*. In this category, the evaluation standards would be concerned with the practicality of evaluation procedures. That is, evaluation designs must meet some criteria and approach the reality of what is feasible politically, cost-wise, and so on.

The final form of the standards is not set nor is the amount of time that will be required to reach agreement on them, because more organizations (then the original sponsoring groups) are involved in the full project. For example, the American Association for School Administrators, the American Federation of Teachers, the American Personnel and Guidance Association, the Association for Supervision and Curriculum Development, the Education Commission of the States, the National Association of Elementary School Principals, the National Education Association, the National School Boards Association, are all involved as well as the original three associations. The final report is expected in 1981, after field testing and national hearings.

In the long run, we feel that the effort to develop and disseminate the evaluation standards should have a healthy effect on the field. We think that it will achieve one of the functions that Shepard specified, that of encouraging the best of practice and discouraging bad practices. As she also noted, the standards also provide an instructional outline for those training evaluators! We see the developments of the standards as providing promise to the field in terms of assisting evaluators to gain consensus on what are acceptable practices, and where we need to go next in improving practice.

REFERENCES

Berman, P. 1977. Congressional testimony on educational innovation. Santa Monica, CA: Rand Corporation.

Cooley, W. W., and Leinhardt, G. 1978. "Design and educational findings of the Instructional Dimension Study." Paper presented at the annual meeting of the American Educational Research Association, Toronto.

Joint Committee on Evaluation Standards and Guidelines. A project to develop guidelines and standards for educational evaluation. Kalamazoo: The Evaluation Center, Western Michigan University. (not dated)

Pondy, L. R. 1977. Two faces of evaluation. In H. W. Melton, and D. J. H. Watson, eds. *Interdisciplinary Dimensions of Accounting for Social Goals and Social Organizations.* Columbus, OH: Grid.

Shepard, L. 1977. "A methodologist's perspective on the need for educational evaluation guidelines and standards." Paper presented at the annual meeting of the American Educational Research Association, New York.

Smith, E. G., Regal, M. L., and Holt, N. L. 1978. "Models for state use in evaluating vocational education: Work in progress." Paper presented at the annual meeting of the American Educational Research Association, Toronto.

Stake, R. 1978. "Using case study methods to study national curricula." Paper presented at the annual meeting of the American Educational Research Association, Toronto.

SELECTED ANNOTATED BIBLIOGRAPHY
Evaluation and Measurement

MARA ZIBRIN | *City University of New York*
CAROL KEHR TITTLE | *University of North Carolina at Greensboro*

The Handbook of Vocational Education Evaluation chapters concentrate on topics and procedures that are currently important for evaluators. Topics vary in the depth of treatment, and some topics important to evaluators have been omitted. With a number of evaluation handbooks, annuals and texts appearing, the editors chose to supplement specific topics with an annotated bibliography for the reader, rather than repeat excellent treatments that are already in print. The references below have been selected to supplement the *Handbook* topics, and are described so that readers will be able to pursue specific topics as they need them.

The bibliography is organized in two sections—the first is *evaluation* and the second *measurement*. In the first section, basic sources such as general handbooks and any texts specific to vocational education are identified, resources related to objectives and task analyses are listed, and annual publications in evaluation (and those including evaluation-related reviews or topics) are also included. The measurement section also includes general texts and references in the field, and sources of test reviews. Two other categories of interest in measurement are included—attitude measurement and observational measures. References are listed in alphabetical order by author within each category.

EVALUATION

a. Basic Sources

AERA Monograph series on curriculum evaluation. American Educational Research Association. Chicago: Rand McNally.

A series of seven monographs devoted to special topics in educational evaluation that started in 1967 and concluded in 1974. Issue No. 1, *Perspectives on Curriculum Evaluation,* has papers by Ralph Tyler, Robert Gagné and Michael Scriven. Issue No. 3, *Instructional Objectives,* contains articles with opposing points of view on operationally stated educational goals, and Issue No. 6, *Classroom Observation,* considers the use of observation in educational evaluation. The final monograph is *Four Evaluation Examples: Economic, Anthropological, Narrative and Portrayal,* and it provides useful contrasts among the several methodological emphases in evaluation.

Albert, K., and Kamrass, M., eds. 1974. *Social Experiments and Social Program Evaluation.* Cambridge, MA: Ballinger.

The proceedings of a symposium sponsored by the Washington Operations Research Council and held at the National Bureau of Standards on March 22, 1972. Deals with evaluation efforts of social programs sponsored at the Federal level. An overview of the varied approaches to evaluation in the different social program areas, as well as case studies of specific programs in income maintenance, manpower, model cities and recreation, are presented.

Anderson, S. B., and Ball, S. 1978. *The Profession and Practice of Program Evaluation.* San Francisco: Jossey-Bass.

As noted in the title, the authors have taken a practical approach to program evaluation. Six purposes of evaluation are distinguished and evaluation methods are usefully categorized for their applicability to a number of evaluation "purposes." Types and sources of evidence associated with major methods of investigating are also summarized. Practical analyses of dissemination of evaluation results are included as are the ethics of evaluation. A survey of evaluators provides a list of most needed skills and a survey of adult technical training programs describes the state of the art for those programs.

Assessing Vocational Education Research and Development. Committee on Vocational Education Research and Development, Assembly of Behavioral and Social Sciences, National Research Council. 1976. Washington, DC: National Academy of Sciences.

A committee formed in 1974 to provide a review and evaluation of vocational education research and development activities sponsored by the Office of Education under the VEA of 1963 and as amended in 1968 and to recommend changes. Cites a lack of information on impact or effectiveness of vocational education. Main topics include the changing focus of vocational education, legislation and funding, assessment and administration of the vocational education R & D program.

Bellack, A. A., and Kliebard, H. M., eds. 1977. *Curriculum and Valuation: Readings in Educational Research.* Berkeley: McCutchan.

One section of the book (Chapter 4, pp. 317-495) deals with the question, "How should curriculum be evaluated?" The various contributors try to look beyond specific methodology to the broad conceptual and ideological issues confronting curriculum evaluation. Some of the areas examined are: course evaluation beyond achievement tests, contrasts between formative and summative evaluation, ways in which process data may contribute toward understanding of educational evaluation, influence of curriculum factors on student achievement, importance of explanatory power vs. correlational data, review of attempts to evaluate post-sputnik curriculum development, and the politics and ideology of evaluation practices.

Bennett, A., and Lumsdaine, A. A., eds. 1975. *Evaluation and Experiment.* New York: Academic Press.

An introductory discussion by the editors identifies major issues in program evaluation. The needs and basis for evaluating social innovations are surveyed through the examination of numerous controlled randomized field tests conducted to ascertain the effects of various innovative programs in the social, socio-medical and medical fields. Some evaluation problems that arise are seen in a review of quasi-experimental evaluations in compensatory education. Further methods are presented in econometric and other nonexperimental approaches, and a series of field trial designs for gauging the impact of fertility planning programs. Finally, the role of evaluation is examined in terms of the feedback that is presented to institutions and its impact on decision making.

Bloom, B. S., Hasting, T., and Madaus, G. F. 1971. *Handbook of Formative and Summative Evaluation.* New York: McGraw-Hill.

Major topics in the book are: Educational Objectives, Learning for Mastery, Summative Evaluation, Evaluation for Placement and Diagnosis, Formative Evaluation, Evaluation Techniques for knowledge and Comprehension, Application and Analysis, Synthesis and Evaluation, and Affective Objectives. Measurement of educational outcomes includes industrial education.

Borich, G. D., ed. 1974. *Evaluating Educational Programs and Products.* Englewood Cliffs, NJ: Educational Technology Publications.

This book is designed to be a guide and handbook for planners, developers, and evaluators of educational programs and products. The work of evaluators is seen as falling into three divisions: establishing perspective, planning the evaluation, and analyzing the data. The first five chapters describe the various settings in which evaluators commonly work and the roles that they perform are identified. The next five chapters present various evaluation models, some of which are appropriate for large scale research, while others represent strategies for evaluating particular educational programs. The final section deals with collecting and analyzing data. Each section is preceded by an introduction that gives the reader a background for the specific topics that follow.

Campbell, D. T., and Stanley, J. C. 1963. Experimental and quasi-experimental designs for research on teaching. In N. L. Gage, ed. *Handbook of Research on Teaching.* Chicago: Rand McNally.

A classic paper conceptualizing types of designs that has been the basis for research and evaluation study design. The validity of sixteen experimental designs is discussed in terms of twelve common threats to valid inference. While committed to "true" experimental designs, the discussion of quasi-experimental design is invaluable for understanding and discussing the validity of conclusions of evaluation research. (See also Cook and Campbell, 1976.)

Cook, T. D., and Campbell, D. T. 1976. The design and conduct of quasi-experiments and true experiments in field settings. In M. R. Dunnette, ed. *Handbook of Industrial and Organizational Psychology.* Chicago: Rand McNally.

This chapter up-dates and extends the Campbell and Stanley (1963) chapter on *Experimental and Quasi-Experimental Designs for Research on Teaching.* Four types of validity are described: statistical conclusion validity, internal validity, construct validity, and external validity. Quasi-experimental designs are categorized as nonequivalent control group designs, cohort designs, regression-discontinuity designs, time-series designs, and correlational designs. Ways of overcoming practical problems in field settings to attain true experimental designs are discussed and illustrated.

Cooley, W. W., and Lohnes, P. R. 1976. *Evaluation Research in Education: Theory Principles, and Practice.* New York: John Wiley.

Presents a view of evaluation research as focused on outcomes of achievement and abilities, derived from the trait and factor theory tradition in psychology. Approach relies heavily on a variety of multivariate analyses and provides a model for the functional relationships among the context of education, student abilities, family, instruction, peer group, and educational outcomes. Concludes with descriptions of a few evaluation studies.

Goldstein, J. H. 1973. The effectiveness of manpower training programs: A review of research on the impact on the poor. In W. A. Niskanen et al., eds. *Benefit-Cost and Policy Analysis.* Chicago: Aldine.

Goldstein analyzes seven studies of five manpower programs (1962-1968) with respect to "the social rate of return," or the benefits derived from the programs in terms of gains vs. costs. No clear conclusions can be drawn due to lack of agreement of specific goals for programs, the different definitions of benefits and costs, and the problems of isolating training, control groups and the length of the observation period associated with evaluation. The first half of the book consists of theoretical considerations of cost-benefit analysis, followed by a cost analysis of two public projects, and investments in people and physical resources. (Annual publications exist for 1971-1974.)

Guttentag, M., and Struening, E. L., eds. 1975. *Handbook of Evaluation Research, Vol. 2.* Beverly Hills: Sage Publications.

The second volume of the handbook deals with politics and values in evaluation research and the cost benefit approach to evaluation. The major portion is devoted to the evaluation of specific social programs, primarily in the mental health field. Chapters four and five deal with cost-benefit analysis. J. Rothberg looks at the difference between decisions in the private and public sectors, the definition of costs and benefits, and the problems ascertaining their values. H.M. Levin compares cost effectiveness analysis with cost-benefit and cost-utility analysis and gives illustrations of the types of data and calculations involved in each. Among the specific evaluation studies is one of new careers programs.

Lecht, L. A. 1974. *Evaluating Vocational Education Policies and Plans for the 1970's.* New York: Praeger.

A book based on a study undertaken by the National Planning Association for the U.S. Office of Education and the National Advisory Committee on Vocational Education. Major chapters include: socio-economic background of students in vocational education, enrollment changes, enrollment and manpower projections, financing, and evaluations of vocational education (by Michael E. Carbine). The evaluation chapter is based on cost benefit analyses by Stromsdorfer and others. This volume also contains an annotated bibliography.

Struening, L. E., and Guttentag, M., eds. 1975. *Handbook of Evaluation Research, Vol. 1.* Beverly Hills: Sage Publications.

The first volume of the handbook emphasizes conceptualization and design strategies of evaluation research. J.C. Nunnally with W.H. Willson and R.L. Durham considers the measurement aspects of evaluation. In Chapter 6, Nunnally discusses the selection and development of measures, and experimental and quasi-experimental designs in the study of change brought about by social programs. Chapter 9 concentrates in greater detail on the development of measures: types of instruments and scales, and the construction of tests. The concepts of reliability, validity and special problems in evaluation research are presented in Chapter 10. The different types of validity, sources of variance and error, and reliability formulas are discussed. Special methods of obtaining evaluation data are illustrated by C.H. Weiss who examines the interview process, and A.S. Weinstein who looks at evaluating general health and mental hygiene programs through the use of medical records and related information systems.

Stufflebeam, D. L., Foley, W. J., Gephart, W. J., Guba, E. G., Hammond, R. L., Merriman, H. O., and Provus, M. M. 1971. *Educational Evaluation and Decision-Making.* Itasca, IL: F.E. Peacock.

This book is aimed at a wide audience, encompassing all who have any role in educational evaluation—teachers, curriculum specialists, evaluators, research methodologists, administrators, organizational theorists, and funding agency personnel. A guide indicates which chapters are most applicable to each position. The material is organized around five major aspects of evaluation: the definition of evaluation, the problem of decision-making, values and criteria to be used, the various administrative levels involved, and research models that will be appropriate for actual evaluation situations. Variables and procedures that would be used in evaluation of educational context, input, process, and product are examined. Finally, the role of the evaluator and the necessary educational training are considered.

Tyler, R. W., ed. 1969. *Educational Evaluation: New Roles; New Means.* The Sixty-Eighth Yearbook of the National Society for the Study of Education. Chicago: University of Chicago Press.

Of particular interest is Chapter 2 by J.C. Merwin. Merwin presents an historical review of educational evaluation dealing with who or what, by whom, how, and to what purpose educational programs are evaluated. In Chapter 3, B.S. Bloom considers some theoretical aspects of evaluation such as the explicitness of specifications, evaluation of nonspecified outcomes of instruction, effects of evaluation, and formative and summative evaluation.

Weiss, C. H. 1972. *Evaluation Research: Methods for Assessing Program Effectiveness.* Englewood Cliffs, NJ: Prentice Hall.

This paperback book is designed as a basic text in evaluation research courses for the evaluation of social programs. Most examples are from social work, mental health, and so on, rather than education. However, the book provides thoughtful analyses of basic topics: the purposes of evaluation, formulating program goals, design, the setting of action programs, and the use of evaluation results. Bibliography included.

Wentling, T. I., and Lawson, T. E. 1974. *Evaluating Occupational Education and Training Programs.* New York: Allyn and Bacon.

The only book on evaluation with a specific focus on vocational education. The authors consider all aspects in the program evaluation process, from the purpose of evaluation to the utilization of the results.

They examine the questions of who or what is to be evaluated, for what purpose, who is participating in the evaluation, at what point of time the evaluation is to be done, what types of data are needed and where and how can they be obtained, how the obtained information is to be analyzed and the results presented, and finally, how the evaluation can be used. Each section contains many examples of procedural outlines, questionnaires, lists of job skills, methods of measuring performance, and ways of presenting data.

Worthen, B. R., and Sanders, J. R. 1973. *Educational Evaluation: Theory and Practice.* Worthington, OH: C. A. Jones.

This is a very comprehensive text suitable both as instructional material in a course as well as a reference for professionals engaged in educational evaluation. It consists of an examination of evaluation as a discipline and its application. Various aspects and approaches are presented by different authors, with an introduction and summary by the editors for each chapter. Some of the topics covered are: methods of evaluation, criteria of educational achievement, measurement and instruments, intrinsic vs. pay-off evaluation, staff utilization and involvement in evaluation, purpose, goals, and roles of evaluation, and decision-making.

b. Evaluation Concepts in Training Programs

Annotated bibliographies of articles, reports, and projects in vocational education. Bibliography Series 36-42. Columbus: The Center for Vocational Education, the Ohio State University, 1976.

This series consists of annotated references in the following areas: Equal Access and Opportunity in Vocational Education; Education and Work Programs; Adult and Post Secondary Vocational Education; Curriculum Management and Instructional Materials for Vocational Education: Personnel Development for Vocational Education; Comprehensive Systems of Guidance, Counseling, Placement and Follow-Through; and Administration of Vocational Education.

Gibbons, A. S. 1977. *A Review of Content and Task Analysis Methodology.* Technical Report Series, Technical Report No. 2. San Diego: Courseware, Inc.

The report deals with the problem of breaking large bodies of subject matter or tasks into smaller and instructionally useful units. It reviews the analysis methods used by various authors, such as Gagné (Hierarchical Organization), Scandura (Rule Analysis), Resnick (Information Processing), Gilbert (Practical Analysis), and many others. The presentation is on a theoretical level, and while general approaches are indicated, there are no instructions for "how to do it."

Schroeder, P. E., ed. 1975. *Proceedings of a Symposium on Task Analysis/ Task Inventories.* Columbus: The Center for Vocational Education, The Ohio State University.

This publication consists of a series of papers by representatives of various organizations (including industry, education, government, and the military) presenting their approaches to task analysis and task inventories.

c. Annual Publications and Journals

Annual Evaluation Report on Programs Administered by the U.S. Office of Education, Fiscal Year 1976. Washington, DC: Capitol Publications, 1977.

Reviews about ninety programs administered by O.E.: (A) Elementary and Secondary; (B) Postsecondary (including college work-study); (C) Programs for handicapped; (D) Programs for career, occupations and Adult Education (Vocational Education for: students with special needs, basic grants to states, research and training, exemplary, consumer and home-making education, cooperative vocational education, work-study, curriculum development, bilingual, adult education grants to states [Career Education]); and E. Developmental programs.

Annual Review of Psychology. Palo Alto, CA: Annual Reviews.

Provides highly useful reviews of major areas in psychology on an annual or systematic basis. Review areas of interest to vocational education evaluation include: personnel-organizational psychology, education and counseling, and research methodology. Review articles also appear on specific topics: instructional psychology, and, in 1976, program evaluation (R. Perloff, E. Perloff, and E. Susna, authors).

Community/Junior College Research Quarterly. Sponsored by the Adult Education Program, Department of Secondary/Post-secondary Education, Virginia Commonwealth University. Washington, DC: Hemisphere Publishing.

Publishes original research in the fields of community and junior college education. Studies are often quasi- or nonexperimental designs. Sample topics include faculty attitudes and perceived teaching effectiveness, evaluation of special services programs, student use of periodicals, and an evaluation of a junior college leadership program.

Evaluation: A Forum for Human Services Decision Makers. Produced by the Program Evaluation Resource Center, Minneapolis, MN (Funded by the National Institute of Mental Health.)

An "experimental magazine" designed to draw together information on evaluation activities from mental health and other human services fields. Sample articles from Volume 4 (1977) include: Federal guidelines for

CMHC evaluations; Evaluation of a community-based clinical program for antisocial youth; The appropriateness of adaptation in the transfer of innovations.

Evaluation and Program Planning. New York: Pergamon Press.

A journal started in 1978 dealing with diverse aspects of evaluation as a topic and the evaluation of different social programs. Includes few articles on educational evaluation thus far.

Evaluation Quarterly: A Journal of Applied Social Research. Beverly Hills: Sage Publications.

This publication is intended for researchers, planners, and policy makers in a wide-range of human services areas: child development, health, education, employment and training, mental health and so on. Includes both empirical evaluation research and new research techniques in evaluation research. "State of the Art" papers are also published and "Research briefs."

Glass, G., ed. 1976. *Evaluation Studies Review Annual, Vol. 1.* Beverly Hills: Sage Publications.

The first third of the book consists of recent essays on the theory and methods of evaluation. Cronbach addresses himself to a special concern in evaluation research, the generalizability of results. Zeckerhauser and House look at values asking respectively the questions of "How much is a life worth?" and "What is the just way of distributing goods and services?" Scriven examines causal investigations where no direct base lines or comparisons exist and evaluation bias and its control, and Boruch advocates randomized field experiments as desirable and feasible. The remainder of the volume is devoted to studies of special programs of education, mental health and public health services, welfare and social services, and crime and justice.

Guttentag, M., ed. 1977. *Evaluation Studies Review Annual, Vol. 2.* Beverly Hills: Sage Publications.

While the entire volume deals with evaluation studies, several sections might be of particular interest: Part 2 (Chapters 5-11) is concerned with evaluation methodology and data integration, covering such topics as using nonexperimental and quasi-experimental data, levels of significance, making decisions in respect to specific goals, and dealing with discrepancies between actual and perceived effects and conflicting studies. Part 3 (Chapters 14-18) concentrates on the relation between evaluation results and their utilization in decision-making, and the type and form of information that might be most useful. Part 6 (chapters 30-32) presents an overall view of the present status of employment policy and looks at the impact of the Public Service Employment Program and the Comprehensive Employment and Training Act.

Journal of Vocational Behavior. New York: Academic Press.

This journal publishes research on a wide variety of topics, including career development, work satisfaction and work values, and vocational interests. Many topics are related to evaluation of vocational education programs; particularly useful for identifying instruments or measurement procedures on these topics.

Review of Educational Research. Washington, DC: American Educational Research Association.

Publishes critical, integrative reviews of research literature bearing on education, including reviews and interpretations of substantive and methodological issues. Often includes topics related to evaluation research, e.g., criterion-referenced testing, instruction, and evaluation of social action programs in education.

MEASUREMENT

a. General Sources

Anastasi, A. 1976. *Psychological Testing.* New York: Macmillan.

The aim of this book is to enable the reader to evaluate psychological tests of any type and to interpret the test results correctly. It covers basic statistical and test theory concepts. Discussions of the different types of test reliability and validity and their measurement are included. The largest part of the book is devoted to an examination of the major types of tests: I.Q., achievement, special abilities, and personality. These are accompanied by many illustrations and a discussion of the type of information that can be obtained, how it is to be interpreted, and its possible use in decision-making.

Buros, O. K. 1972. *The Seventh Mental Measurements Yearbook, Vol. I, II.* Highland Park, NJ: Gryphon Press.

The yearbooks are a continuing series (the eighth is in preparation) of test reviews. Major types of tests reviewed are achievement batteries, character and personality tests, and tests of specific achievement and abilities (English, fine arts, foreign languages, intelligence, and mathematics). A miscellaneous category includes measures in business education, home economics, and industrial arts. The tests reviewed in a vocations category include clerical, mechanical ability, and specific vocations such as accounting, business, computer programming, selling, and skilled trades.

Erickson, R. C., and Wentling, T. L. 1976. *Measuring Student Growth: Techniques and Procedures for Occupational Education.* Boston: Allyn and Bacon.

Part 1 presents measurement concepts on an introductory level. Part 2 presents a highly useful discussion on constructing teacher-made tests, with a wide variety of examples. Especially helpful is the chapter on constructing measures of performance, including work-sample and simulation tests. Part 3 is devoted to standardized instruments, including very brief descriptions of a number of tests used in occupational programs. Part 4 is on obtaining and using measurement information.

Lindquist, E. F., ed. 1951. *Educational Measurement.* Washington, DC: American Council on Education.

This book was written with the purpose of providing students and measurement workers in general with one source for locating everything of major importance that had been learned about the theory and technique of educational test construction, and administration up to that date. The book starts with an analysis of the functions of measurement in education in areas of learning, instruction, counseling, and educational placement. The next section is devoted to the construction of achievement tests, from the initial planning to the final administration of a test. Both paper and pencil and performance tests are included. The last section deals with measurement theory. There is a chapter on reliability by R.L. Thorndike covering sources of variance in test scores. The chapter by E.E. Cureton explores validity of tests from the logical consideration of what a test is to measure through statistical interpretations of validity. The final section deals with units, scores, norms—their interpretation and application.

Lord, F. M., and Novick, M. R. 1968. *Statistical Theories of Mental Test Scores.* Reading, MA: Addison-Wesley.

Develops the mathematical statistical models of test theory. Topics include true and error scores, the classical model for tests of fixed length, composite tests and homogeneous tests of variable length for the classical test theory model. Other topics are reliability, item sampling (matrix sampling), and validity. A section by Allan Birnbaum presents latent trait models and estimating an examinee's abilities.

Nunnally, J. C. 1978. *Psychometric Theory.* New York: McGraw-Hill.

A text that provides a foundation for developing and analyzing educational and psychological tests. Chapters include such topics as scaling models, validity, theory of measurement error, assessment of reliability, construction of conventional and special purpose tests, multivariate statistics, including multidimensional scaling, and measurement of abilities, personality and sentiments.

Standards for Educational and Psychological tests. Washington, DC: American Psychological Association, 1974.

Presents standards for test use as well as test development (manuals), and is intended to guide both test users and test developers. Lists standards for test manuals and reports; standards for reports of research on test reliability and validity; and standards for the use of tests. Prepared by a joint committee of the American Psychological Association, the American Educational Research Association, and the National Council on Measurement in Education.

Thorndike, R. L., ed. 1971. *Educational Measurement.* Washington, DC: American Council on Education.

This book is recognized as a reference work and text for graduate study in the theory and techniques of educational measurement. Of the numerous topics covered the following might be of particular interest. Chapter 13 by J.C. Stanley deals with the reliability of tests. It discusses the sources of true and error variance in testing instruments and in people. Topics such as classical test score theory (dealing with true and observed scores), statistical significance of differences, and various reliability measurement formulas are included. In Chapter 15, L.J. Cronbach considers test validation. Cronbach presents the different types of test validities, the procedures used in validation, and the utilization of these results, with particular attention to content and construct validities. Other topics of interest might be: scales, norms, and equivalent scores; techniques for considering multiple measures; use of measurement in student planning and guidance; and the techniques of test construction.

b. Attitudes

Coughlan, R. J., and Cooke, R. A. 1974. Work Attitudes. In H. J. Walberg, ed. *Evaluating Educational Performance: A Source Book of Methods.* Berkeley: McCutchan.

Example of *teacher attitudes* toward work in low and high performance schools in one community. Suggestions for utilizing surveys in schools.

Chun, K., Cobb, S., and French, J. 1975. *Measures for Psychological Assessment: A Guide to 3,000 Original Sources and Their Applications.* Ann Arbor: Survey Research Center, University of Michigan.

This volume does not present actual instruments, but does provide the original source of each measure and a few references to applications.

Dawes, R. M. 1972. *Fundamentals of Attitude Measurement.* New York: Wiley.

This is an introductory text presenting varied aspects of attitude measurement. The construction of different scales and instruments, and a variety of techniques are described, along with the interpretation of results that might be obtained from their use. Many examples of scales and resulting data make the text easy to follow.

Lindzey, G., and Aronson, E., eds. 1968. *Handbook of Social Psychology, Vol. 2.* Reading, MA: Addison-Wesley.

Chapter 11 on Attitude Measurement presents a theoretical consideration of attitude measurement. Definitions of attitudes and attitude measurement are given, then the characteristics of instruments that are used for attitude measurement, such as forced, multiple choice, or indirect measurement. Scoring and scaling in attitude measurement are reviewed, including the problems of such extraneous determinants as the social desirability of answers and the tendency toward acquiescence. The chapter concludes with the process of instrument construction, detection of contaminated scores, measures of test adequacy, homogeneity, and reliability. An extensive reference list is included.

Robinson, J. P., Athanasiou, R., and Head, K. B. 1969. *Measures of Occupational Attitudes and Occupational Characteristics.* Ann Arbor: Survey Research Center, University of Michigan. 1969.

Provides a systematic review and evaluation of major empirical measures of variables related to a person's occupation. Particular attention is focused on measurement scales, that is, a series of attitude items that attempt to measure the same attitude content. The scales which are reviewed and illustrated fall in the following categories: general job satisfaction and satisfaction with particular occupations and job features, concepts related to job satisfaction, occupational values, leadership styles, other work-relevant attitudes, vocational interest measures, occupational status measures, and measures of social mobility.

Summers, G. F., ed. 1970. *Attitude Measurement.* Chicago: Rand McNally.

This is a collection of articles by many authors who have made important contributions to the area of attitude measurement, including Campbell, Thurstone, Likert, Guttman, Gage, and others. Some of the topics are: attitude scaling, validity and reliability and techniques of measurement. Several studies dealing with specific investigations are included.

c. Observations

Medley, D. M., and Mitzel, H. E. 1963. Measuring classroom behavior by systematic observation. In N. L. Gage, ed. *Handbook of Research on Teaching.* Chicago: Rand McNally.

Reviews early attempts to measure classroom behavior of pupils and teachers, and describes categories and analysis of a number of observation systems, including their own system, OScAR. The combination of description and how data are analyzed is particularly useful for understanding the strengths and limitations of the observation systems. A general design of reliability estimation is developed and an example is provided. The methodology for analyzing these types of data is a highly useful introduction to this area of measurement.

Travers, R. M. W., ed. 1973. *Second Handbook of Research on Teaching.* Chicago: Rand McNally.

The chapter by B. Rosenshine and N. Furst is concerned with the use of direct observation to study teaching, and it summarizes correlational and experimental studies using direct observations of teacher behavior. The chapter also analyzes the content and assumptions of major observation instruments. Other chapters of interest to vocational educators are: Research on Teaching Business Subjects by L.J. West, and Research in Teaching Vocational Skills by C.J. Schaefer, and G.F. Law.

about the
authors
& editors

THEODORE ABRAMSON is Associate Professor of Education at Queens College, City University of New York, and Adjunct Associate Professor in the Educational Psychology doctoral program at the Graduate School and University Center, City University of New York. He is also a Research Associate at the Institute for Research and Development in Occupational Education, Center for Advanced Study in Education, Graduate School and University Center, City University of New York, where he has directed the Instructional Support System in Occupational Education Project for the last two years. His Ph.D. is from Fordham University.

GAIL BANCHIK is a doctoral student in the Educational Psychology Department at City University Graduate Center, and a Research Assistant at the Institute for Research and Development in Occupational Education, part of the Center for Advanced Studies in Education. She worked on the development of curriculum materials in the areas of Food Trades and Building Industries Occupations for the Instructional Support System in Occupational Education. She also serves as consultant to the Jewish Welfare Board, and has co-authored several community reports concerning their Adolescent Growth and Development Study.

MICHAEL BERGER is Chief, U.S. Army Occupational Survey Program at the Army Military Personnel Center, Alexandria, Virginia. He is responsible for the management and operation of the large scale program providing detailed occupational information for use in personnel selection, assignment, skill training, occupational management, and job classification programs. He serves as consultant to military and civilian agencies on survey programs and application of data. He holds a B.A. from Syracuse University and an M.A. from Central Michigan University. Mr. Berger is also President of Social Systems Analysis Group, a consulting firm specializing in educational and training technologies and occupational research and analysis.

DEBORAH GRINA BONNET is Director of Research and Evaluation Programs for New Educational Directions, Inc., Crawfordsville, Indiana. Her recent work has focused on evaluation of career education and vocational education programs, and she directed the 1977 study, "Synthesizing and Communicating Career Education Evaluation Results," funded by the Office of Career Education, U.S.O.E. Ms. Bonnet received her M.S. in Industrial Engineering and Operations Research from Virginia Polytechnic Institute and State University.

EDGAR F. BORGATTA is a member of the faculty of Sociology, and of Personality and Social Psychology at the Graduate School and University Center, City University of New York. He is co-editor of *Sociological Methods and Research,* the new journal, *Research on Aging,* and is the author of many books, monographs, and articles in sociology, social psychology, statistics, and related areas. He received his Ph.D. in Sociology and Social Psychology from New York University.

DAVID BRESNICK is Chairperson of the Department of Public Administration and Associate Professor at Baruch College. He worked for several years at the New York City Board of Education, and is co-author of *Black, White, Green, Red—the Politics of Education in Ethnic America.* He has published articles on education policy in *Educational Administration Quarterly, Urban Education,* and *Western Political Quarterly.* He is particularly interested in the effects of social programs, including vocational education on individual income and life opportunities. He has served as a member of the Dutchess County Manpower Planning Council.

DALE F. CAMPBELL is Dean of Occupational Education, Vernon Regional Junior College, Texas. He was formerly Head of the Public and Support Services Department, Community College of the Air Force, where he supervised twenty-five of the associate degree career education programs of the College. His professional activities include experience at the state and national levels as a consultant and writer on instructional technology, curriculum design, and faculty development. His latest article on future roles of technical instructors appeared in a recent issue of the *American Technical Education Association Journal*. He is presently serving as Treasurer of the Council for Occupational Education of the American Association of Community and Junior Colleges. Mr. Campbell is a Ph.D. candidate at the University of Texas at Austin in the Community College Leadership Program.

LEE COHEN is a Professor with the City University of New York, and founding Director of the Institute for Research and Development in Occupational Education at the Graduate School and University Center. A former teacher, counselor, and chairman of a guidance department within the New York City Board of Education, Dr. Cohen left to undertake district-wide guidance responsibilities with the Long Beach, New York, City School District, and earned his Ph.D. from New York University during that time. He returned to New York City as a Dean involved in the establishment of Manhattan Community College, and subsequently established the Institute.

HENRY H. COORDS is President of Fisher-Price Toys, East Aurora, New York, and a Vice President of The Quaker Oats Company, its parent company. He attended Columbia University and the Program for Senior Executives of M.I.T. In addition to several directorships on the boards of industrial companies, Mr. Coords has been associated for many years with youth related activities. He was president of the Mountain Lakes, N.J. Board of Education; President of the Greater Niagara Frontier Council Boy Scouts of America; is a director of New York State 4-H Foundation and of Children's Hospital at Buffalo. He is presently Chairman of the Niagara Frontier Industry-Education Council.

LOIS-ELLIN DATTA is Assistant Director of the Education and Work Group of the National Institute of Education, Department of Health Education and Welfare, in Washington, D.C. After receiving her Ph.D. from Bryn Mawr College, she conducted basic research on the development of gifted and scientifically talented adolescents at the National Institute of Mental Health. Prior to joining NIE, Dr. Datta was the National Director of Head Start Evaluation for the Office of Economic Opportunity, and then Chief of the Early Childhood Research and Evaluation Branch of the Office of Child Development. Her articles on evaluation have appeared in *Education and Urban Society, Evaluating Social Programs,* and the *Annual Review of Evaluations.*

JOHN W. GALLINELLI is Professor of Industrial Education, The Department of Industrial Education and Technology at Glassboro State College in New Jersey. He co-authored "Methods of Projection, Industrial Arts Future

Alternatives," and served as research associate during the development and field testing of the "Cluster Concept Project" in vocational education of the University of Maryland. Dr. Gallinelli holds a Ph.D. in education from the University of Maryland.

THOMAS A. GONZALES is a Research Assistant at The University of Michigan Rehabilitation Research Institute involved in research on program evaluation in the field of rehabilitation. He received his M.A. in psychology from The University of Michigan where he continues doctoral study in organizational psychology. His areas of interest are the social-psychological factors in the adjustment to work, and relationships between work and health.

ALAN L. GROSS is Associate Professor of Educational Psychology at the Graduate School, City University of New York. He has published in the areas of Applied Statistics and Psychometrics. His recent areas of interest include a Bayesian approach to studies of test bias in selection.

HELMUT H. HAWKINS is Chief of Survey Methods and Management for the U.S. Army Occupational Survey Program at the Army Military Personnel Center, Alexandria, Virginia. He is responsible for methodological innovation in survey techniques and interface with personnel research elements of the Army. He has served as consultant to military and civilian agencies, and held an academic appointment at the University of Maryland. He holds a B.A. and M.A. from the University of Washington, and has completed all but the dissertation in communications at the University of Wisconsin. Mr. Hawkins is also Vice President of Social Systems Analysis Group, consultants specializing in educational and training technologies, and occupational research and analysis.

TEH-WEI HU is Professor of Economics, and Director of the Center for Human Resources at The Pennsylvania State University. He is a co-author of a number of cost-benefit studies of vocational education, such as "Economic Returns to Vocational and Comprehensive High School Graduates," "Economies of Scale in Secondary Schools, By Program," "Theoretical and Empirical Problems in the Analysis of the Economic Costs of Vocational Education," "The Effectiveness of Secondary Vocational Education," and "Vocational Education as an Investment," and so on. He has also written numerous articles of cost-benefit analysis for various social programs. He has a textbook on the introduction of econometrics. Professor Hu has served as a consultant to the National Academy of Sciences, U.S. Department of Health, Education, and Welfare, Urban Institute, and other institutions. He received his Ph.D. from the University of Wisconsin.

MICHAEL H. KEAN is the Executive Director of the Office of Research and Evaluation of The School District of Philadelphia. Prior to accepting that position in 1973, he served for three years as Assistant to the Superintendent of Schools. Dr. Kean is the author of over two dozen journal articles and scholarly papers dealing with such topics as the organization of research and evaluation, the politics of evaluation, and accountability in education. He has served as editor of the American Educational Research Association *Division H (Evaluation and Program Development) Newsletter* since 1976, and is on the editorial board of both *Educational Researcher* and the *Urban Educational Journal.* Dr. Kean is the 1978-1979 chairperson of the Directors of Instructional Research, a group representing the one hundred largest school systems in the United States and Canada. He received his Ph.D. in Educational Development and Administration from The Ohio State University.

HENRY C. LINDSEY is an Education Specialist doing consultant work with the administrative staff of the Community College of the Air Force. He is also President of an Education Consultant Agency, the International Service. Dr. Lindsey formerly served for several years as academic vice president at Ouachita University and Howard Payne University, and has several years of college teaching and research experience in communication. He co-authored, "Telecommunications" for the *Speech Teacher Journal* in 1968, he authored "Adult Education and the Non-Traditional Degree" for the *Educator* magazine in 1973, and has worked as a newspaper drama critic, drama book reviewer, and served for three years as a state editor for *Players* magazine. He also wrote several plays which have been published and produced. Dr. Lindsey received his Ph.D. from the University of Denver.

JONATHAN A. MORELL's chief interests are in the methodology of evaluation, and in the relationship between evaluation research and the planning of social services. He is editor in chief of the journal *Evaluation and Program Planning,* and Associate Director of the Evaluation Training program at the Hahnemann Medical College and Hospital. Currently he is working on a book concerning proper strategies for simultaneously increasing the validity and practical utility of evaluation. Dr. Morell has actively engaged in research and evaluation in the areas of drug abuse, education, and the social impact of mental health legislation. He has also authored a sociological analysis of evaluation as a profession, and has worked at reconceptualizing evaluation as a technological rather than a scientific enterprise. He is an active member of the Evaluation Research Society and the Pennsylvania Evaluation Network. Dr. Morell received a Ph.D. in social psychology in 1974 from Northwestern University.

ANTHONY J. POLEMENI is the Director of the Office of Educational Evaluation, New York City Board of Education. He is Adjunct Associate

Professor in the Educational Psychology doctoral program, and a member of the Executive Board, Center for Advanced Study in Education, Graduate Center, City University of New York. He is also an Adjunct Professor in the Department of Teaching and Curriculum and Urban Studies, Graduate Division, Fordham University. Dr. Polemeni is also National Program Chairman and member of the committee set up by the National Institute for Education for the Safety in Schools Study. He is a member of the Council of Chief School Officers' Committee on Evaluation and Information Systems, and Secretary of Division H, American Educational Research Association. He is the author of a number of publications in the areas of testing, accountability and language development.

ELIZABETH C. PROPER is a social scientist and deputy area manager in the Education Area at Abt Associates Inc., Cambridge, Massachusetts. Her most recent work has included directing the last phase of the national evaluation of Follow Through. She has also been involved in several other evaluation efforts, including evaluations of Title I, Head Start, and Rural Experimental Schools. She is presently completing her doctoral requirements at the University of Massachusetts in the area of educational research, measurement, and evaluation.

ROBERT P. QUINN, a Ph.D. in social psychology, is Associate Research Scientist at The University of Michigan's Survey Research Center. He teaches at Michigan and at National Chengchi University in the Republic of China. During the last decade he has directed the 1969, 1973, and 1977 national Quality of Employment Surveys sponsored by the U.S. Department of Labor; he has also conducted an evaluation study of a pre-employment training program for disadvantaged workers. In addition to his published articles dealing with job satisfaction, he has written two monographs on the topic: *Education and Job Satisfaction—A Questionable Payoff,* and *Job Satisfaction: Is there a Trend?*

DOROTHEA W. STERNE is the Executive Director of the Niagara Frontier Industry Education Council. She was educated at New York University and did graduate work at the State University of New York at Buffalo. She is listed in Who's Who in American Women. Her background includes experience in business as well as in education.

ERNST W. STROMSDORFER is a professor of Economics at Indiana University, and is currently on leave to Abt Associates Inc. in Cambridge, Massachusetts. Prior to that he was Deputy Assistant Secretary for Evaluation and Research in the Office of the Assistant Secretary for Policy, Evaluation and

Research, U.S. Department of Labor. He is the author of *Review and Synthesis of Cost-Effectiveness Studies of Vocational Education.* He is co-author with James Fackler of *An Economic and Institutional Analysis of the Cooperative Vocational Education Program in Dayton, Ohio,* and he is co-author with Kamran Moayed-Dadkhah and Bruno A. Oudet of *An Econometric Analysis of the Costs of Selected Manpower Programs.* He is currently research director on a study of the *Minnesota Work Equity Program,* a study of welfare reform, and a study of the *Youth Incentives Entitlement* Pilot Project, a school-work entitlement program designed to reduce the rate of high school dropout, raise the secondary graduation rate and improve post high school labor market and schooling performance.

CHARLES J. TERYEK is Program Administrator at the Center for Occupational and Professional Assessment, Educational Testing Service (ETS), Princeton, New Jersey. He is responsible for developing measurement programs and conducting evaluation studies in a wide variety of professional and technical areas. Prior to ETS, he was an Assistant Professor at Montclair State College, Montclair, New Jersey, where he taught courses in Industrial Education and Technology. He has written numerous articles and papers on teacher education and teacher evaluation, the most recent being *The NTE and Teacher Accountability and An Investigation of Verbal Interaction Patterns of New Jersey Area Vocational School Educators.* He has also designed an articulation program for Somerset County's Community College and Technical Institute, and he co-authored *Community College and Technical Institute Develop Joint Technological Programs* which describes the program. Dr. Teryek holds an Ed.D. in Educational Administration from Rutger's University.

CAROL KEHR TITTLE is Professor in the School of Education, University of North Carolina at Greensboro. She was previously Adjunct Associate Professor in the doctoral program in Educational Psychology and Senior Project Director at the Institute for Research and Development in Occupational Education, Center for Advanced Study in Education, Graduate School and University Center, City University of New York. Her Ph.D. is from the University of Chicago.

ADRIENNE VOGRIN is the former Assistant Supervising Principal for Curriculum and Instruction at the Fonda-Fultonville Central School and Instructional Support System for Occupational Education Regional Coordinator for Region 4, State of New York. Presently Dr. Vogrin is employed as the Superintendent of Schools, Woodcliff Lake, New Jersey. She is the author of several articles on Curriculum and Instruction. She received her Ed.D. degree from the State University of New York at Albany.

CAROL H. WEISS is Senior Research Associate at the Graduate School of Education, Harvard University. She is the author of *Evaluation Research: Methods of Assessing Program Effectiveness* (1972), *Evaluating Action Programs: Readings in Social Action and Education* (1972), and *Using Social Research in Public Policy Making* (1977). She has published about fifty papers in professional journals and books in her fields of specialization, which include utilization of social science research in policy-making, evaluation of government programs, and survey methods. Prior to joining Harvard in 1978, she spent thirteen years at Columbia University with the Bureau of Applied Social Research and the Center for the Social Sciences. Her next book on decision makers' responses to social science research will be published by Columbia University Press, in 1979.

PAUL G. WHITMORE has been a Principal Scientist with Applied Science Associates, Inc. since 1977 at their Ft. Bliss, Texas field office. He is director of a project to design and evaluate a training management system for Army Air Defense battalions. Prior to this association, he was a Senior Staff Scientist with the Human Resources Research Organization at their Ft. Bliss facility. He is a Certified CRI and IMD Course Manager for Mager Associates, Inc. He has written several research reports dealing with front-end analysis procedures for instructional design. He received his Ph.D. in General-Experimental Psychology from the University of Tennessee.

MARA ZIBRIN is a doctoral student in the Educational Psychology Program of the Graduate Center, City University of New York. She is also a Research Assistant at the Institute for Research and Development in Occupational Education, Center for Advanced Study in Education, City University of New York. She has worked with the project to define the impact of vocational education programs in relation to funding decisions at the state level.

author index

subject index

abilities, in job analysis, 257
accountability, 553-554, 556-557
added benefits, 196
added costs, 196, 204
additive score approach in
    attitude measurement, 378
    additive scores, 384, 394-396
administration and scoring of job satisfaction measures, 427-428
administrative role, 547
adversary evaluation, 152
advisory councils for occupational education, 561-564, 570
Aerospace Education Foundation, 327
affective domain, 383
aggregating data
    state level VEA data, 49
    NCES regulations, 60
    from program evaluations, 66
    and poor measurement in evaluation, 505-506
aircraft maintenance specialist, 307-308, 310-313
air Force specialty description, 307-308
aligned items, 395-396
Alkin's evaluation model, 143-144, 150
ambiguous errors, 389
American College Testing Program Interest Inventory (ACT), 484

American Federation of Labor, 26-27
antecedents, 145-146
apex analysis, 347-348
apprenticeship (also apprentice), 10, 20-22, 26
aptitude by treatment interactions, 136, 153
Arbitrary Implementation Scale (AIS), 187
Assessment of Career Development (ACD), 466-467
attenuation, 218, 223
attitude measurement, 383-402, 399
attitude toward vocational education, 566
attrition, 131, 153, 169, 222, 226-232
    preventing, 227-228

balanced design, 167
Barnard, Henry, 38-39
Base analysis, 347-348
basic academic skills, and measures of, 453
baseline data, 163
Bayesian Decision Theory
    described, 113, 116-124
    vs. MAUT, 114
    local school decision problem, example of, 117-124
    use of interactive computer program, 123, 126